THE PAPERS OF ULYSSES S. GRANT

THE PAPERS OF

ULYSSES S. GRANT

Volume 18: October 1, 1867–June 30, 1868

Edited by John Y. Simon

ASSOCIATE EDITOR

David L. Wilson

ASSISTANT EDITOR

J. Thomas Murphy

EDITORIAL ASSISTANT

Sue E. Dotson

SOUTHERN ILLINOIS UNIVERSITY PRESS

CARBONDALE AND EDWARDSVILLE

Library of Congress Cataloging in Publication Data (Revised)

Grant, Ulysses Simpson, Pres. U.S., 1822–1885.
    The papers of Ulysses S. Grant.

    Prepared under the auspices of the Ulysses S. Grant Association.
Bibliographical footnotes.
    CONTENTS: v. 1. 1837–1861—v. 2. April–September 1861.
—v. 3. October 1, 1861–January 7, 1862.—v. 4. January 8–March 31,
1862.—v. 5. April 1–August 31, 1862.—v. 6. September 1–Decem-
ber 8, 1862.—v. 7. December 9, 1862–March 31, 1863.—v. 8.
April 1–July 6, 1863.—v. 9. July 7–December 31, 1863.—v. 10.
January 1–May 31, 1864.—v. 11. June 1–August 15, 1864.—v. 12.
August 16–November 15, 1864.—v. 13. November 16, 1864–Feb-
ruary 20, 1865.—v. 14. February 21–April 30, 1865.—v. 15. May 1–
December 31, 1865.—v. 16. 1866.—v. 17. January 1–September 30,
1867.—v. 18. October 1, 1867–June 30, 1868.
    1. Grant, Ulysses Simpson, Pres. U.S., 1822–1885. 2. United
States—History—Civil War, 1861–1865—Campaigns and battles
—Sources. 3. United States—Politics and government—1869–1877
—Sources. 4. Presidents—United States—Biography. 5. Generals—
United States—Biography. I. Simon, John Y., ed. II. Wilson, David
L. 1943–. III. Ulysses S. Grant Association.
E660.G756   1967   973.8′2′0924   67–10725
ISBN 0–8093–1693–5 (v. 18)

To Ralph G. Newman

Contents

Introduction

===

IN OCTOBER, 1867, Ulysses S. Grant held the positions of general in chief and secretary of war *ad interim*, the latter as a result of President Andrew Johnson's suspension of Secretary of War Edwin M. Stanton in defiance of the Tenure of Office Act, legislation passed by Congress to prevent Johnson from doing what he then did anyway. When Congress reassembled in December, Grant found himself caught between contending forces as Johnson pursued his rendezvous with impeachment.

When Congress insisted on the reinstatement of Stanton, Grant, recognizing that he might be subject to legal penalties for retaining the War Department, resigned that office. This infuriated Johnson, who had intended to use Grant against Stanton and believed that Grant had agreed to hold office at least long enough to give Johnson an opportunity to place another secretary in office. After Grant instead relinquished the office to Stanton, Johnson accused Grant of dishonesty, inaugurating an acrimonious controversy that destroyed all possibility of future cooperation between the president and the commander of his armies. As Johnson had tried to use Grant's popularity against Stanton, now he tried to use that of Lieutenant General William T. Sherman against Grant by ordering Sherman to Washington, hoping eventually to lure him into the War Department. Grant and Sherman did not always agree on Reconstruction policy, but both abhorred politics and their loyalty to each other proved unbreakable.

Johnson's persistence in attempting to remove Stanton led first to

Johnson's demand that Grant obey no orders from Stanton, then a second attempt to oust him in February, the event that triggered impeachment. As the trial dragged through the spring of 1868, Grant's name and record were frequently mentioned. Grant himself carefully avoided involvement and comment; privately he wrote that Johnson's conviction would "give peace to the country."

Events in early 1868 put Grant to a test more severe than any other since the war ended. After accusing Grant of dishonesty and treachery, Johnson gathered confirmatory statements from cabinet officers; resentful and suspicious of Grant for once supplanting him, Stanton displayed arrogant rudeness in their meetings. The lengthy impeachment trial created uncertainty about the future, while politicians and journalists watched Grant carefully for policy statements as a presidential election loomed. Grant tore up two letters to Sherman that "had run on to the impeachment question" beyond what Grant thought proper. He admitted, however, that the trial was "getting very tedious to us who can be nothing other than victims."

Johnson's irreconcilable quarrel with Grant completed the process of making him the Republican nominee for president. In addition to giving Grant unanimous Republican support, the quarrel gave him reason to believe that duty demanded that he serve lest Democrats surrender the results of victory. If duty led to the White House, personal inclination did not. As Republicans assembled, Grant wrote of "that awful Chicago Convention," and later explained to Sherman that he had been "forced into" nomination "in spite of myself." Staff officers and friendly politicians plotted strategy to maintain Grant's attractiveness as a presidential candidate, but Grant himself did not participate. The documentary record sustains the view that Grant did not seek the nomination, did nothing to enhance his candidacy, and accepted the nomination as an obligation. Neither Lincoln nor Johnson had enjoyed life in the White House, and the victorious Civil War commander hardly needed to enhance his fame and prestige.

Grant's letter accepting the nomination concluded with "Let us have peace." These words, echoing his sentiments about the impeachment trial, reminded voters of Appomattox and caught public imagination. Once a formal candidate, Grant avoided political involvement by fleeing Washington. At the end of June, he planned a trip to St. Louis, the first leg of a journey to the west and back to Galena that would keep him free of public appearances until after the election.

We are indebted to Sara Dunlap Jackson for assistance in searching the National Archives; to Harriet F. Simon for proofreading; and to Dawn Dillard, a graduate student at Southern Illinois University, for research assistance.

Financial support for the period during which this volume was prepared came from Southern Illinois University, the National Endowment for the Humanities, and the National Historical Publications and Records Commission.

JOHN Y. SIMON

January 31, 1990

Editorial Procedure

1. Editorial Insertions

A.   Words or letters in roman type within brackets represent editorial reconstruction of parts of manuscripts torn, mutilated, or illegible.

B.   [. . .] or [— — —] within brackets represent lost material which cannot be reconstructed. The number of dots represents the approximate number of lost letters; dashes represent lost words.

C.   Words in *italic* type within brackets represent material such as dates which were not part of the original manuscript.

D.   Other material crossed out is indicated by ~~cancelled type~~.

E.   Material raised in manuscript, as "4th," has been brought in line, as "4th."

2. Symbols Used to Describe Manuscripts

AD	Autograph Document
ADS	Autograph Document Signed
ADf	Autograph Draft
ADfS	Autograph Draft Signed
AES	Autograph Endorsement Signed
AL	Autograph Letter
ALS	Autograph Letter Signed
ANS	Autograph Note Signed

D	Document
DS	Document Signed
Df	Draft
DfS	Draft Signed
ES	Endorsement Signed
LS	Letter Signed

3. *Military Terms and Abbreviations*

Act.	Acting
Adjt.	Adjutant
AG	Adjutant General
AGO	Adjutant General's Office
Art.	Artillery
Asst.	Assistant
Bvt.	Brevet
Brig.	Brigadier
Capt.	Captain
Cav.	Cavalry
Col.	Colonel
Co.	Company
C.S.A.	Confederate States of America
Dept.	Department
Div.	Division
Gen.	General
Hd. Qrs.	Headquarters
Inf.	Infantry
Lt.	Lieutenant
Maj.	Major
Q. M.	Quartermaster
Regt.	Regiment or regimental
Sgt.	Sergeant
USMA	United States Military Academy, West Point, N.Y.
Vols.	Volunteers

4. *Short Titles and Abbreviations*

ABPC	*American Book-Prices Current* (New York, 1895–)

CG	*Congressional Globe* Numbers following represent the Congress, session, and page.
J. G. Cramer	Jesse Grant Cramer, ed., *Letters of Ulysses S. Grant to his Father and his Youngest Sister, 1857–78* (New York and London, 1912)
DAB	*Dictionary of American Biography* (New York, 1928–36)
Garland	Hamlin Garland, *Ulysses S. Grant: His Life and Character* (New York, 1898)
HED	*House Executive Documents*
HMD	*House Miscellaneous Documents*
HRC	*House Reports of Committees* Numbers following *HED, HMD,* or *HRC* represent the number of the Congress, the session, and the document.
Ill. AG Report	J. N. Reece, ed., *Report of the Adjutant General of the State of Illinois* (Springfield, 1900)
Johnson, Papers	LeRoy P. Graf and Ralph W. Haskins, eds., *The Papers of Andrew Johnson* (Knoxville, 1967–)
Lewis	Lloyd Lewis, *Captain Sam Grant* (Boston, 1950)
Lincoln, Works	Roy P. Basler, Marion Dolores Pratt, and Lloyd A. Dunlap, eds., *The Collected Works of Abraham Lincoln* (New Brunswick, 1953–55)
Memoirs	*Personal Memoirs of U. S. Grant* (New York, 1885–86)
O.R.	*The War of the Rebellion: A Compilation of the Official Records of the Union and Confederate Armies* (Washington, 1880–1901)
O.R. (Navy)	*Official Records of the Union and Confederate Navies in the War of the Rebellion* (Washington, 1894–1927) Roman numerals following *O.R.* or *O.R.* (Navy) represent the series and the volume.
PUSG	John Y. Simon, ed., *The Papers of Ulysses S. Grant* (Carbondale and Edwardsville, 1967–)
Richardson	Albert D. Richardson, *A Personal History of Ulysses S. Grant* (Hartford, Conn., 1868)
SED	*Senate Executive Documents*
SMD	*Senate Miscellaneous Documents*
SRC	*Senate Reports of Committees* Numbers following

SED, SMD, or SRC represent the number of the Congress, the session, and the document.

USGA Newsletter *Ulysses S. Grant Association Newsletter*

Young John Russell Young, *Around the World with General Grant* (New York, 1879)

5. Location Symbols

CLU — University of California at Los Angeles, Los Angeles, Calif.

CoHi — Colorado State Historical Society, Denver, Colo.

CSmH — Henry E. Huntington Library, San Marino, Calif.

CSt — Stanford University, Stanford, Calif.

CtY — Yale University, New Haven, Conn.

CU-B — Bancroft Library, University of California, Berkeley, Calif.

DLC — Library of Congress, Washington, D.C. Numbers following DLC-USG represent the series and volume of military records in the USG papers.

DNA — National Archives, Washington, D.C. Additional numbers identify record groups.

IaHA — Iowa State Department of History and Archives, Des Moines, Iowa.

I-ar — Illinois State Archives, Springfield, Ill.

IC — Chicago Public Library, Chicago, Ill.

ICarbS — Southern Illinois University, Carbondale, Ill.

ICHi — Chicago Historical Society, Chicago, Ill.

ICN — Newberry Library, Chicago, Ill.

ICU — University of Chicago, Chicago, Ill.

IHi — Illinois State Historical Library, Springfield, Ill.

In — Indiana State Library, Indianapolis, Ind.

InFtwL — Lincoln National Life Foundation, Fort Wayne, Ind.

InHi — Indiana Historical Society, Indianapolis, Ind.

InNd — University of Notre Dame, Notre Dame, Ind.

InU — Indiana University, Bloomington, Ind.

KHi — Kansas State Historical Society, Topeka, Kan.

MdAN — United States Naval Academy Museum, Annapolis, Md.

MeB	Bowdoin College, Brunswick, Me.
MH	Harvard University, Cambridge, Mass.
MHi	Massachusetts Historical Society, Boston, Mass.
MiD	Detroit Public Library, Detroit, Mich.
MiU-C	William L. Clements Library, University of Michigan, Ann Arbor, Mich.
MoSHi	Missouri Historical Society, St. Louis, Mo.
NHi	New-York Historical Society, New York, N.Y.
NIC	Cornell University, Ithaca, N.Y.
NjP	Princeton University, Princeton, N.J.
NjR	Rutgers University, New Brunswick, N.J.
NN	New York Public Library, New York, N.Y.
NNP	Pierpont Morgan Library, New York, N.Y.
NRU	University of Rochester, Rochester, N.Y.
OClWHi	Western Reserve Historical Society, Cleveland, Ohio.
OFH	Rutherford B. Hayes Library, Fremont, Ohio.
OHi	Ohio Historical Society, Columbus, Ohio.
OrHi	Oregon Historical Society, Portland, Ore.
PCarlA	U.S. Army Military History Institute, Carlisle Barracks, Pa.
PHi	Historical Society of Pennsylvania, Philadelphia, Pa.
PPRF	Rosenbach Foundation, Philadelphia, Pa.
RPB	Brown University, Providence, R.I.
TxHR	Rice University, Houston, Tex.
USG 3	Maj. Gen. Ulysses S. Grant 3rd, Clinton, N.Y.
USMA	United States Military Academy Library, West Point, N.Y.
ViHi	Virginia Historical Society, Richmond, Va.
ViU	University of Virginia, Charlottesville, Va.
WHi	State Historical Society of Wisconsin, Madison, Wis.
Wy-Ar	Wyoming State Archives and Historical Department, Cheyenne, Wyo.
WyU	University of Wyoming, Laramie, Wyo.

Chronology

═══

OCT. 18.   U.S. acquisition of Alaska completed.

NOV. 5.   Convention convened in Ala., the first under the Reconstruction Acts.

NOV. 29.   Maj. Gen. Winfield S. Hancock assumed command of the Fifth Military District.

DEC. 7.   House of Representatives voted 57–108 against the impeachment of President Andrew Johnson.

DEC. 12.   Johnson asked the Senate to approve the suspension of Secretary of War Edwin M. Stanton.

DEC. 28.   USG issued orders replacing Bvt. Maj. Gen. John Pope in command of the Third Military District with Maj. Gen. George G. Meade.

DEC. 28.   USG exchanged the commands of Bvt. Maj. Gen. Edward O. C. Ord, Fourth Military District, and Bvt. Maj. Gen. Irvin McDowell, Dept. of Calif. Before McDowell's arrival in June, 1868, Bvt. Maj. Gen. Alvan C. Gillem commanded the Fourth Military District.

JAN. 8.   USG asked U.S. Senator Lyman Trumbull of Ill. to represent Ord in *Ex Parte McCardle*.

JAN. 11.   USG and Johnson discussed the consequences if the Senate failed to approve Stanton's removal. Johnson believed that USG promised to remain in office until Johnson could find another secretary of war.

JAN. 12.   USG conferred with Lieutenant General William T. Sherman about War Dept. strategy; as a result, the next day Sherman recommended to Johnson that Jacob D. Cox of Ohio be appointed secretary of war.

JAN. 13.   Senate voted 35–6 to refuse to concur in the suspension of Stanton.

JAN. 13.   Meade removed Governor Charles J. Jenkins of Ga. and replaced him with Bvt. Brig. Gen. Thomas H. Ruger.

JAN. 13.   USG attended a reception at the White House but did not discuss with Johnson his plans to resign the War Dept.

JAN. 14.   USG resigned as secretary of war *ad interim* and handed the keys to the office to Bvt. Maj. Gen. Edward D. Townsend, act. adjt. gen., who then handed them to Stanton.

JAN. 14.   At cabinet meeting, Johnson berated USG for surrendering War Dept.

JAN. 15.   USG and Sherman met Johnson to discuss charges that USG had acted improperly in leaving the War Dept.

JAN. 19.   Visiting Stanton to recommend that he resign, USG realized that this would "incur further his displeasure" and "did not directly suggest it to him."

JAN. 19.   Johnson verbally ordered USG to disobey any orders from Stanton not approved by Johnson. On Jan. 29, at USG's insistence, Johnson repeated these orders in writing.

JAN. 20.   USG visited Richmond.

FEB. 6.   Johnson ordered Sherman from St. Louis to Washington, then withdrew the order.

FEB. 8.   USG ordered Hancock to suspend an order removing nine members of the New Orleans City Council.

FEB. 12.   Johnson again ordered Sherman to Washington.

FEB. 19.   Johnson withdrew his order to Sherman to come to Washington after Sherman protested vehemently.

FEB. 21.   Johnson again suspended Stanton as secretary of war, replacing him with Bvt. Maj. Gen. Lorenzo Thomas, adjt. gen.

FEB. 21.   USG ordered the reinstatement of nine members of the New Orleans City Council removed by Hancock.

FEB. 24.   Through passing a resolution offered by John Covode, the House of Representatives began the process of impeaching Johnson.

MAR. 2. USG instructed Sherman to prepare to abandon forts Phil Kearny, Reno, Fetterman and C. F. Smith to avert hostilities with Indians.

MAR. 2. House of Representatives adopted nine articles of impeachment, two more the next day.

MAR. 10. USG wrote Lewis Wallace a conciliatory letter about his march to Shiloh.

MAR. 13. USG forwarded to Johnson complaints about the Ku Klux Klan in Tenn.

MAR. 14. Hancock removed from command of the Fifth Military District and replaced by Bvt. Maj. Gen. Robert C. Buchanan.

MAR. 27. Hancock assigned to command the Military Div. of the Atlantic.

MAR. 30. Commencement of Johnson's impeachment trial.

APRIL 2. USG ordered Meade to investigate the murder of George W. Ashburn, member of the Ga. convention.

APRIL 4. Bvt. Maj. Gen. John M. Schofield appointed Henry H. Wells as governor of Va.

APRIL 25. USG urged Schofield to decline nomination as secretary of war. Schofield replied the next day that the advice had arrived too late.

APRIL 30. USG recommended restoration of political rights to former C.S.A. Gen. James Longstreet.

MAY 8. USG forwarded a list of officeholders in Tex. who should be removed.

MAY 11. Key vote in the impeachment trial fell one vote short of conviction.

MAY 15. "Impeachment is likely to fail," USG reported.

MAY 21. National Union Republican Convention nominated USG for president.

MAY 26. Following the adjournment of the impeachment trial, Stanton resigned.

MAY 29. USG formally accepted nomination for president.

MAY 29. Schofield confirmed as secretary of war.

JUNE 4. McDowell assumed command of the Fourth Military District.

JUNE 15. McDowell removed Governor Benjamin G. Humphreys of Miss. and appointed Bvt. Maj. Gen. Adelbert Ames.

JUNE 19. USG wrote a letter intended to end his quarrel with U.S. Representative Benjamin F. Butler of Mass.

JUNE 22. Ark. readmitted to Congress.

JUNE 25. Ala., Fla., Ga., La., N.C. and S.C. readmitted to Congress.

JUNE 30. USG left Washington for St. Louis.

The Papers of Ulysses S. Grant
October 1, 1867– June 30, 1868

To William T. Otto

October 1st *1867*.

HON W. T. OTTO,
ACTG. SECY OF INTERIOR
SIR:

In reply to your letter of yesterday's date enclosing a copy of a telegram from General John B. Sanborn of the Indian Peace Commission requesting that this Department turn over to the Commission, as a gratuity, certain army clothing, blankets, &c for distribution among the friendly Indians, I have the honor to state that upon the receipt yesterday of a telegram from Lt. Genl W. T. Sherman making the same request, orders were at once given by telegram to issue the clothing, &c, for the purpose specified.

I have the honor to be, Sir,
Your obedient servant.
U S GRANT
Secretary of War ad int.

Copies, DNA, RG 107, Letters Received from Bureaus; *ibid.*, Letters Sent to the President. On Sept. 30, 1867, Act. Secretary of the Interior William T. Otto had written to USG. "I have the honor to transmit herewith a copy of a telegram dated the 28th inst; from General John B. Sanborn, of the Indian Peace Commission, requesting that the War Department turn over to the Commission, as a gratuity, certain army clothing, blankets &c for distribution among friendly Indians." ALS, *ibid.*, Letters Received from Bureaus. The enclosure is *ibid.* On the same day, Lt. Gen. William T. Sherman, St. Louis, telegraphed to USG. "The Indian Peace Commission could make good use of four or five thousand suits of the Army Clothing to be sold tomorrow at auction at Jeffersonville Indiana, Can you order immediately say five thousand suits except Blouses and Same number of Blankets to be turned over to the order of General Sanborn who is here The price to be charged our appropriation at the average of the

Sale of the balance, Please answer" Telegram received (at 12:40 P.M.), *ibid.*, Telegrams Collected (Bound). At 11:50 A.M., USG telegraphed to Sherman. "Your dispatch received and orders given to turn over clothing for Indians as you recommend." ALS (telegram sent), *ibid.*; telegram sent, *ibid.*; copies, *ibid.*, RG 108, Telegrams Sent; DLC-USG, V, 56.

On Nov. 16, Bvt. Maj. Gen. Daniel H. Rucker, act. q. m. gen., wrote to USG. "I have the honor to submit herewith an account for clothing furnished upon the order of the Secretary of War of September 30th last, to Gen'l John B. Sanborn, Special Indian Commissioner, with copies of the correspondence in the case, and to request that it be transmitted to the proper Department for reimbursement to the QM Department for the supplies furnished." LS, DNA, RG 92, Reports to the Secretary of War (Press). On Nov. 18, USG wrote to Secretary of the Interior Orville H. Browning. "I have the honor to transmit herewith 'an account for *clothing* furnished the *Special Indian Commission*, with copies of the correspondence in the case, and to request that a transfer warrant for the amount ($37,411.88 may be drawn on the appropriations for that Com'n to the credit of the appropriation for the Qr. Mr. Department." Copy, *ibid.*, RG 107, Letters Sent to the President.

To Bvt. Maj. Gens. Edward R. S. Canby and Edward O. C. Ord

[*Oct. 1, 1867, 1:20 P.M.*]

BVT. MAJ. GN. ORD, & CANBY,
VICKSBURG TENN. & CHARLESTON S. C.

Probably second Teusday in November would suit better as day to commence elections.[1]

U. S. GRANT
General

ALS (telegram sent), DNA, RG 107, Telegrams Collected (Bound); telegram sent, *ibid.*; telegram received (at 1:15 P.M., by Bvt. Maj. Gen. Edward R. S. Canby), *ibid.*, RG 393, 2nd Military District, Letters Received. On Sept. 24, 1867, Bvt. Maj. Gen. Edward O. C. Ord had telegraphed to USG. "Registration returns are rec'd from Mississippi Total voters one hundred and thirty six thousand three hundred and eighty five (136,385) Majority of Colored voters about twenty thousand (20000), also returns all in from Arkansas Total sixty six thousand (66000) and odd Colored vote twenty two thousand one hundred and twelve (22112), I am ready to order Election, Prominent Loyal Officials in both States ask delay Shall I issue my order giving forty (40) days time from tomorrow" Telegram received (at 6:00 P.M.), *ibid.*, RG 107, Telegrams Collected (Bound); *ibid.*, RG 108, Telegrams Received; copies (one sent by mail), *ibid.*, Letters Received; *ibid.*, RG 393, 4th Military District, Telegrams

Sent; DLC-USG, V, 55. On Sept. 25, 10:40 A.M., USG telegraphed to Ord. "I would suggest the first Teusday in November as the time for commencing election in both Miss. & Ark." ALS (telegram sent), DNA, RG 107, Telegrams Collected (Bound); telegram sent, *ibid.*; copies, *ibid.*, RG 108, Telegrams Sent; DLC-USG, V, 56. On Sept. 27, 12:15 P.M., USG telegraphed to Canby. "I would recommend that Election orders be prepared in your District for the first Teusday in November as day to commence." ALS (telegram sent), DNA, RG 107, Telegrams Collected (Bound); telegram sent, *ibid.*; telegram received, *ibid.*, RG 393, Dept. of the South, Telegrams Received. On the same day, Canby telegraphed to USG. "If possible the Election will be ordered for the first tuesday but the registration returns may not all be in before the end of next week October sixth (6) This would give less than the thirty (30) days notice required by the Law and allow no time for the apportionment after the Official returns are rec'd" Telegram received (at 5:00 P.M.), *ibid.*, RG 107, Telegrams Collected (Bound); *ibid.*, RG 108, Telegrams Received; copies, *ibid.*, RG 393, 2nd Military District, Letters Sent; DLC-USG, V, 55. On Sept. 28, Ord telegraphed to USG. "Your letter of the twenty second 22 received. will be as heretofore guided by it—No yellow fever in my Dist on account of strict Quarantine—A little Cholera here. Troops generally healthy. No need to move Head Quarters. Election in Dist ordered first tuesday in November" Telegram received (at 5:50 P.M.), DNA, RG 107, Telegrams Collected (Bound); *ibid.*, RG 108, Telegrams Received; copy, DLC-USG, V, 55. See letter to Bvt. Maj. Gen. Edward O. C. Ord, Sept. 22, 1867.

On Oct. 1, Ord telegraphed to USG. "I have issued & distributed my orders for Election in this State & in Arkansas as by telegram for the first (1st) tuesday in November which is generally approved Shall I postpone it" Telegram received (at 4:20 P.M.), DNA, RG 107, Telegrams Collected (Bound); *ibid.*, RG 108, Telegrams Received; copies, *ibid.*, RG 393, 4th Military District, Telegrams Sent; DLC-USG, V, 55. On Oct. 2, 10:35 A.M., USG telegraphed to Ord. "Do not change your election order. I did not know but you might be unable to get it out for first Teusday in ~~October~~ November." ALS (telegram sent), DNA, RG 107, Telegrams Collected (Bound); telegram sent, *ibid.*; copies, *ibid.*, RG 108, Telegrams Sent; DLC-USG, V, 56.

On Oct. 14, Canby telegraphed to USG. "In consequence of the difficulties of communication & serious omissions on the part of Registrars I have been unable to get all the Registration of this state in sooner to order the Election for the second (2nd) tuesday of November They are now all in except one (1) and that will be received tomorrow and the order for this state will at once be issued Some of the returns from the remote Counties in North Carolina are not yet in but I hope to get them in time to order the Election for both states ~~i~~on the same day I go tonight to meet Governors Worth & Orr for conference upon questions of finance in their States and will return tomorrow night" Telegram received (on Oct. 15, 8:25 A.M.), DNA, RG 107, Telegrams Collected (Bound); *ibid.*, RG 108, Telegrams Received; copies, *ibid.*, RG 393, 2nd Military District, Letters Sent; DLC-USG, V, 55. On Oct. 18, Canby telegraphed to USG. "The last Registration returns of North Carolina were received last night and the Election in that State will be ordered today for the ninteenth (19th) & twentieth (20th) of November prox" Telegram received (at 11:30 A.M.), DNA, RG 107, Telegrams Collected (Bound); (at 10:30 A.M.) *ibid.*, RG 108, Telegrams Received; copies, *ibid.*, RG 393, 2nd Military District, Letters Sent; DLC-USG, V, 55. On Oct. 25, Canby wrote to Bvt. Maj. Gen. John A. Rawlins enclosing tabular statements showing the numbers of registered voters for N. C. and S. C. LS, DNA, RG 108, Letters Received.

On Nov. 22, Canby telegraphed to USG. "There is so little telegraphic communication with interior points in this District that returns come in very slowly. So far as reports have been received the Election passed off quietly & without disturbance of any kind" Telegram received (on Nov. 23, 8:20 A.M.), *ibid.*, RG 107, Telegrams Collected (Bound); *ibid.*, RG 108, Telegrams Received; copies, *ibid.*, RG 393, 2nd Military District, Letters Sent; DLC-USG, V, 55. On Nov. 26, Ord telegraphed to USG. "Mississippi & Arkansas is reported by Genl Smith Vote so as to insure Convention, case of McCardle on writ of Habeas-Corpus has been decided by Judge Hill of U. S. District Court He is remanded for trial by Military Commission Trial going on" Telegram received (at 8:30 A.M.), DNA, RG 107, Telegrams Collected (Bound); *ibid.*, RG 108, Telegrams Received; copy, DLC-USG, V, 55. In an undated letter, probably written in early Dec., Ord wrote to USG. "The Elections are over the conventions a fixed fact—I have polled about 75 thousand of the 80 thousand freedmans vote in this state and but little more than enough to secure convention—the total vote is 140 thousand about—Similar are the results in Arkansas—Except that in Miss none but blacks voted for convention—Except a few in each county—in some counties not a vote—I shall assemble the conventions about the last of January—about which time I hope General you will send me my relief—I am & so is Molly considerably used up by our sojourn at Vicksburg we both had fever—and rheumatics begins to warn me to hunt a dryer climate besides I have worked like a good fellow and made few mistakes—I had to arrest the spitfire Editor McCardle who was setting people by the ears—the case is appealed to the Supreme Court but as there are much more aggravated offences which will be appealed on same grounds Soon, I shall release McCardle and let the other cases go up—I am hearily sick of Mississippi—Please send me to Calefornia—! . . . P. S—Molly says she wants to go too—. . . Genl matters of great gravity are occurring now in my District about which I should like to confer with you—great discontent exists among all Classes—and with no resourses but little prospect of being employed— at remunerative rates—the black population have a gloomy prospect before them—" ALS, USG 3. See letter to Henry Stanbery, Jan. 8, 1868.

On Nov. 29, 1867, Canby telegraphed to USG. "The returns from North Carolina indicate a majority for the Convention of between fifty and sixty thousand, ninety six Republicans and ten Conservative delegates elected fourteen Counties yet to be heard from. In South Carolina the Convention has probably failed but the newspapers reports differ so materially from the Official returns that have been received that it is still in doubt" ALS (telegram sent), DNA, RG 393, 2nd Military District, Telegrams Sent; telegram received (at 3:15 P.M.), *ibid.*, RG 107, Telegrams Collected (Bound); *ibid.*, RG 108, Telegrams Received. On Nov. 30, Canby telegraphed to USG. "Returns from thirty four Counties in North Carolina give a majority of twenty four thousand & fifty one for Convention. One hundred & one Republican Delegates & Eleven Conservative Delegates Elected. Eight Counties yet to be heard from as to Delegates further returns from this State indicate that the Convention may have been carried by a small majority" Telegram received (on Dec. 1, 10:30 A.M.), *ibid.*, RG 107, Telegrams Collected (Bound); *ibid.*, RG 108, Telegrams Received; copies, *ibid.*, RG 393, 2nd Military District, Letters Sent; DLC-USG, V, 55. On Dec. 3, Canby telegraphed to USG. "Official returns from fourteen Districts in this State have been rec'd and make it certain that the Convention has been carried by from three (3) to six thousand (6000), In North Carolina the Convention will probably stand One hundred and seven (107) Republicans to thirteen (13) Conservative Delegates" Telegram received (at 11:20 A.M.), DNA, RG 107, Telegrams Collected (Bound); *ibid.*, RG 108, Telegrams Received; copies, *ibid.*, RG 393, 2nd Military District, Letters Sent; DLC-USG, V, 55.

1. At a cabinet meeting on Sept. 24, President Andrew Johnson suggested that elections in the South be held simultaneously. USG believed that this policy would cause difficulty in states where registration had been closed and election day announced. See Howard K. Beale, ed., *Diary of Gideon Welles* (New York, 1960), III, 207.

To William Elrod

Washington, Oct. 2d *18*[*67*][1]

DEAR ELROD,

I have just rec'd your last letter. I am sorry you think of leaving me. I do not you you to stay if you think you can do better and I do not really think you can. [Some] hundred dollars per year is but very little I know out of which to clothe & school a family but that it has been my intention to do much better by you as soon as the place itself produces the means to pay it. You may put down your wages at [Four] hundred from the time you commenced with me and if you stay on I think you will have no reason to regret it.— Except for building a barn and buying additional stock, and some little things of that kind in the way of improvements, I do not want to lay out any money than what comes off the place. All that comes off of it however I want to expend on it. As soon as you may have the means I want all the wood land on the south side of Gravois enclosed and finally all my land enclosed with plank fence.—I intended to tell you in my last letter for you to go on threshing out oats if you thought it best. Sell what ever there is to sell in the way you would if it was your own.—It is not probable that I will get to St. Louis this Fall. I regret it because if I was there for a little while I could explain so much better what I want and could get your views at the same time which might chang[e] mine.

You understand that I want to be very carefull of the timber not for the intrinsic value the timber will have hereafter but because I want the wood land for ornament. I want the whole of it cleared out ultimately so as to leave the remaining trees about the right distance apart to grow thriftily and to look well. This need not be done any faster than the wood is required for fuel.

I am very well satisfied with all you have done so far. Remember me to Sarah Ellen & the children.

Yours Truly
U. S. GRANT

ALS (facsimile), Dr. John T. Bickmore, Dayton, Ohio.

1. On the photostat, the year is overwritten and ambiguous, looking more like "68" than "67." Since USG was in Galena on that day in 1868 and visited St. Louis that fall, William Elrod had not taken over USG's farm in 1866, and the letter is written on military stationery not used by USG in the White House, 1867 is the best date. See letter to William Elrod, Oct. 25, 1867.

To Bvt. Maj. Gen. John M. Schofield

———

Washington, Oct. 4th *1867*,

DEAR GENERAL,

Some time between this and the Va, election, when it may best suit your convenience, say after the 8th inst. I wish you would come to Washington for a personal interview. I wish to see you upon official business though somewhat privately.

I was glad to learn from Maj. Rathbone that you were now recovering from a rather protracted spell of illness and hope this will find you fully recovered.[1] I did not get to pay you the visit I expected to make after my return from the North. The fact is there has been no time since that that I believed it consistent with my duty to be absent from this City.

Yours Truly
U. S. GRANT

To BVT. MAJ. GN. J. M. SCHOFIELD
RICHMOND VA.

ALS, CSmH. On Oct. 5, 1867, Bvt. Maj. Gen. John M. Schofield wrote to USG. "I have just received your letter of yesterday, and thank you for your kind wishes

in reference to my health. I am still improving and hope to escape any further return of my disease. My preparations for the election are about finished, and my Annual report will be completed in a day or two, when I will be comparatively at leisure. I will go to Washington, as you desire, Wednesday or Thursday next."
ADf, DLC-John M. Schofield.

1. On Sept. 11, Schofield, Fort Monroe, had written to USG. "It is my duty to report to you that I have been so sick for the last eighteen days as to be quite unable, most of the time, to attend to any duty. Several of my staff Officers have also been sick much of the time. I must, therefore, ask your indulgence if any thing shall appear to have been neglected. I have, however, succeeded in making out the apportionment, and have prepared an order for an election, of delegates to a State Convention, which order will be published without delay. So that the most important business of my District will progress without interruption." LS, DNA, RG 108, Letters Received. On Sept. 18, Schofield, Richmond, wrote to USG. "I have the honor to report that I have returned to this City, so far re-covered in health as to be able to attend to all my duties." ALS, *ibid.*

To Andrew Johnson

Washington City, D. C., Oct. 7th *1867.*
To the President of the United States
Sir:

Rev. T. B. McFalls, has been appointed Chaplain agreeably to your instructions.

As the law requires chaplains to be assigned to "places most destitute of instruction" his application to be assigned to duty at the post hospital in this city could not be complied with, without detriment to the public service, and he has therefore been ordered to Fort Lyon, C. T., a large post on the frontier greatly requiring the service of a chaplain.

I am, Sir, with great respect
Your obedient servant
U. S. Grant
Secretary of War Ad interim

LS, OFH. On Sept. 26, 1867, Thaddeus B. McFalls, Washington, D. C., had written to USG. "I was chaplain in the Army for four years; and in the Fall of 1865, I contracted a disease, while in the discharge of duty, from which I have not yet sufficiently recovered to enable me to assume charge of a church, or preach an extended sermon. After I was musted out of the service in June 1866,

I continued, at the request of the sick, to visit them at the Washington Post Hospital; and in October of the same year, the Secretary of War directed my employment to render religious services, at the same pay of Hospital chaplains, to be paid out of the contingent fund. Since that time, I have been in daily attendance at the Hospital. The average number of patients per month is about Eighty (80). There are now about fity (50) patients, some of whom are sick unto death. The same reasons exist for my continued employment as existed for my employment at the first. And, believing that some mistake has been made by which the order of the 21st inst. despensing with my services, was issued, I hereby respectfully request a reconsideration of said order" ALS, DNA, RG 94, ACP, 64 1871. On Sept. 30, Bvt. Maj. Gen. Edward D. Townsend noted on the back of McFalls's letter. "call upon him by the usual circular & say what posts are vacant & that under the law he cannot be continued in his present duties." ANS, *ibid.* On Oct. 8, McFalls wrote to USG to accept the appointment. ALS, *ibid.*

To Bvt. Maj. Gen. John Pope

———

Washington, D. C. Oct. 14th *1867*

BREVET MAJOR GENERAL JNO. POPE,
COM'DG 3D MILITARY DISTRICT
GENERAL:

I send the enclosed papers which have just been left with me by B. H. Hill, of Ga.[1] I am well aware of the position held by Mr. Hill towards Congressional legislation touching the rebel States and that personally he cannot have much to ask from officers engaged in the execution of those laws. In this matter however he represents a State interest more than his own and I would suggest whether it would not be well to revoke your order so far as to permit State aid to be continued to the Georgia State Institute

I have advised Mr. Hill to call in person to see you about this matter and hope you will see him when he does call. I would state his argument against the Board of Trustees taking the action you dictate, and also against his resigning which he has expressed a willingness to do, but he can do this verbally.

Very respectfully
Your obe'dt Servt.
U. S. GRANT
General

Copies, DNA, RG 46, Senate 40A–F2, Messages; *ibid.*, RG 108, Letters Sent;
DLC-USG, V, 47, 60. See letter to Bvt. Maj. Gen. John Pope, Oct. 30, 1867.
On Aug. 15, 1867, Capt. George K. Sanderson, Atlanta, had written to Ga.
Treasurer John Jones. "The General Commanding this District directs me to
instruct you to make no further payment on account of the University of Georgia,
from the State Treasury, except on orders approved and countersigned by him,
and that after the appropriations for the present fiscal year are exhausted, no
payments of any kind will be made from the State Treasury of Georgia, unless
on orders approved and authorized as above stated." Copy, DNA, RG 108, Letters Received. On Sept. 22, Bvt. Maj. Gen. John Pope had written to USG. "The
case of the University of Georgia concerning which no doubt many false or partial
accounts have been submitted both to the President and yourself, has reached a
point when it is proper that the facts should be laid before the Government.—
They are briefly these.—Mr B. H. Hill one of the Trustees of the University, immediately after receiving a pardon for his crimes committed against the Government began to flood the State of Georgia with a series of papers which though
filled with absurdities and utterly preposterous in suggestions for the action of
the people, nevertheless had a wide circulation and no doubt more or less influenced the less intelligent and more inflammable portion of the people—He sup-
plemented these papers by a violent inflammatory speech delivered in this city,
in which he advised complete resistance to the Reconstruction Acts; urged the
people to go on and hold elections in spite of Military prohibition both from the
Head Quarters of the Army and of this Military District; counselled every Civil
officer to resist being removed from his office by indictment of the Military Commander, and called upon all citizens 'to fight' for the absurd propositions he laid
down.—In accordance with the course I consider it wise to pursue I did not in any
manner interfere with these individual utterances.—Almost immediately after
the delivery of this violent harangue, he went to Athens in this State to attend
in his official capacity the Commencement Exercises of the University of Georgia.—In the midst of the excitement created by his violent papers and speech he
was elected Law Professor of the University and on the same night delivered to
the students another political speech of the same character as that delivered in
Atlanta.—The next day at the Commencement Exercises, a young man, a protege
of Mr Hill delivered an address before the Board of Trustees, which although
carefully worded, was perfectly understood by the audience and so plainly criti-
cized the course of certain members of the Board of Trustees upon the political
issues of the day, that the audience sympathizing as they did almost unanimously
with his views, cheered him rapturously and showered bouquets upon him; Mr
Hill, present in his official capacity as a member of the Board of Trustees and
Law professor, shook him by the hand and the Band struck up Dixie, thus completing as enthusiastic a rebel demonstration as any disloyal man desired to witness.—Mr Hill's election as Law Professor of the University immediately after
the publication of the notes and speech at Atlanta above referred to; his subsequent speech to the Students and the scene above described fully committed the
University of Georgia to the views he had been promulgating and the seditious
course he had pursued ever since his pardon was secured, and gave him a strength
and influence which personally he could not command.—The whole sequence of
events from the time he issued his first paper to the last incident above indicated,
made it very clear that *his* purpose at least was to bring the University of Georgia
to the support of his political course. His election as Law Professor and the fact
that no official or other action of the University in condemnation of his official

acts as Trustee and Law Professor was taken, very fully confirm the belief that the Board of Trustees and the Faculty of the Institution are not unwilling to be placed in this attitude.—At all events no steps were taken to free them of this well grounded belief.—The State of Georgia gave a large tract of Land many years ago to endow certain Institutions of learning in the State.—Owing afterwards, to difficulty in selling the land or rather in collecting the notes for lands thus sold, the State took up the notes and in lieu of the land donated $100.000 0/100. in money, the interest of which ($8.000 0/000) is paid annually from the State Treasury for the support of the University.—The State has always frowned upon any attempt to make the University or any other Institution of Learning endowed by State bounty, a party to political conflicts or controversies, and in one instance in which there was nothing like so pronounced a case as this, withheld the endowment until a complete change was made in the Board of Trustees.—As the present case not only made the University a party to a political contest, but to a contest in which the laws of the United States were to be resisted; the United States Government brought into contempt; hostility and bitterness created amongst the people toward the Government and people of the United States and all citizens of Georgia who desired pacification and reconstruction under the Acts of Congress, I considered it one in which my interference was absolutely demanded.—I therefore simply followed the precedent established by the State of Georgia itself in a case somewhat similar but in no respect of such gravity and prohibited the farther payment of the endowment until the University by some public and official Act should set the seal of condemnation upon the transactions which have committed it to so injudicious and indefensible a position.—I have conferred freely with a Committee appointed by the Board of Trustees to wait upon me on this subject, and whilst I exact nothing from the University nor require them to comply with any demand, I yet informed the Committee that in my opinion the first step to be taken before any consideration of the matter could be entertained was to dismiss from the Law Professorship the Professor who had abused his office and to pass some resolutions disavowing any sympathy of the University with the course of this unfaithful Trustee.—Thus the matter stands.— I do not doubt that the action I have suggested will be taken, in which case all further trouble will be at an end.—" LS, *ibid.* On Oct. 22, Pope wrote to USG. "I have the honor to acknowledge the receipt of your letter of the 14th Inst with its enclosures.—I will certainly see Mr Hill should he call on me as you suggested to him, but I think I may say with certainty, that in the face of his atrocious speeches in this State he will not do so.—You will remember that he urged the people to disobey my orders as well as yours and to hold the usual elections in Georgia in defiance of the Acts of Congress; that he advised every Civil officer removed to indict me in the State Courts and offered himself as Counsel in all such cases; that he advised the people to *fight* for the maintenance of these propositions; and all this in a public speech of great violence delivered in this City.— Mr Hill, a suppliant to the authorities in Washington for relief from a difficulty in which his outrageous violence and ungentlemanlike abuse of others has involved both himself and the University of Georgia, is not at all the same man as the Mr Hill who rants and raves to disloyal men in Georgia.—It was with the greatest reluctance I took what seemed to me to be absolutely necessary action toward the State University.—If ever education was needed in any part of the world, it is needed here and nothing except what I considered the unavoidable performance of duty, would have induced me to interfere with any educational

institution in this District.—The entire facts of this case are stated in my letter
to you of the 23rd of September.—I have only to say now, that Mr Hill has deceived you with these 'resolutions of the Board of Trustees'.—The influential men
on this Board are Howell Cobb, and Robert Toombs. The speech of the young
gentleman referred to *has* been published in the disloyal papers of this State,
and in sympathizing papers in the North, yet the young man has not even been
reprimanded.—The University is a rebel Institution according to my judgement
and I feel sure will not disavow Mr Hill or his inflammatory speeches except
under the pressure of necessity.—Had this occurrence taken place under ordinary
circumstances in this State the State itself would have withheld its endowment
until not only the Faculty of the University but the Board of Trustees itself was
changed.—I say this because in a case precisely similar where the Students of
the University at the Commencement exercises made a similar demonstration of
preference for Governor Troup over ~~General~~overnor Clarke, both being at the
time Candidates for the Governorship, precisely this action was taken by the
State Authorities.—I have simply followed the precedent thus set.—It is moreover doubtful whether, even in the absence of my order, it would be practicable
to pay this endowment to the University.—That Institution has already drawn
the full amount for the present fiscal year and I presume that no money can be
paid out of the State Treasury on this or any other account without an appropriation by the Legislature.—It is my purpose to lay the whole matter before the
Convention which will no doubt meet by December 5th.—If however you think
it best for me under the circumstances to revoke my order on the subject I will
do so, though I confess with great reluctance, as I believe that the order was
amply warranted by the facts and that its revocation will do great harm to the
public sentiment and to the interests of the State and the Government.—" LS,
ibid.

On Nov. 20, Governor Charles J. Jenkins of Ga., Milledgeville, wrote to
USG. "At a recent meeting of the Board of Trustees of the University of Georgia,
in the absence of the President of the Board I was made the chairman. A copy
of a letter from Genl Pope, commanding the Third Military District to yourself,
relative to his suppression of the endowment of the University, dated October
22d was laid before the Board, and as you will see by the enclosed copy of a
resolution by them adopted, marked paper *A*, it was made the duty of the chairman, to lay before the proper authorities at Washington, the views of the Board
upon the questions discussed in said letter. . . ." Copy, *ibid.* The enclosures are
ibid. On Nov. 21, Jenkins wrote to USG. ". . . When too late, to be remedied,
the mortifying conviction seised upon me that in my haste I neglected to date
the copy I had prepared for you, and still worse to sign it. If this impression be
correct, will you oblige me by inserting for the date the 20th inst. & by attaching
this, and allow my signature to it, to stand as the signature to the document."
ALS, *ibid.*

1. Benjamin H. Hill, born in Ga. in 1823, graduated from the University
of Georgia in 1844 and began to practice law the next year. A Unionist until Ga.
seceded, Hill served in the C.S.A. Senate (1861–65) and became a prominent
opponent of the Reconstruction Acts. See Benjamin H. Hill, Jr., *Senator Benjamin H. Hill of Georgia: His Life, Speeches, and Writings* (Atlanta, 1891); Hay-
wood J. Pearce, Jr., *Benjamin H. Hill: Secession and Reconstruction* (Chicago,
1928).

To Salmon P. Chase

Washington, D. C., Oct. 21st, 1867.

Hon. Salmon P. Chase,
Chief Justice.
Sir:

I have the honor to forward for your information, the enclosed letter from Gen'l Smith, late a Major General in the rebel army; also copies of all papers that have passed through the Head Quarters of the Armies relating to his case. From these you will perceive that no application for the pardon of General Smith has been recommended by me.

I have, however, always held that the paroles extended to rebel officers and soldiers at the close of the late war, so long as they were faithfully observed, exempted such persons from trial for treason, or from punishment for any offenses of a military nature committed during the rebellion, except in violation of the laws of war.

I have not regarded those paroles as exempting the property of such persons from seizure or confiscation, or as relieving them from any political disabilities.

> Very Respectfully,
> Your Obt. Serv't,
> U. S. Grant.
> General.

Copies, DNA, RG 94, Amnesty Papers, Tenn.; *ibid.*, RG 108, Letters Sent; DLC-USG, V, 47, 60; DLC-Andrew Johnson. On Oct. 16, 1867, Gustavus W. Smith, Chattanooga, had written to USG. "I was yesterday visited by the United States Marshal for this district, who informed me that he had come in the performance of a disagreable duty: which was to arrest me & bring me before the United States Court at Knoxville, on a charge of Treason toagainst the U. S. the writ being issued by authority of Chief Justice Chase. The name in the writ was 'Augustus Smith': and of course was informal as to myself. But the Marshal told me it was intended for the person now holding the position of principal officer of the South Western Iron Co. in Chattanooga. And that the clerical error would no doubt be corrected without delay. My understanding has been that my parole, as well as the protection in business accorded me by authority of the President of the United States, issued from your office on the 1st March 1866: would exempt me from arrest or trial on account of acts committed during the war; not contrary to the laws of war. I write for the purpose of asking your opinion and advice in this matter; and your assistance so far as you can give it: consistently with your official duties. I did not recover from the attack of congestion of the brain I had in Washington last winter: and the physicians insisted upon my going to the springs of Va. last summer. I have recently returned improved in health, but still far from well. And 'quiet' is insisted upon by the Physicians as essential to my recovery. Even Ordinary visiting amongst friends has to be foregone. I need not assure you that I have no idea of attempting in any way to evade: or shirk in the matter now before me. Is it impossible to obtain favorable action upon my application for pardon made to the President and recommended by yourself & other military commanders in 1865.—An answer to this will much oblige . . . ." ALS, DNA, RG 108, Letters Received. On Oct. 21, Chief Justice Salmon P. Chase wrote to USG. "The letter of G. W. Smith and the accompanying papers are herewith returned. The writ was, I presume, issued by direction of the United States District Attorney for the Eastern District of Tennessee. All writs from the United States Courts are issued in the name of the Chief Justice which is printed as part of the form. He is, however, seldom—almost never— consulted in relation to the issuing of them, and I know nothing of the writ mentioned in the letter. My impression is that paroles bind only during war. They are military obligations taken by prisoners of war, to observe prescribed conditions and surrender themselves into custody if required. And prisoners who give them are doubtless entitled to protection against any other arrest or imprisonment while the war lasts. But can there be any prisoners of war, or any belligerent rights or obligations when there is no war? If not, why may not treason, committed by levying war against the United States, be punished, if unpardoned, after war has ceased? I give my impression only; having never considered the matter very thoroughly." LS, *ibid.* The enclosures are *ibid.*

On June 19, 1865, Smith, Macon, Ga., wrote to President Andrew Johnson requesting amnesty. ALS, *ibid.*, RG 94, Amnesty Papers, Tenn. On the same day, Bvt. Maj. Gen. James H. Wilson endorsed this letter. "Respectfully forwarded for the action and ordes of the proper authorities. The applicant was educated at West Point Resigned from the U. S. Army in 1854, Resided in NewYork for several years before the war; left there in August 1861; was appointed Maj. Genl. in C. S. army Sept in Sept '61.; resigned Feby 1863; took charge of the Etowah Iron works in Georgia; removed to Macon after these works were destroyed by Genl Sherman; and was subsequently elected Maj. Genl of the Georgia Militia; was called into Service at Atlanta June 1864, and remained in Service till captured and paroled at this place by my command. Since his capture the applicant has in all things deported himself strictly in accordance with his duty, and in act and word has counseled submission on the part of the people & rebel soldiers, to the national authority. His influence has been good in restoring good order, and rendering the rule of Military authority, easy and pleasant. I do not hesitate to say that if allowed the privileges he requests he will be governed in good faith by whatever restrictions the government chooses to impose. The fact that no policy has yet been announced in regard to the 'excepted classes,' and the uncertainty they feel in regard to the future, prevent them from resuming occupations and pursuits by which they may support themselves and families. Unless such privileges as the within, in regard to business, are granted, much suffering must ensue. The applicant requests that this paper may be forwarded through Genl Thomas and Genl Grant. . . . Enclosed, the amnesty oath prescribed, duly sworn and subscribed to before me:" AES, *ibid.* On July 11, USG endorsed this letter. "Respectfully forwarded to the Secretary of War." ES, *ibid.* On Oct. 13, Smith, Lexington, Ky., wrote to USG. "Unofficial . . . I write to thank you for the permission to visit New York &c. and to say that upon your opinion that my presence in Washington at this time, would not facilitate a decision upon my application for pardon under the Amnesty proclamation, I will not come on at present. It will probably be two or three weeks before I go to New York: in the meantime if anything occurs by which I can again resume business, under protection of law in regard to possession of property &c. please communicate with me as before, Care of John R. Viley, at this place." ALS, USG 3.

On Feb. 28, 1866, USG wrote to Johnson. "G. W. Smith, lately a Major General in the rebel service, has applied to me for written assurance that he will not be molested in the performance of his civil pursuits so long as he conducts himself loyally towards the Government of the United States. I would respectfully ask authority to give such assurance." ALS, PHi. On March 1, Bvt. Col. Theodore S. Bowers issued protection papers. "In pursuance of authority from the President of the United, States, G. W. Smith, late a Major General in the Confederate States service will not be molested in the performance of civil pursuits so long as he conducts himself loyally to the Government and laws of the United States" Copies, DLC-USG, V, 47, 109; DNA, RG 108, Letters Sent; *ibid.*, Letters Received.

On Oct. 24, 1867, Smith, Chattanooga, wrote to Col. Adam Badeau. "Your favor of the 21st ins. enclosing copy of letter from Genl. Grant to Chief Justice Chase is recvd. Enclosed with this I send four letters which I would be glad to have filed with the papers. in my case referred to in Genl. Grant's letter, viz— (1) From Gov. Bramlette to the President. (2) M. C. Johnson to the President. (3) James Guthrie to Atty. Genl. Speed. (4.) W. T. Barret, to same. Please say to Genl. Grant that I have never seen the papers since they left Genl. Wilson's office in Macon, Genl. W. gave me a copy of his endorsement, and I afterwards understood both from him & from Genl. Grant, that the difficulty in the way was a rule established against pardoning graduates of West Point. and it seems now that I was not correct in believing that the military commanders had approved & recommended the application for pardon. I regret the mistake; and now request that the enclosed papers be filed with my original application made through Genl. Wilson, Genl. Thomas; and Genl. Grant to the President. By laying this before Genl. Grant you will much oblige . . ." ALS, *ibid.*, RG 94, Amnesty Papers, Tenn. The enclosures are *ibid.* On Dec. 3, USG endorsed Smith's letter. "Respectfully forwarded to the Attorney General" ES, *ibid.*

To Hugh McCulloch

————

October 24th *1867*

HON. H. MCCULLOCH.
SECRETARY OF THE TREASURY
SIR.

In compliance with your request of the 11th instant I have caused the records of the Archive office to be carefully examined.

It is found that the books and papers of the Mechanic's Bank of Augusta, Georgia, have not been received at that office. Its records show that the President of the Bank, Mr. Metcalf, was the "Confederate States Depositary" at Augusta and that he had in his possession at various times several million dollars worth of rebel bonds and notes. I enclose herewith some certificates of deposit which show that during the year 1864 and 1865 he had an amount of coin in his possession. I also enclose copies of the papers giving the history of the seizure of coin belonging to the Bank of Louisiana. These are all the papers found among the records of the archive office bearing upon this subject.

The person by whom the records have been arranged is making farther examination with a view to obtaining information concerning any other transaction by which private parties may have come in possession of funds belonging to the rebel government. The result will be communicated to you as soon as the examination is finished.

> I am, Sir,
> Very Respectfully
> Your obdt. svt.
> U. S. GRANT
> Secretary of War, ad interim

LS, DNA, RG 56, Div. of Captured and Abandoned Property, Letters Received. See letter to Hugh McCulloch, Nov. 1, 1867. On Oct. 25, 1867, Secretary of the Treasury Hugh McCulloch wrote to USG. "I have the honor to acknowledge the receipt of your letter of the 24th instant, inclosing certain documents relative to the taking, by the so-called Confederate Government, of certain coin claimed by some of the banks of New Orleans. I shall be glad to be placed in possession, at any time, of other papers or facts concerning any other transaction by which private parties may have come in possession of funds belonging to or claimed by the rebel government, and now the rightful property of the United States." LS, DNA, RG 94, Letters Received, 352D 1867.

On Oct. 11, McCulloch had written to USG. "I have the honor to enclose herewith a copy of correspondence between this Department and Mr. R. M. Davis concerning information he expected to procure as to large amounts of money once belonging to the late rebel authorities and now supposed to be withheld from the Government by private parties. It appears that you decline to allow him access to examine the archives of the late so-called Confederate Government, but will cause an examination to be made by the officer in charge as to any especial matter at the request of the Head of any Executive Department. I transmit, therefore, the correspondence above alluded to, requesting that an examination may be made as to the subjects described, and the result communicated to me. Is there any objection to allowing Mr. Davis, or some other person familiar with the kind of information desired by this Department, to be present and assist in making the examination, which would probably be thus rendered easier and more effective?" LS, *ibid*. The enclosures are *ibid*.

To Andrew Johnson

October 25th *1867*.

SIR:

In reply to your note of this date, requesting copies of certain reports made to this Department in 1865, by the Honorable John Covode,[1] together with a copy of the instructions under which he was acting when visiting the Southern States, I have the honor to transmit herewith two reports made to this Department dated June 13th 1865, together with a copy of the instructions under which the same were made, dated May 29th 1865.[2]

These reports, after careful search, are all that can be found on file in this Department from Mr. Covode.

> I have the honor to be, Sir,
> Very Respectfully,
> Your obedient servant.
> U. S. GRANT
> Secretary of War ad int

HIS EXCELLENCY ANDREW JOHNSON
PRESIDENT OF THE UNITED STATES.

LS, OFH. On Oct. 25, 1867, President Andrew Johnson had written to USG. "Will the Secretary of War ad interim please furnish me with certain reports made to the War Department, in 1865, by the Honorable John Covode, when visiting the Southern States under authority from that Department, together with a copy of the instructions under which he was at the time acting?" LS, DNA, RG 107, Letters Received from Bureaus.

1. John Covode, born in Pa. in 1808, served as U.S. representative from Pa. (1855–63, 1867–71). In June, 1865, under instructions from Secretary of War Edwin M. Stanton, Covode traveled from Pittsburgh to New Orleans to report on economic and political conditions. Returning to New York on July 11,

Covode began to prepare a report for Stanton and Johnson. On Dec. 18, Johnson wrote to the U.S. Senate stating that he had received no information from Covode. On March 3, 1866, Covode testified before the Joint Committee on Reconstruction that he had presented a complete report to Johnson, who told him to file the material with the War Dept. See *SED*, 39-1-2, p. 2; *HRC*, 39-1-30, part 4, pp. 114–19.

2. A copy of the instructions is in DNA, RG 107, Letters Received, Irregular Series, as is a letter of July 11, 1865, from Covode to Stanton. The other reports have not been found.

To William Elrod

———

Oct. 25th *1867*,

DEAR ELROD,

Your last letter was duly received. You are authorized to give Sarah Ellen One Hundred out of any money of mine you have on hand or may hereafter receive.

I would like very much to have my wood land enclosed but I have no money to to spare now. If you can spare money enough however out of rents from Kesselring, sales of produce &c. to buy posts and plank to fence up the ground South of Gravois creek I would be glad to have it done. In that case I would run a plank fence from in front of Dr. Barrett's house to the creek, and up the creek, North side so as to leave the creek in the enclosure, as far as the land goes. Then with a plank fence on the side of my house next to the school house I think you could get rails enough to fence in the whole of the land on that side of the creek. As I told you I dont expect to draw any money from the land but to spend on it. all it will make, and more too, for years. Dont be afraid to spend all that comes into your hands as you think for the best interest for the farm.

Yours Truly
U. S. GRANT

ALS, Joseph H. Huth, Arlington, Va.

To John Jay

———

Washington, D, C, Oct. 25th *1867*.

JOHN JAY, ESQR,
PRES. UNION LEAGUE,
NEW YORK CITY.
MY DEAR SIR:

Your favor of yesterday informing me that Wm H. Leem [*Lewis*], representing himself as Lt. 1st Inf.y, awaiting order for New Orleans, had presented himself to the Union Club, for relief, with the statement that he had letters from me recommending him, but had lost them, is received. I do not know the man. The enclosed note from Gen. Kelton, A. A. G. who keeps the records of appointments and promotions in the Army, will explain however all that is know of him in this office.

In reply to that portion of your note which expressinges a willingness on the part of the League to give aid where recommended by me I have to thank you and to say that I have no recollection of ever having given such recommendation to any one.

> With great respect,
> your obt. svt.
> U. S. GRANT
> General,

ALS, Columbia University, New York, N. Y. The grandson of Chief Justice John Jay, also named John Jay, born in 1817 in New York City, graduated from Columbia University, practiced law, and helped to organize the Republican Party in New York. A founder of New York's Union League Club in 1863, Jay served twice as its president. On Oct. 24, 1867, Jay, Union League Club, New York City, wrote to USG. "A young man calling himself Second Lieutenant William H. Lewis of the first Regiment U. S. Infantry, & apparently awaiting orders for New Orleans has applied for assistance, saying that he had Served upon y under you, that you had given him *a letter which he had lost*, addressed to the President of this Club, & Commending him to the generosity of the Club. I need not say that any such request from you would be most Cheerfully acceeded to—but we have been approached by so many who altho' supplied with official papers have proved unworthy of Confidence, that before introducing Lieut Lewis to members of the Club in your name, I think it best to ask you if his Statement is reliable, & what assistance you wish us to render him." ALS, DNA, RG 94, ACP, B2171 CB 1867. On Oct. 25, Bvt. Maj. Gen. Edward D. Townsend endorsed this letter.

"The statement made by Wm H. Lewis, and other matters on file in his case, show him to be unfit to hold a commission. His letter of appointment will therefore be recalled & his order for his examination revoked." AES, *ibid.*

On Sept. 26, William H. Lewis, Washington, D. C., had written to USG. "I have the honor to make application for a Commission in the Regular Army (Vet. Reserv Corps) I enlisted as Sergt. in Co "H" 1st New York Mt. Rifles on the 5th of April 1861, and served with said Regt. until the 10th of April 1862 when discharged for reason of expiration of term of service   On the 30th of July 1862 I reinlisted as Sergt. in Co "F" 152 Regt. New. York. Vols, and served with said Regiment until the 3rd of January 1866 when I was mustered out of service as Captain. On the 3rd of June 1867 I inlisted in the Regular Army as Private, and was discharged by reason of Surgeons certificate of Disability (Gun shot wounds recd in line of duty)   I participated in the following engagements viz. Williamsburg, Va   York Town, Va   Battels in front of Richmond, Va   Second. Bull. Run. Va   South Mountain, Md   Antetam, Md   Fredricksburg, Va   Gettysburg Penn, wounded four times   Wilderness Va   Cold Harbor Va   Weldon R Road Va   Petersburg Va wounded twice   Hatchers Run Va and several others. Hoping this application will meet with your favourable consideration, . . ." ALS, *ibid.* On the same day, U.S. Representative John P. C. Shanks of Ind., Washington, D. C., wrote to USG. "Permit me to recommend to your favorable consideration for an appointment, in the service the bearer Mr William H Lewis, formerly a captain in the 152 N York Volunteers and more recently, an orderly Sergeant in the regular army—This captain has good papers and conducts himself properly, and has inteligence   I have herd his statemts touching his Service and Inprisent at Liby with his escape and attempt to relieve other officers—and deeply sympathise with him. I hope you can give him a Commission—" ALS, *ibid.* On Sept. 30, USG endorsed Lewis's application. "Recommended for future vacancy." AES, *ibid.* On Oct. 18, Lewis, New York City, wrote to USG. "I wish you would be so kind as to give me til the 10th of November before I go before the bord of exatioon, as I am at the thime sick in bed. By doing so you will Oblige me verry much" ALS (in another hand), *ibid.* On Oct. 22, Bvt. Brig. Gen. John C. Kelton, AGO, wrote to Bvt. Maj. Gen. Daniel Butterfield, superintendent, recruiting service, New York City. "I have the honor to forward you, herewith, certain letters in regard to W. H. Lewis, appointed 2d Lieutenant, 1st Infantry, October 2d 1867. The Secretary of War ad-interim desires that you will have an ex[a]mination made into the condition and identity of the person who writes under date of October 18. 1867. This letter differing so materially from the application, some investigation is deemed necessary. Please report, at an early day, to the Adjutant General." LS, *ibid.*

On Feb. 17, 1868, George M. Lane, Detroit, wrote to USG. "Herewith I respectfully forward the appointment of 2d Lieut W. H. Lewis, which I have this day received from the Paymaster at this Department Head Quarters in this city viz Major Nelson. Lieut Lewis left this city this morning for Washington, and will doubtless call at your Head Quarters for the enclosure. I forward it to you instead of to the Lieut, thinking there might be some objection to his obtaining possession of it, and also by recommendation of the Paymaster Maj Nelson." ALS, *ibid.* On March 30, Capt. and Bvt. Lt. Col. Loomis L. Langdon, 1st Art., Philadelphia, reported that Lewis, still calling himself an army officer, had been arrested for stealing furs from a hat store. ALS, *ibid.*

To Bvt. Maj. Gen. John Pope

                    Washington D. C. Oct. 30th *1867*

BREVET MAJOR GENERAL JNO POPE
COMDG 3D MILITARY DISTRICT
GENERAL

Your reply to my letter suggesting a revocation of your order suspending state aid to the Ga. University or rather your reply to B. H. Hill (and others') application for such revocation, is received. I am abundantly satisfied myself with your explanation and hope no more will be heard about it. But your reply, which I read to the President and Cabinet, was sent for last evening and may result in some letter, suggestion or opinion.

In your letter you say that the subject of the Ga. University controversy will be submitted to the convention: I would advise that you submit nothing to it officially, except the laws of Congress authorizing the convention and defining its duties. A convention is a sort of original body to enact laws, or rather to frame restrictions and to establish powers within which legislative bodies may act. Under such circumstances it would seem out of place for any authority to submit questions to such conventions as are now being elected in the Military Districts.

                        Yours Truly
                        U. S. GRANT
                        General

Copies, DNA, RG 46, Senate 40A–F2, Messages; *ibid.*, RG 108, Letters Sent; DLC-USG, V, 47, 60. See letter to Bvt. Maj. Gen. John Pope, Oct. 14, 1867.

To Andrew Johnson

Respectfully returned to His Excellency, the President, for his information. In addition to the Military organizations here reported

I understand there are four (4) Comps of White Militia in the
District, raised without authority or objection.[1]

U. S. GRANT

Sec. of War ad int

NOV. 1ST /67

AES, DLC-Andrew Johnson. Written on a report of Oct. 31, 1867, from Bvt.
Maj. Gen. Edward D. Townsend. "Oct. 24, '67, His Excellency, the President,
referred to the Secretary of War an extract from the 'Daily Morning Chronicle'
of Oct. 22, '67, relative to armed organizations of colored persons in this District
for consideration and for information as to the authority under which they have
been raised and to which they are held subject, &c. Referred by Secretary of
War to the Adjutant General, and through him to the Commanding General Dept.
of Washington, for report. Returned by Comdg. Genl. Dept. of Washington,
with a report from Bvt. Brig. Gen. Joseph Roberts, Actg. Asst. Ins. Gen'l. who
reports the following organizations of colored men in the Dist. of Colu. 1st, 'City
Guards of Washington,' a Battalion of 2 cos., designated as cos. A & B—Co. A,
175 men enrolled, about 75 turn out with arms, Co. B, now organizing—is not
uniformed and has but few arms—2nd, 'Washington Guards,' to be also a Battalion of 2 cos.—1 co. now organized about 75 men enrolled—have a few muskets.
3rd, 'Independent Greys'—1 co., uniformed and armed. He says that he learned
that there was a co. in Georgetown, but could procure no information concerning
it, and that in conversation with Gen. Howard he remarked that there were
secret organizations in the District, in which colored & white rebel & union men
had enrolled themselves. Mayor Wallach states that some time since in reply to
an application made by colored men to organize mily. cos. he informed them
that they had as much right as white men to raise companies in conformity with
the militia laws of the District. General Emory, in returning these papers, reports
the following colored mily. organizations, in addition to those named by General
Roberts: 2 cos. of Zouaves; 1 in Washington and 1 in Georgetown—3 cos. in
process of organization on the Island. Gen. Emory does not think there are any
secret organizations worthy of consideration in the District. Says no authority
for these organizations, other than that expressed in the statement of Mayor
Wallach is known to exist. Under the Militia Laws of the Dist. of Columbia
these organizations would be subject to the orders of Maj. Gen. Geo. C. Thomas
(clerk in office of Chf. of Engineers) No authority for organizing such cos. has
been given through this (A. G) office. Two applications have been recd.; one
signed by Jno. M. Brown & 26 others, the other from Andrew Jackson. These
applications were disapproved by the Gen.-in-Chief, who deemed it inexpedient
to authorize militia organizations in the District of Columbia, and the applicants
were so informed by letter from this Office. Respectfully returned to the Secretary
of War, with the foregoing reports." ES, *ibid.*

On Nov. 4, President Andrew Johnson wrote to USG. "I am reliably advised that there are within the District of Columbia a number of armed organizations, formed without authority of law, and for purposes which have not been
communicated to the Government. Being at the present time unnecessary for the
preservation of order or the protection of the civil authority, they have excited
serious apprehensions as to their real design. You will therefore take efficient

steps for promptly disbanding and suppressing all such illegal organizations."
LS, DNA, RG 108, Letters Received. Johnson enclosed a letter of Nov. 1, 1866,
written to Secretary of War Edwin M. Stanton. See *PUSG*, 16, 355. On Nov. 4,
1867, Johnson endorsed this letter. "The within copy of a communication addressed to the War Department on the 1st Novr, 1866, is referred to the Honorable the Secretary of War ad interim, for his attention. As the present posture
of affairs is very similar to that which then existed, if indeed it does not excite
more apprehension in the public mind, I would be pleased to receive an early
report of the number of troops on duty in the Department of Washington, their
distribution, and the name of the officer in command of each post." ES, DNA,
RG 108, Letters Received. On Nov. 5, Bvt. Maj. Gen. William H. Emory, Washington, D. C., endorsed this letter. "The necessary preparations are made for the
execution of this order, but as this District is not under Martial Law, it is respectfully suggested that before proceeding to its execution, to avoid legal complications, that the notice disbanding these organizations shall be served first
by the civil authorities." AES, DLC-Andrew Johnson. On the same day, USG
endorsed this letter. "Respectfully forwarded to the Secy of War." ES, *ibid.*

On Nov. 8, Bvt. Maj. Charles B. Fischer, Washington City Guard, wrote to
USG. "I have the honor to forward to you the following statement in regard to
the Colored Military organizations of this District. The first company was formed
April 25th 1865. and consisted then as all do now, of honorably discharged
Soldiers and Sailors of the United States Army and Navy. We formed at the
same time, the Colored Soldiers and Sailors, National League for whose record,
we can, by permission, refer to Bvt. Brig. Gen. *Chas. H. Howard.* Asst. Commissioner Bureau R. F. and A. L. The objects of our organization are benevolent,
not political. The armed portion of the organization is made up of those men
who purchased from the Government the arms they were permitted to use in its
defense, and we are banded together to resist no law, nor to intimidate any person or persons in the community in which we reside, but to keep up the associations engendered by our companionship in camp. The strength of the armed
organization is as follows: . . . Total 15 Officers. 795. men. The Executive Committee of the League have endeavored to relieve the necessities of the widows and
orphans of our comrades who fell in the late Struggle for Liberty. In making this
Statement we earnestly hope it will, in some degree, correct the erroneous impressions that have gained credence in the minds of some parties, that we are
'Hostile bands of armed negroes'. our object is to show to the world that we are
worthy of the freedom obtained by the late war." LS, DLC-Andrew Johnson. On
Nov. 11, USG endorsed this letter. "Respectfully forwarded to the President for
his information." AES, *ibid.*

1. On May 29 and 30, Maj. Gen. George C. Thomas, D. C. Militia, had
written to USG. "I have the honor to transmit an application for Commissions
for the Officers of a Volunteer Company of Colored men of Georgetown, D. C.
under the style and title of the Independent Zouaves of Georgetown. The requisite number of names for the formation of a company appear upon the Roll, and
a copy of the proceedings, in the election of Officers is furnished. I would respectfully recommend that the Commissions be issued, and am credibly informed
that several other Companies, have been or are about to be organized, and that
applications similar to the one in consideration will soon be made by them for
Commissions for the Officers. In view of the novelty of this question, and the

evident anxiety of the parties, may I ask an early consideration of the subject."
"I have the honor to transmit an application for Commissions for the Officers of
a Volunteer Company of cold men of Georgetown, D. C. under the style and title
of the Independent Guards. I am informed that the requisite number of names for
the formation of a Company have been furnished, and a copy of the proceedings
in the election of Officers for Commission &c. is presented. I would respectfully
recommend that the Commissions be issued, . . ." ALS, DNA, RG 94, Letters
Received, 184T 1867. The enclosures are *ibid.* On May 30, USG endorsed these
letters. "Respectfully forwarded to the Secretary of War." ES, *ibid.* On June 7,
Bvt. Maj. Gen. Edward R. S. Canby endorsed these letters. "There is no apparent necessity for these organizations other than the general militia law of
May 8. 1792 and the special act of Mar 3. 1863 in relation to the organization
of the militia in the District of Columbia. The disqualifications on account of
Color is removed by the 6th section of the Act approved March 2. 1867. and I
see no reason why the class of citizens refered to in these papers should not now
be included in the enrollment, but the necessity for this increase of the militia
~~from~~ of the District is, under the 1st Section of the Act of March 3. 1863, a
question for the discretion of the President. Respectfully returned." AES, *ibid.*

On May 23, John H. Brown and twenty-six other blacks had written to
Stanton requesting permission to form an independent militia co. in D. C. LS,
ibid., 465B 1867. On May 31, Townsend endorsed this letter. "Submitted to Genl
Grant who deems it inexpedient to authorize militia organizations in the D. C. at
present." AES, *ibid.*

On April 10, Thomas had written to USG. "In view of the recent change in
the Militia law in striking therefrom the word 'white', and for other good and
sufficient reasons, I would most earnestly recommend a prompt re-organization
of the Militia of the District of Columbia. It could and should be made a useful
auxilliary to the defences of the Capitol of the Nation." ALS, *ibid.*, RG 107,
Letters Received from Bureaus. On June 11, Canby endorsed this letter. "Respectfully returned. The organization of the Militia of the District of Columbia
is determined by law and by the discretion of the President. The only change
made by the law herein cited is to subject to enrollment a class of persons heretofore excluded by reason of Color, and as a measure of preparation and precau-
tion the enrollment should ~~their enrollment should~~ be made. There is no immediate necessity calling for this, but if it be delayed until the necessity is exhibited
it will then be too late for any practical benefit in that particular emergency. This
may be all done under existing regulations and I do not see that any reorganization is necessary. It may be considered advisable that the organizations of white
and colored militia should be kept distinct and this is recommended." AES, *ibid.*
On June 19, USG endorsed this letter to Stanton. ES, *ibid.*

To Hugh McCulloch

———

November 1st 1862[7].

Hon. H. McCulloch
Secretary of the Treasury.
Sir.

Referring to my letter of October 24th in relation to records of the Archive Office which might throw light upon transactions in the rebel states through which funds rightfully belonging to the United States government have been retained in the hands of private individuals, I now have the honor to transmit additional papers, one of which is a copy of the contract relating to coin belonging to the banks of New Orleans which contract belongs to the papers already furnished you. Another refers to three hundred thousand dollars in specie advanced by the state of Virginia. And three others to certain cotton transactions.

Touching the subject of your letter of the 26th instant I have respectfully to reply that the records of the Archive Office are regarded in the same light as other official records in custody of the War Department. Copies of all such as may be of use to the other Departments of the government, or the originals when they are found not to pertain to the business of the War Department but to some other Department of the Government will be freely furnished to those Departments or the originals will be loaned when necessary. It is however a rule of the War Department from which it is deemed inexpedient to depart in the present instance, not to permit persons unconnected with the War Department to have access to its records for the purpose of a general examination. There is an intelligent clerk in special charge of the Archive records who is thoroughly acquainted with them and who has arranged them under direction of the officer responsible for them. It will, therefore, only be necessary to indicate the character of the papers required to enable this Department to reply promptly to any requisition made upon it, for information which the Archive office can afford.

> I am, Sir,
> Very Respectfully
> Your obedient servant
> U. S. GRANT
> Secretary of War ad interim

LS, DNA, RG 56, Letters Received. The enclosures are *ibid*. See letter to Hugh McCulloch, Oct. 24, 1867. On Oct. 26, 1867, Secretary of the Treasury Hugh McCulloch had written to USG. "I have the honor to inform you that this Department is advised that the War Department has in its possession certain records and papers of the late so-styled Confederate States Government which, it is believed, would be of use and value to this Government in the prosecution of certain suits now in progress, under the joint action of the State and Treasury Departments, looking to the recovery of large amounts of money from former agents of the late rebellious organization above referred to. I have the honor to request, therefore, that you will, if you see no objection to such course, cause these documents to be transferred, either permanently or temporarily, to this Department; or, if you deem that course inexpedient, that you will give such orders as will enable any person designated by me to have access to the same, and to make such examination and copies or other memoranda as may be thought necessary or proper." LS, DNA, RG 94, Letters Received, 352D 1867. On Nov. 14, McCulloch wrote to USG. "I have the honor to acknowledge the receipt of your letter of the 1st instant, transmitting a copy of additional papers from the Archive Office relating to certain coin belonging to the banks in New Orleans, to Three hundred thousand dollars ($300,000 00) in specie, advanced to the late so-styled Confederate States Government by the State of Virginia, and to certain cotton transactions. In further explanation of my letter of the 26th ultimo, to which yours now under notice is a reply, it is proper to say here that my request that you would allow some person designated by me to have access to the Confederate records, was based upon a desire to procure all the information possible bearing upon suits commenced by the United States for the recovery of proceeds of property formerly held by agents of the late so-called Confederate States Government, as well as in suits brought by private individuals against the United States for the recovery of proceeds of captured and abandoned property—each class involving large amounts of money. As these suits include a number of different persons and transactions, it was thought that a person familiar with them detailed from this Department could, if allowed to examine the records in question, glean much that would be of great service, which might not otherwise be obtained, and which might be overlooked if this Department should only undertake to indicate any particular papers wanted. Hence the request made in the form as submitted in my letter of the 26th ult.; but it is possible that everything desired may be accomplished by the plan you propose:—particularly if the person in charge of the Archive Office could receive and act on verbal suggestions in the premises from Mr Samuel A. Duncan, a special agent of this Department." LS, *ibid.*, W1424 1865.

To Bvt. Maj. Gen. Joseph A. Mower

————

Washington, Nov. 2d *1867*. [*11:00* A.M.]

MAJ. GN. MOWER,
NEW ORLEANS, LA.

Please revoke your order appointing Bullitt[1] ~~Mayor~~ Sherriff of
New Orleans. Whilst his name is connected so ~~unfavorably~~ intimately with ~~the~~ Treasury losses I cannot concent to his appointment
to any office over which I have controll. Further particulars by mail.
Unless there is a necessity for the immediate removal of Mayor
Hays[2] I would suggest that no change be made untill Gen. Hancock arrives. Of this be your own judge but report cause of removal.

U. S. GRANT
General,

ALS (telegram sent), DNA, RG 107, Telegrams Collected (Bound); telegram
sent, *ibid.*; copies, *ibid.*, RG 108, Telegrams Sent; DLC-USG, V, 56. On Nov.
2, 1867, Bvt. Maj. Gen. Joseph A. Mower telegraphed to USG. "Will revoke
order removing Sheriff Hays" Telegram received (at 4:30 P.M.), DNA, RG
107, Telegrams Collected (Bound); *ibid.*, RG 108, Telegrams Received; copy,
DLC-USG, V, 55. See telegram to Maj. Gen. Winfield S. Hancock, Nov. 29, 1867.
   On Nov. 1, Harry T. Hays, New Orleans, had telegraphed to USG. "I have
been removed from the Office of Sheriff of the Parish of Orleans by Genl Mower
who tells me he has nothing against me, & Cuthbert Bullitt has been appointed
in my stead. The records of the U. S. Circuit Court in this City show that Cuthbert Bullitt while U. S. Marshall sold the cargo of the Brig 'Dashing Wave', that
instead of depositing the proceeds amounting to two hundred & fifty thousand
(250000) dolls in the U. S. Treasury in conformity with the Law, he deposited
them in the first National Bank, Then he withdrew them without an order of
Court, That he re-deposited them in the same Bank and again withdrew them
without an order of Court & that when the parties entitled to the money under
judgement of the Supreme Court of the U. S. applied for them Bullitt could not
& has not paid the Claimants. British Subjects are now claiming against the
Government of the United States,   I respectfully ask that the order appointing
him may be revoked" Telegram received (on Nov. 2, 8:30 A.M.), DNA, RG
107, Telegrams Collected (Bound); *ibid.*, RG 108, Telegrams Received; copy,
DLC-USG, V, 55. On Nov. 2, Bvt. Brig. Gen. Cyrus B. Comstock wrote to Mower.
"Gen. Grant has telegraphed you today disapproving Bullitts appointment as
Sheriff of NewOrleans, and advising Hays' retention until Gen. Hancock's arrival. He desires me to give the reasons for his disapproval of Bullitts appointment. The Sec. of the Treasury States that the proceeds of the sale of a certain
vessel (amounting it is understood to about $250.000.) after having been de-
posited by Bullitt in the 1st National Bank of NewOrleans, were without authority
transferred by him to New York, retransferred to the Bank in question and again
withdrawn and that now upon order of Court he fails to pay, that money to the

rightful English claimants, who thereupon demand it of the United States. The case is regarded as a bad one against Bullitt and hence the Generals disapproval" Copies, *ibid.*, V, 47, 60; DNA, RG 108, Letters Sent. See *SMD*, 40-2-107. On Nov. 3, Mower telegraphed to USG. "Mr Bullitt has reconsidered his acceptance of the Sheriffalty which leave Mr Hays still in his position" Telegram received (on Nov. 4, 8:30 A.M.), DNA, RG 107, Telegrams Collected (Bound); *ibid.*, RG 108, Telegrams Received; copies, DLC-USG, V, 55; DLC-Andrew Johnson. On Nov. 4, USG endorsed a copy of this telegram to President Andrew Johnson. ES, *ibid.*

On Nov. 17, Mower telegraphed to USG. "I have removed sheriff Hay's as an impediment in the way of reconstruction. The convention meets on the 23d. I am responsible that there shall be no disturbance There was an organization known as 'Hay's Brigade' represented at the 30th of July riot. Should they attempt anything against the convention about to meet their leader should not be a civil officer, and above all a Sheriff—More than this the sheriff should be a loyal man on whom I can rely. I have also removed the clerk of 2nd District Court New-Orleans for malfeasance in office." Telegram received (at 7:55 P.M.), DNA, RG 107, Telegrams Collected (Bound); telegram received (at 8:30 P.M.), *ibid.*, RG 108, Telegrams Received; DLC-Andrew Johnson; copies, DNA, RG 109, Union Provost Marshals' File of Papers Relating to Individual Civilians; 5th Military District Papers, Duke University, Durham, N. C.; DLC-USG, V, 55.

On Nov. 21, Governor Benjamin F. Flanders of La., New Orleans, telegraphed to USG. "Some of the removals of Civil Officers by Gen Mower were inexpedient & his appointment in many cases most objectionable I think the removals & appointments since the tenth (10th) should be disapproved by you until they can have the consideration of Gen Hancock who is hourly expected" Telegram received (at 4:00 P.M.), DNA, RG 107, Telegrams Collected (Bound); *ibid.*, RG 108, Telegrams Received; copy, DLC-USG, V, 55. On Nov. 22, 1:00 P.M., USG telegraphed to Mower. "Suspend your last order making removals of Civil officers until arrival of Gen. Hancock." ALS (telegram sent), DNA, RG 107, Telegrams Collected (Bound); telegram sent, *ibid.*; copies, *ibid.*, RG 108, Telegrams Sent; DLC-USG, V, 56. On the same day, Mower telegraphed to USG. "Telegram received directing suspension of order removing Civil Officers, Will suspend order at once" Telegram received (on Nov. 23, 9:00 A.M.), DNA, RG 107, Telegrams Collected (Bound); *ibid.*, RG 108, Telegrams Received; copies, DLC-USG, V, 55; DLC-Andrew Johnson. On Nov. 25, Mower telegraphed to USG. "I respectfully request authority to remove Governor Flanders for contumacious influence with the Military Authorities here in impeding the removal of Civil Officers who are opposed to the Convention & who from the positions which they occupy *can* and from their known sympathy & antecedents I am fully convinced *will* obstruct the action of the Convention to the full extent of their abilities. Should this request meet with your approval I will appoint temporarily an Officer in the Army to fill the place until the arrival of Gen Hancock" Telegram received (at 3:30 P.M.), DNA, RG 107, Telegrams Collected (Bound); *ibid.*, RG 108, Telegrams Received; copy, DLC-USG, V, 55. On the same day, Comstock telegraphed to Mower. "Your cipher dispatch of 1 30 pm is received. Gen. Grant desires that you suspend all action in the matter till Gen. Hancock's arrival." Copies, *ibid.*, V, 56; DNA, RG 108, Telegrams Sent. On Nov. 27, 9:30 A.M., USG telegraphed to Mower. "Let me know when Gen. Hancock arrives." ALS (telegram sent), *ibid.*, RG 107, Telegrams Collected (Bound); telegram sent, *ibid.*; copies, *ibid.*, RG 108, Telegrams Sent; DLC-USG, V, 56. On the same day, Mower telegraphed to USG. "Gen Hancock passed Vicksburg yesterday and will be here some time tomorrow, Will telegraph his arrival" Telegram received (at 4:15 P.M.), DNA, RG 107, Telegrams Collected (Bound); *ibid.*, RG 108, Telegrams Received; copy, DLC-USG, V, 55. On Nov. 28, Maj. Gen. Winfield S. Hancock, New Orleans, telegraphed to USG. "I have just arrived & will take command at nine (9) oclock tomorrow" Telegram received (on Nov. 29, 8:30 A.M.), DNA, RG 107, Telegrams Collected (Bound); *ibid.*, RG 108, Telegrams Received; copy, DLC-USG, V, 55.

1. Cuthbert Bullitt, born in Ky., a commission merchant in New Orleans, was appointed in 1863 special agent for the collection of customs in New Orleans. In 1864, Bullitt, then U.S. marshal for the eastern district of La., served as a La. delegate to the Union Party Convention. An opponent of Radical Reconstruction, he became a prominent member of the Andrew Johnson Club of La.

2. Harry T. Hays, born in Tenn. in 1820, attended St. Mary's College in Baltimore, became a lawyer in New Orleans in 1844, then served in the Mexican War. In the Civil War, Hays commanded the 7th La., was promoted to brig. gen. in 1862, led the 1st La. Brigade in several major battles, and was severely wounded at Spotsylvania in 1864. He became sheriff of Orleans Parish in 1866.

To Bvt. Maj. Gen. John Pope

Washington Nov. 2d *1867.* [*4:30* P.M.]

Maj. Gn. J. Pope,
Atlanta, Ga,

I would suggest the name of Joshua Hill[1] for Governor when Jenkins time expires if you think it probable that the Constitution will be voted down when submitted to the people. If the office is to be temporary, as it will be if the Constitution is adopted, the matter will become one of less importance,

U. S. Grant
General.

ALS (telegram sent), DNA, RG 107, Telegrams Collected (Bound); telegram sent, *ibid.*; telegram received, Meade Papers, PHi. On Nov. 15, 1867, Bvt. Maj. Gen. John Pope telegraphed to USG. "Will you please answer my letter concerning Mr Joshua Hill" Telegram received (at 4:00 P.M.), DNA, RG 107, Telegrams Collected (Bound); *ibid.*, RG 108, Telegrams Received; copy, DLC-USG, V, 55.

1. Joshua Hill, born in S. C. in 1812, served as U.S. representative from Ga., 1857–61. He supported the Constitutional Union Party in 1860, opposed secession, and declined to participate in the war. An unsuccessful candidate for governor in 1863 and U.S. senator in 1866, Hill was elected U.S. senator in 1868.

Endorsement

Respectfully forwarded to the Secry of War. In addition to the troops reported by Bt. Maj. Gen. Emory in this city is Co. "K" 5th US Cavalry—numbering 121 effective men; Bt. Lt. Col. J. W. Mason, Commandg—which reports direct to these Hdqrs. Orders have also been given for five. Cos. of 29th US Inf., Lt. Col. Buel commanding, which will number about 300 effective men, now at Lynchburg Va., to proceed at once to this city; they are expected to arrive within two or three days.

U. S. GRANT

General

HDQRS. A. U S.

Nov. 5. '67.

ES, DLC-Andrew Johnson. Written on a letter of Nov. 5, 1867, from Bvt. Maj. Gen. William H. Emory, Washington, D. C., to Bvt. Capt. Amos Webster. "In reply to your communication of this date I have the honor to enclose herewith a Return, specifying number and distribution of troops serving in this Department, with the name of the Commanding Officer of each post." LS, *ibid.* The enclosure is *ibid.* See endorsement to Andrew Johnson, Nov. 1, 1867.

On Oct. 22, Emory had written to USG. "From information in my possession, I am induced to believe that unless the Goverment of the united states interposes, a collision between the White poeple and negroes in the city of Baltimore is inevitable which in my opinion will result in the Massacre of a number of the latter race   For some time past, political causes have been operating to bring about this state of things, but more recently the antagonism of parties seems to be assuming more the appearance of a conflict of races, and altho hard to believe I think it is beyond a doubt that there are active persons in each political party who believe their party is to be benefitted by the conflict and are to that extent anxious to precipitate it. One party believes that by the collision in Baltimore the negro race which can be easily crushed in that city if unassisted, will be forever put out of the pale of competition with the white man in Maryland, both in the field of labour and in politics. The other believes that even should the result be disastrous to the negro population in Baltimore it will rouse the North to come to the rescue and recover Maryland from the government of its present rulers. In fact there is every indication that unless some step is taken we are likely to have the occurrence of riots similar to those which took place last summer in New Orleans. I think therefore it is now time, respectfully to recommend that one or two full Regmts of Infantry and a battery of Horse Artillery shall be at once ordered to take post in the vicinity of Baltimore   If they cannot be spared from the Regular Army I recommend that one or two Volunteer Regmts of Infty from Maryland to be selected by the Governmt of the U. S. be mustered into service   I think it proper to state in this connection my belief that there is at present no disposition on the part of either side to place themselves in conflict with the authority of the United States" ALS, USG 3. For an undated draft of this letter, see *PUSG*, 16, 562–63.

On Oct. 29, Bvt. Maj. Gen. John M. Schofield, Richmond, wrote to USG. "I have ordered Lieut. Col. Buell, of the 29th Infantry, with five companies of his Regiment to go to Washington and report to the Commanding officer of that Department for assignment to Winter quarters. I have thought it best to retain Genl Wilcox, with two Companies of his Regiment, for the reasons that I can not well supply his place as Sub-District Commander, that it does not seem prudent to further diminish my force until the State is more quiet, and that I have quarters enough for all that now remain. Please inform me if this arrangement is *not* satisfactory. I will assume that it is so if I do not hear to the contrary." ALS, DNA, RG 108, Letters Received. USG endorsed this letter. "Notify Gn. Emory of the expected arrival of five comps." AE (initialed and undated), *ibid.* On Nov. 4, 2:40 P.M., USG telegraphed to Schofield. "Order the five companies here without delaying for completion of quarters." ALS (telegram sent), *ibid.*, RG 107, Telegrams Collected (Bound); telegram sent, *ibid.*; telegram received, *ibid.*, RG 393, 1st Military District, Telegrams Received. On Nov. 5, USG wrote to the AG. "Direct Gn. Emory to call on Gn. McFerran for tents to quarter 5 Comps. of Inf.y, and officers and to have them put up ready to receive the troops on arrival." AL (initialed), *ibid.*, RG 94, Letters Received, 619A 1867.

On Nov. 7, 10:30 A.M., USG telegraphed to Bvt. Maj. Gen. Edward R. S. Canby, Charleston. "Can you spare the two companies 29th? If so order them to Washington." ALS (telegram sent), *ibid.*, RG 107, Telegrams Collected (Bound); telegram sent, *ibid.*; telegram received (at 12:30 P.M.), *ibid.*, RG 393, 2nd Military District, Letters Received. On the same day, Canby telegraphed to USG. "The order for the movement of the companies will be given at once" LS (telegram sent), *ibid.*, RG 107, Telegrams Collected (Unbound); telegram received (at 2:20 P.M.), *ibid.*, Telegrams Collected (Bound); *ibid.*, RG 108, Telegrams Received. On Nov. 13, Canby telegraphed to Bvt. Maj. Gen. John A. Rawlins. "Under instructions from your office of seventh instant—two companies twenty-ninth Infantry left Florence, S. C., ~~today~~ at three o'clock this P. M. for Washington" Telegram sent, *ibid.*, RG 107, Telegrams Collected (Unbound); telegram received (at 9:00 A.M.), *ibid.*, Telegrams Collected (Bound); *ibid.*, RG 108, Telegrams Received.

To William Elrod

———

Nov. 14th *1867*.

DEAR ELROD,

I enclose you power of Atty. to act for me in all matters except in the sale of real estate. You can get from Sappington all the not[e]s he holds in my favor and collect the money as it falls due. You can also get from him a statement of the land I still own in Jefferson County and pay the taxes on it annually,

In one of your letter you speak of having written to me what you propose to do with the house you now live in? If I got such a letter I do not recollect it. I think the best thing to do is to lock the house up and cultivate the ground and market the fruit yourself. If you think any other course better write to me again and I then will judge.

I was aware that a new road had been made up Gravois Creek but supposed it to be far enough from the bank to admit of a fence between the road and the creek. If this is not the case, and you propose to build the fence I spoke of, I would put the plank fence North of the road and take the rails from there to the South side of the creek. I will not have a barn built until I go out and locate it and give the plans. I want a good one and with accomodations for quite a number of horses and other stock. I do not expect to go largely into horned stock but I do hope to raise a number of fine colts each year. As I told you I have here some fine mares, with foal, that I expect to send out. I will try to be out early in the Spring if not earlyer and start every thing. You will have to have another wagon, if not two of them, and at least three more work horses. Two of these latter I have, much better than any you now have. They cost $800 00 and are about seventeen hands high. All these, with harness, I will get when I go out. I have no old harness to send you but may be able to get it. I will probably send you a box containing some things by express in the course of a week or two. If I do you will find them with Mr. Ford, United States Ex. Co.

U. S. GRANT

ALS, Dorothy Elrod, Marissa, Ill.

To Lt. Gen. William T. Sherman

———

Nov. 21st *1867.*

MY DEAR GENERAL,

I congratulate you on your speach to the society of the Army of the Tenn.[1] I read it with great pleasure and defy any of our Statesmen to beat that portion of it which touches upon the condition of our country and our duties as a citizen. When I read that part of your spech which said that Western emigration would after a while turn South &c. I smiled at the coincident of having made the same remark, though in different language, after the paper was brought containing your speach but before I had opened it. Mr. Dent in his usual rebel style was predicting all sorts of disasters to the Country and that in the next fight a Million of men would go from the North to help the South. I told him I thought so, but they would go with brain in their heads, money in their pockets, ~~and~~ strength and energy in their limbs, and would make the South bloom like the rose untill the old inhabitants would wonder why they had not done so before. You will find that you will not be assailed on that speech. Some extreeme men might take issue with you for even hinting that it was possible that some portion of blame might be attached to the North for the begining of our troubles. But if they do it will be a class of men whos enmity is always more desirable than their friendship.

I see you are not to be here untill the first week in December; and want then to get back to St. Louis as soon as you can. I think there will be such a condition of affairs here that Mr. Johnson will not insist on your remaining. But I have not given up the idea of getting away from here for a couple of months during the Winter. If I go you will have to take my place.

Please present my respects to Mrs Sherman and the children.

Yours Truly,

U. S. GRANT

To LT. GN. W. T. SHERMAN,
U. S. ARMY,

ALS, PHi. On Oct. 29, 1867, Lt. Gen. William T. Sherman, St. Louis, wrote to Bvt. Maj. Gen. John A. Rawlins. "I am very anxious to be at the meeting of the Army of the Tennessee here on the 13 & 14 of November, next, as you know. If General Grant and the President are willing, I can get Genl Augur to go on under his present orders to represent me at the Indian Councils at North Platte & Laramie, and after our meeting here, I can go up and join them in time to take part in what I consider the most important part of this business viz, the final Consultations and Report to Congress. I already know all that can transpire at North Platte & Laramie through our Military Reports, so that I will feel as able to act in the final recommendations to Congress as if present at Laramie, for we had already agreed substantially on the true policy as to the Northern Indians in our August & September Conferences. Please see General Grant & the President & telegraph me substantially the result that I may be prepared to act when the Commissioners come here. I have a despatch from Comr Taylor in which he advises me that they will leave Medicine Lodge on the 27th inst—They ought to reach here by Friday Novr 1. & must then proceed via Chicago to Omaha so as to reach North Platte & Laramie as soon after the times fixed for these Councils as possible. I should know by Friday or Saturday at furthest." ALS, DNA, RG 108, Letters Received. On Nov. 1, 2:45 P.M., USG telegraphed to Sherman. "The President authorizes you to delay joining the Indian Commission as suggested in your letter to Gen Rawlins dated Oct. 29th /67—" Telegrams sent (2), *ibid.*, RG 107, Telegrams Collected (Bound); copies, *ibid.*, RG 108, Telegrams Sent; DLC-USG, V, 56. On Nov. 2, Sherman telegraphed to USG. "Dispatch received. I will go with the Indian Peace Commission tomorrow via Chicago and Omaha as far as Cheyenne, but will return here by November thirteenth—(13th)—Tell General Rawlins" Telegram received (at 11:10 A.M.), DNA, RG 107, Telegrams Collected (Bound); *ibid.*, RG 108, Telegrams Received; copy, DLC-USG, V, 55.

On Nov. 9, Saturday, Bvt. Maj. Gen. William A. Nichols, St. Louis, telegraphed to USG. "I have just received the following dispatch from Lieut Genl Sherman   Hillsdale Colorado   June 8th 1867   Commissioners started for Laramie today,   All well   Road done to within five (5) miles of Cheyenne,   Very few Indians at Laramie,   No Treaty will probably be made till Spring. I start now for St Louis & will reach there on wednesday next if possible   Report this to General Grant" Telegram received (at 2:30 P.M.), DNA, RG 107, Telegrams Collected (Bound). On Nov. 14, 3:20 P.M., USG telegraphed to Lt. Col. Lewis M. Dayton. "I regret my inability to be with the Society of the Army of the Tenn. at the banquet this evening, but hope to be more fortunate ~~at~~ on the occasion of ~~your~~ its next meeting. I wish you a happy reunion and know that it will prove a harmonious one." ALS (telegram sent), *ibid.*; telegram sent, *ibid.*

1. For text, see *New York Times*, Nov. 17, 1867.

To Joseph W. McClurg

Washington City, Nov 27th 1867

HON. J. W. MCCLURG,
CHAIRMAN OF SELECT COMMITTEE ON SOUTHERN RAILROADS
HOUSE OF REPRESENTATIVES
SIR:

In reply to your letter of the 11th inst. requesting that the Committee on Southern Railroads be furnished with a statement of the amount paid by each of the *Railroads* in the States lately in rebel-

lion on their indebtedness to the U S. Government, in cash or otherwise, with dates of payments, so as to show the balance due upon
their bonds up to as recent a date as information in possession of
the Department will admit, I have the honor to enclose, herewith,
a statement of the indebtedness of the respective Railroads on Nov.
1st 1867, from which it appears that the total appraised value of
the property sold was $7.456.396.39/100   The total payments to
Nov. 1st 1867 were $3.459.344 29/100 as follows:—

By cash $2.169.546.48

By transportation of Govt. troops &
   and supplies   708.569.42

By Mail service   581.228.39

The payments were made at various dates between Nov. 30th
1865 and Nov. 1st 1867—and the total balance due the U. S. Nov.
1st 1867 including interest, was $4.884.500 62/100

> Very respectfully, Your obedient servant.
>
> U. S. GRANT
>
> Secy of War ad int.

Copies, DNA, RG 92, Consolidated Correspondence, Southern Railroads; *ibid.*,
RG 107, Reports to Congress. See *HRC*, 40-2-3. On Nov. 11, 1867, U.S. Representative Joseph W. McClurg of Mo., chairman, Select Committee on Southern
Railroads, had written to USG. "I have the honor to state that I am instructed by
the Committee on Southern Railroads to request that you will furnish the Committee a Statement of the Amount paid by each of the Railroads, in the States
lately in rebellion, on their indebtedness, to the United States Government, and
whether in Cash or otherwise, with dates of payments; so as to show the balance
due, if any, upon their bonds, up to as recent a date as information in your possession will enable you." ALS, DNA, RG 92, Consolidated Correspondence,
Southern Railroads. On Nov. 26, Bvt. Maj. Gen. Daniel H. Rucker, act. q. m.
gen., wrote to USG enclosing a report on the indebtedness of southern railroad
cos. LS, *ibid.*
    On Aug. 21, Bvt. Maj. Gen. Edmund Schriver, inspector gen., had tele-
graphed to Bvt. Col. Samuel R. Hamill. "The Acting Secy of War directs that
you suspend for a reasonable time the taking possession of the East Tennessee &
Virginia Rail Road for failure to pay its indebtedness to the U. S & report by
mail in the case" ALS (telegram sent), *ibid.*, RG 107, Telegrams Collected
(Bound); copy, *ibid.*, Letters Sent. On Sept. 20, Governor William G. Brownlow
of Tenn., Knoxville, wrote to USG. "This note will be handed to you by John R.
Branner, President of the Tennessee & Virginia Railroad, who visits you on the
business of the Road. You can confide in any statments that he may make—he
will state facts as they are, and so will President Calloway, of the Road below
here. These two Roads are owned by the State, and by loyal Stockholders, for the
most part, and ought not to stand on a footing with the *Rebel* Roads of Middle

and West Tennessee. I could and would say much more on behalf of these two Roads, but I expect to see you in person the coming winter." ALS, *ibid.*, Letters Received, T149 1867. On the same day, U.S. Representative Horace Maynard of Tenn., Knoxville, wrote to USG. "John R. Branner Esq. is the President of the East Tennessee & Virginia Rail Road & goes to Washington in its behalf to urge payment for property of the Road furnished to the Government during the War— The subject underwent some examination last winter by a Committee of the House of Representatives, whose Report is printed, & constitutes 'Report No. 34. 2nd Session 39th Congress' May I invite your attention to the testimony of L. S. Trowbridge p 21, of J. B. Hoxie p. 36, of P. Dickinson p 44, of John Williams p. 52, & Mr. Secretary Stanton p. 266. I hope this matter will receive an attentive & favorable consideration." ALS, *ibid.*, M496 1867. On Sept. 23, Schriver wrote to Rucker. "It is within the personal knowledge of the Sec'y. of War, ad int. that the *East Tennessee and Virginia R. R.* passes through a thoroughly loyal part of Tenn., is owned by loyal people and was during the war, through the agency of loyal directors, made most useful to the U. S. Govmt. He therefore regards it in different light now from many other R. R. Cos whose Roads &c became the property of the Govm't. by conquest. He is disposed to treat this Co. with more consideration and for this purpose directs that the accompanying accounts for property taken and used by the U. S. be examined with a view to a report as to the value of of the articles therein enumerated, and any other information which it is desirable for the Sec'y. of War to know. The question as to the propriety of their being allowed as an offset to the debts due the U. S. from the Company need not be entertained by you. The papers will be returned." Copy, *ibid.*, Letters Sent to the President. On Sept. 30, Rucker wrote to USG. "I have the honor to return herewith the papers in the claim of the East Tennessee and Virginia Railroad Company. This claim is for Railway-track, Bridges, Depot-buildings, Water-tanks, Locomotive-Engines and Cars destroyed while in the possession of the Company: for Engines, Cars and other property surrendered to the United States; and for the use of Engines & Cars while in the possession of the United States. . . ." LS, *ibid.*, RG 92, Reports to the Secretary of War (Press). On Oct. 12, Rucker wrote to USG enclosing Hamill's report concerning the questionable loyalty of John R. Branner, president, East Tennessee and Virginia Railroad Co. LS, *ibid.* See *HED*, 40-2-73.

On Oct. 19, Rucker wrote to USG. "I have the honor to return herewith the letter of Thos. H. Calaway, President East Tennessee and Georgia Railroad, dated September 28th 1867, complaining of the delay in settlement of the accounts of that Company for mail service, and suggesting that all payments be made through the office of Bvt Col. S. R. Hamill, A. Q. M., Louisville, Ky. . . . The rule of this Department is to credit the indebted Railroads with the amount found due for transportation services other than mail, from the date of the receipt of those accounts in this office, thus saving the Railroad Companies harmless from loss of interest during the period necessary for the examination and adjustment of their accounts. It is therefore recommended that no change be made in the manner of settling the accounts of indebted Railroads, either for postal or other transportation services for the Government, but that the present method be adhered to." LS, DNA, RG 92, Reports to the Secretary of War (Press).

On Oct. 28, Brownlow wrote to USG. "The State of Tennessee has a lien under the laws of the State on all the rail roads in Tennessee for the paymt of the interest on the state bonds issued to the roads, and for the redemption of the bonds so issued. Most of the roads were either destroyed or materially damaged during the rebellion, and when the present State government took charge of affairs, a large amount of interest on the bonds had accumulated and was due the State, and the roads were prostrated, and unable either to resume operations or pay the accumulated and accruing interest on the bonds. The Legislature under my recommendation promptly aided the roads by the issuance of additional State bonds, which enabled all of them to resume operations. The success which has attended these Enterprises has demonstrated the wisdom of the policy pursued by the Legislature, for in a short time it is beleived the roads will be enabled to pay the entire amount of interest due the State. *Just at this juncture in our affairs* it would be seriously detrimental to the Credit of the State if the Government of the United States should seize the machinery &c of the roads in Tennessee on which the United States has a lien, for it would prevent the roads from paying the interest due the State on the 1st Jany proxo and tend greatly to paralize our Efforts in Tennessee to carry on the State government successfully. I learn from a communication shown me, that ~~it~~ there has been referred to you recently the question of the propriety of taking charge for the United States, of the Nashville & Northwestern Rail Road. I trust this will not be done, at least until the Committee appointed by Congress, to look into the Condition of the Rail Roads on which the United States has a lien for rolling Stock have examined into the matter as to the Tennessee roads, and until the merits of the matter as to the particular road I have named is looked into." LS, *ibid.*, RG 94, Letters Received, 334T 1867. On Nov. 1, 2:10 P.M., Schriver telegraphed to Maj. Gen. George H. Thomas, Louisville. "The Secretary of War directs that you suspend action against all the Rail Road companies in Tennessee for non-payment of indebtedness to the United States until the examination into their affairs ~~shall be~~ by the Congressional Committee shall have taken place & until further orders from this Department." ADfS, *ibid.*; ALS (telegram sent), *ibid.*, RG 107, Telegrams Collected (Bound); copy, *ibid.*, Letters Sent.

On Dec. 13, Rucker wrote to USG. "I have the honor to transmit herewith a communication from Geo. H. Hazlehurst, President of the Macon & Brunswick Rail Road Company, dated Nov. 16 1867, addressed to Bt. Col. S. R. Hamill, a. q. m., in which he proposes to pay the indebtedness of that Company by installments of $1000. per month, with interest, said payments to commence on the 1st of January 1868. . . . Mr. Hazlehurst to be informed that any failure on the part of the Macon and Brunswick R. R. Co., to comply with the terms of payment proposcd by him in his letter to Col. Hamill of the 16th. ulto. and now recommended, will result in the immediate enforcement of the provisions of the bond, and the sale of the Company's property, as therein provided." LS, *ibid.*, RG 92, Reports to the Secretary of War (Press).

On Dec. 21, Rucker wrote to USG. "I have the honor to return herewith the report of Bt Col. S. R. Hamill, a. q. m. relative to the indebtedness of Southern Rail Roads for R. R. property purchased of the United States. . . ." LS, *ibid.* On Jan. 4, 1868, USG wrote to Speaker of the House Schuyler Colfax. "I have the honor to send, for the information of the Select Committee on Southern *RailRoads*, a report made to this Department by the officer of the Quartermasters Department, who, under the orders of Major General G. H. Thomas, has had charge of the subject of the indebtedness to the US. of some of the Rail Road Companies in the Southern States." Df, *ibid.*, RG 94, Letters Received, 993C 1867; copy, *ibid.*, RG 107, Reports to Congress. Printed as *HED*, 40-2-73.

On Oct. 16, 1867, McClurg wrote to USG inquiring about land grants to

Southern railroads. LS, DNA, RG 92, Consolidated Correspondence, Southern Railroads. On Jan. 13, 1868, Rucker wrote to USG reporting at length on the subject. LS, *ibid.*, Reports to the Secretary of War (Press). Printed in *HED*, 40-2-101.

To Maj. Gen. Winfield S. Hancock

Washington Nov. 29th *1867*. [*9:30* A.M.]

MAJ. GN. W. S. HANCOCK,
NEW ORLEANS, LA.

You are authorized to revoke or sustain all orders for the removal and appointment of civil officers in your district since the 10th of Nov. I direct however the removal of Judge Cutler[1] either by revocation of the order appointing him or by other selection as you deem proper. ~~Report~~ In the case of Sherriff removed by Gn. Mower report to me your recommendation ~~in the~~ whether his order should be sustained.

U. S. GRANT
General,

ALS (telegram sent), DNA, RG 107, Telegrams Collected (Bound); telegram sent, *ibid.*; telegram received (at 9:30 A.M.), *ibid.*, RG 393, 5th Military District, Telegrams Received. See telegram to Bvt. Maj. Gen. Joseph A. Mower, Nov. 2, 1867.

On Nov. 29, 1867, Maj. Gen. Winfield S. Hancock telegraphed to USG. "I have assumed Command, Back to what date did you intend to suspend the order of Gen Mower removing Officers By your telegram of the twenty second (22) inst Your dispatch says 'Your' his' last orders" Telegram received (on Nov. 30, 8:40 A.M.), DNA, RG 107, Telegrams Collected (Bound); *ibid.*, RG 108, Telegrams Received; copy, DLC-USG, V, 55.

On Nov. 26, Governor Benjamin F. Flanders of La., New Orleans, had written to USG. "On the 22d inst, I had the honor to send you the following despatch viz. 'Some of the removals of Civil officers by Gen'l Mower were inexpedient and his appointments in many cases, most objectionable. I think the removals and appointments since the 10th should be disapproved by you until they can have the consideration of Gen'l Hancock, who is hourly expected.' I now enclose a copy of special orders issued by Gen'l Mower, bearing date the 23d, in compliance it is presumed, with instructions from you. The order does not however include two of his most obnoxious appointees. I refer to R King Cutler appointed Judge of Court, to fill a vacancy and R L Shelly to be clerk of the Probate Court, in place of incumbent removed. These appointments are regarded by the community, and I think justly, as an affront to their moral sense and intelligence. Cutler formerly resided in Massac County Illinois. He was there indicted for burglary, fled from justice, forfeiting his bonds. His career in this State has not mended his reputation. He was an original Secessionist—he made inflammatory speeches in support of the rebellion and raised a confederate military Company, which bore the name of the 'King Cutler Guards.' When the overthrow of the rebellion seemed assured, he Cutler set himself up as an original Union man and claimed to have been loyal throughout the war. With this pretense and by the art of a demagouge, he got elected to the Convention in 1864, and subsequently by a Legislature composed largely of police officers, and men like him, was elected to Congress. In spite of his rebel record, he deliberately takes an oath, in order to qualify as Judge, that he has never given Voluntary aid or support to the rebellion. In view of the more serious objections to his moral Character, it is scarcely necessary to urge his deficiency of legal qualifications for the position of Judge. This is so notorious, that his elevation to the bench is regarded by the members of the bar as a slur on their profession. Shelly came to this city as reporter for a New York paper. He was ordered out of the department by Gen'l Canby, for what offense I do not know, but the fact that it was done by Gen'l Canby affords assurance that it was not without adequate cause. Shellys character may be inferred from the fact, that his domicil is a public house of prostitution. I do not deem it necessary to go into detail as regards the character of the appointees of Genl Mower which have been suspended. The sweeping removals of State officers were inexpedient and a majority of the persons selected by him to take their places, had no recommendations, either as regards competency or loyalty. Like Cutler, the most of them would have to forswear themselves in order to qualify. Gen'l Hancock, who has been detained by low water will probably reach here to morrow. His presence is much needed, and I trust, that under his administration the work of reconstruction will be pushed forward to completion." LS, DNA, RG 108, Letters Received.

On Dec. 2, R. King Cutler, New Orleans, telegraphed to USG. "Gen Hancock revoked order appointing me Judge to fill vacancy. Is this Law or right Must I submit or not?" Telegram received (on Dec. 3, 9:00 A.M.), *ibid*., RG 393, 5th Military District, Telegrams Received. On Dec. 3, USG endorsed this telegram. "This despatch has just been rec'd but no reply has been made to it nor will there be. Cutler may think however your order revoking the order appointing him a violation of orders issued by me soon after your assignment to the command of the 5th Military Dist. If you desire to correct this impression you can do so by furnishing him an extract from my dispatch of the 30th of Nov." AES, *ibid*. On Dec. 9, Hancock wrote to USG. "Your endorsement upon the dispatch of R. King Cutler, has been received. When I see him, if that occurs, I will inform him that his removal was by your order. However, since the receipt of your dispatch, I read your original order to Govr Flanders—supposing in that way at least he would know in time, the basis of my action. I understand the point, and had I thought of it at the time of issuing my order, the reasons would have been expressed. I believed however, that you did not desire rule invoked, and I was ready to assume the responsibility. I fully recognize your orders without questioning them further than to know the fact, and shall always be pleased to have your orders or advice. . . . P. S. Judge Cazabat declined the Judgeship vacated by Cutler—because he could not take the oath. The laws make it necessary that he should." ALS, USG 3.

On Dec. 2, Hancock had telegraphed to USG. "Yesterday I wrote a letter to you requesting that as soon as Genl Buchanan should arrive in this District, he should be placed on duty with his Brevet rank with a view of relieving General Mower as Comd'r. of the District of Louisiana. I also suggested in my letter if Genl Buchanan was not approved or available the name of Genl L. P Graham as a suitable officer to relieve General Mower if he was ordered here; On account of Genl Mower's usefulness being impaired here as a means of reconstruction I think it would be well to relieve him as soon as possible. If he is made relieved as Commander of the District it would be well to detail another officer as Assistant Commissioner B. R. F and A. L. State of Louisiana." LS (telegram sent), DNA, RG 107, Telegrams Collected (Bound); telegram received (on Dec. 3, 10:00 A.M.), *ibid.*; *ibid.*, RG 108, Telegrams Received. On Dec. 3, 11:30 A.M., USG telegraphed to Hancock. "Your telegram received. General Buchanan is ordered to report to you without delay to relieve General Mower in command of the Sub. District of Louisiana, and as assistant commissioner Freedmen Bureau. You can if you deem best order the next officer in rank to Genl Mower to relieve him until Buchanan arrives. He has asked General Howard to have him relieved immediately." LS (telegram sent), *ibid.*, RG 107, Telegrams Collected (Bound); telegram sent, *ibid.*; telegram received, *ibid.*, RG 393, 5th Military District, Telegrams Received. On Dec. 3, Hancock wrote to USG. "Your dispatch in reference to the removals and appointments made by General Mower, was received yesterday, and will be attended to. It will take time, however, before I can be satisfied in all cases. I have called upon General Mower for the reasons and evidence which governed him in said removals, and also for the evidence of fitness of character in his appointments. The cases will be taken up individually, and so acted upon. In the cases of one or two appointments, at least, there is scarcely, I imagine, a doubt but that prompt action should be taken. I shall be as careful as possible to have men of high character selected, and those who are as far as possible free from objection. I am inclined to believe, from what I hear, that, as a general rule, General Mower's appointments were not of the best. I think his conduct was indelicate to me, for I wrote to him from St. Louis that I would start to New Orleans on the 15th, and would be there about the 24th, and it does not appear that there were any especial reasons for the greater portion of his removals, which did not exist when General Sheridan was here, as well as prior to the action of General Mower during his own administration, and which could have been deferred until my arrival. I believe it will be found that General Mower's action has been, at least, injudicious, and that his usefulness as a means of reconstruction, is seriously impaired. As soon as General Buchanan arrives in this District I shall request that he be placed on duty according to his brevet rank, with the view to relieving General Mower from duty as Commander of the District of Louisiana. I believe General Buchanan ranks General Mower both by lineal and brevet rank, and therefore is an appropriate officer to relieve him. Or General L. P. Graham, 4th U. S. Cavalry, would be a suitable officer for the Command of the District of Louisiana, in case he is ordered to this District." LS, *ibid.*, RG 108, Letters Received.

On Dec. 4, Hancock wrote to USG. "I desire to know if, in appointing municipal officers to fill vacancies, I am absolutely restricted to those who can take the oath prescribed by the Act of Congress approved July 2d 1862, and published in General Orders No 80, from the War Department, A. G. O., July 16th 1862—The municipal offices of the city, especially, are in a lamentable condition.

Many of the best men, having the interests of the city at heart, are, I believe, inclined to cooperate with me in restoring its affairs, but if I am restricted in this matter to those who can take the oath indicated, it will be impossible, I believe, to find a sufficient number of the best persons, otherwise good men, whose services can be relied on. The poor here are the sufferers. Earnest and pressing demands are made for relief. The great difficulty is in the mode. It would be folly in me, I believe, to enter into details—assuming to the military the responsibility of any failure in regulating the currency by arbitrary orders affecting it in details. I know of no better remedy, at present, than in filling the councils with the best men of the city, and yet those who have no disloyal sentiments. This matter of the currency, in New Orleans, is of the last importance, and my attention to it has been demanded from all sources,—from the Governor, the mayor and city councils and the public. Before action, I desire information, and an early reply is requested." LS, *ibid*. On Dec. 11, Hancock wrote to USG. "In connection with my letter of Dec 4th, I desire to state that in making appointments I have been entirely guided by the provisions of section 9 of the Supplementary Reconstruction Act, and have selected only such men as have been represented to me as able to take the oath prescribed by Act of Congress, approved July 2nd 1862. This appears to me to be the only proper interpretation of the section referred to. In my letter of the 4th inst I omitted to state that such had been my course of action. It is however true that in restricting my appointments to those able to take this oath, I exclude some of the very best men, who by experience and ability are in many instances particularly qualified for certain positions, which it becomes my duty to fill. I shall however continue to require all persons appointed by me to civil offices in this District to take the oath referred to, until and unless I hear from you that a proper interpretation of the Supplementary Reconstruction Act, would permit me to depart from my view in exceptional cases, as referred to in my previous letter on this subject." LS, *ibid*.

On Dec. 22, Charles Deléry, New Orleans, wrote to USG. "I feel warrented by late events to recur to you in a matter, which personally important to me, should not intrude on the time of a public officer, already absorbed in higher concerns; were I not convinced that no claim of justice can come before you without its duu share of attention   In order to save time, therefore, I shall endeavor to be as brief as the necessities of my statement comport. By order of Genl. Mower, No 192, I was on the 21st of November ultimo, removed from my elected office of Coroner of the Parish of Orleans on the ground that, I am an 'impediment to reconstruction.' On the following day, Nov 22d 1867 an order issued at Washington City, suspended the execution of Gen. Mower's order of the 21st of the same month. What was the nature of charges, brought forward against me, under cover of misrepresentations—of slanders—, it may be, I have never been able to compass. Equally uninformed am I, to the present day, of the nature of any pretended proof, that may have swayed the constituted authorities in the Fifth Military District, to proceed to these extremities, which now affect my standing as a law abiding Citizen, and I trust, a not unhonored Officer of the City of New Orleans. I reiterate, General, that the nature of my offence—could I have offended in the discharge of my duty, is utterly uncommunicated to me; and that the proof of the offence—if there can be proof of that which does not exist—has not been intimated to me. Secret charges, General, coming from secret, or interested accusers, have heretofore belonged to the darkest ages of despotism. In ours they can exert no influence with men, whose record is one of justice &

integrity. And yet so strong seems to be the charge which may have been against me, that the General now commanding this Military District, has not considered himself at liberty to recede from the Order of General Mower, prescribing my removal from the office of Coroner. An office, to which I hold it to be some measure of self-gratification, to have been elected by a community, now disposed, within every concession, that honorable men are not only ready to make, but which they do actually proffer to pacify the asperities of the past and smooth the way to a better future. In addressing you, General, I am not moved merely by my own sense of your appreciation of what is right; but I am also encouraged by a courteous suggestion of the General, who now so worthily commands our Military District, to come before you with the statement, which I have the honor to enclose to you through the proper channels. That suggestion, General, from an Officer of the Federal Government, who has won over many a reluctance and prepared more than one way to the end, to which we all look, in sincerity and hope, I freely submit to one, who deservedly holds so high a place, in the general esteem of fellow citizens North & South. To you, therefore, I most respectfully commend these hasty considerations, with the trust that a public officer conscious of no wrong, and unattainted by any substantial dereliction of duty, shall not be condemned on what may prove to be erroneous impressions, or malicious information. Especially so, on the mere denunciation, it may be; of some secret enemy should not an American Citizen, a tried officer who has, to the best of his fidelity, discharged his duties, even to the satisfaction of political adversaries, be so condemned as to bear, hereafter, a mark of public reproval. Enclosed, General, I have the honor to transmit to you, signatures of some of our most respectable citizens, who have known me for now long years, accompanied by the assurances of the very great respect, . . ." Copy, *ibid*.

On Dec. 23, Hancock wrote to USG. "In reply to your telegram of November 29th, requesting me to report to you my recommendation as to whether General Mower's order removing Sheriff Hays should be sustained or not, I have the honor to state after mature investigation of the matter, that notwithstanding Mr Hays antecedents during the late war, I am of the opinion that there was no evidence against him which should have warranted his removal as an obstruction to the Reconstruction Acts, at the time he was displaced. From all I have been able to learn on this subject, Mr Hays gave entire satisfaction in his office to the great mass of the people here, and was an active and efficient officer in the discharge of his duties. He was the choice of the people for that office by election, and from my present knowledge, I certainly would not have removed him. There was no objection made against him as far as I can learn by General Sheridan while he was in command of this District, nor by General Mower, until he issued the order displacing him; nor do I now know of any allegations against him which did not then exist. I am of the opinion that with proper guidance, Mr Hays would have been a valuable officer here at this time, and I consider that it would have been the wiser course not to have removed him. Whether it would be judicious to restore him notwithstanding the circumstances under which he was displaced and those antecedent thereto, is a question to be taken into consideration; but having been removed and his successor having acted, I would consider it as a *new* appointment to place Mr Hays now in that office, and not simply a revocation of General Mower's order; and therefore requiring him to take the oath, which I believe he cannot consistently do; and if such is a proper interpretation of the Law, Mr Hays cannot be legally appointed. The successor of Mr Hays, Dr G. W. Avery has been an Officer of the Army on the Medical staff, and I am informed has resided here since 1863. I have no evidence that he is not a proper person for the office, nevertheless I do not consider him the best selection for the Sheriffalty of a great city like New Orleans, especially in the present condition of affairs here; and as I have before stated that I do not believe the charges upon which Mr Hays was removed can be sustained under all the peculiar circumstances of the case, I would suggest that, as final action on this subject, if Mr Hays be not restored, a new appointment should be made; and with this end in view, I would suggest the name of the present Deputy Sheriff, Mr Edward S. Wurzberger, who has held his present position for eight years past, and is represented to me by many of the best citizens here as being a faithful, capable and efficient Officer, whose antecedents show him to have been obedient to the laws. I am of the opinion that he would be the most suitable selection, in case you do not think it well to restore Mr Hays, or judicious to retain Mr Avery as Sheriff. In appointing men to offices, I have felt it was necessary to be guided by the Reconstruction acts, which require that they shall take the oath. Notwithstanding this fact however, I am of the opinion that there are many conscientious men and good citizens who cannot take the Oath, and who are more subordinate to the laws than many who do. That Oath refers more particularly to what is in the past, but the usefulness of citizens here refers especially to their present status. Herewith I enclose a letter addressed to me by Mr J. Ad. Rozier, a prominent Lawer and well known Union man of this city, which about represents the spirit of other letters I have had on the same subject, and probably exhibits quite accurately the feeling of this community concerning the matter, that is, of citizens who have always been considered as Union men without being swayed by other interests." LS, *ibid.* The enclosure is *ibid.* On Dec. 30, Bvt. Maj. Gen. John A. Rawlins wrote to Hancock. "Your communication of date Dec. 1867 in reply to telegram of the General Commanding U. S. A. of date Nov. 29th 1867, relating to the removal of Sheriff Hays, is received Upon information of the removal of Sheriff Hays and appointment of Mr. Bullitt, the General Commanding, by telegram of date Nov. 2d, 1867, directed Gen. Mower to revoke the order appointing Mr. Bullitt, and suggested that unless there was a necessity for the immediate removal of Sheriff Hays, no change should be made until your arrival; of that necessity Gen. Mower was to be the judge. As the matter was determined by him in the appointment of Dr. G. W. Avery, and no evidence having been presented that Avery is not a proper person for the office, the General Commanding deems it judicious that he be retained. Your interpretation of the Reconstruction acts, that all appointees under them must take the oath, is concurred in by the General Commanding." Copies, DLC-USG, V, 47, 60; DNA, RG 108, Letters Sent. On Jan. 15, 1868, Hancock wrote to USG. "I have the honor to forward herewith for your information, copies of the following papers, relative to removals from office in the State of Louisiana, by Brevet Major General Mower: . . ." LS, *ibid.*, Letters Received. The enclosures are *ibid.*

1. R. King Cutler, born in Va., was a lawyer in Orleans and Jefferson Parishes. A former slaveholder, he was a conservative Unionist and a member of the La. constitutional conventions in 1864 and 1866. In 1864, Cutler was elected U.S. senator from La., but Congress refused to seat the La. legislators. See *PUSG*, 16, 294, 560.

Concerning Lewis Dent

———

Judge Lewis Dent now of Friar's Point, Miss. is an applicant for the appointment of Minister to Mexico. He is a man of education, went to California with the first troops that crossed the continent during the Mexican War, settled there, was a member of the Constitutional Convention that formed the Constitution under which the State was admitted, or received, into the union. He speaks the Spanish language thoroughly, and writes it. If desirable he can come here to see the President.

U. S. GRANT
General

WASHINGTON, D, C,
NOV. 30TH 1867,

ALS, DNA, RG 59, Applications and Recommendations, Lincoln and Johnson. USG's recommendation accompanied a letter of Nov. 29, 1867, from Thomas Cottman, Washington, D. C., to President Andrew Johnson. "At a meeting of your friends in New Orleans on the 22nd instant it was decided that they recommend for the Mission to Mexico, Judge Lewis Dent and I was deputized to personally express to you their sentiments of the fitness of the Judge for the position & the hope that their recommendation might be favorably recieved" ALS, *ibid.*

To Andrew Johnson

———

[*Nov. 1867*]

SIR:

I have the honor to submit the following and accompanying, reports of the operations of the Army and Bureaux under the War Dept. since the ~~report of the Sec. of War last year.~~ last Annual report of the Sec. of War.

I assumed the duties of Sec. of War, *Ad.* int. August 12th /67 in pursuance ~~of~~ to the following instructions from the President, towit:

(Here Presidents letter of apt.)

On receipt of the above ~~the~~ I ~~addressed a note to the Sec. of War~~ notified the Sec. of War, ~~firs verbal of the~~ it, first verbally, and then, at his suggestion, by letter of which the following is a copy.

(Letter)

To the this the Sec. of War made this reply.

(Letter of Sec.)

Immediately after this ~~chan~~ exchange of notes I commenced upon the duties of the office assigned to me, in addition to the duties of General of the Army. A long War had entailed upon the Army practices of extravigance totally unjustifyable in times of peace, and as the increase of the ~~Arm~~ Regular Army since 1860, (now almost the entire Army) is officered by men whos Army experience does not go back of that period, (and therefore ~~do~~ they may not know but their indulgences at the expense of the general Government are all legitimate) retrenchment was the first subject to attract my attention. During the ~~War~~ Rebellion Ambulances and mounted orderlies at every Hd Qrs. down as low as Brigade Hd Qrs. certainly, had come into use; and since the ~~War~~ rebellion they have been continued, if not at every post of a single company, at least generally throughout the Army. A discontinuance of this evil is necessary both to the discipline and efficiency of the Army and to the relief of the Treasury. Orders were given both for breaking it up and seeing to its execution.

The Bureau of Rebel Archives was transfered ~~was transfered~~ to the Adj. Gen's Department, as was also the Bureau for the Exchange of Prisoners &c. thus relieving from ~~em~~Government employment ~~the~~ a large number of Clerks and several Officers who had, to that, date been continued in service.

Supplying large Armies for a period of Four years of hostilities necessarily led to an accumulations of stores of all sorts far beyond the wants of our present establishment for many years ~~of peace.~~ to come. These stores being borne on the returns of officers accountable for them they had to be stored and guarded though the cost of care, per annum, might be greater than the value of the article. Under my direction all surplus ~~stores~~ and useless stores in the Qr. Mrs. Dept. are being sold and the balance distributed for issue to troops as they may be wanted. This releases a large amount of

store houses for which rent is being paid, and also discharging̶e̶s a
large number of civil employees of Govt.

During the last Summer and Summer before I h̶a̶v̶e̶ caused inspections to be made of the various routes of travel and supply
through the territory between the Missouri River and the Pacific
Coast. The cost of maintaining troops in that section is so inormous
that I desired, if possible, to reduce them. Some benefit has been
derived, in the way desired, from these inspections, but for the
present the Military establishment between the lines designated
must be maintained at a great cost per man. It is to be hoped that
the completion of the rail-roads to the Pacific will r̶e̶d̶u̶c̶e̶ almost
settle the question of Indian Hostilities. Their completion will materially reduce the cost per man o̶for supporting the Army, and will
also reduce materially the number of men to be kept b̶e̶t̶w̶e̶e̶n̶ on the
plains.

T̶h̶e̶ ̶P̶e̶a̶c̶e̶ ̶C̶o̶m̶m̶i̶s̶s̶i̶o̶n̶e̶r̶s̶ ̶n̶o̶w̶ ̶n̶e̶g̶o̶t̶i̶a̶t̶i̶n̶g̶ ̶w̶i̶t̶h̶ ̶t̶h̶e̶ ̶I̶n̶d̶i̶a̶n̶s̶ ̶o̶f̶
t̶h̶e̶ ̶P̶l̶a̶i̶n̶s̶,̶ ̶a̶c̶t̶i̶n̶g̶ ̶u̶n̶d̶e̶r̶ ̶d̶i̶r̶e̶c̶t̶ ̶a̶u̶t̶h̶o̶r̶i̶t̶y̶ ̶o̶f̶ ̶C̶o̶n̶g̶r̶e̶s̶s̶,̶ ̶a̶r̶e̶ ̶i̶n̶ ̶n̶o̶ ̶w̶a̶y̶
c̶a̶l̶l̶e̶d̶ ̶u̶p̶ ̶t̶o̶ ̶r̶e̶p̶o̶r̶t̶ ̶t̶h̶r̶o̶u̶g̶h̶ ̶t̶h̶i̶s̶ ̶D̶e̶p̶a̶r̶t̶m̶e̶n̶t̶.̶ ̶B̶u̶t̶ ̶a̶s̶ ̶t̶h̶e̶ ̶C̶o̶m̶m̶i̶s̶-̶
s̶i̶o̶n̶ ̶i̶s̶ ̶c̶o̶m̶p̶o̶s̶e̶d̶ ̶i̶n̶ ̶p̶a̶r̶t̶ ̶o̶f̶ ̶o̶f̶f̶i̶c̶e̶r̶s̶ ̶o̶f̶ ̶t̶h̶e̶ ̶A̶r̶m̶y̶,̶ ̶a̶n̶d̶ ̶a̶s̶ ̶n̶o̶ ̶o̶t̶h̶e̶r̶
D̶e̶p̶a̶r̶t̶m̶e̶n̶t̶ ̶o̶f̶ ̶t̶h̶e̶ ̶G̶o̶v̶e̶r̶m̶e̶n̶t̶ ̶i̶s̶ ̶s̶o̶ ̶d̶i̶r̶e̶c̶t̶l̶y̶ ̶i̶n̶t̶e̶r̶e̶s̶t̶e̶d̶ ̶i̶n̶ ̶a̶l̶l̶

I̶t̶ ̶i̶s̶ There is also good reason to hope that negotiations now
going on with the hostile tribes of Indians will result, if not in a
permanent peace at at least to a suspension of hostilities untill the
rail-roads h̶a̶v̶e̶ ̶b̶e̶e̶n̶ are pushed through that portion of the Indian
Territory where they can give the most trouble.

From the report of the Commissioner of the Bureau of F̶r̶e̶e̶d̶-̶
m̶e̶n̶, Refugees, Freedmen & Abandoned Lands I make the following Synopsis:

No changes have been made (Here abstract of Gn. Howards
report)
This gives but a very brief e̶x̶t̶r̶a̶c̶t̶ abstract of the report of the
Commissioner of Refugees, Freedmen & abandoned lands. Special
attention to the report itself, accompanying this, is respectfully
invited.

The report of the Adj. Gn. of the Army Shows (Here Synopsis)

~~It is believed~~ Attention is called to the great number of desertions and the necessity ~~of~~ for a change in the present system of Courts Martial and of punishment to abate the evil. It is well to remark too that in a large number of cases where punishment is awarded, to both officers and enlisted men, they find the most influential citizens ready to intercede for a remission of sentence. I would recommend an increase of Three ~~to the Adj. Gens. Dept~~ Asst. Adj. Gens. ~~to give~~ This would ~~give~~ enable the assignment of one to each of the Major Generals & Brigadier Generals of the Army and avoid the necessity of detaching officers from their legitimate duties to act. as Asst. Adj. Gns.

During the year There has been no change in the Inspector Gens. Dept. except

(Here follows synopsis of In. Gn. report. The Chief of the Bureau Justice reports that in (Insert Abstract)

The Quartermaster General submits (synopsis to be inserted)

I ~~would recom~~ respectfully recommend a repeal of that portion of the Act of Congress of (date & title of act) which requires the ~~erection of Head~~ placing of stone or Iron ~~Hd~~ Head Boards at the head of each grave. The National Cemeteries are laid out with great regularity. A plat and register of ~~the~~ each will be kept at the Qr. Mr. Generals office in Washington, and each Keeper of a Cemetry will have a plat and register of the Cemetry he has charge of. Streets and graves being numbered a reference to these will shew the visitor or friend of the ~~deceased~~ soldier exactly where to find the resting place of any deceased looked for. It is a question whether many claims for the arrears due to deceased soldiers have not been fraudulently pressed from data obtained by taking names and dates from head stones.

~~No changes have been made (Here abstract of Gn. Howards~~

The Commissary General of Subsistence reports that (Here follows synopsis of report of Comy Gn.)

The recommendation of the Commissary General for the appointment of Thirty-two Asst. Commissaries is recommended. It is absolutely necessary that there should be, and there is, an officer acting as Commissary at every post garrisoned by troops. The only bonded officers to act in such capacity are the officers of the Subsistence Department and the Regimental Quartermasters. The same bonds should be required from Asst. Commissaries as is required to be given by ~~Regimental Quartermasters~~ the latter. The additional pay would only be allowed when ~~they were performing~~ the duty of Asst. Com.y was performed and they would never perform that duty at a post of less than a full regiment where there was present either a Commissary or a Regimental Quartermaster.—I would recommend that no provision be made to carry out the law abolishing Sutlers.

From the report of the Surgeon General it will be found that (Here abstract of report)

The Paymaster General reports that

(Here synopsis.

(Here synopsis of Chief Eng'r' report)

(Synopsis of report of Chief of Ordnance)

(Here abstract from report of Signal officer)

(Inspector of Military Academy's report)

(Total estimates,)

The foregoing estimates for the approaching fiscal year are taken from the estimate of the different Bureaux Chiefs, without change or examination into the items. They may have been based upon expenditures for the current year, and, if so, will in all probability exceed the amount which will be required. A season of peace with the Indians on the plains alone will diminish materially the disbursments in the Qr. Mr. Dept. and, by justifying a reduction in the number of enlisted men to a company, also the expenditures in the Pay and Subsistence Dept. Further attention will be given to this subject hereafter.

The small regular Army sustained ~~in time of peace~~ by the United States prior to ~~the War~~ rebellion 1861, ~~in time of peace,~~ was kept well supplied with officers educated at the National Military Academy. ~~With the increase of this standing force found necessary since the rebellion, which is not likely to be materially decreased~~

~~hereafter~~, After the rebellion however it was found necessary to increase this standing force about four fold. The War ~~had~~ educated soldiers to fill well, ~~with~~ by judicious selections, this increase to the Army to start with, but not to keep up the supply. Once filled, as is the case at present, all appointments, to fill vacancies, must go in at the foot of the Army register. The time has passed, or soon will, when efficient Volunteer officers, ~~will of~~ educated in the rebellion, will accept such positions, or will be of an age making it advisable to accept them. While the Army has been so much increased no addition has been made to the number of Cadets admitted at West Point. I would now respectfully recommend an increase to the full number that can be accomodated ~~in~~ without additional ~~profs~~ buildings. The present number of Cadets is limited by the number of representatives and deligates in the lower house of Congress, and ten, *at Large*, each year, appointed by the President. Four hundred Cadets can be accomodated without increase of expense to the Goverment further than ~~their own~~ the pay to the additional number. The manner of making these appointments I would suggest should be by adding three, *at large*, additional to be appointed by the President, and by regarding a vacancy as existing in each Congressional District when the Cadet representing it enters the Second Class.

I would recommend the continuance for another year of the additional pay allowed to officers of the Army by the last Congress.

The 37 Sec. of the Act of July 28th 186~~7~~6 appropriates $20,000 00/100 for the procurement of an Equestrian Statue of Lt. Gn. Winfield Scott. It has been found that the work cannot be contracted for for less than from three to four times the appropriation, hence no contract has been entered into.

Special report will be submitted hereafter of plans and estimates that have been prepared for the erection of new War Department buildings.

By Act of Congress the ten southern states ~~that~~ which have no representation in in the National Councils has been divided into Five Military Districts, each Commanded by an officer of the Army

of not less rank than Brigadier General. The powers of these commanders are both civil and Military. So far as their Military duties
are concerned they are under the same subordination to the General
of the Army and Sec. of War that Department Commanders are.
In their Civil capacity they are entirely independent of both the
Gen. and sec. except in the ~~single~~ matter of removals, apointments
and detail ~~of offi~~ where the General of the Army has the same
powers as have District Commanders. It is but fare to the District
Commanders however to state that while they have been made thus
independent in their Civil duties there has not been one of them
who would not yeald to a positively expressed wish, in regard to
any matter of Civil administration, from either of the officers placed
over them by the Constitution ~~and~~ or Acts of Congress, so long as
that wish was in the direction of a proper execution of the law
which they, alone, were made responsible for the execution of. I am
pleased to say ~~these~~ the commanders named for the five Military
Districts have executed the difficult trust submitted to their care
faithfully and without ~~judging for them~~ byas from any judgement
of their own as to the merit or demerit of the law they were executing.

No report has yet been received from Gen. Mower, Commanding the 5th Military District, but it is expected in time to present
to Congress.

~~By direction of the President~~

The following orders of the President relieved Gns. Sheridan &
Sickles from the Command of the 5th & 2d Districts.

(Here orders)

These officers being relieved before the period for submitting
their annual reports none have been received from them. They have
however been called on recently to submit reports which may be
expected before the meeting of Congress.

The ~~balance of~~ territory of the United States not embraced in
the five military districts is divided into Military Divisions, they
subdivided into Departments, and Departments   (Here synopsis
of Dept. reports)

~~This report~~ Acting in the double capacity of Sec. of War and Gn. of the Army this report is made to embrace both.

U. S. GRANT

sec. of War ad int.

ADfS, DLC-USG, III. USG probably wrote this draft in early Nov. after receiving reports prepared by the bureau chiefs and the div., dept., and district commanders. His expanded final report was dated Nov. 1867. LS, DNA, RG 94, Letters Received, Annual Reports, 1867. *HED,* 40-2-1, II, part 1, pp. 1–30. On Nov. 20, USG wrote to President Andrew Johnson. "Enclosed I have the honor to send you Abstract of my report as Sec. of War, ad int. and General in Chief of the Army. The Summary is lengthy and touches every subject of which mention is made in the report itself." ALS, DLC-Andrew Johnson. The sixteen-page enclosure is *ibid.*

On Oct. 1, Bvt. Maj. Gen. John Pope, Atlanta, wrote to USG. "In compliance with your order, I have the honor to enclose my Report, of operations Civil, and Military, in this District, since I assumed command April. 1st 1867." LS, DNA, RG 94, Letters Received, Annual Reports, 1867. On Oct. 21, Pope telegraphed to USG. "Have you received my Official report sent you by Express on the ninth (9) of October" Telegram received (at 1:00 P.M.), *ibid.,* RG 107, Telegrams Collected (Bound); *ibid.,* RG 108, Telegrams Received; copy, DLC-USG, V, 55. At 1:45 P.M., Bvt. Brig. Gen. Frederick T. Dent telegraphed to Pope. "Your report is received" ALS (telegram sent), DNA, RG 107, Telegrams Collected (Bound); telegram sent, *ibid.*; copies, *ibid.,* RG 108, Telegrams Sent; DLC-USG, V, 56.

On Oct. 19, Col. Albert J. Myer, chief signal officer, wrote to USG. "I would like to delay my Annual Report until Nov 1st if this can be permitted—in order that I may then include the action taken in both the Army and Navy in my branch. I returned from the Naval Academy at Annapolis last night and the report cannot be complete if sent in today." ALS, DNA, RG 107, Letters Received from Bureaus. On Oct. 21, USG wrote to Myer. "You have permission to delay sending in your report as Chief of Signal Office until the time and for the purpose specified in your note of the 19th instant." Copies, *ibid.*; *ibid.,* Letters Sent to the President. On the same day, 1:10 P.M., USG telegraphed to Maj. Gen. George G. Meade, Philadelphia. "When can you forward your annual report." Telegrams sent (2), *ibid.,* Telegrams Collected (Bound); telegram received (at 2:10 P.M.), *ibid.,* RG 393, Dept. of the East, Letters Received. On Oct. 22, Meade, New York City, telegraphed to USG. "Report will be sent in on friday the twenty fifth (25th) inst   Has been delayed to complete Inspection which will be finished today" Telegram received (at 12:40 P.M.), *ibid.,* RG 107, Telegrams Collected (Bound); *ibid.,* RG 108, Telegrams Received; copy, DLC-USG, V, 55.

On Nov. 22, Bvt. Maj. Gen. Edward O. C. Ord, Holly Springs, Miss., telegraphed to USG. "Thomas B Connoy telegraphs for my Annual report saying he has your permission to publish it,   Is that so?" Telegram received (on Nov. 23, 8:20 A.M.), DNA, RG 107, Telegrams Collected (Bound); *ibid.,* RG 108, Telegrams Received; copy, DLC-USG, V, 55. On Nov. 23, 12:50 P.M., USG telegraphed to Ord. "Your report can be given to the press here." ALS (telegram sent), DNA, RG 107, Telegrams Collected (Bound); telegram sent, *ibid.*; copies, *ibid.,* RG 108, Telegrams Sent; DLC-USG, V, 56.

On Dec. 4, Secretary of State William H. Seward wrote to USG. "I shall feel obliged, if you can without inconvenience, send to me for the use of the officers of this government abroad, one hundred and fifty copies of your report to Congress." LS, DNA, RG 107, Letters Received from Bureaus.

To Hugh McCulloch

December 4th *1867*

HON. HUGH MCCULLOCH,
SEC'Y. OF THE TREASURY.
SIR,

Orders issued from this Dept. since the date at which the estimates for the Military service for the fiscal year ending June 30th 1869 were prepared and sent to the Treasury Department modify those estimates so materially, that I now transmit others to be considered in lieu of them.

Under the head of Army Proper the estimated amount required was $51,039,134.20 and is now reduced to $37,511,512.20 which is caused by suspending enlistments until the Army is brought to its authorized minimum strength, at which it is now proposed to keep it.

The letter of the Chief of Engineers herewith, explains the decrease in his estimates for "Fortifications &c", "Surveys of the Northern and North Western Lakes", and "Purchase & Repairs of Instruments" to $632,500. from $2,507,000. which sum included $2,245,000 for Fortifications &c $242,000. for surveys of Northern and North Western Lakes and $20,000. for purchase and repairs of Instruments.

His estimates for Harbor and River Improvements, for Public Buildings and Grounds and for the Washington Aqueduct are left, unchanged, to the judgment and consideration of Congress.

The estimate for Armories, Arsenals &c has been reduced from $1,533,084. to $1,093,202. and that for Signal Service from $27,000. to $15,000.

The sum of all these makes an aggregate reduction in the

Estimates for the Military service for the next fiscal year of $15, 842,004.

Very Respectfully,
Your obt. servant,
U. S. GRANT,
Sec'y. of War, ad int.

Copies, DNA, RG 46, Senate 40A–E1, Appropriations; *ibid.*, RG 203, Letters Sent by the Secretary of War to the Secretary of the Treasury. On Dec. 4, 1867, USG wrote identical letters to U.S. Senator John Sherman of Ohio, chairman, Committee on Finance, and U.S. Representative Robert C. Schenck of Ohio, chairman, Committee on Ways and Means. "I have the honor to transmit herewith for the information of your Committee, a copy of a letter from this Department to the Secretary of the Treasury, with supplemental estimates for the Military service for the fiscal year ending June 30. 1869." LS, *ibid.*, RG 46, Senate 40A–E1, Appropriations; copies, *ibid.*, RG 107, Reports to Congress; *ibid.*, RG 203, Letters Sent by the Secretary of War to the Secretary of the Treasury.

On Aug. 14, J. A. Graham, act. register, Treasury Dept., had written to USG requesting estimates of War Dept. expenses. LS, *ibid.*, RG 107, Letters Received from Bureaus. On Sept. 18, USG wrote to Secretary of the Treasury Hugh McCulloch. "I have the honor to transmit herewith my estimates for Salaries and Contingent Expenses of the War Department for the fiscal year ending 30th June 1869." Copy, *ibid.*, RG 203, Letters Sent by the Secretary of War to the Secretary of the Treasury. The enclosure is *ibid.* On Nov. 7, USG thrice wrote to McCulloch. "I have the honor to transmit herewith the estimates of this department for the military services and for public buildings and grounds, and Washington aqueduct, for the fiscal year ending June 30th, 1869. The estimates for the army proper are based upon the maximum strength of the army authorized by law. Should the Indian difficulties in the west be settled, as it is confidently expected they will be, by the treaties now being made with them, then the army will be gradually decreased to its minimum strength, and the expenditures for recruiting and for the pay and quartermaster department will be materially reduced below the amounts estimated for, probably ten millions of dollars. The amount asked for fortifications is $2.245.000. Whether that sum will be expended, if appropriated, depends upon the question, not yet determined, of changing the present system of defence to one better calculated to resist modern projectiles. The amounts estimated for rivers and harbors are only what is actually required for the improvements needed at the diferent points named; but it is not anticipated that the full amount will be given." "I have the honor to submit to you an Estimate of additional appropriations required for the service of the War Department for the present fiscal year ending 30th June 1868 This Estimate is necessitated by a deficiency arising in consequence of no appropriation having been asked for or made on account of the Quartermasters Department for the fiscal Year ending 30th June 1868, and in consequence of large expenditures growing out of the Indian disturbances on the western and north-western frontier" "I have the honor to submit to you an Estimate of additional appropriations required for the Contingencies of the office of the Chief of Engineers and Government Building Cor. of F & 17th St. for the fiscal year ending 30th June 1867 and 30th June 1868" Copies, *ibid.* The enclosures are *ibid.* See *HED*, 40-2-3, pp. 8–9, 201–50.

On Nov. 21, USG wrote to McCulloch. "I have the honor to transmit, herewith, for your information, a copy of a letter from the Paymaster Gen'l., stating that the deficiency in the appropriations for the execution of the '*Reconstruction*' laws amount to $1,152.254.12 for which an early appropriation is necessary." Copies, DNA, RG 107, Letters Sent to the President; *ibid.*, RG 203, Letters Sent by the Secretary of War to the Secretary of the Treasury. The enclosure is *ibid.* On Dec. 16, Bvt. Maj. Gen. Benjamin W. Brice, paymaster gen., wrote to USG. "I have the honor to transmit herewith a deficiency Estimate of $5000—indispensably necessary to meet the contingent expenses of this Office, during the remainder of the current fiscal year ending July 1. 1868. . . ." Copy, *ibid.*, RG 99, Letters Sent. On Dec. 20, USG wrote to McCulloch. "I have the honor to submit to you an estimate of additional appropriations required for Contingencies of the Office of the Paymaster General and for the Government Building corner of F and 15th Sts. for the present fiscal year ending 30th June 1868." LS, *ibid.*, RG 56, Letters Received. The enclosure is *ibid.*, RG 203, Letters Sent by the Secretary of War to the Secretary of the Treasury. See *HED*, 40-2-69. On Dec. 9 and 12, USG wrote to Speaker of the House Schuyler Colfax. "I have the honor to send herewith, for the consideration of the proper committee, a communication of the 6th inst. from the Paymaster General, being another estimate for funds for *Registration* purposes in the 1st military District." "I have the honor to enclose, herewith, for the consideration of the proper Committee a communication from the Paymaster General of Dec 11th reporting a necessity for the appropriation of a further sum of $50.000 for *Reconstruction* purposes in the 3d military District and invite attention to the Paymaster Generals suggestion that an appropriation of $1.400,000 be asked for to guard against possible further demands that may be made." Copies, DNA, RG 107, Reports to Congress. See *HED*, 40-2-41.

To William Coffin

————

Dec. 12th *1867.*

My Dear Sir:

Your favor of yesterday enclosing Mr. Baugh's check for $400 00/100, for rent to ~~Oct~~ Nov. 30th 1867, is received.

Yours Truly

U. S. Grant

To Mr. Wm Coffin,
Phila Pa.

If you are willing to take so much trouble for me I will leave the matter of renewing the lease of my Phila house to Mr. Baugh, or renting it to other parties, as you think best and for what you think it ought to bring. I am willing that is should be leased for three or five years from first of Jan.y or May 1868.

I regret to hear that you have had so long and severe a spell of sickness. Hope it will be succeeded by a long period of health and every other blessing. I have been wanting for several months to pay a short visit to Phila but it seems impossible for me to get away.

Please present Mrs. Grant's and my compliments to Mrs. Coffin, and daughter, and accept the same for yourself

Yours Truly,

U. S. GRANT

ALS, Free Library of Philadelphia, Philadelphia, Pa. See *PUSG*, 15, 388–89.

To Schuyler Colfax

———

Washington, D. C., Dec. 17th 1867.

HON. SCHUYLER COLFAX
SPEAKER OF THE HOUSE OF REPRESENTATIVES
SIR:

In answer to the resolution of the House of Representatives of date Nov. 26th 1867, I have the honor to submit the following:

First—All the correspondence in the matter of the removal of Hon. E. M. Stanton, Secretary of War, of Gen'l P. H. Sheridan, Commander of the 5th Military District, and of Gen. D. E. Sickles, Commander of the Second Military District. . . .

Second—Correspondence and orders showing the condition of the Fifth Military District prior to the passage of the military reconstruction bill, and recommendations made thereon with the action of the civil authorities on such recommendations so far as known to me, together with explanatory remarks and the action it was deemed necessary to take from time to time, in the premises. . . .

Washington, Nov. 22nd 1866.

HON. E. M. STANTON, SEC OF WAR,

Enclosed please find copy of communication addressed to Major Gen. Sheridan under date of Oct. 17th 1866, . . .

(Sgd) U. S. GRANT. Gen'l

To the foregoing communications[1] no answer was ever received; but in answer to a Senate resolution dated Jany. 8th 1867, asking for information in relation to violations of the Act entitled "An Act to protect all persons in the United States in their civil rights and furnish the means of their vindication" and what steps had been taken to enforce the same, the President with his message of Feby. 19th 1867, submitted among other papers, Order No. 44, which led me to suppose that he regarded it as still in force. At this time Congress was discussing and maturing plans of legislation for the maintenance and enforcement of law and order in the States lately in rebellion. I therefore deemed it unecessary to take further action in the premises but await the result of Congressional action.

The preceding correspondence and orders show briefly and generally the condition of the Fifth Military District (Florida, Louisiana and Texas) prior to the passage of the military reconstruction bill. As the basis in part of this correspondence, and exhibiting more in detail the condition of affairs in different localities, the reports of subordinate commanders, so far as they are on file in this office, are also herewith submitted. All of these reports have reached here through the regular military channels

Third—Correspondence in regard to the difficulties in Baltimore touching the Police Commissioners and other matters prior to the election in 1866. . . .

Fourth Correspondence in regard to a proposed mission of the General of the Army to Mexico in the year 1866. . . .

I have the honor to be
Very respectfully
Your obt. servt.
U. S. GRANT
General

Copies (ellipses in original), DLC-USG, V, 47, 60; DNA, RG 108, Letters Sent. Printed in full as *HED*, 40-2-57. On Nov. 26, 1867, Edward McPherson, clerk, U.S. House of Representatives, wrote to USG. "On motion of Mr. Blaine   Resolved, That the General commanding the Armies of the United States be directed to communicate to this House any and all correspondence addressed by him to the President of the United States, upon the subject of the removal of Hon. E. M. Stanton, Secretary of War, and of Gen. P. H. Sheridan commander of the Fifth Military District, and of Gen. D. E. Sickles commander of the Second Military District; and also any correspondence or orders in his office showing the condition of the Fifth Military District prior to the passage of the Military Reconstruction bill, and any recommendations that he may have made thereon; and what steps, if any, were taken by civil authority in regard to such recommendations. And also all correspondence in regard to the difficulties in Baltimore touching the Police Commissioners and other matters prior to the election in eighteen hundred and sixty-six; and further, all correspondence in regard to a proposed mission of the General of the Army to Mexico in the year eighteen hundred and sixty-six" LS, DNA, RG 108, Letters Received. On Nov. 27, USG endorsed this letter as secretary of war *ad interim* and gen. "Case of Resolution of Congress calling for certain correspondence . . . Referred to Bvt. Maj. Gn. J. A. Rawlins, Chief of Staff of the Army." "Refered to Chief of Staff of the Army to collect the correspondence called for by the within resolution of Congress." AES, *ibid.*

On Nov. 30, President Andrew Johnson signed identical letters to each cabinet member, including USG. "You no doubt are aware that certain evil disposed persons have formed a conspiracy to depose the President of the United States, and to supply his place by an individual of their own selection. Their plan of operations seems to contemplate certain accusations against the President which are to take the form of articles of impeachment; and that thereupon, before hearing or trial, he is, under color of law, to be placed under arrest, and suspended or removed from office. The first intention apparently was to proceed by regular impeachment, in the mode prescribed by the Constitution. This however, required some credible evidence of an official act, criminal in its nature, and of a grade high enough to justify such a proceeding before an enlightened and impartial public. Failing to obtain, after efforts of the most extraordinary and unscrupulous character, any plausible ground for such an accusation, the persons engaged in this scheme discover that, to accomplish their purpose, they must now resort to a revolution changing the whole organic system of our Government. Such a design has been openly and publicly avowed, in language un-ambiguous in meaning by persons of great notoriety and much influence. While it is hoped that their declarations may be the mere ebullition of intense party excitement, it must be remembered that at the present time the temper of many political leaders is desperate and extremely reckless, and that the most prominent and influential among them have admitted and proclaimed that the constitution has been set aside and repudiated by Congress. The temptation to join in a revolutionary enterprise for the overthrow of our institutions is extremely strong at the present moment. A combination of men directing the operations of Government, without regard to law, or under a Constitution which they hold themselves authorized to repudiate at pleasure, would be absolute masters of all the wealth of a country, the richest in the world, and they could hold at their mercy the life and liberty of every individual within our territorial limits. Supreme and irresponsible power is always dangerous and seductive; but here, in the present condition

of American affairs, with our large Army, our powerful Navy, and our vast resources, it is a prize so dazzling that we cannot wonder if a desire to grasp it
should overcome the public virtue of some ambitious men. The coveted power,
once usurped, would easily find means to make itself perpetual. It cannot be
doubted that nine-tenths of the American people are true to the Constitution and
the free institutions established by the wisdom of their fathers. So, in 1861, were
the people of the South, yet they were mis-led by a few designing men and forced
into a disastrous revolution. A revolutionary party once in full possession of the
Government, with the entire control of the monetary affairs of the country and
the immense revenues now paid annually into the Treasury, with universal Negro
suffrage, and Military supervision of elections, might even maintain by force and
fraud, some external show of popular approbation for its worst excesses. Without
attempting to set forth all the facts and circumstances which tend to establish
the existence of a formidable conspiracy for the overthrow of the Government by
the deposition of the Chief Executive Magistrate, it is clear that those who are
engaged in it regard the present Executive as the main obstacle to the assumption
and exercise by them of unwarranted and arbitrary authority over the people. It
is believed that if the Executive had united with the majority of Congress in the
passage of measures, which he deemed subversive of the fundamental principles
of free government, he would have had their approbation. Their unqualified
animosity has been excited by the efforts he has made faithfully to fulfill his
solemn obligations. It has never once occurred to him, however, that upon the
mere demands of illegal and revolutionary violence, he could surrender his office
to a usurper, and thus yield the high duty imposed upon him by his oath 'to preserve, protect, and defend the Constitution'. To do so would be to betray the most
sacred trust ever committed to human hands. I cannot deliver the great charter
of a Nation's Liberty to men who, by the very act of usurping it, would show
their determination to disregard and trample it under foot. The strong probability that such a demand will be made, and the certainty that, if made, it must,
from a high sense of official obligation on my part, be resisted with all the legal
and constitutional means at the disposal of the President—thus bringing on a
conflict between co-ordinate branches of the Government—make it absolutely
necessary that the Executive and the Heads of the several Departments should,
upon a question so momentous, understand one another without any reserve
whatever. To that end, I request your separate opinions in writing on the following questions: 1. Can the President be removed from Office in any other mode
than that prescribed in the Constitution, viz 'On impeachment for and conviction
of treason, bribery, or other high crimes and misdemeanors?' 2. Pending impeachment and before conviction and judgment, can the President, by act of
Congress or otherwise, be suspended from Office, and the President pro-tempore
of the Senate, or other officer provided by law, be authorized to act as President
during such suspension? 3. If a law providing for such suspension and such
exercise of the office by any officer other than the President should be passed,
would it be the duty of the President to surrender his Office or withdraw from
the exercise of his official duties, or to continue to exercise them and to maintain
his authority? 4. Whether such deposition or arrest of the President, and the
transfer of his official functions to another person, would be less a violation of the
organic law if attempted or done by Members of Congress, or at their instigation,
than if attempted or effected by private parties?" LS, DLC-Andrew Johnson. Instead of delivering these letters, Johnson read a copy aloud that day at a cabinet
meeting. USG stated that Johnson should not submit to suspension under *ex*

post facto legislation unless the Supreme Court sustained the law. Howard K. Beale, ed., *Diary of Gideon Welles* (New York, 1960), III, 237–38.

1. See *PUSG*, 16, 389–90.

To Bvt. Maj. Gen. Edward R. S. Canby

Washington, D, C,
Dec. 18th 1867. [*11:00* A.M.]

MAJ. GN. CANBY,
CHARLESTON S, C,

Do you not think it better to keep troops scattered in S. C. untill after contracts are all made and people quietly settled to work? Orders are issued revoking musterout of Gn. Scott.

U. S. GRANT
General,

ALS (telegram sent), DNA, RG 107, Telegrams Collected (Bound); telegram sent, *ibid.*; copies, *ibid.*, RG 108, Telegrams Sent; DLC-USG, V, 56. On Dec. 18, 1867, Bvt. Maj. Gen. Edward R. S. Canby telegraphed to USG. "I had already suspended the movement of the Companies at Darlington & Georgetown until further orders designing to keep them as they are until after the holidays. At the other Stations, Charleston Columbia & Aiken by reason of the Rail Road and water communication they will be more effective than if they were scattered. I believe that every District in this state wishes to have Troops not only on account of the feeling of Security it gives but on account of the money that is disbursed but it will be necessary to have some in reserve & I think that Charleston & Columbia are the best points. I could very well use four additional Companies in this State & would bring the remainder of the eighth Infantry down if an equivalent force could be Sent to Raleigh" Telegram received (at 4:00 P.M.), DNA, RG 107, Telegrams Collected (Bound); *ibid.*, RG 108, Telegrams Received; copies (one sent by mail), *ibid.*, Letters Received; *ibid.*, RG 393, 2nd Military District, Letters Sent; DLC-USG, V, 55.

On Dec. 12, Canby had written to Bvt. Maj. Gen. John A. Rawlins. "I have the honor to recommend that the muster-out of service of Brigadier General R. K. Scott, U. S. Volunteers—may be suspended until the thirtieth of June, 1868, or, if this is not practicable, until the thirty-first of March. There is a very general feeling of uneasiness both among whites and blacks in this State—as to the events of the coming winter, and Genl Scott's administration of the bureau matters in this State has been such as to secure the confidence of all classes and especially of the colored population, and to give him an influence that could not be acquired by any one else in many months. The cry of—'negro insurrection' has been so much used in this State for political effect that it has created much real uneasiness on the part of the whites, and this in turn has re-acted upon the blacks,

so that each now fears and distrusts the other. I enclose copies of some correspondence with Governor Orr, which will show the extent to which the feeling
prevails in the western part of the State, where the colored population is not
largely in excess of the white, and it exists in still more exaggerated form in those
parts of the State in which the white element is comparatively small. The great
danger will be between the end of this month and the resumption of labor on the
plantations—about the first of April—and if the muster-out of Genl Scott cannot
be suspended for a longer period, I hope that it may be postponed, at least—until
the thirty-first of March." LS, DNA, RG 94, ACP, S335 CB 1868. On Dec. 17,
USG wrote a note. "The President authorizes a revocation of the order mustering
out of service Brig. & Bvt. Maj. Gn. Scott, Vols. Make the order." AN (initialed),
ibid. On March 12, Maj. Gen. Oliver O. Howard had written to USG. "I have the
honor to recommend Bvt. Major General R. K. Scott U. S. Vols. for the colonelcy
of any regiment when a vacancy may occur by the non-acceptance of appointment. Gen. Scott was a brigade comdr. in the Army of the Tennessee, distinguished himself in many battles, is able & worthy in every respect as an officer.
He has done himself great credit since the war as an administrative officer in
S. C. His state is Ohio." ALS, *ibid.*

On Dec. 20, Canby wrote to Rawlins. "I had the honor sometime since to
invite attention to the destitution and suffering likely to result, from the almost
total failure of the Crops (Rice and Sea Island Cotton) in the seaboard districts
of this State, and to request that authority might be given, to meet that contingency by special issues of food as the occasions might arise. Since then the
subject has been one of serious concern and inquiry, and as the result I am satisfied that the stock of food in those districts will, in the main, be exhausted by the
end of next month, (January 1868), that the Planters, with few exceptions, will
be without the means of supplying and paying, or even feeding the laborers required in carrying on their plantations, for another year, and that capitalists are
so much discouraged by the failures of the past two years, that no further advances can be expected from them. Without aid from some quarter I am convinced, that by the end of next month there will be at least 30.000 (of all classes)
of the colored population of those districts without employment, and consequently without the means of procuring food. The same difficulties will exist in
other sections of the State, and of North Carolina, but they will be of comparatively small importance, and the suffering that will result, may be met by the
local authorities. In the Sea Islands, and so much of the mainland, as is embraced
in the operation of General Sherman's order, the local civil authority has not yet
been reorganized, so as to be of any practical use in cases of this kind, and some
extraordinary means will be necessary to prevent suffering, or the theft, disorder, and violence, that may naturally be expected from a population, idle from
necessity, and impelled by hunger. How this danger may best be averted, is a
question of the gravest character. If direct issues of food are made, we incur the
risk of encouraging idleness, and its attendant vices, and of creating a proletarian
population, that will look to the Government for relief, whenever misfortune,
want of thrift, or idleness reduces them to want: If, on the other hand, there
should be any Governmental interference, by which employment is provided, the
precedent established will be almost as dangerous. I am clearly of the opinion,
that except to the infirm and helpless, there should be no gratuitous issues, that
whatever relief is given, should be in the shape of advances, or loans, to be repaid
when the next crop is gathered, and that these advances should be limited to the
poor only, and in such quantities as may be needed to prevent suffering. These

advances should, moreover, be a lien upon the crop, not only to assure the Government against loss, but to impress upon them, to whom they are made, habits of industry, and thrift, by considerations of interest, as well as, of morals. As far as practicable, these advances should be made to such of the colored people as are cultivating land for themselves, and when this cannot be done, to such planters, or owners of land, as are without the means of giving employment to laborers unless they are assisted, and who can be relied upon to deal fairly with the people employed by them. There will of course be some practical difficulties in the application of any system of relief, but with the knowledge, that we now possess of the people in those districts, or can procure through the officers of the Army and the Agents of the Freedmen's Bureau, I think that the one, just indicated, of giving it by loans, or advances of food, will be liable to the present objections or abuses. Any estimate of the quantity required will, of course, be conjectured, but I am of the opinion, that from the 1st of February until the 1st of September 1868, there will be thirty thousand of the colored people of those districts that will require assistance, to a greater, or less extent. Of this number ⅖s, or 12000 will be adults, and the remainder (18000) children under fourteen years of age. For the adults there will be required an average of corn for each, or a total of 120.000 bushels, and 60 pounds of bacon for each— total 720.000. pounds. For the children half the allowance for adults, making 90.000 bushels of Corn and 540.000 pounds of bacon; making a grand total of 210.000 bushels of corn and 1.260.000. pounds of bacon. I have stated what I believe to be the extreme limit. If the corn and vegetable crops of the next season should be at all favorable the necessity for issues will diminish in an increasing ratio during the months of June, July and August, and if there should be such a revival of confidence as to induce capitalists to make their usual advances; the necessity will in a great measure be obviated. At present the prospects are gloomy and it will be prudent to prepare for the worst. I will endeavor, by establishing labor agencies, and by disseminating information among the colored people in search of employment, and among the planters, who may need laborers, to diminish, as far as possible, the necessity of either issues, or advances, but it is recommended that authority be given to meet the contingency in one, or the other, of the ways suggested." LS, *ibid.*, RG 108, Letters Received.

On Dec. 23, Canby wrote to Rawlins. "I have the honor to transmit a copy of a letter which I have just received from Governor Orr, and of my reply thereto. While I do not share the apprehensions entertained by the Governor, I have thought it proper to submit his communication for the consideration of the General of the Army with my own remarks. South Carolina with reference to its colored population, may be properly divided into four Districts. The first is the Sea board: a District in which the adult male population is about as follows: Whites, 16000—Blacks, 36000. Nearly one fourth of this white population is congregated in this City; leaving in the District of Beaufort 1 White man to 7 Blacks. In the District of Berkeley 1 White to 9 Blacks; In the District of Colleton 1 White to 3 Blacks; In the District of Georgetown 1 White to 6 Blacks, & in the District of Williamsburg 1 White to 2 Blacks. In the others the black population is not largely in excess. The communication with different points of this District must be almost entirely by water, and this City is the only point where the requisite facilities for the movement of Troops can be found. The second is the Central District in which the adult male population is about as follows: Whites 17000, Blacks 26000. In two of the State Districts the white population is in excess. In the others the proportion of Blacks ranges from a bare majority to three to one in Sumter District. The centre of this District so far as facilities for the movement of Troops is concerned is Columbia and there is Railroad communication with the greater part of it. The third is the Savannah river District, and the adult male population is about as follows: Whites 7000 Blacks 12000. Aiken is the proper centre of this District, and is in direct Railroad communication with Charleston & Columbia. The fourth is the Western or Mountain District and the adult male population is about as follows: Whites 12000— Blacks 8000. Only one of the State Districts (Laurens) has a preponderance in black population. In the arrangement of Troops in this State I have assigned to the first District, where the black population is most largely in excess, eight Companies; to the second District where the black population is next in importance, Six Companies; to the third, a comparatively small District, two Companies, and to the fourth where the white population is considerably in excess of the black, two Companies. In making these arrangements the relative numbers of the two classes, the disposition of the people and the means of communication, were all fully considered. It would no doubt have been a much more satisfactory arrangement to the people of the State to have established a small guard in every town and have relieved them of their Ordinary Police duties, but this would have rendered the Command entirely useless if any serious difficulties should be threatened. I do not find thus far that there has been any increase in the number of serious crimes, but pilfering has largely increased within the last thirty days, and there is much force in the Governors Suggestions that it may lead to graver disorders, unless it can be prevented by finding employment for the Negroes or making issues of food to prevent suffering. The apprehensions expressed by the Governor are entertained by many others whose opinions are entitled to consideration and they are shared by the colored population to a very considerable extent. This mutual apprehension & distrust may of itself bring about some of the troubles we hope to avoid. To quiet these apprehensions as well as to guard against the possibility of danger, I recommend that four Companies be ordered to report to me. This will enable me to establish two additional Garrisons at points that are most difficult of access, and to which Troops could not be sent as rapidly as is desirable. Will you please advise me by telegraph of the Generals action." LS, *ibid.* USG endorsed this letter. "The Subsistence Dept. has been ordered to turn over to the Bureau of R. F & A. about Thirty Million rations of dessicated vegitables to relive suffering in the South. The distribution of this, which will commence without delay, may arest the danger apprehended. If Gn. Canby still thinks it necessary to have more troops however they will have to be ordered from here. In that case order them from 12th Inf.y." AE (initialed and undated), *ibid.* See telegram to Bvt. Maj. Gen. Edward O. C. Ord, Dec. 23, 1867.

On Jan. 4, 1868, 12:20 P.M., Rawlins telegraphed to Canby. "Your communication of the 23d December, and enclosures, received. The Freedmen's Bureau is authorized to issue sufficient rations to all classes of destitute persons, which will avoid much of the apprehended troubles. Will you still require the additional troops you ask for?" Telegrams sent (2), DNA, RG 107, Telegrams Collected (Bound); copies, *ibid.*, RG 108, Telegrams Sent; DLC-USG, V, 56. On the same day, Canby telegraphed to Rawlins. "Telegram rec'd. I do not myself apprehend any serious trouble but there is a general feeling of uneasiness among both Whites and Blacks and this feeling will be kept up for Political purposes, To allay this is to give it best assurances of quiet and order, and to this end I think it desirable that the force in the District should be increased by four (4) Companies of Infantry" Telegram received (on Jan. 5, 10:00 A.M.), DNA, RG 107, Telegrams Collected (Bound); *ibid.*, RG 108, Telegrams Received; copies, *ibid.*, RG 94, Letters Received, 5M 1868; (sent by mail) *ibid.*, RG 108, Letters Received; DLC-USG, V, 55. On Jan. 6, Maj. George K. Leet endorsed a copy of this telegram. "The Adjutant General will direct Bvt. Maj. Gen. W. H. Emory, Comd'g Dept. Washington, to send four companies of the 12th Infantry, by rail, to report to Bvt. Maj. Gen. E. R. S. Canby, Comd'g. 2d Military District; Notice to be given Gen. Canby by telegraph when the troops leave Wash'gton." ES, DNA, RG 94, Letters Received, 5M 1868.

On Dec. 27, 1867, Canby had telegraphed to USG. "I sent my Provost Marshal General to investigate troubles in Jones County North Carolina, Upon his recommendation I will authorize County Court to organize a Local Police force to be composed of Loyal whites and blacks of good character and standing, Expense of the force to be charged upon County Treasury, Same Course may be necessary in Pitt & Onslow Counties. Have also suspended movement of Company of Eighth (8th) Infantry from Newbern Its Commander will Co-operate with Civil authorities. Of three (3) murders Committed two (2) were by the same band, One (1) has been arrested and I have hopes of securing the others" Telegram received (at 11:00 A.M.), *ibid.*, RG 107, Telegrams Collected (Bound); *ibid.*, RG 108, Telegrams Received; copies (one sent by mail), *ibid.*, Letters Received; *ibid.*, RG 393, 2nd Military District, Letters Sent; DLC-USG, V, 55.

On Jan. 6, 1868, Canby wrote to Rawlins. "I have the honor to transmit a copy of a Special Order, which I have issued, as one of the means adopted to meet the existing difficulties in the counties of Jones, Craven, Lenoir, and Pitt, North Carolina. I have adopted this course with some hesitation, because there is still, in many parts of North Carolina, a feeling of bitterness among the actual rebellious, that influences any party that may be in power, to use that power as against their former enemies, and present political opponents. This experiment, however, will be watched very closely, and if any improper tendency cannot be fully controlled, the authority will be withdrawn, and a regular force substituted. The difficulties in these counties originated at a period considerably anterior to the close of the Rebellion, and is referable to the spirit of revenge and retaliation for the execution of a number of Union men as deserters from the Rebel Service. In addition to the outrages, that were tracable to political excitement were many, that were due to personal animosities, or committed purely for the sake of plunder. These troubles have had periodical recurrences, requiring the assistance of the Military to suppress them. On learning of the murder of Colonel Northercutt I apprehended a renewal of the former troubles, and immediately sent the Provost Marshal General of the District, to investigate the subject, and institute the most effective measures, for the detection and punishment of the criminals. The movement of the Company from Newbern was suspended, and mounted detachments from it are now cooperating with the Civil authorities in the attempt to arrest the murderers. A copy of General Hink's report is transmitted herewith. The present difficulties do not appear to have any political origin, but committed for purposes of plunder." LS, DNA, RG 108, Letters Received. The enclosures are *ibid.*

To Hamilton Fish

Washington, D, C,
Dec. 18th 1867.

MY DEAR GOVERNOR,

Your letter of enquiry as to whether I would attend the Richmond meeting of Trustees for the Peabody Fund was duly received. It is my intention now to attend that meeting. It is possible public duties may prevent my doing so but I do not apprehend any thing of the kind.

Mrs. Grant feels disappointed that your letters gives no promise that your daughters will accompany Mrs. Fish and yourself to pay us a visit. Why can they not come on with you and remain with Mrs. Grant whilst we go to Richmond?

Yours Truly
U. S. GRANT

GOV. H. FISH
NEW YORK, CITY.

ALS, ICarbS. On Jan. 22, 1868, USG attended the meeting discussed. *Proceedings of the Trustees of the Peabody Education Fund* (Boston, 1875), I, 58–59.

To Henry Wilson

Washington City, D. C., December 18th *1867*.

HON HENRY WILSON
CHAIRMAN OF THE MILITARY COMMITTEE OF THE SENATE
WASHINGTON D. C.
SIR,

In reply to the resolution of the Military Committee of the Senate, of December 16th 1867, calling for "a list of the appointments made in the Army, from civil life, since March 4. 1867, and

the names of the persons by whom such appointments are recommended, and to state, also, under what law persons, who have not
served in the Army, are appointed officers and assigned to 'original
vacancies', created by the Act of July 28, 1866"—I have the honor
to enclose a list of all civilians—appointed in the Army since March
4. 1867, with the names of the persons by whom they have been
recommended—

The Act of July 28. 1866, (section 2) provides that "the first,
second, third and fourth regiments of Artillery shall have the same
organization as is now prescribed by law for the fifth regiment of
Artillery," which, by the Act of July 29. 1861, was allowed, for its
minimum, *twelve* and for its maximum, *twenty four* Second Lieutenants. Section 2, Act of July 28. 1866, further provides, that the
regimental Adjutants, Quartermasters & Commissaries shall be
extra lieutenants. By this legislation *fourteen* vacancies of 2d Lieutenants were created in each of the first four Artillery Regiments,
and *two* in the fifth. The section of the Act authorizing this increase
in the Artillery, does not require that the original vacancies be filled
by selection from among the volunteers, thus leaving it to the discretion of the President to appoint civilians to fill original vacancies
of 2d Lieutenants in the Artillery Arm of the service. It may here
be remarked, that the greater part of the graduating class of the
Military Academy of West Point for 1867, were appointed to original vacancies in the Artillery regiments, and were confirmed by the
Senate, June 17th 1867.

Two Officers, Lt Frank M. Gibson, 7th Cav'y & Lieut James
Calhoun, 32d Infantry, have been erroneously nominated "to fill
original vacancies." The vacancies to which they were appointed
were *not original* & a new nomination in their case has been submitted. A number of Officers were nominated to the Senate, *as of
different States*, their volunteer rank not being known.

This information has since been ascertained, and the names of
these officers appear on the accompanying list, with their rank &
regiment attached.

I have therefore to inform you that all of the original vacancies created by the Act of July 28. 1866, have been filled in accordance with the requirements of that Act.

> I am, Sir, Very Respectfully
> Your Obedient Servant,
> U. S. GRANT
> Secretary of War, *ad interim.*

LS, PHi. The resolution is in DNA, RG 94, ACP, S1569 CB 1867.

To Bvt. Maj. Gen. John Pope

> Hd Qrs. Army,
> Dec. 219th *1867.* [*noon*]

MAJ. GN. J. POPE,
ATLANTA GA.

I had not thought of reversing any of your orders of removals and appointments and should not do so without getting your report.

> U. S. GRANT
> General,

ALS (telegram sent), DNA, RG 107, Telegrams Collected (Bound); telegram sent, *ibid.*; copies, *ibid.*, RG 108, Telegrams Sent; DLC-USG, V, 56. On Dec. 18, 1867, Bvt. Maj. Gen. John Pope had telegraphed to USG. "I see it circulated in the papers that I have removed a number of Judicial & Ministerial Officers in Alabama for political purposes & have replaced them by violent partizans; It is impossible for me to correct all the slanders and falsehoods thats circulated Every Civil Officer I have removed, I have removed for good & sufficient cause on record in this Office & I am prepared when called on by proper authority to furnish the facts. It is unjust and unfair to lend attention or think of taking action in such matters without the Official facts or without calling upon the Officer concerned for a report. I do not know that this is being done but I must infer something of the kind if I am to believe what I hear" Telegram received (on Dec. 19, 10:00 A.M.), DNA, RG 107, Telegrams Collected (Bound); *ibid.*, RG 108, Telegrams Received; copy, DLC-USG, V, 55.

On Dec. 21, Pope telegraphed to USG. "I had no purpose of indicating that action in certain ~~eases~~ matters in this District would be taken by you without report of facts from me, but was and am led to think that report of a different sort & from another source based wholly upon *Ex parte* or rather Rebel statements was contemplated I trust I may be wrong" Telegram received (at 10:30 A.M.), DNA, RG 107, Telegrams Collected (Bound); *ibid.*, RG 108,

Telegrams Received; copy, DLC-USG, V, 55. On Dec. 22, Bvt. Brig. Gen. Cyrus B. Comstock wrote to Pope. "I enclose herewith papers sent to General Grant by the President in reference to frauds alledged to have been committed in the late election for delegates to a convention for forming a constitution for the state of Georgia. General Grant desires that you will report to him fully the facts in the cases referred to and return these papers with the report" Copies, *ibid.*, V, 47, 60; DNA, RG 108, Letters Sent. On Dec. 27, Pope wrote to USG. "I have the honor to acknowledge the receipt of a letter from General C. B. Comstock dated December 22nd written by your order and transmitting to me a memorial complaining of frauds in the late election in Alabama, accompanied by a private letter from A. Edwards representing himself to have been a Judge of Election and to be Register of the United States Land Office. I have sent these papers to General Swayne Commanding in Alabama, with orders to examine into the complaints set out in the Memorial referred to and to make full report of the facts,—Sending with his report all instructions received from me or issued by him concerning the conduct of the election in Alabama.—As soon as this report is received I will forward it to you.—I cannot of course undertake to say that there was no fraudulent voting in Alabama.—I presume it would be hazardous to say as much for any election held in the United States.—I *can* say however that so far as it was in my power, I omitted no measures, which seemed necessary to prevent fraud.— I have given no instructions or orders concerning the elections in this District except such as have been sent you—Necessarily most of the details of the elections were left in the hands of the immediate Commanders in the State concerned and I think it will be found difficult to make any one believe that an officer of the high and pure character of General Swayne, would be guilty of or privy to any fraudulent act whatever.—I enclose the only election order for Alabama issued by me from which you will see that the detailed instructions to the Superintendents of election (Boards of Registration) were directed to be made and were made by General Swayne. You will also observe that the 4th Section of the Supplementary Act of March 23 1867 simply commands the District Commander, 'to open the returns made by the Boards of Registration ascertain the persons elected as Delegates *according to the returns of the officers who conducted said election* and make proclamation thereof.'—This simple duty I performed literally and no complaints of fraud have been made to me until the receipt of the Memorial referred to in the beginning of this letter.—Neither is it clear to me that under the Reconstruction Acts, I have any right to investigate complaints of fraudulent voting.—The paragraph of the Supplementary Act of March 23 above quoted, seems to restrict me to the specific acts therein mentioned, and I have therefore referred to the Conventions themselves all questions pertaining to qualifications of Delegates or claims to seats contested on any ground whatever.—I have not assumed to decide or even to express an opinion on any such questions.—Concerning the private letter from me to General Swayne of which your Memorialists profess to give a copy I do not know that I need say any thing I think the copy is a true copy of a private letter written by me to General Swayne as far as it goes, but there is one whole paragraph omitted, perhaps purposely, which would show still more clearly its entirely private character.—Nevertheless it is difficult to understand what cause of complaint is found in the letter even had it been official.—I express in it certain doubts about my power to order payment to the Convention out of the State Treasury but express my willingness to sanction such payment on certain conditions.—My sanction was necessary as I have issued orders that no money should be paid out of the State Treasury except for the expenses of the Civil Administration.—As I made no order however on the subject and as the same question has arisen in Georgia and been referred to Washington for decision, I do not see that the opinion in my letter to General Swayne has any significance whatever.—I also express the opinion that the Convention ought to finish its work as soon as possible and to vote itself the very smallest compensation barely enough to pay expenses.—This private opinion even had it been officially given to the Convention can hardly be found fault with by sensible men of any political party.—I farther State to General Swayne my opinion that the success of Reconstruction depends upon the retention of power for several years by the political party which passed the Reconstruction Acts.—But this opinion is a platitude.—It has been openly proclaimed by all the Rebel papers in the South and the Democratic papers in the North for months past. There is perhaps objection to the expression of this opinion, that it indicates my own political opinions.—I have only to say to this that I have never concealed my opinions on the general politics of the day but have expressed them in conversation on all proper occasions. I am free to say that so far as Reconstruction is concerned I am entirely in sympathy with the political party which passed the Reconstruction Acts. If it be an offence to entertain political opinions on one side of this question it is surely equally a cause of offence to entertain opinions of an opposite nature and I think and hope it would be difficult to find an officer of sufficient rank to command one of these Military Districts who does not entertain very decided opinions on the subject.—It is not to be supposed that the President of the United, States, would select an officer to execute a law of the United, States, on account of his personal opinions of its wisdom or that in his official action he would consider it an offence to think one way and not an equal offence to think another.—All this however is of purely a private character and in common with every other citizen of this country I must claim the right to hold such opinions as best suit me on public questions.—Whenever it shall be charged against me that I have committed any specific act in violation of or beyond the limits of the law; that I have wronged or oppressed any man; that I have taken any action or issued any order not manifestly necessary to the faithful execution of the Law; or that I have in any manner used my official position to force my political opinions on any body and I fail to refute such a charge to the satisfaction of the Government, I shall hold myself liable to censure.—But until this is the case I consider myself free from self reproach or the censure of the Government.—For my official Acts I hold myself responsible to the proper Authorities,—but my opinions are a different matter altogether and for them I am officially responsible to no man.—" LS, DLC-Andrew Johnson. The enclosure is *ibid*. USG endorsed this letter. "REFERRED TO The President of the United States" AES (undated), *ibid*.

To Henry Wilson

———

War Department
Washington City
December 19, 1867.

HON. HENRY WILSON
CHAIRMAN MILITARY COMMITTEE U. S. SENATE.
SIR.

In compliance with your request for my views on the proposed Joint Resolution for the relief of certain officers of Ullmans Brigade I make the following remarks:

The necessity for such a Resolution arises from the fact that quite a number of enlisted men were nominated by Gen. Ullman for commissions in his Brigade *in excess of the number* of officers *allowed by law.* Having reported in good faith they were put on duty by Gen. Ullman as officers but could not be mustered in until vacancies occurred. In some instance they served in this manner from five to nine months before being mustered.

The Department had power in case they were not mustered exactly at the time a vacancy occurred to change the date of muster to that of the vacancy. But it could not go behind the date of vacancy without authorizing a greater number of officers than the law allowed to Regiments.

In order to pay such persons for the full time that they were actually on duty as commissioned officers, if such be th[e] object, I suggest the following amendment to the Joint Resolution: —Strike out all after the word "of," line 12, and before the word "deducting"—line 18, and substitute therefor as follows: "there being no legal vacancy or from other cause beyond his control and without his own fault or neglect was not mustered in as a commissioned officer of the date he reported at Genl. Ullman's Headquarters, the War Department, after an examination of the facts in each case shall allow him full pay and emoluments for the rank to which he was assigned and in which he served from the date on which he reported at the aforesaid Headquarters."

I think it best in all cases like this that legislation should be in such a form as to admit of decision on each individual case being made on its own merits. The distinctions between just and improper claims are often too nice to be safely entrusted to legislation which would cover a whole class.

I am, Sir,
Very Respectfully
Yr. obt. svt.
U. S. GRANT
Sec. of War ad. int.

Copies, DNA, RG 107, Letters Received, W489 1867; *ibid.*, Reports to Congress. In March, 1863, Brig. Gen. Daniel Ullmann received orders to recruit a brigade of black troops in La.; in Sept., Brig. Gen. Lorenzo Thomas revoked those orders when Ullmann proposed to appoint black officers. *O.R.*, III, iii, 14, 101–3, 766, 787.

To Henry Wilson

War Department
Washington City
Decr. 19, 1867.

HON. HENRY WILSON
CHAIRMAN MILITARY COMMITTEE U. S. SENATE.
SIR.

In reply to your request for my views as to the Joint Resolution passed the 11th inst. by the House of Representatives directing the Secretary of War to furnish certain muster Rolls to the different states, I have respectfully to inform you that there are on file in the Adjutant General's office applications from State authorities for copies of 11.428 muster Rolls each containing from 80 to 150 names. The following are only a few of the objections to furnishing these Rolls:

The clerical force of the office is kept down to the lowest number consistent with the prompt discharge of its duties, and every room in the many buildings occupied by the clerks is already too crowded. Forty good clerks extra and at least eight more rooms would be required for one year to make all these copies. The regular force of the office cannot possibly be diverted from its business for this purpose without suspending other important operations daily arising. Beside that there is no room where persons employed by the states could be accommodated in making these copies, the Rolls themselves are referred to for information necessary to answer claims and enquiries of a legal nature so frequently that they cannot be spared for any other purpose; and the greatest care has to be taken in handling them because they are so frequently used. But there is another still more serious objection to permitting copies of these Rolls to go out of the possession of the War Department. The information they contain is precisely what Claim Agents most desire to get. Once in possession of these names and dates they would send circulars far and wide, as in fact they do now, inviting people to call upon them for settlement of claims and many of them, as we know from daily experience, would not hesitate to make up and forge papers and powers of attorney through which stupendous frauds would be practised against not only the Government but against lawful claimants.

The adjutant General's office will probably be for years to come ~~particularly~~ patiently and laboriously occupied in tracing out all reliable facts of the military history of every officer and soldier who has ever been in the service. It affords promptly and completely to individuals *who have a right to it*. all the information which can possibly be of use to them   It furnishes states copies of such rolls as they need in settling their own business. It aids the Treasury Department not only in settling claims but by the peculiar character of its information it enables the Treasury officers to have some check against fraudulent claims. To furnish copies of its rolls which would be sure to be published in military histories, State Reports, and other works, would be to remove the only check the Government now possesses against forgery and fraud. The experience of years ago upon which the present Regulations concerning giving information were based has been abundantly confirmed by the experience of this war.

I trust in view of these facts that no legislation will be had re-
laxing the Rules now in existence for I am sure it could not *benefit*
any one, but would on the contrary be detrimental to many.

> I am Sir, Very Respy,
> Yr. obt. svt.
> U. S. GRANT
> Sec. of War ad. int.

Copies, DNA, RG 107, Letters Received, W481 1867; *ibid.*, Reports to Congress.

Endorsement

Respectfully forwarded to the Secretary of War, disapproved, as
no good to the service could result from granting the application.
In justice to Genl. Carleton I would state that having received unfavorable reports of the condition of military affairs in New Mexico,
I directed Bvt. Brig. Gen., (then Bvt. Col.) A. J. Alexander, Major
9th US. Cavalry, to make a thorough inspection of that District,
which he did; and pertinent to the subject matter of this communication, reported as follows:

"I do not find any of the grave charges against Genl. Carleton
by the citizens sustained by evidence so far as his official conduct
is concerned. . . . The principal feature of his rule in New Mexico
was the subjugation of the Navajoe Indians, the most powerful and
dangerous tribe in the mountains.—In this he was perfectly successful and although the advantage to the inhabitants is incalculable, there are many, particularly the Indian Agents and contractors, who have never ceased to heap abuse on him since the Indians
were captured. These agents are, with few exceptions, utterly
worthless and abandoned, and their whole object is plundering the
Indians. It makes a vast difference in the perquisites of their office
whether they distribute goods to 20,000, or 30,000 Indians running

wild in the mountains, or 7550 on a Reservation, that are counted regularly, and where the distribution is supervised by reliable officers...."[1]

U. S. GRANT
General.

HDQRS. A. U S.
DEC. 23. '67.

ES (ellipses in original), DNA, RG 94, Letters Received, 304C 1867. Written on a letter of March 26, 1867, from Bvt. Brig. Gen. James H. Carleton, Santa Fé, to Bvt. Maj. Gen. John A. Rawlins. "I have received an order relieving me from the command of the District of New Mexico. This order, taken in connection with what was said of me in the United States Senate by the Hon. *John Conness*, [see the enclosed copy of the 'Daily Globe' of March 9. 1867.,] leads me to believe that the calumnies which have been so unsparingly heaped upon me by unscrupulous political demagogues, and by low people here—have had weight in creating an unfavorable impression of me at the Head Quarters of the Army and elsewhere. Feeling sure that I do not deserve this, and feeling that not only my own reputation but that of the Army, demands that the truth should be known, and these calumniators forever be put to shame, I hereby beg that General Grant will order a Court of Inquiry to meet here, *before I go from this country*, to examine into ALL matters pertaining to my administration of affairs in New Mexico—and to report the facts and the opinion of the Court in the premises. I desire the most thorough and searching scrutiny:—and trust, that after nearly five years hard labor here, I may not be permitted to depart from New Mexico, with the idea attached to me, unless it be true, that I have acted in bad faith as an officer, or dishonestly as a man. I appeal to General *Grant* if this is not due to me as an old soldier.... Note: I also enclose herewith a copy of a letter which I this day sent to the Hon. John Conness in relation to documentary evidence against me which he says he holds in his hands." LS (brackets in original), *ibid.* The enclosures are *ibid.* On Oct. 21, Carleton wrote to Rawlins renewing his request. ALS, *ibid.*, RG 108, Letters Received. See telegram to Lt. Gen. William T. Sherman, Feb. 25, 1867.

On June 18, Bvt. Brig. Gen. Andrew J. Alexander, Washington, D. C., had written to Rawlins. "I have the honor to hand you herewith Inspection Reports of the following named posts viz Fts Bascom, Sumner, Stanton, Bliss, Selden, Bayard, Cummings, McRae, Craig, Wingate, Albuquerque Marcy, and Union, the latter including that portion of the garrison stationed at Maxwells In order to make this inspection it became necessary for me to travel over (1700) Seventeen hundred miles in ambulances & on horseback, across swolen streams and through hostile Indians I have endeavored to report all irregularities as briefly as possible and all my statements can be substantiated That the Reports will be found deficient in many aspects I do not doubt, but I beg to call your attention to the fact that the duties were entirely new to me Trusting that they may serve the purposes intended . . ." ALS, DNA, RG 159, Letters Received, M19 1867. On June 21, USG endorsed this letter. "Respectfully forwarded to the Secretary of War, with recommendation that copies of so much of these reports as relates to Indian matters be furnished the Secretary of the Interior." ES, *ibid.* On Aug.

29, USG wrote to Secretary of the Interior Orville H. Browning. "I have the honor to send herewith for your information an extract from *Colonel Alexander's Inspection report* made to this Dept. relative to certain *Indians in New Mexico.*" Df, *ibid.*, RG 107, Letters Received from Bureaus; copy, *ibid.*, Letters Sent to the President. On Sept. 2, Act. Secretary of the Interior William T. Otto wrote to USG acknowledging his letter. LS, *ibid.*, Letters Received from Bureaus.

On Dec. 23, G. W. Messenger, Boston, wrote to USG. "I had the honor on the occasion of your visit to Boston to tender to you the hospitalities of our city— and perhaps from this fact I am induced to take the liberty of addressing you on the subject of a brave and meritorious officer who thinks he has not received justice at the hands of the Committee on Military affairs of the U. S. Senate—I allude to Genl James H Carleton recently commanding in the department of New Mexico—the facts of the case are these—under date of Decr 1. 1866 he was notified by Hon Mr Stanton, Secy of War that the President of the U. S. had appointed him for meritorious services during the war a Major General by Brevet in the U. S. Service to rank as such from the '13th March 1865' The Senate confirmed this in February but afterwards the list was recalled—and not reported again until March 4th—when Genl Carletons name was left off—so Senator Foster wrote Genl Carleton—and I have reason to think some enemies of Genl Carleton prejudiced certain members of the Senate by raising doubts as to his loyalty—Now I happen to have a relative a most reliable, truthful man who served under Genl Carleton during the war who assures me that a *braver, more loyal meritorious* officer, in his judgment, could not be found—and in addition I have seen officers of the army who know him well who would testify to the same effect—I am therefore desirous that Genl Carletons name should again be sent to the senate as Major General by Brevet to date from March 13 1865—and should this be done I have good reason to think the nomination would *now* be confirmed by the Senate pray excuse the liberty I have taken . . ." ALS, *ibid.*, RG 94, ACP, 5058 1872. On Jan. 3, 1868, USG endorsed this letter. "Not approved" ES, *ibid.* On the same day, U.S. Delegate Charles P. Clever of New Mexico Territory, Washington, D. C., wrote to USG. "As Delegate from New Mexico I feel it due to myself and the people I have the honor to represent to endorse in the fullest manner the wisdom, energy and fidelity with which General James H, Carleton managed the affairs of New Mexico during his occupation of the position of Commanding General of the Department of New Mexico. The Brevet rank of Major General given to him and then, by the malicious efforts of personal enemies withdrawn, I hope will be again tendered to him, as a just and well merited compliment for his long and faithful services in New Mexico in subduing and colonizing the Navajoe Indians and laboring to advance the prosperity of that Territory.—" LS, *ibid.* On Jan. 6, USG unfavorably endorsed a letter of Dec. 6, 1867, from Bvt. Maj. Gen. John Pope, Atlanta, to USG. "I have the honor to recommend that Bvt. Brig Genl James H Carleton U. S. A be brevetted Major Genl in the Army for distinguished & valuable services in command of the District of New Mexico in the Dept of the Missouri, of which Dept I was in command—I esteem Genl Carleton' services very highly & I trust his claim to the Brevet promotion I ask for him may be favorably considered by the Genl in chief—" ES and ALS, *ibid.*

On June 8, 1868, Carleton, Bangor, Maine, wrote to Rawlins. "I see by the dispatches published by the Associated Press that on the 6th instant, I was confirmed as Brevet Major General in the Army. This, of course, is gratifying to myself and to my friends, as it is an official vindication on the part of the Government of my labors in New Mexico, where all commanders who do their duty, are sooner or later more or less maligned by certain classes of men whose interests or whose ambitions do not harmonize with what he may consider to be right and for the best interests of the United States. I became especially obnoxious to those classes and was the object of their vituperation. Many of my staff, who stood manfully by me, suffered directly or indirectly in reproaches unsparingly heaped upon myself. This point above all others caused me much chagrin. My labors to conquer hostile Indians,—to protect the people,—and to develop these resources of that great country, never could have had success but for the hearty coöperation of the officers to whom I have alluded. If credit is therefore due to any one it is certainly due to them more than to myself. . . ." ALS, *ibid.,* C161 CB 1868.

1. Quoted from a lengthy confidential report of May 5, 1867, from Alexander to Rawlins. USG omitted the second sentence by ellipses: "I think he made a great mistake in using the influence created by his official position to influence the elections, in devoting the Govt. money and soldiers to the development of the Country and particularly that portion of it where he and his staff had large pecuniary interests." Copy, *ibid.,* RG 159, Letters Received, M19 1867.

To Bvt. Maj. Gen. Edward O. C. Ord

———

Dec. 23d *1867.* [*9:40* A.M.]

Maj. Gn. E. O. C. Ord,
Holly Springs, Miss.

If Gn. Gillem has not started countermand your order sending him to Washington. He has received instructions how to prevent suffering in the Miss. Valley. Your order of the 19th I fear will do great harm and would advise its revocation.

U. S. Grant
General

ALS (telegram sent), DNA, RG 107, Telegrams Collected (Bound); telegram sent, *ibid.*; telegram received, *ibid.*, RG 393, 4th Military District, Letters Received. On Dec. 19, 1867, Bvt. Maj. Gen. Edward O. C. Ord had written to USG. "I send enclosed report of the Election Returns from this State and Arkansas— from which you will see that if the votes not cast in favor of Conventions are cast against ratifying any constitutions made by them—the constitutions will not be ratified in Arkansas—and may fail in this State if the opposition as I expect will be lively—The reports of Freedmen without food or work—and of danger from insurrection are multiplying—they can not be ignored and will certainly lead to a war of races if some thing is not done soon Genl Gillem coroborates the reports I have from the counties with large surplus freed population—of burning Cotton Gins—and armed bands plundering ~~with~~ I have given him what papers are on file here on the subject and directed him to proceed to Washington to confer with you and the President on the subject—The measures I am taking General to prevent insurrections—may affect the vote on ratifying a convention   would it not be well General to have an Officer here by that time who believed in the *Policy*—as well as the right—of Congress to reconstruct on negro suffrage basis—I dont—and if the constitutions fail—as they will—my motives are likely to be misconstrued—and I held responsible for the failures—I shall abide by your judgement in the matter of remaining here Genl and do my best— though you should know the facts—and my opinions   I would be glad however if you would try and impress upon Congress the necessity of prompt action in this Social question of starvation on the freedmen—"   ALS, *ibid.*, RG 108, Letters Received. The enclosures are *ibid.* On Dec. 24, Ord telegraphed to USG. "Genl Gillem is now probably in Washington   ⅋ do not know what order of the nineteenth referred to   none issued that day—my order ~~no~~ nos 22 & 24 for arbitration of claims affecting freedmans share of crops, protect him from landlords who as crop was small were taking it all—"   ADfS (telegram sent), *ibid.*, RG 393, 4th Military District, Letters Received; telegram received (at 9:30 A.M.), *ibid.*, RG 107, Telegrams Collected (Bound); *ibid.*, RG 108, Telegrams Received.

On Dec. 7, Ord had twice telegraphed to USG. "In the River Counties but little corn has been raised for the past two crops, Cotton has not paid expenses There is no inducement to employ Freedmen to make it and there is but little else for them to do,   *They have spent* the results of this years work,   Are in large numbers armed and plundering for food,   Owners are leaving the Country for Safety and there is reason to fear a War of Races if the blacks are not fed, From all sides appeals reach me for Troops to protect the Whites,   The blacks must be disarmed. An appropriation of half a million to repair levees from Tunica to Vicksburg by blacks might avert this disaster if made now   There is no time to lose"   "Add to my telegram of this morning that this is not a question of Politics with Planter or laborer but cotton does not pay and the laborer is discharged"   Telegrams received (the first at 4:40 P.M., the second on Dec. 8, 10:45 A.M.), *ibid.*, RG 107, Telegrams Collected (Bound); *ibid.*, RG 108, Telegrams Received; copies, *ibid.*, RG 105, Letters Received; DLC-USG, V, 55. On Dec. 9, Bvt. Brig. Gen. Eliphalet Whittlesey, Bureau of Refugees, Freedmen, and Abandoned Lands, wrote to Maj. George K. Leet. "I have the honor to acknowledge the receipt of copies of telegrams from General Ord, reporting great distress in the river counties of Mississippi, and to inform you that I have directed General Gillem, Asst. Commissioner, to furnish all the relief possible in the case   The means at his disposal are limited, but he will be able, I trust, to meet the present pressing wants of the people." Copy, DNA, RG 105, Letters Sent.

On the same day, Ord wrote to USG. "I telegraphed yesterday concerning the numerous and increasing applications received at these Headquarters, for troops to protect the property of whites, from unemployed freedmen, and stated that, there ~~being~~ was but little demand for labor for the cultivation of cotton, ~~and~~ on account of the bankruptcy of those who have engaged in its culture ~~is why that culture~~ which culture is now ceasing. The blacks share in the ruin and general despondency; many of them have left off work, others work just enough in the picking to obtain rations; the result is the unemployed laborer must starve or plunder, for he has nothing to live on; and by reference to the enclosed reports of Judge Hill, U. S. District Judge, who has just decided the reconstruction acts to be valid, and Judge Shackelford appointed under the act of Congress, Circuit Judge, about the most reliable union men I could find in this section; of Governor Sharkey, of Governor Humphry's, of Sheriff Mounman [*Moorman*], and many others,—(and every planter and merchant that I have conversed with, endorses this statement), from which it will be seen that the freedmen have commenced plundering. As the blacks are armed, and are indisposed to submit to either Civil or military laws, unless they are fed or employed, there are reasons to fear a war of races, which can only be prevented—if they are not fed,—by disarming them The question is one of food, the freedmen I think, if they had reason to expect good wages, or a good price for their cotton, would work as well as they have at any time since the war; the planters could they get the provisions to supply the hands, would employ them, they are in many cases offering them the use of lands gratis, but these offers can but seldom be accepted, because the freedmen have no corn laid up, no meat, no money or credit. Such is the condition of affairs in the river counties; for that of the prairie Counties, on the Alabama border, I refer you to the clear and truthful report of Mr John R. Gillylen, Clerk of the Board of Police for Monroe County. Two of the reports of plots among freedmen to rise on the whites are enclosed. When such men as Judge Sharkey and Governor Humphry's, who a year since, were indignant at the ordering of a few troops into the state as an insult to a loyal people, are calling on me for more U. S. troops, to protect the whites against the freedmen, no doubt can be entertained as to their sincerity, or of the immenent danger. I have endeavored to prevent crime, and suffering, and provide as far as possible against a war of races, by requesting the Governor of Mississippi to issue a proclamation cautioning the citizens against taking the law into their own hands, assuring them that the Military would contribute their share to protect lives and property, and would interpose by force of arms, to put down any attempts of freedmen to seize the property of the whites. In every case coming to my knowledge of cruelty, or killing even when the latter occurred under great provocation and in self defense, I have caused the arrest of the offender against the freedmen, and have in several cases directed trials and approved sentences so as to afford the freedmen no just cause of provocation. The crimes are by no means confined to the white population, who believing, as they do, that there is an intention to place the control of affairs in the hands of their late slaves, have conducted themselves with commendable forbearance. The majority of black over white voters registered in this state is about twenty thousand (20.000) and in some counties the black outnumber the whites, four or five one; in such localities they, I am informed, expect a division of the property, and in case they are disappointed, with arms in their hands, they will probably attempt to take what they want, that this is the belief of the whites is clear. To meet these dangers I recommend immediate action of Congress, First. to employ and feed as many of the freed people in the counties on the Mississippi river, as possible, by appropriating at least a million dollars for the repair of the levees from Tunica, South, which were cut by U. S. troops during the war, and have never recovered. Second. and most important in every sense, to build up a loyal white laboring population who can provide for themselves, and have proved their ability to maintain a republican form of government; as well as to protect the whites, and freedmen from each other—I recommend that at least ten thousand (10.000) white volunteers be called out from the north west, with their wives, to occupy and as soon as they can locate to be discharged, so as to colonize each of the six cotton states, with provision made for the support of their families, provided they remain in the country at least a year after their discharge. Such a military colonyies would have been looked upon a year ago as an insult, they would now be welcomed and would settle the question of reconstruction. I enclose among other papers, extract from a letter from the Commanding Officer of Arkansas, who reports similar destitution among the freedmen of the rich cotton counties of that state, and the probable abandonment of those lands. It will be seen that my recommendation for prompt employment on the levies, of the freedmen in the river counties is in accordance with the recommendations of the inclosed petition of Judge Hill, to Congress, this accordance was entirely without previous knowledge of the opinions of the other by either of us. There are a number of other reasons why a loyal white population should occupy the southern states as soon as possible, which will suggest themselves to an intelligent observer in this country. I hope the General Commanding will through the proper channel present the subject for the early consideration of Congress." LS, *ibid.*, RG 108, Letters Received. The enclosures are *ibid.* On Dec. 13, Ord wrote to USG. "I have the honor to forward herewith report of Genl Gillem on the condition of the Freed men in his Sub Dist—The report presents matters of vital importance to the peace and welfare of the country and which in connection with my report I beg to call to the attention of the Secy of War" ALS, *ibid.*, RG 94, Letters Received, 1818M 1867. The enclosure is *ibid.*

On Dec. 27, Maj. Gen. Oliver O. Howard, Washington, D. C., wrote to USG. "With your approbation, I believe, under the present Acts of Congress supplies may be issued to a limited extent,—that is to the extent of the means that can be appropriated thereto,—to prevent extreme want in the southern and southwestern states. There is no method except to issue to individuals or families that are absolutely in need; but I know nothing to prevent a single Agent being held responsible for the relief of one hundred families, more or less. If the Agent be chosen carefully having in view his responsibility and integrity, and a lien be taken upon the next crop whenever the issue is upon a farm or plantation or upon other products that the recipients may not consider themselves as paupers, there will be no violation of law and little danger of loss to the Government. I would not issue anything but the simplest necessaries, corn and meat. If this method of relief meets your approbation until the whole subject can be brought before Congress, I would be glad to have your formal endorsement with any additional instructions you may wish to give." LS, *ibid.*, RG 105, Letters Received. On Dec. 30, USG favorably endorsed this letter. AES, *ibid.* On Dec. 31, Howard wrote to USG. "I have the honor to request that such quantity of Mixed and Deseccated vegetables, now on hand in Subsistence Department, as are not required for issue to the Army may be transferred to this Bureau for distribution to the destitute people of the South. The terms upon which this transfer is to be made to be settled by the Commissary General of Subsistence and myself" LS, *ibid.*, RG 94, Letters Received, 347F 1867. On the same day, USG endorsed this letter. "Approved." AES, *ibid.* On Jan. 2, 1868, Howard wrote to USG. "Please find enclosed herewith reports of Generals Ord, Gillem, Hancock, Canby, Scott, and other officers bearing upon the destitution present and prospective in the southern states,—also, a statement and request made by Mr. William Whaley on behalf of the planters of South Carolina. Since my last annual report, reports from military officers, Bureau Agents, and citizens from different parts of the south, have considerably changed in their tone. The sudden fall in the price of cotton together with the failure of the crops in large sections where a good yield was anticipated— this latter misfortune being occasioned by heavy rains causing overflows in some sections, also by the caterpillar and other causes—have produced great depression, anxiety and apprehension. It is generally believed by those who have communicated with this office that there will be great suffering from want of food in portions of Louisiana, Mississippi, South Carolina and in limited sections of other states before the close of the present winter, and that relief in some shape, must be furnished to prevent the anarchy that many apprehend. I call your special attention to these reports, and recommend that the attention of the President and Congress be called to them with a view to some thorough and practical mode of relief that will not have a tendency to pauperise the people. Could a fund be established from which employers might draw on paying reasonable interest it might afford temporary if not permanent relief. General Canby favors relief through such a fund, or through the issue of provisions taking a lien upon the crops for security. Mr Whaley recommends a loan of thirty millions in currency to be secured by bonds and mortgage and other good security for the benefit of all the states in extreme need. Generals Ord and Hancock suggest the repairing of the levees of the Mississippi by the Government, and make other suggestions and recommendations   I do not feel prepared, after giving these reports a full consideration, to suggest any complete method of relief, or offer any detailed plan. I am fully aware that certain politicians have taken advantage of the suffering in the regions where destitution prevails to further their own peculiar views or interests. They are trying to reduce the price of labor to board merely, to get control of those who are impoverished, and to check or hinder the exercise of the rights of the latter as citizens. Still the reports that I forward speak for themselves, and I recommend a thorough consideration of the subject presented with a view to prevent the evils that are feared and predicted by so many witnesses. Enclosed please find also copies of dispatches and letters giving instructions to Assistant Commissioners to enable them to meet any sudden emergency—" LS, *ibid.*, RG 107, Letters Received from Bureaus. On Jan. 4, Howard wrote to USG. "Understanding that there is quite a quantity of desiccated mixed vegetables on hand in the Commissary Department which may be made use of to relieve present destitution so extensively complained of in the South, I recommend that the attention of Congress be called to it, with a view to its transfer to this Bureau for use. As it will bring very little if sold, I recommend that it be not made a charge against the Freedmen's Bureau." Copy, *ibid.*, RG 105, Letters Sent. On Jan. 10, USG wrote to Speaker of the House Schuyler Colfax. "I have the honor to send, herewith, for the consideration of the proper Committee, a communication of January 4th from the Commissioner of Freedmen, recommending that authority be granted by Congress, for the transfer, without cost, to the Bureau of Refugees, for distribution to the destitute in the South, a quantity of *desicated mixed vegetables* now on hand in the Subsistence Department. The Commissary General of Subsistence concurs in the recommendation and this Department approves the passage of a Joint Resolution for that object—a draft of which is respectfully sent herewith—" Df, *ibid.*, Letters Received; copy, *ibid.*, RG 107, Reports to Congress. See *HED*, 40-2-95.

On Dec. 20, 1867, I. N. Maynard, St. Francisville, La., had written to USG. "I had the honor some weeks since of addressing you a few lines from the City of New Orleans, relative to the *then* condition of our affairs in this section. Will you permit me to add a few more reflections and state a few more *facts* as they exist here *today*. Public Officers like yourself ought to have *correct* information, not only from your offices—(which you doubtless receive) but from the *people* also—it is not presumed you are pleased to hear, on all questions affecting their peace and welfare. This *presumption* emboldens me to write you. One of the most *vital* questions now upon us here in this section—and I believe it is *universal* over the South—is, how are we to feed and clothe the Colored people of the South—to say nothing of the poor and utterly impoverished *white* people also. The Crops having so lamentably failed during the last *two* years, from causes, which you are well aware of—demoralized Negroes—lack of labor—brought on by 'Radical teachings'—*unfavorable* Seasons—'Army Worms' &c. &c.—that *everybody* finds themselves—both *White* and *Black*, completely impoverished, and *destitute* of the means of support. This state of things is *unniversal* with us—all over the South, Louisiana has suffered perhaps *more* than any Southern State, the past *two* years, by the overflow of the Mississippi and *tributaries*, destroying every vestage of a crop of any kind. Our uplands have yielded from other causes—scarcely more than a *bale* or *two*—at the outside—on an average—of Cotton—to the *hand*, and with Cotton down to 12½¢ to 15¢—pr 'ordinary' to 'strict middling', and that the *awful killing* 'Cotton tax' of 2½¢ to the *pound*—with Pork and Corn at *ruinous high prices*, you can easily see for yourself, without my going *into figures*, what a lamentable *failure* has followed the planter in that staple. The effort has beggared every man who has touched it since the War, The 'Cotton tax' has come in to take the *last dollar*. It was this measure—so *unjust* and unconstitutional—(at least so believed by eminent jurists) which has 'broken the Camel's back,' and crushed us to earth. The result is seen in all its *horrors* today, all around us, *universal poverty* and *universal want*,—and I may add with *truth, almost universal despair*! What are we to do, General, in this awful extremity? Our only hope is in *Congress*. They *must* come to the relief of this people. The Colored people cannot be *put to work*, by any means to be procured with us or in New Orleans. The Cotton Factors are as a body—completely 'used up,' to use a *common* but very *appropriate* and *expressive* phrase. They will not receive but a *pittance* of their advances to the planter the present year. The proceeds of a bale of 400 pounds of Cotton at PRESENT *prices* will yield but *Thirty* or *Thirty four* Dollars at the most, when all the charges are deducted. We cannot look to these Merchants as heretofore for assistance to set the hands to work *again* in the fields. The Planter has no means of *his own* to do so. The Negroes would willingly—thousands of them men women & children—go to work today, for their *food* & *clothing*, but no one has the ability to offer them *that*, so *utterly* impoverished are the *white* people of the Country. Famine, General, cruel and widespread *famine* is *almost upon* us, and will *certainly* overtake us To avoid *this* and all its attendant *horrors*, I have had the honor to suggest to the Hon'l. Schuyler Colfax, Speaker of the House and Hon'l. Mr. Fessenden of the Senate, that Congress make appropriations to purchase provisions in the Cities, and distribute them to Planters, after they have *employed* and enrolled their hands, the necessary Corn and *Pork*. to set them at work, the Government taking a lien on the Crop for its reimbursment in the Fall. These statements of the Planters must be verified by an oath or affirmation that he is not able to obtain supplies in any other way, nor has any means to feed and clothe the Freedmen *employed* or *on his* place. I can conceive of no other plan by which we can put the Colored people to work. The Government cannot afford thus to *feed them* in *idleness*, for they *will not work, if they can help it*. All the *live* stock of the Country is now nearly *destroyed* by these *thieving vagabonds*, who constantly prowl about the plantations—and *soon* they will have nearly or *quite* the *whole*; This stock is the *only hope* and *sustenance* of the *white* people, without this, there would be *wholesale famine now—everywhere*. I appeal to you therefore General, as Commander in Chief to do all you can to preserve *life*—to set the negro to work—to help the poor and distressed of both races,—and thus *preserve* the *peace* and *good order* and   of society. All these things—troubles, poverty—and universal painful apprehensions of the *Future*, compose the unwise measures of Congress, towards the South. It *must* be so. You can trace them by regular gradations up to Washington   Cannot Congress be induced, when they behold the effects of their measures, upon the general prosperity of the Country—*recede* from their legislation—repeal the 'Cotton tax,'—and all the 'Reconstruction Acts' especially that one of *July*, and let us *into* the Union upon fair and honorable terms? I *hope* so. I trust General, that no considerations of *Public favor*—nor the blandishments of Power—will ever swerve you from giving, us the full benefit of your advice and unbiassed judgment, in our present most *lamentable* condition, Politically & *Materially*. . . . Would be pleased to receive a reply to this at your leisure." Copy, DNA, RG 105, Letters Received. On Jan. 4, 1868, Howard endorsed this letter. "The enclosed letter of *J. N. Maynard* having been referred to me is respectfully returned to the *Secty* of *War ad interim*.—The representations of destitution are probably in the main correct. But the charges that freedmen will not work, and that they are fed by the Government in idleness are not believed to be true. If any coercive measures are adopted to enforce labor, it is recommended that they apply to the idle whites as well as blacks." Copy, *ibid*.

To Andrew Johnson

December 24th *1867*.

To The President.
Sir:

In the matter of the claim of *William Rayne*, (Trustee) for rent of a building in Alexandria, Va., used and occupied by the United States from 1861 to 1865, and for damage caused by such use and occupation, referred to me for examination and report, by you, on the 19th instant, I have the honor to report that it appears from the papers and evidence on file in this Department that this claim comes within the prohibitory act of February 19th 1867, which provides that previous legislation "shall not be construed to authorize the settlement of any claim for . . . occupation of, or injury to, real estate . . . by the military authorities or troops of the United States, where such claim originated during the war for the suppression of the rebellion, in a State, or part of a State, declared in insurrection by the Proclamation of the President of the United States, dated July 1st 1862, or in a State which, by an ordinance of secession, attempted to withdraw from the United States government."— The claim, therefore, cannot be liquidated.

> I am, Very Respectfully
> Your obedient Servant
> U. S. GRANT
> Sec. of War, ad int.

LS (ellipses in original), DLC-Andrew Johnson. In an undated letter, Marian E. Bayne had written to President Andrew Johnson. "May it please Your Excellency to grant unto your memorialist favorable consideration. Your memorialist is the daughter of the late Purser Speiden of the U. S. Navy, and the widow of Geo. H. Bayne who departed this life in the year 1858 leaving infant children of very tender age, and devising to their uncle William Bayne in trust for these orphans the rent of a certain warehouse in the City of Alexandria Virginia. This warehouse was taken possession of by the United States and used used as a hospital for a long period of time as appears from the papers filed herewith. The rent of this building was the only income of these orphan, children, and of this they have been cruelly deprived. The claim for rent was referred to the claims commission, whose judgement was that it came within the purview of the Act of Congress, forbidding the payment of claims originating in those states which passed ordinances of secession. May it please Your Excellency—to allow me to plead that thes little children are innocent and helpless and that the Governmt should not wrong them by thus withholding what is acknowledged to be their due, and by the withholding of which they have already been greatly injured. May it please Your Excellency to do justice in the premises and Your Memorialist as in duty bound will ever pray &c" ALS, *ibid.* On Nov. 8, 1867, Bvt. Maj. Gen. Daniel H. Rucker, act. q. m. gen., had written to USG. "I have the honor to return herewith the enclosed communication of H. O. Claughton, requesting that the War Department reconsider the petition of Wm Bayne, Trustee of the children of Geo H. Bayne, deceased, for rent and damage of property at Alexandria Va. stated at $300. and also requesting copies of the papers &c, and to report. That all the papers connected with the claim referred to, were returned April 5th 1867 from this Office to the War Department for *file*, in obedience to the order of the Secretary of War." LS, DNA, RG 92, Reports to the Secretary of War (Press).

On March 3, 1873, Asst. Secretary of the Treasury William A. Richardson wrote to USG. "I have the honor to return herewith H. R. 3166, 'An Act for the relief of William Bayne, trustee &c' and inform you that I know of no objection to its receiving your approval." Copy, *ibid.*, RG 56, Letters Sent to the President.

To William H. Seward

Washington City,
Dec. 24th 1867

Hon. W. H. Seward, Sec'y.
Sir,
Referring to your com'n. dated yesterday, requesting information in respect to the Military record, services and character of *Record O. S. Burke*, late of the 15th Regt. N. Y. Vols. Eng'rs., now charged with being concerned in the Fenian Conspiracy, I have the honor to inform you as follows:

Record O. S. Burke, was promoted from Qr. Mr. Ser'gt. 15th N. Y. Vol. Eng'rs. and appointed 2d Lt. in the same Regt. in Jan'y. or Feb'y. 1863, he was on detached service from Mch. 1863 to Sept. 22d 1863 as Brigade Qr. Mr., when he was mustered into service as 1st Lt., and detached as Regimental Qr. Mr. on which duty he continued until Aug. 26th 1864 when he was returned to his Co. in arrest, and tried by Genl. Court Martial, the proceedings of which were promulgated in Gen'l. Court Martial Orders No. 34, Sept. 14th 1864 from Hd. Qrs. Army of the Potomac (copy herewith). He was in command of Co. "G", from Sept. 26th 1864 to Dec. 26th 1864 when he was placed in charge of fortifications, and continued on that duty to Jan'y. 22d 1865, when he was granted leave of absence—returned to duty Feb 6 /65   He was in command of Co. "I" from April 24th 1865 and mustered into service as Capt. of Co. "I" May 29th 1865 and honorably discharged with his Co. June 13th 1865.

His Milty. record in the volunteer service of the U. S., is deemed an honorable one, and no milt'y. charges appear against him, except as set forth in the Gen'l. Court Martial Order No. 34 Army of the Potomac, series of 1864 hereinbefore referred to.

I have the honor to be, Very Resp'y.
Your obt. servant,
U. S. Grant,
Sec'y. of War, ad int.

Copies, DNA, RG 107, Letters Sent to the President; *ibid.*, Letters Received, W482 1867.

To Albert G. Riddle

Dec. 26th 1867

SIR:

It is my desire that the arrangement made by my predecessor, to hav[e] cases desided against the U. States appealed, and your services retained, be continued.

U. S. GRANT
sec. of war ad int

TO HON. A. G. RIDDLE

ALS, OClWHi. Albert G. Riddle, born in 1816, served as prosecutor in Chardon, Ohio (1840–46), in the Ohio legislature (1848–50), as U.S. representative (1861–63), and consul at Matanzas, Cuba (1863–64), then returned to Washington, D. C., to practice law.

On Nov. 22, 1867, Riddle had written to USG. "I am under the advice of the War Dept. Counsel for Gen A. H. Terry in the case of Buckly vs Terry in the Sup. Court of this Dist. set for trial Dec 30 prox. The case grows out of the matter refered to and covered by the enclosed letter The papers therein re-fered to will be necessary to the defence of Gen. Terry on the trial I have to request official copies of all, the papers for his defence" ALS, DNA, RG 94, Letters Received, 271B 1865. The enclosure is *ibid.* On Dec. 9, Bvt. Maj. Gen. Alfred H. Terry, Washington, D. C., wrote to USG. "In June or July 1865 while I was in command of the department of Virginia and exercising all the powers of a military commander in a district when martial law prevails it became my duty to decide upon the right of possession to certain lands between a lessee of the Treasury of the U. S. and a lessee of the rebel owner of the property. I decided in favor of the lessee of the Treasury. Whereupon the other party brought a suit against me in the courts of the District of Columbia for damages for the eviction which followed my decision. This case is now set down for trial on Decr 30th My Attorney advises me that the presence of Bvt. Lt. Col. E W Smith one of my aides is desirable both on the trial and in the preparation of the case. Col. Smith was Adjutant General of the Dept. of Va. both duig Genl Ords command & my own, the transaction on which the suit in question is founded commenced under General Ord, & Col Smiths recollection of facts not of record will be valuable to me The suit arises purely & solely out of official action & I therefore respectfully ask that Col Smith may be ordered to report to me here." ALS, *ibid.*, 456D 1867.

On Dec. 6, Riddle wrote to USG. "Mr. Jno H. Garrett writes me to make enquiries as to his claim for the distruction of his barn It was burned by Col. Conger at the time of the death of Booth & the capture of Herrold He claims that he was loyal and innocent and the property burned under circumstances that entitles him to compensation The claim was made some two years ago—" ALS, *ibid.*, RG 107, Letters Received, R225 1867.

On March 10, 1869, Riddle wrote to USG. "I understand that Louis J. Weichmann, of Philadelphia, will apply for some place under the government. In his behalf, I beg to say that I made his acquaintance while acting as counsel for the United States in the trial of John H. Surratt in 1867. Mr. Weichmann was so situated in reference to the case that he was compelled to act a very conspicuous, delicate, and painful part, and one which severely tried his mental and moral qualities. He acquitted himself in an admirable manner, which gained him the entire confidence of both Judge Pierrepont and myself, and aside from testifying, his services in other respects were valuable to us. I think him entitled to the most favorable consideration of the government." Louis J. Weichmann, *A True History of the Assassination of Abraham Lincoln and of the Conspiracy of 1865* (New York, 1975), p. 399.

Later, Riddle wrote to USG. "I have to request that you will see the bearer Mrs Barney Woods whose husband is to be executed at the jail on the 27th inst. I commend her to your kindest consideration" ALS (written to USG as president, dated only Nov. 21), ICarbS.

To Maj. Gen. Winfield S. Hancock

Dec. 27th *1867.* [*11:30* A.M.]

Maj. Gn. W. S. Hancock,
New Orleans La.

Three or four companies have been ordered from the 3d District to report to you.

U. S. Grant
General

ALS (telegram sent), DNA, RG 107, Telegrams Collected (Bound); telegram sent, *ibid.*; telegram received, *ibid.*, RG 393, 5th Military District, Telegrams Received. On Dec. 18, 1867, Maj. Gen. Winfield S. Hancock had written to the AG requesting an additional regt. of white troops. Copy, *ibid.*, RG 107, Letters Received from Bureaus. On Dec. 23, 12:30 P.M., Hancock telegraphed to USG. "I send this day by mail a report by Lieut Colonel Wood Commanding District of Louisiana and Asst Commissioner Bureau R. F and A. L., together with various other papers representing a condition of affairs in the State of La, calculated to excite serious apprehension and demanding prompt action on the part of the Government. I have already partially represented this condition of things in a letter of the Eighteenth (18th) inst, asking for additional white troops to prevent disorders and disturbances from these causes. Troops have been and will continue to be sent to the districts in which disturbances are threatened as far as practicable   Destitution and threatened famine, principally on the part of the freedmen, together with imperfect ideas of their rights, prompt them to the commission of theft of food, ~~principally~~ generally so far by killing cattle, and hogs—retaliation follows. The worst passions of both classes are excited and if not soon prevented, the most lamentable consequences will follow.—The localities most affected are the river towns, into which the freedmen are congregating, and the lately inundated sections where the crops haveing failed or proven unremunerative, the laborers are unpaid, and are without work or sufficient food.

If it should be determined to issue rations to the destitute, they might be required to work, on rebuilding the destroyed, and mending the unsafe Levees, in such places and under such regulations as may be prescribed. Neither the State nor private individuals are now able to do this work and nothing that can be done in or for the State can at present compare in importance respecting its material interests with this" LS (telegram sent), *ibid.*, Telegrams Collected (Bound); telegram received (at 5:20 P.M.), *ibid.*; *ibid.*, RG 108, Telegrams Received. The report is *ibid.*, Letters Received.

On Dec. 23, 1:00 P.M., USG telegraphed to Bvt. Maj. Gen. John Pope, Atlanta. "If you can possibly spare them send four companies of troops from your command to New Orleans to report to Gn. Hancock. If they cannot be spared otherwise you might diminis the garrisons in forts." ALS (telegram sent), *ibid.*, RG 107, Telegrams Collected (Bound); telegram sent, *ibid.*; copies, *ibid.*, RG 46, Senate 40A–F2, Messages; *ibid.*, RG 108, Telegrams Sent; DLC-USG, V, 56. On Dec. 24, Pope telegraphed to USG. "I will endeavor to send a part at least of the troops you indicate to New Orleans I may get three Co's but with the understanding that they are to be returned to Georgia by February 20th in time for the Election and I cannot spare a man from Ala—until after Feby 4th There is & will be such Excitement here until these Elections are over that I am fearful of weakning the force too much. There are Co's of Arty—at Ft Jefferson some of which might be sent but as they were stationed there by the express orders of the Genl in Chief I do not feel authorized to remove them" Telegram received (on Dec. 25, 10:30 A.M.), DNA, RG 107, Telegrams Collected (Bound); *ibid.*, RG 108, Telegrams Received; copy, DLC-USG, V, 55. On Dec. 26, 11:30 A.M., USG telegraphed to Pope. "The return of troops can't be promised. You can however send any Artilery companies that you think can be spared from present duties. Answer." ALS (telegram sent), DNA, RG 107, Telegrams Collected (Bound); telegram sent, *ibid.*; copies, *ibid.*, RG 46, Senate 40A–F2, Messages; *ibid.*, RG 108, Telegrams Sent; DLC-USG, V, 56. On the same day, Pope telegraphed to USG. "Have ordered by Telegraph two (2) companies of Artillery from Fort Jefferson—Will reach New Orleans about fifteenth (15th) January—One company of Infantry from Georgia will proceed immediately" Telegram received (at 6:30 P.M.), DNA, RG 107, Telegrams Collected (Bound); *ibid.*, RG 108, Telegrams Received; copies, *ibid.*, RG 46, Senate 40A–F2, Messages; DLC-USG, V, 55. On Dec. 27, Bvt. Brig. Gen. Cyrus B. Comstock telegraphed to Hancock. "Two (2) companies of Artillery from Fort Jefferson have been ordered to you and one (1) company of infantry from Georgia." ALS (telegram sent), DNA, RG 107, Telegrams Collected (Bound); telegram sent, *ibid.*; copies, *ibid.*, RG 108, Telegrams Sent; DLC-USG, V, 56.

General Orders

[*December 28, 1867*]

By direction of the Pres. of the U. S. the following orders are made. Bvt. Maj. Gn. E. O. C. Ord will turn over the command of the 4th Mil. Dist. to Bvt. Maj. Gn.　　　　Gillem and proceed to San Francisco Cal, to take command of the Dept. of Cal.[1]

On being relieved by Bvt. Maj. Gn. Ord, Bvt. Maj. Gn. I. Mc-Dowell will proceed to Vicksburg Miss and relieve Gen. Gillem of the Comd of the 4th District.

Bvt. Maj. Gn. J Pope is hereby relieved of the command of the 3d Mil. Dist. ~~and will turn over the command to the officer next in rank in the command until~~ and will report at Hd Qrs of the Army for further orders

Maj. Gn. G. G. Meade is assigned to the Command of the 3d Mill Dist. and will ~~proceed~~ assume it, without delay.[2] The Dept. of the East will be commanded by the senio[r] officer now ~~in it~~ on duty in it untill a commander is named by the President.

Bvt. Maj. Gn. W Swayne is hereby relieved from duty in the Bureau of R. F & A. and will proceed to Nashville, Tenn. and assume command of his regiment.

ADf, DNA, RG 94, Letters Received, 991W 1867. Issued with no significant alterations as AGO General Orders No. 104, Dec. 28, 1867. Copy (printed), *ibid.*, 523E 1867.

1. On Dec. 28, 3:00 P.M., USG telegraphed to Bvt. Maj. Gen. Edward O. C. Ord, Holly Springs. "Orders made to-day sending you to Cal. to relieve Gn. McDowell." ALS (telegram sent), *ibid.*, RG 107, Telegrams Collected (Bound); telegram sent, *ibid.*; copies, *ibid.*, RG 108, Telegrams Sent; DLC-USG, V, 56. On Nov. 30, Ord had telegraphed to USG. "Expect to be absent for some days, have much difficult business, Can I retain Major Green his health is better & I would be glad to keep him till I am relieved" Telegram received (on Dec. 1, 10:20 A.M.), DNA, RG 107, Telegrams Collected (Bound); *ibid.*, RG 108, Telegrams Received; copy, DLC-USG, V, 55. On Dec. 2, noon, USG telegraphed to Ord. "You are authorized to retain Col. Green as long as you need his services." ALS (telegram sent), DNA, RG 107, Telegrams Collected (Bound); telegram sent, *ibid.*; copies, *ibid.*, RG 108, Telegrams Sent; DLC-USG, V, 56. On Dec. 30, 11:05 A.M., USG telegraphed to Ord. "Your order requires you to turn over command to Gn. Gillem on his arrival. You can stay where you like untill Mrs. Ord can travel." ALS (telegram sent), DNA, RG 107, Telegrams Collected (Bound); telegram sent, *ibid.*; telegram received, Ord Papers, CU-B. On Dec. 30, Ord telegraphed to President Andrew Johnson. "Before going to California I wish to see you can I be directed to come to Washn" Telegram received, DNA, RG 108, Letters Received. On Dec. 31, Johnson endorsed this telegram. "RESPECTFULLY REFERRED TO General U. S. Grant Secretary of War ad-interim, who will please issue necessary Order granting request of Gen'l Ord—" ES, *ibid.* On Jan. 2, 1868, 9:20 A.M., USG telegraphed to Ord. "When relieved by Gn. Gillem report to Army Head Qrs." ALS (telegram sent), *ibid.*, RG 107,

Telegrams Collected (Bound); telegram sent, *ibid.*; copies, *ibid.*, RG 108, Telegrams Sent; DLC-USG, V, 56.

On Feb. 29, Ord wrote to USG. "Mrs Ord gave me another daughter on the 13th—the Mother is getting along slowly—caught cold and was set back but is convalescing again she tried going out most too soon—I expect to start from here about the 15th Mar—and from N York about the 21st or the Steamer next after—I presume it is not necessary for me to say that I am as I have always been—ready to support the Congress and its laws, unless the latter should be declared unconstitutional, ~~and~~ by competent court—and such declaration be generally deferred to—by them I hope all serious difficulties will be settled by competent tribunals, and not allowed to go to the subordinate officers of the Army— Mr Brinkley—whose wife & mine are old friends asked me when I was in Washington what I thought would be the course of Army officers if the President should by any accident or other wise Call on them to support him as against the Congress—and I told him that nine tenths or perhaps more of the officers would Certainly support Congress—and gave him by my reasons to know that I would be with that 9/10ths At the same time tho I shall stand by Congress and the laws—I think the negro suffrage policy will as a policy, prove mistaken, and injurious to the interest of the republicans and to the whole country—I wrote Sherman, from whom I had a letter since his return that I thought we officers had better let the politicians fight out their own battles—and that as long as I could find out what the laws were & who was my command'g officer (under them) I didnt expect to have any trouble—my kindest regards to Mrs Grant—and love to Nellie & Jess—My Brother Maj Ord—1st Lt 1st Infy is too poor to pay the expense of his large family out to Cal and so has to decline going as my aid ~~as~~. I requested ~~he~~ I might be ~~ordered~~ authorised to take him & was—by you, so that I shall order him to his Company at N Orleans—which makes a vacancy on my staff which I shall fill by detail from troops in Cal—If there is any probability of my destination being changed by present or to be expected events—I hope you will let me know it before I start Your orders no matter how they interfere with privt affairs will be obeyed with alacrity—" ALS, USG 3.

On May 3, Ord, San Francisco, wrote to Bvt. Maj. Gen. John A. Rawlins. "private—Show some of this to the Genl—. . . Am here at last—I write to say that Minister Burlingame, (who will reach home about the time of this letter)— has had a flattering ovation here by all parties united—He means to help U S interests in China and can do so but his reception abroad partly depends on the honor shown him by the U S—his mission to bring China into intercourse with the rest of the world, is the great commercial move of the time, and his selection by the Chinese is what we can all feel proud of—I told him I knew Genl Grant would take pleasure in doing his mission Special honor—If on his arrival he could receive a grand military reception twould impress the mandarins with him and put the U S well forward in their Books—which they are making to send the Emperor—The democrats here have put a Strong spoke into our wheel by sending rebel sympathysers to their national Convention who will stick to Pendleton or some anti war man I shall inspect my Dept soon and write you about condition of affairs—please say to the Genl if he can—to approve ~~permiss~~ application for 'Spring' Waggon to run to Black Point and fetch Officers who want to live there if they can get to Town—where they are on duty—the Commutation &c which will be saved to Govt if they can have the waggon will amount to *4733* dols—the waggon is on hand & horses & to run it will cost only the Extra duty

pay of driver—three officers now live by the way   I wish he would authorise *me* as Dept Commander to ~~make some~~ comfortably house the men ~~ion~~ these frontiers they are at so[me] posts now in miserable holes and dens & have to hut—forage— water—wood—blacksmith—& carpenter &c &c &c &c &c for themselves—So that it takes two thirds or three fourths their time and labor *to take care of them- selves*—during which their is *no* Indian hunting done—and as they are miserably cared for; in some instances *two thirds* of whole compan[ies] have deserted—in Miss I found the only way *and the cheapest* to prevent desertions was to make the men so comfortable that they didnt want to quit—I did it and desertions went down from 230 or 40 per ct to 3 & 5—"   ALS, DNA, RG 108, Letters Received.
   2. See endorsement to Maj. Gen. George G. Meade, Jan. 6, 1868.

To Henry M. Cist

———

Washington, D. C., January 2, 1868.

MY DEAR SIR:

   Your favor of the 30th of December, extending to me, on the part of the committee to make arrangements for the organization of the "Society of the Army of the Cumberland," an invitation to meet them in Cincinnati, on the 6th of February, is received. It is not probable that my duties will permit of my absence from this city at that time, otherwise I would accept with great pleasure.

   I am glad to see the Army of the Cumberland organizing such a society, and would equally like to see each of the distinctive armies of the Union against rebellion organize such societies. Each may be proud of their record during the rebellion, and annual reunions will tend to keep up a brotherly feeling, cemented by hardships and dangers endured by all the members in our great patriotic cause.

   Hoping you will meet with success in the objects of your meet- ing, I subscribe myself,

                                        Your obedient servant,
                                        U. S. GRANT,
                                        General.

To HENRY M. CIST,
Corresponding Secretary, etc.

Report of the First Meeting of the Society of the Army of the Cumberland, . . .
(Cincinnati, 1868), p. 102. Henry M. Cist, born in Cincinnati in 1839, entered
the Civil War as private, 6th Ohio, and left as maj. and adjt.

To Maj. Gen. George G. Meade

Respectfully returned—

The Convention is authorized, by the Act of Congress passed
March 23rd 1867 supplementary to an act entitled "An Act to provide for the more efficient government of the rebel States" of March
2d 1867, to levy upon and collect a sufficient amount of taxes on the
property of the State, as was necessary to pay the expenses of the
same. The Ordinance passed by the Convention for this purpose and
the order of the Military Commander to the State Treasurer endorsed thereon, is in conformity to the letter and spirit of said Acts,
and the Act supplementary thereto of July 19. 67

The Government under the Constitution of the State of Georgia
adopted in 1865 which said Treasurer sets up as a bar to his compliance with said ordinance, is, by the said Acts of Congress, specif-
ically declared, with the governments of other States lately in rebellion, therein named to be "not legal State governments; and that
thereafter said Governments, if continued, were to be continued,
subject in all respects to the Military Comman[d]ers of the respective districts, and the paramount authority of Congress

Section 11 of the said supplementary act of July 19th provides
"That all the provisions of this Act and of the Acts to which this is
supplementary shall be construed liberally, to the end that all the
intents thereof may be fully and perfectly carried out"

It is clear from the correspondence between Genl Pope and the
Treasurer that the proper administration of the Military Reconstruction Acts require the removal of said Treasurer, and the appointment of some person in his stead under Section 2d of said Supplementary Act of July 19th who will respect the authority of Congress, the orders of military commanders, and the Ordinance of the
Convention under the same

Should the Comptroller General of the State, as Genl Pope seems to fear he may, decline to execute the Ordinance of the Convention, then he too should be removed

U. S. GRANT

General

HD QRS AUS

JANY 6 68

Copies (2), DLC-Andrew Johnson; Meade Papers, PHi; DNA, RG 46, Senate 40A–F2, Messages; *ibid.*, RG 108, Letters Received; *ibid.*, Register of Letters Received. Written on a letter of Dec. 26, 1867, from Bvt. Maj. Gen. John Pope, Atlanta, to USG. "I have the honor to transmit enclosed an Ordinance passed by the Georgia Convention now in session in conformity to the Reconstruction Acts with my endorsement thereon and a letter in reply to the Ordinance from the Treasurer of the State. I also enclose a copy of my order to the Treasurer dated October 25th and his answer thereto, which will explain to you why my endorsement on the enclosed Ordinance was made The letter of the State Treasurer dated December 21st simply means that he denies the authority of the Convention to exercise any control over the State Treasurer. It is altogether probable that substantially the same grounds will be taken by the Comptroller General of the State who is ordered to levy the special tax provided in the Ordinance as well as the Tax Collectors whose duty it is to collect it. Of course under the Reconstruction Acts my own power over the State Officers is not disputed but in a matter of this kind, I have not been willing to resort to military force unless I can be clear concerning the meaning of the Law. I therefore present the subject to your consideration with the request that I be furnished with the views of the Government, and such instructions as may be considered necessary. It is manifest that without the means to pay its daily expenses, there is every probability that the Convention must dissolve. The special tax authorized by the Reconstruction Acts cannot be collected in much less than six months, even if the Tax Collectors willingly collect it at all—This will be altogether too late for the necessities now pressing. Whether the Convention has control enough over the State Treasury to maintain its own existence, I must leave to be decided after the facts are presented. In Alabama no trouble arose from this cause for the simple reason that the Governor and State Officers were in favor of Reconstruction. In Georgia the opposite is the fact and the question I have now the honor to ask is this. Is it my duty to exercise such control over the State Treasury as will suffice to prevent the Officers of the Provisional State Government above referred to, from defeating the execution of the Reconstruction Acts? If there be no money in the State Treasury of course none can be had, but it is understood that there is more than sufficient for the purpose as the sum collected to pay the Legislature which would have met last month, if elections for the purpose could have been held under the Reconstruction Acts, is understood to be in the State Treasury, The Convention in conformity to the Acts of Congress has directed the Comptroller General of the State to levy a special tax necessary to pay its expenses and if he does so and the Tax Collectors are required to collect it, the whole amount will be returned to the State Treasury during the present fiscal year. The legality of this special tax will not be disputed so long as the Reconstruction Acts are recognized and enforced   That far then the Convention has the right to go, and as the enclosed Ordinance provides fully for reimbursement to the State Treasury for the expenses of the Convention, it is not so much a question whether or not the Convention has power to command the Provisional State Officers in this matter as whether the Military Commander of this District having power in the case, must not exercise it, to secure the execution of the Acts of Congress, or rather to protect the execution of these Acts against the obstruction set up by the officers of the Provisional State Government of Georgia. This is a peculiar and important question and one upon the decision of which the execution of the Reconstruction Acts will largely depend   I therefore respectfully ask as speedy a decision as possible, as matters are pressing. The Ordinances passed by the Alabama Convention as also by the Georgia Convention, (except that providing for the compensation of members and necessary expenses of these Conventions,) I have not considered to possess any validity until the constitutions are ratified by the people and approved by Congress and have therefore declined to enforce them or allow them to be enforced." Copies (2), DLC-Andrew Johnson; Meade Papers, PHi; DNA, RG 108, Letters Received. USG endorsed this letter. "Referred to Gn. Rawlins for careful reading, and examination of re-construction acts on the points at issue touched upon within and prepare endorsement. Other information shews that the present Treas. of Ga. found no difficulty in finding law to pay the rebel convention which passed the state out of the Union and also the convention called to ratify the amendments to state constitution dictated by the President. Question whether the best solution would not be the removal of present state Treas. and apt. of one who has always been loyal." AE (undated), *ibid.*

On Dec. 21, Pope had telegraphed to USG. "Convention in Alabama and Georgia have passed ordinances of relief to debtors which the Civil Officers will not obey or recognize   What is considered to be my duty in the case" Telegram received (at 4:30 P.M.), *ibid.*, RG 107, Telegrams Collected (Bound); *ibid.*, RG 108, Telegrams Received; copies, *ibid.*, RG 46, Senate 40A–F2, Messages; DLC-USG, V, 55. On Dec. 23, noon, USG telegraphed to Pope. "The constitutions adopted by the conventions now in session are not the law of the states untill submitted to the people and ratified by them, and accepted by Congress. I do not see therefore how you can enforce laws enacted by them untill so ratified." ALS (telegram sent), DNA, RG 107, Telegrams Collected (Bound); telegram sent, *ibid.*; telegram received, Meade Papers, PHi. On Dec. 24, Pope telegraphed to USG. "General Dunn will leave here for Washington tomorrow night to lay before you the action of the Georgia Convention concerning the payment of its expenses & also certain action of this and the Alabama Convention,   No action in any of these matters will be taken by the Military Authorities until General Dunn reports to you all the facts, and the views of the Government are known" Telegram received (at 11:50 A.M.), DNA, RG 107, Telegrams Collected (Bound); *ibid.*, RG 108, Telegrams Received; copy, DLC-USG, V, 55. On Dec. 31, Bvt. Brig. Gen. William M. Dunn, Sr., Washington, D. C., telegraphed to Pope. "Was John Jones the Treasurer who paid the Delegates to the convention of 1865." Telegram sent, DNA, RG 107, Telegrams Collected (Bound). On the same day, Pope telegraphed to Dunn. "John Jones is the state Treasurer who paid the Sesession Convention in 1861 and the convention in 1865 also, on the order of those conventions respectively" Telegram received (on Jan. 1, 1868, 9:30 A.M.), *ibid.*; *ibid.*, RG 108, Telegrams Received; copy, DLC-USG, V, 55.

On Dec. 23, 1867, 11:00 A.M., USG had telegraphed to Maj. Gen. George G. Meade, Philadelphia. "You will please report to the President, in person, without delay." ALS (telegram sent), DNA, RG 107, Telegrams Collected (Bound); telegram sent, *ibid.*; telegram received (at 11:15 A.M.), *ibid.*, RG 393, Dept. of the East, Hd. Qrs., Letters Received. On the same day, Meade telegraphed to USG. "Telegram rec'd. Will report tomorrow morning" Telegram received (at 4:35 P.M.), *ibid.*, RG 107, Telegrams Collected (Bound); (at 8:20 P.M.) *ibid.*, RG 108, Telegrams Received; copies, *ibid.*, RG 393, Dept. of the East, Letters Sent; DLC-USG, V, 55.

On Dec. 27 and 28, Pope wrote to USG. "I have the honor to transmit enclosed a copy of a letter just received from General Swayne. It sets out clearly the determined purpose of the disloyal element to foment disturbance and to misrepresent the condition of affairs in Alabama to suit their own purposes.— The entire associated Press is in the hands of disloyal men and is used for purposes hostile to the peace of the South and to the well being of the Country.— The indications now are that the managers of the disloyal faction in the South will succeed in breaking down every General who performs his duty. The result will be deplorable especially to Union men and Freedmen in this District.— The perplexities and difficulties of a Military Commander in the South are such that he must have the support of the Government to execute the laws.—If he cannot have that it is next to impossible for him to discharge the duties of his office.—The vaguest and the most reckless charges against him are sent or carried to Washington and are first made known to him through the Newspapers in the North.—I still hope that the Government will sustain its officers in the performance of their duties and that unless for some specific act of wrong which they cannot refute they will be supported in their position.—Unless this is done the Reconstruction Acts and all other laws of the U. S. bearing upon the South will prove but a dead letter.—If the President has not confidence in the officers Commanding in the South it would be best to send others at once who can rely upon his support and whom he will support.—The constant reports from Washington about the removal of Military Commanders in the South on account of the stories carried there by disloyal or troublesome men unsettle confidence and impair the standing and authority of the General concerned to such an extent that he is obliged at times to use arbitrary measures to do what the law requires him to do and what under other circumstances would be accomplished without force.— Under these circumstances it is best to have some officer in command whom the President will trust and not leave the execution of so important a law of the U. S. to an officer who is not sustained by the President and bitterly opposed by the disloyal faction in the South, for whose control the Reconstruction Acts were passed." "I have the honor to enclose a copy of General Order No 109. which should have accompanied my letter of yesterday in reference to the parading of a Colored Militia organization at Montgomery, Ala, on Christmas Day." LS, DNA, RG 108, Letters Received. The enclosures are *ibid.*

On Dec. 29, Meade telegraphed to USG. "General-order number one hundred & four (104) recd. Have telegraphed Brevet Maj Genl Sherman to report here at once. Will turn over Command to him in a few days after he reaches here, will then proceed to Atlanta. Brevet Brig General Drum assistant adjt Genl & Brevet Col Sanders assistant Judge Advocate are willing to accompany me & I would esteem it a great relief & a personal favor if I could be authorized to take them with me particularly Gen'l Drum." Telegram received, *ibid.*, Telegrams Received; copy, DLC-USG, V, 55. See General Orders, *Dec. 28, 1867.* On Dec. 30, 9:20 A.M., Bvt. Brig. Gen. Cyrus B. Comstock telegraphed to Meade. "In reply to your telegram of yesterday Gen. Grant authorises you to take General

Drum & Col Sanders with you to Georgia." ALS (telegram sent), DNA, RG 107, Telegrams Collected (Bound); telegram sent, *ibid.*; telegram received, *ibid.*, RG 393, Dept. of the East, Hd. Qrs., Letters Received. On Dec. 31, 1:00 P.M., Bvt. Brig. Gen. Frederick T. Dent telegraphed to Meade. "Gen Grant wishes to see you as you pass through this city" ALS (telegram sent), *ibid.*, RG 107, Telegrams Collected (Bound); telegram sent, *ibid.*; telegram received, *ibid.*, RG 393, Dept. of the East, Hd. Qrs., Letters Received. On the same day, Meade telegraphed to Dent. "Dispatch recd. Will stop thursday evening in Washington to see the General" Telegram received (at 3:20 P.M.), *ibid.*, RG 107, Telegrams Collected (Bound).

On Dec. 30, 11:35 A.M., USG telegraphed to Pope. "Order Gen. Shepherd to Washington to report for instructions. Gen Swayne will remain on his present duties untill Gn. Shepherd returns." ALS (telegram sent), *ibid.*; telegram sent, *ibid.*; copies, *ibid.*, RG 108, Telegrams Sent; DLC-USG, V, 56. On the same day, Pope telegraphed to USG. "I hope you will remember that it will be exceedingly painful to me to be ordered to the Pacific Coast, and that it would be nearly impossible for me for private reasons to go there. In addition my relations to Genl Halleck are very unpleasant and it would be as disagreeable to him as to me" Telegram received (at 6:00 P.M.), DNA, RG 107, Telegrams Collected (Bound); *ibid.*, RG 108, Telegrams Received; copy, DLC-USG, V, 55. On Dec. 31, Pope wrote to USG. "I am just in receipt of the order relieving me from the command of this District & shall leave here on the 2d January for Washington, via Cincinnati where I must leave my family—I will be in Washington on Tuesday next—I do not know in the least the immediate cause of this order nor indeed the remote cause—The only allegation against me of which I have any knowledge or which has ever been referred to me for explanation was the Memorial from certain citizens of Montgomery Ala. about frauds in the election alleged to have been committed in that County, but as my reply to it had not reached Washington until after the order of removal was issued, I infer that the removal was made for other causes of which I am in profound ignorance—Genl Dunn has doubtless made you acquainted with every thing concerning affairs here & so I need write nothing about them—I need not say to you that it takes a great weight off my mind to be relieved of this command—Under any circumstances even if I had been warmly supported by the Executive, the duty would have been very difficult, & full of perplexity, but as matters stand it had become almost unbearable—I shall leave here with a sense of relief which I have never experienced before. I telegraphed you yesterday about not sending me to the Pacific Coast—As you know my feeling on that subject I feel quite easy on that point—I wish Meade every success here—He will have a troublesome time & if he can interfere less than I have done with the Civil Administration & perform his duties under the law I shall be both surprised & gratified—I think however, unless he surrenders entirely to the Rebels, he will be warred upon as I have been—The Rebellion is as active & so far as the people of this Dist are concerned, nearly as powerful as during the War—I fear there will be sad calamities here unless this fiendish & malignant spirit is quelled or entirely conetrolled—You can scarcely form an idea of the spirit of malice & hatred in this people—It is a misnomer to call this question in the South a political question—It is *War* pure & simpl-;e—that is as far as war is permitted to be made by the Military authorities—The question is not whether Georgia & Alabama will accept or reject reconstruction—It is, shall the Union men & Freedmen, be the slaves of the old negro rebel aristocracy or not? or rather shall the former be permitted to live in these states at all or the latter (the negroes) as Free men—I hope much from the convention in this state—It will make a reasonable & moderate Constitution which will be ratified unless there is farther interference from without—I hope to see you next week & to have the opportunity of talking farther with you on this subject—" ALS, USG 3. On Jan. 6, 1868, Bvt. Col. H. Clay Wood, Atlanta, telegraphed to USG. "Please assign me with General Pope I know he will apply for me" Telegram received (at 2:20 P.M.), DNA, RG 107, Telegrams Collected (Bound). On Jan. 13, USG wrote a note. "Order Gn. Pope to command of Dept. of the Lakes," AN, *ibid.*, RG 94, Letters Received, 34W 1868.

On Jan. 8, 10:00 A.M., USG telegraphed to Meade. "Please take no action on the removal of Mayor and Council of Augusta untill charges are fully investigated" ALS (telegram sent), *ibid.*, RG 107, Telegrams Collected (Bound); telegram sent, *ibid.*; telegram received, *ibid.*, RG 393, 3rd Military District, Letters Received.

Also on Jan. 8, Meade telegraphed to USG. "The passages of ordinances by the conventions of Alabama & Georgia enacting ~~stay~~ relief laws, are producing great suffering in these states, by causing expedition to be used in making levys in anticipation of these ordinances having the force of law ~~on the adoption of the constitutions—Hence during that~~ advantage is being taken of the interval of time before these ordinances are laws to hurry levys & executions thus causing these ordinances intended as a measure of relief to become in reality the means of increasing & greatly aggravating the burdens of the people—I am therefore inclined to ~~give~~ adopt these ordinances as the act of the military athority & declare them to have force *until* the question is settled as to the adoption or rejection of the constitutions enacting them—I refer to you because your telegram of Decr 23d is adverse to enforcing any of the ordinances of the conventions prior to the adoption of the constitutions—and to obtain your approval of my proposed action—answer immediately.—" ALS (telegram sent), Meade Papers, PHi; telegram received (at 4:30 P.M., misdated Jan. 9), DNA, RG 107, Telegrams Collected (Bound); *ibid.*, RG 108, Telegrams Received. On Jan. 10, 11:00 A.M., USG telegraphed to Meade. "As District Commander I think you will be perfectly justifidable in adopting as your own order the stay laws proposed in the Constitutions to be submitted to the people of Ala. & Ga. This course is different from adopting as law the provision of the constitutions in advance of their ratification." ALS (telegram sent), *ibid.*, RG 107, Telegrams Collected (Bound); telegram sent, *ibid.*; telegram received, Meade Papers, PHi.

On Jan. 9, Meade telegraphed to USG. "I have had a conference with Govr Jenkins & exerted all my influence to induce him to consider, the appropriation by the Convention, as an appropriation made by law and not inconsistent with the provisions of the Georgia Constitution, and ~~require~~ urged him to sign the warrant required by the Treasurer—The Govr declined, and there is no alternative, but the exercise of my power to obtain control of the State Treasury—To avoid making any more changes than are required to effect the object, and also the difficulty of finding a suitable person & the questions of bonds I propose to remove only the Treasurer and to assign to the duty Brevt Brig Genl. Ruger—with instructions to continue payments as heretofore in accordance with the existing laws of the state & to make such payments to the convention as I shall authorise—checking thus un-necessary expenditures. I see no other mode of supplying the wants of the convention, and its continuance in session is dependant on its wants being immediately supplied—It is probable other steps may have to be taken, before the money can be secured, as it is intimated that an issue will be

made, with a view of testing the validity of my powers.—Your approval or disapproval is asked at once." ALS (telegram sent), *ibid.*; telegram received (on
Jan. 10, 10:30 A.M.), DNA, RG 107, Telegrams Collected (Bound); (on Jan.
10, 7:00 A.M.) *ibid.*, RG 108, Telegrams Received. On Jan. 10, 3:00 P.M.,
USG telegraphed to Meade. "Plan proposed in your dispatch of last evening to
remove State Treasurer of Ga. is approved." ALS (telegram sent), *ibid.*, RG
107, Telegrams Collected (Bound); telegram sent, *ibid.*; telegram received,
Meade Papers, PHi.

On Jan. 13, Meade wrote to USG. "Upon my arrival in, and assumption of
command of this District, one of the first questions which required action on my
part, was the providing of means to enable the Constitutional Convention of
Georgia to discharge the duty, imposed on it by the Reconstruction laws—You
are apprised of the steps taken by my predecessor, the papers relating to which,
are herewith appended that the record in the case may be complete. Finding that
the State Treasurer based his refusal to pay on the ground that he required the
warrant of the Governor, endorsed by the Comptroller General, I addressed an
official communication to the Governor urging a compliance with the form as
prescribed by the Constitution of the state of Georgia & requesting that my
views & wishes should be laid before the Comptroller General for his action
also—In reply I received a letter from the Governor declining to accede to my
wishes & arguing in extenso against my request. Being satisfied from this letter,
and from a personal interview held with the Governor, and from a letter written
by this officer to the Solicitor General of the Tallapoosa Circuit in which he declines to pay him his salary, on the ground of the illegality of his appointment by
my predecessor, that there was no possibility of harmonious co-operation between
the Governor & myself, in executing the Reconstruction Act. I felt it my duty
under the law to remove him as also the State Treasurer & to appoint in their
places Bvt Brig Gen'l Thos H Ruger to act as Governor & Lt Rockwell as State
Treasurer. The correspondence between the Govr & myself—the Governors letter
to the Solicitor General.—the notification to the Governor & State Treasurer of
their removal & the order issued on this subject are herewith appended." LS,
DNA, RG 108, Letters Received.

On Dec. 21, 1867, George Opdycke, New York City, had written to USG.
"I understand efforts are making to procure the removal from office of Gov.
Jenkins, of Ga. I am satisfied that this would be most impolitic. Gov. J., as I am
reliably assured, is a gentleman of integrity and of great purity of character;
that these qualities, combined with his business capacity, have placed the finances
of that State in a prosperous condition, and elevated its credit in this city were
many of its bonds have recently been negotiated on advantagious terms to the
state. The material interests of the southern people are already sadly depressed,
and it would seem to be both unwise and improper to depress them still more
by the proposed removal, unless other public considerations imparatively demand
it. Gov. J., I am assured, opposed secession, and, also, that he has not, since
joining in the movement to test the constitutionality of the reconstruction Act,
done any thing in opposition to the Government; and further, that he will not
hereafter. I have requested my friend Senator Conkling to confer with you on
this subject, and to submit some papers relating to it that have been placed in my
hands." ALS, Meade Papers, PHi. On Dec. 23, USG endorsed this letter. "Respectfully forwarded to Gn. Pope. It seems to me, in view of the near approach
of the election in Ga. that it is advisable to retain in office all the present incumbents untill that time unless removed for palpable misconduct." AES, *ibid.*

To Frederick Dent Grant

––––––

Washington D, C,
Jan.y 7th /68

DEAR FRED,

I have just received from Capt. Boynton the report of your examination in Mathematics and see that you stand Nineteen. In French you will be much nearer the other end of the class than you are to the head of it in Mathematics but I hope you will get through. If your eyes keep well you must try to get up hereafter. If your eyes trouble you relieve them by doing your studieng in the day time.

Your Ma has just written to you and I suppose told you that the family are all well and send you a great deal of love.

Your Affectionate
U. S. GRANT

ALS, CSmH.

To Henry Stanbery

––––––

January 8th *1868*.

SIR:

In reply to your letter of December 31st, suggesting the propriety of this Department employing counsel to represent the parties having McCardle[1] in custody, the case No. 380 on the Supreme Court Calendar entitled exparte McCardle, I have the honor to send you a copy of a telegram received from Major General Ord, from which it will be seen that he has directed the Judge Advocate who conducted the case to confer with the Attorney General.

Very respectfully
Your obedient Servant
U. S. GRANT
Secretary of War ad int.

THE HONORABLE THE ATTORNEY GENERAL.

LS, DNA, RG 60, Letters Received, War Dept. The enclosure is *ibid*. On Dec. 31, 1867, Attorney Gen. Henry Stanbery had written to USG. "I beg leave to call your attention to case No. 380 on the calendar of the Supreme Court of the United States for this term, entitled *Ex parte McCardle*. It appears that McCardle was arrested by the military authorities in Mississippi for publishing certain articles in a newspaper of which he was the editor, alleged to be in violation of the Reconstruction Acts. Being in military custody, a military commission was ordered to try him. He made application to the District Court of Mississippi for a writ of *habeas corpus*. The writ was granted, a return made by the officer having him in custody, and a hearing had, and the decision of the District Judge was that he should be remanded into the custody of the military authorities. From this decision, McCardle has taken an appeal to the Supreme Court of the United States. Mr. Black, who appears as counsel for McCardle, yesterday made a motion before the Sup. Ct. to have the case advanced upon the docket in order to a speedy hearing. No action has yet been taken by the court upon the motion. I do not propose to appear in the case. As the matter appertains to your Department, I will suggest to you the propriety of employing counsel to represent the parties having McCardle in custody, so that the case may receive proper attention before the Supreme Court." LS, *ibid*., RG 94, Record & Pension Office, 670220.

On Nov. 18, Bvt. Maj. Gen. Edward O. C. Ord, Holly Springs, Miss., had written to USG. "I have the honor to enclose herewith copies of letters from Generals Smith and Gillem, stating that writs of Habeas Corpus had been served on them for certain prisoners. I have directed the writs complied with; in the case of Old, in Arkansas, my telegraphic order (enclosed) reached General Smith after adjournment of the Court. General Gillem, in obedience to my orders, will respond with the body of McCardle on the 21st, after he shall have been arraigned before a Military Commission, and Judge Burwell of Vicksburg has been requested to act as associate counsel to defend the arrest and order for trial. I enclose copy of telegraphic orders for arrests of persons inciting hostility of races. &c." LS, *ibid*., RG 108, Letters Received. The enclosures are *ibid*.

On Jan. 4, 1868, Bvt. Maj. Gen. Edmund Schriver, inspector gen., telegraphed to Ord. "The secretary of war wishes to know whether it is advisable to employ the same council that managed the McCardle case in Mississippi to appear for the United States in the appeal to the supreme court here" ADfS (telegram sent), *ibid*., RG 107, Telegrams Collected (Bound); telegram received (at 7:30 P.M.), *ibid*., RG 393, 4th Military District, Letters Received. On Jan. 8, USG wrote to U.S. Senator Lyman Trumbull of Ill. "The case, exparte *W. H. McCardle*, appealed from the circuit court of So. Dist. of Miss. to the Supreme Court of the United States it is believed may soon be called up. The Attorney General of the United States having expressed his intention not to appear in the case this Department desires to engaged your professional services for that object. The case is numbered 380 & a transcript of the Record together with a copy of the Atty General's letter on the 31st ultimo on the subject, to this Department, is herewith enclosed." Df, *ibid*., RG 94, Record & Pension Office, 670220; copy, *ibid*., RG 107, Letters Sent. On Jan. 11, Trumbull wrote to USG. "Agreeably to your request, I will appear in behalf of the United States in the case of Ex parte W. H. McCardle now pending in the Supreme Court; but should desire to have other counsel associated with me, about which I will confer with you at an early day." ALS, *ibid*., RG 94, Record & Pension Office, 670220.

1. William H. McCardle, editor, Vicksburg *Times*, wrote a series of articles denouncing the Reconstruction Acts and military authority. On Nov. 8, 1867, Ord arrested McCardle and charged him with libel, disturbing the peace, and impeding Reconstruction. See Sever L. Eubank, "The McCardle Case: A Challenge to Radical Reconstruction," *Journal of Mississippi History*, XVIII, 2 (April, 1956), 111–27; Stanley I. Kutler, *Judicial Power and Reconstruction Politics* (Chicago, 1968), 99–110.

To Maj. Gen. George G. Meade

(Cipher)   Washington, D, C,
                                                    Jan. 13th 1867̶8. [*2:30* P.M.]

MAJ. GEN. G. G. MEADE,
ATLANTA GA.

You will perceive ~~that~~ by the re-construction acts that "Conventions are to frame Constitutions and Civil Govt. for their respective States." which clearly implies authority to order the election of officers thereunder; and in fixing the day of election Ala. has only followed a well established prescedent.

The Governments elected can not assume authority except under orders from the Dist. Commander or after action of Congress upon their Constitution

U. S. GRANT
General,

ALS (telegram sent), DNA, RG 107, Telegrams Collected (Bound); telegram sent, *ibid.*; telegram received (at 7:00 P.M.), Meade Papers, PHi. On Jan. 11, 1868, Maj. Gen. George G. Meade, Atlanta, telegraphed to USG. "The convention of Alabama—~~nominated a ticket~~ ordained that when the election for the ratification of the Constitution should be held, the people should vote to fill all the offices created by the constitution & for members of Congress—Genl Pope in his order authorises the officers of the election to receive the votes cast in conformity with this ordinance—Govr Patton ~~of~~ & many influential citizens advocate strongly the withdrawal of this authority—alleging it will affect injuriously the question of ratification, & that the nominees mostly members of the convention, are not such as the people would put in nomination if they had a fair chance.—Genl. Swayne admits some of the objections ~~but objects to now withdrawing~~ but strongly reports against the revocation on the grounds that it would be disastrous to reconstruction—that it would require additional elections greatly to be deprecated and that tho not required explicitly by the Reconstruction act, the power exercised by the convention is implied in these acts. My own judgement, would be against authorising this election, were the questions submitted ab initio—as the order has been issued, there are reasons against any change provided the order is legitimate. The ordinance contemplates the whole of the state machinery—going into effect so soon as the constitution is ratified, but I do not think the officers elected can take office without my authority, as until the constitution under which they are elected receives the approval of Congress—But there will undoubtedly be great pressure brought to bear to obtain my authority, and recent action in Congress would seem to indicate a desire to place the state governments in the hands of the conventions—I should be glad to have your views—and as the urgency is immediate I ask for instructions them by telegraph.—" ALS (telegram sent), *ibid.*; telegram received (at 9:00 P.M.), DNA, RG 107, Telegrams Collected (Bound); *ibid.*, RG 108, Telegrams Received.

On Jan. 12, Meade twice telegraphed to USG. "Unless the pending bill in Congress, directing military commanders to fill all the offices in the states under their commands rescinds the test oath & provides for selection from qualified voters, I am informed its execution in this District will be entirely impracticable" "Genl. Swayne, upon further reflection, & fuller information as to the character of the nominees; withdraws the objections, reported in my despatch of yesterday, to the postponement of the election of State officers in Alabama on the 4th of Feby proxo—" ALS (telegrams sent), Meade Papers, PHi; telegrams received (at 10:00 P.M.), DNA, RG 107, Telegrams Collected (Bound); *ibid.*, RG 108, Telegrams Received. On Jan. 13, 3:00 P.M., USG telegraphed to Meade. "I would not advise interference with elections ordered by the Ala. Convention unless very satisfactory reasons exist for doing so." ALS (telegram sent), *ibid.*, RG 107, Telegrams Collected (Bound); telegram sent, *ibid.*; telegram received (at 8:00 P.M.), Meade Papers, PHi. On Jan. 14, USG wrote to President Andrew Johnson. "I have the honor to enclose herewith copy of a telegram received from Maj. Gen. Geo. G. Meade, Comdg. 3d Military District." LS, DLC-Andrew Johnson. USG enclosed a copy of the first Meade telegram of Jan. 12.

On Jan. 14, Governor Robert M. Patton of Ala. telegraphed and wrote to USG. "Genl Meade informs me that the revocation of Gen Popes order authorizing Election for State Officers does not meet with your approval. I respectfully request a suspension of your opinion until I can communicate with you by letter Please acknowledge" Telegram received (at 4:20 P.M.), DNA, RG 107, Telegrams Collected (Bound); *ibid.*, RG 108, Telegrams Received; copy, DLC-USG, V, 55. "To-day I had the honor to telegraph you in regard to the election of State officers in Alabama. In accordance with the intimation contained in the dispatch, I now have the honor to send herewith a copy of a communication which I recently addressed to Major General Meade, upon the same subject. It may be proper to observe, also, that I have had personal conferences with Gen. Meade, and Gen. Hayden, who commands in this State; and they both concur with me in the opinion that it would greatly promote the public good to have the election of State officers postponed, so that a separate vote could be had upon the question of ratifying the constitution. Gen. Swayne was of the same opinion before he left this military district, and so advised Gen. Meade, though he formerly entertained a different view. I beg to add still another reason in favor of separating the vote for State officers from that of ratifying the constitution. Under the proposed constitution all officers are to be elected by the people—from Governor down to bailiff, and from Supreme Judges down to Justices of the Peace. Bailiffs and Justices are chosen by the voters of their respective beats, of which there are from twelve to twenty-five in each county. Under the reconstruction acts, and the existing circumstances in this State, it will be impracticable to hold elections at more than two or three places in a county. This being the case, it is quite reasonable to assume that, from a large number of beats—possibly a majority—there will be very few voters in attendance at any of the voting places, while from many of them there would be none at all. Hence, most of the beat officers will be chosen by an insignificant number of voters, and not a few of the beats will have no officers elected. These, and many other anomalies, to say nothing of serious evils and complications, may be avoided by having the election of officers postponed until after the constitution shall have been definitely acted upon by the people, and by Congress." LS, DNA, RG 108, Letters Received. On Jan. 15, 9:45 A.M., USG telegraphed to Patton. "Your dispatch of 14th received." ALS (telegram sent), *ibid.*, RG 107, Telegrams Collected (Bound); telegram sent, *ibid.*; copies, *ibid.*, RG 108, Telegrams Sent; DLC-USG, V, 56.

On Jan. 18, 11:00 A.M., USG telegraphed to Meade. "Tell me whether you think the election for Civil officers in Ala. should take place as now ordered or not? It looks to me better that it should but being present you can tell better than I can." ALS (telegram sent), DNA, RG 107, Telegrams Collected (Bound); telegram sent, *ibid.*; telegram received, Meade Papers, PHi. On the same day, Meade telegraphed to USG. "I have nothing to add to my telegrams of the Eleventh & Twelfth instants in relation to postponement of Alabama election— My own judgement was in favor of rescinding Genl Pope's order authorising it, but your despatches of the Thirteenth instant were so conclusive, and the delicacy I have in regard to Genl Pope's orders, caused me to notify Govr Patton that I should take no action—It is now in my judgement as the election is so near too late to make any change.—" ALS (telegram sent), *ibid.*; telegram received (at 7:30 P.M.), DNA, RG 107, Telegrams Collected (Bound); *ibid.*, RG 108, Telegrams Received.

To Andrew Johnson

Washington, D. C. Jan.y 14th *1868.*

HIS EXCELLENCY, A. JOHNSON,
PRESIDENT OF THE UNITED STATES,
SIR:

I have the honor to enclose herewith, copy of official notice received by me, last evening, of the action of the Senate of the United States in the case of the suspension of the Hon. E. M. Stanton, Secretary of War.

According to the provisions of Section 2 of "An Act regulating the Tenure of certain Civil offices" my functions as Secretary of War, ad interim, ceased from the moment of the receipt of the within notice.

> I have the honor to be,
> Very respectfully,
> Your obt. svt.
> U. S. GRANT
> General.

ALS, DLC-Andrew Johnson.

    On Jan. 14, 1868, William S. Hillyer wrote to President Andrew Johnson. "I had a short conversation with Gen Grant this morning and a long conversation with Gen Rawlins. The conversations to a large extent were confidential I can therefore only say to you as ~~sufficient~~ supplemental to the remarks of yesterday, that I am now *fully satisfied that Gen Grant never had any conversation or collusion with Mr Stanton in regard to his (Stantons) restoration to the War office.* that Grant never expected that Stanton would resume the duties of the war office: that Grant has no sympathy with the present radical measures pending before Congress that Grant does not think that the President has any right to judge of the Constitutionality of the laws of Congress, *nor that any subordinate officer has any right to question the legality of the orders of the Constitutional Commander in chief of the army.* You will understand me not to state the conversations but my own impressions derived from these conversations." ALS, *ibid.*

To Maj. Gen. George G. Meade

———

(Cypher)   Washington, D, C. Jan. 17th *1868* [*1:00* P.M.]
MAJ. GEN. G. G. MEADE,
ATLANTA GA.

    Congress unquestionably can determine upon the questions presented by the Governor of Florida whatever may be the authority of District Commanders over such cases. Gen. Pope having practically settled the matter complained of by his action before you assumed command of the 3d Dist, it is deemed judicious not to interfere with the meeting of the Convention at the time ordered by him but leave the whole matter to Congress in its final action.

> U. S. GRANT
> General.

ALS (telegram sent), DNA, RG 107, Telegrams Collected (Bound); telegram
sent, *ibid.*; telegram received, Meade Papers, PHi. On Jan. 15 and 16, 1868,
5:40 P.M., Maj. Gen. George G. Meade telegraphed to USG. "The Governor of
Florida, has laid before me & endorsed the same, a petition ~~of~~ numerously signed,
asking that the order of Genl Pope calling together the constitutional convention
on the 20th inst be suspended, for a period sufficiently long to enable me to decide on the questions raised by them invalidating the election of the members—
The points raised, are the violation of the Reconstruction laws by Genl Pope first
in the manner of districting the state—secondly in the registration thereof—
thirdly in the conduct of the election.—There is not time for me to deliberately
examine these points but there is prima-facie evidence justifing me in the belief
that perhaps, according to my judgement, the reconstruction laws have not been
strictly adhered to, or at least there are grave questions raised—Under this view
I am disposed to postpone the meeting of the convention for 30 days but in this
as in all cases refrain from acting until advised that you do not disapprove my
proposed action—Please reply immediately.—" ALS (telegram sent), *ibid.*; telegram received (at 7:30 P.M.), DNA, RG 107, Telegrams Collected (Bound);
ibid., RG 108, Telegrams Received; DLC-Andrew Johnson. "Has a district
commander any authority under the law to correct infractions of the law? ~~He~~
Has he any power, supposing he is satisfied that an election had not been properly conducted, or that great frauds existed, to set the election aside, and order
another? My own opinion is that he has not, and that the only appeal in cases of
improper districting, or fraudulent elections, is to be found in Congress, when
the constitutions are acted on. Answer to these questions are important, because
if I cannot correct the evils charged in the case of Florida there is no occasion
to postpone the meeting of the convention." LS (telegram sent), Meade Papers,
PHi; telegram received (at 7:30 P.M.), DNA, RG 108, Telegrams Received.
On Jan. 15, 9:30 P.M., Bvt. Brig. Gen. Adam Badeau telegraphed to Meade.
"Telegram to General Grant received. He ~~replies~~ replies—Act according to your
own judgment about postponing convention" ALS (telegram sent), *ibid.*, RG
107, Telegrams Collected (Bound); telegram sent, *ibid.*; telegram received (on
Jan. 16), Meade Papers, PHi.

On Jan. 21, Meade telegraphed to USG. "I have received, thro' the President
of the U. S. a communication from the Govr of Florida, relating to the meeting
of the convention—May I ask you to shew to the President my telegrams on this
subject with your replies—I am advised today by telegraph that the convention
met yesterday and organised.—" ALS (telegram sent), *ibid.*; telegram received
(on Jan. 22, 9:30 A.M.), DNA, RG 107, Telegrams Collected (Bound); *ibid.*,
RG 108, Telegrams Received. On Jan. 24, USG wrote to President Andrew
Johnson. "I have the honor to transmit herewith copy of a telegraphic dispatch
from Maj. Gen. Geo. G. Meade, Commanding the 3d Military District, dated the
21st instant, and copies of telegrams therein referred to." LS, DLC-Andrew
Johnson.

To Lt. Gen. William T. Sherman

January 19th. 1868.

DEAR SHERMAN,

I called on the President and Mr. Stanton to-day, but without any effect.

I soon found that to recommend resignation to Mr. S. would have no effect unless it was to incur further his displeasure and therefore did not directly suggest it to him. I explained to him however the course I supposed he would pursue, and what I expected to do in that case, namely, to notify the President of his intentions and thus leave him to violate the "Tenure of Office Bill." if he chose, instead of having me do it.

I would advise that you say nothing to Mr. Stanton in the subject unless he asks your advice. It will do no good and may embarrass you. I did not mention your name to him, at least not in connection with his position or what you thought upon it.

All that Mr. Johnson said was pacific and compromising. Whilst I think he wanted the constitutionality of the "Tenure Bill" tested, I think now he would be glad either to get the vacancy of Secretary of War, or have the office just where it was during suspension.

Yours truly,
U S. GRANT

Copies (2), DLC-William T. Sherman. Dated Jan. 29, 1868, in *Memoirs of Gen. W. T. Sherman* (4th ed., New York, 1891), II, 424.

On Jan. 14, Bvt. Brig. Gen. Adam Badeau had written to Lt. Gen. William T. Sherman. "General Grant directs me to inform you that he would like to see you at these headquarters today, after your board adjourns—" ALS, DLC-William T. Sherman. On Jan. 15, USG and Sherman called on President Andrew Johnson, inaugurating a series of meetings during which Johnson offered Sherman the office of secretary of war. Sherman, *Memoirs*, II, 423–28; M. A. De-Wolfe Howe, ed., *Home Letters of General Sherman* (New York, 1909), pp. 365–70.

On Jan. 18, Sherman wrote to USG. "On the point of starting, I have written the above and will send a fair copy of it to the President. Please retain this, that in case of necessity, I may have a copy. The President clearly stated to me that he relied on us in this category. Think of the propriety of your putting in writing what you have to say tomorrow—even if you have to put it in the form of a letter to hand him in person, retaining a copy. I'm afraid that acting as a go-between for three persons, I may share the usual fate of meddlers, at last get kicks from all. We ought not to be involved in politics, but for the sake of the Army we are justified in trying at least to cut this Gordian Knot, which they do not appear to have any practicable plan to do." Copies (2), DLC-William T. Sherman. Misdated Jan. 28 in Sherman, *Memoirs*, II, 424. On the same day, Sherman had written to Johnson. "I neglected this morning to say that I had agreed to go down to Annapolis to spend Sunday with Admiral Porter. General Grant also has to leave for Richmond on Monday Morning at 6. a. m. At a conversation with the General after our interview, wherein I offered to go with him on Monday Morning to Mr Stanton and to say that it was our joint opinion he should resign, it was found impossible by reason of his going to Richmond, and my going to Annapolis. The General proposed this course. He will call on you tomorrow, and offer to go to Mr Stanton to say for the good of the service, and of the Country, he ought to resign—this on Sunday. On Monday I will again call on you. And if you think it necessary I will do the same call on Mr Stanton and tell him he should resign. If he will not, then it will be time to contrive ulterior measures In the mean time it so happens that no necessity exists for precipitating matters." ALS, DLC-Andrew Johnson. Misdated Jan. 28 in Sherman, *Memoirs*, II, 423–24. On Jan. 19, 9:00 A.M., USG telegraphed to Dr. Alexander Sharp, Richmond. "I leave here for Richmond via. Aquia. Creek by morning boat to-morrow." ALS (telegram sent), DNA, RG 107, Telegrams Collected (Bound); telegram sent, *ibid*.

On Jan. 27, Sherman wrote to USG. "At your request, I will endeavor to recall the events within my observation at and about the time you vacated the office of Secretary of War ad interim, and when Mr. Stanton reëntered. During the week preceding this event I saw you almost daily, as the Board of which I am a member occupied the room in the building next the office of the Secretary of War. On Saturday, the 11th of January you told me that within the past few days you had read carefully the Act of Congress known as the Tenure of Civil Office Bill, that it was different from what you had supposed; that it was so worded that in case the Resolution reported by Mr. Howard should pass the Senate, Mr. Stanton would be restored, and that, if you held on or did any act as Secretary of War you would incur a liability of ten thousand dollars and imprisonment for five years, a risk you did not feel inclined to run. We then knew the Resolution was being debated in the Senate and was likely to pass at any time. I think I asked you if you had not promised to give notice to the President, and also what course you intended to pursue. You said you supposed after the Resolution had passed the Senate, Mr. Stanton would pursue towards you the same order of proceedings as he had required of you on taking the office at the time of his suspension, viz: that he would write you a letter demanding the office, and would give you one or two days to act. But you said you would also go to the President right away, and tell him how you felt. At 3 p. m., our Board adjourned and by appointment with General Pope, I took him (General Pope) to the Executive mansion to pay his personal and official respects to the President. Mr. Johnson received General Pope very courteously, and after a few minutes conversation in which both appeared well pleased, General Pope withdrew, and the President detained me to show me some paper, and at that moment you entered. After a minute, I also withdrew, leaving you and the President alone together. This was about 4 p. m. of Saturday, the 11th instant, and I supposed of course you had gone to the President, at that unusual hour, expressly to tell him your conclusion about the office you then held as Secretary of War ad interim. I knew that both the President and the Army would be embarrassed by the restoration to the office of Secretary of War, of Mr. Stanton, after the strong feelings generated by past events, and saw no solution, except for the President to submit to the Senate the name of some good successor, likely to be confirmed by the Senate. The name of Governor Cox of Ohio rose to my mind as being the very man for the place. A gentleman in the highest sense of the term, of fine address and education, of a perfect war record, who had filled every commission from that of Colonel to that of Corps Commander, who had lost favor with the Republican party by reason of his opposition to universal negro suffrage, and whose term of office in Ohio was to expire on the following Monday. I had not seen Governor Cox since the close of the war, and did not know that he would accept if named, but proposed to use my influence to that end. That evening, I dined by invitation with Mr. Reverdy Johnson, to whom I mentioned my thoughts. He said it was the very thing, that he would himself call on the President the next morning, Sunday, and as he had to go to Annapolis that evening, he would drop me a note telling me the result of his interview with the President. On Sunday, I saw several gentlemen and some Senators to whom I mentioned the circumstance and all approved; I then called on you at your house about 3 p. m. of Sunday, the 12th, and you not only approved, but urged me to push the matter all I could, saying that Governor Cox was perfectly acceptable to you, and to the Army generally. When I got to my room, I was disappointed to find no note from Reverdy Johnson. On Monday morning, the 13th, early, I again came to this room where our Board sits, and you soon came in and asked me what was the result of the matter. I answered that Mr. Reverdy Johnson had not written me as I expected, and that I inferred that his application to the President had met with no success. You then urged me to go at once to the President and use your name, as not only consenting, but urging that course. I did go to the President about 11 a. m., and after waiting some time was admitted. I asked the President if Mr. Reverdy Johnson had been there the day before, and if he had named Governor Cox in connection with the office of Secretary of War. The President answered 'Yes,' and that he had a good opinion of Governor Cox, but made no intimation of a purpose to send his name to the Senate. Satisfied the President had given the matter his thoughts, I did not deem it proper for me further to urge the matter, only stating that I thought General Cox in every way qualified, and that I knew from you personally that his appointment would be most acceptable. At this time it was almost certain that the Senate would pass Mr. Howard's Resolution, and I supposed the President was fully prepared for it. I believed that you had in the interview of the previous Saturday given the President your frank statement of your intentions in this connexion. I left the President and came straight to you and told you the result, and that, though the President had not said to me what he would do, he left me to infer he would not send the name of General Cox to the Senate. Tuesday came and with it Mr. Stanton. He came into the room where Generals Sheridan, Augur and I were sitting, and was very friendly in his greeting. He said he wanted to see me when at leisure; and about 10½ a. m., I went into his office through the side door, and found you and him together. I stayed but a moment, and said to Mr. Stanton that I was close by, and would come in whenever he called me; ~~and~~ I then left you two together. I afterwards was called in by Mr. Stanton who spoke to me very kindly, but not a word about his tenure of office. I saw you again that afternoon, in your office of General-in-Chief, and you told me that you did not like at all the manner in which Mr. Stanton had resumed the office, that he had sent for you in a rather discourteous mode, that at the time you had relieved him, he had required you to make your demand in writing, and had taken two or more days to clear out the office before letting you in, and that you thought he would have acted towards you as he had required you to act towards him, that by his course he had compromized you and you did not like it at all. I think I suggested that we should go together to the President, and have a clear understanding about the matter to which you promptly assented, but as it was then late in the day you said you would come to your office at 9½ a. m., and we could go to the President the first thing next morning. That was agreed to, and we met at your office as appointed. You remarked that since you had read an article in the 'Intelligencer' of that morning, you did not feel inclined to go as far as you had intended, as facts were stated therein that could hardly have reached the Editor excepting from one or more of the Cabinet. I was then shown by General Badeau, the article which before I had not seen. I gave it but a casual glance, when you and I went to the President's house together. He received us promptly and kindly. We were all seated. Nobody in the room but the President, yourself and myself. You first began by telling of certain matters in Georgia and Alabama, which seemed to be the continuation of a former conversation, after which you said substantially:—Mr. President,—'Whoever gave the facts for the article of the Intelligencer of this morning has made some serious mistakes, &c.' The President promptly interrupted,—'General Grant, let me interrupt you just there. I have not seen the Intelligencer of this morning, and have no knowledge of the contents of any article therein.' General Grant resumed,—'Well, the idea is given there that I have not kept faith with you. Now, Mr. President, I remember when you spoke to me on this subject last summer, I did say that like the case of the Baltimore Police Commissioners I did suppose Mr. Stanton could not regain his office except by a process through the Courts.' To this the President assented saying he remembered the reference to the case of the Baltimore Commissioners, and you, General Grant, resumed. You said that if you changed your opinion you would give the President notice, and put things where they were before your appointment as Secretary of War ad interim. Here a general conversation ensued in which General Grant said he had taken the office simply because it seemed better that he should be there than anybody who would likely be nominated by the President and confirmed by the Senate. And the President referred to his past conduct to show how desirous he had always been to manifest friendship and confidence in General Grant, stating that at a former period he had used his power as Commander-in-Chief to secure to General Grant the exercise of certain functions of his office which from practice had been exercised by Secretaries of War, &c. After which General Grant resumed and related to the President how Mr. Stanton had got the key of the room usually occupied by the Secretary of War and gone into possession of the office, sending to him a blunt message to come to him in the 'old style,' at which he said he was not at all pleased; and he then stated strongly that there had been no understanding with Mr. Stanton on his part; and that he had acted as Secretary of War ad interim, in the interest of the Army, and not of Mr. Stanton, that Mr. Stanton's being in the office did not make him Secretary of War any more than if he were to make his office in his own Library Room at his own private house. At all which the President expressed himself gratified and pleased. I took no part in that conversation, but as we rose and walked towards the door, General Grant said,—'Mr. President, you should make some order that we of the Army are not bound to

obey the orders of Mr. Stanton as Secretary of War,' which the President said
he would do. After you had finished, I merely said in general terms that I did
not profess to know the law of the case, but on the score of honor I did not see
how any one could hold a Cabinet office without the full confidence of the President. This is all I can recall as having occurred about that time, and I confess I
have been surprised to see the statements of late in the newspapers as emanating
from the Cabinet. Surely I thought that your explanation, of Wednesday, after
that Cabinet council, was satisfactory to the President on every point touching
your action in this matter, only he thought if you had been more positive on
Saturday he might have put some one in the office who would have resisted the
entry of Mr. Stanton into that particular room; but I thought that your explanation, that Mr. Stanton's being in that particular room did not make him lawful
Secretary of War, was conclusive. The real question is, does the Secretary of
the Treasury honor his warrants as Secretary of War, because he signs his
name in that office, or because of the legal effects of the Resolution of the Senate
declaring the reasons for his removal insufficient under the Tenure of Civil Office Bill   I do think the Army should be spared these conflicts in cases purely
legal." Copies (2), DLC-William T. Sherman.

Sherman, along with Maj. Gen. Philip H. Sheridan and Bvt. Maj. Gen.
Christopher C. Augur, comprised a board revising the Articles of War, and
USG endorsed approval of their report on Jan. 28. Copy, DNA, RG 108, Letters
Received. On Jan. 29, USG wrote to Stanton. "I have the honor herewith to
forward 'Articles of War' as proposed by the Board of distinguished officers of
the Army, convened to revise the same, and the Army Regulations, and to request that they be forwarded to Congress, for its action, should the President
approve the same." ALS, *ibid.*, RG 94, Letters Received, 723A 1866.

On Feb. 10, Sherman, St. Louis, wrote to USG. "I am back safe at my post,
and glad am I that I am out of that City of yours. The publication of yours & the
Presidents letters followed my departure sooner than I expected, but no doubt
after you had resolved on that course. Of course I dont want to be drawn into the
controversy, and should be almost driven to resignation if the President should
force me to come to Washington in any capacity likely to draw me into the
vortex. As soon as I get all my papers I will have the copies you asked for made
and sent to you. We had at Cincinati a good meeting, much larger and more
enthusiastic than I expected. You have doubtless seen and read as much about
it as you feel inclined, and I need not attempt a description. There has been a
great deal of sickness here in all the army families—and at this momt the wife of
Paymaster Brown is in danger. I hope however she will recover. Nichols has
been very sick but is now well. All my folks are well excepting the youngest girl
Rachel who looks pale & feeble, but not really down sick. I think all this resulted
from the long dry fall, which made a miasmatic poisoned air. I dont want to
come again to Washington unless you resolve to be President. In that case I
would if promoted have to come, and then would build on that lot out by Columbia College and remove my family there. You know how expensive a family is in
these days and that I cannot well afford to keep house here and be myself somewhere else at expense. My best regards to Mrs Grant and all yr family." ALS,
USG 3.

On Feb. 12, Sherman wrote to USG. "I now enclose you copies of the two
papers that you asked of me before I left Washington. These are the ones just
preceding your visit to Richmond. I remember well the fact that on the previous
Saturday, viz 11th of January, in your office at Army HeadQuarters you called

my attention to the terms of the 'Tenure of Civil Office Bill' which would have
made you liable to the penalties therein prescribed, if you had held on to the
office of Sec. of War, ad interim, after you had notice of the passage by the
Senate of the Resolution then pending, pronouncing that the reasons assigned for
the Removal of Mr Stanton were insufficient, and you said you would go right
over to the President and so inform him.—Shortly after I went with General Pope
to see the President, and you came in before I left, and you two were together
when I withdrew. I presumed as a matter of course you were then with the President for the express purpose of telling him your conclusion. Of course I have
seen the letters that have passed between you and the President, touching this
subject and regret excedingly that any difference should have arisen in consequence of the manner in which you relinquished the office of Sec of War, but
as the whole point of difference arises from your understanding of the agreemt
at that time, I do not think you need more than your own assertion as to the fact."
ALS, *ibid*.

To Edwin M. Stanton

Respectfully forwarded to the Secretary of War, with the recommendation that if the money referred to by Gen. Meade has not
passed out of the control of the War Department and it can be done
without violation of law, a temporary return be made as he suggests.

I can see no reason why the auditing and settlement of the
accounts of the superintendent of the State road referred to by
Gen. Meade could not be transferred to an officer of the Quartermaster Department in the State of Georgia, and it is therefore
recommended.

U. S. GRANT
General.

HDQRS. A. U. S.
JAN. 24. '68.

ES, DNA, RG 393, 3rd Military District, Letters Received. Written on a copy
of a telegram of Jan. 19, 1868, from Maj. Gen. George G. Meade, Atlanta, to
USG. "The conduct of the officials of Georgia embarrasses me in procuring
funds for immediate purposes—I am informed the Georgia State road, under instructions from the Govr & doubtess in anticipation of existing condition of affairs, has recently without regard to the wants of the State Treasury paid large
sums to the Quarter Master Genl on account of its indebtedness to the Government It has occurred to me, that if this money has not yet reverted to the

Treasury, and is under the control of the War Dept that a temporary return of a portion of it might be made to the Treasurer of Georgia or myself, for immediate wants, and when the present difficulties are overcome, & the revenue of the state, derived from the regular Sources this loan could be returned.—If this is practicable, I would most urgently recommed it—as if I can only get money the officials are flanked.—I am further advised by the Supdt of the state road, who is faithfully co-opera[ting] with me, that if the auditing & settlemen[t] of his accounts, could be transferred from Col Dana at Washington to an officer here either Genl Saxton or Capt Farnsworth that the settlement would be greatly expedited and the revenue derived from the road placed in the state Treasury in a much shorter time. This is very desirable and I would urge Said transfer be authorised.—" ALS (telegram sent), Meade Papers, PHi; telegrams received (2—on Jan. 20, 11:00 A.M.), DNA, RG 107, Telegrams Collected (Bound); *ibid.*, RG 108, Telegrams Received. On Jan. 23, Meade telegraphed to USG. "The importance of the subject and the very great embarrassment I find myself in, owing to the financial condition of this state—authorise & compel me to call your attention to my telegram of the 19th inst & to urge immediate action thereon—" ALS (telegram sent), Meade Papers, PHi; telegram received (at 4:15 P.M.), DNA, RG 107, Telegrams Collected (Bound); *ibid.*, RG 108, Telegrams Received. On Jan. 24, 3:00 P.M., USG telegraphed to Meade. "I have recommended the adoption of your suggestions about Georgia rail-road and funds." ALS (telegram sent), *ibid.*, RG 107, Telegrams Collected (Bound); telegram sent, *ibid.*; telegram received (at 6:00 P.M.), Meade Papers, PHi.

On Jan. 18, Meade had telegraphed to USG. "The state Treasurer & Comptroller General of this state, have not only removed beyond my jurisdiction, all the funds in their charge, but all the books & records of their offices, hoping by these means to force a resort to civil process. As these acts are not only in violation of the statutes of Georgia, but clear cases of contempt of the power & authority of the United States, I have ordered the arrest & if necessary confinement of these derelict officers, and their trial by Military commission, for malfeasance in office & contempt of my authority.—" ALS (telegram sent), *ibid.*; telegram received (at 5:00 P.M.), DNA, RG 107, Telegrams Collected (Bound); *ibid.*, RG 108, Telegrams Received.

On Jan. 21, Meade wrote to USG. "I have already advised you by telegraph, and communicated by mail, that I had removed from office the Provisional Governor and State Treasurer of the State of Georgia, and appointed to their places Bt Brigadier General T. H. Ruger, and Bt Captain C. F. Rockwell; I have now to report that the Comptroller General having declined to acknowledge my authority, I have removed him, and appointed provisionally Captain Charles Wheaton 33d Infantry. I have also advised you by telegram of these officers having assumed the duties of their offices, but that the State Treasurer Captain Rockwell found the office completely stripped of all its records, and that it was believed the office of the Comptroller General was in the same condition, and that all the funds of the State were either expended or placed beyond his control. I furthermore am advised by a letter this day received from General Ruger, that the taxes ordered to be levied amounting to over $600,000.00. had as far as he could ascertain been all collected, and paid into the State Treasury except about $75,000.00, this amount has yet to be collected, and a deduction of perhaps $25.000 00 should be made for insolvent citizens. Since the change of officials I have been able to get possession of only $5000,00: in hands of the depository at this place; and the Superintendent of the State Road at my request, has advanced me $10,000.00. out of the anticipated nett earnings of the road for the present month. It is impossible to form any idea of what amount of funds, if any, that should be in the Treasury, have been removed therefrom. The revenues of the State have hitherto been derived from the nett earnings of the State Road, and from the taxes levied by each legislature for the support of the civil list, and the payment of interest on the state debt. The legislature met in November— the tax levied in the succeeding spring, and its collection required by the month of December. The fiscal year terminated on the 20th of October and each legislature provided for its successor and for sufficient means in addition to the anticipated revenue from from the State Road; to enable the machinery of the State to be kept in operation, till the tax levied by its successor could be made available. Therefore under ordinary circumstances although the period specifically provided for by the last legislature sitting in 1866, expired last October, yet as provision was made for a legislature in November 1867 not convened, and as it was usual always to provide for a portion of the fiscal year beginning in October 1867, there should have been a considerable sum in the Treasury on the 1st January, inst, but as there may have been incoming bonds requiring liquidation, and the necessity of paying off the indebtedness of the State Road to the U. S. was pressing, it is not impossible that the balance that should have been in the Treasury may have been thus diminished. The fact however that there is on hand not more than $15,000 cash with prospective collection from the people of $50,000 more renders some immediate measure of relief absolutely essential, and in searching for such measure my attention has been called to the large amount recently paid to the U. S. by the State on account of the indebtedness of the State Road, which led to my telegram of the 19th inst, asking that if this amount had not reverted to the Treasury, and was yet under the control of the Department, that a temporary return of a portion of it say 1 or 200,000.00 be made to myself or the State Treasurer, to meet the immediate wants of the Treasury—said loan to be returned so soon as the tax about to be levied is collected, and the proceeds made available Should this money be beyond the control of the Department, I would then suggest an appeal to Congress to authorize the proposition here made. Unless some immediate relief is obtained from some source, not only will the civil list, the charitable institutions of the State, have to be materially cut down, but the ability of the State to meet the interest on its debt be jeopardized, and the constitutional convention be greatly embarrassed if not obstructed, for want of means. I trust therefore that you will give this subject your earnest attention and prompt action," LS, *ibid.*, Letters Received.

On Jan. 31, 5:00 P.M., Meade telegraphed to USG. "I am sorry to seem to be importunate but the convention presses me with their wants, and are making various propositions to raise money, which in the event of any action being had on my telegram of the (19) Nineteenth inst—I am reluctant to accede to—I therefore would like to know what probability there is of my proposition & your recommendation being acted on—" ALS (telegram sent), Meade Papers, PHi; telegram sent, *ibid.*, RG 94, Letters Received, 461A 1868; telegram received (at 7:15 P.M.), *ibid.*, RG 107, Telegrams Collected (Bound); (at 7:30 P.M.) *ibid.*, RG 108, Telegrams Received. On Feb. 1, 10:30 A.M., USG telegraphed to Meade. "Report of action on your dispatch of 19th Feb.y was sent by mail several days ago. There is scarsely a hope of aid from here of a pecuniary nature." ALS (telegram sent), *ibid.*, RG 107, Telegrams Collected (Bound); telegram sent, *ibid.*; telegram received, Meade Papers, PHi.

To Andrew Johnson

Washington, Jan. 25th *1868*

His Excellency A. Johnson
President of the U. S.
Sir:

Referring to your communication of the 21st instant, relative to Col. C. W. Foster, of the Q. M. Department, I have the honor to transmit herewith copy of a letter from Bvt Maj. Gen. D. H. Rucker, Acting Q. M. Genl., dated January 23d '68, which contains a correspondence between Gen. Rucker and Bvt. Maj. Gen. R. Allen, relating to the subject matter of your communication.[1] Also copy of a letter from Mr John Mullan, to the Qr. Mr. General, dated Dec. 30th 1867, on the same subject.[2] From Gen. Allen's letter it appears that the public interests require the retention of Col. Hoyt on duty in San Francisco. Both the officers named—Cols. Foster and Hoyt—are not needed there. I therefore await further instructions before ordering the retention of Col. Foster.

Very respectfully
Your obed't serv't
U. S. Grant
General.

LS, DNA, RG 94, Letters Received, 787P 1867. On Jan. 21, 1868, President Andrew Johnson had written to USG. "Unless the public interests require otherwise—in which case be good enough to let me know—please issue instructions that Colonel C. W. Foster, of the Quartermaster's Department, be retained on duty at San Francisco, California, as originally ordered, in lieu of Colonel Hoyt." LS, *ibid.*, RG 108, Letters Received. On Jan. 27, Johnson endorsed USG's letter of Jan. 25. "Let Colonel Hoyt be relieved from duty at San Francisco by the assignment of Colonel C. W. Foster." AES, *ibid.*, RG 94, Letters Received, 787P 1867. On Feb. 26, William G. Moore, secretary to Johnson, wrote to USG. "The President directs me to say, that he would be pleased to have you revoke the order which relieves Captain Hoyt from duty as Quartermaster at San Francisco, California." ALS, *ibid.*

On May 6, 1867, Bvt. Maj. Gen. Irvin McDowell, San Francisco, had written to the AG protesting the transfer of Bvt. Maj. James T. Hoyt from the Dept. of Calif. to Minn. LS, *ibid.*, 469C 1867. On May 28, U.S. Senator Cornelius Cole of Calif., San Francisco, wrote to USG. "I am fully convinced that Major James T. Hoyt A. Q. M. in this place has passed the time of his usefulness here—A very few persons may be anxious that he shall remain longer, but not the people, nor more than a handful in the military service. My information is *all* from civilians, but very rerliable. I understand he has been ordered away but that it is alleged he cannot be spared. I assure you he *can* be spared & ought *not* to remain *longer*." ALS, *ibid*.

On June 1, "Veritas," San Francisco, telegraphed to USG. "The interferance of Gen McDowell in his letter of May 10th. and Senator Conness to have the order assigning Qr Master Hoyt to Saint Paul rescinded is not warranted in any sense for the good of the service. By referring the matter to Genl Allen Ass't Qr Mr General here you can get the correct state of officers" Telegram received (on June 7, 2:00 P.M.), *ibid*., RG 107, Telegrams Collected (Bound). On June 25, U.S. Senator John Conness of Calif., San Francisco, telegraphed to USG. "Please rescind order assigning Captain James L Hoyt A Q M. to Dacotah. Genl's Halleck & McDowell want it & I ask it as personal to me." Telegram received (on June 26, 11:00 A.M.), *ibid*., RG 108, Telegrams Received; copy, DLC-USG, V, 55.

On Nov. 29, 10:45 A.M., USG telegraphed to Maj. Gen. Henry W. Halleck, San Francisco. "Suspend the order removing Capt. Hoyt untill Jan. 1st." ALS (telegram sent), DNA, RG 107, Telegrams Collected (Bound); telegram sent, *ibid*.; copies, *ibid*., RG 108, Telegrams Sent; DLC-USG, V, 56.

1. On Jan. 23, 1868, Bvt. Maj. Gen. Daniel H. Rucker, act. q. m. gen., wrote to USG. "On the 29th November 1867 in accordance with the verbal Orders of the General Commanding the Army, the following letter was addressed to Brevet Major General Robert Allen, Chief Quartermaster Military Division of the Pacific referring to Special Order 463 A. G. O. Oct 8th 1867 (Par 4) assigning Captain J. T. Hoyt A. Q. M to duty in the Department of Dakota. 'BREVET MAJOR GENERAL ROBERT ALLEN assistant Quartermaster General USA Chief Qrmr Mil Divn of the Pacific San Francisco, Cal. GENERAL: Referring to the order of Oct 8th 1867 relieving Captain J. T. Hoyt asst Qrmr U. S. A. from duty at San-Francisco Cal, I am directed by the General, Comdg the Army to inform you that the congressional delegation from California are divided as to the propriety of keeping Captain Hoyt still on duty there or of relieving him therefrom. Before taking final action in the case, he desires you to report at once to the Quartermaster General whether in your opinion the interest of the Government and Service will be best promoted by relieving him from duty there, or by retaining him in his present position. You are directed to postpone the execution of the order above referred to, and to retain Captain Hoyt on duty in his present position until you shall receive notification as to the action of the General Commanding the Army on your report in the case.' Very respectfully Your obedient servant *sd* D. H. RUCKER acting Qrmr General Bvt major General U. S. Army. On the 20th instant the following reply of General Allen was received. 'Office of Chief Quartermaster Military Division of the Pacific San Francisco 18th Dec 67. BREVET MAJOR GEN'L D. H. RUCKER acting Qrmr. General U. S. A Washington D. C. GENERAL: I have your letter of November 29th in reference to relieving Captain J. T. Hoyt a. q. m from duty at this place, and requiring me to report for the information of the General Commanding the Army, whether his removal to another Post would promote the interests of the service. Although Captain Hoyt was originally assigned to, and has been maintained in, a position, by political influence, that he was not entitled to by his rank, I do not think that the interests of the public service now, would be promoted by his removal. His duties are not confined to the Department of California, for he is in fact, the

principal purchasing and shipping Officer for the Division, and the business of his Office is, accordingly complex and responsible. He has knowledge of the country, of the routes over which supplies have to be transported and a general acquaintance with the markets: all of which, can only be acquired by a stranger after years of experience. He is competent and attentive to his duties. Very respectfully Your obedient servant *sd* Rb't ALLEN asst Qrmr General In addition to the above, I respectfully enclose a letter from John Mullan, San Francisco, Cal for the information of the General Commanding, in connection with previous action of this Office upon this subject." LS, DNA, RG 108, Letters Received.

    2. On Dec. 30, 1867, John Mullan, San Francisco, had written to Bvt. Maj. Gen. Montgomery C. Meigs. "Nothing less than a sense of duty that I owe myself as a citizen of California; and my regard for the simpler days of the Nation—when compliance on the part of the inferiors with orders received from Military Superiors characterised our Army, and when our national affairs were administered with every respect on the part of the individual officer for economy and integrity; warrant my addressing you officially upon a subject that demands your attention I desire to bring to your ~~attention~~ notice the case of the further military presence on the Pacific Coast of Capt & Bvt Major James T. Hoyt Asst Qr Master USA This official has more than once been relieved in military orders from your Dept from further duty on this Coast and transferred to other Military Districts—in compliance with the long and *well* established regulations that govern the movements of our entire army—But as often ordered—so often have the Telegraphic wires transmitted a petitions to the political partizans serving in *temporary* positions in Washington city requesting that he be retained in this particular Military Division—and the orders have been countermanded. The citizens of California have a right to ask and do ask if there be any special reason behind this, prompting so nefarious a military course? Its effect is but too plainly seen and openly commented upon in the City of San Francisco. Its tendency is to bring the military—that arm of the nation hitherto rightfully kept aloof from partizan manipulation—into discredit and into suspicion—. This man—who before being appointed to fill his present position of Quarter Master—was a citizen of insignificant pretensions and moderate means—suddenly found to be the possessor in this city of extensive possessions of city Railroad Stock—ornamented grounds—house silver &c becomes the willing aider and abetter of politicians whose presence would be a good riddance from our midst.—'It is not who he is, or what he is—but whose he is, ~~that~~ of which we complain.' And though there be abuses & wrongs committed by persons in official trust that the individual citizens cannot reach &—hence cannot remedy—, Yet there are others—that need but be referred to their superiors in position in order to have ended The citizens & Taxpayers in California have a right to ask and do ask the question, why it is that such things are tolerated in our military regime in this City? To us, the reason *seems* at least plain The Qr Masters staff on this Coast in the judgement of well advised citizens could well dispense with any officer comprising its force—when ordered to other localities for duty—and it would seem that both General Halleck and General McDowell so fully imbued as they are, with the spirit & the principle that has so long characterized our Army—would hesitate long before deciding or recommending to the contrary. I desire therefore thus briefly to bring this matter to your very special and official attention" ALS, *ibid.*

To Andrew Johnson

———

Washington, D, C, Jan.y 28th *1868*

His EXCELLENCY, A. JOHNSON
PRESIDENT OF THE UNITED STATES
SIR;

On the 24th inst. I requested you to give me, in writing, the instructions which you had previously given me verbally not to obey any order from Hon. E. M. Stanton, Sec. of War, unless I knew that it came from yourself.[1]

To this written request I received a message that has left doubt in my mind of your intentions. To prevent any possible misunderstanding therefore I renew the request that you will give me written instructions, and till they are received will suspend action on your verbal ones.

I am compelled to ask these instructions in writing, in consequence of the many and gross misrepresentations, affecting my personal honor, circulated through the press for the last fortnight, purporting to come from you, the President, of conversations which occurred either with the President privately in his office, or in Cabinet meeting. What is written admits of no misunderstanding.

In view of the misrepresentations refered to, it will be well to state the facts in the case. Some time after I assumed the duties of Sec. of War, ad int. the President asked me my views as to the course Mr. Stanton would have to pursue in case the Senate should not concur in his suspension, to obtain possession of his office. My reply was in substance, that Mr. Stanton would have to appeal to the courts to reinstate him, illustrating my position by citing the ground I had taken in the case of the Baltimore Police Commissioners. In that case I did not doubt the technical right of Governor Swann to remove the old Commissioners and to appoint their successors. As the old Commissioners refused to give up however, I contended that no recourse was left but to appeal to the Courts.

Finding that the President was desirous of keeping Mr. Stanton out of office whether sustained in the suspension or not, I stated that I had not looked particularly into the "Tenure of Office Bill," but that what I had stated was a general principle and if I should change my mind in this particular case, I would inform him of the fact.

Subsequently, on reading the "Tenure of office Bill" closely, I found that I could not without violation of the law refuse to vacate the office of Sec. of War the moment Mr. Stanton was reinstated by the Senate. Even though the President should order me to retain it, which he never did.

Taking this view of the subject, and learning on Saturday, the 11th inst. that the senate had taken up the subject of Mr. Stanton's suspension, after some conversation with Lt. Gen. Sherman, and some members of my staff, in which I stated [t]hat the law left me no discretion as to my action should Mr. Stanton be reinstated, and that I intended to inform the President, I went to the President for the sole purpose of making this decission known and did so make it known. In doing this I fulfilled the promise made in our last preceding conversation on this subject.

The President however instead of accepting my view of the requirements of the "Tenure of Office Bill" contended that he had suspended Mr. Stanton under the authority given by the Constitution, and that the same authority did not preclude him from reporting, as an act of courtesy, his reasons for the suspension, to the Senate. That having appointed me under the authority given by the Constitution and not under any Act of Congress, I could not be governed by the act. I stated that the law was binding on me, constitutional or not, until set aside by the proper tribunal. An hour or more was consumed, each reiterating his views on this subject, until getting late, the President said he would see me again. I did not agree to call again on Monday nor at any other definite time, nor was I sent for by the President until the following Tuesday.

From ~~that time~~ the 11th to the Cabinet meeting on the 14th inst. a doubt never entered my mind about the President fully understanding my position, namely, that if the Senate refused to concur in the suspension of Mr. Stanton, my powers as Sec. of War, ad int. would cease, and Mr. Stanton's right to resume at once the functions of his office would under the law be indisputable, and I acted accordingly. With Mr. Stanton I had no communication, direct or indirect on the subject of his reinstatement during his suspension.

I knew that it had been recommended to the President to send in the name of Governor Cox, of Ohio, for Sec. of War, and thus save all embarassment, a proposition that I sincerely hoped he would entertain favorably, Gen. Sherman seeing the President at my particular request to urge this, on the President

On Tuesday, (the day Mr. Stanton reentered the office of Sec. of War) General Comstock who had carried my official letter announcing that with Mr. Stanton's reinstatement by the Senate I had ceased to be Sec. of War, ad int. and who saw the President open and read the communication, brought back to me from the President a message that he wanted to see me that day at the Cabinet meeting, after I had made known the fact that I was no longer Sec. of War, ad int.

At this meeting, after opening it as though I were a member of the Cabinet, when reminded of the notification already given him that I was no longer Sec. of War, ad int. the President gave a version of the conversations alluded to already. In this statement it was asserted that in both conversations I had agreed to hold on to the office of Sec. of War until displaced by the Courts, or resign so as to place the President where he would have been had I never accepted the office.

After hearing the President through I stated our conversation substantially as given in this letter.—I will add that my conversation before the Cabinet embraced other matter not pertinent here and is therefore left out. I in no wise admitted the correctness of the Presidents statement of our conversations though to soften the evident contradiction my statement gave, I said (alluding to our first conversation on the subject) the President might have understood me in the way he said, namely that I had promised to resign if I did not resist the reinstatement. I made no such promise.

> I have the honor to be,
> Very respectfully
> Your obt. svt.
> U. S. GRANT
> General,

ALS, DLC-Andrew Johnson. A draft in the hand of Bvt. Brig. Gen. Cyrus B.
Comstock contains insertions by USG, including "which he never did" at the
conclusion of paragraph six, "nor was I sent for by the President until the following Tuesday" at the conclusion of paragraph eight, and "and I acted accordingly" in the penultimate sentence of paragraph nine. Df, DLC-Cyrus B.
Comstock. On Jan. 31, 1868, President Andrew Johnson wrote to USG. "I have
received your communication of the 28th instant, renewing your request of the
24th, that I should repeat, in a written form, my verbal instructions of the 19th
instant, viz: That you obey no order from the Honorable Edwin M. Stanton, as
Secretary of War, unless you have information that it was issued by the President's direction. In submitting this request, (with which I complied on the 29th
instant,) you take occasion to allude to recent publications in reference to the
circumstances connected with the vacation, by yourself, of the office of Secretary
of War ad interim; and, with the view of correcting statements which you term
'gross misrepresentations,' give at length your own recollection of the facts under
which, without the sanction of the President, from whom you had received and
accepted the appointment, you yielded the Department of War to the present
incumbent. As stated in your communication, some time after you had assumed
the duties of Secretary of War ad interim, we interchanged views respecting the
course that should be pursued in the event of non-concurrence, by the Senate, in
the suspension from office of Mr. Stanton. I sought that interview, calling myself
at the War Department. My sole object, in then bringing the subject to your
attention, was to ascertain definitely what would be your own action should such
an attempt be made for his restoration to the War Department. That object was
accomplished; for the interview terminated with the distinct understanding that
if, upon reflection, you should prefer not to become a party to the controversy, or
should conclude that it would be your duty to surrender the Department to Mr
Stanton upon action in his favor by the Senate, you were to return the office to
me prior to a decision by the Senate, in order that, if I desired to do so, I might
designate some one to succeed you. It must have been apparent to you that had
not this understanding been reached, it was my purpose to relieve you from the
further discharge of the duties of Secretary of War ad interim, and to appoint
some other ~~person~~ other person in that capacity. Other conversations upon this
subject ensued, all of them having, on my part, the same object, and leading to
the same conclusion as the first. It is not necessary, however, to refer to any of
them, excepting that of Saturday, the 11th instant, mentioned in your communication. As it was then known that the Senate had proceeded to consider the case
of Mr. Stanton, I was anxious to learn your determination. After a protracted
interview, during which the the provisions of the 'tenure of office bill' were freely
discussed, you said that, as had been agreed upon in our first conference, you
would either return the office to my possession in time to enable me to appoint a
successor before final action by the Senate upon Mr. Stanton's suspension, or
would remain as its Head, awaiting a decision of the question by judicial proceedings. It was then understood that there would be a further conference on
Monday, by which time I supposed you would be prepared to inform me of your
final decision. You failed, however, to fulfill the engagement, and on Tuesday
notified me, in writing, of the receipt by you of official notification of the action
of the Senate in the case of Mr. Stanton, and at the same time informed me that,
according to the act regulating the tenure of certain civil offices, your 'functions
as Secretary of War ad interim ceased from the moment of the receipt of the
notice.' You thus, in disregard of the understanding between us, vacated the

office without having given me notice of your intention to do so. It is but just, however, to say that in your communication you claim that you did inform me of your purpose, and thus 'fulfilled the promise made in our last preceding conversation on this subject.' The fact that such a promise existed is evidence ~~of the existence~~ of an arrangement of the kind I have mentioned. You had found, in our first conference, 'that the President was desirous of keeping Mr. Stanton out of office, whether sustained in the suspension or not.' You knew what reasons had induced the President to ask from you a promise. You also knew that in case your views of duty did not accord with his own convictions, it was his purpose to fill your place by another appointment. Even ignoring the existence of a positive understanding between us, these conclusions were plainly deducible from our various conversations. It is certain, however, that even under these circumstances you did not offer to return the place to my possession, but, according to your own statement, placed yourself in a position where, could I have anticipated your action, I would have been compelled to ask of you, as I was compelled to ask of your predecessor in the War Department, a letter of resignation, or else to resort to the more disagreeable expedient of superseding you by a successor. As stated in your letter, the nomination of Governor Cox, of Ohio, for the office of Secretary of War, was suggested to me. His appointment, as Mr. Stanton's successor, was urged in your name, and it was said that his selection would save further embarrassment. I did not think that in the selection of a Cabinet officer I should be trammelled by such considerations. I was prepared to take the responsibility of deciding the question in accordance with my ideas of constitutional duty, and having determined upon a course which I deemed right and proper, was anxious to learn the steps you would take should the possession of the War Department be demanded by Mr. Stanton. Had your action been in conformity to the understanding between us, I do not believe that the embarrassment would have attained its present proportions, or that the probability of its repetition would have been so great. I know that with a view to an early termination of a state of affairs so detrimental to the public interests, you voluntarily offered, both on Wednesday the 15th instant, and on the succeeding Sunday, to call upon Mr. Stanton, and urge upon him that the good of the service required his resignation. I confess that I considered your proposal as a sort of reparation for the failure, on your part, to act in accordance with an understanding more than once repeated, which I thought had received your full assent, and under which you could have returned to me the office which I had conferred upon you, thus saving yourself from embarrassment, and leaving the responsibility where it properly belonged—with the President, who ~~alone~~ is accountable for the faithful execution of the laws. I have not yet been informed by you whether, as twice proposed by yourself, you have called upon Mr. Stanton, and made an effort to induce him voluntarily to retire from the War Department. You conclude your communication with a reference to our conversation at the meeting of the Cabinet held on Tuesday, the 14th instant. In your account of what then occurred, you say that after the President had given his version of our previous conversations, you stated them substantially as given in your letter, that you in no wise admitted the correctness of his statement of them, 'though, to soften the evident contradiction my statement gave, I said (alluding to our first conversation on the subject,) the President might have understood me in the way he said, namely: that I had promised to resign if I did not resist the re-instatement. I made no such promise.' My recollection of what then transpired is diametrically the reverse of your narration. In the presence of the Cabinet, I asked you—First, If, in a conversation which took place shortly after your appointment as Secretary of War ad interim, you did not agree either to remain at the Head of the War Department and abide any judicial proceedings that might follow non-concurrence by the Senate in Mr. Stanton's suspension; or, should you wish not to become involved in such a controversy, to put me in the same position with respect to the office as I occupied previous to your appointment, by returning it to me in time to anticipate such action by the Senate. This you admitted. Second. I then asked you if, at our conference on the preceding Saturday, I had not, to avoid misunderstanding, requested you to state what you intended to do, and, further, if, in reply to that inquiry, you had not referred to our former conversations, saying that from them I understood your position, and that your action would be consistent with the understanding which had been reached. To these questions you also replied in the affirmative. Third. I next asked if, at the conclusion of our interview on Saturday, it was not understood that we were to have another conference on Monday, before final action by the Senate in the case of Mr Stanton. You replied that such was the understanding; but that you did not suppose the Senate would act so soon; that on Monday you had been engaged in a conference with Gen'l. Sherman, and were occupied with 'many little matters,' and asked if Gen'l. Sherman had not called on that day. What relevancy Gen'l. Sherman's visit to me on Monday had with the purpose for which you were then to have called, I am at a loss to perceive, as he certainly did not inform me whether you had determined to retain possession of the office, or to afford me an opportunity to appoint a successor, in advance of any attempted re-instatement of Mr. Stanton. This account of what passed between us at the Cabinet meeting on the 14th instant widely differs from that contained in your communication; for it shows that instead of having 'stated our conversations as given in the letter' which has made this reply necessary, you admitted that my recital of them was entirely accurate. Sincerely anxious, however, to be correct in my statements, I have to-day read this narration of what occurred on the 14th instant to the members of the Cabinet who were then present. They, without exception, agree in its accuracy. It is only necessary to add that on Wednesday morning, the 15th, you called on me, in company with Lieutenant General Sherman. After some preliminary conversation, you remarked that an article in the 'National Intelligencer' of that date did you much injustice. I replied that I had not read the 'Intelligencer' of that morning. You then first told me that it was your intention to urge Mr. Stanton to resign his office. After you had withdrawn, I carefully read the article of which you had spoken, and found that its statements of the understanding between us were substantially correct. On the 17th I caused it to be read to four of the five members of the Cabinet who were present at our conference on the 14th, and they concurred in the general accuracy of its statements respecting our conversation upon that occasion. In reply to your communication I have deemed it proper, in order to prevent further misunderstanding, to make this simple recital of facts." LS, DNA, RG 108, Letters Received; Df, DLC-Andrew Johnson. See letter to Andrew Johnson, Feb. 3, 1868.

1. On Jan. 24, USG had written to Johnson. "I have the honor, very respectfully, to request to have, in writing, the order which the President gave me, verbally, on Sunday, the 19th inst. to disregard the orders of the Hon. E. M. Stanton, as Sec. of War, until I know, from the President himself, that they were his orders." Copies (2), DLC-Andrew Johnson; DNA, RG 108, Letters Sent; DLC-USG, V, 47, 60. On Jan. 29, Johnson endorsed this letter. "As re-

quested in this communication, General Grant is instructed, in writing, not to obey any order from the War Department, assumed to be issued by the direction of the President, unless such order is known, by the General commanding the armies of the United States, to have been authorized by the Executive." Copies (2), DLC-Andrew Johnson. See letter to Andrew Johnson, Jan. 30, 1868.

To Hamilton Fish

Washington, D. C. Jany 29th *1868*.

MY DEAR GOVERNOR.

Mrs. Grant has some visitors she expects to remain with her all of next week which will preven[t] our going to New York City at the time we expected, next Friday[1] week. As soon as we can however, after they leave, we will go to stay four or five days, spending from Saturday to Monday either at Ravenswood or West Point. The balance of the time we will avail ourselves of your kind invitation, or Mrs. Fishes, to accept your hospitalities. It is likely now that we will not be able to get off much, if any, before Lent. Please present Mrs. Grant's and my kind regards to Mrs Fish and the family.

Yours Truly
U. S. GRANT

ALS, DLC-Hamilton Fish.
   1. Feb. 7, 1868.

To Andrew Johnson

Washington January 30th *1868*

HIS EXCELLENCY A. JOHNSON
PRESIDENT OF THE U S.
SIR:

I have the honor to acknowledge the return of my note of the 24th inst. with your endorsement thereon, that I am not to obey any order from the War Department, assumed to be issued by the direction of the President unless such order is known by me to have

been authorized by the Executive; and in reply thereto to say—
That I am informed by the Secretary of War that he has not received from the Executive any order or instructions limiting or im-
pairing his authority to issue orders to the Army as has heretofore
been his practice under the law, and the customs of the Department.
While this authority to the War Department is not countermanded
it will be satisfactory evidence to me that any orders issued from
the War Department by direction of the President are authorized
by the Executive

I have the honor to be,
Very respectfully
your obt. svt.
U. S. GRANT
General,

LS, DLC-Andrew Johnson. See letter to Andrew Johnson, Jan. 28, 1868, note 1.

To Elihu B. Washburne

Washington, Jan. 30th *1868*

DEAR WASHBURN,

This will introduce to you Gen. Bolles, Solicitor & Judge Advocate Gen. of the Navy, who desires to speak to you on business personal to himself as well as of public interest.

Gen.l Bolles is brother-in-law of Gen. Dix, our able Minister to
France. He is a gentleman who I can vouch for. As to the matter of
business he wishes to speak about I can say that, in my opinion, the
office which he holds in the Navy is of the same importance as the
office of Judge Advocate General in the Army.

Yours Truly
U. S. GRANT

ALS, DLC-USG, I, B.

On Dec. 22, 1868, USG wrote to U.S. Representative Frederick A. Pike of
Maine. "I would respectfully recommend to the favorable consideration of your
Comee the importance of legislating for the continuance of the office of Judge Advocate General of the Navy. Trials by Courts Martial, both in the army and navy,
are necessarily conducted by officers who cannot be expected to have a thorough

knowledge of law, and it looks as though their proceedings should at least be submitted to the scrutiny of a law officer to secure justice." Copy, CSmH. USG endorsed this copy to U.S. Senator James W. Grimes of Iowa. "The inclosed is copy of ~~of~~ a letter addressed to Hon. F. A. Pike, of the House, in behalf of ~~appropriating money~~ legislating to retain the office of Judge Advocate, of the Navy, which I respectfully submit to you as Chairman of Com. on Naval Affairs in the Senate. Please give the subject such consideration as you may deem it deserves." AES, *ibid.* Congress reauthorized the position of solicitor and judge advocate, U.S. Navy, which John A. Bolles retained until his death in 1878. Documents concerning reauthorization are in DNA, RG 46, Senate 40A–E1, Appropriations.

To Andrew Johnson

Washington, February 3d *1868.*

His Excellency A. Johnson
President of the U S.
Sir:

I have the honor to acknowledge the receipt of your communication of the 31st ulto., in answer to mine of the 28th ulto. After a careful reading and comparison of it with the article in the "National Intelligencer of the 15th ulto. and the article over the initials "J. B. S." in the "New-York World" of the 27th ulto., purporting to be based upon your statement and that of the members of your Cabinet therein named, I find it to be but a reiteration—only somewhat more in detail—of the "many and gross misrepresentations" contained in these articles, and which my statement of the facts, set forth in my letter of the 28th ulto. was intended to correct; and I here reassert the correctness of my statements in that letter, anything in yours in reply to it to the contrary notwithstanding.

I confess my surprise that the Cabinet Officers referred to should so greatly misapprehend the facts in the matter of admissions alleged to have been made by me at the Cabinet meeting of the 14th ulto. as to suffer their names to be made the basis of the charges in the newspaper articles referred to, or agree in the accuracy, as you affirm they do, of your account of what occurred at that meeting.

You know that we parted on Saturday, the 11th ulto., without any promise on my part, either express or implied, to the effect that I would hold on to the office of Secretary of War *ad interim* against the action of the Senate, or, declining to do so myself, would surrender it to you before such action was had; or that I would see you again at any fixed time on the subject.

The performance of the promises alleged by you to have been made by me would have involved a resistance to law, and an inconsistency with the whole history of my connection with the suspension of Mr. Stanton.

From our conversations, and my written protest of August 1st 1867 against the removal of Mr. Stanton, you must have known that my greatest objection, to his removal or suspension, was the fear that some one would be appointed in his stead who would, by opposition to the laws relating to the restoration of the Southern States to their proper relations to the Government, embarrass the Army in the performance of duties especially imposed upon it by these laws; and it was to prevent such an appointment that I accepted the office of Secretary of War *ad interim*, and not for the purpose of enabling you to get rid of Mr. Stanton by my withholding it from him in opposition to law, or, not doing so myself, surrendering it to one who would, as the statement and assumptions in your communication plainly indicate was sought.

And it was to avoid this same danger, as well as to relieve you from the personal embarrassment in which Mr. Stanton's reinstatement would place you, that I urged the appointment of Governor Cox, believing that it would be agreeable to you and also to Mr. Stanton—satisfied as I was that it was the good of the country, and not the office, the latter desired.

On the 15th ulto., in presence of General Sherman, I stated to you that I thought Mr. Stanton would resign, but did not say that I would advise him to do so. On the 18th I did agree with General Sherman to go and advise him to that course, and on the 19th I had an interview alone with Mr. Stanton, which led me to the conclusion that any advice to him of the kind would be useless, and I so informed General Sherman.

Before I consented to advise Mr. Stanton to resign, I understood from him in a conversation on the subject immediately after his reinstatement that it was his opinion, that the Act of Congress entitled "An act temporarily to supply vacancies in the Executive Departments in certain cases", approved Feb. 20th 1863, was repealed by subsequent legislation, which materially influenced my action. Previous to this time I had had no doubt ~~but~~ that the law of 1863 was still in force, and notwithstanding my action, a fuller examination of the law leaves a question in my mind whether it is or is not repealed, this being the case, I could not now advise his resignation lest the same danger I apprehended on his first removal might follow.

The course you would have it understood I agreed to pursue, was in violation of law, and without orders from you; while the course I did pursue and which I never doubted you fully understood, was in accordance with law, and not in disobedience of any orders of my superior.

And now, Mr. President, where my honor as a soldier and integrity as a man have been so violently assailed, pardon me for saying that I can but regard this whole matter, from the beginning to the end, as an attempt to involve me in the resistance of law, for which you hesitated to assume the responsibility in orders, and thus to destroy my character before the country.

I am in a measure confirmed in this conclusion by your recent orders directing me to disobey orders from the Secretary of War—my *superior* and your subordinate—without having countermanded his authority to issue the orders I am to disobey.

With assurances, Mr. President, that nothing less than a vindication of my personal honor and character could have induced this correspondence on my part

> I have the honor to be
> Very respectfully
> Your obedt servt
> U. S. GRANT
> General.

LS, DLC-Andrew Johnson. An incomplete two-page draft primarily in USG's hand with both pages numbered "3" may represent material considered for the Feb. 3, 1868, letter to President Andrew Johnson. "or resign so as to place the President where he would have been had I never accepted the office. After hearing the President through I stated our conversations substantially as given by me in this letter. The only ~~possible~~ words spoken by me that I can possibly conceive of giving ground for [the] statements said to be made by *four* Cabinet Ministers are that, (alluding to our first conversation), I said the President might have understood me in the way he ~~did~~ said. This was said ~~apologetically and not confirmatory. Our statements were so contradictory that I felt an apology to be necessary.~~ in defference to his office [and not in admmission of the statements.] ~~I will state here that after our conversation of the 14th I meditated seriously how I could leave the President free to violate resist the 'Tenure of Office Bill' himself if he chose without making me a party to the action. The plan arrived at was to notify the President as soon as relieved by the act of the Senate, and, when notified by Mr. Stanton of his readiness to assume the functions of his office to forward that notice to the President. In as much as Mr. S. had required me to notify him, in writing, of my willin acceptance of the office of Sec. of War, ad int. after he had received, officially, notice of his suspension and my appointment, I supposed he would extend the same courticy to me.~~ This version of our two conversations was ~~all gone over~~ repeated by me on Wednesday, the 15th inst. in presence of General Sherman, where the President not only did not dissent from it but ~~denied knowing anything about what had appeared in the National Intelligencer that morning.~~ clearly conveyed the impression to me that the Article in the Intelligencer of that morning, reflecting on my course in this matter was entirely without his authority or knowledge. ~~I cannot believe the President gave out the newspaper articles which assert they are by authority, but~~ All the facts occurring when they should have been held sacred, unless official action was deemed necessary, one word of contradiction by the President to any one of the correspondents visiting the 'White House' would have set this whole matter at rest. If the President has authorized the s[ta]tements made *by authority*, as stated in the Press I would respectfully request [I have now stated the facts in the case & have the I have honor to enclose a copy of a letter from Gen Sherman in reference to that part of these facts known to him.] I will add that my ~~statement~~ conversation before the Cabinet embraced other matter ~~as to my intentions (formed after the last interview with the President) in case Mr. Stanton should be reinstated to his office. This however is~~ not pertinent here and is therefore left out. ~~In conclusion I have to ask that should the President have further complaints to make against me that I be furnished the grounds of the complaint direct, and not through the press as stated by anonymous writers for the press. After hearing the President through, I stated our conversations substantially as they occurr.~~" ADf (bracketed material not in USG's hand), DLC-Cyrus B. Comstock. See letter to Andrew Johnson, Feb. 11, 1868.

To Maj. Gen. Winfield S. Hancock

Feb 3, 1868 [12:30 P.M.]

To Major General W. S. Hancock
comdg 5th Military district
New Orleans.

Please report what steps you have taken looking to the establishment of a new line of posts from the Rio Grande to the Red River If a commission have been appointed to examine and recommend new sites, send forward its report and your action without delay. Telegraph any changes made in Military routes, so that the Post office department may be informed.

U. S. Grant
General,

LS (telegram sent), DNA, RG 107, Telegrams Collected (Bound); telegram sent, *ibid.*; telegram received, *ibid.*, RG 393, 5th Military District, Telegrams Received. On Feb. 3, 1868, Maj. Gen. Winfield S. Hancock telegraphed to USG. "Telegram concerning military posts in Texas received. I have just returned from Texas, where I gave personally to Genl Reynolds the general directions for the establishment of the frontier line of posts Troops are now in, or moving to the places selected. The detailed orders will be issued as soon as a little more information can be forwarded by Genl Reynolds. Will telegraph orders as soon as made and will telegraph immediately, information in detail if required Will forward immediately by mail report of commissions" Telegram received, *ibid.*, RG 107, Telegrams Collected (Bound); *ibid.*, RG 108, Telegrams Received; copies (one sent by mail), *ibid.*, Letters Received; DLC-USG, V, 55.

Also on Feb. 3, George W. McLellan, 2nd asst. postmaster gen., had written to Secretary of War Edwin M. Stanton. "It has been represented to this Department that in October last a military commission was appointed, to settle upon some general plan of defence for the Texas frontiers, and that the said commission has made a report recommending a line of posts from the Rio Grande to the Red River. An application is now pending in this Department for a change in the course of the San Antonio and El Paso mail, so as to send it by way of Forts Mason, Griffin, and Stockton, instead of by Camps Hudson and Lancaster. This application requires immediate decision; but before final action can be had thereon, it is desired to have some official information as to the report of the commission above referred to. Accordingly, I have the honor to request that you will cause this Department to be furnished, as early as possible, with the information desired in the premises, and also with a copy of the report, if any has been made by the commission." LS, DNA, RG 108, Letters Received. On the same day, Stanton endorsed this letter to USG, and USG added his endorsement. "The enclosed dispatch contains all that is known at these HdQrs. on the subject of the P. M. Gn's enquiries." AES, *ibid.* USG then transmitted a copy of Hancock's telegram. Copy, *ibid.*, RG 107, Letters Received from Bureaus.

On Feb. 6, Hancock telegraphed to USG. "The following S. O. was issued today and is sent in accordance with promise in dispatch of the third 3d Inst. I request in this connection authority to purchase the wire and material for building Telegraph lines connecting the posts on the line with each other and with San Antonio and to employ two (2) experienced telegraphers until soldiers can be instructed as telegraphers—about eight hundred (800) miles of wire will be required. Report of the board and status of the new posts mailed today. . . ." Telegram received (at 6:15 P.M.), *ibid.*, Telegrams Collected (Bound); *ibid.*, RG 108, Telegrams Received; copies (one sent by mail), *ibid.*, Letters Received; DLC-USG, V, 55. On Feb. 7, USG endorsed a copy of this telegram. "Respy forwarded to the Sec of War for his information and instructions—I cannot recommend the building [o]f 800 miles of telegraph unless Congress should authorize it—though it would be of great service and the [wo]rk being done by troops, could be done without further out lay than for materials—" Copy, DNA, RG 108, Register of Letters Received. On Feb. 15, USG again endorsed a copy of Special Orders No. 27. "Respectfully returned to the Secretary of War. I recommend that the names herein given to the new posts be approved, and that par 6, of this order, be disapproved. I cannot recommend the erection of the telegraph lines, unless Congress makes an appropriation for that purpose." Copies, DLC-USG, V, 44; Babcock Papers, ICN. On Feb. 6, Hancock wrote to USG. "I have the honor to transmit herewith, copies of Report of Board of Officers convened for the examination of sites for frontier posts, &c., together with report of General Reynolds, and accompanying papers, and a copy of an order establishing the posts, which was also sent you by telegraph today." Copy, *ibid.* Copies of the enclosures are *ibid.*

To Maj. Gen. George G. Meade

Cypher   Washington, D, C, Feb.y 6th *1868* [*10:40* A.M.]
MAJ. GN. G. G. MEADE,
MOBILE ALA.

Dispatches are received here saying that floods, and embarassments thrown in the way of voters getting to the polls by opposers of reconstruction makes the time given for voting too short to get out all who wish to vote. There should be a fare chance for all who are entitled ~~to~~ to express their will by their ballot. No doubt you are looking into this matter and will do what is right but I inform you of this for your information.

U. S. GRANT
Gen.l

If there is no Cyher operator at Mobile this will be sent out of Cyher.

U. S. G.

ALS (telegram sent), DNA, RG 107, Telegrams Collected (Bound); telegram sent, *ibid.*; copies, *ibid.*, RG 108, Telegrams Sent; DLC-USG, V, 56. On Feb. 6, 1868, Maj. Gen. George G. Meade telegraphed to USG. "I have extended the time of election one day   The weather is now clear and this will give three 3 days of good weather including today & two days of bad weather   The bad weather did not begin till the day of the election. I [*think*] this extension will be sufficient"   Telegram received (at 12:50 P.M.), DNA, RG 107, Telegrams Collected (Bound); *ibid.*, RG 108, Telegrams Received; copies, DLC-USG, V, 55; (2) Meade Papers, PHi.

On Jan. 25, 2:00 P.M., USG had telegraphed to Meade. "Will it not be well to extend the number of days the polls ~~will~~ are to be kept open at the Alabama election in order to give full opportunity to all who register to vote? Two days will hardly give sufficient time.   ~~and~~ It would be better to amend Gen. Pope's order now than after the election had commenced." ALS (telegram sent), DNA, RG 107, Telegrams Collected (Bound); telegram sent, *ibid.*; telegram received, Meade Papers, PHi. On Jan. 26, Meade, Atlanta, telegraphed to USG. "After reference to C. O. in Alabama I have modified Genl Order No one hundred and one (101), so as to allow (4) Four days for voting, and confined the number of precincts to not more than three (3) in in any one county.—" ALS (telegram sent), *ibid.*; telegram received (on Jan. 27, 10:20 A.M.), DNA, RG 107, Telegrams Collected (Bound); *ibid.*, RG 108, Telegrams Received.

To Hamilton Fish

———

Washington, Feb.y 6th *1868*

MY DEAR GOVERNOR,

Your favor asking Mrs. Grant and myself to visit New York so as to be present at Miss Fish's wedding on Tuesday next is received. I regret it is so that we can not go at that time. Mrs. Grant has several lady friends visiting her now who will not be gone by that time, and more have written from Chicago and Michigan that they will also be here to pay us a visit. I think it will be near the 20th before all will be gone.

Please allow me to express my congratulations to Miss Fish in advance, and wish her a long and happy life.

Mrs. Grant sends her love to Mrs. Fish and the young ladies.

Yours Truly
U. S. GRANT

HON. H. FISH

ALS, DLC-Hamilton Fish. Susan Fish married 2nd Lt. William E. Rogers, USMA 1867, on Feb. 13, 1868.

To Alexander T. Stewart

Washington, D, C, Feb.y 6th *1868.*

A. T. STEWART, ESQ,
MY DEAR SIR:

This will introduce to you the Hon. E. B. Washburne, Member of Congress from Ill. who, you know probably, has stood steadfastly as my friend during the dark days of the rebellion, when efforts were made for my removal from command. I will say however, in this connection, that I never asked aid though feel none the less gratful for it. Mr. Washburne visits New York, I know not what for exactly, and I take the liberty of writing you this letter to ask for him an interview, and to say that you may rely upon him as being a sincere, patriotic man who desires the welfare of the whole country, and one who would betray no confidence reposed in him[.]

Yours Truly
U. S. GRANT

ALS, IHi. Alexander T. Stewart, born in Ireland in 1803, opened a lace shop in New York City in 1823. In 1862, when he opened the largest retail store in the world, he had numerous other lucrative commercial interests. On Dec. 16, 1867, Stewart wrote to USG. "It is with great pleasure I communicate to you in an official form the proceedings of our Great Popular demonstration in favor of placing you in nomination for President of the United States. The newspapers have told you truly, that the Vast Hall of the Cooper Institute was incapable of holding more than a Fifth of those who sought admittance; but you may not have been assured of the fact, that the Class of People who composed the meeting, and who filled the Hall nearly an hour before the time appointed, were plainly of that kind who act and think for themselves uncontrolled by party leaders. It was, indeed, an assemblage well worthy of the occasion. I feel warranted in saying here, that this is but the beginning of a movement which plainly indicates, that our Country is disposed to give a Unanimous call upon you for help to restore by your sound Judgement, the Government you have saved by your Valor. I need scarcely add, that we will be delighted to see you here, and as it is now about the time you appointed to visit us, may I ask, when you intend carrying into effect your purpose." LS, USG 3. The enclosure, dated Dec. 5, is *ibid.* Copies of a printed broadside, dated Jan. 1, 1868, issued by Stewart, calling for USG's election, are in James Lawson Kemper Manuscripts, ViU; OFH; DLC-Andrew Johnson.

To Maj. Gen. Winfield S. Hancock

Washington, Feb.y 7th *1868* [*12:30* P.M.]

MAJ. GN. W. S. HANCOCK,

NEW ORLEANS, LA.

Report ~~by mail~~ the reasons for removal of Baker, street commissioner, and result of investigation of his conduct.

U. S. GRANT

General.

ALS (telegram sent), DNA, RG 107, Telegrams Collected (Bound); telegram sent (at 1:00 P.M.), *ibid.*; telegram received, *ibid.*, RG 393, 5th Military District, Telegrams Received. On Feb. 7, 1868, Maj. Gen. Winfield S. Hancock telegraphed to USG. "Despatch asking reasons for removal of Baker Street Commissioner received. I explained reasons in a despatch sent yesterday. About forty five days ago I referred charges against him for malfeasance in office, to the Mayor for investigation. A Committee of the City Council commenced the investigation, the evidence adduced soon satisfied me that his Office had been improperly administered by Baker but the investigation was tardy and obstructed apparently for the purpose of continuing it until I might be removed from command. Being myself perfectly satisfied of this, and of Bakers unfitness for the Office under the circumstances I removed him. I will send the charges and evidence as soon as they can be prepared. If more details are required by telegraph please inform me" Telegram received (on Feb. 8, 10:00 A.M.), *ibid.*, RG 107, Telegrams Collected (Bound); *ibid.*, RG 108, Telegrams Received; copies (one sent by mail), *ibid.*, Letters Received; DLC-USG, V, 55.

On Feb. 5, Hancock had telegraphed to USG. "I have removed Wm Baker street commissioner of this city, military appointment, being satisfied that he has been using his office for corrupt purposes, to the public scandal. This action was taken under that clause of the reconstruction act, which directs military appointments to be made from time to time for the performance of the said duties of such officer or person so suspended or removed. Mr Baker was an appointment made by General Sheridan" Telegram received (on Feb. 6, 9:00 A.M.), DNA, RG 107, Telegrams Collected (Bound); *ibid.*, RG 108, Telegrams Received; copies (one sent by mail), *ibid.*, Letters Received; *ibid.*, RG 393, 5th Military District, Telegrams Sent; DLC-USG, V, 55.

On Feb. 8, William Baker, New Orleans, wrote to USG. "I beg leave to lay before you, for your information, the following facts, and most respectfully ask that you will take such action as may be necessary to secure me a fair opportunity of defending myself against false and malicious charges. On the 3d day of June 1867, I was appointed street Commissioner of this city, by Maj Gen P. H. Sheridan then commanding the 5th military district. I took the oath required by the Act of Congress, gave the bonds required by the City Charter, and on the 5th day of June entered upon the duties of my office, in which position I continued up to the 4th day of Feb. 1868, when I was removed from office, by Special Order No 26, issued by Maj Gen Hancock, under the following circumstances: On the 17th day of December 1867 Mr Frank Marquez, a city contractor, made a written complaint to Maj Gen Hancock, alleging that one of my deputies and my chief clerk had been guilty of extorting money from him, and that I was cognizant of and a party to it. Maj Gen Hancock immediately forwarded the complaint to the Hon. E. Heath, Mayor, with instructions to investigate the charges. The Mayor fixed a time for making the investigation, which was to have been public—but the City Attorney raised a doubt as to the power of the Mayor to make the investigation, urging that under the city charter, the Board of Assistant Alderman was the proper body to investigate, and more particularly as Maj Gen. Hancock, had in an order announced that the civil law would be permitted to take its course. The subject was referred back to Maj Gen Hancock for instructions, when he immediately approved the recommendation of the city attorney, and directed the investigation to be had in accordance with the provisions of the city charter. The papers were forwarded to the Board of Assistant Aldermen, who appointed a 'committee to ~~examine~~ investigate and report' on the charges. The on the next day proceeded to perform the duty assigned them. The proceeded vigorously with the investigation, until the evening of Feb 4, when the party making the charge having produced all the evidence they could, then withdrew, declining to take any part, when the evidence for the defence was to be heard. Over forty witnesses were permitted to testify, against me and only a few have been heard in my defence. On Feb 4 Maj Gen Hancock issued an order stopping the investigation of the Committee, and dismissing me from office; thus declaring me guilty and that before I had had an opportunity of defending myself. I think I am fully justified in asking you General to at least suspend the order of Maj Gen Hancock in dismissing that committee and removing me from office—on *ex-parte* testimony. While the committee, which Gen Hancock had recognized as the proper authority under the law, were examining the subject, referred to them, and without any allegation that they in any manner had failed to do their duty under the law, and at the very moment when my defence is to be heard, that Committee is dismissed, I am deprived of a the chance to rebut the charges against me. The charges against me have not been proven, yet I am by this high handed outrage upon my rights as an American city, without any redress under the law. Under the law of the city I am wrongfully removed from office. I claim that my appointment to the office of street Commissioner was confirmed by Sec 4 of Act of Congress No 27 passed—July 1867, and that I can only be removed from office, in the event of it appearing that I am disloyal, or that I hinder and obstruct the work of reconstruction. I am, and always have been loyal to the Government of the U. S.—have taken an active part in the work of Reconstruction—I was a member of the first Free State Committee ever organized in this state. I had the honer to be chairman of the Board of Registers of the parish and city of New Orleans. At the present time I am the treasurer of the Central Executive Committee of the Republican party of Louisiana. These things mentioned to show you that I am know to and have the confidence of the loyal people here—I also refer you to Maj Gen P: H Sheridan Hon Thomas J. Durant, Judge Kelley, and Senator Wilson If, General, I have been guilty of any offence as a public officer, which I deny the charter of the city provides for the proper mode of dealing with me,—I have given bonds in the sum of $10,000 for the proper performance of my duties. I therefore earnestly, but most respectfully ask that you will at least suspend the order of Maj Gen. Hancock, removing me from office, until such time as I shall have a fair opportunity of defending myself from the charges made against me, and until I shall be proven to guilty under the law." ALS, DNA, RG 108, Letters Received. Louis C. d'Homergue wrote an undated letter to USG. "On the 10th day of June 1867 I was appointed Deputy Street Commissioner of New Orleans under the recommendation of Major Gen'l P H Sheridan & was in accordance with the City Charter duly commissioned & my appointment approved by the Common Council. On the 21st of December last I was notified by the Mayor that charges had been preferred against Mr Wm Baker and myself through Genl W. S. Hancock by one Frank Marquez which Genl Hancock forwarded to the Mayor for investigation. The document marked "A" is a copy of same. On being notified of this I immediately demanded an investigation and wrote to that effect to Genl Hancock the original of which with its endorsement please examine—marked "B." The preliminary examination resulted in the Mayor coming to the conclusion that he had no authority in the premises guided in this by the opinion of the Corporation Counsel Judge Buchanan. The prosecuter was represented by Judge Collins a man well known for his anti Union sentiments. This meeting was adjourned by the Mayor so as to consult Genl Hancock who on being shown the law which provides that all charges against Municipal offiscirs shall be examined by the Asstt Board of Alderman previous to impeachment and trial by the Upper Board, ordered the investigation to be thus conducted. In accordance with his order the Asst Board appointed a Committee of five of their members to investigate the charges viz. Messers. Joubert Straight Marie Sterry and Gauche all men of reputation and wealth. The investigation in accordance with our request was made public. On the evening of their first meeting the prosecuter was examined when he swore to the charges he had previously made in writing to Genl Hancock. His evidence & cross examination please find on paper marked "C." It will be found that therein he gratuitously insults Genl Sheridan Genl Mower and the Council by admitting the reasons he did not complain before were that he felt assured he could get no redress from those parties but preferred to await for months the arrival of Genl Hancock. This Marquez was a Confederate soldier and his partner Correjolles was engaged in erecting the rebel works at Chalmette. The second evening of the meeting of the Committee these parties were represented by additional Counsel Judge Alexander Walker a prominent man in secession times and now it is said a confidential adviser of Genl Hancock and a writer for the N. O. Times: The proceedings are herein inclosed of the succeeding meetings up to the last. It will be found on perusal that the prosecution did not confine itself to the charges and the committee in their anxiety to get at the truth allowed them to introduce evidence not bearing on the case. In so doing the prosecution had full opportunity of procuring such evidence as they would desire in a community hating Union men and especially those appointed by Genl Sheridan to office. My counsel objected on the start against this evidence well knowing from an experience of thirty years as a criminal lawyer that with such latitude as the Committee gave the prosecution and with the known unscrupulousness of the parties themselves that they could summon up a host of irevalent witnesses. As we foresaw this occurred. During this trial the room was densely filled by just such a class of people as caused the riot of the 30th of July 1866. & such was the feeling of bitterness expressed that frequent applause & other marks of approbation would be made in favor of the prosecution. Our counsel were insulted & intimidated openly during the trial until at last a request was made to the Mayor to have a force of Police there to protect the peace, which being done this class of people were observed to discontinue their presence whilst their organ the N. O Times commenced to write editorials against the Mayor for having police in attendance. On two different

occasions the Counsel for the prosecution notified the Committee they had finished
their case when hardly would we have time to examine a witness when they
would ask the Committee to allow them to resume their case on the ground of
important witnesses who upon being examined testified to nothing touching the
charges made But in this they had a purpose—they wished to embarrass and
delay the defense and by the introduction of a large number of witnesses cause
us to summon an equal number for rebutting evidence so as to consume time. It
will be seen on reading the evidence of Marquez and Correjolles and comparing
it with others for the defense that these parties have sworn falsely—the first in
swearing that he always promptly attended to the orders I and my assistant's
gave him, while these assistants so far as I have had the opportunity of examining have all sworn to the contrary & the enclosed certificate marked "D" signed
by a majority of the members of the Committee, the Mayor and Surveyor of the
City after a personal inspection of the roads fully corroborates the testimony of
my subordinates. Correjolles swore positively that the official order book in
which I wrote orders to these parties to fulfil under their contract was the most of
the time looked up in the desk of my private office. The evidence so far proves
that such was not the case inasmuch as this book was always kept as proven in
the public office accessible to all and at all times during office hours. They endeavored to prove the filthy condition of that portion of the City under my charge,
but the evidence of the Health Officer of my district a Professer of one of our
Schools of Medicine fully sets that aside. His official report to the Board of
Health marked "E" is hereby submitted. The enclosed Certificate marked "F"
is also forwarded to prove by citizens of standing the disposition I made of dirt
at my disposal. The enclosed letter of the assistant Treasurer of the City marked
"FG" fully exonerates me from having received any money from him on Marquez
account as he Marquez swore to. This evidence owing to the action of Genl Hancock I have not been permitted to present. Now General I am a very humble
individual filling a [v]ery humble place but as an American Citizen I am entitled
to be heard in defense of my reputation which is all I have and which the law of
the land guarantees protection to. I have been assailed by men who as contracters
have endeavored to rob the City by non fulfilment of contract and by preferring
these charges to cause my removal as an obstruction to their plans of robbery of
the City Treasury. The Tribunal before which I was being tried has been ordered
to cease its investigations at the close of witnesses for the prosecution and I am
prevented from making my defense. If I go now to the Courts of Justice owing to
the feeling against loyal men fostered by the conduct of Gen'l Hancock—I feel
confident before a jury I would not get justice especially as all the evidence for
the prosecution has been made public—the Press for weeks during the trial filled
with articles ridiculing us or violently denouncing us and by this course inflam-
ing the public mind. On the other hand a complaint of mine before the Criminal
Courts owing to the large amount of cases could not be reached before next Fall
& I wish to leave this City in the Spring. The document marked "H" is a copy
of my letter to Genl Hancock protesting against his action in this matter. It is
evident the course of this officer advised by his surroundings—men well known
for their an[ta]gonism to the policy of Congress, is to throw the direction of affairs on the slightest pretense in the hands of Rebels & their sympathizers to
defeat re-construction in this state. As a loyal man as one who since his arrival
in New Orleans has extended the most hearty hospitality to the Army and Navy
Officers of our Government whose house & purse were always open to relieve

those who suffered by the acts of Rebels and Traitors I simply ask for justice. To you Sir I appeal directly as my only recourse. Trusting General that you will condescend to notice my case . . ." ALS, *ibid.*

On Feb. 17, Hancock wrote to USG. "In the case of William Baker, Street Commissioner, it is believed that the testimony established beyond all question or doubt, a deep and systematic corruption and extortion in the Street Commissioners office; that Contractors were in the habit of paying that official and his Deputies, large sums of money, in order to obtain certificates that their work was done according to the specifications and ordinances of the city; that a large number of men were put on the pay rolls, and received pay from the City, who were not on the time rolls, and did not work for the city; that some were put on the rolls for political or electioneering purposes, who did not work; that the men and vehicles employed and paid by the city, were permitted to work for individuals during the time for which they were paid by the city; that both laborers and materials of the city were diverted from their proper use and occupation, to the private use and profit of the Street Commissioner and his friends; that the Public Pounds which are under the charge of the Street Commissioner, were made the sources of great corruption and oppression by the Street Commissioner and his deputies; that animals belonging to the Citizens, impounded, were appropriated or purchased for a nominal sum, and in some cases, were without the formality of a sale, forfeited to these officials; that sums were demanded and extorted from Citizens, for the influence and aid of the Street Commissioner. The testimony in these and in other points, indicating vast loosness, venality and corruption in this important office, was presented to the investigating Committee. Upon this evidence, the committee should have found a report or presentment, so that a trial could be had before a competent Judicial tribunal. But they determined on a course, which would have protracted the investigation indefinately. It had already consumed six weeks, and was not approaching a close. It was obvious that a committee composed of citizens engaged in their private affairs, and in their aldermanic duties, could not perform these judicial functions in a satisfactory manner, and within a reasonable time, and after they had concluded their functions, the examination would have been had 'de novo' before the tribunal to which the case might be committed for trial. Meantime this official would be left in his office, armed with its large patronage and influence, with an immense retinue of followers and servitors and dependants, to sustain, defend and bolster up his reputation and obstruct the prosecution. There being a law of the state making the offences charged against the Street Commissioner, cognisable by the Grand Jury now in session, it was proper that the matter should be handed over to that tribunal and the Criminal Court, when the accused and the State would meet on terms that would ensure a speedy and satisfactory trial" LS, *ibid.*

On Feb. 24, Thomas J. Durant, Washington, D. C., wrote to Bvt. Maj. Gen. John A. Rawlins. "I have just received the enclosed letter from William Baker, Street Commissioner of Neworleans, removed by General Hancock. I know nothing of the charges upon which General Hancock ordered Baker to be tried by the N. O. Aldermen. I can testify in the most unreserved manner, from personal knowledge, as to Bakers loyalty to the United States during the rebellion and until the present time: I know him also to be a warm and active supporter of the congressional reconstruction policy. His character for integrity and good business habits has always been excellent in Neworleans. To break of the trial before the aldermen before the evidence was closed, and dismiss him from office, as if found guilty, is apparently an act of injustice which no man would like to have Committed on himself, and therefore should not suffer to be done to another. The General—H—has we are informed ordered Baker to be tried before a jury in the Criminal Court of Neworleans; I do not know on what charge: but the jury lists have been modified in Louisiana, in violation of U. S. law, by striking from them all the citizens of african, descent, and with such juries as will be empanelled, it will be almost, if not impossible for such a Man as Baker to have an impartial trial. Under these circumstances I cordially unite in the prayer of Mr Bakers letter to General Grant of 3. inst, . . ." ALS, *ibid.* Durant enclosed a letter of Feb. 19 from Baker to Durant. "Pardon the liberty I take in addressing you—I enclose you a copy of the statement of my case which is in the hands of General Grant. I know your love of justice too well to believe that you will think it too much trouble, or that it is a demand that should not be made of you, to ask you to use your influence to secure me a fair opportunity of defending myself—I beg to assure you *I do not* for one moment *ask you to commit yourself to my innocence,—give me the chance, I will prove that*—The abuse which I have labored under daily for many months, has only culminated just now when it is desirable that the rebels should if possible disorganize the Republican party, for the purpose of defeating the constitution which is soon to be submitted to the people. The removal of eight of the best men in the Common Council is only part of the same programme. It is not, sir, that I have been guilty of any offence that I am removed from the office of street Commissioner,—it is because I am the first man who appointed colored men to positions of trust and honor—it is that I have given the poor colored laborers a share of the city work of cleaning the streets,—as you might know by the frequent sneers of the newspaper to 'Baker's nigger squad' Lest there should be any doubt as to the object of my removal—it is plainly enough seen when I tell you that in the few days since my removal every colored man employed as Assistant Deputy has been removed from office, in violation of city law, without any charges against them—simply—'you are relieved from any further duty in this department' The conservative party claim to have rec'd from the north a large sum of money for the purpose of defeating the ratification of the constitution Excuse my trespass on your time, I know you are too well informed to misconstrue my purpose in writing to you—I am ready and willing at any moment to meet any charges against me either private or public—I only want a fair field and no favor." ALS, *ibid.*

On Feb. 28, Rawlins wrote to Hancock. "Your report of date the 17th inst. in response to a telegram of the General-in-Chief dated the 7 inst., in the matter of the removal of William Baker, street commissioner of the City of New Orleans, is received. A communication from Mr. Baker on the same subject has also been received. It appears that on the 17th Dec. '67, Frank Marquez laid before you a complaint and charges in writing against William Baker, street commissioner of New Orleans and his deputies, S. H. Brown, and L. C. d'Hormague which on the 20th of same month, was referred by you to the Mayor of the City of New-Orleans endorsed as follows 'Respectfully transmitted to His Honor E. Heath, Mayor of New-Orleans for investigation and remark'—and by the Mayor was, with your knowledge and approval transmitted to the Board of Assistant Alderman of said city, for investigation and procedure under the charter of the city of New Orleans. This investgation was conducted by a committee duly appointed by the Board of Assistant Alderman, and continued until all the witnesses produced against the accused were heard, and a few in their defence, when the counsel for the prosecution after first stating 'that there was no fault found with the Committee by the prosecution for the general manner in which they had discharged the duties assigned them,' withdrew ostensibly for reasons set forth in their written communication to the Committee, which appears to be based upon representations made by Frank Marquez, the prosecuting witness and accuser, in a communication to you, dated Feby. 3d, 1868, This latter communication concluded with the assertion that the examination ordered by you could not be satisfactorily conducted so long as E. Heath remained in the office of Mayor and Wm. Baker in that of street commissioner; and asked that you would afford such relief in the premises as the nature of the case required. Whereupon you issued your Special Order, No. 26, dated Feby. 5th, 1868, paragraph 4 of which summarily terminated the investigation which had been ordered by you, without giving the accused an opportunity to present their full defense, and also removing the said Wm. Baker, Street Commissioner for the City of New Orleans, from office, and appointing George D. Field in his place While the civil government of the city of New Orleans is continued under military authority and jurisdiction is accorded them to correct such evils and punish such offences as are complained of, and they are disposed and willing to comply with every requirement of law and military orders, as in this case they were, the proper enforcement of the reconstruction acts did not require the issuance of par. 4 of said Special Order, No. 26, dated Headquarters, 5th Military District, Feby. 5th, 1868. In view of these facts, and in justice to the accused, so much of par. 4, of said order as removes Wm. Baker, Street Commissioner for the city of New Orleans and appoints Geo. D. Field in his place, is hereby disapproved and revoked; and the said Wm. Baker, is hereby reinstated, and will resume the duties of said office of Street Commissioner for the city of New Orleans, the same as if said order of removal had not been made. You will please carry this order into effect" Copies (3), USG 3; DLC-USG, V, 47, 60; DNA, RG 108, Letters Sent.

On March 5, Rawlins telegraphed to Hancock. "General Grant, directs that your order [r]emoving William Baker, Street Commissioner for the City of New Or[l]eans be revoked; and that said William Baker be reinstated [a]nd resume the duties of said office, the same as if said order of removal had not been made." Copy, *ibid.*, RG 393, 5th Military District, Telegrams Received.

To Lt. Gen. William T. Sherman

————

Washington, February 10, 1868.

DEAR GENERAL,

I have received at last the President's reply to my last letter. He attempts to substantiate his statements by his Cabinet. In this view it is important that I should have a letter from you, if you are willing to give it, of what I said to you about the effect of the "Tenure of Office Bill," and my object in going to see the President on Saturday before the installment of Mr. Stanton. What occurred after the meeting of the Cabinet on the Tuesday following is not a subject under controversy now; therefore if you choose to write down your recollection (and I would like to have it) on Wednesday when you and I called on the President, and your conversation with him the last time you saw him make that a separate communication.

Your order to come east was received several days ago, but the President withdrew it, I supposed to make some alteration; but it has not been returned.[1]

Yours truly,
U. S. GRANT.

Copies (3), DLC-William T. Sherman. On Feb. 14, 1868, Lt. Gen. William T. Sherman, St. Louis, wrote to USG. "Last evening, just before leaving my office, I received your note of the 10th, and had intended answering it according to your request; but after I got home I got your despatch of yesterday, announcing that the order I dreaded so much was issued. I never felt so troubled in my life. Were it an order to go to Sitka, to the Devil,—to battle with rebels or Indians, I think you would not hear a whimper from me, but it comes in such a questionable form that, like Hamlet's Ghost, it curdles my blood and mars my judgment. My first thoughts were of resignation, and I had almost made up my mind to ask Dodge for some place on the Pacific Road, or on one of the Iowa Roads, and then again various Colleges ran through my memory; but hard times and an expensive family have brought me back to staring the proposition square in the face, and I have just written a letter to the President, which I herewith transmit through you, on which I will hang a hope of respite till you telegraph me its effect. The uncertainties ahead are too great to warrant my incurring the expense of breaking up my house and family here, and therefore in no event will I do this till I can be assured of some permanence elsewhere. If it were at all certain that you would accept the nomination (of President) in May I would try and kill the intervening time, and then judge of the chances, but I do not want you to reveal your plans to me till you choose to do so. I have telegraphed to John Sherman to oppose the nomination which the papers announce has been made of me for Brevet General.—I have this minute received your cipher despatch of to-day, which I have just answered and sent down to the Telegraph Office, and the clerk is just engaged in copying my letter to the President to go with this. If the President or his friends pretend that I seek to go to Washington, it will be fully rebutted by letters I have written to the President, to you, to John Sherman, to Mr. Ewing, and to Mr. Stanbery. You remember that in our last talk you suggested I should write again to the President. I thought of it, and concluded my letter of January 31st, already delivered, was full and emphatic. Still I did write again to Mr. Stanbery asking him as a friend to interpose in my behalf. There are plenty of people who know my wishes, and I would avoid if possible the publication of a letter so confidential as that of January 31st, in which I notice I allude to the President's purpose of removing Mr. Stanton by force, a fact that ought not to be drawn out through me if it be possible to avoid it. In the letter herewith, I confine myself to purely private matter, and will not object if it reaches the public in any proper way. My opinion is the President thinks Mrs. Sherman would like to come to Washington by reason of her father and brothers being there. This is true, for Mrs. Sherman has an idea that Saint

Louis is unhealthy for our children, and because most of the Catholics here are tainted with the old Secesh feeling. But I know better what is to our common interest, and prefer to judge of the proprieties myself. What I do object to is the false position I would occupy as between you and the President. Were there an actual Army at or near Washington, I could be withdrawn from the most unpleasant attitude of a 'go-between', but there is no Army there nor any military duties which you with a host of subordinates can not perform. Therefore I would be there with naked, informal and sinecure duties, and utterly out of place. This you understand well enough, and the Army too, but the President and the politicians who flatter themselves they are saving the country, cannot and will not understand. My opinion is the country is doctored to death, and if President and Congress would go to sleep like Rip van Winkle, the country would go on under natural influences and recover far faster than under their joint and several treatment. This doctrine would be accounted by Congress and by the President too as High Treason, and therefore I don't care about saying so to either of them, but I know you can hear anything and give it just what thought or action it merits. Excuse this long letter, and telegraph me the result of my letter to the President as early as you can. If he holds my letter so long as to make it improper for me to await his answer, also telegraph me. The order when received will I suppose direct me as to whom and how I am to turn over this command, which should in my judgment not be broken up as the three Departments composing the Division should be under one head. I expect my staff officers to be making for me within the hour to learn their fate. So advise me all you can as quick as possible." Copies (2), *ibid.*

1. On Feb. 6, President Andrew Johnson had written to USG. "You will please issue an order creating a Military Division, to be called the Military Division of the Atlantic, to be composed of the Department of the Lakes, the Department of the East, and the Department of Washington, and to be commanded by Lieutenant General William T. Sherman, with his headquarters at Washington You will direct Lieutenant General Sherman to assume command of the Military Division of the Atlantic as early as may be practicable, and will, until further orders from the President, assign no officer to the permanent command of the Military Division of the Missouri" LS, DLC-Andrew Johnson; Df, *ibid.* On Feb. 7, William G. Moore, secretary to Johnson, wrote to USG. "The President directs me to request the return of his communication of yesterday, in reference to the establishment of a Military Division, to be called the Military Division of the Atlantic." LS, DNA, RG 108, Letters Received. On Feb. 12, Johnson wrote to USG. "You will please issue an order creating a Military Division to be called the Military Division of the Atlantic, to be composed of the Department of the Lakes, the Department of the East, and the Department of Washington, and to be commanded by Lieutenant General William T. Sherman, with his headquarters at Washington. Until further orders from the President you will assign no officer to the permanent command of the Military Division of the Missouri." LS, Forbes Magazine Collection, New York, N. Y.
On Feb. 13, 4:35 P.M., USG telegraphed to Sherman. "The order is issued ordering you to Atlantic Division." ALS (telegram sent), DNA, RG 107, Telegrams Collected (Bound); telegram sent, *ibid.*; copies, *ibid.*, RG 108, Telegrams Sent; DLC-USG, V, 56; (3) DLC-William T. Sherman. On Feb. 14, Sherman telegraphed to USG. "Your dispatch informing me that the order for the Atlantic Division was issued, and that I was assigned to its command. I was in hopes I

had escaped the danger, and now were I prepared, should resign on the spot, as it requires no forsight to predict such must be the inevitable result in the end. I will make one more desperate effort by mail, which please await." Telegram received (at 11:30 A.M.), DNA, RG 107, Telegrams Collected (Bound); *ibid.*, RG 108, Telegrams Received; copies, DLC-USG, V, 55; (2) DLC-William T. Sherman. At 10:00 A.M., USG telegraphed to Sherman. "I think it due to you that your letter of Jan. 31st to the President should be published to correct misapprehensions in the public mind about your willingness to come to Washington. It will not be published against your will." ALS (telegram sent), DNA, RG 107, Telegrams Collected (Bound); telegram sent, *ibid.*; copies, *ibid.*, RG 108, Telegrams Sent; DLC-USG, V, 56; (3) DLC-William T. Sherman. On the same day, Sherman telegraphed to USG. "Despatch of today received. Please await a letter I address this day through you to the President, which will in due time reach the public, covering the very point you make. I dont want to come to Washington at all." Telegram received (at noon), DNA, RG 107, Telegrams Collected (Bound); *ibid.*, RG 108, Telegrams Received; copies, DLC-USG, V, 55; (3) DLC-William T. Sherman. On Feb. 14, Sherman wrote to Johnson. "It is hard for me to conceive you would purposely do me an unkindness unless under the pressure of a sense of public duty, or because you do not believe me sincere. I was in hopes, since my letter to you of the 31st of January, that you had concluded to pass over that purpose of yours, expressed more than once in conversation, to organize a new command for me in the East with Headquarters in Washington; but a telegram from General Grant, of yesterday says that 'the order was issued ordering you' (me) 'to Atlantic Division,' and the newspapers of this morning contain the same information, with the addition that I have been nominated as 'Brevet General.' I have telegraphed to my own brother in the Senate to oppose my confirmation, on the ground that the two higher grades in the Army ought not to be complicated with Brevets, and I trust you will conceive my motives aright. If I could see my way clear to maintain my family, I should not hesitate a moment to resign my present commission, and seek some business wherein I would be free from those unhappy complications that seem to be closing about me, spite of my earnest efforts to avoid them; but necessity ties my hands and I must submit with the best grace I can till I make other arrangements. In Washington are already the Headquarters of a Department, and of the Army itself and it is hard for me to see wherein I can render military service there. Any staff officer with the rank of Major could surely fill any gap left between these two military offices; and by being placed in Washington I will be universally construed as a rival to the General in Chief a position damaging to me in the highest degree. Our relations have always been most confidential and friendly, and if unhappily any cloud of difficulty should arise between us, my sense of personal dignity and duty would leave me no alternative but resignation. For this I am not yet prepared, but I shall proceed to arrange for it as rapidly as possible that when the time does come (as it surely will, if this plan is carried into effect) I may act promptly. Inasmuch as the order is now issued, I cannot expect a full revocation of it, but I beg the privilege of taking post at New York or any point you may name within the new Military Division, other than Washington. This privilege is generally granted to all Military Commanders, and I see no good reason why I too may not ask for it, and this simple concession, involving no public interest, will much soften the blow, which, right or wrong, I construe as one of the hardest I have sustained in a life somewhat checkered with adversity" LS, DLC-Andrew Johnson. On Feb. 19, USG endorsed this letter to Johnson, and endorsed a copy to Secretary of War

Edwin M. Stanton. AES, *ibid.*; ES, DNA, RG 107, Letters Received from Bureaus. On the same day, Johnson telegraphed to Sherman, sending a copy to USG. "I have just received, with General Grant's endorsement of reference, your letter to me of the 14th instant. The order to which you refer was made in good faith, and with a view to the best interests of the country and the service. As, however, your assignment to a new military division seems so objectionable, You will retain your present command." Copy, *ibid.*, RG 108, Letters Received. At 10:10 A.M., USG telegraphed to Sherman. "Your admirable letter to President just received. Dont leave St. Louis until you hear from me again." ALS (telegram sent), *ibid.*, RG 107, Telegrams Collected (Bound); telegram sent, *ibid.*; copies, *ibid.*, RG 108, Telegrams Sent; (2) DLC-William T. Sherman; (misdated Feb. 18) DLC-USG, V, 56.

On Feb. 18, Sherman telegraphed to Bvt. Maj. Gen. Edward D. Townsend. "General Orders number ten 10 are this moment received. General Sheridan is now absent from the limits of the Division, but is expected at any moment. A[s] soon as he relieves me I will start for Washington. If there be occasion for unusual haste please notify me" Telegram received (at 11:40 A.M.), DNA, RG 108, Telegrams Received; copy, DLC-USG, V, 55. At 2:45 P.M., USG telegraphed to Sherman. "I think tThere is no necessity for you starting to Washington until Sheridan relieves you. Your letter of which you notified me by telegraph on Friday has not yet been received." ALS (telegram sent), DNA, RG 107, Telegrams Collected (Bound); telegram sent, *ibid.*; copies, *ibid.*, RG 108, Telegrams Sent; DLC-USG, V, 56; (2) DLC-William T. Sherman. On Feb. 19, Sherman telegraphed to USG. "Your dispatches of yesterday and today are received. I await Gen'l Sheridans coming and your further or[d]ers" Telegram received (at 2:30 P.M.), DNA, RG 107, Telegrams Collected (Bound); *ibid.*, RG 108, Telegrams Received; copy, DLC-USG, V, 55. On Feb. 20, Sherman telegraphed to USG. "The President telegraphs that I may remain in my present command. I write him a letter of thanks through you today. Congress should not have for publication my letters to the President unless the President himself chooses to give them" Telegram received (at 3:15 P.M.), DNA, RG 107, Telegrams Collected (Bound); *ibid.*, RG 108, Telegrams Received; copies, DLC-USG, V, 55; (3) DLC-William T. Sherman. At 3:15 P.M., USG telegraphed to Sherman. "Please inform Gen. Sheridan that the Presidents authority for you to remain where you are revokes so much of General Orders No ten (10) as assign him to command of Mil. Div. of Mo." ALS (telegram sent), DNA, RG 107, Telegrams Collected (Bound); telegram sent, *ibid.*; copies, *ibid.*, RG 108, Telegrams Sent; DLC-USG, V, 56. On Feb. 21, Bvt. Brig. Gen. Cyrus B. Comstock wrote to U.S. Senator John Sherman. "By Gen. Grants direction I enclose a copy of a dispatch from Gen. Sherman, seeming to indicate his preference that the correspondence in question should not now be made public." ALS, DLC-William T. Sherman.

On Feb. 20, Lt. Gen. Sherman wrote to Johnson. "I received your telegraphic despatch of the 19th last evening, and replied to it at once I again beg to thank you for your decision in this matter. I do not question the motives that actuated you, but on the contrary beg to assure you of my obligations for your personal kindness to me on many occasions, indeed on all occasions since I first had the honor to meet you as President in May 1865. I have always taken strong ground against Brevets in the Army, unless conferred for acts of Extraordinary Gallantry on the Field of Battle. Recently Brevets have been lavished on all, even on non combatants, so that the principal officers of our Army favor the utter abolition of the whole system, and the Board of which I was recently a member adopted a

Resolution, that stript Brevet Rank of all its value save when the assignmt to duty was made by the President himself. My views on this subject are so well known to the whole Army, that were I silently to have accepted a Brevet I would have stood convicted of insincerity In my former letters of January 31, and February 14 I endeavored in the most respectful manner possible to point out the dangers I apprehended to myself and the harmony of the service, in my exercising a Command that would keep me in Washington. It is hardly to be expected that you whose experiences lay in another branch of Public service, could remember the sad effects to the Army of the personal differences that unhappily existed between General Jackson and General Scott; between Genl Scott and Genl Gaines; and between Genl Scott, and Jefferson Davis, but we of the Old Army remember them too well. I too have had my own troubles, but they bring no feelings of pride or satisfaction, and I sincerely wish to avoid them in the future. If in this matter I have wrongly foreseen what was not likely to happen, I hope you will at least credit my purpose. I did not allow myself to hope for the abrogation of the order in toto, though I confess I am very much pleased at it and think I can do more good service on the Plains than any where else in the present situation of public affairs. I do believe that all the orders you may give for the Army, will be promptly and fairly executed by General Grant. The unhappy difficulty existing in relation to the office of Secretary of War ought to be settled by the Supreme Court, and Lawyers are far better qualified to discover the mode of making up a Case, than we can possibly be. I admit that my feeling about Politics in their ordinary meaning, amounts to a Prejudice, and I cannot foresee any combination of affairs that will induce me to take part in them. I hope that the Election for which all our People now seem to be preparing, will quietly settle the dangerous questions that agitate the Country, and which have resulted from the Civil War. Any decision, even if wrong in principle if submitted to will be far better than a renewal of strife Again assuring you of my firm belief that in this matter you have been moved by considerations of the utmost kindness to myself, . . ." ALS, DLC-Andrew Johnson.

On Feb. 26, Sherman telegraphed to USG. "General Sheridan has not yet come. Where is he?" Telegram received (at 12:10 P.M.), DNA, RG 108, Telegrams Received. At 2:40 P.M., USG telegraphed to Sherman. "I do not know where Sheridan is. Supposed he would be in St. Louis yesterday." ALS (telegram sent), *ibid.*, RG 107, Telegrams Collected (Bound); telegram sent, *ibid.*; copies, *ibid.*, RG 108, Telegrams Sent; DLC-USG, V, 56.

To Jesse Root Grant

———

Washington, D, C, Feb.y 10th *1868*

DEAR FATHER:

The memorandums you left with me relative to bounty due two needy persons in Covington I attended to soon after you left here. The answer of the Paymaster Gen.l being that under no circumstances could he take up claims for bounty out of turn, therefore not satisfactory to you, I neglected to answer at the time and the matter escaped my memory until now.

I spoke to Sec. McCulloch about giving Mrs. Porter a clerkship in the Treasury and he promised me he would do it, but has not yet. Now I fancy I would not have much influence and if I had would be very careful about using it.

The family are well and send much love to Mother Jennie and yourself.

Yours Truly
U. S. GRANT

ALS, Berg Collection, NN.

To Andrew Johnson

———

Washington, D. C., Feby 11th *1868*

HIS EXCELLENCY A. JOHNSON
PRESIDENT OF THE US.
SIR:

I have the honor to acknowledge the receipt of your communication of the 10th inst., accompanied by statements of five Cabinet Ministers of their recollection of what occurred in Cabinet meeting on the 14th of January. Without admitting anything in these statements, where they differ from anything heretofore stated by me, I propose ~~now~~ to notice only that portion of your communication wherein I am charged with insubordination. I think it will be plain to the reader of my letter of the 30th of January that I did not propose to disobey any legal order of the President, distinctly given, but only gave an interpretation of what would be regarded as satisfactory evidence of the President's sanction to orders communicated by the Sec. of War. I will say here that your letter of the 10th inst. contains the first intimation I have had that you did not accept that interpretation.

Now for reasons for giving that interpretation: It was clear to me before my letter of Jany 30th was written that I, the person having more public business to transact with the Sec. of War than any other of the Presidents subordinates, was the only one who had been instructed to disregard the authority of Mr. Stanton where his authority was derived as agent of the President.

On the 27th of January I received a letter from the Sec. of War, (copy herewith) directing me to furnish escort to Public treasure from the Rio Grande to New Orleans &c, at the request of the Sec. of the Treasury to him.[1] I also send two other enclosures showing recognition of Mr. Stanton as Sec. of War by both the Sec. of the Treasury[2] and the Post Master General,[3] in all of which cases the Sec. of War had to call upon me to make the orders requested or give the information desired, and where his authority to do so is derived, in my view, as agent of the President

With an order so clearly ambiguous as that of the President here referred to, it was my duty to inform the President of my interpretations of it and to abide by that interpretation until I receive other orders.

Disclaiming any intention, now or heretofore, of disobeying any legal order of the President, distinctly communicated, I remain

Very respectfully
Your obt. serv't
U. S. GRANT
General

LS, DLC-Andrew Johnson. On Feb. 10, 1868, President Andrew Johnson had written to USG. "The extraordinary character of your letter of the 3d. instant would seem to preclude any reply on my part, but the manner in which publicity has been given to the correspondence of which that letter forms a part, and the grave questions which are involved, induce me to take this mode of giving, as a proper sequel to the communications which have passed between us, the statements of the five members of the Cabinet who were present on the occasion of our conversation on the 14th ultimo. Copies of the letters which they have addressed to me upon the subject are accordingly herewith enclosed. You speak of my letter of the 31st ulto. as a reiteration of the 'many and gross misrepresentations' contained in certain newspaper articles, and reassert the correctness of the statements contained in your communication of the 28th ulto, adding—and here I give your own words—'anything in yours in reply to it to the contrary notwithstanding.' When a controversy upon matters of fact reaches the point to which this has been brought, further assertion or denial between the immediate parties should cease, especially where, upon either side, it loses the character of the respectful discussion which is required by the relations in which the parties stand to each other, and degenerates in tone and temper. In such a case, if there is nothing to rely upon but the opposing statements, conclusions must be drawn from those statements alone, and from whatever intrinsic probabilities they afford in favor of or against either of the parties. I should not shrink from this test in this controversy, but, fortunately, it is not left to this test alone. There were five Cabinet officers present at the conversation, the detail of which, in my letter of the 28th ultimo, you allow yourself to say, contains 'many and gross misrepresentations.' These gentlemen heard that conversation and have read my statement. They speak for themselves, and I leave the proof without a word of comment. I deem it proper, before concluding this communication, to notice some of the statements contained in your letter. You say that a performance of the promises alleged to have been made by you to the President 'would have involved a resistance to law, and an inconsistency with the whole history of my connection with the suspension of Mr. Stanton.' You then state that you had fears the President would, on the removal of Mr. Stanton, appoint some one in his place who would embarrass the army in carrying out the Reconstruction Acts, and add 'It was to prevent such an appointment that I accepted the office of Secretary of War *ad interim*, and not for the purpose of enabling you to get rid of Mr. Stanton by my withholding it from him in opposition to law, or, not doing so myself, surrendering it to one who would, as the statements and assumptions in your communication plainly indicate was sought.' First of all, you here admit that from the very beginning of what you term 'the whole history' of your connection with Mr. Stanton's suspension, you intended to circumvent the President. It was to carry out that intent that you accepted the appointment. This was in your mind at the time of your acceptance. It was not, then, in obedience to the order of your superior, as has heretofore been supposed, that you assumed the duties of the office. You knew it was the President's purpose to prevent Mr. Stanton from resuming the office of Secretary of War, and you intended to defeat that purpose. You accepted the office, not in the interest of the President, but of Mr. Stanton. If this purpose, so entertained by you, had been confined to yourself,—if, when accepting the office, you had done so with a mental reservation to frustrate the President, it would have been a tacit deception. In the ethics of some persons such a course is allowable. But you cannot stand even upon that questionable ground. The 'history' of your connection with this transaction, as written by yourself, places you in a different predicament, and shows that you not only concealed your design from the President, but induced him to suppose that you would carry out his purpose to keep Mr. Stanton out of office, by retaining it yourself after an attempted restoration by the Senate, so as to require Mr. Stanton to establish his right by judicial decision. I now give that part of this 'history', as written by yourself in your letter of the 28th ulto. 'Sometime after I assumed the duties of Secretary of War *ad interim*, the President asked me my views as to the course Mr. Stanton would have to pursue, in case the Senate should not concur in his suspension, to obtain possession of his office. My reply was, in substance, that Mr. Stanton would have to appeal to the courts to reinstate him, illustrating my position by citing the ground I had taken in the case of the Baltimore police commissioners' Now, at that time, as you admit in your letter of the 3d inst., you held the office for the very object of defeating an appeal to the courts. In that letter you say that in accepting the office one motive was to prevent the President from appointing some other person who would retain possession, and thus make judicial proceedings necessary. You knew the President was unwilling to trust the office with any one who would not, by holding it, compel Mr. Stanton to resort to the courts. You perfectly understood that in this interview 'sometime' after you accepted the office, the President, not content with your silence, desired an expression of your views, and you answered him that Mr. Stanton 'would have to appeal to the courts.' If the President had reposed confidence *before* he knew your views, and that confidence had been violated, it might have been said he made a mistake; but a violation of confidence reposed *after* that conversation was no mistake of his, nor of yours. It is the fact only that needs be stated, that at the date of this conversation you did not intend to hold the office with the purpose of forcing Mr. Stanton into court, but did hold it then, and had accepted it, to prevent that course from being carried out. In other words, you said to the President, 'that is the proper course,' and you said to yourself, 'I have accepted this office, and now hold it, to defeat that course.' The excuse you make in a subsequent paragraph of that letter of the 28th ulto, that afterwards you changed you views as to what would be a proper course, has nothing to do with the point now under consideration. The point is, that *before* you changed your views you had secretly determined to do the very thing which at last you did—surrender the office to Mr Stanton. You may have changed your views as to the law, but you certainly did not change your views as to the course you had marked out for yourself from the beginning. I will only notice one more statement in your letter of the 3rd inst—that the performance of the promises which it is alleged were made by you 'would have involved you in the resistance of law.' I know of no statute that would have been violated had you, carrying out your promises in good faith, tendered your resignation when you concluded not to be made a party in any legal proceedings. You add: 'I am in a measure confirmed in this conclusion by your recent orders directing me to disobey orders from the Secretary of War, my *superior* and your subordinate, without having countermanded his authority to issue the orders I am to disobey.' On the 24th ulto, you addressed a note to the President, requesting in writing an order given to you verbally five days before, to disregard orders from Mr Stanton as Secretary of War, until you 'knew from the President himself that they were his orders.' On the 29th, in compliance with your request, I did give you instructions in writing 'not to obey any order from the War Department assumed to be issued by the direction of the President, unless such order is known by the General commanding the armies of the United States to have been authorized by the Executive.' There are some orders which a Secretary of War may issue without the authority of the President; there are others which he issues simply as the agent of the President, and which purport to be 'by direction' of the President. For such orders the President is responsible, and he should therefore know and understand what they are before giving such 'direction.' Mr. Stanton states, in his letter of the 4th inst. which accompanies the published correspondence, that he 'has had no correspondence with the President since the 12th of August last,' and he further says that since he resumed the duties of the office he has continued to discharge them 'without any personal or written communication with the President;' and he adds, 'No orders have been issued from this department in the name of the President with my knowledge, and I have received no orders from him.' It thus seems that Mr. Stanton now discharges the duties of the War Department without any reference to the President, and without using his name. My order to you had only rference to orders 'assumed to be issued by the direction of the President.' It would appear from Mr. Stanton's letter that you have received no such orders from him. However, in your note to the President of the 30th ulto., in which you acknowledge the receipt of the written order of the 29th, you say that you have been informed by Mr Stanton that he has not received any order limiting his authority to issue orders to the army, according to the practice of the Department, and state that 'While this authority to the War Department is not countermanded, it will be satisfactory evidence to me that any orders issued from the War Department by direction of the President are authorized by the Executive.' The President issues an order to you to obey no order from the War Department, purporting to be made 'by the direction of the President,' until you have referred it to him for his approval. You reply that you have received the Presidents order, and will not obey it, but will obey an order purporting to be given by his direction, *if it comes from the War Department.* You will not obey the direct order of the President, but will obey his indirect [o]rder. If, as you say, there has been a practice in the War Department to issue orders in the name of the President without his direction, does not the precise order you have requested and have received change the practice as to the General of the Army? Could not the President countermand any such order issued to you from the War Department? If you should receive an order from that department issued in the name of the President to do a special act, and an order directly from the President himself not to do the act, is there a doubt which you are to obey? You answer the question when you say to the President, in your letter of the 3d inst., the Secretary of War is 'my superior and your subordinate;' and yet you refuse obedience to the superior out of deference to the subordinate. Without further comment upon the insubordinate attitude which you have assumed, I am at a loss to know how you can relieve yourself from obedience to the orders of the President, who is made by the Constitution the Commander-in-Chief of the Army and Navy, and is therefore the official superior, as well of the General of the Army as of the Secretary of War." Copy, *ibid.*; Df (dated Feb. 4), *ibid.* Johnson enclosed supporting letters from Secretary of the Interior Orville H. Browning, Secretary of the Treasury Hugh McCulloch, Postmaster Gen. Alexander W. Randall, Secretary of State William H. Seward, and Secretary of the Navy Gideon Welles. Copies, *ibid. HED,* 40-2-168.

On Feb. 10, USG wrote to Secretary of War Edwin M. Stanton. "Will you do me the favor to give me a copy of the letter of the Sec. of the Treas. to you requesting an escort for public funds from the Rio Grande to New Orleans, dated somewhere from the 20th to the 25th of Jan.y, and also copy of a letter from the P. M. Gn. to you, about same date, requesting report of Commission to settle line of defence along the N. W. boundary of Texas?" ALS, DNA, RG 107, Letters Received from Bureaus. On the same day, Stanton wrote to USG. "Your letter of this date asking for a copy of the Secretary of the Treasury's letter requesting an escort for public funds from the Rio Grande to New Orleans; and also for a copy of the letter from the Postmaster General requesting a report of Commission to settle line of defence along the Northwest boundary of Texas, has been received. The original of the latter letter is sent herewith. No letter was received from the Secretary of the Treasury, but a personal application for the escort was made by Mr Coleman, Clerk of the Secretary of the Treasury, who has been accustomed to make such applications to this Department personally, and who furnished the memorandum copy of which is herewith enclosed. Personal application on this subject was also had with the Secretary of the Treasury by a clerk of this Department. Communications from other Heads of Department relating to business connected with the War Department have also been received, and the action of this Department communicated to them by me in usual course. as Secretary of War." LS, *ibid.,* RG 108, Letters Received.

On Feb. 12, USG wrote to U.S. Representative John A. Bingham of Ohio. "In reply to your note of this date I have to state that I am very certain Mr. Johnson did not state in our 'Saturday' interview that he would assume the fine & imprisonment &c, but did make that statement at the Cabinet meeting on Tuesday the 14th ult." Copy, DLC-Adam Badeau.

1. On Jan. 27, Stanton had written to USG. "The Secretary of the Treasury has requested this Department to afford A. F. Randall, Special Agent of the Treasury Department such military aid as may be necessary to secure and forward for deposite, from Brownsville, Texas, to New-Orleans, public moneys in possession of Custom-House Officers at Brownsville, and which are deemed insecure at that place. You will please give such directions as you may deem proper to the Officer commanding at Brownsville to carry into effect the request of the Treasury Department, the instructions to be sent by telegraph to Galveston, to the care of A. F. Randall, Special Agent, who is at Galveston waiting telegraphic order, there being no telegraphic communication with Brownsville, and the necessity for military protection to the public moneys being represented as urgent. Please favor me with a copy of such instructions as you may give, in order that they may be communicated to the Secretary of the Treasury." LS, DNA, RG 108, Letters Received. On the same day, USG telegraphed to the commanding officer, Brownsville, "Care A. F. Randall, . . . You will afford A. F. Randall, Special Agent Treasury Dept., the necessary military aid to secure and forward, ~~for deposit~~ from Brownsville to New Orleans, ~~La.~~, public moneys in possession of CustomHouse Officers at Brownsville." Telegrams sent (2), *ibid.*, RG 107, Telegrams Collected (Bound); copies, *ibid.*, RG 56, Letters Received from Executive Officers; (certified by USG) *ibid.*, RG 107, Letters Received from Bureaus; *ibid.*, RG 108, Telegrams Sent; DLC-USG, V, 56.

2. On Jan. 29, McCulloch wrote to Stanton. "It is represented to this Department that a band of robbers has obtained such a foot hold in the section of country between Humbolt and Lawrence Kansas, committing depradations upon travellers both by public and private conveyance, that the safety of the public money collected by the Receiver of the Land Office at Humbolt requires that it should be guarded during its transit from Humbolt to Lawrence—I have therefore the honor to request that the proper commanding officer of that district may be instructed by the War Department, if in the opinion of the Honorable Secretary of War it can be done without prejudice to the public interests, to furnish a sufficient military guard to protect such moneys as may be in transitu from the above office for the purpose of being deposited to the credit of the Treasurer of the United States. As far as we are now advised such service will not be necessary oftener than once a month. Will you please advise me of the action taken that I may instruct the Receiver and the Commissioner of the General Land Office in the matter." LS, DNA, RG 108, Letters Received. On Feb. 5, Bvt. Maj. Gen. Edmund Schriver, inspector gen., referred this letter to USG. AES, *ibid.*

3. See telegram to Maj. Gen. Winfield S. Hancock, Feb. 3, 1868.

To Edwin M. Stanton

Respectfully refered to the Sec. of War. The boy spoken of is
Cadet U. G. White who was dismissed for having over One Hundred demerit for the half year and in whos behalf I sent a recommendation some weeks ago to have him restored.

Except in the matter of getting demerit I believe Cadet White
stands well at the Academy, and as he has been there one & a half
years I think it better to give him another trial than to make the
vacancy for a new appointment.

U. S. GRANT
General

FEB.Y 11TH 1868.

AES, DNA, RG 94, Cadet Applications. Written on a letter of Feb. 6, 1868,
from Carr B. White, Georgetown, Ohio, to USG. "I have just learned from Col.
D. W. C. Loudon, that my son has been dismissed from the Military, Academy,
for deficiency in conduct. This I much regret; but must say it was not unexpected,
as the monthly reports received from the Inspector, General, foreshadowed such
results. His conduct has been a source of much anxiety to both his mother, and
my self, since he has been at the 'Point;' and we have written him frequently,
admonishing him of the results that have followed. Col. L. says; you have kindly
offered your influence to secure his reinstatement. I hope it may be done; but
should you fail, his mother and myself, will not be less thankful to you, for your
efforts to save us and our boy this great affliction. I have no apology to offer in
his behalf for the demerits he has received; he could do better if he would; and
on no principle of justice, or right, can I ask his reinstatement; but as an act of
mercy to the boy, to spare him the disgrace of dismissal; and his mother and
myself, the grief attending the dishonoring our only son; I beg you to use all
your influence to get him reinstated; and should you succeed, I hope his after
conduct will be such as never to cause you to regret it. I am sure any influence
we may have over him will be used to that end. He has never written us a word
about this matter. I suppose he hoped to get it fixed up before we found it out."
ALS, *ibid.*

On Jan. 24, USG had written on an envelope. "Will the Ins. Gn. please see
Cadet White and hear his explanation. As his standing, in studies is fare if he can
be relieved of the disability to his going on with his class I should like it." ANS,
ibid. On Jan. 28, Ulysses G. White, West Point, telegraphed to USG. "Cannot
get the recommendation of Academic Board, Tell me what to do" Telegram
received (at 2:00 P.M.), *ibid.*, RG 107, Telegrams Collected (Bound). On Jan.
29, 9:30 A.M., USG telegraphed to Bvt. Brig. Gen. Thomas G. Pitcher, superintendent, USMA. "Cant Cadet White get off demerit to retain him? He promises
well if allowed to stay. Tell him to await there for final action." ALS (telegram
sent), *ibid.*; telegram sent, *ibid.*; copies, *ibid.*, RG 108, Telegrams Sent; DLC-

USG, V, 55. On Jan. 29, Pitcher telegraphed and wrote to USG. "Yours of this date received. I will look into cadet White's case at once and will do what I can for him. Respectfully suggest his case is beyond my control. Letter by mail" Telegram received (at 2:00 P.M.), DNA, RG 94, Cadet Applications; *ibid.*, RG 107, Telegrams Collected (Bound). "Your telegram of this date relative to Cadet White is received. You ask me if 'Cadet White can't get off demerit to retain him'? In reply I would state, that it is perfectly, competent for the Supt to remove his demerit, but if I did it, that would not restore him, as the action of the Board has been approved, and the order published discharging him—His case is therefore beyond our control, unless the Secty should order us to reconsider it—He has recorded against him up to the 6th Decr for the six months preceeding 180 demerit of which number I removed 25 early in the fall, leaving 155 standing against him Decr 6th—There are doubtless many that he could have gotten off, had he taken the trouble to have written explanations, but he did not—Carelessness and indifference was his trouble—He is a bright, manly boy, and I have never discovered any thing vicious to him, but he was utterly indifferent to his military duties—I cautioned him early, what would be the result of his course—In fact sent for him three different times and talked with him, as if he had been my own son, but all to no affect—I will take up his record, and see what can be done for him—Will send for him and tell him to look over his record, and to write explanations for every report recorded against him, which he thinks ought to come off, and if I can possibly reduce his number below *the Hundred*, will do so, and in the mean time, you will have to get an order for the Board to reconsider his case—I would however suggest that the shortest way to get him back, would be to get the Secty, to rescind the order discharging him, and to disapprove the proceedings of the Board, and direct him to continue on with his class, as he has done in several instances heretofore—" ALS, *ibid.*, RG 94, Cadet Applications. On Jan. 29 and 31, USG endorsed the telegram and letter. "Respectfully refered to the Sec. of War. This is in reply to a dispatch from me asking if some of the demerit of Cadet White cannot be excused to enable him to go on with his class. As he is proficient in his studies, and has no reports for special bad conduct, I would like him to be permitted to go on with his class." "Respectfully refered to the Sec. of War, and recommend that the order approving the recommendation of the 'Academic Board' dismissing Cadet White be rescinded and he be ordered to go on with his class." AES, *ibid.*

On March 21, U.S. Representative Reader W. Clarke of Ohio endorsed to USG a letter from Carr B. White asking the reappointment of his son to USMA. "The within letter from Col White of Georgetown Ohio in relation to his son, I request you to read, and inform me if any thing can be done in his behalf—I am willing to do any thing in my power to restore the young man even to re-appoint him if that is allowable.   your attention to this will be a great kindness to Col. White who feels deeply the embarrasment that it occasions to the success of his son." AES, *ibid.* On March 28, the academic board, USMA, recommended the readmission of Cadet White. DS, *ibid.* White graduated in 1871.

To Maj. Gen. George G. Meade

[( )Cipher)   Washington, D, C.
                                              Feb.y 12th 1868 [*10:15* A.M.]

MAJ. GN. G. G. MEADE,
ATLANTA GA.

Your dispatch stating that you would investigate causes for
nonholding of election in parts of Ala. and of nonextension of time
in others, and determination to give time hereafter is right. We
have nothing to do with defeat or success of the Constitution of
Alabama but it is the duty of the Military to see that all who are
entitled to should have an opportunity to express their will in the
matter at the polls.

                                                  U. S. GRANT
                                                     General

ALS (telegram sent), DNA, RG 107, Telegrams Collected (Bound); telegram
sent, *ibid.*; telegram received, Meade Papers, PHi.

On Feb. 10, 1868, 10:20 A.M., USG had telegraphed to Maj. Gen. George
G. Meade. "Tell me the probable result of Alabama election." ALS (telegram
sent), DNA, RG 107, Telegrams Collected (Bound); telegram sent, *ibid.*; telegram received, Meade Papers, PHi. On the same day, Meade telegraphed to USG.
"I returned from Alabama yesterday—The election passed off without disorder
of any kind—It is not practicable as yet to form any accurate opinion of the vote,
but indications would seem to shew that it will not be greater than the vote cast
for convention, perhaps less and if the registered vote has been much increased,
the Constitution may be lost.—In some of the counties no polls were opened—
cause as yet unknown—In others neither of the orders extending time of election
were received—I am having a thorough investigation of these cases, and wherever
I am satisfied, the facilities required by the law, have not been furnished—I shall
re-open the polls, or have polls opened for a sufficient length of time to enable
all who desire to vote to do so—" ALS (telegram sent), *ibid.*; telegram received
(at 2:00 P.M.), DNA, RG 107, Telegrams Collected (Bound); *ibid.*, RG 108,
Telegrams Received.

On Feb. 14, Meade wrote to USG. "I have already advised you by telegraph
of all that I know of the recent election in Alabama. Upon my return to this
place, I sent instructions to the Commanding Officer in that state, to have made
a thorough investigation of the manner in which the election had been conducted
in each county and to report the facts to me, that I might judge of the propriety
of reopening the polls at any place, where from the evidence adduced, the proper
number of boxes had not been kept open the whole term (five (5) days) authorized by existing orders. I also directed him to retain the returns and not
make the same public until this investigation was completed and the returns re-

ceived from the re-opened polls. Up to the present moment the Commanding Officer in Alabama has reported two counties as not having any polls opened, and two counties, where after the polls had been partially opened, the ballot boxes had been stolen at the close of the election. In these four counties therefore there will be a new election but I do not propose to issue any order, until the whole State has been thoroughly examined, and as some of the counties are remote from main lines of travel, it will require some time to obtain the facts in all cases. So far as I can judge from such returns, as have gotten into the public press, I am of the opinion that the vote will fall short of the number required to ratify the constitution. This is to be accounted for by several reasons 1st It is due to a determined, vigorous and effecient organization on the part of the opponents of Reconstruction, who have resorted to every means within the letter of the law, to dissuade and prevent voters from going to the Polls. This organization and action, has been greatly assisted by the demoralization produced by the Northern elections, and the prevailing opinion that the Supreme Court will pronounce the Reconstruction Laws unconstitutional. The fear that reconstruction was, or is to be set aside, has deterred many white voters from taking part in the election. Again the obstracism socially and through business relations brought to bear on white voters and the threats of discharging and the actual discharging of employees on account of voting has had great influence in keeping persons of both colors from the Polls. In illustration of this, I may state, I was informed at Montgomery that whilst they had at one time over (500) five hundred rebublican voters, they did not expect to poll over (50) fifty white votes at the election. The same fact was told me in other parts of the State. 2nd The merits of the Constitution per se had an injurious effect. The oath required to be taken by voters, and the disfranchisement of a much larger number of citizens than the laws of Congress require, together with other obnoxious details, served together with the reasons indicated above to prevent voters going to the Polls. Added to this was the discontent produced by the character of the nominees for office— many of whom, are reported not to be such as were likely to add any strenght to the vote—besides the effect of the cooling influance produced on disappointed candidates. Charges are made of improper conduct on the part of the managers of the election on which I can form no opinion till pending investigations are terminated. Major General Pope had prohibited candidates for office being Judges of Election, and as the revision of the registration had as much to do with the vote, as the actual casting of votes, I deemed it my duty to prohibit candidates for office being Registrars. It has subsequently appeared that this ruling on my part, required the removal of some twenty Registrars, out of over two hundred previously appointed. The change of these officers, together with the change of Superintendent of Registration and Military Commander, right on the eve of the election, doubtless was unfortunate as for want of experience, many difficulties were not foreseen that otherwise might have been avoided. The dereliction of so many managers of the election, as have occurred, could have been provided against if known in time. Whilst I was at Mobile on the third day of the election a gentleman from Baldwin County, situated on the opposite side of the bay, called to tell me that no polls had been opened in that county. I inquired how many precincts they had intended to have polls open at, before my order extending time of election and limiting precincts to three was issued. He replied five precincts. I inquired if they had provided the number of Judges fifteen at least to open these polls to which he answered, yes! and yet he could not or did not account for their inability to get these out of these fifteen to open boxes at one place. I immediately found qualified Judges in Mobile. Ordered the Government Steamer to take them at once across the bay and polls were opened for the last two days. I only mention this fact to shew the apathy on the part even of these who are presumed to be heartily interested in the election. Besides the reasons given above for this indifference, is one which I am satisfied has had great influence on the managers of the election, and that is they were not only insufficiently paid for their services, Judges of election under General Popes order getting only two dollars a day whilst actually engaged, but owing to the insufficiency of Generals Pope's estimate, the funds gave out, and noone has as yet been paid anything for the election held in Alabama in the fall for the Convention. When I arrived here I found that both Generals Pope and Swayne, had given all the orders necessary for the election, and presuming the machinery of the last election was in full working order, my occupation with affairs in Georgia caused me to rely with confidence on everything being right in Alabama, and it was not until the eve of the election that I was enabled to go there. But I do not now believe any precautionary measures would have had any effect beyond having polls opened in these counties, where the managers have proved derelict and this can readily be overcome hereafter. I shall leave for Florida to night, and must leave any further action on Alabama affairs till my return, when all the data necessary for correct action will be received." LS, *ibid.*, Letters Received. On Feb. 20, USG endorsed a copy of this letter. "Respectfully forwarded to the Secretary of War for his information." ES, *ibid.*, RG 107, Letters Received from Bureaus.

To Henry Stanbery

Washington, D, C. Feb.y 13th *1868*

Hon. H. Stanbery,
Atty. Gen.
Sir:

Your favor of the 12th inst. informing me that a motion has been made in the Supreme Court to file a bill in that court in favor of the state of Georgia against myself is the first notice that I have had in the matter. Seeing in the newspapers however that the Sec. of War had retained counsel to defend Gen. Meade, and others, defendents, I have made enquiry of him to ascertain what has been done in the matter. He informs me that counsil has been employed and will appear to-morrow to defend our case.

I have to thank you for your kind offer to appear for us, but under the circumstances it does not appear necessary that you should do so.

> I have the honor to be
> Very respectfully
> your obt. svt.
> U. S. GRANT
> General

ALS, DNA, RG 60, Letters Received, War Dept. On Feb. 12, 1868, Attorney Gen. Henry Stanbery had written to USG. "A motion has been made in the Supreme Court by Mr. Black to file an original bill in that court in favor of the State of Georgia against yourself, General Meade, General Ruger, and Captain Rockwell. It charges all of you with unauthorized violations of the rights of the State of Georgia in taking possession of certain real estate, railroad conveyances and moneys belonging to the State, and seeks to enjoin you from further interference with the State authorities, and to compel you to surrender the property so taken. The motion for leave to file this bill will be made on Friday next, and should be resisted. The rules of court require that you should receive notice of this application, which, I presume, has been given you, and been sent to the other defendants by the counsel for the State of Georgia. As the bill is apparently brought against you and the other defendants, in your individual capacity, I feel somewhat embarrassed in appearing in opposition to this motion without knowing your wishes on the subject. In the cases at the last term brought against the Secretary of War and yourself, I was advised by Mr. Stanton that he, as well as yourself, wished me to appear in my official capacity to argue the motions then made. Upon the present motion, I feel no sort of embarrassment in resisting it in consequence of my known opinions as to the constitutionality of the Reconstruction Acts, as that question is not necessarily involved in this motion. But, as in the further progress of the case, if the bill should be filed, that question may arise, it is very proper that you should be represented by special counsel of your own selection who may not feel the same embarrassment which I do in reference to it; and I beg, therefore, to suggest to you the propriety of requesting the Secretary of War to retain such counsel. It may also be proper, especially on behalf of the other defendants, to ask a postponement of the hearing of the motion, to allow them the opportunity of being heard by counsel of their own selection. I beg you to advise me in the premises at your earliest convenience, that I may understand what course you wish to be pursued." LS, *ibid.*, RG 108, Letters Received.

On Jan. 13, Maj. Gen. George G. Meade issued General Orders No. 8 replacing Governor Charles J. Jenkins of Ga. with Bvt. Brig. Gen. Thomas H. Ruger and replacing Ga. Treasurer John Jones with Bvt. Capt. Charles F. Rockwell. On Jan. 17, Meade issued General Orders No. 12 replacing Ga. Comptroller John T. Burns with Capt. Charles Wheaton. Jenkins then served notice on USG, Meade, Ruger, Rockwell, and Wheaton of a suit before the U.S. Supreme Court for relief. See *ibid.*, RG 94, Letters Received, 161M, 162M, 1868. See letter to Andrew Johnson, Feb. 18, 1868.

To Maj. Gen. George G. Meade

Washington, D, C, Feb.y 13th *1868* [*10:30* A.M.]
MAJ. GEN. G. G. MEADE
ATLANTA GA.

I suggest that you advise Florida Convention that their acts cannot be recognized unless they are ~~adopted by~~ the acts of an undoubted quorum of the whole number of delegates elected. Unless such a quorums join in their acts in a reasonable time I would refer the whole matter, with all facts, to Congress. It will be well for you to go to Florida as soon as possible.

U. S. GRANT
General.

ALS (telegram sent), DNA, RG 107, Telegrams Collected (Bound); telegram sent, *ibid.*; telegram received, Meade Papers, PHi. On Feb. 12, 1868, Maj. Gen. George G. Meade had telegraphed to USG. "Out of Forty Six delegates elected to the Convention of ~~Georgia~~ Florida & ordered by Genl—Pope to assemble at Tallahasee Forty appeared and organised—Subsequently dissensions arose—principally on the question of distribution of offices—when Eighteen of the members withdrew from the Convention—The Twenty two left proceeded to form a constitution & have notified me of their having done so & ask an order for an election,—& await my action prior to adjournment.—In the mean time the Eighteen Seceders joined by Three of the delegates who failed to appear at the original organisation making 21 elected members, have organised and send a protest against the action of the original body & claim they have Twenty four members present—Up to this time I have declined to interfere with their discussions or to allow the military power to intervene in aid of one or the other party   deferring any action till their procedings required it on my part—I must now decide on the legality of the acts of the Twenty two who present a constitution   If this party had a ~~quorum~~ majority of the original ~~organisation~~ number elected, I should have no doubt of their status—but they have not—They have a ~~qu~~majority of the members present at the organisation, but three ~~have~~ are known to have since joined & the seceders claim that Six have joined them—In other words are Twenty two members of a body to which Forty Six were elected—Forty organised—& three subsequently appeared—competen[t] to discharge the functions assigned by law to the Convention   I should have gone to Florida but for the Alabama election, and will now go so soon as affairs in Alabama will permit—I have used every effort by recommendations to produce harmony, and perhaps, unless otherwise advised by you—shall continue to refuse any action, until sufficient number of the seceders shall return to the original body, so as to make their number a majority of the number elected—This will require the return of Two of the seceders—Your views are asked as soon as possible—" ALS (telegram sent), *ibid.*; telegram received (at 4:50 P.M.), DNA, RG 107, Telegrams Collected (Bound); *ibid.*, RG 108, Telegrams Received.

On Feb. 13, 10:30 A.M., USG telegraphed to Meade. "Haves not the Convention of Fla. expelled some of the members elect as inelegible to seats? If so is not twenty-two members a quorum? and are not expelled members among the ceceders?" ALS (telegram sent), *ibid.*, RG 107, Telegrams Collected (Bound); telegram sent, *ibid.*; telegram received, Meade Papers, PHi. At 11:30 P.M., Meade telegraphed to USG. "No member has been expelled from the Convention—One of the delegates elected and announced in Genl Pope's order was named Geo W. Walker. No such person has appeared nor is there any reason to believe any such person exists. There is a man living in the County named George Walker who is presumed to be the individual voted for but he positively declines qualifying. A person named Butler who had the most votes claimed Walkers seat and his claim was denied by the Convention. This is stated to be the origin of the difficulty   Butler appealed to me and asked to have Genl Pope's order modified and he declared elected; this I declined, having no right to go behind the returns of the Board of Registrars. Since sending my telegram of yesterday I have received Copy of the proceedings of the twenty two. I find out of forty six 46 elected delegates that only twenty nine 29 were present at the organization and election of Officers. Subsequently twelve 12 delegates appeared and qualified, making the number forty one 41, when the question of the admission of Butler, which stood twenty 20 for & twenty one 21 against produced the outbreak at the meeting. Only twenty two 22 who were present then have continued to meet and form a Constitution. Forty three 43 delegates have been sworn in altogether. The Seceeders in their telegram to me claim twenty four 24 as with them but as Walker has never turned up and Butler refused admittance—it is probable that they have included him as he was here trying to get me to order his admission— they therefore cannot have more than twenty three 23. Of the twenty two 22 Seven 7 are white and of the twenty one 21 Seceeders three 3 are black. What do you think of referring both Constitutions to the people of Florida to decide between the parties? I will leave for Florida tomorrow but there are certain matters in Alabama and others here that require immediate attention on my part but which I can arrange by that time." Telegram received (on Feb. 14, 9:00 A.M.), DNA, RG 107, Telegrams Collected (Bound); *ibid.*, RG 108, Telegrams Received; copy, DLC-USG, V, 55. On Feb. 14, 4:35 P.M., USG telegraphed to Meade. "I dont think I would submit two Constitutions to voters of Fla. When you get there you may harmonize matters and be able to tell better what to do." ALS (telegram sent), DNA, RG 107, Telegrams Collected (Bound); telegram sent, *ibid.*; copies, *ibid.*, RG 108, Telegrams Sent; DLC-USG, V, 56.

On Feb. 19, Meade, Tallahassee, telegraphed to USG. "The Convention have reconciled their differences and are now in harmonious action in one body" Telegram received (at 10:45 A.M.), DNA, RG 107, Telegrams Collected (Bound); *ibid.*, RG 108, Telegrams Received; copies, DLC-USG, V, 55; Meade Papers, PHi. On Feb. 21, Meade, Atlanta, wrote to USG. "I have already advised you by telegram of the existence of dissentions in the Florida Convention, and of my refusal to take any action in regard to the same, till I could obtain all the facts in the case. So soon as my duties permitted, I proceeded to Tallahassee arriving there on the 17th inst—where I found the condition of affairs as follows—On the 20th day of January of the 46. elected members called together by G. O. No. 110. from these Hd Qrs—30 assembled and organized. That soon after meeting a contest arose in the Convention on the question of iligibility of members and the power of the Convention to decide thereon—That on Feby 1. the number of members having increased to 41.—on a test vote they stood 21 to 20, that on Feby 3rd 18 members withdrew leaving 22 in attendance, who proceeded to form a Constitution, and frame a civil government for the state of Florida. Completing their labors on 8th inst, when they adjourned to the 15th inst, awaiting my action and orders. In the meantime the seceding party left Tallahassee and proceeded to Monticillo, but returned on the 10th inst and taking possession of the hall hitherto occupied by the other party, organized themselves into a separate Convention, which at the time of my arrival numbered 25 members—2 of the other party after signing the constitution having gone over to the seceders—This last body claimed recognition from me as the legal Convention composed of the majority of the elected members. Immediately on my arrival I called together committees from both bodies and stated to them, that up to Feby. 3rd I recognized the Convention presided over by Mr. D. Richards, as the legitimate convention, and its acts up to that date as legal—but that being on that date reduced to a number below 24 the majority of the whole number elected.—I considered it without a quorum and all its acts void, except its adjournment from day to day till it could get a quorum.—That the seceders had in my judgement no legal status, nor would their acts be of any avail without my authority—That it was out of my power to decide the several questions submitted by each party, and therefore unless they harmonized and came together, I should feel myself compelled to adjourn both, and refer the difficulty to Congress.—in the mean time I should be glad to receive propositions from both sides and to act as a mediator between them—after many interviews, I received on the 18th inst a proposition in writing from the seceders, which as I considered reasonable I submitted to the Richards party, urging its acceptance, and requesting Mr. Richards to resign, at the same time intimating to Mr Richards, that if this proposition was refused, inasmuch as I was satisfied, there was no possibility of his getting a quorum in view of the great delay involved in a reference to Congress—I might feel myself called upon to recognize the majority and organize them into a Convention. Mr Richards after consultation with his friends, sent me his resignation under protest. Mr. Jenkins the President of the seceders having sent me his, I directed Col. Sprague Commdg Sub-District of Florida to convene both parties and with the aid of the Secretary to reorganize the Convention—This was done on the 18th inst. and when I left on the 19th the Convention with 45 members present were actively engaged in their duties" Copies, *ibid.*; DNA, RG 108, Letters Received.

On Feb. 29, Meade telegraphed to USG. "The Florida convention have submitted to me an ordinance relating to the Ratification of the Constitution & election of ~~state~~ officers under it—This ordinance provides that when the election is held under my orders for ratification, that the judges, inspectors & other officers shall provide separate ballot boxes, poll books, &c and shall receive the ballots for ~~state~~ congressional state & county officers of all persons qualified to vote under the provisions of the Constitution. Or in other words the votes of persons not registered under the Reconstruction Laws, are to be allowed to vote for ~~all~~ these officers.—Is this election of officers, under the constitution, & only to take office on the adoption of the constitution, to be considered as an election for officers under the Provisional Government referred to in Section Six of Act—apprd Mar. 2./67 and all non registered voters, excluded by this section at first election held under the new constitution.—Again the Ordinance designates certain days in May for holding the election—Since adjourning the President of the Convention on behalf of a majority of its members, applyies to have the date of election advanced to some time in April—Does Section Four of Act—Approved Mar. Twenty third Sixty Seven authorise District Commander to fix day of election, or change the same after the convention has designated a day." ALS (telegram sent), Meade Papers, PHi; telegram received (on March 1, 8:00 A.M.), DNA, RG 108, Telegrams Received. On March 2, 12:30 P.M., USG telegraphed to Meade. "The election proposed by the convention for officers under the new constitution I do not consider as an election for officers under the provisional government referred to in Section Six of the Act Approved March 2d '67   It is clear to my mind that a proper construction of Sec. 4 of Act Approved March 23 '67 does not authorize District Commanders to fix or change the day of election after it has been designated by the convention." LS (telegram sent), *ibid.*, RG 107, Telegrams Collected (Bound); telegram sent, *ibid.*; telegram received (misdated Feb. 2), Meade Papers, PHi.

On March 14, 11:00 A.M., USG telegraphed to Meade. "If you think it advisable to authorize the Fla. election to take place in Apl. do not permit anything in my dispatch on that subject to keep you from it." ALS (telegram sent), DNA, RG 107, Telegrams Collected (Bound); telegram sent, *ibid.*; telegram received (misdated March 13), Meade Papers, PHi; copies (misdated March 15), DNA, RG 108, Telegrams Sent; DLC-USG, V, 56.

To Sidney Perham

Washington, D, C, Feb.y 14th *1868*

CHAIRMAN COMMITTEE ON PENSIONS,
HOUSE OF REPRESENTATIVES,
SIR:

I have the honor to recommend that the pension heretofore granted Mrs. Wallace, widow of Brig. Gen. W. H. L. Wallace, who fell mortally wounded whilst gallantly leading a Division of troops, in the battle of Shiloh, Apl. 6th 1862, be increased to Fifty (50) dollars per month. The same favor has been granted in several other cases and I am sure a more deserving case does not exist. Gen. Wallace I regarded the equal of the best, if not the very best, of the Volunteer Generals with me at the date of his death. He went into the war at the first call for troops and was soon followed by three brothers, his father-in-law, and two brothers of his wife, all the brothers and brothers-in-laws that he had that I know of. All of these relatives except one brother who had previously lost his life, were in the battle when the General fell, and his wife was at the very time, if I am not mistake, under fire of the enemy ministering to the wants of wounded men as they were carried in.

I think this a most deserving case, and one which does not establish a wrong precedent.

> I have the honor to be,
> With great respest,
> your obt. svt.
> U. S. GRANT
> General,

ALS, IHi. U.S. Representative Sidney Perham of Maine, chairman, Committee on Invalid Pensions. On Sept. 8, 1869, USG wrote an unaddressed letter. "Mrs. W. H. L. Wallace, the bearer of this letter, is the widow of one of the most gallent, efficient and respected Union Officers of the late rebellion. He fell a Martyr to the cause which he so honestly believed in whilst gallantly leading his division, on the memorable 6th of Apl. 1862, mourned by his command, the Army with which he was serving, and his country. The bereaved widow, who is now traveling in Europe, was worthy of such a husband, and is entitled to the sympathy of a grea[t]ful country, and to all the attention she may receive abroad or at home." ALS, *ibid.*

To Eli A. Collins

Feb.y 15th *1868*

DEAR COLLINS;

With this I enclose you a letter of introduction to Gen. Hancock. I do not know any one in Memphis to whom I could give you a letter. The few weeks I spent in Memphis in /62 and again in /63 was so much occupied with public business that I did not make acquaintance with citizens so as to know their standing or to justify me in presuming to address them letters of introduction.

> Yours Truly
> U. S. GRANT

ALS, ICarbS. USG enclosed a letter of Feb. 15, 1868, to Maj. Gen. Winfield S. Hancock. "This will introduce to you Mr. E. A. Collins of Davenport, Iowa, a friend of mine from my boyhood, and for many years a partner in business with my father. Any attention shewn Mr. Collins will be appreciated by him and will be regarded as a personal favor to me." ALS, George V. Rountree, Chicago, Ill.

On July 10, 1866, Jesse Root Grant had written to Eli A. Collins. ". . . You say something about my Soldier Boy. I forget what, but I believe you say you want to go WASHINGTON when he is inaugurated President, and ask me if I will go with you. Oh, yes, certainly I will go, and hope we may have a nice time of it. Stranger things than that have happened, but not more strange things than that would have been four or five years ago. You know ULYSSES is not and never was an aspirant for any personal favor or promotion. When the war broke out he felt that as the Government had educated him for a soldier, and as it was likely soon to need his services he would not withhold them, so he was among the first to volunteer for the war, and to say the very least of it, his career has been a very remarkable one. You know he never asked for an office, a promotion or a command, or agreed to accept such when consulted. But when appointed, promoted, or ordered, he took right hold and has commanded larger armies, fought more battles, taken more prisoners and more ordnance than any other General history gives any account of. You may have noticed that the Government and the people fully appreciated all he has done and a good deal more. He was promoted from a private up to Brigadier-General in a few months, and all the time placed in important commands. He was promoted, until there was no longer any rank to promote him to. Then the Congress created a new rank of Lieutenant-General, and he was again promoted to that rank. No satisfied with that, Congress has created a still higher rank, of what is called a full General, and yesterday the Senate confirmed his appointment to that rank. I suppose they will have to be content, as there is no other rank which can be created. But that is not all. The people have moved in every way; besides the promotions I have described, and the large substantial testimonials he has received, the people everywhere are disposed to do him honor. Take that altogether, don't that seem a little strange to you? It does to me. Now there is another thing which seems equally strange; the most ultra Radicals, the worst Copperheads, the desperate secesh, and the true Union men, all say: 'Give us GRANT, we want no other platform than that he has written with his sword.' You know enough about ULYSSES to know that to accept the Presidency would be to him a sacrifice of feeling and personal interest. He could not well stand the trial of being a candidate for public favor; and his present position is every way a much better one than that of President. But if there should seem to be the same necessity for it two years hence, as now, I expect he will yield." *New York Times*, Sept. 24, 1866.

On Feb. 5, 1867, Grant wrote to Collins. ". . . You say you & Thompson are going east—That you want a fat office, & want me to go with you to Washington—Well come on prepared to stop here a day or two get rested & shined up nice, & I will consult with you about an office, & give you directions where to find good refreshments & a good Barber—But I cant go such a journey any more at this season of the year, for I am now in my 74 year, & it is time to consult my physical strength on such subjects . . . As to that large Boy reaching the Presidency, that is further along. If it were evan possible, it would be every way a sacrafice to him, & although he might, & probably to the Nation. Alth would make a good president, still the Nation might be a large loss. For it is much more easier to find material for a President, than an efficient Gen And that the Nation migh suffer more in the loss of a Gen, than it would gain in a President . . ." ALS, ICarbS. On Feb. 12, Collins, Davenport, Iowa, telegraphed to USG. "I have bought property and moved to this place—Can I get collectorship for this district which office is vacant? Will be there in few days—" Telegram received (at 5:00 P.M.), DNA, RG 107, Telegrams Collected (Bound).

To Rutherford B. Hayes

———

Washington, February 15th *1868*.

GOVERNOR R. B. HAYES.
EX-OFFICIO CH'RM'N, O. M. ASSOCIATION
SIR:

Your letter of date January 31st 1868, relating to the memorial in honor of the Soldiers of Ohio and in memory of Mr. Lincoln is received.

The only officers of the confederate army present at the conference of July 3d 1863 between Generals Grant and Pemberton which resulted in the surrender of Vicksburg July 4th 1863 were Lieut Genl. J. C. Pemberton, Maj. Gen. John S. Bowen, and Lieut. Col. Louis M. Montgomery, (a volunteer aid on Pemberton's staff.) On the Union side were Generals U S Grant, J. B. McPherson, E. O. C. Ord, John A. Logan, A. J. Smith, and several other subordinate and staff-officers. The usual mounted orderlies accompanied the commanders on either side. As to the accessories of the scene, the tree &c, I quote from a letter written at the time by a correspondent [of the New York Herald],[1] who was present; which is correct and probably sufficiently elaborate for your purpose—

"At three o'clock precisely, one gun, the prearranged signal, was fired and immediately replied to by the enemy. General Pemberton then made his appearance on the works in McPherson's front, under a white flag, considerably on the left of what is known as Fort Hill. General Grant rode through our trenches until he came to an outlet leading to a small green space which had not been trod by either army, here he dismounted and advanced to meet General Pemberton, with whom he shook hands and greeted familiarly.

    Scene.

It was beneath the outspreading branches of a gigantic oak that the conference of the generals took place. Here presented the only space which had not been used for some purpose or other by the contending armies. The ground was covered with a fresh, luxuriant verdure, here and there a shrub or clump of bushes could be seen standing out from the green growth on the surface, while several oaks filled up the scene and gave it character. Some of the trees in their tops exhibited the effects of flying projectiles, by the loss of limbs or torn foliage, and in their trunks the indentations of smaller missiles plainly marked the occurrences to which they had been silent witnesses."

The rebel lines ran at the point where the conference was held nearly parallel to the road, less than two hundred feet from it. The Union lines were some distance farther off, and both were covered with unarmed men, in different attitudes, standing, sitting and lying. The sky was slightly overcast with clouds.—There was no formal surrender of his sword by Pemberton. There were no papers of any description passed between the parties: hence whether a scroll in the hands of either party would be appropriate, is a matter of taste in which the artist and the Association are the best judges.

> Very respectfully
> Your obedient servant
> U. S. GRANT
> General.

LS, OFH.

1. Words erased and barely decipherable. The passage following is quoted accurately from De B. Randolph Keim's letter from Vicksburg, July 4, in *New York Herald*, July 15, 1863.

To Andrew Johnson

Washington, February 18th *1868*

HIS EXCELLENCY A. JOHNSON,
PRESIDENT OF THE US.
SIR:

I have the honor to acknowledge the receipt of your communication of the 17th inst., and in answer thereto respectfully submit herewith a copy of General Meade's report, with enclosures referred to by him, in the matter of the removal of Governor Jenkins and State Treasurer Jones. This embraces all the correspondence on the subject.

The only part of it that seemed to be clearly called for by the Senate resolution, viz. my endorsement dated January 6th 1868, on letter of General John Pope dated December 27th 1867, in the matter of the refusal of the State Treasurer of Georgia to pay the members of the convention, was transmitted with my communication of the 12th inst.

> Very respectfully
> Your obedt servt.
> U. S. Grant
> General.

LS, DLC-Andrew Johnson. On Feb. 17, 1868, President Andrew Johnson had written to USG. "The correspondence which accompanies your communication of the 12th instant embraces telegrams referring to the removal of the Treasurer of the State of Georgia, but contains no papers relating to the removal at the same time, of Governor Jenkins. If there was any correspondence upon that subject between yourself and Genl. Meade, should it not accompany the papers furnished with your communication of the 12th instant, for transmission to the Senate?" Copies (2), *ibid.* See letter to Henry Stanbery, Feb. 13, 1868.

On Feb. 22, Maj. Gen. George G. Meade, Atlanta, wrote to USG. "On the 18th inst. I received the telegram of which the enclosed is a copy—and deem it proper to report to you that in compliance with the request of the President I forwarded yesterday to his address copies of my telegram to you of the 9th of January and your reply by telegraph of 10th January also of the letter to you dated Jany. 13th and accompanying papers being my report of action in the cases of Governor Jenkins and others." LS, DNA, RG 108, Letters Received. Meade enclosed a copy of a telegram of Feb. 18 from Johnson to Meade. "Please send me at once copy of correspondence if any between Genl Grant and yourself respecting removal of Governor Jenkins" Copies, *ibid.*; Meade Papers, PHi.

On Feb. 28, 3:30 p.m., USG telegraphed to Meade. "If any notice, subpoenʏa or other ~~notice~~ paper is served on you in the Georgia case give no answer whatever other than to refer any party or paper to our council, care of the Sec. of War. Give the same notice to Ruger and Rockwell." ALS (telegram sent), DNA, RG 107, Telegrams Collected (Bound); telegram sent, *ibid.*; telegram received, Meade Papers, PHi.

On March 27, Matthew H. Carpenter wrote to USG. "The motion for injunction in the Georgia case, has been continued to the next Decr Term; and that too without our having to use either of the affidavits made by you. The hearing of all these questions is thus transferred, where it belongs, to the people; and the application will be determined at the polls the 1st Monday of November next." ALS, USG 3.

To Lt. Gen. William T. Sherman

Private   Washington, D, C, Feb.y 18th *1868*

MY DEAR GENERAL:

Your letter to the President which you informed me, by telegraph, on Friday last had been mailed, through me, has not yet
come to hand. It may come to-day. The course you have pursued
has given immense satisfaction so far as I have heard any expression of opinion. The dispatch you sent to Senator Sherman has not
been published, but it is understood to be the ground of his action
in the senate.—You see by the papers Mr. J. has been expressing
surprise at your action, saying that his course was understood between you before you left, and that you did not seem to disapprove
of it.—Of course I do not expect to make any use of the letters which
you have written, in my own vindication, but I thought your letter
to the President might set you right in the estimation of people who
do not know you as well as I do, and might possibly suppose from
the fact that you had been in Washington and in direct communication with the President, that you had consented to aid him in his
plans to offer me an indignity. I would be very glad to have you
here if the public was not losing by bringing you away from where
you are, and if not for the annoying position it would place you in.
I have heard that Mr. Johnson said to some of his intimate friends
that he intended to have you and me knock our heads to-gether.—
Your intimation that you would resign under any circumstances has
called out an expression that you should not be placed in a position
to make it necessary even if it took legislation to prevent the contingency. This of course is an individual expression of opinion. But
I would say under no circumstances tender even a contingent resignation. You do not owe Mr. Johnson any thing and he is not entitled to such a sacrifice from you.

Please present my kindest regards to Mrs. Sherman and the
children.

Yours Truly
U. S. GRANT

TO LT. GN. W. T. SHERMAN,
ST. LOUIS, MO.

ALS, DLC-William T. Sherman. On Feb. 22, 1868, Lt. Gen. William T. Sherman wrote to USG. "I have received your letter of Feby 18th, written before the receipt of my letter of the 14th, to the President, which your telegram pronounces elegant, and therefore it suits me. Events have come along so fast, and I am out, so I will await the result. You are in possession of evry letter I ever wrote to the President, but I leave him to publish them as he pleases, or not. I don't much fear he can do me serious harm, and am willing to bear it in the spirit of peace. He seems to me friendly and I don't care about being drawn into any contro- vercies, for times are delicate and his position one not to be envied. It may be that he has made this state of things himself, and should bear the consequences, but I don't want to become involved one way or the other. I feel a little curious to know if Geo H Thomas will take what I declined. I would not object to Congress providing by law for one (1) General and three (3) Lieut Genls. But I will op- pose any brevets to those grades for reasons which you will understand. My des- patch to John Sherman was simply to oppose my confirmation because I thought the two higher grades should not be complicated with brevets. If the President asserts that I acquiesced in his intention, I need not say to you that he did inti- mate such a course, but my letter of January 31st was designed to meet them as positively and as courteously as any one should speak to the President. Sheridan is not here yet—Augur telegraphs me from Chicago en-route to Omaha—. I sup- pose ere you get this all my Dep't Com'drs will be at their Posts." Copies (2), *ibid.*

To Bvt. Maj. Gen. Edward R. S. Canby

(Cypher)   Washington D, C,
                                                                Feb.y 20th 1868. [*11:30* A.M.]

Maj. Gn. E R. S. Canby,
Charleston, S, C,

Would it not be well to order the 6th Inf.y to N. C. and replace them by troops from that state?

U. S. Grant
General,

ALS (telegram sent), DNA, RG 107, Telegrams Collected (Bound); telegram sent, *ibid.*; telegram received (at noon), *ibid.*, RG 393, 2nd Military District, Letters Received. On Feb. 20, 1868, Bvt. Maj. Gen. Edward R. S. Canby tele- graphed to USG. "I think that any general change of troops until after the next election would be productive of greater embarrassment than of good results. Is there any objection against the character or conduct of the troops in either state?" Telegram received (at 7:00 P.M.), *ibid.*, RG 108, Telegrams Received; copies (one sent by mail), *ibid.*, Letters Received; *ibid.*, RG 393, 2nd Military District, Letters Sent; DLC-USG, V, 55. USG drafted his reply of Feb. 20 at the foot of the telegram received. "You are best judge whether anything is wrong with troops in your command. Complaint was made against some of 6th Infantry but I know nothing of character of complainants." ADfS, DNA, RG 108, Telegrams Received; telegrams sent (2—at 8:00 P.M.), *ibid.*, RG 107, Telegrams Collected (Bound); telegram received (at 11:30 P.M.), *ibid.*, RG 393, 2nd Military District, Letters Received. On Feb. 21, Canby telegraphed to USG. "There is nothing wrong with the troops which I cannot correct without change and a change at this time would be embarrassing. I presume that I know the character of the complaints, but the charges are exceptional and apply to any other troops, as well as to the 6th Infantry, and can be controlled. Fuller report by mail" Telegram received (at noon), *ibid.*, RG 107, Telegrams Collected (Bound); *ibid.*, RG 108, Telegrams Received; copies (one sent by mail), *ibid.*, Letters Received; *ibid.*, RG 393, 2nd Military District, Letters Sent; DLC-USG, V, 55. On the same day, Canby wrote to USG's hd. qrs. "I have the honor to report, in relation to subject of the telegrams received yesterday from the General of the Army, that complaints of the action of the troops in this District, have frequently been made, but it has generally been found upon investigation, that the complaints originated in an imperfect knowledge of the facts existing in the particular case, and that if any improper action had been taken it was susceptible to easy correction—It is no doubt true, that there are officers whose prejudices, or feelings, are against the Reconstruction Acts of Congress, but I do not know of any, whose action would be determined by that feeling to such an extent, as to impair the strict and impartial enforcement of any of the provisions of those laws, and in no instance have I found a disposition to question, or evade, the instructions given by the District Commander—The short period that will elapse between the adjournment of the Conventions and the election upon the question of adopting the Constitution, makes it important that no important changes should be made until after that election has been held—At the last, it was found almost impracticable to secure a sufficient number of competent and qualified inspectors and managers of elections, and this difficulty made it necessary to reduce the number of polling places in many of the election Districts, and before this could be effected so little time remained, that the reasonable notice of the changes made, could not be given, and at some precincts no elections were held, for the reason, that the notice did not reach the places until the time for holding the elections, had passed—For these reasons several thousand registered voters in each state were unable to vote—In the arrangements that are now being made, I hope to be able to establish a polling precinct at every registration precinct, and place it in the power of every registered voter, to deposit his ballot at the place at which he was registered—The officers now on duty in the districts of both states, are in communication with the Registrars and other local officials, for the purpose of making these arrangements, and are familiar with the localities and necessities of the districts, or counties, within their commands; and any change at this time would be productive of serious embarrassments, and probably in some of the remote districts involve a repetition of the difficulties encountered at the last election—" LS, DNA, RG 108, Letters Received.

Also on Feb. 21, Canby wrote to USG's hd. qrs. transmitting papers concerning the arrest of Mayor P. C. Gaillard of Charleston. LS, *ibid.*

On April 16, Canby telegraphed to USG. "I propose to send three companies of the 6th Infantry into North Carolina, and to carry out the suggestions made in your telegram, of February 20th, by bringing down the 8th Infantry, after the election, and sending up the remainder of the 6th. If there be any reason why the permanent change should not be made now please advise me" Telegram received (on April 17, 9:00 A.M.), *ibid.*, RG 107, Telegrams Collected (Bound); (on April 17, 9:30 A.M.) *ibid.*, RG 108, Telegrams Received; copy, DLC-USG, V, 55. On April 17, 10:45 A.M., USG telegraphed to Canby. "There is no objection to the transfer of troops from South to North Carolina proposed in your dispatch of this date." ALS (telegram sent), DNA, RG 107, Telegrams Collected (Bound); telegram sent, *ibid.*; telegram received (at 12:30 P.M.), *ibid.*, RG 393, 2nd Military District, Letters Received.

To Hamilton Fish

Washington, D, C, Feb.y 20th *1868*

DEAR GOVERNER;

General Comstock and myself leave here for New York tomorrow evening, to be absent probably until Friday of next week. Mrs. Grant will not accompany me this time, and as I shall go directly through New York to West Point to spend Saturday & Sunday, and as I have already accepted invitations to dine out for Tuesday, Wednesday & Thursday evenings, I think it will be better for me to stop at a public house, and defer my acceptance of your hospitalities until later in the season when Mrs. Grant does accompany me.

Mrs. Grant and the children send their love to Mrs. Fish & Miss Julia and also their kindest regards to yourself.

Please present my complements to the ladies.

Yours Truly

U. S. GRANT

To GOVERNER HAMILTON FISH,
NEW YORK CITY,

ALS, Columbia University, New York, N. Y.

On Feb. 18, 1868, Tuesday, USG had telegraphed to Alexander T. Stewart, New York City. "Mrs. Grant will not be with me. I accept your invitation for Tuesday with pleasure." ALS (telegram sent), DNA, RG 107, Telegrams Collected (Bound). On Feb. 21, 2:55 P.M., USG telegraphed to Stewart, Edwards Pierrepont, and Henry E. Davies, New York City, "Copy to Gn. Pitcher, West Point, N. Y." "Important public duty will prevent my going to New York for the present." ALS (telegram sent), *ibid.*; telegram sent, *ibid.*

On Feb. 19, USG telegraphed to Robert Bonner, editor, *New York Ledger.*

"Please not publish the article announced for February 24th till you see me. I will be in [New York] Saturday." LS (telegram sent), *ibid.*; telegram received, DLC-USG, I, B. On the same day, Bonner wrote to USG. "I have just received your telegram. I should have acquainted you before of my intention to publish the sketches, but I wished to be able to say with absolute truth that *you* knew nothing about them until you saw the announcement in the newspapers. They are excellent, and will add to your previously great popularity immensely. The most sagacious counsellor that Abraham Lincoln had in this city says that it is impossible to conceive of anything else so well calculated to promote your election. The letters are all written with great ability; and Henry Ward Beecher was so impressed with them that he said to me, (I quote his exact words) 'the old man must be a splendid old fellow.' I send you an advance copy, of which a large edition is already printed. Our edition is so large that we consume over a week in the printing. The letters, as you will see, are very judiciously written. There is not a line in them, which the most cautious friend of yours could want omitted or altered, or I should not have printed them. They make a most favorable impression in regard to you, and also in regard to your father. His very portrait shows to everybody that he is a superior man. I shall be glad to see you on Saturday, and shall, if you desire it, be happy to show you the rest of the letters, though perhaps you will ~~prefer~~ prefer to be able to say of them all, as you can of the first, that you never saw them until they were in print. . . . N. B. If Edward Everett,—over-cautious as every body knows him to have been, could say to me, as you will find by the enclosed extract, '*I feel as if I could think aloud to you,*' you may feel safe in trusting to my judgment about these articles." ALS, USG 3. On Feb. 22, Jesse Root Grant wrote to Bonner. "When Mr Bartlett was here looking after incidents in the life of Gen Grant; I furnished him freely with such as I thought would interest the public—But at that time I had no thought of the matter being published over my name—And when Mr Bartlet read the letters to me for my approval & signature, I felt, & expressed misgivings about the propriety of leting them appear before the public over my name. Mr B. however quieted my misgivings to some extent, & I signed them—As I feared other papers & writers have seized upon your notice of the publication and are trying to make some capital out of them; last evening I read a letter from the Gen, asking me to have the publication stoped—Also a letter from a Gentleman in N Y to a member of his Staff, suggesting the same thing—I would therefore respectfully ask that the letters be with held from publication. If however you wish to publish the facts you can do so, by so changing the language as to be written by Mr B. or by *Annonimos*, & so entire with hold my name—You know the Gen is rather modest, and does not wish it infered that he is s[ee]king the Presidency; for really he would rather decline it, if he were to consult his own personal interest and feelings—If he consent to run, it will be through a sense of duty to the country, & not through any personal ambition—My respects to Mr Bartlett . . ." ALS, DLC-USG, I, B. On Feb. 26, Bonner wrote to Grant. "I recd your letter of the 22nd Inst. this evening. Your letters in the Ledger are very much praised by people & by the newspapers, & are doing Genl Grant a great deal of good. I have seen but one exception & that is the Cin. Com. a mean contemptible Chase paper, which lies in saying that I ever applied to Genl Grant himself to write. I recd a telegram from Genl Grant a week ago yesterday at the same time he wrote to you, & I enclose you a copy of the letter I sent to him in reply. This letter I have no doubt convinced him that the articles would do him good, as, after he recd it he made no further objection to their publication. I suppose the trouble at Washington confines the General there, as he telegraphed me he would be here last Saturday. He is in the habit of calling upon me when he visits the city; & I should like to have him stop in just now, & see the piles of newspapers from different parts of the country which I have, containing favorable notices of your account of his early life   The letters are all printed but two, as you will see from the enclosed *advance* copy; & if we did not print the last two, it wd be an injury to the Genl. The letters would not have done him a hundredth part of the good they do, if they had been published anonymously, even though dictated as they are by you. They are very satisfactory to the public, & being genuine they put an end to the silly & injurious trash which wd otherwise be printed & circulated about him. They are not liable to objection on the ground of writing him up as a Presidential candidate, for you made no reference to politics whatever, & no one could tell from your letters to which party he belongs. The press is all in our favor, & the spiteful envious Com. even if there were a dozen such, wd amount to no more than a drop in the bucket. . . . N. B. On the opposite page, I place a few of the notices. You will see that one of the literary papers—the *Evening Mail*—compares your history of the Genl's early life to Queen Victorias interesting account of her ~~going~~ journey through the Highlands, which she has recently published;—a number of people have said that your articles are the best of the two." ALS, *ibid*. On March 6, Bonner wrote to USG. "I enclose an advance copy of the *Ledger*, containing the last of the Letters. Now that they are finished, do you not agree with me that they are excellent, and that it was better that you should not have seen them until they appeared in print?" ALS, USG 3. See "The Early Life of Gen. Grant By his Father," printed in three weekly installments in the *Ledger*, reprinted in *USGA Newsletter*, VIII, 1–2 (Oct., 1970–Jan., 1971), 5–19.

To Maj. Gen. Winfield S. Hancock

Washington, D, C, Feb.y 22d *1868*. [*4:15* P.M.]

MAJ. GN. W. S. HANCOCK,
NEW ORLEANS, LA,

In relation to your ordr of the 19th of Feb.y I would call your attention to the seventh (7) section of the Act. of Congress of March 2d 1867. making appropriation.

The publication of the registry in other states has not been resorted to and looks like an unnecessary expense.

U. S. GRANT
General,

ALS (telegram sent), DNA, RG 107, Telegrams Collected (Bound); telegram sent, *ibid.*; telegram received (at 4:30 P.M.), *ibid.*, RG 393, 5th Military District, Telegrams Received. On Feb. 22, 1868, Edward McPherson, clerk, U.S. House of Representatives, wrote to USG. "The Newspapers of the 21st contain a telegram dated New Orleans, February 20th, stating that General Hancock issued an order on the 19th that the 'last revised registry in each parish in Louisiana shall be published once in the newspaper having the greatest circulation in each parish; fifty hand-bills of each list shall also be published by the same paper and posted in the most conspicuous place in each parish, under direction of the sheriffs. The lists for publication will be furnished from the office of the Secretary of Civil Affairs *who will pay the expenses*.' General Hancock has issued this order—which, if executed, will involve an enormous expense,—in evident ignorance of the provisions of the Seventh section of the Act of March 2, 1867, (a copy of which I enclose). This Act directs where these lists,—if to be printed at all,—shall be printed, viz: in the papers selected thereunder; and prohibits the payment of the expense of any printing in the districts named, except that ordered in pursuance of these provisions. I have the honor to request that General Hancock's attention be called to this law." LS, *ibid.*, RG 108, Letters Received. On Feb. 23, Maj. Gen. Winfield S. Hancock telegraphed to USG. "Your telegram of yesterday is received. Some time since I ordered the publication of the Registry lists in Texas, to cover accidents by loss of Records, (so widely distributed as these Records are,) and as a basis to prevent fraud, knowing that such precautionary measures have been habitually practised in the Northern States. Preparatory to an election about to take place (I presume) in Louisiana, and in accordance with the wisdom of good men here, I ordered the publication of the Registry in Louisiana as well. It being a usual custom, and knowing no evil could grow out of it, I concluded the small expense of publication would be well bestowed in preventing and exposing fraud, and in satisfying the people that the laws were honestly executed. I do not suppose another publication absolutely necessary, although it would be proper, previous to each election. If the expense is a paramount question, it may be omitted. I think, however the publication recently ordered should proceed. The lists are ready for publication and will be published unless you order to the contrary. Section 7, of the act to which you refer, does not apply to the Army or to the Reconstruction acts, but relates to the civil branch of the Government and to its Executive officers. The New Orleans Republican purports to be the only official paper of this State to which the act referred to applies. Notice was sent to the Editors, of that paper, two days since, that the Registry lists would be furnished them for publication. I beg to refer you to Sec. 7, of the Reconstruction act of March 23d 1867, which was passed subsequent to the act to which you refer." LS (telegram sent), *ibid.*, RG 107, Telegrams Collected (Bound); telegram received (on Feb. 24, 9:00 P.M.), *ibid.*, RG 108, Telegrams Received. On Feb. 25, 10:00 A.M., USG telegraphed to Hancock. "In the matter of publishing registry lists you are the sole judge of the law and the necessity. My dispatch was suggestive only." ALS (telegram sent), *ibid.*, RG 107, Telegrams Collected (Bound); telegram sent, *ibid.*; telegram received (at 10:30 A.M.), *ibid.*, RG 393, 5th Military District, Telegrams Received.

On Feb. 10, Thomas J. Durant, Washington, D. C., had written to USG. "I have just received a letter from Neworleans, dated the 4th inst. addressed to me by my friend Henry C. Warmoth, who has been nominated by a convention of the Republican party as their Candidate for the office of Governor of the State of Louisiana under the Constitution framed by the Convention assembled under the reconstruction acts of Congress. From this letter I beg leave to call your attention to the following extract: — 'It is important that the bill now before the Senate should pass at an early day. Hancock I fear will not cooperate with the Convention in holding the election for State officers at the same time the vote is taken on the constitution.' The Louisiana Convention has adopted an ordinance, similar to that which passed the Alabama Convention, directing that on the same occasion with the vote of the Registered voters on the question of the ratification of the Constitution, they shall also vote for Governor and other State officers, members of state Legislature and members of Congress. This ordinance, it is respectfully submitted, is within the powers of the Convention; in harmony with the provisions and spirit of the reconstruction acts; is one which the District Commander ought to aid in the execution of; and one with regard to which the General of the army has by law the right to interpose his superior authority, in case the District Commander misapprehends his own duty of assisting the Convention. . . . It is to be hoped, then, should the District Commander in Louisiana think proper to interfere with the orders of the convention for the election of state officers, Legislature and members of Congress, and in this way to *delay and obstruct* the consummation of the congressional plan, that the General of the Army may find the proper means to control him, and enforce obedience to the laws. The undersigned cannot refrain from expressing his deep solicitude upon this subject; *the defeat of the Constitutions in Alabama and Louisiana, if permitted to remain defeats*, must necessarily shatter the confidence of the people in the wisdom and energy of that party whose principles are alone calculated to save the nation; must place us in great jeopardy, paralyse our friends, encourage and elate our opponents; and while it postpones reconstruction, subjects us to a train of evils not too much to be apprehended." ALS, *ibid.*, RG 108, Letters Received.

On March 13, Stephen B. Packard, chairman, Board of Registration, New Orleans, wrote to USG. "The Board of Registration, appointed by the late Constitutional Convention to look after the subject of election for the ratification of the Constitution and election of Civil officers respectfully beg leave to present the enclosed official acts of the convention upon which all their acts are predicated. Also to enclose a copy of the late orders of Gen. Hancock relative to Registrars and the election for the ratification of the Constitution. The Committee beg leave to state that they ~~have~~ telegraphed you on the 13th inst (to day) and thought best to forward the enclosed Orders   We most earnestly desire your interference in behalf of the loyal people of Louisiana, as Gen Hancock's aim seems evidently to be the defeat of their hopes in reconstructing this state. His removal from this district and the appointmt of some such gentleman as Gen. Sheriden, or Gen. Mower would gladden the heart of every loyal man in our state, and secure the triumph of loyalty at the coming state election as well as greatly assist the hopes of all loyal men in regard to the next presidential election. Hoping that our petition for relief will not be disregarded . . . The mass of the registrars appointed by Hancock are notorious rebels, and open enemies to reconstruction." ALS, *ibid.* The enclosure is *ibid.* On the same day, Packard and other registrars telegraphed a protest to U.S. Senator Henry Wilson of Mass., who endorsed the telegram to USG. AES, *ibid.*

To John Sherman

Washington, D, C, Feb.y 22d *1868*

HON. J. SHERMAN,
U. S. SENATE:
DEAR SIR:

The National Intelligencer of this morning contains a private note which Gen. Sherman sent to the President whilst he was in Washington, dictated by the purest kindness, and a disposition to preserve harmony, and not intended for publication.[1] It seems to me the publication of that letter is calculated to place the General in a wrong light before the public, taken in connection with what correspondents have said before, evidently getting their inspiration from the White House. As Gen. Sherman afterwards wrote a semi official note to the President, furnishing me a copy, and still later, a purely official one sent through me, which place him in his true position, and which have not been published, though called for by the "House," I take the liberty of sending you these letters to give you the opportunity of consulting Gen. Sherman as to what action to take upon them. In all matters where I am not personally interested I would not hesitate to advise Gen. Sherman how I would act in his place. But in this instance, after the correspondence I have had with Mr. Johnson, I may not see Gen. Shermans interest in the same light others see it, or that I would see it in if no such correspondence had occurred. I am clear in this however: the correspondence here enclosed to you should not be made public except by the President, or with the full sanction of Gen. Sherman. Probably the letter of the 31st of Jan.y, marked Confidential, should not be given out at all.

Yours Truly
U. S. GRANT

ALS, DLC-William T. Sherman.

1. "In connection with the recent imbroglio in which the President, General Grant, and General Sherman were parties, we publish the following lette[r] from General Sherman to the President, which speaks for itself: 'WASHINGTON, Saturday, January 18. I neglected this morning to say that I had agreed to go down to Annapolis to spend Sunday with Admiral Porter. General Grant also has to

leave for Richmond on Monday, at 6 A. M. At a conversation with the General, after our interview wherein I offered to go with him on Monday morning to Mr. Stanton, and to say that it was our joint opinion he should resign, it was found impossible, by reason of his going to Richmond and my going to Annapolis. The General proposed this course. He will call upon you to-morrow, and offer to go to Mr. Stanton, to say, for the good of the service and of the country, he ought to resign. This on Sunday. On Monday I will again call on you, and, if you think it necessary, I will do the same—call on Mr. Stanton, and tell him to resign. If he will not, then it will be time to contrive ulterior measures. In the meantime it so happens that no necessity exists for precipitating matters. Yours truly, W. T. Sherman, Lt Gen.' " *National Intelligencer*, Feb. 22, 1868. On Feb. 22, 1868, U.S. Senator John Sherman wrote to the editors. "The publication in your paper yesterday of General Sherman's note to the President, and its simultaneous transmission by telegraph unaccompanied by subsequent letters withheld by the President because they were 'private,' is so unfair as to justify severe censure upon the person who furnished you this letter, whoever he may be. Upon its face it is an informal private note dictated by the purest motives,—a desire to preserve harmony,—and not intended for publication. How any gentleman receiving such a note could first allow vague but false suggestions of its contents to be given out, and then print it, and withhold other letters because they were 'private,' with a view to create the impression that General Sherman in referring to ulterior measures suggested the violent expulsion of a high officer from his office, passes my comprehension. Still I know that General Sherman is so sensitive upon questions of official propriety in publishing papers, that he would rather suffer from this false inference than to correct it by publishing another private note; and as I knew that this letter was not the only one written by General Sherman to the President about Mr. Stanton, I applied to the President for his consent to publish subsequent letters. This consent was freely given by the President, and I therefore send copies to you and ask their publication. These copies are furnished me from official sources; for while I know General Sherman's opinions, yet he did not show me either of the letters to the President, during his stay here, nervously anxious to promote harmony, to avoid strife, and certainly never suggested or countenanced resistance to law—or violence in any form. He no doubt left Washington with his old repugnance to politics, politicians, and newspapers very much increased by his visit here." Rachel Sherman Thorndike, ed., *The Sherman Letters: Correspondence Between General Sherman and Senator Sherman from 1837 to 1891* (New York, 1894), pp. 309–10.

To Maj. Gen. George G. Meade

Washington, Feb. 24th *1868* [*11:00* P.M.]

Maj. Gn. G. G. Meade,
Atlanta Ga.

Gen. Shepherd is the senior officer belonging to the State of Alabama and would have been in command from the time Gen.

Sywayne was relieved only that he asked leave of absence. Hayden could not be kept in command only by keeping Shepherd, a good officer, away from his regiment. There is no objection to Gn. Hayden carrying on the investigations he is engaged in and exercising such authority in the matter of elections as you deem proper. Gen. Shepherd is instructed to report to you in person at Atlanta.

U. S. GRANT
General,

ALS (telegram sent), DNA, RG 107, Telegrams Collected (Bound); telegram sent, *ibid.*; telegram received, Meade Papers, PHi.

On Jan. 10, 1868, USG had written to the AG. "The Adj. Gn. will extend to Gn. Shepherd, now in Washington under orders, permission to delay joining his post for sixty days from this date. Mail order to New Port, R. I." ALS, DNA, RG 94, Letters Received, 29W 1868. On Feb. 18, USG wrote to the AG. "You will please order Gen. O. H. Shepherd, Col. 15th Inf.y back to his regiment and to assume command of the sub District of Ala. on his arrival there." ALS, *ibid.*, 107S 1868.

On Feb. 22, 1:00 P.M., USG telegraphed to Maj. Gen. George G. Meade. "During your absence in Fla. I ordered Gn. Shepherd back to his regiment and to the command of subdistrict of Ala. He leaves here to-day." ALS (telegram sent), *ibid.*, RG 107, Telegrams Collected (Bound); telegram sent, *ibid.*; telegram received, Meade Papers, PHi. On Feb. 23, Meade telegraphed to USG. "I regret you ordered Col Shepherd here without a reference to my views—I fear you have been misled, by reports from interested parties, in regard to Genl—Hayden—That officer may have committed errors of judgement but I am satisfied his motives & intentions were good & right—and I deem it but justice to him to ask that I be authorised to suspend the order placing Col Shepherd in command until the investigations now being carried on by Genl—Hayden are closed & the election conducted by him settled.—" ALS (telegram sent), *ibid.*; telegram received (at 10:00 A.M.), DNA, RG 107, Telegrams Collected (Bound); *ibid.*, RG 108, Telegrams Received.

To Maj. Gen. Winfield S. Hancock

Washington D. C. Feby. 29th *1868*

MAJ. GEN. W. S. HANCOCK,
COMDG. 5TH MIL. DISTRICT
GENERAL:

Your telegraphic dispatch of the 27th inst., in reply to my order revoking your order displacing a portion of the City Council of New Orleans, and appointing their successors is received. There was nothing in my order which doubted your authority to make removals and appointments when the public exigency requires it. I only exercised an authority given to me as General of the Army, under which law both of us find our authority to act in such matters. Your order of removal was based on certain charges which I did not think were sustained by the facts as they were presented to me.

Dispatches of such length as yours should be sent by mail when there is not a greater necessity for prompt reply than seems to exist in this case.

> Very respectfully
> Your obt. servt.
> U. S. GRANT
> General

Copies, DLC-USG, V, 47, 60; DLC-Andrew Johnson; DNA, RG 108, Letters Sent. On Feb. 27, 1868, Maj. Gen. Winfield S. Hancock, New Orleans, had telegraphed to USG. "Your letter of the 21st inst. is this day received, disapproving and revoking my orders (S. O. number 28) which removes the Alderman and Asst Aldermen of the City of New Orleans, therein named and appointing others in their stead; also reinstating the members of the Boards of Aldermen removed by said order, and directing that they will resume their duties as Aldermen and Assistant Aldermen, the same as if said order had not been issued. My action in the removal of the members of the city Council of New Orleans, who are reinstated by your order, was adopted after grave deliberation and, as I believe, was the result of a necessity imposed on me, which could not have been avoided without a disregard of the interest of the public service and of the obligations imposed on me by the Reconstruction Act, and by the orders of my predecessor. It is in substance declared, in the Reconstruction Acts, that the Government of the Rebel states, if continued, are to be continued subject in all respects to the Military Commander of the respective Military Districts &c. In section 6th of the act passed March 2nd, 1867, it is enacted that, until the people of said Rebel States shall be by law, admitted to representation in the congress of the United States any civil government, which may exist therein, shall be deemed provisional only and in all respects subject to the paramount authority of the United States, at any time to abolish, modify, control or superceed the same; under the authority of that section my predecessor, in command of this District, issued special orders No. 7, dated March 28, 1867, in which, he prohibited the holding of any elections for state, parrish, municipal or judicial officers in the state of Louisiana until the provisions of the laws of Congress shall have been complied with. The office of Recorder, for the 2nd District in the city of New Orleans, is a judicial office of great importance to the administration of criminal justice. By the laws of the state that officer is elected, and is to be so, by a vote of the people of the District. Since the order of my predecessor was issued I am not aware that any election by the people has been holden in the state to fill any office, nor am I aware that the city Council has, by its action filled any office other than such as the Council is authorized to fill under the law creating the City Government. The City Attorney referred to in your letter is an officer appointed to transact the legal business of the City and he is, by law, to be chosen by a vote of the City Council. The selection of a person to fill that office is a part of the duty imposed on the City Council, by its charter after it once becomes an original body. The office of Recorder for one of the Districts, into which the City is divided, is not an office created by law for the administration of municipal business, but is one in which the people of the City at large, and the public in general are, interested. It is, therefore by law, filled in the ordinary condition of things, by an election by the people and the City Council has no authority to act in relation to it except it be to provide temporarily to prevent a vacancy in it during the interval between the election provided for by law. It is in no sense an office with which the City Council has any concern in the administration of the municipal business and, in my opinion, was clearly embraced in the terms of the order of the 28th March 1867, issued by my predecessor The Jefferson City Council was removed by Genl Mower because they ordered an election to be held for the appointment of their successors. This action on the part of the City Council was in direct contravention of the order referred to and in my view the action of the members of the City Council of New Orleans in attempting to fill the office of Recorder for the 2d District of the City was, not only in violation of that order, but was also an assumption on their part of the right to exercise the authority to fill offices of a general nature which is, by the Reconstruction Acts, specially delegated to the District Commander. It is true that General Orders No. 40, issued by me, to which you refer declares, that when insurrection—any force has been overthrown and peace established and the City Authorities are ready and willing to perform their duties the military power should cease to lead and the civil administration resume its natural and rightful dominion, and I conceive that no violence was done to the principles enunciated and declared when I gave effect to the order of my predecessor and restrained the members of a municipal body from doing an act for which no existing law gave them any authority. In conclusion I will only observe that I entertain serious apprehensions that the revokcation of my order, and the reinstatement of the Council removed by me, will be injurious to the public interest and increase the embarrassments under which the community is now laboring. Your order will be immediately executed" Telegrams received (2—on Feb. 28, 1:00 P.M.), *ibid.*, RG 107, Telegrams Collected (Bound); *ibid.*, RG 108, Telegrams Received; copies (one sent by mail), *ibid.*, Letters Received; *ibid.*, RG 393, 5th Military District, Telegrams Sent; DLC-USG, V, 55; DLC-Andrew Johnson. On Feb. 21, Bvt. Maj. Gen. John A. Rawlins had written to Hancock. "Your report of date the 15th inst, in response to a telegram of the General Comdg the Army, dated the 8th inst, in the matter of the removal of certain Aldermen & Asst Aldermen of the City of New Orleans for contempt of Military Orders, is received. In the same matter there has also been received a memorial from said Alderman and Assistant Aldermen. From the report and memorial, and your previous telegrams, the following facts appear. The Office of Recorder of the City of New Orleans is elective by the people, but in case of a vacancy, it is made the duty by law of the Boards of Aldermen and Assistant Aldermen in joint meeting to elect *viva voce* a person to fill the vacancy. The Office of Recorder of the 2d District of New Orleans, was by the Supreme Court of

Louisiana adjudged vacant, and the City of New Orleans was ordered to be notified to proceed according to law to elect a Recorder for said District, which judgment was made final Jany 20th 1868. In pursuance of this order of the Court the Boards of Aldermen and Assistant Aldermen met in joint session on the 4th day of February 1868 to elect a recorder for said Second district. At this session was read a communication written by Captain Chandler Assistant Sect'y Civil Affairs, and purpoting to be by your direction, inviting attention to the first and Second Sections of the supplementary Reconstruction Act of Congress passed July 19th 1867, and to paragraph 2 Special Orders No 7 from Hdqrs. 5th Milt District dated March 28th, 1867   At the date of this communication, viz—Jany 25th 1868 and before any action of either branch of the Council had been had relative to the election therein referred to, you were absent from the City of New Orleans, in the State of Texas   This communication did not in terms forbid the election, neither did the section of the Act to which it referred, except as it might be inferred from the Second Section wherein the District Commander is empowered under certain restrictions 'to fill vacancies occasioned by Death, resignation or otherwise:' Section 9 of this Act, as well as the original reconstruction act, of March 2d 1867, recognizes the right of the State and Municipal Authorities to appoint and elect Officers under certain restrictions & limitations; but the exercise of this right is subject to the Authority of the District Commander. Subsequent to the issuing of Special Orders No 7 referred to, and during the administration of Generals Sheridan and Mower, the City Council of New Orleans, did in some cases fill vacancies in Corporation Offices under the provision of Section 24 of the city charter of New Orleans, in the same manner as is provided for filling a vacancy in the office of Recorder. And after you assumed command, the Office of City Attorney was filled under the same authority and in the same manner. No exception was taken in any case by any of the District Commanders to such action. On assuming command of the of the District, you announced in General Orders No 40 of Nov 29th 67, that it was your purpose to preserve peace and quiet in your command and that as a means to this great end, you regarded the maintenance of the Civil Authorities in the faithful execution of the laws as the most efficient, under existing circumstances'—also that when 'the civil authorities are ready and willing to perform their duties, the military power should cease to lead, and the civil administration resume its natural and rightful dominion.' Under this statement of facts, the City Council of New Orleans might reasonably have presumed it to be their right and duty, especially so under the order of the Court, and your order No 40, to fill the vacancy in the Office of recorder, as it appears they did from from your report in this case dated Feby. 15 1868. The same facts too, in connection with the printed report of their proceedings embraced in your report of Feby 15th, 68, precludes the presumption of any intended contempt of the Military Authority by the members of the City Council. The case of 'Jefferson City Council,' is not deemed a paralell one, in this, that they had not their own unquestioned acts in similar cases, nor the order of the District Commander to justify them. There being no contempt of Military Authority intended by the Boards of Aldermen & Asst Aldermen of the City of New Orleans, removed by Special Orders No 28 Head Quarters 5th Military District, dated Feby. 7th 1868, and a proper administration of the reconstruction acts, not requiring their removal, said Special Order removing the Alderman and Asst Aldermen therein named and appointing others in their stead, is hereby disapproved and revolked, and the Members of the Boards of Aldermen and Asst

Aldermen removed by it are hereby reinstated and will resume their duties as Aldermen and Asst Aldermen of the City of New Orleans the same as if said order had not been issued. You will please carry this order into effect." Copies, DLC-USG, V, 47, 60; DLC-Andrew Johnson; DNA, RG 108, Letters Sent.

On Feb. 7, Hancock had telegraphed to USG. "I have removed nine 9 members of the City Council two white & seven 7 colored for contempt of the orders of the Military Commander in proceeding to an election for a recorder for the second District & which is an elective office under the laws by the people & not by the council the attempt to hold the election was made while I was absent in Texas but the Council was referred to Gen'l sheridans order forbidding elections until reconstruction was completed without the authority of the commanding General neverthelesss, these members voted for an immediate election & the project was carried the election was about to be Completed when one 1 or two 2 members more timed than these left & broke the quorum a case in point is the order of Gen'l Mower S. O. of oct fifteenth sixty seven 67 removing the Jefferson City Council for a like offence my action in this matter was in accordance with the power granted by the reconstruction act which allows the district commander to suspend or remove persons from office & provide from time to time for the performance of the duties of persons removed by appointment &c" Telegram received (at 7:35 P.M.), *ibid.*, Telegrams Received; copies (one sent by mail), *ibid.*, Letters Received; *ibid.*, RG 393, 5th Military District, Telegrams Sent; DLC-USG, V, 55; DLC-Andrew Johnson. On Feb. 8, USG, Willard's Hotel, telegraphed to Hancock. "Suspend your order removing City Council of New Orleans until full report of reasons is sent. Answer by mail." ALS (telegram sent), DNA, RG 107, Telegrams Collected (Bound); telegram sent, *ibid.*; telegram received, *ibid.*, RG 393, 5th Military District, Telegrams Received. On Feb. 9, 2:30 P.M., Hancock telegraphed to USG. "Your despatch of the eighth February directing me to suspend my orders number twenty eight of seventh December removing certain members of the city council of New Orleans until full report of the reasons therefor should be sent to you, was received at ten P. M. today. I request that you may reconsider your action and that my order in the premises be not suspended until you have the full report of the reasons called for by you. I telegraphed you at the moment the order was issued giving as full a statement of my reasons for action as I thought could be made. I referred you to the orders of General Sheridan forbidding elections which you have on file at your Head Quarters, and stated that the city council had been previously notified of this order by me I also referred you to an order of General Mower issued in October last which set forth a parallel case and which you have on file. In that case an appeal was taken to you for a reinstatement of the Council removed by General Mower, which appeal you have not sustained the present case was in defiance of that example of Genl Sheridans order and of my own letter cautioning the council to desist in this election and forwarded to you printed copy January twenty sixth. it was also illegal under the law by which they claimed to act. I was astonished at the action of the Council and could not account for it except in the fact that they had been instigated to it by designing men who believed, if I dared to make those removals that it would end in my own removal from this place and that they would be protected—At any rate my self respect as Commander of this District made it absolutely necessary that I should take summary measures regardless of the consequences with which partisans might threaten me I do not know what fuller report could be furnished in this case for all the papers explaining my action have been sent to you To suspend my order would be to destroy my usefulness here and in such event a sense of what I consider due to me and my position in this matter would necessitate a respectful request to be relieved from my present command. Although I have been here seventy days this is the second occasion I have taken on my own responsibility to make a removal the first one two days previous to this both for grave causes reported to you in detail by telegraph and while I fully recognize the power of the General in Chief to disapprove my action I respectfully request that as I have acted upon a full knowledge of the facts the General in Chief may delay his action until he can inform me what further papers or information he may desire in addition to what has been already furnished for a full understanding of the case under consideration. My action in the premises was originally based on the first Supplementary Reconstruction Act of July nineteenth 19th 1867. I await your reply before issueing the order" LS (telegram sent), *ibid.*, RG 107, Telegrams Collected (Bound); telegram received (at 3:30 P.M.), *ibid.*; (on Feb. 11, 9:00 A.M.) *ibid.*, RG 108, Telegrams Received. On Feb. 11, 11:55 A.M., USG telegraphed to Hancock. "If your order removing City Council has been executed and new appointees are in you need not suspend orders as directed." ALS (telegram sent), *ibid.*, RG 107, Telegrams Collected (Bound); telegram sent, *ibid.*; telegram received (at 12:30 P.M.), *ibid.*, RG 393, 5th Military District, Telegrams Received. On the same day, Hancock telegraphed to USG. "The change in the city council was an accomplished fact when your dispatch of February ninth (9th) was received several of the appointees had already filed copies of their oaths of office in my selections I have appointed the best men to office without regard to their political sentiments. All must take the required oath or the change will be of immense advantage to the city as the poor of which the city is principally composed are dependent upon the public Confidence" Telegram received (on Feb. 12, 9:00 A.M.), *ibid.*, RG 107, Telegrams Collected (Bound); *ibid.*, RG 108, Telegrams Received; copies (one sent by mail), *ibid.*, Letters Received; *ibid.*, RG 393, 5th Military District, Telegrams Sent; DLC-USG, V, 55; DLC-Andrew Johnson. On Feb. 15, USG wrote to Speaker of the House Schuyler Colfax. "In compliance with Resolution of the House of Representatives of February 14th, 1868, I have the honor to transmit herewith copies of the correspondence between General Hancock and myself in relation to the removal by General Hancock of councilmen in the City of New Orleans." Copies, DLC-USG, V, 47, 60; DNA, RG 108, Letters Sent. USG transmitted all communications contained in this paragraph.

On March 10, USG wrote to Colfax. "In compliance with the Resolution of the House of Representatives of March 9th, 1868, I have the honor to transmit herewith copies of all correspondence received at these Headquarters, since February 15th, 1868, in relation to the removal of the City Council of New Orleans. All the correspondence prior to that date was furnished to the House under its resolution, dated February 14th, 1868. Copies of all the correspondence in relation to the Jefferson City Council are also herewith transmitted." Copies, *ibid.* Documents transmitted on Feb. 15 are printed as *HED*, 40-2-172; those on March 10 as *HED*, 40-2-209.

On March 3, Maj. Gen. Philip H. Sheridan, Fort Leavenworth, had written to Rawlins. "I see from the papers that General Hancock gives as a reason for the removal of certain Councilmen in New Orleans a violation of an order issued by me when in command of that District. I wish to place myself right by saying that the order referred to never was intended to cover such cases; but was an order forbidding elections by the people." LS, DNA, RG 108, Letters Received.

On March 8, W. F. McLean, New Orleans, wrote to USG. "I would respectfully call your attention to the following facts in relation to my removal from the office of *Second Justice* of *the peace* for the parish of Orleans and City of New Orleans, believing that you will do me justice in the premises. In the month of October 1867 George H. Braughn second justice of the peace was charged by Mr John A. Cheevers an Attorney at law, and by others with malfeisance in office. This charge was duly brought to the notice of Brevet Maj-Genl Joseph A. Mower then commanding this District and resulted in the removal of Justice Braughn and the appointment of the undersigned in his stead. This appointment was popular among Lawyers, and soon after I took my seat the business of the Court rapidly increased. The appointment too met the approbation of the Citizens among whom I have lived so long, and of the press of the City, save the notoriously venal 'New Orleans Times'. The secret of the animosity of the 'Times' was that W. H. C. King the present Editor and one of the proprietors had dealt with me in the most unfair and dishonest manner during my absence from the city to the north, and I have taken frequent occasion to expose him to my friends. At the time of the unfair and dishonest practices of King I was attached to the Times, and withdrew from the paper in consequence of his acts. The attacks of King professed to be based upon information given by one Pennyman who had to leave St Louis for his conduct while clerk at the Planters Hotel. He was turned out of the International Hotel in San Francisco for like acts, *Petit Larceny*, and was twice arrested by the proprietors of the City Hotel of New Orleans for the same offence. On the 20th day of December 1867 I was removed by Major Genl Hancock and Paris Childers succeeded me, justice Childers was a few days since arrested on a *charge* of *perjury* for taking the test oath having been, under Genl Butlers Military Administration, a registered enemy. My removal was brought about by the misrepresentations and falshoods of the aforesaid King and Pennyman, who made every effort both personally and thrugh the columns of the Times to defame me and influence Head-Quarters. It is probable that other reasons have been furnished you for my removal. If so, I can only say that the facts above stated can be easily proven, and I hold in my possession sundry documents which will readily place me right if they should be necessary. For any information touching me personally, or my fitness for the position from which I was expelled, I respectfully refer you to Major General P. H. Sheridan. Although Genl Hancock gives no reason for turning me out in his order, I am convinced there were two: one was that he does not like Genl Mower, and the other and important was, that I rendered justice to the late enfranchised portion of our people and without doing injustice to the whites. I have been informed that he has said that I gave too much weight and consideration to negro testimony in cases where white and colored parties were contestants. I hope that you will give my case an early consideration and put me in the position that I was ejected from by the malicious influence of notorious rebels who appear to be some of the leading advisers and councillors at Head Quarters. . . . Capt Chandler Secretary of Civil affairs informs me that he sent you a Copy of my answers to the Interogatories that General Hancok propounded to me. Should you desire recommendations as to my fitness and Loyalty, I can get the endorsement of the Republican State and Congressional nominees, Judge Warmouth at the head as candidate for Governor. General Sheridan gave me letter of introduction & recommendation to Genl Hancock." ALS, *ibid*.

USG received a letter of March 12, signed "Scheck Catholic Priest" written in German with accompanying translation. "Will you gratiously grant, to order Genl Hancock that he will compel the City authorities of New Orleans to borrow

4 Millions United States Currency according to the lately established rules and to exchange at once their City Srib for this currency at par, that the daily increasing suffering of the poor workmen will cease. Every workman is paid here with this City Scrib and businessman will not take it in pay for their goods; therefor the poor laboror is compelled to exchange the Scrib at the Broker's at from 15-20 p cent discount: Every measure of Mayor Heath only makes the evil worse." ALS, *ibid.*

On March 31, Thomas J. Durant, Washington, D. C., wrote to Rawlins. "I have received from Neworleans, with a request to transmit to you, the enclosed letter from Dr. C. Déléry, dated at Neworleans on the 21st inst. The case he presents is this. Dr Déléry was elected coroner of the city of Neworleans, in 1865: and removed from office, in company with several other local officers of various functions elected at the same time, by General Mower whose order was suspended by directions from General Grant. Soon after General Hancock took command of the Fifth Military District, all the officers removed by General Mower were reinstated, with the single exception of Dr. C. Delery the coroner: who was not restored, but replaced by General Hancock's appointment of Thomas Bradford, special order No. 214 Head Quarters Fifth Military District, Neworleans 19, 1867. Dr Delery affirms that he knows no reason why he should have thus been singled out, but the fact seems to imply that some special reason is applicable to him, which did not fit the other office holders, who were all restored. It is true he was informed a few days after by General Hancock that the ground of exception in his case was, that 'he had caused himself to be registered as an enemy of the United States, and then embarked for Havana, on board of a spanish Man-of-war,' but this he explains. It was upon this that Dr. Delery made the appeal to General Grant, that was forward to the Head Quarters of the Army in December last. Col. Lee was kind enough under your direction, General, to look up these papers when I called at Head Quarters in the begining of March, and he then informed me, that had not been up to that time considered or acted upon. Among these papers, as Dr Delery informs me, is a certificate signed by several respectable persons, to the effect that Dr. Delery called at the office of Col. Kilbourn, then Provost-Marshal in Neworleans, and protested against his being inscribed as an enemy of the United States; and this protest he claims shows that the inscription was against his will, and should not therefore be permitted to weigh against him. What the merits of Dr Delery's case may be I do not take it upon myself to advise or determine; but I second with pleasure the application he makes to have his case considered, under an impartial view of the circumstances, and to have upon it the enlightend opinn and order of the General of the Army." ALS, *ibid.* The enclosure is *ibid.*

A petition to USG of March 21, with some 3,000 signatures, defending Hancock's policy of removals in New Orleans, delivered to USG on March 30, is printed in the *National Intelligencer*, April 7, 1868.

To Lt. Gen. William T. Sherman

Washington D. C. March 2nd 1868.

GENERAL;

I think it will be well to prepare at once for the abandonment of the Posts Phil. Kearney, Reno & Fetterman and to make all the capital with the Indians that can be made out of the change. In making this removal it may be necessary to establish a new line of posts to protect travel from the railroad North from some point West of Cheyenne   Your knowledge of the country will enable you to fix this to the best advantage. I would advise that but little confidence be placed in the suggestions of citizens who have their homes in the territories in selecting points to be occupied by troops. My experience is, and no doubt it is ~~born~~ borne out by your own, that these people act from selfish and interested motives. We will have to, hereafter, rely upon inspections by competent officers to govern us in our distribution of troops and dealings with the Indians. This advice is probably more applicable to myself than to you. I am where a President, a Secy of War, Secy. of the Interior and Supt. of Indian affairs can all be approached by politicians in the interest of traders, agents and speculators. I will try to embarrass you as little as possible by their suggestions.

I recommend this early movement in the abandonment of the Posts referred to, because I fear that, by delay, the Indians may commence hostilities and make it impossible for us to give them up.

Very respectfully
Your obt. servt
U. S. GRANT
General

To LT. GEN. W. T. SHERMAN
COMDG. MIL. DIV. OF THE MO.

Copies, DLC-USG, V, 47, 60; DNA, RG 108, Letters Sent. On March 3, 1868, 11:00 A.M., USG telegraphed to Lt. Gen. William T. Sherman. "Add Ft. C. F. Smith to my letter of March 2d/68." ALS (telegram sent), *ibid.*, RG 107, Telegrams Collected (Bound); telegram sent, *ibid.*; copies, *ibid.*, RG 108, Telegrams Sent; DLC-USG, V, 56. On March 3, Sherman, St. Louis, telegraphed to USG.

"Despatch received. If your letter of second contemplates breaking up the powder river road, negotiate with Indian Bureau for the purchase of such buildings and property as we must leave behind. The change can best be made in June" Telegram received (at 2:30 P.M.), DNA, RG 107, Telegrams Collected (Bound); *ibid.*, RG 108, Telegrams Received; copy, DLC-USG, V, 55. On March 7, Sherman wrote to USG. "I have the honor to acknowledge the receipt of your letter of March 2nd, with the despatch of the same date, qualifying the letter by including Fort C. F. Smith as one of the number to be broken up. I rather think that we may have to retain Fort Fetterman, which is not properly on the Powder River road, but rather on the old California or Sweetwater road, and will still be needed in connection with the overland system of posts. Inasmuch as the Pacific Railroad will be pushed rapidly west, I doubt the propriety of making any new line of posts intermediate between the route now proposed to be abandoned, and the one commonly travelled from Salt Lake. Still, on this point I will consult General Augur. It may be that the Commissioners intend to treat with the Sioux and Northern Cheyennes this spring at or near Fort Phil. Kearney, and that they would prefer that we should delay giving up the post till the treaty is over. I think you had better give Mr. Commissioner Taylor and Mr. Senator Henderson notice that we propose to draw off our troops very soon unless they give us official notice that the Indian Peace Commission want us there, up to some certain date for their protection. Also Mr. Taylor spoke to me and offered to buy of us the buildings at Forts Phil. Kearney and C. F. Smith for use as Indian agencies. If we can realize any money by the sale of the buildings and fixtures, it could be applied by us for the erection of quarters for our men at their new stations. I will send a copy of your letter to General Augur, with instructions to begin the preparations for this change and I expect to go up there myself before the transfer is complete." LS, DNA, RG 108, Letters Received. On March 10, USG endorsed a copy of this letter to Secretary of War Edwin M. Stanton. ES, *ibid.* See letter to Edwin M. Stanton, March 10, 1868.

To Andrew Johnson

Washington, March 5th 1868.

His Excellency A. Johnson
President of the US.
Sir:

I have the honor to acknowledge the receipt of your communication of the 3d inst, concerning Bvt. Maj. Gen. D. E. Sickles, Col. 42d US. Infantry. In reply thereto I would respectfully state that after being relieved from the command of the 2d Military District,

Bvt. Maj. Gen. Sickles was ordered to New York City to await further orders. He has not since been ordered to duty.

Very respectfully

Your obed't serv't

U. S. GRANT

General.

LS, DLC-Andrew Johnson. On March 3, 1868, William G. Moore, secretary to President Andrew Johnson, had written to USG. "If Brevet Major General Sickles has been ordered to duty, please direct him to take command of his regiment, at its Headquarters, Sackett's Harbor, New York." Copies (2), *ibid.*

To Edwin M. Stanton

Respectfully forwarded to the Secretary of War. In addition to the correspondence transmitted by Major General Hancock I enclose copy of my letter to him of date Feb. 29th 1868, in reply to his telegram of the 27th, and subsequent to the date of the within communication, and copy of sections 15 & 24 of city charter of New Orleans.

U. S. GRANT

General.

HDQRS. AUS.

MARCH 5. '68.

ES, DLC-Miscellaneous Manuscripts. Written on a letter of Feb. 27, 1868, from Maj. Gen. Winfield S. Hancock, New Orleans, to Bvt. Maj. Gen. Lorenzo Thomas. "I have the honor to transmit herewith copies of my correspondence with the General-in-Chief in reference to my recent action concerning the removal from office of certain Aldermen and Assistant Aldermen of the Council of the city of New Orleans, made by me 'for contempt of the orders of the District Commander.' I request that the same may—in the appropriate manner—as explanatory of my action, and for his information—be laid before His Excellency the President of the United States, with this—my request to be relieved from the command of this Military District, where it is no longer useful or agreeable for me to serve. When relieved, should the exigencies of the service permit, it would be most in accordance with my inclinations to be sent to Saint Louis, Missouri, there to await further orders." LS, *ibid.* On March 7, President Andrew Johnson wrote to USG. "Please send to me Major Gen'l Hancock's application to be relieved from the command of the Fifth Military District, together with the accompanying correspondence." Copies (2), DLC-Andrew Johnson; DNA, RG 107, Letters Received from Bureaus. On the same day, USG again endorsed Hancock's letter. "Respectfully forwarded to His Excellency, the President." AES, DLC-Miscellaneous Manuscripts.

On Feb. 28, 7:30 P.M., Bvt. Brig. Gen. Horace Porter, New Orleans, had telegraphed to Bvt. Lt. Col. George K. Leet. "Arrived yesterday after a series of delays. City Council of New Orleans reinstated. Gen. Hancock very bitter. He will send by mail tomorrow request to be relieved, accompanied by documents which will however throw no new light on the subject. All loyal men approve Gen. Grants course—details by mail." Telegram received, DNA, RG 108, Telegrams Received; copy, DLC-USG, V, 55. On March 2, Porter wrote to "General," presumably USG. "After a careful investigation of the recent action of Gen. Hancock, in the removal of certain members of the council of this city, I have arrived at the following conclusions. Gen. H. appears to justify his course upon the following grounds: viz; 1st That an order of Gen. Sheridan's, at the time in force, prohibited all elections, of whatever kind. 2d That the Council had been specially directed not to proceed to the election of a recorder. 3d That it did proceed to hold Such election, in contempt of the District Commander's Authority. 4th That the removal of the Council of Jefferson City, by Gen. Mower, and sustained by Gen. Grant, was a parallel case. 5th That the election of the City Attorney, by the Council, was not a parallel case. 6th That there was no legal vacancy in the office of recorder. In reply to these reasons, I submit, briefly, the following facts. 1st It was intended by Gen. Sheridan that his order should apply to elections by the people, only, and one member of the Council, at least, had been so informed by him. Besides, it is unreasonable to suppose that he would, in general orders, limit the functions of his own appointees, and deprive them of privileges granted to them by charter when they were persons specially chosen by him on account of their fitness for performing the duties devolving upon them. The Council felt still more Secure in exercising the rights legally delegated to it, inasmuch as Gen. H. had recently announced the Supemacy of civil law. 2d The only notification received by the Council, of its having no authority to elect a recorder, was a letter from one of the staff officers of Gen. H. written during his absence, ~~and~~ addressed to the Mayor, and by him forwarded to the council, merely calling attention to a portion of the Reconstruction Act, and the above-mentioned order of Gen. Sheridan's. 3d Indefinite as this notification was, it had the desired effect of preventing the holding of the election, two of the members absenting themselves and depriving the body of the necessary quorum. 4th The Jefferson City case was a very different one from that under discussion. There the existing council (not appointees of the District Commander) proceeded to call an extraordinary election, *by the people*, for a Mayor, and other city officers, the Mayor whom they wished thus to displace being an appointee of the District Commander. 5th The Authority to elect a city Attorney and a recorder to fill a legal vacancy are alike conferred by charter on the City Council; and, although the duties of the former are much more closely connected with those of the Council, still the *authority* for their election is the same in both cases. 6th The existence of a vacancy in the office of Recorder of the Second District had been declared by the Court, and its decision was sufficient authority for the Council to act upon. It should be stated, in favor of Gen. H's course, that those whom he appointed were Unionists, with probably one exception, and good men, who represented the interests of the city very fairly. I have also examined into the practical workings of Gen. Buchanan's order affording assistance to planters, and furnishing employment to freedmen. It provides for an issue of provisions to all planters not having sufficient capital, and not employing more than 15 hands, the value to be refunded upon the sale of the crop, the Government taking a lien on the property, crop &c, as well as requiring bonds for Security. Gen. B. has about $100 000. of the Freedems Bureau funds, which, thus employed, will afford work, he estimates, for about 3000 freedmen. I am satisfied the order was published with the best intentions, and, though of questionable practicability, will, no doubt, afford some relief. The only objection is a probability that it might enable the planter to control his hands at the polls. This, however, I think, will not amount to a Serious objections. He will, at least, exert a less influence over them than if he provided for them out of his own means: for he is here brought more directly under the eye of the Bureau Agent, and, having been compelled to make a definite contract with his hands, he cannot punish them by discharge unless they violate the contract. But few have yet taken advantage of the measure, and the limited funds will, at best, confine its action to a small sphere. I shall leave here day after tomorrow, 4th inst. and stop a day at Atlanta. I have seen all classes, conditions and colors here, and I think have ascertained the true state of affairs. The 'Conservatives' are rallying for a tremendous effort, and the Unionists are apparently depressed but will lose no opportunities. There is great poverty, and there have been heavy losses in property, wherever I have been, but all owing to the people attempting to work for a *fortune* instead of a *living*. I find the mass of the residents are *war* democrats i. e. in favor of a war upon Congress if it doesn't legislate to suit them. I exclose a few amiable articles to illustrate the beauties of the freedom of the press." AL (initialed), DNA, RG 108, Letters Received.

On Feb. 28, three New Orleans editors telegraphed to USG. "In behalf of the loyal men of Louisiana, we respectfully ask the appointment of General Sickles in place of Gen. Hancock" Telegram received (at 4:50 P.M.), *ibid.*, RG 107, Telegrams Collected (Bound). Also on Feb. 28, J. M. G. Parkes, president, Pioneer Grant Club, New Orleans, and Lionel A. Sheldon, president, Union A & N Association, telegraphed to USG. "We earnestly request the appointment of General Sickles vice Hancock." Telegram received (on Feb. 29, 9:00 A.M.), *ibid.*

To Edwin M. Stanton

Washington, D, C, March 10th *1868*,

Hon. E. M. STANTON,
SEC. OF WAR;
SIR:

The line of Military posts known as Forts. Fetterman, Reno, Phil. Kearny and C. F. Smith, intended originally to cover an emigrant road to Montana, are found to pass through a country so desirable to the Indians for its game that no use can be made of the road thus covered except the traveler is protected by an escort sufficient to meet any band of Indians that may be on the War path. These posts are kept up at great expense and without any benefit. I propose to abandon them this Spring or Summer and have instructed Gen. Sherman accordingly. He suggests that as the buildings erected at them will not pay for removing them that they, or such of them as may be wanted, be disposed of to the Indian Bureau. I respectfully recommend that this suggestion be carried out.

> Very respectfully
> Your obt. svt.
> U. S. GRANT
> General,

ALS, DNA, RG 108, Letters Received. See letter to Lt. Gen. William T. Sherman, March 2, 1868.

To William Elrod

———

Washington, D, C,
March 10th 1868,

DEAR ELROD:

I should have been in Mo. by this time but for the impeachment of the President.[1] Whilst the trial lasts I presume it will be necessary for me to remain in this City. If it is over in time I will take my family out and spend two or three weeks in Mo.—I went yesterday to make arrangements for shipping two horses to you. If I can send them they will probably start from here about Monday next. Go on with farming the best you can until I do go out. You did well to save what was coming from Kasselring. When you can it will be well to increase the number of Cows on the place, so as to make butter or milk an object. I can not spare money however to do what I expected. If you can sell the notes you hold on Jefferson Co. property without too much discount you had better dispose of them.

You will not require a mowing machine until about the time you will be selling something so that by getting sixty or ninety days time you can pay for it from the crop. I enclose you two hundred dollars to work along with for the present. I will make your own wages better for this year than last and hope in the end you will be able to accumulate something for each of your children.

Yours Truly
U. S. GRANT

Can you not sell some corn and hay? It seems to me you must have some to spare.

U. S. G.

ALS, Illinois Historical Survey, University of Illinois, Urbana, Ill.

1. On Feb. 13, 1868, President Andrew Johnson had written to USG. "I desire that Brevet Major General Lorenzo Thomas resume his duties as Adjutant General of the Army of the United States." Copies, DNA, RG 107, Letters Received from Bureaus; (2) DLC-Andrew Johnson. On Feb. 14, Bvt. Brig. Gen. Cyrus B. Comstock wrote to Bvt. Maj. Gen. Lorenzo Thomas. "Gen. Grant directs me to say that the Presdt of the U. S. desires you to resume your duties as Adjt General of the Army." ALS, DNA, RG 94, Letters Received, 57A 1868.

On Feb. 15, Secretary of War Edwin M. Stanton wrote to USG. "I will thank you to furnish me with copies of any and all orders in your possession given by the President, since the 12th day of August last, to yourself, as Secretary of War *ad interim*, or as General commanding the Army of the United States, and to any of the commanding officers of the Military Districts, touching their duties &c. under the reconstruction acts." LS, *ibid.*, RG 107, Letters Received from Bureaus. On the same day, USG endorsed this letter. "Respectfully returned to the Secretary of War with the information that there are no orders in my possession of the character herein referred to. During the time mentioned the President's orders were addressed to me as Secty of War *ad interim*, and they were all filed in the War Department." ES, *ibid.*

On Feb. 21, William G. Moore, secretary to Johnson, endorsed to USG a copy of a letter of the same day from Johnson to Stanton. "By virtue of the power and authority vested in me, as President, by the Constitution and Laws of the United States, you are hereby removed from office as Secretary for the Department of War, and your functions as such will terminate upon receipt of this communication. You will transfer to Brevet Major General Lorenzo Thomas, Adjutant General of the Army, who has this day been authorized and empowered to act as Secretary of War ad interim, all records, books, papers, and other public property now in your custody and charge." Copy, *ibid.*, RG 108, Letters Received. Moore also enclosed a letter of the same day from Johnson to Thomas. "The Honorable Edwin M Stanton having been this day removed from office as Secretary for the Department of War, you are hereby authorized and empowered to act as Secretary of War ad interim, and will immediately enter upon the discharge of the duties pertaining to that office. Mr. Stanton has been instructed to transfer to you all the records, books, papers, and other public property now in his custody and charge." Copy, *ibid.*

On Feb. 22, Stanton wrote to USG. "In order to protect the archives and public property in the War Department building, occupied by the Secretary of War, and in his charge, you will please direct a competent officer, such for instance as Gen Carr, to go on duty at the War Department building, reporting to me, at seven o'clock this evening, and to remain until relieved by my order. If you are not engaged I will be glad to see you at the War Department at as early an hour as convenient this evening." LS, *ibid.* On the same day, Comstock wrote to Bvt. Maj. Gen. William H. Emory. "In compliance with the request of the Secretary of War and for the purpose of protecting the archives & public property in his charge, you will detail Gen. Carr or other suitable officer to report to the Secretary of War at the War Department at seven o'clock this, evening, to remain till relieved." ALS, *ibid.* On Feb. 24, the U.S. House of Representatives began the process of impeaching Johnson on eleven charges, most of them concerning the replacement of Stanton with Thomas.

On March 10, Thomas, as secretary of war *ad interim*, wrote to USG. "The President of the United States directs that you issue an order requiring that all orders and communications from Chiefs of bureaux and other officers intended either for himself or the Secretary of War be sent to me. This is not intended to interfere with any communication you may desire to bring to the notice of the President personally. For the present I shall transact the duties of the War Department at my residence No 446. H. Street corner of 10th." Copy, DLC-Andrew Johnson. There is no evidence that Thomas himself drafted this letter or that it was sent to USG.

On March 16 and 23, Edwards Pierrepont, New York City, wrote to USG. "I assure you that the people and all the earnest men who love peace and their Country are with you—But this trial must not fail—Imagine the President *acquitted*!!! The Department of the Atlantic filled by a willing tool & where would Congress be?—Let no man be deceived—This is the trial of an issue which determines whether true men or rebels shall rule—If the President is acquitted even by the lack of one necessary vote to Convict, Congress will be dispersed & in that event, it ought to be, as it will prove unfit to govern—" "I have this moment learned that Dana's Paper contains a letter from Washington stating that I had been retained by the President, & that lately while in Washington he consulted me at the White House—In the papers of to-morrow the refutation of the slander will appear I have not been inside the White House nor seen the President for more than a year & a half—He never retained me nor consulted me The lie is without the shadow of excuse—" ALS, USG 3.

On April 1, U.S. Representative John A. Bingham of Ohio wrote to USG. "The Managers on the part of the House of Representatives to conduct the impeachment of Andrew Johnson, President of the United States, request you to appear and bring with you or to send by the bearer, all letters and communications addressed to you by the President, touching the suspension and removal of Hon E. M. Stanton from the office of Sec.y of War, especially the letter of 10th Feb. 1868, and the order directing you to disobey the orders of said Stanton." LS, DNA, RG 108, Letters Received. On July 25, B. D. Whitney, clerk, wrote to USG. "The managers of the impeachment trial of the President having been discharged at their request by the Ho of Representatives, I have the honor to return herewith certain original papers which were furnished by you for the information of the managers during the trial." ALS, *ibid.* The enclosures are *ibid.*

To Lewis Wallace

————

Washington, D. C., March 10th *1868*.

MY DEAR GENERAL:

Enclosed herewith I return you letters from officers of the Army, who served with you at the battle of Shiloh, Tenn., giving their statement of your action on that occasion. I can only state that my orders to you were given verbally, to a staff officer, to communicate, and that they were substantially as given by Gen. Badeau in his book. I always understood that the staff officer referred to, Capt. Baxter, made a memorandum of the orders he received and left it with you. That memorandum I never saw.

The statements which I now return seem to exonerate you from the great point of blame, your taking the wrong road, or different road from the one directed, from Crumps Landing to Pittsburg Landing. All your subsequent military career showed you active and ready in the execution of every order you received. Your promptness in moving from Baltimore to Monocacy, Md., in 1864, and meeting the enemy in force far superior to your own, when Washington was threatened, is a case particularly in point. There you could scarcely have hoped for a victory. But you delayed the enemy and enabled me to get troops from City Point, Va., in time to save the City. That act I regarded as most praiseworthy. I refer you to my report of 1865 touching your course there.

In view of the assaults made upon you now I think it due to you that you should publish what your own staff, and other subordinate officers, have to say in exoneration of your course.

Yours Truly

U. S. GRANT

General,

To MAJ. GEN. L. WALLACE
CRAWFORDSVILLE INDA.

LS, InHi. On Feb. 28, 1868, Lewis Wallace, Washington, D. C., had written to USG. "About a year after the battle of Pittsburg Landing, it came to my knowledge that I was suffering, in your opinion, from erroneous information upon the subject of my conduct and movements, as commander of the 3rd. Division of your army, during the first day of the battle named. To place myself right in your estimation, and in that of the army generally, I asked a ~~e~~Court of Inquiry, by letter to the Sec. of War (Mr. Stanton,) July 17, 1863. After several months, during which the application received no attention from the Secretary, I withdrew it by advice of friends, Gen. Sherman, amongst others. The course I then resolved upon, that counseled by Gen. Sherman, was to carry my explanation directly to you; and such continued my intention until the battle of Monocacy, after which your treatment of me became so uniformly kind and considerate, that I was led to believe the disagreements connected with Pittsburg Landing forgotten; a result to which I tacitly assented notwithstanding the record of that battle as you had made it, in the form of an endorsement on my official report, was grievously against me. A recent circumstance, however, has made it essential to my good name, which I cannot bring myself to believe you wish to see destroyed, ~~has made it essential~~ to go back to my former purpose; in pursuance of which, the object of this letter is simply to introduce certain statements of gentlemen lately in the army, your friends as much as mine, in hopes that the explanations to be found therein will be sufficient to authorize you to give me a note of acquittal from blame, plain enough to allay the suspicions and charges to which I have been so painfully subjected. The statements are in the form of extracts, pertinent to the subject, from letters now in my possession, from Gen. Fred. Knefler, Gen. Geo. McGinnis, Col. James R. Ross, Gen. Danl Macauley, Capt. A. D. Ware, Genl Jno. A. Strickland, and Gen. Jno. M. Thayer, now U. S. Senator from Nebraska—all of my command on the day in question, present with me, well known to you, and of unimpeachable honor. I could have obtained many other letters of like purport, but selected these because their authors had peculiar opportunities for information upon points considered of chief importance. It is possible that my explanations of the matter would be sufficient for the object in view; however that may be, it is my judgment now, that the charges against me have gone so far, and been put in such grave form, that public opinion may require an exoneration, though it come from your hand, to be based upon the testimony of others. Permit me to say further, that as to the order you started to me by Capt. Baxter, I do not understand there is any question of veracity between us. You tell me that, from the battle field, you despatched a verbal order, by the officer named, to be delivered to me at Crump's Landing, directing me to march my division to *Pittsburg Landing, by the road paralell with the river*; and supposing, as you did, that the order would reach me by 11 o'clock, A. M., you reasonably calculated that my command would be on the field by 1 o'clock, P. M. Now, in all candor, if you have been, as I am informed, of opinion that I received that order as it was given, and at the time stated, (11 o'clock, A. M.,) and that for any reason such as personal feeling against you, or that I lost my way, or took the wrong road, or lingered on the march, making but five miles in seven hours, it must be admitted that you were justified in any, even the most extreme, judgment against me; and I must myself confess that your moderation was greater than mine would likely have been had our positions been reversed. I do not flinch from that conclusion at all; but what I do say, in defense, is that the opinion, and the conclusion, which is its corollary, are both wrong, because the order admitted to have been despatched was not *not delivered to me in form or substance as despatched*; on the contrary, the order I received from your messenger was in writing, unsigned, and contained substantially the following instructions—'You will leave a force at Crump's Landing sufficient to guard the public property there; then march the rest of your division, and effect a junction *with the right of the army*; after which you will form your line of battle at right angles with the river, and act as circumstances dictate.' This order was read by Col. Ross under circumstances well calculated to impress it upon his memory. It was given, also, to Col. Knefler, then my Adj. Genl, and by him read and unfortunately lost. Finally, its purport, as stated by the above, is vouched for by Capt. Ware, at the time my A. D. C. To refuse credit to my version of its contents will be very hard indeed, corroborated as it is by so many gentlemen of unquestionable veracity, and such excellent opportunity for information on the point. I think myself warranted now in asserting upon the credit of the three officers just named, as well as my own, that by the terms of the order as it was delivered to me, the objective of my march was not Pittsburg Landing, as you intended, but the right of the army, resting when the battle opened in the morning, at a point quite three miles out from that Landing on the road to Purdy. As a general principle, it must be admitted that, when you entrusted the order to a proper messenger for delivery to me, your responsibility ceased; but I turn, and ask you, appealing to your experience and justice, how am I to be held responsible for the execution of the order, if it never reached me? Or if it reached me conveying an idea radically different from that originally given? Of necessity, I was accountable for the execution of the order only *as it was received*;? and if was not received in a form to convey your true design, but was promptly executed, neither of us is responsible for the result—it was not your mistake, nor was it mine. Having established the purport, at least, of the order as it came to my hand, the next inquiry is, Did I proceed to execute it? And how? On these heads all the letters filed are applicable; they show, as I think, that I took measures anticipatory of the order you gave me personally on your passage up the river to the battle field; viz., to hold myself in readiness for orders to march in any direction; that my brigades were ordered to concentrate at the place most proper and convenient for a prompt execution of the orders whatever they might be, because it was at the junction of two roads, one leading to Pittsburg Landing, the other to the right of the army; to one of which points, it may be added, I was sure of being ultimately sent, if the exigencies of the battle should require the presence of my command; that after you parted from me going up the river, I took measures to forward your messenger to me instantly upon his arrival, (see Col. Ross' letter,) then rode to the place of concentration, and waited impatiently and anxiously the expected instructions; that they came to hand about 12 o'clock, (my own remembrance is 11:30, A. M.); and that the officer who brought them, also brought the news that you were driving the enemy all along the line. (See letters of Gen. Knefler and Col. Ross.) Up to that time, therefore, I certainly was blameless. But let me ask you to stop here, and consider the effect upon my mind and subsequent movements of the information, thus reliably obtained, that the battle was won. What inducement could I have had to march away from, or linger on the road to, a victory? Upon the hypothesis that the good news was true, how could I have imagined, had there been so much as a doubt as to the intent of the order received, a necessity for my command at Pittsburg Landing? But proceeding—The letters further establish that, immediately upon receiving the order, I put my column *en route* to execute it. Now come the questions, Did I take the right road to effect the junction with the right of the army? Or one leading to Purdy, away from the battle? Pertinent to these enquiries, Gen. Knefler says that the road chosen for the movement had been patrolled and piquetted by my cavalry; by their reports, if nothing else, I must have been posted as to its terminus; in corroboration of this assertion, please notice that ~~Col.~~ Gen. Macauley, Gen. Strickland, Gen. Thayer, and Gen. Knefler all allude to the fact that the head of the column was approaching, not going away from, the firing, when the countermarch took place. Consider further that ~~one of~~ the most imperative necessities of my situation, isolated as it had been from the main army, were to know all the communications with that army, and to keep them clear, and in order for rapid movement. Not only did I know the road, but every step my division took from the initial point of the march up to the moment of the change of direction, was, as is well known to every intelligent soldier in the column, a step nearer the firing, and therefore a step ~~nearer~~ toward the battle. While on this enquiry, let me add, that the report of my being set right, after marching upon the wrong road, has in it this much truth, and no more—When about a mile from the position which had been occupied by the right of the army, (Gen. Sherman's division,) Capt. Rowley overtook me, and told me that you had sent him to hurry me up, and that our lines had been carried by the enemy, and the army driven back almost to the river—a very different story from that brought me by Capt. Baxter! Capt. Rowley set me right as *to the condition of the battle*, not as to *the road I was following*. Col. McPherson and Maj. Rawlins, the other officers of your staff mentioned as having been sent to me, met me after the countermarch, when my command was on the river road, moving to Pittsburg Landing. Concerning the countermarch, I would remark that the condition of the battle, as reported by Capt. Rowley, made it prudent, if not necessary. My column was only five thousand men of all arms. Reflecting upon it now, I am still of opinion that it did better service next day in your new line of battle, than it could have done operating alone and unsupported in the rear of the whole rebel army, where I was certainly taking it when 'set right,' by the Captain. Instead of making the change of direction, when it was resolved upon, by a countermarch, the result proved that it should have been effected by a general right about. The former maneuver was chosen, however because I was confident of finding a cross road to the river road long before the head of the column doubled upon its foot (See Col. Ross' statement of the effort made to accomplish that idea.) One of the results I confidently anticipate from a reading of the letters submitted is, that you will be satisfied of the wrong done me (unintentionally, I believe) by Col. Badeau, when, in his book, he describes me as consuming seven hours in marching five miles in the direction of the battle. The march actually performed in that time was not less than fifteen miles over an execrable dirt road. Your opinion, as advanced in your letter to the War Office, July 13, 1863, that Gen. Morgan L. Smith, had he been put in command, could have had the division in the battle by 1 o'clock P. M., is, in direct terms, based upon the condition that Gen. S. received your orders as you supposed them communicated to me. But suppose he had not received the orders as originally given; suppose, on the contrary, the orders actually received by him had the effect to ~~sent~~ send him in another direction than Pittsburg Landing; and suppose that, on approaching his objective, he had found himself in the rear of the whole rebel army, and in his judgment compelled, by that circumstance, together with the bad fortune of our own army, to a further movement of quite ten miles,—all which were terrible realities in my case,—I am sure you are too just a man to have held him accountable for the hours, however precious, thus necessarily lost. With these remarks I place the letters of the officers named in your hands. They will satisfy you, I think, that the exoneration I seek will be an act of simple justice. The many misconceptions which have been attached to my movements on that bloody Sunday, have, it must be confessed, made me extremely sensitive upon the subject; you can imagine, therefore, with what anxiety your reply will be waited." ADfS and LS, *ibid*. See *PUSG*, 5, 68–70; *ibid*., 8, 59–62.

On March 23, Wallace, Crawfordsville, Ind., wrote to USG. "The friendly spirit of your letter cannot be mistaken, and I thank you for it very heartily. Only on one point have I a suggestion to make. The words 'seem to,' in the opening sentence of the second paragraph, have the effect, I fear, to make the exoneration so indefinite that, while it will not do me all the good intended, it may subject you to unfriendly criticisms. I submit, therefore, whether the words mentioned may not be stricken out. If you think not, I then submit whether it would not be better for your interests, (just at this time of paramount importance to us all,) that the publication should be withheld at least for the present. Whatever your conclusion on the point may be, I beg you to understand that, with the exception of the words quoted, your letter is in the highest degree satisfactory." ALS, USG 3.

To William Coffin

Washington, D, C, March 11th *1868*

MR. WM COFFIN,

DEAR SIR:

Your letter inclosing check for quarters rent, and receipt for taxes paid, on my house is rec'd. I think in making new lease it ought to bring the same rent it does now independent of taxes and repairs. This matter however I leave entirely to you.

Mrs. Grant and myself expected to visit Phila. about this time and to spend a week there. Complications here will prevent our doing so now.

Please present Mrs. Grant's and my compliments to to Mrs. Coffin and your daughter, and believe me,

Yours Truly

U. S. GRANT

ALS, Free Library of Philadelphia, Philadelphia, Pa. See *PUSG*, 15, 388–89.

To Andrew Johnson

Respectfully forwarded to the Presid't of the U S. for his information and instructions.

U. S. GRANT
General

HDQRS A. U S.
MARCH 13. '68.

ES, DNA, RG 94, Letters Received, C178 1868. Written on two items of correspondence forwarded by Maj. Gen. George H. Thomas, Louisville, the first a
letter from Tenn. Representative W. Bosson, March 5, to Thomas. "I write to
say, that our State is greatly exercised by the presence in many localities, of an
organised body of men, who, without provocation & in violation of Law—seemingly desperate in purpose are scouring the country by night—causing dismay &
terror to all—Our civil authorities are powerless—& terror struck themselves not
only fail to arrest, but are silent & inactive—No information is had of the number, or ultimate purpose, of the organization, It certainly is not peaceful They
overide the Law, & defy its administrators—& with consumate daring ride over
the land with menace & threats—In this extremity, what is to be done? The
public sentiment, does not only encourage, by its silence, the works of a set of
desperate men, but in many forms affords direct sympathy I am advised that it
will not be in the line of your duty, without authority, to place a military force
in the State; but I would say just that without its presence, there is iminant
danger of a bloody colision—A body of sixty mounted men last night passed my
house—with crys of 'murderer' & in her terror my wife came here to day, fearing
that I would return home & fall a victim to the threats of of these men—The assault of Saty last at Murfreesboro was unprovoked. In my address to a large meeting I studiously avoided, offensive, or inflamatory language but yet, the occasion
was sought to bring on & execute a bloody attack, on an unarmed & peaceful &
unsuspecting crowd—I remark again—the executors of the Law are panic struck,
& powerless, & the commission of crime goes unpunished & with defiant boldness
seeks new victims—What can be done?" ALS, *ibid.* The second enclosure: a
letter of Feb. 27 from E. D. Lyons, q. m. agent, Bridgeport, Ala., to Bvt. Maj.
Gen. Thomas Swords, Louisville. "I. have the honor to inform you that I. can
probaly give you information, regarding the *lawless* depredations of that *rebel*
order Known as the *Ku Klux Klan*—While investgating—at Pulaski a few days
I. obtained information—which is as follows—That in *Pulaski Tenn.* the order
is in full blast and *negroes* with white men, who chance to differ with them in
politics are subjected to severe treatment and in many cases Union men are
forced to leave. Col Harrison—has been their object for some time. And one
night, only a few days ago, (while I. was present,) they drew a revolver and had
it not been for friends being at hand, He would have been shot. What business I.
do there, is done in the night. If any information is wanted I. refer to D. A.
Welburne and E Molene, sound Union men of that City—They can give any
amont of information. They know the *ringleaders.* And let me say that the most
lawless of the *Ku Klux*—resides in the City of Pulaski, Giles, *Co* Middle *Tenn
That City is the Headquarters, of the rebel order.*" ALS, *ibid.* On March 9,

Thomas endorsed this correspondence. "Respectfully forwarded to the Adjutant General for the information of the General-in-Chief. He will see by this as he doubtless has already learned from other sources that the enemies of the present state Government in Tennessee are organizing for resistance to the laws. This resistance to the laws is an outgrowth of the rebellion and means as well oppression and hostility to everything representing patriotism, and devotion to the best interests of the country although as yet it has not taken the form of open resistance to the U. S. Government. As Tennessee is a fully constructed state I consider that the state authorities should deal with and suppress this organization of lawless desperate men and I have not to the present time considered myself authorized to take active measures against them. I shall be glad to receive any orders or instructions you may see fit to give in the premises" ES, *ibid*. On March 14, President Andrew Johnson endorsed this correspondence. "Returned to the General commanding the Army of the United States. The Constitution provides that the United States shall protect each State, 'on application of the Legislature, or of the Executive, (when the Legislature cannot be convened,) against domestic violence.' As the Legislature of Tennessee is now in session, and as no application for Federal aid has been received from that body, or any information communicated by the Governor of the State, it is not at this time deemed within the province of the Executive to give any instructions upon the subject to which these papers refer." ES, *ibid*.

On March 20, Thomas wrote to USG. "I was very much gratified to receive your letter of the 15th by yesterday's mail, although I had not for one moment supposed that the absurd rumors set afloat—no doubt to subserve the ends of those who started them—in Washington regarding my report of the condition of affairs in parts of Tennessee, had been started from your Office—Whatever may have been the object of the author of these rumors I cannot perceive that he has succeeded in disproving the facts which will be substantiated by the investigations which seems to have been inaugurated by the newspapers outside of Tennessee. If the disaffected of Tennessee will play the Divil they ought not to object to receive the reward of their labors. By an examination of Genl Carlen's Report on the affairs of the Freedmen in Tennessee for February you will be satisfied that Mr Bosson's statement is not at all exaggerated—" ALS, USG 3.

To Maj. Gen. Winfield S. Hancock and Bvt. Maj. Gen. Alvan C. Gillem

———

Washington, D, C,
March 13th 1868 [*10:00* A.M.]

MAJ. GN W. S. HANCOCK,
NEW ORLEANS, LA,
& BVT. M. G. A. C. GILLEM HOLLEY SPRINGS, MISS.[1]

The last amendatory reconstruction act is now law. It provides that majority of votes actually cast determine adoption or rejection of Constitution, also that the electors may at the same time vote for Members of Congress and all elective offices provided for by said Constitution.

U. S. GRANT

General,

ALS (telegram sent), DNA, RG 107, Telegrams Collected (Bound); telegram sent, *ibid.*; telegram received, *ibid.*, RG 393, 5th Military District, Telegrams Received; *ibid.*, 4th Military District, Telegrams Received. Copies of this telegram were sent to Bvt. Maj. Gen. Edward R. S. Canby, Charleston, and Bvt. Maj. Gen. John M. Schofield, Richmond. Telegram received, *ibid.*, 2nd Military District, Telegrams Received; *ibid.*, 1st Military District, Telegrams Received. On March 14, 1868, Canby telegraphed to USG. "Your telegram of Yesterday has been received. The election in South Carolina has been ordered for the fourteenth 14. fifteenth 15th and Sixteenth 16 of April and the provision of the law so far as present action is concerned have been embraced in the order" Telegram received (at 10:15 A.M.), *ibid.*, RG 107, Telegrams Collected (Bound); *ibid.*, RG 108, Telegrams Received; copies (one sent by mail), *ibid.*, Letters Received; (misdated March 16) *ibid.*, RG 393, 2nd Military District, Letters Sent; DLC-USG, V, 55.
On March 9, Maj. Gen. Winfield S. Hancock telegraphed to USG. "Has new Reconstruction Bill providing for Election of Members of House of Representatives and other State Officers at time of voting upon the Ratification of the Constitutions Become a Law yet. if So please Send official copy of the Law by Telegraph." Telegram received (on March 10, 10:00 A.M.), DNA, RG 107, Telegrams Collected (Bound); (on March 9, 5:35 P.M.) *ibid.*, RG 108, Telegrams Received; copies, *ibid.*, RG 393, 5th Military District, Telegrams Sent; DLC-USG, V, 55. On March 10, 9:55 A.M., USG telegraphed to Hancock. "New Reconstruction act not yet law. Send you copy by to-days mail." ALS (telegram sent), DNA, RG 107, Telegrams Collected (Bound); telegram sent, *ibid.*; telegram received, *ibid.*, RG 393, 5th Military District, Telegrams Received. On March 13, Hancock telegraphed to USG. "I am waiting for the official or authentic copy of the law before issuing an order meeting its requirements. I presume it will be received in a day or two. In election order I have announced that when the law passed further orders would issue. My order was in press when the telegraph announced that the bill was a law. I presumed it would become a law and therefore referred to it in my order" Telegram received (at 3:00 P.M.), *ibid.*, RG 107, Telegrams Collected (Bound); *ibid.*, RG 108, Telegrams Received; copies (one sent by mail), *ibid.*, Letters Received; *ibid.*, RG 393, 5th Military District, Telegrams Sent; DLC-USG, V, 55. The copy of the law arrived on March 17. Copy, DNA, RG 393, 5th Military District, Letters Received. See following telegram.

1. On Feb. 26, 10:30 A.M., USG had telegraphed to Bvt. Maj. Gen. Alvan C. Gillem, Vicksburg. "Is there an effort being made to postpone the election in Arkansas? I advise that the military do not suggest a change of time from that ordered by Convention." ALS (telegram sent), DNA, RG 107, Telegrams Collected (Bound); telegram sent, *ibid.*; telegram received (at 11:00 A.M.), *ibid.*, RG 393, 4th Military District, Letters Received. On Feb. 27, 1:00 P.M., Gillem

telegraphed to USG. "No such effort is being made. Election ordered to be given March thirteenth 13 the day designated by Convention   See General Order number seven 7 from my Head Quarters   Correct copies forwarded today"   Telegram received (on Feb. 28, 9:00 A.M.), *ibid.*, RG 107, Telegrams Collected (Bound); *ibid.*, RG 108, Telegrams Received; copies (one sent by mail), *ibid.*, Letters Received; *ibid.*, RG 393, 4th Military District, Letters and Telegrams Sent; DLC-USG, V, 55.

On March 31, 1:00 P.M., USG telegraphed to Gillem. "When returns from Ark. election are received please forward all the papers to these Hd Qrs. with your own views whether Constitution has been carried in accordance with law, but for Congress to decide should their be doubt." ALS (telegram sent), DNA, RG 107, Telegrams Collected (Bound); telegram sent, *ibid.*; telegram received (on April 2, 4:00 P.M.), *ibid.*, RG 393, 4th Military District, Letters Received. On April 4, Gillem telegraphed to USG. "Your dispatch received. The course indicated will be pursued. Full returns not yet in"   Telegram received (at 4:45 P.M.), *ibid.*, RG 107, Telegrams Collected (Bound); *ibid.*, RG 108, Telegrams Received; copies, *ibid.*, RG 393, 4th Military District, Letters and Telegrams Sent; DLC-USG, V, 55. On April 17, 12:05 P.M., USG telegraphed to Gillem. "Have you got returns from Ark. election yet?" ALS (telegram sent), DNA, RG 107, Telegrams Collected (Bound); telegram sent, *ibid.*; telegram received (on April 20, 5:00 P.M.), *ibid.*, RG 393, 4th Military District, Letters Received. On April 21 and 22, Gillem telegraphed to USG. "Despatch of seventeenth (17) received. Not all in yet. Telegraph & special messenger being used to get them. There will be no delay at my Office"   "Returns all in. Will be forwarded tomorrow"   Telegrams received (on April 21, 3:25 P.M., and April 22, 4:50 P.M.), *ibid.*, RG 107, Telegrams Collected (Bound); *ibid.*, RG 108, Telegrams Received; copies, *ibid.*, RG 393, 4th Military District, Letters and Telegrams Sent; DLC-USG, V, 55. Also on April 22, Gillem addressed a lengthy report of the election to USG. Copy, DNA, RG 393, 4th Military District, Letters and Telegrams Sent.

On May 1, USG wrote to Secretary of War Edwin M. Stanton. "I have the honor to forward herewith Gen. Gillem's report, with accompanying documents, of the election held in the State of Arkansas on the adoption of the Constitution framed by the Convention assembled in accordance with the reconstruction acts of Congress. I would respectfully request that the same be transmitted to Congress." LS, *ibid.*, RG 159, Letters Received. On May 4, USG wrote to Speaker of the House Schuyler Colfax. "I have the honor to acknowledge the receipt of resolution of the House of Representatives of the 2nd inst., directing me to communicate a statement of the number of votes cast for and against the State Constitution at the recent election in Arkansas; and in answer thereto I respectfully submit herewith Bvt. Maj. Gen. A. C. Gillem's report of said election, and accompanying documents which contain the information called for." Copies, DLC-USG, V, 47, 60; DNA, RG 108, Letters Sent. The enclosures are printed in *HED*, 40-2-278; *ibid.*, 40-3-1, III, part 1, pp. 531–36.

To Maj. Gen. Winfield S. Hancock

Washington, March 14th *1868* [*5:15* P.M.]

MAJ. GEN. W. S. HANCOCK,

NEW ORLEANS, LA,

The President directs that you report in Washington without delay. Turn over your command to the officer next in rank in your District.

U. S. GRANT

General,

ALS (telegram sent), DNA, RG 107, Telegrams Collected (Bound); telegram sent, *ibid.*; telegram received, *ibid.*, RG 393, 5th Military District, Telegrams Received. On March 14, 1868, President Andrew Johnson wrote to USG. "Referring to the application of Major General Hancock, to be relieved from the command of the Fifth Military District; I have to request that you will telegraph him to report in person at Washington, without delay." LS, *ibid.*, RG 108, Letters Received. On March 15, Maj. Gen. Winfield S. Hancock telegraphed to USG. "Your despatch received. The order will be obeyed but I desire to know if the transfer of my command to the senior officer here is a permanent one, in order to enable me to make personal arrangements before leaving. Your despatch is not clear on that point. Please reply without delay" Telegram received, *ibid.*, RG 107, Telegrams Collected (Bound); (at 11:15 A.M.) *ibid.*, RG 108, Telegrams Received; copies, DLC-USG, V, 55; (2) DLC-Andrew Johnson. On the same day, USG endorsed this telegram. "Respectfully refered to his Excellency, the President, for instructions. Enclosed herewith is a copy of despatch sent to Gen. Hancock." AES, DNA, RG 108, Telegrams Received. On the same day, Johnson endorsed this telegram. "The question referred to by General Hancock cannot be determined until he reaches Washington." ES, *ibid.* At 11:45 A.M., USG telegraphed to Hancock. "The Presidents letter to me reads substantially 'Refering to Gen. Hancock application to be relieved from the Command of the 5th District I have to request that he be ordered to report here without delay.' I will refer to the President for fuller instructions." ALS (telegram sent), *ibid.*, RG 107, Telegrams Collected (Bound); telegram sent, *ibid.*; copies, *ibid.*, RG 108, Telegrams Sent; *ibid.*, RG 393, 5th Military District, Telegrams Received; DLC-USG, V, 55; DLC-Andrew Johnson.

At 2:00 P.M., Hancock telegraphed to USG. "Your last telegram just received. Has General Buchanan been assigned as Major General as requested in his late application? I leave for Washington on the first train North." LS (telegram sent), DNA, RG 107, Telegrams Collected (Bound); telegram received (marked as sent at 3:30 P.M., received on March 16, 9:15 A.M.), *ibid.*; (on March 15, 9:15 P.M.) *ibid.*, RG 108, Telegrams Received. On March 16, 9:30 A.M., Bvt. Brig. Gen. Cyrus B. Comstock telegraphed to Hancock. "Gen. Grant directs me to say that your question as to the permanence of the transfer of your command having been referred to the President, is answered by him as follows: 'The question referred to by Gen. Hancock cannot be determined until he reaches

Washington' " ALS (telegram sent), *ibid.*, RG 107, Telegrams Collected (Bound); copies, *ibid.*, RG 108, Telegrams Sent; DLC-USG, V, 56; DLC-Andrew Johnson.

On March 21, Johnson wrote to USG. "Please furnish me with a copy, of the telegraphic correspondence which has passed between yourself and Major Gen'l Hancock since the date of my request that he be ordered to Washington." Copies (2), *ibid.* On the same day, USG wrote to Johnson. "In compliance with your direction of this date I have the honor to transmit herewith a copy of the telegraphic correspondence which has passed between Gen. Hancock and myself since the date of your request that he be ordered to Washington." LS, *ibid.* The enclosed correspondence is printed above. On the same day, Johnson wrote to USG. "Please send me the application of General Buchanan to be assigned as Major General, referred to in the telegram addressed to you by Major General Hancock under date of the 15th instant." LS, PHi. On March 23, USG wrote to Johnson. "In compliance with your communication of the 21st inst., I have the honor to send herewith copy of Gen. Buchanan's application to be assigned to duty according to his Brevet rank, and copy of Gen. Hancock's letter, referring to his endorsement thereon. The action upon Gen. Buchanan's application was not had until after the receipt of Gen. Hancock's letter. The originals of these papers were forwarded to the War Department February 15th 1868." LS, DNA, RG 94, ACP, B333 CB 1870. On the same day, Johnson endorsed this letter. "Returned to the General commanding the Army of the United States, who will please assign Genl Buchanan to duty according to his brevet rank, and notify him by telegraphic despatch." ES, *ibid.*

On Feb. 3, Bvt. Maj. Gen. Robert C. Buchanan, New Orleans, had written to Bvt. Maj. Gen. George L. Hartsuff, adjt., 5th Military District. "Having learned that Brvt: Maj. Genl J. J. Reynolds, commdg: Dist. of Texas, has been assigned to duty according to his Brevet of Major General, I respectfully request that the same assignment be made in my case. I am the senior of Genl Reynolds both by brevet and regular commission as Colonel, and under my present assignment as Brigadier General, am liable to fall under his command." LS, *ibid.* On Feb. 15, USG endorsed this letter. "Respectfully forwarded to the Secretary of War, disapproved." ES, *ibid.* On Feb. 6, Hancock wrote to the AG. "Referring to endorsement on application of Bvt Maj. Gen. Buchanan, to be assigned to duty according to his Brevet Rank of Major General, endorsed by me with a recommendation that Generals Reynolds, and Buchanan, be assigned by brevet in the same grade, the character of their duties being the same, it is proper to state that if Bvt Maj. Gen Buchanan should be assigned to duty according to his Brevet rank of Major General, he will be senior to me, unless I should also be assigned to duty according to my brevet rank." Copy, *ibid.*

On March 24, Hancock, Washington, D. C., wrote to the AG. "I desire to visit a Son at New Haven Conn. and request permission to be absent from here for a few days not exceeding four for that purpose." ALS, *ibid.*, Letters Received, 147H 1868. On the same day, USG endorsed this letter. "Respectfully refered to the President. Gen. Hancock being in this City upon the order of the President I do not feel authorized to grant this request, but recommend its approval." AES, *ibid.* On the same day, Johnson approved the request. AES, *ibid.*

To Maj. Gen. George G. Meade

Cipher   Washington, March 16th *1868* [*noon*]
MAJ. GEN. G. G. MEADE
ATLANTA, GA.

Section two of the last amendatory reconstruction act provides
the same qualifications for. voters for members of congress and the
elective officers provided for by the constitution submitted as are
prescribed for voters on the ratification of the constitution. Voters
on the ratification of the constitution cannot under the law be required to take the oath prescribed by the convention, and in my
opinion it would be in contravention of the acts of congress to require voters for congressmen and other elective officers to take it.

Section second referred to is applicable to the Florida election

U S GRANT
General.

Telegrams sent (2), DNA, RG 107, Telegrams Collected (Bound); telegram
received, Meade Papers, PHi. On March 13, 1868, 11:00 A.M., USG had telegraphed to Maj. Gen. George G. Meade. "The last amendatory reconstruction
act is now law." ALS (telegram sent), DNA, RG 107, Telegrams Collected
(Bound); telegram sent, *ibid.*; telegram received, Meade Papers, PHi. On March
14, Meade telegraphed to USG. "Georgia Convention in ordering election of
Members of Congress & State officers, after prescribing that at these elections the
qualifications for voters shall be the same as prescribed by acts of Congress for
voters on ratification, require voters to swear they will support the Constitution
submitted, and that they have not prevented or attempted to prevent any one from
voting—Is this permitted by the Law of March 12./68 which prescribes that at
these elections registered voters may vote—If permitted do you think any oath
should be required of registered voters, for officers under the Constitution which
is not required of voters on the Constitution.—" ALS (telegram sent), *ibid.*;
telegram received (at 5:00 P.M.), DNA, RG 107, Telegrams Collected (Bound);
(at 5:50 P.M.) *ibid.*, RG 108, Telegrams Received.

On March 20, Bvt. Brig. Gen. Horace Porter wrote to Meade. "Gen Grant
has received your order providing for the Georgia Constitutional election, with
which he is very much pleased. He can suggest no change in any of its provisions,
except as to the right of challenge as specified in paragraph VII as follows:
'When he offers to vote in the County where he was registered, and his name
appears upon the list of registered voters, he shall not be subject to question or
challenge, except for the purpose, of identification, or as to residence.' It appears
to him that if *any one* present at the polls is allowed to challenge, parties may
collect there, and, under pretence of exercising this right, intimidate the freedmen, delay the voting, and otherwise interfere with the election. He therefore

directs me to write to you and ask whether you do not think it would be well to confine the privilege to the judges of election, who are sworn officers of the Government, and can be held responsible for their interest." Copies, DLC-USG, V, 47, 60; DNA, RG 108, Letters Sent. On March 23, Meade wrote to Porter. "Your's of the 20th is received—The subject you refer to, the right of challenge has received my consideration—To give this right to the managers would not be fair—First because these managers *are all on one side*, and naturally biassed— Again they have not the knowledge of voters sufficient to enable them to detect fraudulent voting—In order however to meet the objections raised I have issued an explanatory order copy enclosed—from which you will see the Challenger has to swear he has cause for belief for his action & that he does not challenge simply to obstruct the election—This oath & that to the voter, will be administered verbally and will take but little time, and parties will soon find that they can not accomplish their object, if it is to delay & will give it up.—" ALS, *ibid.*, Letters Received.

To William Elrod

————

Washington, D, C,
March 17th 1868,

DEAR ELROD,

Tomorrow morning the two horses I send from here start by rail to the care of C. W. Ford of the U. S. Express Company, St. Louis. They will probably reach St Louis in about one week. One of these animals is a mare, very large and kind in all kinds of harness. I think about June you had better breed her to some large fine horse. . . . very strong. Work any place you put him, single or double, near or off side. The mare is the same. The horse strained his right hind ancle very badly over two months ago and may not be fit to work this Sumer. If he recovers entirely you will find him a superb horse and he ought to bring $1000 00 readily for his speed. He is ten years old. The mare I do not know the age of. The cost of the mare and her mate that died was $800 00.

AL (incomplete), Illinois Historical Survey, University of Illinois, Urbana, Ill.

To Lt. Gen. William T. Sherman

————

Washington, March 18th *1868*

DEAR GENERAL,

Your favor of the 16th is received. I will set for Mr. Healy any time he selects.[1] I expected to be in ~~Washington~~ Chicago before this and to see him there. Events here, (which you have been very fortunate to escape) keep me here however, and will until they terminate one way or the other.

I have written you two private letters but on reading them over I found that I had run on to the impeachment question further than I might think after awhile that I ought so tore them up. This constant jaring is getting very tedious to us who can be nothing other than victims.

Yours Truly
U. S. GRANT
General

ALS, DLC-William T. Sherman.

1. On Jan. 17, 1868, 1:00 P.M., Lt. Gen. William T. Sherman had written to USG. "Healy of Chicago wants to paint your portrait to make a picture of yourself, Mr. Lincoln and myself as we sat in the steamer at City Point. Are you willing? What shall I answer Healy?" Marie de Mare, *G. P. A. Healy: American Artist* (New York, 1954), p. 238. USG endorsed this letter. "I have sat so often for portraits that I had determined not to sit again. The object Mr. Healy has is such, however, that I may change my mind in this case, but before giving a positive answer I will see when it will be convenient for him and me both. Answer that I will reply to his dispatch soon." *Ibid.*, pp. 238–39. On May 29, 1867, Isaac N. Arnold, Chicago, had written to Sherman proposing that George P. A. Healy paint a picture of the meeting at City Point, and on Jan. 5, 1868, Healy wrote to Sherman on the subject. ALS, DLC-William T. Sherman. See also Arnold to U.S. Representative Elihu B. Washburne, Jan. 29, ALS, DLC-Elihu B. Washburne. On Jan. 13, Sherman wrote to Healy providing recollections of the meeting aboard the *River Queen*. De Mare, *Healy*, pp. 239–41.

On April 30, USG wrote to Healy. "Your favor of the 28th inst. is at hand. I shall probably not leave Washington for more than a few days at a time before the middle of June. Will give you as many sittings as you require at any time previous to that date. I will probably be able to go to ~~At~~ Annapolis to give them." ALS (facsimile), Madigan Collection, NN. USG wrote an undated note to Julia Dent Grant. "Please send me my best uniform coat and vest. I want it to have a photograph in for Healy to paint his picture from. I will take the money up to you this afternoon." ANS, USG 3.

To Charles W. Ford

———

Washington, D, C,
March 18th 1868.

DEAR FORD,

I have shipped to-day, to your care, a pair of horses to go to my farm. I have written to Elrod to call for them. Please have them taken care of when they arrive until called for.

One of these horses is one that I have driven for the last two & a half years called "Butcher Boy." He can trot inside of 3 m when he will and paces as fast as he pleases. Over two months ago, driving at night when it was dark and muddy, he strained his ancle and I fear will not recover from it for a long time. If he does recover I will have him on my farm to use when I visit there.

What is thought about impeachment out with you? My impression is that it will give peace to the country. I will be out to see you as soon as the question is settled.

Yours Truly
U. S. GRANT

ALS, DLC-USG.

To Henry Wilson

———

Washington, D. C.
March 20th 1868.

HON. HENRY WILSON,
CHAIRMAN COMMITTEE ON MILITARY AFFAIRS
U. S. SENATE.

DEAR SIR:

General Myer, Chief Signal Officer of the Army, informs me, that the appropriation for the Signal Service ($5.000), which has passed the House, in the Army Bill, has been Stricken out in the Senate Bill, as reported.

The duties of the Signal Office are unusually extensive this year: embracing the equipment and Supply of the whole Army, in which the instruction is now general, and will require more than this amount, in addition to any balance on hand.

I regard this item as for the interest of the Service; and I hope it may be retained and increased. I have regarded the original estimate as not too much.

Very respectfully,
Your obedient Servant,
U. S. GRANT,
General.

Copy, DNA, RG 46, Senate 40A–E1, Appropriations.

On Feb. 17, 1868, USG had written to U.S. Representative Elihu B. Washburne. "This will introduce to you Gn. Myer of the Signal Corps who wishes to speak to you about the matter of nonappropriation for the Signal Corps. 1 think there should have been an appropriation for one clerk at least, and some more appropriation for the support of the Corps than has been favorably reported by the Committee." ALS, NNP. On Feb. 18, Bvt. Brig. Gen. Albert J. Myer wrote to USG. "I beg to represent to you, with the view of bringing the Subject before the Committee, the necessity for the appropriation for the two Clerks in this office. . . . I judge from the 'Globe,' that this appropriation ($2800) was stricken out because there was no one in the House informed as to its necessity; and I hope the estimate may be permitted to remain. It cannot be lost without Seriously embarrassing the duties of this office under your orders. I am disposed to reduce every expenditure I can, but this is not real economy." Copies, DNA, RG 46, Senate 40A–E1, Appropriations; *ibid.*, RG 111, Letters Sent.

To Charles W. Ford

Washington, March 25th *1868*

DEAR FORD,

Enclosed I send you a slip that has just come to my notice. Please ask Lackland if he knows what it means. I supposed I had finished with White. Is it possible that he may have avoided the necessity of giving security for the amount of judgement against him by giving up possession and then taken an appeal without my, or my Counsil, knowing it?

The rail-road company promised to have the horses I sent delivered to you by Saturday evening last. I hope they have got through safely before this.[1]—Impeachment seems to be in a fare way of going through speedily. I hope it will give peace and quiet to the country.

Yours Truly,
U. S. GRANT

ALS, DLC-USG. USG enclosed a clipping. "GEN. GRANT's LAWSUIT.—In the Supreme Court yesterday, the case of U. S. GRANT *vs.* JOSEPH W. WHITE was submitted on brief. The decision will probably be rendered on Monday next. The suit is for the possession of a farm in Dent's settlement, which had been sold by Gen. GRANT to Mr. WHITE, but not fully paid for. The case first came before Justice CUNNINGHAM, and was gained by WHITE. Gen. GRANT took an appeal to Judge LORD's court, where he obtained a judgment in his favor, and WHITE took it to the Supreme Court.—*St. Louis Democrat. March 20.*" On March 25, 1868, USG telegraphed to Charles W. Ford. "I see by St. Louis paper that my suit with White was submitted to Supreme Court. Please ask Lackland if he knows anything about it." ALS (telegram sent), DNA, RG 107, Telegrams Collected (Bound). On March 30, W. H. Lackland, St. Louis, telegraphed to USG. "The case of Grant vs. White is affirmed" Telegram received (at 3:15 P.M.), *ibid.*

1. On March 24, Tuesday, Ford had telegraphed to USG. "By what route were the horses shipped and when should they be here" Telegram received (at 2:45 P.M.), *ibid.* At 3:35 P.M., USG telegraphed to Ford. "Horses were sent by Balt. & Ohio road to Cincinnati & from there to St Louis by Ohio & Miss. road. They should have reached St Louis Sunday morning" Telegram sent, *ibid.* On March 27, Ford telegraphed to USG. "The horses came yesterday Were the charges prepaid or the price agreed Answer" Telegram received (at 3:30 P.M.), *ibid.* USG drafted his reply at the foot of the telegram received. "I made no agreement for shipment of horses." ADfS, *ibid.*

To Bvt. Maj. Gen. William H. Emory

———

Washington D. C. March 26 1868

GENERAL:

Enclosed I send you a dispatch just received from Baltimore. Mr. Fulton, the writer, I do not know. It will be well probably to ask General Brooks to be on the lookout and notify you of what transpires; though I can scarcely think it possible there will be anything more than talk.

U. S. GRANT
General

To Bvt. Brig. Gen Emory
Comd.g. Dept of Washington

Copies, DLC-USG, V, 47, 60; DNA, RG 108, Letters Sent. The enclosure has not been found; eleven items of correspondence, March 12–22, 1868, involving Bvt. Maj. Gen. William H. Emory, New York City Police Superintendent John A. Kennedy, Washington, D. C., Police Superintendent A. C. Richards, and agents sent to investigate reports that armed men in Md. planned to disrupt the trial of President Andrew Johnson are in USG 3.

To Edwin M. Stanton

Washington D. C. March 27. 1868

Hon. E. M. Stanton
Sec. of War,
Sir:

Herewith I have the honor to enclose to you a report from Maj. Gen'l G. G. Meade, Comdg. 3d Mil. Dist. upon the subject of the election held in the State of Alabama for the ratification of the Constitution submitted to them. In view of action now pending in Congress looking to the admission of Alabama notwithstanding the defeat of the constitution and the clearness with which Gen. Meade has set forth all the facts connected with the election, I would recommend that his report with accompanying papers be furnished to the House of Representatives.

Gen. Meade has furnished me this report in triplicate, so that if it is deemed advisable to accept my suggestion this copy could be sent and one of the remaining copies furnished for the files of the War Department

Very respectfully
Your obt. servt
U. S. GRANT
General

Copies, DLC-USG, V, 47, 60; DNA, RG 108, Letters Sent. On March 23, 1868, Maj. Gen. George G. Meade, Atlanta, had sent to USG a lengthy report on the Ala. election with fourteen enclosures, ten subenclosures. LS, *ibid.*, RG 107, Letters Received from Bureaus; *ibid.*, RG 108, Letters Received. The report is printed as *HED*, 40-2-238.

On March 6, Meade telegraphed to USG. "Can you not send me an official or certified copy of the Supplementary Reconstruction act recently passed by Congress—I mean the one authorising election for state officers at same time that Constitution is submitted for ratification.—" ALS (telegram sent), Meade Papers, PHi; telegram received (at 7:30 P.M.), DNA, RG 108, Telegrams Received. On March 7, 3:00 P.M., USG telegraphed to Meade. "Law asked for by you sent by mail. U. S. G̶R̶A̶N̶T̶ When may your report on Ala. election be looked for?" ALS (telegram sent), *ibid.*, RG 107, Telegrams Collected (Bound); telegram sent, *ibid.*; telegram received, Meade Papers, PHi. See telegram to Maj. Gen. George G. Meade, March 16, 1868.

On March 9, 3:30 P.M., USG telegraphed to Meade. "Telegraph me the number of votes cast for C̶o̶n̶v̶e̶n̶t̶i̶o̶n̶ Constitution, the number against, and the total number registered. Resolution of Congress calls on me for this information." ALS (telegram sent), DNA, RG 107, Telegrams Collected (Bound); telegram sent, *ibid.*; telegram received, Meade Papers, PHi. At 11:45 P.M., Meade telegraphed to USG. "I have only today received report on Alabama election—Vote for constitution 70,812—against it—1,005.—Total vote cast 71,817. Total vote cast for Convention 91,808.—White vote for constitution 6.702—Do for Convention 18,553.—Vote on constitution lacks for ratification 13,550.—Out of 62 counties Twenty voted four days—Thirteen voted two days, and Two had no election—the balance Twenty seven voted Five days.—I am satisfied the constitution was lost on its merits, and I think the best thing to do, would be for Congress to reassemble the convention to revise the constitution & then resubmit it to the people under the new law giving a majority of votes cast the power to ratify.—I do not see much use in re-opening the polls as I proposed as there is no possibility the votes that would be cast affecting the result—As soon as I can get away from here I shall go to Montgomery to decide this question In the mean time, as soon as I can have prepared the data, I will send you a report, shewing the election as it took place this will require perhaps a week.—" ALS (telegram sent), *ibid.*; telegram received (on March 10, 7:00 P.M.), DNA, RG 107, Telegrams Collected (Bound); *ibid.*, RG 108, Telegrams Received. On March 10, Meade telegraphed to USG. "I telegraphed yesterday the result of Alabama election—By adding the amt—vote on constitution fails of ratification, to that vote, & doubling you will get amount of registered votes—viz one hundred & ninety thousand Seven hundred and thirty four—but I should explain that this amount is partly estimated as some of the counties had not all sent in their revised registration—Again this amount includes registration in those counties where no election was held which ought not in my judgement to be included— All these points I will give you when my written report goes on—I telegraphed yesterday only the substance of Haydens report.—" ALS (telegram sent), Meade Papers, PHi; telegram received (at 5:00 P.M.), DNA, RG 107, Telegrams Collected (Bound); (at 7:00 P.M.) *ibid.*, RG 108, Telegrams Received. On March 11, USG wrote to Speaker of the House Schuyler Colfax. "In compliance with resolution of the House of Representatives, of March 9th 1868, I have the honor to state that Gen. Meade reports the total number of votes cast under the reconstruction laws up to the present time for the adoption of the constitution for the

State of Alabama to be 70.812 Against its adoption [*1,005*]—" LS, *ibid.*, RG
233, 40A–F29.8. On March 12, Meade telegraphed to USG. "Alabama election
Returns shew that the vote on Governor is Eleven hundred and eighty six 1186
less than vote on Constitution and vote on Probate Judges is Seven hundred and
forty two 742 less than vote for Constitution. I send these because it has been
charged that gross frauds were perpetrated, in mutilating the tickets of colored
men by tearing off the vote on the Constitution, & it was predicted that the vote
for Probate Judges would exceed the vote on the Constitution by many thousands. I am of the opinion that most of the charges of extensive frauds will prove
as illusory as the above—There were undoubtedly irregularities in the election
sufficient to justify its being set aside as recommended, and I believe a more
liberal constitution would command a majority of votes—In this state & Florida
where the constitutions do not go beyond the requirements of Congress but fully
comply with them—there seems to be no doubt among all parties but that the
people will ratify them by large majorities.—The Georgia Convention adjourned
yesterday & the election for ratification will be held on the Twentyeth (20)
proximo.—" ALS (telegram sent), Meade Papers, PHi; telegram received (misdated March 13, received at 3:30 P.M.), DNA, RG 107, Telegrams Collected
(Bound); *ibid.*, RG 108, Telegrams Received.

On April 29, Meade endorsed papers concerning the readmission of Ala.
"Respectfully forwarded to the General in Chief for his information and action,
and inviting his attention to the views expressed in my report on the Alabama
election. The bill recently passed by the House of Representatives meets with my
approval, inasmuch as it submits the Constitution to the revision of the legislature
and subsequently enables the people to vote on it under the new law.—I should
have preferred a new election for officers under it because I am satisfied that
many of those recently elected, are not judicious nominations and can not qualify
by giving bonds &c. Whenever it has been necessary to remove any officer I
have appointed the person elected on being satisfied there was no objection to
him personally but I have not made a sweeping change as urged upon me, awaiting
action on the part of Congress." ES, *ibid.*, RG 94, Letters Received, 535M 1868.
On May 1, USG endorsed these papers. "Respectfully forwarded to the Secretary
of War, with recommendation that these papers be transmitted to Congress." ES,
ibid.

On May 27, Meade wrote to USG. "I have the honor to transmit, herewith
enclosed, a copy of the report of the Superintendent of Registration for Alabama,
relative to the election held in that State, and which I desire should be considered
as part of my report of March 23rd 1868. The Superintendents report was not
received at these Head Quarters until quite recently; hence the delay in forwarding
it." Copy, Meade Papers, PHi. On June 1, USG wrote to Secretary of War John
M. Schofield. "I have the honor to forward herewith copy of report from General
Meade, Commanding 3d Military District, relative to the election in Alabama,
which the General requests may be made a part of his report on the same subject,
transmitted to the Hon. Secretary of War from these Headquarters, ~~May~~ March
27, 1868. If said report has been furnished the House of Representatives, it is
recommended that this also be sent, to be made a part of it." Copies, DLC-USG,
V, 47, 60; DNA, RG 108, Letters Sent. See *HED*, 40-2-303.

To Andrew Johnson

Washington, D, C, March 28th *1868*,

HIS EXCELLENCY, A. JOHNSON,
PRESIDENT OF THE UNITED STATES;
SIR;

I have the honor to acknowledge the receipt of your direction of the 27th inst. to relieve Maj. Gen. W. S. Hancock from the command of the 5th Mil. Dist. and to assign him to the command of the Mil. Division of the Atlantic. These directions indicate no successor to Gen. Hancock to command the 5th Dist. and as the law of Congress creating these Districts require that they should be commanded by Army officers of rank not less than Brigadier General, I respectfully ask who shall be named in the order to relieve Gen. Hancock.

Very respectfully
Your obt. svt.
U. S. GRANT
General,

ALS, DLC-Andrew Johnson. On March 27, 1868, President Andrew Johnson had written to USG. "You will please issue an order relieving Major General Winfield S. Hancock from the command of the Fifth Military District, and assigning him to the command of the Military Division of the Atlantic" LS, DNA, RG 94, Letters Received, 145P 1868. USG endorsed this letter. "By direction of the President of the United States Maj. Gn. W. S. Hancock is hereby relieved from the Command of the 5th Military District, and assigned to the Command of the Mil. Div. of the Atlantic, created by Gn. Orders No 10 of Feb.y 12th 1868. . . . Issue above order and circulate without delay, furnishing Copy to the President." AE, *ibid*. On March 28, Bvt. Maj. Gen. Edward D. Townsend issued General Orders No. 17, virtually repeating USG's words. Copy, *ibid*.

On March 28, Johnson wrote to USG. "I am in receipt of your communication of this date, in which reference is made to my letter of the 27th inst., and instructions requested as to the designation of an officer to succeed Major Genl. Hancock in the command of the Fifth Military District. Until further orders, the duties of commander can be discharged by Brevet Major General Buchanan, who I understand is the senior officer in the Fifth District. He has been assigned to duty according to his brevet rank, and is therefore 'not below the rank of Brigadier General'—thus fulfilling the requirement of the second section of the act of Congress passed March 2d, 1867. If in your opinion, however, such a designation is not in accordance with a proper construction of the law, I would be pleased to receive any suggestions you may deem proper to submit upon the subject." LS, *ibid*., RG 108, Letters Received.

To Maj. Gen. Philip H. Sheridan

Private   March 31st *1868*
MY DEAR GENERAL,

Enclosed I send you further statements in the Van Hook matter. I find I was wrong in my statement that the debt was created to furnish Dunn with a start, but it will be proper I think to let some one investigate the matter and advise whether Dunn should be turned out or not. Let Forsythe, or some member of your staff take the papers and make such recommendation as he thinks proper.

Impeachment seems to grow in popularity, and indications are that the trial will not be protracted. I know when removal takes place, as every one seems to think it will, there will be a great desire to send you back to New Orleans to complete the work which you commenced so well. If this arrangement is greatly against your will write to me in advance so that I may aid you. I confess that I would like to see you there for a while, but at the same time feel that you can do substantial good where you are.

Yours Truly
U. S. GRANT

ALS, DLC-Philip H. Sheridan. On April 12, 1868, Maj. Gen. Philip H. Sheridan, Fort Leavenworth, wrote to USG. "On my return from a trip with the Indian Commission as far as Cheyenne, I found your letter of March 31st. I will have the matter of Dunn investigated at once, & will report the result. In reference to my assignment to duty in the 5th Militry. District, I will make no objections if you desire me to go. I might be able to help along that which I consider of great importance to the safety of the country, & of every officer, prominent in suppessing the rebellion—It would be hard for us to have to apply for pardon to those who attempted to destroy the goverment, & such will be the case should they again get into power. I would not like to remain longer in New Orleans than next winter I have been there the last three consecutive summers, & with much peril from cholera, & yellow fever the coming one would be my 4th but I am always willing, satisfied, & happy, to be of service under your directions— Under them this world has been a good world to me, & I will strive hard not to disappoint you." ALS, USG 3. On April 30, Sheridan wrote to USG. "I have the honor to forward a report of the affairs of Dunn, sutler at this Post agreeable to the request made in your letter to me of March 31st There has been some delay in forwarding this report from my being absent on the frontier when your letter was received and again being absent when the investigation and report was made." Copy, DLC-Philip H. Sheridan.

On March 13, Sheridan had telegraphed to USG. "Mr Dunn, Sutler at this Post, declines to pay the claim of Mr Van Hook." Telegram received (at 4:20 P.M.), DNA, RG 107, Telegrams Collected (Bound); copies (2), DLC-Philip H. Sheridan. On the same day, Michael L. Dunn, Fort Leavenworth, telegraphed to USG. "I have seen General Sheridan. I can explain. Please await my letter of this date" Telegram received (at 4:20 P.M.), DNA, RG 107, Telegrams Collected (Bound). See *PUSG*, 16, 169, 430–33.

To Maj. Gen. George G. Meade

(Cipher)   Washington, Apl. 2d *1868* [*11:00* A.M.]
MAJ. GN. G. G. MEADE,
ATLANTA GA.

I suggest that the murder of Dr. Ashburton, in Columbus Ga. be investigated ~~promptly~~ and justice be meeted out promptly by Military Commission if the Civil Courts cannot be relied on.

U. S. GRANT
General

ALS (telegram sent), DNA, RG 107, Telegrams Collected (Bound); telegram sent, *ibid.*; telegram received, Meade Papers, PHi. On April 3, 1868, Maj. Gen. George G. Meade telegraphed to USG. "I have just returned from Florida & find your despatch in relation to the murder of Mr. Ashburne—Capt—Mills Comdr at Columbus reports he is doing every thing in co-operation with the civil authorities, to detect & arrest the murderers and if any are caught I intend trying them by military commission—" ALS (telegram sent), *ibid.*; telegram received (at 8:35 P.M.), DNA, RG 107, Telegrams Collected (Bound); (at 8:45 P.M.) *ibid.*, RG 108, Telegrams Received.

On April 4, Meade wrote to USG. "You have been advised of the assassination of Mr. G. A. Ashburn recently a member of the Constitutional Convention of this state—The event took place during my absence in Florida, but the Asst—Adj—Genl—at Hd Qrs immediately sent instructions to the Comdg officer at Columbus to use every means within his power to discover & arrest the guilty parties—I transmit herewith the reports received to date, by which you will see that the military & civil authorities are harmoniously co-operating to detect the criminals who if arrested will be promptly brought to trial before a military commission—I regret to report that within the last ten days, a spirit of disorder & violence has manifested itself in both this state & Alabama—Anonymous placards & letters threatening the lives & property of union citizens have been circulated— the assassination of Mr Ashburn is the first murder—tho there have been reported several cases of lynching—I have thought proper to issue a stringent order, a copy of which is enclosed and I shall execute it promptly as far as the forces under my command will admit, but I deem it proper to make known, that if this evil is carried to the extent, to which appearances now indicate—that the force is in this

District is inadequate to its suppression, and that it will be absolutely necessary, that a larger military force be given me, if it is expected that I am to protect life & property in the whole District—On this point I would call your attention the fact, that whilst I command the largest District geographically, I have the smallest force to enforce law & order—So long as the moral power of the Govt was respected, I had sufficient force—but if it becomes necessary to use *physical* force my command must be increased to enable me to occupy all parts of the states enforce my orders & compel submission I have this day telegraphed you on this point & desire this communication to be considered in connection with this telegram.—" ALS, *ibid.*, Letters Received. The enclosures are *ibid.* Also on April 4, Meade telegraphed to USG. "There are unmistakeable signs of disorder in this state & Alabama from secret organisations, such as have disturbed Tennessee I am about issueing a very stringent order and shall take very summary measures to check this evil if practicable, but the force under my command is insufficient to control all parts of these states, and in view of the approaching elections, I would be much relieved, if the forces here could be temporarily increased—say an additional regiment for two months—The moral effect of reinforcements would be very great, besides the actual benefit of additional forces—The people are becoming alarmed—the negroes getting excited & threatening retaliation, and affairs within the last ten days assuming a serious aspect The object seems to be to drive obnoxious men out of the country & intimidate voters.—. . . If you can not spare a regiment—any companies you could send will be of great value.—" ALS (telegram sent), Meade Papers, PHi; telegram received (marked as sent on April 5, received on April 6, 9:00 A.M.), DNA, RG 107, Telegrams Collected (Bound); (marked as sent on April 5, received at 9:00 P.M.) *ibid.*, RG 108, Telegrams Received. See telegram to Maj. Gen. George G. Meade, April 7, 1868.

On April 6, 10:30 A.M., USG telegraphed to Maj. Gen. George H. Thomas, Louisville. "Can you send four Companies to report to Gn. Meade, Answer." ALS (telegram sent), DNA, RG 107, Telegrams Collected (Bound); telegram sent, *ibid.*; copies, *ibid.*, RG 108, Telegrams Sent; (misdated March 6) DLC-USG, V, 56. On the same day, Thomas telegraphed to USG. "Can spare temporarily, one Company from Paducah, one from Humboldt, one from ~~Vinton~~ Memphis and one from Nashville" Telegram received (at 4:10 P.M.), DNA, RG 107, Telegrams Collected (Bound); (at 4:30 P.M.) *ibid.*, RG 108, Telegrams Received; copies (one sent by mail), *ibid.*, Letters Received; DLC-USG, V, 55. On April 7, 9:30 A.M., Bvt. Brig. Gen. Cyrus B. Comstock telegraphed to Thomas. "Gen. Grant wishes you to send the four companies spoken of in your despatch of yesterday, temporarily to Gen. Meade, who will inform you where he wants them." ALS (telegram sent), DNA, RG 107, Telegrams Collected (Bound); telegram sent, *ibid.*; copies, *ibid.*, RG 108, Telegrams Sent; DLC-USG, V, 56. At 10:00 A.M., Comstock telegraphed to Meade. "Gen. Thomas will send you temporarily four companies of infantry, ~~one~~ from Paducah, Humboldt, Vinton Memphis & Nashville, respectively. Gen Grant wishes you to telegraph Gen. Thomas where to send them." ALS (telegram sent), DNA, RG 107, Telegrams Collected (Bound); telegram sent, *ibid.*; telegram received, Meade Papers, PHi.

On April 6, 10:30 A.M., USG telegraphed to Bvt. Maj. Gen. Alvan C. Gillem, Vicksburg. "Can you not send a regiment or battalion from Ark. to report to Gn. Meade." ALS (telegram sent), DNA, RG 107, Telegrams Collected (Bound); telegram sent, *ibid.*; copies, *ibid.*, RG 108, Telegrams Sent; DLC-USG, V, 56. On April 10, Gillem telegraphed to USG. "Your despatch received today. I can send four (4) companies and a field officer of the nineteenth (19) Infantry Where shall they report." Telegram received (at 4:35 P.M.), DNA, RG 107, Telegrams Collected (Bound); *ibid.*, RG 108, Telegrams Received; copy, DLC-USG, V, 55. At 10:00 A.M., USG telegraphed to Gillem. "Gen. Meade will inform you where to send troops." ALS (telegram sent), DNA, RG 107, Telegrams Collected (Bound); telegram sent, *ibid.*; copies, *ibid.*, RG 108, Telegrams Sent; DLC-USG, V, 56. At the same time, USG telegraphed to Meade. "Gen. Gillem can send you four Companies. Inform him by telegraph where to send them." ALS (telegram sent), DNA, RG 107, Telegrams Collected (Bound); telegram sent (marked as sent at 10:00 P.M.), *ibid.*; telegram received, Meade Papers, PHi. On April 11, Meade telegraphed to USG. "Have requested Genl Gillem to send companies at once to this place—These with those from Thomas will answer all purposes so far as can be anticipated—Matters have become, in appearance— much quieter since issueing general orders number fifty one.—" ALS (telegram sent), *ibid.*; telegram received (on April 12, 10:00 A.M.), DNA, RG 107, Telegrams Collected (Bound); (on April 11, 7:15 P.M.) *ibid.*, RG 108, Telegrams Received. On April 13, Gillem telegraphed to USG. "Your dispatch of the tenth (10) reads G. H. Thomas. Was it so intended" Telegram received (at 4:30 P.M.), *ibid.*, RG 107, Telegrams Collected (Bound). At 6:52 P.M., USG drafted his response at the foot of the telegram received. "My dispatch should read Gn. Meade." ADfS, *ibid.*; telegram sent, *ibid.* On April 20, Gillem wrote to USG. "A few days since I received a Telegram from you asking, whether I could not send 'a Regiment or Battalion from Arkansas to Genl Meade,' and in reply I informed you that I could spare four Companies of the 19 Inf. The day after the receipt of your dispatch I received one from Genl Meade informing me that you had notified him that I would send four companies to him—and further stating that he should not require them longer than the end of the month (April) and requesting that they might be sent as soon as practicable—Perceiving at once that to delay until the troops could arrive from Arkansas, would be to render them useless for the service required by Genl Meade—I ~~therefore~~ at once ordered the Garrisons at Holly Springs (2 comps 34 Inf) & at Corinth (2 comps 34 Inf) to proceed to Atlanta. I consider this explanation necessary, in view of the fact that I changed the troops which I intended to send, and which you had been notified would be sent. This communication is ~~d~~ sent to you direct, on account of yours having been transmitted in *cypher* and regarded as confidential. The election returns from Arkansas are not all in, and the vote is so close that the result can not be predicted—Fraud is charged by both parties. so soon as the returns are all in—All the papers will be forwarded for the action of the proper authorities. The Mississippi Convention will I think adjourn by the 1st of May. I have Telegraphed—and sent special Messengers for missing election returns from Arkansas. Everything perfectly quiet in Miss. and Arkansas." ALS, *ibid.*, RG 108, Letters Received.

On April 6, Bvt. Maj. Gen. Robert C. Buchanan, New Orleans, telegraphed to USG. "It is of great importance that I be permitted to retain three companies belonging to Third Military District until after the election in Louisiana which occurs on the seventeenth (17th) and eighteenth (18th) instants. I will return them immediately afterwards. If they cannot be so retained by me, Please notify me" Telegram received (marked as sent on April 7, received on April 8, 9:15 A.M.), *ibid.*, RG 107, Telegrams Collected (Bound); *ibid.*, RG 108, Telegrams Received; copy, DLC-USG, V, 55. On April 8, 10:10 A.M., Bvt. Maj. Gen. John

A. Rawlins telegraphed to Buchanan. "You are authorized to retain the three companies belonging to third (3d) district until after Louisiana election" Telegrams sent (2), DNA, RG 107, Telegrams Collected (Bound); copies, *ibid.*, RG 108, Telegrams Sent; DLC-USG, V, 56.

To William Elrod

Washington, D. C., Apl. 2d *1868*

DEAR ELROD,

I believe I mentioned it to you before, but lest I may not of done so now mention it again that I want all my mares put to a blooded horse. Legal Tender will be a good horse. The last mare I sent out, from a blooded horse, should raise the finest kind of carriage horses. The three mares from here, with those you have, will give you a good start. Brood mares will not do for heavy work but they will do all the light. These I send from here I shall never wish to have hitched to a load. They will do to go to a light market wagon and such work as that. In a year I will probably have my own horse to breed from. Put the mares early.

Yours
U. S. GRANT

ALS, Illinois Historical Survey, University of Illinois, Urbana, Ill.

To John Sartain

Washington, D, C, Apl. 2d *1868*

JOHN SARTAIN, ESQ,
DEAR SIR:

Your favor of the 26th of March, asking for the portraits of myself and family, by Cogswell, to put in the Academy of Art, Philadelphia, during the approaching exhibition, was duly received. I owe you an apology for not responding earlyer. Your letter does not contain the name of the Guilder, or Artist, who was to put up the picture for shipment, and I have forgotten the name which was in some other letter on the same subject, which I cannot now find. If you will telegraph me the name I will attend to the matter at once. I sent a note to Mr. Cogswell this morning requesting him to select some one to pack the picture for shipment but have received no reply from him whether he can do it or not.—It affords me pleasure to respond to any request from the Citizens of Philadelphia to whom I am under so many obligations.

> With great respect,
> your obt. svt.
> U. S. GRANT

ALS, ICarbS. On April 3, 1868, John Sartain, Philadelphia, telegraphed to USG. "The Academy has arranged with Cogswell to select the Gilder" Telegram received (at 1:30 P.M.), DNA, RG 107, Telegrams Collected (Bound). Sartain, born in London, became a prominent engraver in Philadelphia. William Cogswell's 1867 painting of the Grant family, now in the National Portrait Gallery, Smithsonian Institution, is reproduced in color in *Gateway Heritage*, 6, 3 (Winter, 1985–86), p. 20.

To Bvt. Maj. Gen. John M. Schofield

Washington, April 3d *1868*

BT. MAJ. GEN. J. M. SCHOFIELD
COMDG. 1ST MILTY DISTRICT
GENERAL:

I have the honor to acknowledge the receipt of your letter of the 2d inst., enclosing your G. O. No. 33 and draft of G O No. —. I have carefully read them and in reply would say: That I approve of G O 33 and concur fully with the views expressed by you respecting the importance of appointing to offices the most respectable and competent persons that can be found, who at the same time can take the test-oath required by the Acts of Congress and will not retard the restoration of the State to its proper relations with the Government under the reconstruction acts.

Without discussing your authority to make removals, I would suggest that no removals be made "except for cause" until Order 33

be fully executed. From the effect and influence that order may
have, you will be enabled better to judge of the expediency of further removals and appointments, and also as to whether they are required to a proper administration of the reconstruction acts "to the
end that all the intents thereof may be fully and perfectly carried
out."

As to the removal of Gov. Pierpoint[1] and appointment of Gen.
Wells to his place, I would simply say that in that matter you must
be the judge. The form of order you propose issuing is a good one,
and if issued, from any information I now have, will not be interfered with by me.

From my limited acquaintance with the people of Virginia, I
know no one who would probably accept the office that I would
sooner name than Gen. Wells to succeed Gov. Pierpoint in case of
his removal.

> Very respectfully
> Your obed't serv't
> U. S. GRANT
> General.

LS, DLC-John M. Schofield. On April 2, 1868, Bvt. Maj. Gen. John M. Schofield,
Richmond, had written to USG. "I have the honor to invite your special attention
to an order issued on the 30th of March, of which I enclose a copy, providing for
appointment of officers to fill vacancies caused by expiration of terms of service.
I have endeavored to make it accord with what I believe to be a fair and just
construction of the Acts of Congress, but am well aware that it falls short of the
wishes of many of the friends of the congressional measures in Virginia. I have
heretofore carried out the requirements of sections *Two* and *Four* of the Act of
July 19th 1867 in all cases where evidence could be obtained sufficient to justify
action acording to the terms of the law. In the belief that only a short time would
probably elapse after the expiration of terms of elective offices before an election
could be properly held I at first determined to permit elective officers to hold over,
as an authorized by the State law, except in cases where their removal is required
by the Acts of Congress, and thus avoid the attempt to do what seems almost
impossible, Viz:—to find competent persons, who can take the test oath, to fill all
offices. The fact that a very large proportion of those who are competent to fill
important offices and can take the oath are quite as objectionable to the radical
party as persons who can not take that oath, also adds greatly to the embarassment. The fact is the Congressional Oath is now no test of loyalty whatever—No
matter by what *present* standard the word loyalty may be interpreted, and hence
displacing disfranchised officers and appointing in their stead persons who can
take the oath, although it may be in strict conformity to the law, does not necessarily satisfy anybody except the persons appointed. There are many important

offices in the State now held by disfranchised persons whose terms of service have not expired. They are, in general, the offices most desired by the radical party, and I am strongly importuned to remove the present incumbents and appoint other persons who have been recommended to me. Some such offices could be filled by persons well qualified in all respects, but the majority of them, in my opinion, could not. Section 2 of the Act of July 19th 1867, gives power to 'the Commander of any district' . . . *'Whenever in the opinion of such Commander the proper administration of said act shall require it'* to suspend or remove from office, &c. and Section 4 of the same Act makes it his *duty* to remove, &c for certain specified causes. I understand that it is not only not my duty, but that *I have not the power* to remove from office except where the reasons exist which are specified in the Acts of Congress, and which I have above quoted or referred to. It must often be a question of opinion, upon which people will differ according to their political views and interests, and the point of view from which their opinions are formed, whether in any particular case 'the proper administration of said acts.' requires the removal of an officer. There are two important and distinct objects to be accomplished by the proper administration of the Acts of Congress. One is good government under the provisional system, and the other the formation of a loyal State government for restoration to the union. Unfortunately it is often difficult, if not impossible, to secure the efficient coöperation toward the accomplishment of both these objects. The men who are most zealous in their support of colored suffrage and most clamorous for office, although they have acquired a very extended influence over the colored voters are in many cases entirely unfit for the offices they aspire to. It is my intention, as a rule to appoint republicans in all cases where respectable and competent persons of that party can be found. This will be but just to all parties from the fact that most of the offices are now held by 'Conservatives.' If by this course I incidentally give additional strength and influence to respectable republicans as against the lower class of men who have acquired control over the mass of colored voters, I am sure I shall thereby render the country an important service and not be justly subject to the charge of partizanship. I would be glad to have your opinion and advice as to whether I have power, and whether it is expedient, to go further than my order of March 30th proposes, and remove all disfranchised officers whose terms of service have not expired. Meanwhile I shall have as much as I can possibly attend to in carrying out what I have proposed. There is one case of special importance under my late order, upon which I respectfully request your advice,—That is of Governor Pierpoint. He has been holding over since the first of January under the very doubtful authority derived from the old Constitution, which says 'Judges and all other officers whether elected or appointed shall continue to discharge the duties of their offices after their terms of service have expired, until their successors are qualified.' The Constitution of Virginia has always made the Governor ineligible to the same office for term next succeeding that for which he was elected.' The Convention now in session has retained that clause in the Constitution they are framing. However little binding force the old constitution may have upon my action the general *principle* of which the clause above quoted is but the expression, is an exceedingly wise and salutary one, as is well illustrated in this particular instance. Governor Pierpoint is holding over and using his official position for no other apparent purpose than to secure his renomination and election to the same office, for which it is no secret he is a candidate, and that in spite of the constitutional prohibition I have quoted. I do not hesitate to say that Govr Pierpoint has by his official conduct and influence, though of course unintentionally, done more to prevent the proper execution of the acts of Congress than all the disfranchised office-holders in Virginia combined. If the Governor were still serving out his constitutional term I would hesitate, for obvious reasons, to remove him. But as his term has expired I am convinced it is my duty to appoint a successor who is eligible under the laws of the State as well as under the Acts of Congress, who will be more acceptable to the people, and who can and will aid me, instead of being a dead weight, or worse, in the work of reconstruction. After consultation with a number of leading republicans, I have selected Genl H. H. Wells of Alexandria, who is I believe known to you personally, and unless otherwise advised by you, intend to appoint him in a few days. I will of course cheerfully follow your advice in the matter without the official order which the law empowers you to make in all such cases. I do not wish this letter to be regarded as official, or made public, especially the portion of it relating to Governor Pierpoint, unless the propriety of my action be hereafter officially questioned, when I shall be prepared to justify it. . . . Note: —I propose to announce the change in the Executive in the following form—General Orders No   The Office of Governor of Virginia having become vacant by expiration of the term of service of His Excellency Francis H. Pierpoint, and the Governor being 'ineligible to the same office for the term next succeeding that for which he was elected,' His Excellency _____ _____ has this day been appointed Provisional Governor of Virginia and will be obeyed and respected accordingly. By Command &c   This will avoid giving ground for the pretext that I have removed the Governor from office." LS, DNA, RG 108, Letters Received.

On March 20, Bvt. Lt. Col. George K. Leet wrote to Bvt. Brig. Gen. Orville E. Babcock. "You will proceed without delay to Richmond, Va. under the orders verbally communicated to you by the Gen. of the Army. Upon the completion of this duty you will rejoin these Headquarters." Copies, DLC-USG, V, 47, 60; DNA, RG 108, Letters Sent. On March 21, Babcock, Richmond, telegraphed to USG. "I shall return tonight. I have a letter with me, relating to special tax, from General Schofield" Telegram received (at 7:25 P.M.), *ibid.*, RG 107, Telegrams Collected (Bound). On the same day, Schofield wrote to USG. "In compliance with the request of a Committee of the Virginia Constitutional Convention, I have the honor to invite your attention to the following facts, in order that you may take such action in the premises as you may deem expedient—The Act of Congress, passed March 23rd 1867, authorized the Convention to assemble in each of the ten 'rebel states', to levy and collect a special tax to defray their expenses—Subsequent to the passage of that Act, the Virginia legislature provided, in the regular tax bill of that year, for the collection of one hundred thousand dollars for the same purpose—When the Virginia Convention assembled, I ordered its expenses to be paid out of the Treasury, from the money collected under the Act of Assembly, for the purspose, as stated at the time, of saving the people the burden of a special tax, and collection of the same, in a time of general depression—Under my order, the whole sum of one hundred thousand dollars has been paid to, and expended by, the Convention, and now they have passed an Ordinance directing the levy and collection of a special tax to the amount of about one hundred thousand dollars, and have appointed a committee to negociate a loan of ninety thousand dollars, for the use of the convention, to be reimbursed from the proceeds of this special tax—The Act of Congress of March 23rd does not limit the Amount of tax which the convention may levy, and hence they may go on levying and collecting as long as the people can be forced to pay, and borrow money on the credit of the unlimited Authority given them by Congress, as long as any one can be found to loan them money—The sums already expended ought to have been ample,—more than was necessary, to defray all their expenses; And having accepted that sum from the treasury, they ought, in my opinion, to be debarred from the exercise of the Authority given them by Congress to levy and collect a special tax—I have been requested by the committee upon this subject to sign the ordinance passed March 18th 'Providing additional means to pay the expenses of the Convention', upon which approval by me it is expected that a loan may be negociated, and the Committee further desire to know whether in the event of their failure to negociate a loan, I will be willing to sign an ordinance, making certificates issued in payment of expenses of the Convention receivable in payment of taxes and other liabilities due the State of Virginia—I have suggested to the Committee of the Convention, that the members ought to be content with certificates of indebtedness, to be paid after the ratification by the people of the Constitution they are framing—If the work of the Convention be satisfactory to the people, and be ratified by them, the extra expense may not be seriously objectionable—If on the contrary the Convention fail to make a Constitution which the people will ratify, it seems to me they have already been paid quite enough for such services—Not being able, consistently with my sense of duty, to comply with the wishes of the Convention, I have consented upon the request of the Committee to refer the matter to you, for such action as you may deem expedient—I have the honor to enclose herewith all correspondence had with the Convention on this subject—" LS, USG 3. The enclosures are *ibid.*

On March 27, Schofield wrote to Babcock. "I have determined, in accordance with the General's advice, to arrange for payment of the Convention up to April 6th, and am negociating a loan for that purpose. This I can manage very well if Congress will appropriate the money to pay the cost of vote on the Constitution and registration preceding it. I have today written a letter to the Adjutant General on this subject Please ask General Grant to give it a favorable consideration In addition to the money necessary for the Convention, which will be about $50,000, I will have to borrow in a few days $.50,000 more to meet interest on state debt and other liabilities. This will be about all we can carry. So that unless Congress gives the appropriation asked for I shall be very much embarrassed to raise money to pay my registering officers &c—Please let me know what the General thinks about it." ALS, *ibid.* On March 31, Babcock wrote to Schofield. "Your letter of the 27th reached me this morning. I have submitted it to Genl Grant who directs me to inform you that he will assist you in securing ~~any~~ the appropriation you ~~may~~ wish for the First Mil Dist. Genl Hancock is to day assigned to the Mil Div of the Atlantic Head Qrs here. No one named by the President for the 5th Mil Dist." Copy, *ibid.*

On April 18, Schofield twice wrote to USG. "I have the honor to forward herewith a copy of the Constitution framed by the Virginia Convention which adjourned yesterday, and a copy of the Ordinance providing for submitting that constitution to the people for ratification or rejection, on the 2d of June next, and for election of officers at the same time. On the 13th of March last I sent to the Convention a communication, a copy of which I enclose herewith, asking an appropriation to defray the expenses of the anticipated election. The Convention failed to take any action on the subject. As you are aware I sent to Washington on the 8th of Jany. last an estimate of funds for the same purpose, and again on the 27th of March asked attention to that estimate, and requested an appropriation by Congress; basing that request upon the large and unexpected increase of

expenses of the Convention arising from the prolongation of its session. I am informed that my estimate has been laid before Congress, but that no appropriation
has yet been made. There is at this time no money in the state Treasury to defray the expenses of an election, and there will not be any for a long time unless
it be taken from funds collected and needed to meet other liabilities of the state.
This I do not feel authorized to do. I must, therefore, postpone ordering an election, or revision of registration, until Congress makes the necessary appropriation. There is ample time for Congress to act upon my application before it will
be necessary to issue my order, even if the election take place at the time indicated by the Convention, June 2d, and I suppose a later day could be substituted
if the action of Congress were delayed. Fortunately, the Constitution which it is
proposed to submit to the people of Virginia having been framed, Congress will
know, in making the appropriation, exactly for what it is made. I shall regard
the action, or failure to act, of Congress as indicating my duty in this matter."
"Unofficial . . . In spite of every effort that could be made to prevent it, the Va.
Convention has adhered to its proscriptive measures, or rather to the most objectionable of them. After every other means had failed, I even went so far as to
visit the Convention and urge the repeal of the test oath. But what I said seemed
not to have the slightest influence. I enclose a newspaper report, which is a pretty
accurate one, of what I said, and which will show that I have at least done my
duty in that regard, if not more. The same baneful influence that secured the
election of a majority of ignorant blacks and equally ignorant or unprincipled
whites to the convention has proved sufficient to hold them firmly to the original
purpose. They could only hope to obtain office by disqualifying every body in the
State who is capable of discharging official duties, and all else to them was of
comparatively slight importance. Even the question whether their constitution
will be ratified or rejected they treat with indifference. Congress, they say, will
make it all right any way. There is some division of opinion among intelligent
men as to what will be the result of an election. Some of the friends of reconstruction seem hopeful of the ratification of the constitution and think it may
possibly be made to work by electing to the legislature men pledged in advance
to remove the restrictions. But I observe that persons of that hopeful disposition
are generally from sections of the State where the whites are in a large majority
and there are original union men enough to hold all the offices. Men like Judge
Rives and Judge Snead, from the 'darker' sections of the State, say they can not
possibly support the constitution and are very despondent. Of course I may be
mistaken, but my opinion is that the constitution must be rejected. This would
not be a serious matter if it (the constitution) were a good one and good officers
could be elected under it. But it seems hardly possible that the union party can
organize upon a satisfactory basis for the election. The negroes and their associates will doubtless insist upon unqualified endorsement of the constitution by
their nominees. This the respectable whites will not give. Hence the late Convention will be reproduced in the legislature, a large majority being either worthless radicals, white and black, or bitter opponents of reconstruction upon the
congressional plan. The danger is that we will have on our hands, not only one
big elephant in the constitution, but a host of little ones in the shape of officers
elect who are not fit to be installed, Aa prospect not very encouraging at best.
My impression is that the wisest course would be to let the thing fall and die
where it is—Not submit it to the people at all. We can then go on putting union
men in office and reorganizing the provisional government upon a loyal basis until the friends of reconstruction get control of the State. Then a convention can

be called which will frame a constitution fit to be ratified by the people of the State and approved by Congress and the country at large. If Congress would give a little more latitude in the selection of officers, by modifying the test oath, there would be no difficulty in filling all the offices in the State by men who would aid restoration. Without some such change the work of reorganization can not be carried very far. The view of the question which I have given above is, of course, the local one. But it seems to me the national one leads to the same conclusion. I cant see how the endorsement of such a constitution as this one by the republican party can be otherwise than damaging to them in the North. Would it not be wiser for Congress to say at once, 'We reject, once and for all, proscriptive constitutions'? I have written this letter merely to suggest points that occur to me as worthy of very careful consideration. I suppose Congress alone can determine what is to be done. As explained in my official letter today I feel bound to await the action of Congress before ordering an election. The nominating conventions of the two parties meet in Richmond on the 6th and 7th of May. Perhaps it may be best for Congress to await their action before determining the question." LS and ALS, DNA, RG 108, Letters Received. On April 19, Schofield wrote to USG. "Unofficial . . . In addition to what was said in my letter of yesterday, I desire to call attention to other features of the proposed Virginia Constitution which seem to me very objectionable although perhaps they would not be fatal if the test oath were not added. The most notable of these features are, first the election by the people of city town and county officers. The Negroes have a majority of voters in more than half the cities, towns and counties. Unless their temper changes very greatly from what it now is they will elect persons of their own race who can neither read nor write to fill a majority of those offices. Some Negroes have already announced themselves as candidates for Congress and the State Legislature, and they expect as a matter of course to appropriate to themselves a large proportion at least of the minor offices. Will the country at large endure such a government in Virginia? Second—They have adhered to the cumbrous county organization, by division into townships, with a multitude of officers, entirely disproportional to the number and wealth of the people. These township officers, even including justices of the peace, are all to be elected by the people. Third—The retroactive portion of the homestead clause, Article XI, is I believe clearly repugnant to the Constitution of the United States. The defects above noted seem worthy of consideration in connection with the questions suggested in my letter of yesterday." ALS, *ibid.*

On May 8, Schofield twice wrote to USG. "I have the honor to forward herewith a corrected copy of the Constitution framed by the Virginia Convention, and to recommend that when said Constitution is submitted for ratification to the qualified voters, Section 9. Article III, which prescribes an additional oath of Office, may be submitted separately. I have also the honor to recommend that a time be appointed by Congress for the election in Virginia, not less than forty days from the date of the Act making the necessary appropriation." Copy, *ibid.*, RG 393, 1st Military District, Letters Sent. "*Unofficial* . . . I have today addressed you an official letter, recommending that Congress authorize a separate vote on the test-oath in the Virginia Constitution, and appoint a time for the election. As you will recollect my opinion was that some other sections of the proposed constitution ought also to be submitted separately. But so far as I have been able to learn the friends of the Constitution generally prefer to have a separate vote taken on the test-oath only, and seem very united on that. I have delayed my recommendation for the purpose of ascertaining as far as practicable the views and wishes of leading citizens of the State, and have limited my recommendation to what I understand to be their views and wishes, so as not to produce discord among the friends of reconstruction. I understand that the gentlemen referred to will communicate directly with the reconstruction Committee of Congress on the subject," ALS, USG 3.

On May 15, Schofield twice wrote to USG. "I have the honor to invite your attention to a matter which I understand to be of great importance and which, if I am correct, will demand the early attention of Congress. I suppose the Amendment to the Constitution of the United States proposed by the Thirty Ninth Congress, & Known as aArticle Fourteen, will soon be declared to have been ratified and become a part of the Constitution; and I understand the effect will be to at once remove from Office all persons who are disfranchised by that Amendment. If I am right in the above supposition and in my understanding of the effect of the proposed Amendment it becomes a matter of great importance to determine what is to be done in those states whose governments are still 'provisional only.' In the states which shall have been readmitted to representation in Congress no serious difficulty will exist for the reason that in those states the only disqualification for office will be that contained in the Constitutional Amendment, and hence an ample field will be left for the selection of persons to fill all the vacant offices except perhaps the higher Judgships but in the states not readmitted to representation the oath prescribed by Act of Congress of July 2d 1862 will still be required of all persons elected or appointed to any office—I have called for reports which will give the number of offices of the various grades in Virginia who will be displaced by operation of the Constitutional amendment and will forward the specific information when obtained. For the present I can only state that the number will probably be several thousands, and that only a small proportion of the vacancies thus created can possibly be filled by persons possessing the necessary qualifications including ability to take the present test oath—In the Judiciary Department to dispense with the test oath even would probably be insufficient, for nearly all lawyers of sufficient experience to fit them for the bench held some office before the War, and hence are disqualified by the Constitutional Amendment. I have already appointed in Virginia nearly five hundred officers and would have appointed more if qualified persons could be found. It is important to observe that the large majority of City town and County officers receive little or no compensation for their services   Hence men who possess the necessary qualifications cannot be induced to accept such offices, except in the places where they reside and own property or have substantial interests. Reports have been received from several portions of the State that no person can be found even to fill vacancies that now exist. When the Constitutional Amendment takes effect a large number of important offices must become vacant and remain so, until restoration is completed unless some relief is afforded by Congress." "I have the honor to submit herewith an estimate by the Paymaster of this Military District of funds necessary to pay expenses incident to the Military Government in Virginia. If Congress make the appropriation of $75.000, required for an election for ratification of the proposed Constitution in a short time hereafter and the Constitution be ratified, the funds herein asked for can be dispensed with. Otherwise about the sum estimated, three thousand dollars per month will be necessary during the Continuance of the Military Government, for incidental expenses not provided for in the general Army appropriation." Copies, DNA, RG 393, 1st Military District, Letters Sent; DLC-John M. Schofield.

1. In Dec., 1867, Schofield drafted a letter to USG proposing to act as governor of Va. after removing Governor Francis H. Peirpoint. Copy, *ibid*. The imprecise date, lack of other records or copies, and absence of a reply indicate that Schofield probably never sent the letter.

To Charles W. Ford

Washington, D. C., Apl. 4th *1868*

Dear Ford,

Your last letter come duly to hand and would have been immediately answered but that the principle point in it had been stated by Benton in a letter received only the day before yours was, and was answered, I hope satisfactorily, as soon as read. Benton has no doubt told you what I wrote?[1] Of course I will do what I can for you and had thought of the same thing before receiving either of your letters.

Elrod writes to me that White has commenced suit again! ~~Does he mean appealed to the~~ Does he refer to the appeal which has just been decided in my favor?

Please ask my lawyers about it and if a new suit has been commenced I think I will either get some other lawyer to attend to the case or to associate with them. If White does commence again it seems to me he can be made to give security for costs and damages.

Yours Truly
U. S. Grant

ALS, DLC-USG.

1. On March 30, 1868, USG had written to W. H. Benton. "Your letter of the 26th inst. in relation to Ford is just received. The matter you speak of I had thought of before, and intended, without saying a word about it, to ask for his appointment to the best place I could think of in St. Louis Co. in the event of a change of Administration. Ford is one of the men I have known for a long time that I would be willing to trust in any position of responsibility. He has always had my confidence and can rely on my friendship whether it benefits him or not. I will speak to Drake, Henderson and the member from his district about it without delay." Sotheby's (London) sale, May 27, 1986, no. 454; Joseph M. Maddalena, Catalog 8 [1989], no. 41.

To Bvt. Maj. Gen. John M. Schofield

Apl. 5th *1868*

DEAR GENERAL

Governor Pierpont is here, brought by his removal from office, and will be to see me in the morning, reinforced by all the backing he can get from Members of Congress by his representations, and those of opposers to his removal. He indicates that the appointment of Wells is in the interest of the anti-reconstructionest. This seems querr to me for I had supposed that Wells was an open advocate of ratification: Is this not so?—I have no doubt but strong efforts will be made to get me to order postponement of the inaugeration of Wells, with the view of putting it off all together. Now as it is but a few week until the election takes place when a Governor will be elected by the people, who will probably be installed in office whether the Constitution is ratified or not, I do not see what difference it makes to Pierpont whether he goes out now or then, unless he is likely to be the choice of the people for re-election. I do not understand that he is likely to be even a candidate.—I do not propose to interfere with the course you have pursued, from any information I now have, but if you think proper to change your determination, or to postpone action, do so. I would like you to postpone the inaugeration of Wells until I see the Governor and his friends to-morrow, and telegraph you the substance of what they have to say. I will telegraph you as early as possible in the morning.

Yours Truly
U. S. GRANT
General

TO BVT. MAJ. GN. J. M. SCHOFIELD,
COMD.G FIRST DISTRICT,
RICHMOND, VA.

ALS, CSmH. On April 5, 1868, 2:30 P.M., USG telegraphed to Bvt. Maj. Gen. John M. Schofield. "Please await receipt of letter from me just mailed before having Governor inaugerated." ALS (telegram sent), DNA, RG 107, Telegrams Collected (Bound); telegram sent, *ibid.*; telegram received, DLC-John M. Schofield.

On April 4, Schofield had written to USG. "Col. Wherry informs me that you suggested Judge Rives as being perhaps one whose appointment of Governor would have been more appropriate. I think I ought to inform you, what I thought Col. Wherry knew and would have told you, that I offered the appointment to Judge Rives when I first determined to make the change. The Judge decidedly declined to be a candidate either for appointment or election, saying he much preferred his present position. He would have been invaluable to the Union Cause in the office of Governor, yet it would be impossible to fill his present office if it were to be vacated, and I am not sure but he will be of even more service to the State where he is. The appointment of Genl Wells will I am sure give very general satisfaction." ALS, DNA, RG 108, Letters Received.

On April 6, Schofield telegraphed to USG. "Your telegram and letter of yesterday are received. I understand Genl Wells to be one of the strongest advocates of reconstruction in Virginia. The practical question at this time is not, who will support the constitution for the vital parts of that instrument are yet to be determined. The question now, is whether the friends of reconstruction can be united in harmonious action, and the constitution be so framed that the adoption will be either possible or desirable. They have at length almost unanimously agreed upon Genl Wells for Governor and have petitioned me to appoint him. I believe his inaüguration is the last hope of harmonious action, among the friends of reconstruction and of the success of that measure this year. I will delay the inauguration of Gen Wells until you are satisfied on the subject. He has not yet arrived in Richmond" ADf (telegram sent), DLC-John M. Schofield; telegram received (at 10:00 A.M.), DNA, RG 107, Telegrams Collected (Bound); *ibid.*, RG 108, Telegrams Received. At 12:25 and 2:45 P.M., USG telegraphed to Schofield. "I see nothing special to report to you from interview of this morning. My dispatch and letter need not delay your action longer." "Governor Pierpont's request [i]s to suspend action in the removal question until he can show it has been made in the interest [o]f the rebels to defeat adoption of Constitution. He [d]eclines making his statements in writing unless I will suspend your action, which I declined doing, but he will make them to Congress. ~~You will probably have a stir and and may want to prepare ordinances~~ [for] ~~it~~." ALS (telegrams sent), *ibid.*, RG 107, Telegrams Collected (Bound); telegrams sent, *ibid.*; telegrams received, DLC-John M. Schofield.

To Maj. Gen. George G. Meade

(Cipher)   Washington, Apl. 7th *1868* [*3:45* P.M.]
MAJ. GN. G. G. MEADE,
ATLANTA GA.

Will it not be well to remove all the civil officers in Columbus, and all other places where like outrages occur, and appoint true men in their place? In Alabam where outrages are committed the men elected might be installed.

U. S. GRANT

General

ALS (telegram sent), DNA, RG 107, Telegrams Collected (Bound); telegram sent, *ibid.*; telegram received, Meade Papers, PHi. See telegram to Maj. Gen. George G. Meade, April 2, 1868. On April 9, 1868, Maj. Gen. George G. Meade telegraphed to USG. "I have not removed civil authorities of Columbus, because Capt—Mills Comdr there reported they were acting in concert with him & evinced every disposition to ferret out murderers. I did not send any board to investigate, because Mills & his subordinates were doing every thing it was practicable to do—I have been fully alive to the necessity of action, but am waiting till I see the time, when action will be available—Capt Mills has made some Ten arrests principally of people, whom he has reason to believe have knowledge of the perpetraters of the deed—I have sent Maj. Smythe of the Judge Advocate Genl Dept to assist in the investigation, and have written to Mills to get his judgement on expediency of making removals of the civil officers—There will be difficulty just now in finding people willing to assume the responsibilities & dangers of the positions—" ALS (telegram sent), Meade Papers, PHi; telegram received (at 11:00 A.M.), DNA, RG 107, Telegrams Collected (Bound); (at noon) *ibid.*, RG 108, Telegrams Received.

On April 13, Meade telegraphed to USG. "I desire to have sent to me without delay, an expericienced detective to aid in detecting the Ashburn murderers He should report to me in person at this place—& Can such a person be sent.—" ALS (telegram sent), Meade Papers, PHi; telegram received (on April 14, 9:00 A.M.), DNA, RG 107, Telegrams Collected (Bound); (on April 13, 7:00 P.M.) *ibid.*, RG 108, Telegrams Received. On April 14, 1:45 P.M., USG telegraphed to Meade. "Your request for a man will be complied with." ALS (telegram sent), *ibid.*, RG 107, Telegrams Collected (Bound); telegram sent, *ibid.*; telegram received, Meade Papers, PHi. On April 20, Meade telegraphed to USG. "H. C. Whitley now in Kansas, and under the orders of the Commissioner of the Internal Revenue, is very much wanted here in connection with the Columbus Murder— I beg therefore the Comr may be urged to order him here at once to report to me.—" ALS (telegram sent), *ibid.*; telegram received (at 4:00 P.M.), DNA, RG 108, Telegrams Received. On April 23, 1:45 P.M., USG telegraphed to Meade. "Whitley can start for Atlanta on the 28th" ALS (telegram sent), *ibid.*, RG 107, Telegrams Collected (Bound); telegram sent, *ibid.*; telegram received, Meade Papers, PHi.

On May 2, Meade telegraphed to USG. "Ryland Randolph Editor of the Tuscaloosa Monitor, whose paper has been frequently sent to you as well as myself, recently assaulted with intent to kill a freedman in that town. The disordered condition of the state, the influential position of the criminal, induced Genl Shepherd to have Randolph arrested & to prefer charges against him, which I have ordered tried by military commission.—Judge Busteed of the U. S. Dist Court has granted a writ of Habeas Corpus returnable on the fifth instant—Under my orders G. O. No 11 this writ will be obeyed so far as presenting the body in court & making respectful return setting forth the ground and authority of arrest. It is not known whether Judge Busteed will acknowledge the authority or admit the justification on the grounds set forth—Should he order the discharge of the prisoner, your opinion of the course to be pursued is solicited." ALS (telegram sent), *ibid.*; telegram received (at 9:25 P.M.), DNA, RG 107, Telegrams Collected (Bound); (at 10:00 P.M.) *ibid.*, RG 108, Telegrams Received. On May 4, 11:00 A.M., USG telegraphed to Meade. "Randolph being taken before a United States Court I advise ~~yielding~~ submission to decission of that Court. ~~right or wrong~~." ALS (telegram sent), *ibid.*, RG 107, Telegrams Collected (Bound); telegram sent, *ibid.*; telegram received, Meade Papers, PHi. On May 4, Richard Busteed, Mobile, telegraphed to Bvt. Brig. Gen. Adam Badeau. "Yours of yesterday received here. All will be well if others act discretely." Telegram received (at 2:00 P.M.), DNA, RG 107, Telegrams Collected (Bound).

On Friday, June 5, 5:00 P.M., USG telegraphed to Meade. "If you can reach Washington by Tuesday morning I would like to see you here." ALS (telegram sent), *ibid.*; telegram sent, *ibid.*; copies, *ibid.*, RG 108, Telegrams Sent; DLC-USG, V, 56. On June 6, Meade, Huntsville, Ala., telegraphed to USG. "Cannot reach Washington by Tuesday morning, but can be there by Wednesday morning. Will that do? Answer to Atlanta" Telegram received (at 2:00 P.M.), DNA, RG 107, Telegrams Collected (Bound); (forwarded to Annapolis) *ibid.*, RG 108, Telegrams Received; copies, DLC-USG, V, 55; Meade Papers, PHi.

On June 26, Meade, Atlanta, telegraphed to Secretary of War John M. Schofield. "I deem it of the utmost importance not only for the ends of justice, but for my personal vindication that the Ashburn murderers should be tried by military commission and I have accordingly, ordered the trial for monday next.— Before going north, I retained ex-Govr Jos Brown as counsel for the Govt—I deem his services of great importance not only for his legal ability but for the influence his position in the state will give the prosecution.—He has been actively employed during my absence, but today on my asking him what his fee would be he replied Five thousand dollars—I stated I did not feel authorised to pay such an amount without the sanction of superior authority—He expressed his willingness to withdraw & not to communicate any information he had obtained   In view of the great importance of the case of the value of Govr Browns services— of the fact that a large fee will have to be paid him for what he has done—I would strongly recommend my being authorised to pay the amount asked, as I am satisfied he would have received double, if not quadruple the amount from the other side—who approached him after I had retained him, and said any amount of money could be raised—I should mention the prisoners have engaged over a dozen of the best lawyers of the state and that besides my Asst Judge Advocate Genl I have only Govr Brown—The evidence accumulated is of the most positive ground and leaves no doubt of conviction of the principal actors in the tragedy.—Please advise me, as soon as possible & if authorised & there is no fund available, have an item introduced into pending bill to cover th~~is~~e expenses of this trial.—" ALS (telegram sent), Meade Papers, PHi. See Louise Biles Hill, *Joseph E. Brown and the Confederacy* (Chapel Hill, 1939; reprinted, Westport, Conn., 1974), pp. 284–86.

On June 30, Meade telegraphed to Schofield and USG. "When I left Washington, I was of the opinion that the trial of all civil prisoners might be & should be left to the civil authorities on the admission of the state—Since my arrival owing to the developments in the Ashburn murder case, the intense excitement produced by the same, and the false and malicious statements made for political purposes, I deem it most urgent that this trial should be carried on to the end by the military authorities—Col Schofield will apprise you, of the character of the evidence, but every conceivable obstacle, is being resorted to, to produce delay with the intention of taking the prisoners, out of my hands by writ of habeas corpus, so soon as the state is supposed to be admitted—I think therefore for the purposes of justice—some action should be had in Congress—continuing the trial of all cases by military commission pending at the time the state is admitted Can not this be done?—" ALS (telegram sent), Meade Papers, PHi; telegram received (at 4:00 P.M.), DNA, RG 107, Telegrams Collected (Bound); *ibid.*, RG 108, Telegrams Received. On June 30, John W. Shaffer, "Capitol," Washington, D. C., telegraphed to Bvt. Maj. Gen. John A. Rawlins or Bvt. Brig. Gen. Horace Porter. "Reconstruction Committee will take action" Telegram received (at 2:00 P.M.), *ibid.*, RG 107, Telegrams Collected (Bound). On July 1, 4:00 P.M., Rawlins telegraphed to Meade. "In the absence of Genl Grant, your dispatch of yesterday was today submitted to the Secy. of War, and it is his opinion that the suggested Congressional action cannot be had." LS (telegram sent), *ibid.*; telegram sent, *ibid.*; telegram received, Meade Papers, PHi. On July 2, Rawlins wrote to Meade. "*Unofficial* . . . After submitting your dispatch of the 30th ult. to the Secretary of War, and before answering it, at his suggestion, I took it to Senator Trumbull, Ch'rm'n of the Senate Judiciary Committee, who expressed the opinion, that when the State had complied with the conditions of the reconstruction acts, the jurisdiction of the military tribunals authorized by said acts would cease. Senator Trumbull consulted with Senators Edmunds and Frelinghuysen, also of the Judiciary Committee. Edmunds agreed with him, but Frelinghuysen was of opinion that, where a case was on trial before a military tribunal at the time of the compliance of a State with the conditions of said acts, its jurisdiction would hold until the determination of such trial. In this latter opinion Representatives Boutwell and Lawrence, of the House Judiciary Committee strongly concur. The Secretary of War and Senator Trumbull thought there was weight in this latter view. It is therefore suggested that the trial proceed to its determination, or at least until the civil courts properly claim and determine the question of jurisdiction. None of those above named believe that any thing can be done in time by further legislation to help the matter." LS, *ibid.*

On July 21, Meade wrote to USG. "The numerous malicious and false statements, that have been given to the public, through the press, for political and partisan purposes—in relation to the trial, and the treatment of witnesses and prisoners, implicated in the murder of Mr. G. W. Ashburn of Columbus, require on my part a special report, which is herewith made, and to which I beg to ask I may be authorized to give that publicity which my vindication requires. The accompanying papers contain all the instructions, orders and telegrams that have emanated from these Head Quarters and the replies made thereto. A careful perusal of these papers will give an accurate history of the whole transaction, and will exhibit the part taken by each individual whether military or civil under my control. A Brief Synopsis of these papers, and a succinct statement of the facts of the case is herewith submitted—On the 30th of March last, a little after midnight, G. W. Ashburn ex member of the Constitutional Convention of Georgia was assassinated at a house where he was boarding in the town of Columbus. Immediately on receiving notification I instructed the Commanding Officer at Columbus Captain Wm Mills 16th Infantry to make every effort in co-operation with the civil authorities to detect and arrest the criminals—Captain Mills having reported the civil authorities were disposed to act with energy, I declined the frequent recommendations of parties to remove them but subsequently Capt. Mills reporting, that the energy of the civil authorities, was all show and merely assumed, and that he could place no reliance on them—I removed the Mayor and Board of Aldermen—together with the Marshall and his deputy—appointing others and appointing Captain Mills, Mayor—. About the 6th of April, nearly a week after the assassination, Capt. Mills having obtained sufficient evidence to warrant his action, arrested by my order some Ten citizens of Columbus, either as participators, accessories, or for having some knowledge of the facts of the case. These persons were subsequently relased on bonds to appear and stand their trial—Finding, that owing to the character of this crime, in a great measure political as well as social, there was no effort on the part of the community where it was committed—either through the authorities or among the citizens, to ferret out the guilty—I deemed it proper to ask of the War Department that a competent detective officer should be sent to report to me, that he might assist Captain Mills in his researches—On the 18th of April Mr. Reed having arrived from Washington was sent to Columbus to report to Captain Mills. On Mr. Reed reaching Columbus and being made acquainted with the evidence then procured, he earnestly urged I should send for a Mr. Whitely, then in Kansas in the service of the Internal Revenue Department—My application to Commissioner Rollins being courteously received and acceded to Mr. Whitly arrived about May 1st and was immediately sent to Captain Mills—Soon after his arrival at Columbus Mr. Whitely reported he was satisfied Capt. Mills was on the track of the criminals and had arrested some of the principals but that it was utterly impracticable to obtain any testimony, from any party in Columbus, as their lives would be forfeited if they dared to dis-close what they knew—and he recommended that certain parties whom he believed had a knowledge of the affair, should be removed to some secure place, where being protected they could without fear dis-close such facts as were in their possession—Upon receipt of this communication I authorized the transfer of the parties named to Fort Pulaski, and directed the Commanding Officer of the Post to permit the Detectives Whitely and Reed to have free access to the prisoners, and to have a general direction of their treatment—at the same time I cautioned the Detectives, that in their efforts to extract the facts as known to these parties, no unusual or cruel or physical means should be resorted to—The result of this movement was the dis-closure of most important facts by several parties who had not dared to speak out, until under the protection of the Government—From the statements made by these prisoners a number of others were arrested and brought to Atlanta early in June.—Being compelled to go North myself and other circumstances—delayed the organization of the Military Commission 'till late in June. Finding on my return, the most false and exaggerated statements in regard to the treatment of prisoners and witnesses—I called on General Sibley Commanding Sub-District of Georgia for a report on their treatment at this Post, Atlanta, and on Captain Mills and Captain Cook, for reports as to the treatment of those confined at Columbus and Fort Pulaski—respectively—I also called on Mr. Whitely the Detective for a report on the same subject—All these reports are herewith submitted, and it will be seen from them, and from the affidavit of the prisoners themselves attached to Mr. Whitely's report, that the exaggerated statements which for political purposes, the press have given circulation to are all false and have no foundation beyond the fact admitted by Mr. Whitely that he did operate on the fears of two negroes Wells and Stapler, whom he believed knew something, but that soon finding they knew nothing—they were released and with the exception of threatening to shave their heads, and confining them for some hours; in a cell at Fort Pulaski previously arranged for the punishment of refractory soldiers—they were well treated—and were in no wise injured.—The trial has been in progress now some Twenty days, and the evidence for the prosecution made public—It is for the Department and the people of the Country to judge whether with the evidence as adduced on the trial, I was not only justified, but compelled to arrest and bring to trial the parties implicated—My conscience is free that throughout the whole transaction, I have been animated by but one purpose, which was to secure the ends of justice and vindicate the law—The character of the crime—the social status of parties implicated in its commission—and the doubts, as to the guilt of the several parties—had no influence on me except to increase my determination to bring the facts out, even at the risk of for a time putting persons to inconvenience who might subsequently prove innocent—Hence many arrests were made of parties, who were subsequently released, on its being proved they were neither participators or had any knowledge of the case—In all these cases, these parties were well treated, and on being dis-charged were paid the usual witness fees for the period they were removed from their business. Had the civil authorities acted in good faith and with energy, and made any attempt to ferrit out the guilty—or had the people of Columbus evinced or felt any horror of the crime and co-operated in any way in detecting its perpetrators—much that was seemingly harsh and arbitrary—might have and would have been avoided—but the case required prompt and decided measures, which I did not hesitate to take, and am satisfied now, that when the whole truth is made public, as it will be by the documents accompanying this Report, and the evidence on the trial—that every right-thinking man will justify me." LS (dated "July"), DNA, RG 107, Letters Received from Bureaus; copy (dated), Meade Papers, PHi.

To Jesse Root Grant

Washington, Apl. 7th *1868*

DEAR FATHER,

Your letter of the 2d inst. asking a letter of introduction for Dr. Whitacre abroad is received. Enclosed I send you a letter for him addressed to our Minister to France. The Dr. need not deliver this to Gen. Dix unless he chooses but can shew it to any of our Ministers he meets. I think your prediction about the nomination of Mr. Johnson in a certain event very absurd. If deposed he will not be elegible, and, out of office, he would have no strength with the Democratic party.

The family are all well. I hope to get West in June to stay some weeks, six or more. I will stay most of the time on my farm and in Galena, but expect to spend two or three days with you.

John Simpson[1] has made strong friends of the Officers and

citizens who know him. He is a man of sterling good sence, great simplicity and truthfulness, and a student. At Thirty-five he will be regarded as educated, refined and acomplished. It is a great pity that in the reorganization of the Army we did not get more such men.

Yours Truly

U. S. GRANT

ALS, Williams College, Williamstown, Mass.

1. See *PUSG*, 13, 298. USG's cousin, John Simpson, was appointed 2nd lt., 4th Art., as of Aug. 17, 1867.

To Maj. Gen. George G. Meade

Washington April 9 1868

MAJ. GEN. G. G. MEADE
COMDG. 3D DIST
GENERAL

Enclosed I send you a letter which explains itself. It seems to me Maj. Russell (I believe of the 7th Infy.) should be held up to scorn in his regiment and forced to resign if the facts disclosed in the ~~written~~ within letter are true. I think it will be well to send the letter to the Col. of his regiment for such investigation, and action, as he may deem proper. Without the consent of the young lady however I would not advise the publicity of a trial.

Very respectfully

Your obt. Servt

U. S. GRANT

General

Copies, DLC-USG, V, 47, 60; DNA, RG 108, Letters Sent. Written in response to a letter of March 24, 1868, received at USG's hd. qrs., from Miss A. L. Fernald, St. Augustine, Fla. "Give an account of an 'unfortunate ride' with Capt Samuel A. Russell 7th U. S. Infantry—and the gross conduct of the aforesaid Captain Russell—same being verified by Miss Peolazzi." *Ibid.*, Register of Letters Received.

On Feb. 16, 1867, USG had written to Judge Abraham D. Russel, New York City, thanking him for "the pipe and tobacco . . . when I travel, I will not forget the beautiful tobacco pouch . . . Please thank Mrs. Russel for remembering me in the kind manner she has . . ." Charles Hamilton Auction No. 47, Feb. 3, 1971, pp. 34–35. On Jan. 15, 1871, Sallie Russel, Fort Shaw, Montana Territory, wrote to USG. "You no doubt will be surprised in receiving a letter from me, but oh, General I [*know*] you would pity me if you knew how much I have suffered for the last two days. My darling Father, Judge A. D. Russel of New York, died on the twenty fifth of last April, and you can imagine my sorrow at the loss of the most adored Parent   all we had in the world to depend on was my Brother Capt S. A. Russel of the Seventh Infantry. My Mother and myself joined him here three months ago, at a great expense,   day before yesterday we heard that my Brother was to be discharged the Service. I assure you General it cast a gloom over the whole Garrison for no Officer is more beloved or can show a better record than he. If you remember one time at dear old West [*Point*] you said any request I might ask you would grant   now dear General please reinstate my Brother. our *all* depends upon your answer   he will come on to Washington and bring letters from all his Commanding Officers to shew what I assert is true   Oh! General if you will only grant my request my prayers will nightly ascend in your behalf. Write me if but a line for our *all* depends upon *your* answer" ALS, DNA, RG 94, ACP, 589 1871. Capt. and Bvt. Maj. Samuel A. Russel, 7th Inf., had been mustered out as of Jan. 1. On July 8, Russel, New York City, wrote to USG. "I have the honor to respectfully solicit a commision in one of the Infantry Regements of U. S. Army. Eighth Regement preferred—" ALS, *ibid.* On Sept. 19, Bvt. Maj. Gen. Rufus Ingalls, New York City, wrote to USG. "I desire to commend to your consideration the case of Major S. A. Russell, who was mustered out of service under the operations of the late Army Bill. The case is a serious and embarrassing one, and if Maj. R. could be given an original appointment as Second Lieutenant, it would please me—as well as his many friends." LS, *ibid.* On Sept. 23, Mary L. Lanier, Brooklyn, wrote to USG requesting her brother's reappointment. ALS, *ibid.* On March 14, 1873, Mrs. E. M. Russel, New York City, wrote to USG. "When I last saw You at the Fifth Avenue Hotel You were kind enough to say You would do all You could for me. I learn through the Secretary of War that the five Reapointments were bye Your orders. I know Your kind heart will prompt You to make the sixth. *You* are all powerful and God has placed it in Your power to dispense happiness. And to reappoint my Son Captain S A Russel will be an Act I shall be truly grateful for." ALS, *ibid.* On Oct. 20, 1876, Sallie Russel Bomford, New York City, again wrote to USG requesting her brother's reappointment. ALS, *ibid.* No action followed.

To Charles W. Ford

Washington, D, C,
Apl. 21st 1868,

DEAR FORD,

Enclosed find check for $66 00, amt. of charges paid by you on my horses to St. Louis. Your letter asking if you had better take further steps to secure recommendations for the office held by Able was duly received! I do not know what to advise in that matter. I should think all the support you would want would be the senator and representative from St. Louis. You have been advised of what I will do.

I shall go out to St. Louis just as soon as I can and remain there two or three weeks.

Yours Truly
U. S. Grant

ALS, DLC-USG.

To Bvt. Maj. Gen. John M. Schofield

Washington, D. C., April 25 1868.

Dear General

Under the circumstances I advise you to decline the Secretary Ship in advance

U. S. Grant.
General

Maj Gn Jno M Schofield
Com'g 1st Mil District

Telegram sent, Washington University, St. Louis, Mo. On April 26, 1868, Bvt. Maj. Gen. John M. Schofield, Richmond, twice wrote to USG. "Confidential . . . I regret exceedingly that your advice comes too late. I have already promised not to decline the nomination in advance of any action of the Senate." "I see from the papers that the President has nominated me to the Senate as Secretary of War. You are aware that I do not want that office; Yet, under existing circumstances, if the Senate should wish me to serve I could not decline. I presume my nomination will not be confirmed, but have no right to act upon such presumption." ALS, USG 3. See Schofield, *Forty-Six Years in the Army* (New York, 1897), pp. 413–18.

On May 29, 7:15 P.M., USG telegraphed to Schofield. "Your nomination confirmed." ALS (telegram sent), DNA, RG 107, Telegrams Collected (Bound); telegram sent, *ibid.*; telegram received, DLC-John M. Schofield.

To William Elrod

————

Washington, D, C,
Apl. 28th 1868,

Put all three

DEAR ELROD,

Have all three of my mares put to a blooded horse. What one I leave entirely to your own judgement. If Legal Tender is standing I think it would be well to try him again, but I am not particular. I have two colts here, one of which I hope to raise for a stallion to put on my farm. I also have one in Wisconsin to raise for the same purpose, both well bred both on Syire and dam side.

I shall unquestionably go to Mo. soon after the impeachment trial closes.

Yours Truly
U. S. GRANT
Gen.l

P. S. Cant you make pork enough this year to put up about twenty hams to send to me?

U. S. G.

ALS, Illinois Historical Survey, University of Illinois, Urbana, Ill.

To Maj. Gen. George G. Meade

————

Washington, Apl. 29th *1868* [*noon*]

MAJ. GN. G. G. MEADE,
ATLANTA GA.

I have carefully read your letter of 16th Apl. and its enclosures. I see nothing in them to change my opinion as expressed to you in my dispatch of March 2d 1868. The officers elected under the new Constitution of Georgia are not officers of the provisional government refered to in the reconstruction acts, nor are they officers elected under any so called state authority, and are not therefore required to take the oath prescribed in section 9 Act, Act of July 19th 1867. The eligibility to hold office must be determined by

the new Constitution and the amendment to the Constitution of the
United States designa[ted] as Article fourteen.

U. S. GRANT

General

ALS (telegram sent), DNA, RG 107, Telegrams Collected (Bound); telegram
sent, *ibid.*; telegram received (at 3:30 P.M.), Meade Papers, PHi. On April 29,
1868, Maj. Gen. George G. Meade telegraphed to USG. "Election passed off as
quietly as could be expected—one or two serious outbreaks only.—Many complaints of fraud from both sides & some applications based on them for re-
elections—these will be thoroughly investigated & action predicated on result of
investigation.—Official returns come in slowly—No accurate judgement can as
yet be formed, but the probabilities are—that the Constitution is ratified by a very
large majority—Bullock republican elected by a small majority, and Democrats
carried a majority of the Legislature.—No acknowledgement has been received
by me of my letter to you of the 16th inst, and I would be relieved to know at the
earliest moment your views on the points raised therein—" ALS (telegram sent),
ibid.; telegram received (at 11:00 A.M.), DNA, RG 107, Telegrams Collected
(Bound); *ibid.*, RG 108, Telegrams Received.

On April 16, Meade had written to USG. "The Georgia Convention in its
Ordinance requiring the election of Federal and State Officers on the same days
as the election for ratification provided as follows: 'And Major General Meade is
respectfully requested to give the necessary orders to carry into effect the foregoing provisions, and cause due returns to be made, and certificates of *election* to
to be issued by the *proper* officers.' This duty of issuing certificates of election,
was one I should never voluntarily have assumed, but unfortunately my attention
was not called to it, 'till after the adjournment of the Convention too late to have
the Ordinance modified and have the returns, sent either to the President of the
Convention as was the case in Alabama, or to a board of Canvassers as is provided in the ordinance of the Florida Convention. The objection to discharging
this duty, is that it imposes on me the necessity of enquiring into the qualifications and eligibility of those officers, who are not members of bodies competent
themselves to adjust such questions; as for instance the Governor. On the 3d inst.
a letter was handed to me by: a committee of gentlemen—asking of me an expression of opinion, on a given statement of facts, as to the eligibility of the Hon
D. Irvin as a candidate for Governor—to which letter I replied giving my opinion
and stating that if a person with such a status was elected, I should not feel myself authorized to permit him to take office. I considered that in view of the duty
imposed on me by the convention, it was due to the voters of the State, if I had
settled opinions, and would be governed by them, that I ought not to decline
making them public, in advance of being required to act, though I now regret
I did not assume this position and decline. A copy of my letter in reply, and of
the one of enquiry in the case of Judge Irvin, are herewith transmitted. The
consequence of this letter was the withdrawal of Judge Irvin and the putting in
nomination by another party of General Gordon—whose friends likewise addressed me a letter enquiring as to his qualifications under the acts of Congress.
Finding General Gordon had never held office before the rebellion, and had never
taken an oath to support the Constitution, before entering the military service
of the Confederate States I considered he was not excluded by the 14th Article.
Constitutional Amendments, which in my judgment then, and *now*, was the test

by which qualifications for office holders was to be tested. Correspondence in the case of Gen. Gordon herein transmitted. Finding the publicity of the fact that I had to issue certificates of election, and to decide on the eligibility of candidates, was involving me in letters from almost every candidate, I thought proper to issue an order (copy herewith transmitted) announcing the parts of the reconstruction acts bearing on the qualifications for office, and stating what offices would be voted for. In preparing this order I advised with the Assistant Judge Advocate General of the army on duty at these Headquarters, whose clear judgment on such points has been of great assistance to me, and on which I have principally depended since being here. Since the nomination of General Gordon, his eligibility under the Reconstruction Laws has been impeached, on the ground, that until the State is admitted to representation, all government is only provisional, and that no one can be elected or appointed to office under any provisional government unless they can take the test oath. This point is very ingeniously argued by one opposed politically to General Gordon as will be seen by reference to the enclosed extract from a paper published here. If this point is fairly raised my opinion of April 4th and subsequent order are both wrong, but I am not disposed to acquiesce in its correctness, and for the following reasons: First—I am of the opinion from a careful perusal of the several reconstruction acts, that the officers elected under the Constitutions framed in accordance with these acts, were not considered or intended to be considered as provisional governments within the meaning of the term as used in section 6 of the Act of March 2, 1867—nor are they to be considered 'as elected under any so-called State authority' as referred to in section 9 of act of July 19, 1867. They are elected to office under the authority of the reconstruction acts themselves and are not entitled to hold office until, all the steps required by said acts are fully complied with—and the only qualification for holding office, is—the qualification required by the 14th Article Constitutional Amendment. This has been my opinion since first taking command and so fully impressed was I with it, that prior to the Alabama election, I urged the postponement of the election of state and County officers, until after the adoption of the Constitution by Congress, on the ground that until the state was restored to its proper relations, these offices had no existence and did not require to be filled by election. It is true those elected could be appointed by me, as officers of a provisional government—or as in the case of Alabama where the Constitution failed of ratification they could be legislated into office, as it is now proposed to do by bill in Congress, and this bill is in my judgment a vindication of the position I herein assume, that the governments elected under the Constitutions submitted to Congress, said Constitutions are adopted, and said governments go into operation, are not provisional—nor do they emanate from any so-called state authority, because this bill in legislating into office the persons elected, when the Constitution failed of ratification, distinctly declares they are to be considered a provisional government, and that the reconstruction laws are to continue in force until certain steps are taken. Now if all governments are provisional until the state is represented, there was no occasion for reiterating this provision—the reiteration confirms me in the opinion it was made because Congress designed the governments created by their acts to be considered permanent and were being an exception—viz: a government created by Congress, but not in accordance with the reconstruction acts—Congress does, what it did not do before, makes it a provisional government, and subject to the authority of the District Commander. Hence I conclude that the officers to be elected in Georgia, under the new Constitution, if they are not put into office, before the adoption of the Constitution by Congress, and the adoption by the State of the 14th Article, are not officers elected under any so-called State authority, and not therefore required to take the oath prescribed in section 9 act July 19. 1867. Now as the members of the legislature, will be called together, either by myself or by the Provisional Governor, in order to adopt the 14th Article, this preliminary step may be considered as under a Provisional Government, and the power of the members be considered as derived from my authority, and therefore under section 9. July 19, 1867, these members may be required before they can complete this preliminary step to the admission of the state, to take the oath prescribed in said section for appointees of the District Commander. In view of this contingency and in order to set myself right on the record, I issued order No 61. copy of which is herewith transmitted. Having thus given my reasons for the opinion as set forth, I desire to add, 2ndly, That this opinion has already been submitted to you and my views confirmed—You will remember that the ordinance of the Convention in Florida prescribed that the election for state and county officers should be held on the same day, as the Constitution was submitted to the people, and this Constitution enfranchised every citizen. This being before the recent act of Congress authorizing these elections to be held in advance of the adoption of the Constitution, I was in doubt as to the proper action to be pursued. If the position maintained by the writer in the 'New Era' is correct, that the government elected under the new Constitution, and in pursuance of the reconstruction act, is a Provisional Government then none but registered voters could vote for the officers, hence I telegraphed you as follows on February 29, 1868: 'GENERAL U. S. GRANT Washington, D. C. Is this election of officers under the Constitution and only to take office on the adoption of the Constitution to be considered as an election for officers under the provisional government referred to in section 6 of Act of March 2, 1867 and are non-registered voters excluded by this section at first election held under the new Constitution.' To which I received your reply under date of March 2d 1868. 'The election proposed by the convention for officers under the new Constitution I do not consider as an election for officers under the provisional government referred to in section 6 of act of March 2d, 67. (Signed) U. S GRANT General.' Subsequently Congress sustained us in our opinion by passing a bill authorizing elections in advance of adoption of Constitution, and as previous laws had defined the qualifications for voters, Congress to prohibit the *exclusion* of registered voters, prescribes that at these elections registered voters may vote—Congress again doing an act inconsistent with the theory of the writer in the 'New Era', because if the persons elected at these elections were by previous acts members of provisional governments why reiterate what previous laws required that only registered voters should vote. You will thus perceive that the opinions given in the cases of Judge Irvin and General Gordon were predicated on the conviction that the 14th Article contained the only qualifications prescribed by the Reconstruction Acts, and the correspondence of the 29th of February by telegram, had settled me in the opinion that these governments to be elected were not provisional or to be considered as deriving their authority from any socalled state authority—and that this question fortunately for me had been raised in advance of its application to any individual or political consideration. I have now given you a full statement of the manner in which I became involved in giving construction to the laws and also the construction given—to which unless overruled I shall adhere—It is true Congress can at any moment pass an amendatory or explanatory act—which shall require the test oath to be taken by persons elected under the new Constitution, but I should greatly regret such action for two reasons First. That it would be considered as an additional condition, and imposed for special purposes. 2ndly. It will be very difficult to carry out, as I have already advised you at the time it was proposed to require a complete change in office-holders. The question however is important and should be settled—It evidenty has never been understood, in the light that it is now attempted to be thrown on it, for if it had the members of the Constitutional Convention should certainly have been required to take the test oath, and I am not aware that it was ever required of any of them. Elections are now coming off both in this state and Florida—and pending bill in Congress requires those elected recently in Alabama to be installed in office—the question is, are all these officers, under existing laws required to take the test oath—those in Alabama being members of a provisional government as declared by statute I presume will be required—but I see no reason these in Georgia and Florida should be so required. An early answer desired." Copies, *ibid.*, Letters Received; Meade Papers, PHi.

On April 17, Rufus B. Bullock, Atlanta, and Foster Blodgett, Augusta, telegraphed separately to Charles A. Tinker, Washington, D. C. "Say to the proper party that it is of the utmost importance that the General should decide that the Reconstruction Act requires that all persons to be eligible at this election shall be able to take the test oath under Section nine of Supplemental Act of July. Large majority of our candidates can take it and the opposition for Governor and Legislature cannot. If opposition Governor and Legislature should be decided eligible they would refuse Constitutional Amendment and defeat the whole plan of reconstruction. It is important that Commander here should be so ordered by Telegraph at once—Election commences on Monday—Telegraph me in cipher if anything is done." "Say to General Grant that General Meades order '61' issued yesterday requires members elected to the Legislature to take the test oath. Nothing said about Governor. Will not General Grant by telegraph suggest to General Meade ~~and~~ an amendment including Governor and other state officers? See and let me know immediately—answer in cipher" Telegrams received, DNA, RG 108, Letters Received. USG endorsed the Blodgett telegram. "Please look at law and see if Gov.r is required to take test oath and advise Gn. Meade if you think best. I go to West Point to-night. Will be back Monday morning." AE (initialed), *ibid.* On April 18, Bvt. Maj. Gen. John A. Rawlins wrote to Tinker. "Messrs. Bullock and Blodgett must apply to General Meade for the amendment they desire to his order. He is judge of the law governing his action. It is not deemed advisable to send any suggestions on the subject from here." Copy, *ibid.*

To Thaddeus Stevens

Washington, D, C, Apl. 30th *1868.*

Ch. Com. on Reconstruction
House of Representatives,
Sir:

I have the honor to recommend to the Hon. Congress of the United States the removal of the disabilities, imposed by the reconstruction acts, on James Longstreet, of Huntsville, Ala, and T. Ochiltree of Galveston Texas.[1] The course pursued by Gen. Longstreet since the surrender of the rebel army, and his high character always, both before and since the rebellion, entitle him to the confidence of all good Citizens. Mr. Ochiltree I have no personal acquaintance with to enable me to speak of him from my own knowledge. He is well and responsibly recommended however, and, as I understand, publishes a paper which he wishes to make the advocate of reconstruction, peace & good will between all sections of the country, industry and prosperity in his own state, all of which can be better done if he is relieved from the disabilities he is now laboring under.

Respectfully, your obt. svt.
U. S. GRANT.
General,

ALS, DNA, RG 233, 40A–F29.8.

On April 11, 1868, James Longstreet, Huntsville, Ala., had written to Bvt. Brig. Gen. Frederick T. Dent. "Your esteemed favor of the 6th instant is just received. Your letter to N. O. was received at this place after I wrote you. I have also just received a letter from Maj. Ochiltree of Texas who is now in Washington. He speaks of an appointment that he had mentioned to Gen Grant for me; which the Genl. recd favorably; if you find yourself in condition to aid the matter I trust that you will do so—So far as the test oath is concerned, I had hoped that my political disability had been removed. If it has not I beg that you will say a good word to Senator Wilson. He intimated when I saw him in N. O. that these political disabilities would be removed: and I am inclined to believe that it would be done at once—if you could make it convenient to speak to him about it. I dont know the Mr Hiram Barney of whom you speak, as a New York man, nor do I know his business or address. Please make my respectful salutations to Gen Grant and family, and the members of your own family, not omitting your father. I hope to hear from you when you have an idle moment to spare" ALS, ICarbS.

1. Thomas P. Ochiltree, born in Nacogdoches, Tex., the son of a prominent lawyer-politician, fought Indians with the Texas Rangers, practiced law, edited a newspaper, and served in the C.S. Army as staff officer. After the war, he spent time in Europe and edited the Houston *Daily Telegraph*. On March 25, 1868, Longstreet wrote to USG introducing Ochiltree. Doris Harris catalogue, [1966], no. 68.

To Alexander T. Stewart

[*May 4, 1868*]

Owing to my absence from this City . . . your favor of the first is only just now come to hand. In the matter of Sec. of the Treas. in case of the removal of Mr. Johnston, I have heard but little said, and have not thought myself who will make a good one. Mr. Ward, of whom you speak, Mr. Chandler might recommend, but beyond him I doubt whether any one else has ever thought seriously about such a selection. Mr. W. has been eminently successful in managing his private affairs, but, I believe, he is entirely inexperienced in public matters. I think Mr. Wade will be glad to see you and consult with you, in case he should come into the presidential chair, about this matter and other matters of appointment. For myself, I want to keep as clear as I can from having any thing to do with civil appointments now, but upon this matter I will talk with you when you visit the City. . . .

Parke-Bernet Sale No. 2190, April 23, 1963, no. 208; Robert K. Black, Catalogue 94; Sotheby's, March 27, 1985, no. 171.

On June 15, 1868, USG wrote to Alexander T. Stewart. ". . . I would like very much to meet you as well as other friends in New York, and expected to have done so on my way to West Point. The violent storm of Wednesday last, the day spent at Ravenswood, prevented." Autograph catalogue clipping, NN.

To Edwin M. Stanton

Washington May 6th 1868

Hon. E. M. Stanton
Secretary of War
Sir:

I have the honor to forward herewith a communication from Brevet Major Gen'l E. R. S. Canby, Comdg. 2nd Military District of date May 4th 1868, relating to Section 3d of the Constitutional Amendment Known as Article 14, as it affects the eligibility of some of the officers elected under the recently ratified constitutions of the States of North Carolina and South Carolina, and to the applicability of Section 9, of the supplementary reconstruction Act of July 19th 1867, to the officers elected under said constitutions. I also forward in connection therewith and relating to the applicability of said Section 9, of the Act of July 19th 1867, to officers elected under the constitutions adopted in pursuance of the reconstruction laws. The correspondence with accompanying enclosures between Major General G. G. Meade, Commanding 3d Military District and myself.[1]

In view of the importance of the subject to which they relate and the necessity for immediate action, I respectfully recommend that they be submitted to Congress at the earliest opportunity.

> Very respectfully
> Your obt. servt.
> U. S. GRANT
> General

Copies, DLC-USG, V, 47, 60; DNA, RG 108, Letters Sent. On May 4, 1868, Bvt. Maj. Gen. Edward R. S. Canby, Charleston, had written to Bvt. Maj. Gen. John A. Rawlins. "I consider it my duty to ask that the attention of the General of the Army may be invited to an obstacle about to be encountered in the organization of the new Governments under the Constitutions recently adopted in the States of North Carolina and South Carolina. In my judgment some action by Congress will be needed in order to remove this embarrassment. One of the most serious impediments that has been met with in the execution of the Reconstruction laws, has grown out of the enforcement of the provision requiring all appointees of the District Commander to take, what is known as the test-oath. In both States there are many active and zealous friends of the Union, and of restoration, who have been technically debarred by this oath from any official participation in the work of reconstruction and many others who could take the oath have declined to do so, from a sensitive fear that their motives would be misconstrued. A large number from these classes have been chosen to office at the recent elections, and the difficulty heretofore encountered, again presents itself, and in still greater magnitude. The provisions of law which lead to these complications, may be briefly recapitulated as follows: By the third section of the amendment to the Constitution of the United States, known as article XIV, the disabilities imposed upon certain individuals for participation in the Rebellion, are extended to State officers. The 5th Section of the law of March, declares the conditions upon which the Rebel States shall be admitted to representation in the Congress of the United States. The 6th Section of the same law enacts 'That until the people of the said Rebel States shall be by law admitted to representation in the Congress of the United States, any civil government which may exist therein, shall be deemed provisional only' . . . and no person shall be eligible to any office under any such provisional governments who would be disqualified for holding office under the provisions of the third article of the said Constitutional

Amendment.' The 9th Section of the law of July 19th, 1867, supplementary to
the foregoing, directs 'That all members of said boards of Registration, and all
persons hereafter elected, or appointed to office under any so called State or
municipal authority, or by detail or appointment of the District Commander shall
be required to take and subscribe the oath of office prescribed by law for officers
of the United States.' At the recent elections in the two States, several persons
have been chosen as Representatives in the Congress of the United States, who
are disqualified by the third Section of the Constitutional Amendment; and quite
a large number as State Executive and Legislative officers, who labor under the
same disqualification; while there is a still greater number of both classes, who
cannot take the oath prescribed by the law of July 2nd, 1862. If these new State
Governments did not go into operation until after the people of the States had
been declared by law to be entitled to representation in the Congress of the
United States, the question involved would be limited to the cases of those who
are disqualified under the third section of the proposed Amendment; but a part,
at least, (the Legislative Department) of the new Government must go into
operation before the State can be admitted, and there are many reasons why the
whole should be, so soon as Congress has passed upon and approved the Constitutions, that have been adopted. So far as the question affects the members elect of
the House of Representatives, the decision does not rest with the District Commander, but with the House, which is the judge of the election returns and qualifications of its own members; but as concerns the State officers, all who are disqualified under the third section of the amendment, must necessarily be excluded,
unless the disability is removed by Congress: and, so long as the Government
remains provisional, all must take the oath of office prescribed by the law of July
2nd, 1862. In North Carolina, not only the Executive and Legislative and the
Judicial officers, but the county officers have been elected, and the new Constitution provides that the term of office of the judiciary shall commence, upon
the approval of the Constitution by Congress; of the county officers five, of the
Executive officers ten, and of the Legislative fifteen days after that approval. In
South Carolina only the Executive and Legislative officers were elected; and the
Constitution makes no provision for the inauguration of the new Government.
An ordinance passed by the Convention on the 16th day of March, provides for
the meeting of the Legislature on the 12th day of May, instant, but I propose, if
Congress shall not in the mean time otherwise direct, that the Executive Of-
ficers elect shall enter upon their duties ten days after the approval of the Constitution by Congress, provided they are not disqualified by the third section of
the Constitutional amendment, and can take the oath prescribed by the law of
July 2nd, 1862. In North Carolina, two of the most important Executive Officers, (Governor and Lieutenant Governor) several of the Judicial Officers, and a
number of the members of the General Assembly, are disqualified under the
Constitutional Amendment, and, unless the disability be removed by Congress,
cannot enter upon their duties. A still greater number cannot take the oath prescribed by the law of July 2nd 1862, but can take that prescribed by the new
Constitution, if it should be approved by Congress. The same circumstances obtain in South Carolina, but not to so great an extent. None, I believe, of the
Executive Officers are disqualified by the Constitutional Amendment, and only
two or three by the law prescribing the oath. In the General Assembly, there will
probably be a number. The meeting of the Legislature (for the purpose of adopting the Constitutional Amendment) is a necessary prerequisite to the admission
of the State to representation. The organization of the other branches of the

State government, though less essential, is in every way, extremely desirable, and should be complete and self sustaining, previous to the withdrawal of the military authority; otherwise efforts might, and no doubt would, be made to embarass, delay, or prevent such organization. Under the laws as they now stand, none of the officers elect, who are disqualified by the Constitutional Amendment, or who are unable to take the oath prescribed by the act of July 2nd, 1862, can enter upon the discharge of the duties of the offices to which they have been elected, until, in the first case, the disability has been removed by Congress, or, in the second case, the provisions of the Reconstruction Laws, shall have become 'inoperative' by the admission of the State to representation in Congress The embarrassment that will result from even the temporary suspension of any officer, or provisional appointments until the question of removing the disability be determined, or until the provisions of the 9th Section of the law of July 19th, are no longer operative may readily be appreciated, and as it is presumed that the action of Congress upon questions of disability under the Constitutional amendment, will be upon individual cases, and not upon classes, it is recommended that the 9th Section of the law of July 19th be so modified as to permit persons elected to office under the new Constitution, who are not disqualified by the Constitutional amendment, to enter upon the duties of the officers to which they have been chosen, upon taking the oath of office prescribed by the Constitution of the State in which they have been elected. If there were any personal considerations prejudicial to the individual officers elect, it would be inexpedient to dispense with the requirement, which I desire to see relaxed. But no such objections are known to exist; on the contrary, in many instances there is the best ground for believing that such legislation would be a public benefit by securing the services of capable men, devoted in good faith to the interests of reconstruction, whose influence would not be limited to the immediate communities in which they live. To continue the disabilities which exclude these persons is to deprive the Government still further of the services of intelligent and well disposed men, whose technical disqualification is their only fault, and whose aid is essentially important to the speedy organization and successful working, of the new State Governments. The removal of the disabilities, while it will not jeopardize any interest which it is the policy of the Government of the United States to conserve and foster, will, in my judgment, not only meet the approval of a large majority of the people of the two States but will disarm much of the opposition, which the new State Governments must expect to encounter, and contribute greatly to the permanent success of the work of reconstruction." Copy, *ibid.*, Letters Received.

On May 9, USG wrote to Secretary of War Edwin M. Stanton. "I have the honor to forward herewith General Canby's letter relating to an ordinance of the South Carolina Convention, with enclosures, and to request that they be laid before Congress as matter of information." LS, *ibid.*, RG 46, Senate 40A–G3, War Dept. Reports. USG enclosed a letter of May 7 from Canby to Rawlins with several enclosures, concerning the government of S. C., printed as *SED*, 40-2-55.

1. See telegram to Maj. Gen. George G. Meade, April 29, 1868. See also *HED*, 40-2-276.

To Charles W. Ford

———

Washington, D. C., May 7th *1868*,

DEAR FORD,

Enclosed I send you a notice which I received yesterday. I presume this relates to one piece of the land purchased from L. Dent. Will you do me the kindness to settle this and send the bill to me. I think now it will be safe to cancel the deed of trust which you hold. Heretofore I have been afraid to have it canceled lest there might be something against the land that I knew nothing of. It is a matter of surprise to me that the Dents ever retained anything. The fact is they have not retained anything clear from all embarassment.

Yours Truly

U. S. GRANT

ALS, DLC-USG.

To Benjamin F. Wade

———

Washington, D. C., May 7th *1868*

HON. B. F. WADE,
PRESIDENT US. SENATE.
SIR:

I have the honor to acknowledge the receipt of Senate resolution of date Dec. 5th 1867, calling upon me for a statement of the number of white and colored voters registered in each of the States subject to the reconstruction acts of Congress, the number of white and colored voters voting for and against the calling of a convention, the number of white and colored voters who failed to vote either for or against the calling of a convention, and as far as practicable the number of white and colored persons disfranchised and rendered incompetent by the reconstruction acts to vote for a convention, and the number of white persons entitled to be registered but who did not apply for registration.—Not having the facts necessary to enable me to furnish the statement required, I referred the Resolution to the several District Commanders for the information called for so far as related to their several Districts; and in answer thereto I respectfully submit herewith their several reports.

Very respectfully

Your obedt. Servt.

U. S. GRANT

General.

LS, DNA, RG 46, Senate 40A–G3, War Dept. Reports. See *SED*, 40-2-53.

To Bvt. Maj. Gen. Robert C. Buchanan

———

Washington May 8th 1868

BVT. MAJ. GEN R. C. BUCHANAN

COMDG. 5TH MILITY DISTRICT

GENERAL:

The following list of office holders in the State of Texas has been submitted to me as obstacles to reconstruction in that State; and certain names have been suggested as proper persons to succeed the present incumbents, which is also herewith sent.[1] You will please refer this communication to Bvt. Maj. Gen'l. J. J. Reynolds, Commanding District of Texas, for his report, which you will return to these Headquarters with your recommendation on the same.

Galveston County

E. T. Austin, County Judge, to be succeeded by Jessee Stancel

John G. Walker, Dist. Atty. for Galveston and Harris counties to be succeeded by Ridge Paschal.

Oscar Farish, County Clerk, to be succeeded by J. Spencer Smith

John S. Jones, Dist. Clerk, to be succeeded by Wm E. Parker.

Frank Dirks, Sheriff, to be succeeded by J. R. Romain.

Geo. Mason, Just. Peace, prect. No. 1, to be succeeded by Wm. Easton.

R. D. Johnson, Just. Peace, prect. No. 2, to be succeeded by by G. T. Ruly

Constables—
Vacancy in prect. No. 1, to be filled by C. P. Gardner.
Vacancy in prect. No. 2, to be filled to J. P. Kissane.
O. B. Chapin prect. No. 3, to be succeeded by H. H. Swanston.
Vacancy in prect. No. 4, to be filled by Geo. S. Beale
City officers for Galveston—
R. D. Johnson, Recorder, to be succeeded by Wm. J. Lewis
J. G. Sewall, Clerk, to be succeeded by Robt. L. Sherrard
Sidney Scudder Assessor & Collector, to be succeeded by Oscar
F. Hunsaker
David Wakelee, Treasurer, to be succeeded by Sanford Mason
M. F. Mott, Attorney, to be succeeded by A. Waitz
Aldermen—
Barnard Turnan, 1st Ward, to be succeeded by R. K. Smith
Oscar Farish, 1st Ward, to be succeeded by John DeBruhl
N. B. Yard, 2nd Ward, to be succeeded by Dr. Geo. Beale
E. L. Ufford, 3d Ward, to be succeeded by J. Kuhne.
P. H. Hennessey, 4th Ward, to be succeded by T. G. Nichols
Houston, Harris County.
A. McGowan, Mayor, to be succeeded by J. S. Bachelder.
Washington County—
F. A. Baber, Sherriff, to be succeeded by E. T. Randle
Robt. Harris, Assessor & Collector, to be succeeded by T. S.
Post
J. J. Stockbridge, Dist. Clerk, to be succeeded by B. J. Arnold.

> Very respectfully
> Your obt. servt
> U. S. GRANT
> General

Copies, DLC-USG, V, 47, 60; DNA, RG 108, Letters Sent. On June 22, 1868, Bvt. Maj. Gen. Robert C. Buchanan, New Orleans, endorsed this letter. "I enclose letter of E. M. Pease, Gov of state of Texas of date June 6th '68. Neither he nor Gen Reynolds thinking proper to make any recommendation—I do likewise." Copy, *ibid.*, Register of Letters Received.

On May 4, 11:00 A.M., USG had telegraphed to Buchanan. "Why has not Constitutional Convention of Texas been convened?" ALS (telegram sent), *ibid.*, RG 107, Telegrams Collected (Bound); telegram sent, *ibid.*; telegram received (at 10:30 A.M.), *ibid.*, RG 393, 5th Military District, Telegrams Received. At 1:00 P.M., Buchanan telegraphed to USG. "Despatch received—Orders convening Constitutional Convention of Texas were issued April 13th—Copy sent to Adjutant General of the Army April 14th—Complete returns of election for delegates have not yet been received—" ALS (telegram sent), *ibid.*, RG 107, Telegrams Collected (Bound); telegram received (at 3:40 P.M.), *ibid.*; (at 4:30 P.M.) *ibid.*, RG 108, Telegrams Received.

On May 5, 11:45 A.M., USG telegraphed to Buchanan. "I would suggest that the convention in Texas be ordered to convene June 1st instead of 15th as now ordered." ALS (telegram sent), *ibid.*, RG 107, Telegrams Collected (Bound); telegram sent, *ibid.*; telegram received (at 11:15 A.M.), *ibid.*, RG 393, 5th Military District, Telegrams Received. On the same day, Buchanan telegraphed to USG. "I will order the Convention in Texas to convene June 1st, but do not think that the order will reach the remote Counties in season—The election for Members took place Febr 10th to 14th and complete returns have not yet been received—" ALS (telegram sent), *ibid.*, RG 107, Telegrams Collected (Bound); telegram received (at 3:30 P.M.), *ibid.*; *ibid.*, RG 108, Telegrams Received.

On May 9, 4:00 P.M., Buchanan telegraphed to USG. "The count of the returns of [t]he late election in this state shows: For the Constitution (66152) Sixty six thousand, one hundred & fifty two   Against the Constitution (48739) Forty eight thousand seven hundred & thirty nine   Majority for the Constitution (17413) Seventeen thousand four hundred & thirteen   The count of the other returns not yet completed" ALS (telegram sent), *ibid.*, RG 107, Telegrams Collected (Bound); telegram received (at 8:00 P.M.), *ibid.*; (at 6:30 P.M.) *ibid.*, RG 108, Telegrams Received. On May 21, Stephen B. Packard, chairman, Board of Registration, New Orleans, telegraphed to USG. "The Constitutional Convention authorized this board to promulgate the result of the election for Civil Officers including members of General assembly. See article one hundred fifty seven (157) Constitution. Gen Buchanan refuses to recognize the Board with the returns. Will you furnish the same or order Gen Buchanan to do so, or promulgate the result of the election that the general assembly may be convened and state Government inaugurated" Telegram received (at 5:20 P.M.), *ibid.*, RG 107, Telegrams Collected (Bound); (at 9:30 P.M.) *ibid.*, RG 108, Telegrams Received; copy, DLC-USG, V, 55. On May 22, 12:35 P.M., USG telegraphed to Buchanan. "In your dispatch of the 9th inst. reporting the result of the vote on the constitution in La, you say 'the count of the other returns not yet completed.' Is there any objection to furnishing the count of those returns when completed to the board of registration so that they may promulgate the same as provided by the convention, or will you promulgate them yourself" LS (telegram sent), DNA, RG 107, Telegrams Collected (Bound); telegram sent, *ibid.*; telegram received, *ibid.*, RG 393, 5th Military District, Telegrams Received. On the same day, Buchanan telegraphed to USG. "Dispatch received. I notified the Board of Registration yesterday that I would promulgate the result as soon as the count was finished" Telegram received (at 3:15 P.M.), *ibid.*, RG 107, Telegrams Collected (Bound); *ibid.*, RG 108, Telegrams Received; copies, *ibid.*, RG 393, 5th Military District, Telegrams Sent; DLC-USG, V, 55.

1. On May 7, Oscar F. Hunsaker, Washington, D. C., president, Republican Association of Tex., with endorsements of support from others, including George W. Paschal, wrote to USG. "I have the honor to transmit to you a list of names, asking their removal from office, as being opposed to reconstruction, and active in trying to defeat the laws of office congress, also a list of names to supply their places, towit, . . ." ALS, DNA, RG 108, Letters Received. USG incorporated Hunsaker's list in his letter to Buchanan.

To Edwin M. Stanton

———

Washington, D. C., May 9th *1868*

HON. E. M. STANTON
SECRETARY OF WAR
SIR:

I have the honor to forward herewith a corrected copy of the Constitution framed by the Virginia Convention, as furnished by General Schofield, together with his recommendations; and to request that they be laid before Congress.

Very respectfully
Your obedt serv't.
U. S. GRANT
General.

LS, DNA, RG 46, Senate 40A–G3, War Dept. Reports. On May 8, 1868, Bvt. Maj. Gen. John M. Schofield, Richmond, had written to USG. "I have the honor to forward herewith a corrected copy of the Constitution framed by the Virginia Convention, and to recommend that when said Constitution is submitted for ratification to the qualified Voters, Section 7 Article III, which prescribes an additional oath of office, may be submitted separately. I have also the honor to recommend that a time be appointed by Congress for the election in Virginia, not less than forty days from the date of the Act making the necessary appropriation" ALS, *ibid.* See *SED*, 40-2-54.

To Maj. Gen. George G. Meade

———

(Cipher)   Washington, May 9th *1868* [*10:15* A.M.]
MAJ. GN. G. G. MEADE,
ATLANTA GA.

Do you not think it advisable to appoint Civil officers elected at late election in Georgia to relieve all Army officers heretofore appointed by you?

U. S. GRANT
General

ALS (telegram sent), DNA, RG 107, Telegrams Collected (Bound); telegram sent, *ibid.*; telegram received, Meade Papers, PHi. On May 11, 1868, Maj. Gen. George G. Meade telegraphed to USG. "It was not my intention to put in office, any of the civil officers recently elected until Congress had acted on the Constitution—The only army officers detailed are the Governor, Comptroller & Treasurer—The Governor if put in office could not appoint any one, and would have to appoint evey one through me—I do not desire any such position, and doubt if it would result harmoniously—Again all appointees would have to take the test oath & I question whether many of the elected can do this—I have been greatly embarrassed in the few appointments I have made to find men who could take this oath.—When the Constitution is sent to Congress, if they authorise the Civil government going into office in advance of the admission of the state, and on the same terms, as if the state had been admitted, that is without requiring the test oath, I think this would be well.—I am not disposed to relieve Gov. Ruger at present, as there are certain financial & other questions originating under him which it is due to him, he should have time to adjust and settle.—I perhaps ought to explain, what I mean by want of harmony, between the Governor elect & myself.—Of course you will understand his appointments will be made on political & party grounds, and will be undoubtedly from his standpoint on good & sufficient reasons, but I have nothing & wish to have nothing to do with these matters & if he makes appointments thro me, the responsibility of concurrence if nothing more must rest on me.—" ALS (telegram sent), *ibid.*; telegram received (at 5:30 P.M.), DNA, RG 107, Telegrams Collected (Bound); *ibid.*, RG 108, Telegrams Received.

On May 11, 2:45 P.M., USG telegraphed to Meade. "Telegraph total number of votes, for & against Constitution, in Georgia" Telegrams sent (2), *ibid.*, RG 107, Telegrams Collected (Bound); telegram received, *ibid.*, RG 393, 3rd Military District, Telegrams Received. On the same day, Meade telegraphed to USG. "Official returns from all counties in which election was held, show total vote cast, one hundred and sixty thousand three hundred and sixteen, (160.316), Majority for the constitution, seventeen thousand six hundred and ninety nine (17,699) Majority for Bulloch, Governor seven thousand one hundred and ninety seven (7.197) I have issued an order proclaiming Constitution ratified under act, March twelfth (12th) sixty eight (68) and President of Convention will at once transmit it to congress." Telegram received (at 5:00 P.M.), *ibid.*, RG 107, Telegrams Collected (Bound); *ibid.*, RG 108, Telegrams Received; copies, DLC-USG, V, 55; Meade Papers, PHi. On May 12, Meade wrote to USG. "I herewith transmit an official copy of the Constitution of the State of Georgia recently ratified by the people of the state by a majority which you will see in the accompanying order proclaiming the same" ALS, DNA, RG 108, Letters Received. See letter to Schuyler Colfax, May 15, 1868. On May 26, Meade wrote to USG. "I have the honor to transmit, herewith inclosed, a report, showing the total registration of the State of Georgia, as also the vote cast at the recent election for and against the Constitution, and for Governor." Copy, Meade Papers, PHi. On June 1, USG wrote to Speaker of the House Schuyler Colfax. "In further answer to House Resolution of the 13th May, 1868, I have the honor to transmit herewith the report, just received, of Gen'l Meade, Comdg. 3d Military District, of the vote cast at the recent election for and against the constitution, and for Governor, in the State of Georgia. Also two General Orders from Gen. Canby,

Comd'g 2d Military District, proclaiming results of election in North Carolina and South Carolina" Copies, DLC-USG, V, 47, 60; DNA, RG 108, Letters Sent. See *HED*, 40-2-300.

To Schuyler Colfax

Washington, May 12, 1868

HON SCHUYLER COLFAX
SPEAKER OF THE HOUSE OF REPRESENTATIVES

In compliance with Resolution of the House of Representatives of May 11th., 1868, I have the honor to submit the following statement of the number of votes cast for and against the Constitutions of North Carolina, South Carolina, Georgia Louisiana and Alabama as reported by the several District Commanders

North Carolina
Votes for Constitution	92,590
Votes Against Constitution	71,820

South Carolina
Votes for Constitution	70.758
Votes Against Constitution	27.288

Georgia
Votes for Constitution	89,007
Votes against Constitution	71,309

Louisiana
Votes for Constitution	66.152
Votes against Constitution	48.739

Alabama
Votes for Constitution	69,807
Votes against Constitution	1,005

U. S. GRANT
General

Copies, DLC-USG, V, 47, 60; DNA, RG 108, Letters Sent.

To Bvt. Maj. Gen. Edward R. S. Canby

(Cypher)   Washington, May 13th *1868*, [*May 14, 10:30* A.M.]
MAJ. GN. E. R. S. CANBY,
CHARLESTON S. C.

Would it not be well to withdraw interference to the assembling of the Legislatures in N. & S. Carolina and leave it to Congress to recognize or reject their acts as they see fit? I would not advise formal recognition but do not see that it will not be well to leave the Legislatures elect to take the responsibility as they did in Arkansas.

U. S. GRANT
General

ALS (telegram sent), DNA, RG 107, Telegrams Collected (Bound); telegram sent, *ibid*.; telegram received (at 11:20 A.M.), *ibid*., RG 393, 2nd Military District, Letters Received. On May 14, 1868, Bvt. Maj. Gen. Edward R. S. Canby telegraphed to USG. "Telegram received. Constitution of North Carolina provides, that Legislature shall meet fifteen days after Constitution has been approved by Congress. The day for its meeting, in this State, was fixed for the 12th of May, under supposition that Congress would, before that time, have approved the Constitution. Finding that this was not probable, everyone became satisfied that there would be complications and embarrassments that should be avoided if possible. The most serious of these results arose from fact that, by the new Constitution, the judiciary must be recognized and judicial officers elected by the Legislature. This might be remedied by the adoption of the new Constitution by a military order, and the appointment of provincial judges; but the first would be, not only disrespectful to Congress, but would probably be regarded as an usurpation of a power which that body has reserved to itself; and the last would greatly embarrass the Legislature when it comes to pass upon that question. The order postponing the meeting of the Legislature was concurred in by the President of the Convention, the Governor elect, and a number of the other newly elected officers, and, thus far, I have heard no objection to it." Telegram received (at 4:00 P.M.), *ibid*., RG 107, Telegrams Collected (Bound); (at 3:45 P.M.) *ibid*., RG 108, Telegrams Received; copies (one sent by mail), *ibid*., Letters Received; *ibid*., RG 393, 2nd Military District, Letters Sent; DLC-USG, V, 55.

From April 16 to May 5, Canby sent ten telegrams to USG reporting election results in N. C. and S. C.; all are printed in *HED*, 40-[2]-291, pp. 1–4. On May 11, 3:30 P.M., USG telegraphed to Canby. "Telegraph ~~num~~ total number of votes, for & against Constitution, in South Carolina" Telegrams sent (2), DNA, RG 107, Telegrams Collected (Bound); telegram received (at 3:50 P.M.), *ibid*., RG 393, 2nd Military District, Letters Received. On the same day, Canby telegraphed to USG. "South Carolina total vote for the constitution seventy thousand, seven hundred and fifty eight (70.758)   Total vote against the constitution twenty seven thousand, two hundred and eighty eight (27.288)" Telegram received (at 4:30 P.M.), *ibid.*, RG 107, Telegrams Collected (Bound); *ibid.*, RG 108, Telegrams Received; copies, *ibid.*, RG 393, 2nd Military District, Letters Sent; DLC-USG, V, 55.

On May 6, Canby had telegraphed to USG. "General Scott, Governor elect of South Carolina, has informed me that it was expectation of the Legislature to organize new Government at meeting of Legislature on 12th instant, whether Congress has voted upon new Constitution or not; that much feeling is expressed against the order which fixes date of organization thirteen days after approval of Constitution by Congress, subject, of course, to a different direction by that body. My action, taken, either by Legislature, or by District Commander, to give effect to new Constitution, or to organize a government under it before it has been approved by Congress would be a direct usurpation of a power that rightfully belongs to Congress, and is expressly reserved, by that body, by 5th. Section, law March 2nd. 1867. The meeting of Legislature for purpose only of adopting the Constitutional Amendment, as it may hasten restoration of the State, and appears to be warranted by law, I do not regard objectionable, but any attempt to take possession of office and property of State before Constitution is approved would be unlawful and in contempt of authority of Congress. It would have been better, as in North Carolina, to have deferred meeting of new Legislature until after Congress has approved Constitution. I report more fully by mail" Telegram received (at 3:15 P.M.), DNA, RG 107, Telegrams Collected (Bound); *ibid.*, RG 108, Telegrams Received; copies (one sent by mail), *ibid.*, Letters Received; *ibid.*, RG 393, 2nd Military District, Letters Sent; DLC-USG, V, 55. See *SED*, 40-2-55. On May 7, Canby telegraphed to USG. "I have postponed the meeting of the Legislature until after Congress has approved the Constitution. This settles satisfactorily any questions that might have arisen" Telegram received (on May 8, 9:00 A.M.), DNA, RG 107, Telegrams Collected (Bound); *ibid.*, RG 108, Telegrams Received; copies (one sent by mail), *ibid.*, Letters Received; *ibid.*, RG 393, 2nd Military District, Letters Sent; DLC-USG, V, 55.

On May 15, 3:30 P.M., USG telegraphed to Canby. "I would suggest that all elections for officers of rail-roads in which the states have an interest, in your district, be suspended until the organization of State governments recently elected." ALS (telegram sent), DNA, RG 107, Telegrams Collected (Bound); telegram sent, *ibid.*; telegram received (at 4:30 P.M.), *ibid.*, RG 393, 2nd Military District, Telegrams Received.

To Bvt. Maj. Gen. Robert C. Buchanan

Washington, May 145th *1868.* [9:40 A.M.]

Bvt. Maj. Gn. R. C. Buchanan,
New Orleans, La,

Chairman La. Board of Registration reports murders in many parts of the state and no protection afforded by the Military or

Civil government.[1] If Civil government fails to protect the Citizen Military government should supply its place. What is the state of affairs?

U. S. GRANT

General,

ALS (telegram sent), DNA, RG 107, Telegrams Collected (Bound); telegram sent, *ibid.*; telegram received (at 10:00 A.M.), *ibid.*, RG 393, 5th Military District, Telegrams Received. On May 16, 1868, Bvt. Maj. Gen. Robert C. Buchanan telegraphed to USG. "Dispatch received. Seventeen (17) homicides in all reported in Louisiana since I assumed command of the 5th Military District. In every instance, as far as I am informed the matter has been investigated by the Civil authorities. When Civil authority fails to act, Military authority is interposed From the information received by me I do not believe all of these homicides were committed solely on account of political differences although in many instances they may have grown out of them" ALS (telegram sent), *ibid.*, RG 107, Telegrams Collected (Bound); telegram received (on May 17, 10:30 A.M.— misdated 1867), *ibid.*; *ibid.*, RG 108, Telegrams Received.

1. On May 14, Stephen B. Packard, chairman, Board of Registration, New Orleans, telegraphed to USG. "Loyal men are being murdered in many parishes. General Buchanan refuses to interfere to stop the massacre. He affects to believe that civil law is amply able to protect our people. He declares he will not govern Louisiana by military rule. revenge and murders are rampant in our state. Can nothing be done to protect our Lloyal people from assassination?" Telegram received (on May 15, 9:00 A.M.), *ibid.*, RG 107, Telegrams Collected (Bound); *ibid.*, RG 108, Telegrams Received; copies, DLC-USG, V, *55*; DLC-Andrew Johnson. On May 15, USG endorsed a copy of this telegram to President Andrew Johnson. ES, *ibid.*

To Schuyler Colfax

———

Washington, May 15, 1868,

HON. SCHUYLER COLFAX
SPEAKER OF THE HOUSE OF REPRESENTATIVES
SIR:

I have the honor to acknowledge the receipt of House resolution of the 12th inst. severally directing the Secretary of War and the General of the Army to communicate to the House the reports of the several District Commanders of the elections held for and against the ratification of the proposed constitutions in the States of Georgia, North Carolina, South Carolina and Louisiana, and for the elections of officers thereunder in said States, together with all the accompanying papers forwarded by them or any of them, touching said elections or the revised registration authorized by the reconstruction Acts of Congress." In answer thereto I respectfully transmit herewith copies of all dispatches received from District Commanders for any of the above States bearing upon the points embraced in the resolution, and of all orders issued by them touching the elections and the revised registrations in said States, also an official copy furnished by Gen. Meade for these Head quarters of the Constitution of the State of Georgia recently ratified by the people of the State by a majority, with General Meade's order proclaiming the same. No other reports have as yet been received at these Headquarters.

> Very respectfully
> Your obt servt.
> U. S. GRANT
> General

Copies, DLC-USG, V, 47, 60; DNA, RG 108, Letters Sent. The enclosures are printed in *HED*, 40-2-291. On June 2, 1868, USG wrote to Speaker of the House Schuyler Colfax. "In further answer to House Resolution, of the 13th May, 1868, I have the honor to transmit herewith an abstract just received from Gen. Canby, Comdg. 2nd Milty. Dist, of the votes cast for members of the House of Representatives of the Congress of the United States at the recent elections held in the States of North Carolina and South Carolina." Copies, DLC-USG, V, 47, 60; DNA, RG 108, Letters Sent. The enclosure is printed in *HED*, 40-2-301.

To Charles W. Ford

———

> Washington, D, C,
> May 15th 1868,

DEAR FORD,

Enclosed I send you my check for $39 87/100, the amount of taxes which you were kind enough to pay for me. I sent you some time ago check for freight which you paid on my horses which I hope was duly received.

Impeachment is likely to fail, though more will probably be known on the subject before you receive this. A great deal of anxiety is felt here on the subject.

I expect to go to Mo in June and to remain there for several weeks. I have been so often disappointed however that I shall not feel certain of my movements untill I actually start.

Yours Truly
U. S. GRANT

ALS, DLC-USG.

To Lt. Gen. William T. Sherman

Washington, May 19, 1868

LT. GEN. W. T. SHERMAN
CARE BVT. MAJ. GEN. C. C. AUGUR,
OMAHA, N. T.
GENERAL:

Your letter of the 8th of May, from Fort Laramie,[1] is received, and will be submitted to the Secretary of War for his approval of the course proposed by you. I of course approve. Any expense, or course, that will preserve peace with the Indians is to be commended.

I think your proposition to build cheap barracks at Omaha to accommodate a regiment of troops a good one. A reserve at that point can be maintained cheaply and will be available to send against hostile Indi[an]s wherever they may break out.

Your Peace commission may accomplish a great deal of good, beside that of collecting the Indians on reservations, by attracting the attention of the Indians during the season practicable for making war, and also of our white people, who seem never to be satisfied without hostilities with them. It is much better to support a

Peace commission than a campaign against Indians. I do not mean
to insinuate that real and lasting good may not also result from
your labors. On the contrary I believe it will; but the incidental
good is a compensation

> With great respect
> Your obt. servt.
> U. S. GRANT
> General

Copies, DLC-USG, V, 47, 60; DNA, RG 108, Letters Sent. On June 7, 1868,
Lt. Gen. William T. Sherman, Santa Fé, wrote to USG. "I have from Genl
Nichols at Saint Louis a copy of your letter of May 19, and am well satisfied at
your general approval of our acts up to the North. I must now ask a similar share
of liberality to another similar step just taken as to the Navajos. I found the
Bosque a mere spot of green grass in the midst of a Wild desert, and that the
Navajos had sunk into a Condition of absolute poverty & despair. To allow them
to remain was to assume an annual cost of their maintainence for *Ever*, of about
half a million. To move them East ward was impossible by reason of their strong
prejudices, and no alternative was left but to give them a part of their old
Country, and move them there at once. When I come East I will come fortified
by facts that will satisfy most people, but Carleton & friends are half crazy on
this Bosque Redondo question, and it is the only vital question of New Mexico—
One feature is that the few Rancheros East of the Rio Grande are sadly disappointed at this change as the Establishmt consuming so much public money was
of profit and advantage to them. Whereas the People West of the Valley favor
the change back to the Old Country for a similar reason. Now if the Navajos
were a hostile or dangerous tribe of Indians the very reverse would be the Case,
but General Getty and all the officers here say the Navajos if left alone will be
peaceful, and as peonage is pretty well broken up, the Mexicans will no longer
invade the Navajos to steal children which was one of the provoking causes of
War in former times. Of this more at length, if a Controversy should arise. The
only Indians who give trouble out here are the Apaches, who are scattered all
over Western Texas, Southern New Mexico & Arizona, but they operate in small
parties. General Getty says four (4) armed men can go anywhere in NewMexico,
and that is as high a measure of safety as the Military can give. It was never
contemplated that our soldiers, should be employed in hunting down sniper murderers & thieves, but this seems to have been their habitual use here for twenty
years. When a Citizen loses a horse, or some cattle or sheep, instead of calling on
his neighbors to go and help find them, he rides fifty or a hundred miles to some
Military post, to report the fact, and forthwith publishes some paragraph to the
Effect that the Regular troops are of no account. Take away the Troops from this
Country and it will be poor indeed. The only profitable mines in NewMexico,
have their base in the U S. Treasury in Washington. General Getty however is
universally Esteemed and is as good an officer as we could have out here. I will
start Eastward tomorrow but cannot travel as fast as the Mail. I must stop at
Fort Union, and at Maxwells, to see the Utes who are there. After that I will
come by stage to Fort Lyon, cross over to Fort Wallace, and down the Smoky
Hill, looking at our Military interests in that Quarter. If without neglecting

material interests I can reach St Louis by the 24 I will attend Mary Shermans Wedding at Cleveland Ohio, on the 26, of June I agree with you, that the Chief use of the Peace Commission is to kill time, which will do more to settle Indians than any thing we can do—" ALS, *ibid.*, Letters Received. Enclosed correspondence between Sherman and Bvt. Maj. Gen. George W. Getty is *ibid.* On June 18, USG endorsed a copy of Sherman's letter to Secretary of War John M. Schofield. ES, *ibid.*, RG 94, Letters Received, 793M 1868. Related papers are *ibid.*

On April 23, Sherman, St. Louis, had telegraphed to USG. "Just arrived— news from Laramie shows that the Grand Council will not be held on the first of May, so I will stay here till Sunday and can reach Cheyenne in four 4 days." Telegram received (on April 24, 9:00 A.M.), *ibid.*, RG 107, Telegrams Collected (Bound); (on April 23) *ibid.*, RG 108, Telegrams Received; copy, DLC-USG, V, 55. On May 2, Sherman, Fort Russell, Dakota Territory, telegraphed to USG. "Yesterday I went to end of track which is within three (3) miles of Fort Sanders, and will reach there today. I start this morning for Fort Laramie. Nothing definite as to indian affairs" Telegram received (marked as sent on May 3, received at 10:20 A.M.), DNA, RG 107, Telegrams Collected (Bound); *ibid.*, RG 108, Telegrams Received; copy, DLC-USG, V, 55.

On May 9, Bvt. Maj. Gen. William A. Nichols, St. Louis, telegraphed to USG. "The following telegram just received: Fort Laramie, May 5th 1868. Received at St Louis Mo. May 9th, 10.30 A M. To GEN. W. A. NICHOLS Head Quarters. Arrived yesterday. Snow storm prevailing. Commissioners now in session. They are positive that the recent killing and depredations along the railroad have been committed by small bands of Minneconjous of which they had *notice.* The Commissioners believes the bulk of the Sioux can be peaceably removed to the Missouri River on the reservation slected last year, after which we may have to war with the malcontents. We hold council with the Crows tomorrow. The Upper Cheyennes are in, and the Arrapahoes are near at hand, but Red Cloud is uncertain. Signed W. T. SHERMAN" Telegram received (at 3:15 P.M.), DNA, RG 108, Telegrams Received; copy, DLC-USG, V, 55. On May 13, Sherman, Fort Russell, telegraphed to USG. "Just arrived from Laramie things proceeding about as well as we can expect will be here & at Denver till next Monday when will start by stage for New Mexico beyond reach of telegraph if there is anything I should know let some one telegraph me at Denver by Sunday" Telegram received (at 9:25 P.M.), DNA, RG 108, Telegrams Received; copy, DLC-USG, V, 55. On May 14, Nichols telegraphed to USG. "I have a dispatch from Genl Sherman dated Fort Russell thirteenth (13th). He says. Indian matters progressing as well as can be expected. The General will leave Denver next monday for New Mexico, from which time he will be away from the telegraph for a month; mail matters addressed to Fort Union will reach him." Telegram received (at 12:40 P.M.), DNA, RG 107, Telegrams Collected (Bound); *ibid.*, RG 108, Telegrams Received; copy, DLC-USG, V, 55.

1. On May 8, Sherman, Fort Laramie, had written to USG. "It is proper I should keep you advised of the condition of affairs on this Frontier, that you may judge of the probabilities in the Future. I was of opinion, and still am of opinion that this Peace Commission should do little or nothing more till our Report to Congress of last December, with the Bill reported by Mr Henderson have been fully and freely discussed in Congress, and action taken in the form of Law. But we find Congress at a dead Lock by reason of the Impeachment Trial, and the

Indians finding our General promises not sustained by facts, are naturally tending to the conclusion that the Treaties we make, and the promises held out, are of the same nature ~~and kind~~ as others of like kind in former times. Still as a rule those whom we met last year seem to act on their promises of Peace, whereas others whom we did not meet, and have not yet seen, are as mistrustful and seemingly hostile as Ever. Several murders and robberies have occurred along the Line of the Railroad, and the People generally ridicule our Efforts at Peace, and think we are deliberately deluded, and deceived even by those who have signed Treaties. I arrived here last Monday and found here Generals Harney, Augur & Terry, and Genl Sanborn. Mr Commissioner Tappan came with me, so that we are now Six Commissioners Present. We have had several meetings, and have canvassed all the questions, and have concluded it is best to persevere in the course begun, if only to gain time, and to withdraw from hostility a considerable part—Before my arrival a Treaty had been signed by the Brulé Band of sioux in which they Engage, on certain very liberal terms to remove to the Reservation indicated in our Report, (on the Missouri River); and as many of these were encamped last winter at North Platte on the Railroad, we have concluded it best for them, and for us that they should move at once over to the Missouri River near Fort Randall, even if we the Military must furnish them subsistence till Congress provides the necessary means to the Indian Dept to fulfil the Treaty stipulations. With the Brulés will go scattered parts of other Bands, including some Half Breeds, that have usually lingered about this Fort (Laramie). Yesterday we signed a Treaty with the Crow Nation which is represented to have always been friendly, and we have given them a Reservation of limited Extent in Montana, South of the Yellowstone, a Reservation that I think will be temporary, and that in due time they too will find it to their interest to go down the Missouri River and settle among the Sioux. Today and tomorrow we hold Councils with the fragments of Northern Cheyennes and Arapahos, and will insist on their becoming a part of the Sioux Nation, or returning to their old tribes located in the Reservation back of Arkansas. This will close out all Indians now here, but will leave out the Ogallallas, and Minneconjous who have been our worst Enemies on the Powder River Road. From these we have varied accounts. Some want to come in for Peace, but the young warriors contend that they will wait to see if we are honest in our resolve to withdraw those Posts, which they assert were the Cause of the War. I have long since given an order for the withdrawal of these posts, but it is impracticable till Summer. On the 1st of June, all the public stores & property which cannot be moved at Fort C. F. Smith will be sold at auction, to People who are willing to buy and remove back into Montana. The Garrison will move them to Fort Phil Kearney. From that Post we will remove every thing portable & abandon the Post & remove to Reno, and then the same to Fort Fetterman and Laramie. This will bring in the Regiment of Jno. E. Smith, with which General Augur designed to build a new Post on the head of Wind River, at the Mouth of Popage Creek, above fifty miles north of St Marys Station on the Old Emigrant Road, or about 80 miles north of the Pacific Railroad. After full reflection I have instructed General Augur not to build that Post, and not to complete the Post of Fort Fetterman begun last year, but rather to protect the Railroad by detachments posted along the Railroad itself, or temporary stations near it—This will leave us to build only Quarters for ~~four~~ 4 Companies on the Railroad where it crosses the North Platte, intermediate between Fort Sanders and Fort Bridger. General Augur will keep the troops in summer in tents, and may send a Couple of Companies to the Wind River to give protection to the People who have gone to the newly discovered Gold Mines there, but will bring in all to the Posts already finished or to the Rail Road Stations for winter. Still this will leave Genl Augur short of quarters for one Regimt the coming winter. We have never had reserves in hand for the clamors that always open with Spring, and instead of pushing our troops out so far, I am convinced we should have a Regimt at Omaha in winter to send out on the Railroad to meet these cases. Instead of building these Expensive Posts out here, I will recommend that we build cheap barracks for one Regimt in or near Omaha. Parties there have more than once offered the necessary land, and Genl Augur will on his return to Omaha Endeavor to secure a site of about 100 acres near Omaha, and proceed to build there quarters for a Regimt. We have already there all the necessary store houses, leaving necessary only the Barracks. He will have plenty of time to make plans & Estimates to be submitted to you and the Quarter Master General for approval. I am satisfied this will prove more Economical, and more Efficient than to rebuild one or more new Posts out here, to replace those to be abandoned. On Monday next we will have concluded with all the Indians who have come in, when Gen Augur, Gen Terry Mr. Tappan and myself will return to Cheyenne, leaving Generals Harney & Sanborn here some days longer to await the return of some messengers, who have gone out to 'Red Cloud,' and the 'Man afraid of his horses,' who represent the hostile Indians. If they come in here these two Commissioners can conclude with them a Treaty similar to the one already made with the Brulés I and Mr Tappan will go by stage to Denver and Fort Union in New Mexico and thence to the Navajos to see if we can make any solution of that most troublesome case. General Augur after looking to matters pertaining to his command will go out to Fort Bridger to conclude a Treaty with the Shoshonees or Snakes, who are represented as 'Willing and Waiting' General Terry will go up to Ft Randall and Fort Sully to make preperation for the Sioux to be moved over to that neighborhood, and be prepared to join Generals Harney and Sanborn who will go up the Missouri River as high as Fort Rice, to conclude with the River Indians, who are also represented as perfectly willing to remove within the Reservation marked out for them West of the River, and above Nebraska. Thus you will see we have cut out work for all summer, although I expect to get in the latter part of June, from NewMexico, and will await the Return of the other Commissioners from their various Errands before we all meet again, at some agreed on place, to conclude our Work. I do not apprehend any general War this year, only the predatory bands of thieving or murdering Indians ~~for~~ which the People in this vast uninhabited Region should be prepared to resist. In time we must take these Wild Indians in hand—and give them a devil of a thrashing They deserve it now, but they are ~~now~~ so scattered, and so mixed up, that even if we were prepared, we would hardly know which way to strike. I will do all that is possible to give general protection especially to the rapid progress of the Pacific Railroad, but it were idle to undertake to run down every horsethief, or to protect what are termed the Ranches scattered at wide distances along the Roads, occasionally traversed by trains of wagons. The Pacific Railroad does not make settlements in the strict sense, of the Term. Every twenty miles is a Station where a few men are kept as Repair parties, but they are so dispersed that they are a weakness instead of strength. They are all clamoring for protection, and Genl Augur has been forced to ~~station~~ place soldiers at nearly Every station outsid of Omaha. The great advantage of the Railroad is that it gives us rapid communication, and cannot be stolen like the horses and mules of trains as of old, but the People along it are much Exposed to depredating bands of hostile Indians. They always charge their losses to the Friendly Indians who have been collected near, and it is for this reason that I deem it so essential to remove them at once, even— at our Military Expense, without awaiting the lawful but slow action of Congress. Asking yours and the Secretary of War's approval in these matters I will act at once. Please reply in General terms by letter and telegraph to General Augur, as by the time this reaches you I will probably be beyond Denver." ALS, DNA, RG 108, Letters Received. On May 20, USG endorsed a copy of this letter. "Respectfully forwarded to the Secy of War, inviting special attention to those portions of the letter which relate to the removal and subsistence of Indians at military expense, requesting to be informed as early as practicable whether the Secretary sanctions such expenditure. Gen. Sherman's recommendation that cheap barracks for one regiment be built in or near Omaha is approved." ES, *ibid.*

To Vice Admiral David D. Porter

Washington, D, C,
May 25th 1868,

My Dear Adm.l

Your telegram informing me that Healy will be at Annapolis tomorrow is received. I would like to take Mrs. Grant up and spend a few days with you whilst he is there, but one of her sisters who she has not met for a long time has just arrived, and then too a Committee from that awful Chicago Convention will meet here on Friday,[1] and, under all the circumstances, I must be here to meet it. I see no chance now but for Mr. Healy to come to Washington. You and he had better come down here. I will give Mr. H. a place in my office to work.

Yours Truly
U. S. Grant

ALS, CtY. See letter to Lt. Gen. William T. Sherman, March 18, 1868.

1. See letter to Joseph R. Hawley, May 29, 1868.

To William Elrod

———

Washington, D, C,
May 27th/68

DEAR ELROD,

I want you to take possession of W. Dent's, and Gen. Dent's, lands, collect the rents, and as soon as possible get all tenants off the places. Next year we will put their cleared lands in oats and clover if you think best. If they are rich enough you can put in wheat and timothy this fall.

I will be out to the farm just as soon as possible.—I will take out with me, if I do not send before, power of Attorney for you to act for the Messrs. Dent.

I am pleased to know you have the farm all enclosed! After a while we will have stock enough to eat all the grass. In time I hope you will have cows enough to make it an object. When the crop comes into market you may be able to buy a few heifer calves to help along a little. My expenses are so great that I can spare but little money out of pocket to put in the farm. You of course understand that I intend your salary for this year to be $500 00 besides what Sarah Ellen and the children can make off of chickens? After this year I hope they will be able to make Three or Four Hundred that wa[y].

AL (signature clipped), Illinois Historical Survey, University of Illinois, Urbana, Ill.

To Joseph R. Hawley

———

Washington, D, C. May 29th *1868*,

GENERAL JOSEPH R. HAWLEY,
PRESIDENT NATIONAL UNION REPUBLICAN CONVENTION.

In formally accepting the nomination of the "National Union Republican Convention," of the 21st of May, inst. it seems proper that some statement of views, beyond the mere acceptance of the nomination, should be expressed.

The proceedings of the Convention were marked with wisdom, moderation and patriotism, and, I believe, express the feelings of the great mass of those who sustained the Country through its recent trials. I endore their ~~proceedings~~ resolutions.

If elected to the office of President of the United States it will be my endeavor to administer all the laws, in good faith, with economy, and with the view of giving peace, quiet and protection every where. In times like the present it is impossible, or at least eminently improper, to lay down a policy to be adhered to, right or wrong, through an Administration of four years. New political issues, not foreseen, are constantly arising; the views of the public on old ones are constantly changing, and a purely Administrative officer should always be left free to execute the will of the people. I always have, ~~and always shall~~, respected that will, and always shall.

Peace, and universal prosperity, its sequence, with economy of administration, will lighten the burden of taxation, while it con-stan[tl]y reduces the National debt. Let us have peace.

With great respect,

your obt. svt.

U. S. Grant

ALS, Roswell Hawley, Hartford, Conn. USG's draft of this letter was also dated May 29, 1868. "In formally accepting the nomination of the National Union Republican Convention, of the 21st of May, inst. it seems proper that some ~~pledge~~ statement of views, beyond the mere acceptance of the nomination, should be expressed.—The proceedings of the Convention were marked with wisdom, moderation and patriotism, and, I believe, express the feelings of the great mass of those who sustained the Country through its trials. I endors those proceedings. ~~generally, and give more than an endorsement to those clauses touching upon repudiation and the protection of our Citizens, native or naturalized, at home or abroad.~~ If elected to the office of President of the United States it will be my endeavor to administer all the laws, in good faith, with economy, and with the view of giving peace, quiet and protection every where. At the earlyest moment practicable I want to see all ~~distinctions~~ disfranchisements, on account of the rebellion, ended, and every man ~~made~~ left to feel that he too is a citizen, with all the rights of any other citizen, ~~in~~ of this growing nation. When reconstruction, as provided for by those who alone have the wright and the power to dictate the terms, is completed, this, it seems to me, may be safely, and speedily effected. A few years of peace, with economy of Administration, will drive out of sight questions ~~of repudiation~~ of burden of taxation. Let us have peace. In times like the present it is impossible, ~~for~~ at least eminently improper, to lay down a policy to be adhered to, right or wrong, through an administration of four years. New political ~~immergeneics~~ issues, not foreseen are constantly arising; ~~and~~ the views of the public on old ones are constantly changing, and a purely administrative officer should always be left free to execute the will of the ~~sovreign of the Nation, the people~~ people. I always have, and always shall, respect ~~theat laws of this sovreign~~ will. ~~Peace~~ Quiet, and universal prosperity, its sequence, with ~~and~~ economy of administration, will lighten the burden of taxation while it constantly reduces the National debt. ~~Twenty years of peace will develope this great country to such greatness, extent, great and will develope such resources, that, to pay the entire national debt in one year then would not tax the peope of that day as their resources were taxed in one year of the war.~~ Let us have peace." ADf, USG 3. On June 5, Joseph R. Hawley, Hartford, wrote to USG. "I have the honor to acknowledge the receipt of your letter accepting the nomination tendered by the National Union Republican Convention. It was delayed a day by being directed to New Haven instead of Hartford, but as it had already been given to the public no practical inconvenience resulted therefrom. Permit me to add my voice to that of the public in general in expressing profound satisfaction with its terms." ALS, *ibid.*

A Soldiers' and Sailors' National Convention that endorsed USG's nomination on May 19 presented resolutions of support to him on May 29. USG responded: "GENTLEMEN OF THE SOLDIERS' AND SAILORS' CONVENTION— I will say, while it was never a desire of mine to be a candidate for political office, it affords me great gratification to feel that I have the support of those who were with me in the war. If I did not feel that I had the confidence of those I would feel less desirous of accepting the position. The acceptance of the office is not a matter of choice but of duty. Hoping, having accepted the nomination, I will receive your aid till next November, I must thank you, gentlemen, for the honor you have conferred upon me." *New York Tribune,* May 30, 1868.

Also on May 29, USG responded to the notification committee of the Republican Convention. "MR. PRESIDENT AND GENTLEMEN OF THE NATIONAL UNION CONVENTION: I will endeavor in a very short time to write you a letter accepting the trust you have imposed upon me. Expressing my gratitude for the confidence you have placed in me I will now say but little orally, and that is to thank you for the unanimity with which you have selected me as a candidate for the Presidential office. I can say in addition I looked on during the progress of the proceedings at Chicago with a great deal of interest, and am gratified with the harmony and unanimity which seem to have governed the deliberations of the Convention. If chosen to fill the high office for which you have selected me I will give to its duties the same energy, the same spirit, and the same will, that I have given to the performance of all duties which have devolved upon me heretofore. Whether I shall be able to perform these duties to your entire satisfaction, time will determine. You have truly said, in the course of your address, that I shall have no policy of my own to interfere against the will of the people." *New York Times,* May 30, 1868.

On May 21, William Orton, Chicago, telegraphed to USG. "I have the pleasure to announce your nomination by the National Republican Convention, now in session, for the office of President of the U. S. unanimously and by acclamation" Telegram received, ICarbS. Bvt. Brig. Gen. Frederick T. Dent noted on the telegram: "This telegram first announced to Gen Grant his nomination" AES, *ibid.* On the same day, USG addressed a crowd gathered outside his house. "GENTLEMEN: Being entirely unaccustomed to public speaking, and without the desire to cultivate that power, it is impossible for me to find appropriate language to thank you for this demonstration. All that I can say is, that to whatever position I may be called by your will, I shall endeavor to discharge its duties with fidelity and honesty of purpose. Of my rectitude in the performance of public duties you will have to judge for yourselves by my record before you." *New York Times*, May 23, 1868.

On May 22, Maj. Gen. Philip H. Sheridan, Fort Leavenworth, wrote to USG. "I feel very happy over the result of the Chicago. Convention I can now. see peace & prosperity for the Country—& the period is not distant when loyalty to the governmt will not. be considered a crime at the White House. I will not Congratulate you because I believe you are sacrificing personal interest & comforts. to give to the Country a civil victory which will be fatal to the Rebels North & South—" ALS, USG 3.

On the same day, John G. F. Holston, Zanesville, Ohio, wrote to USG. "Permit me to offer my congratulation In the lonely tent on the banks of the Tishemingo (Corinth), I dimly saw the rising star, beginning to emerge from the cloud. Three years ago, when I took the liberty of questioning you on the subject, I advocated and felt certain, of what the Telegraph yesterday, flashed over the length & breadth of the land. The people will ratify the action of the Chicago Convention, and I shall see, my ardent wish crowned, by beholding you at the Zenith of human glory. May God protect and guide you, and like your prototype Washington, may you be 'First in war, first in peace and first in the hearts of your countrymen." ALS, *ibid.*

On May 25, Bvt. Maj. Gen. John M. Schofield, Richmond, wrote to USG. "I hope you will not think it out of place for me to tender you my hearty congratulations upon the action of the Chicago Convention. The perfect unanimity and great enthusiasm of your nomination were certainly highly gratifying, as being a formal ratification of the popular endorsements of your public record which have heretofore been made throughout the country. But your unanimous nomination was long pre-determined, and was but the fulfilment of universal expectation. On the other hand, when the Convention met there was ground for apprehension that its action in other respects might not be so wise. But this apprehension has, at least in a great degree, been dispelled. The judicious selection of Mr. Colfax as second on the ticket, and the general practical wisdom displayed in framing the platform; that is, in laying down practical rules of action based upon the necessities of the country instead of abstract political theories, have greatly increased the probabilities of success and, at the same time, made that success the more to be desired I have always believed that the union could be fully restored only by the man who put down the rebellion, while I have not been without serious apprehension that by forcing upon the country extreme radical theories the stability of the government might be endangered. Great reforms require time for their full development—time in which theories may be analyzed and that which is sound and of practical utility separated from the unsound and chimerical. Wisdom and moderation in Congress will now give the country restoration and peace. Your election to the Presidency will be the end of our political troubles as your accession to the command in chief of the Army was the end of the Southern rebellion." ALS, *ibid.*

On the same day, Maj. James S. Brisbin, Lexington, wrote to USG. "*Private & Confidential* . . . I congratulate you on the unanimous nomination at Chicago by your old comrads and the citizen delegates to an office that no man ever before reached, except Washington, without opposition. If I had been a delegate I would have felt constrained to vote for brave old Ben Wade for the second place on the ticket but in Colfax we have a first rate man and now the next thing is to elect you and Schuyler, Notwithstanding your overwhelming popularity we must work day and night from now until the election or we will be defeated I have closely watched ~~and~~ or participated in every great political contest since 1844 and if my judgement is worth anything there never was a time when there was greater need of untiring vigilance and labor. The revenues of the Country are in the hands of the enemy and the whiskey ring alone can raise from now until the close of the canvas a million a day should they need so much for political purposes. If impeachment fails finally I beg you to urge Congress to at once repeal the whiskey tax and thus cut off the corrupting influences of the 'Ring'. I fear more than anything else the effect of money aganst us in the next Campaign and especially in the South. An active corps of good white and black speakers should be got early into the field in the South and kept at work. Some of our speakers will no doubt be hung or shot in the back counties of Kentucky during the Campaign but we will make an active canvas at all hazards. The rebels are more afraid of me than any man in the state and for that reason I wish to be left on duty here until after the election. Cash Clay is coming home and we will take care of the rebellion in Kentucky. When you are elected I will ask you to be for us a good President and stand firmly by our republican principles, and victories in the field but what will be most agreeable to you I will never ask you for any political office not being a politician, and having no ~~friends~~ partisans to reward nor enemies to punish Wishing you well General . . ." ALS, *ibid.*

On the same day, Carl Schurz, St. Louis, wrote to USG. "*Private* . . . I beg leave to offer you my sincerest congratulations on the unanimity with which you have been nominated for the Presidency and the general enthusiasm called forth by the event. Let me ask you to listen to a few suggestions concerning the coming campaign. Although we have a very strong ticket, I do not look upon our success as absolutely certain. We shall have to work vigorously and incessantly, and in order to do that we must put the *working force* of the party in the right spirit. All that is necessary is that you should in your letter of acceptance express ~~the~~ your approval of the platform upon which you have been nominated, in clear and emphatic terms That letter will be your first political manifesto, I believe, and it ought to silence all those who have found fault with you for keeping your own counsel and not indulging in any political declarations. A strong and decided endorsement of the platform will not frighten any of the timid and quiet gentlemen who are ready to follow your lead anyhow and with whom your name alone is a tower of strength; but it will inspire the working men of the party for the task before them. I doubt not, you have found the platform just in sentiment and moderate in tone; it is at the same time liberal enough to take the wind out of any 'Chase-movement,' if such a thing be attempted to divide us. All that is wanted, is your emphatic endorsement. The second suggestion I wish to offer is the following: One of the principal elements of strength of the Democratic party in the coming contest will be the whisky ring. It will furnish the money, and probably very large sums, perhaps large enough to become dangerous to us. There is a simple way to knock the bottom out of that concern. Congress should pass a bill reducing the tax on whisky to 50 or even 25 cents. Such a measure would increase the revenues of the government, stop that source of corruption and put an end to the whisky ring. The thing ought to have been done long ago. I suppose your influence upon members of Congress would at present go very far to bring it about in time to have an effect upon the campaign. But it ought to be done very soon. Please, General, do not consider these suggestions as an attempt to force myself upon your notice. They come from one who is going to devote his whole energies to the work before us and who has the success of the cause and the candidates sincerely at heart." ALS, *ibid.*

On June 1, Silas Miller, Cincinnati, wrote to USG. "Allow me to congratulate you on your unanimous nomination as the candidate of the great Republican party as their standard bearer in the election for President, and allow me here to say that there is but one obstacle in the way of your triumphant election, and that can be removed by Congress, with or without the consent of the acting President,   To insure your election it is only necessary for Congress to repeal the Whisky Tax, which is the great lever of success with the corrupt Democratic party,   With your personal influence you can have it repealed, and thereby save the Country and secure your election, if not I tremble for both. We are now paying 25 Millions annually to collect 13 Millions and putting into Democrats and corrupt Republicans pockets 80 Millions' to ruin the country and the Repulican party. If this Tax is not repealed or put so low that they cannot afford to buy up the Revenue officers, Grant & Colfax will be defeated in November, and in less than four years thereafter the country as a Repulican form of government ended. I therefore as an ardent friend of yours and the Republican party urge you to use your influence with the present Congress to repeal this Tax. With every wish for your success, through life . . ." ALS, *ibid.*

USG received letters and telegrams of congratulation dated May 21 from George C. Bates, Chicago, George C. Boker, Union League House, Philadelphia, H. W. Corbett, Chicago; dated May 22 from Governor Alexander Bullock of Mass., Worcester, William Frishmuth, Philadelphia, J. H. Humphreys, Richmond, Stephen Miller, Philadelphia, J. N. Osborn, Vicksburg, Hugo Schauer, Philadelphia, G. Howland Sinclair, Brooklyn, George H. Stuart, Pittsburgh; dated May 23 from H. C. Alleman, Philadelphia, George W. Gibbons, New York City; dated May 25 from R. W. White, Savannah; dated May 28 from Edward R. Brink, Wilmington, N. C., Charles W. Glaser, Fort Lee, N. J., C. H. Hopkins, Savannah, R. L. Laski, Memphis, Wade McDonald, Huntsville, Ala., Charles W. Rooth, New York City; dated May 30 from George N. Eaton, Baltimore; dated June 1 from J. B. Corey, Braddock's Fields, Pa., Governor Lucius Fairchild of Wis., Madison; dated June 2 from Elliott F. Shepard, New York City, Henry E. Turner, Lowville, N. Y.; dated June 3 from R. H. McCurdy, New York City; dated June 4 from S. C. Norvell, Mobile; dated June 5 from Joshua Hill, Madison, Ga.; dated June 6 from J. H. Bailey, Boyds Corners, N. Y., George H. Chapman, Indianapolis; dated June 8 from A. G. Mackey, Charleston, S. C.; dated June 22 from Alvin P. Hovey, Lima, Peru. *Ibid.*

To Andrew Johnson

Washington, D. C., June 1st, *1868*

THE PRESIDENT:
SIR:

Your letter of the 30th of May directlying me to immediately suspend, by telegraphic dispatch, the order relieving Col. Eddy as

Chief Quartermaster for the Department of Oregon, and designating Col. Hodges as his successor, and report to you the reasons
which led to the change, was duly received. Your letter was the
first intimation I had of the existence of such an order. The Departments being closed on Saturday, the day your letter was received,
I could not ascertain about the existence of the order referred to by
you, and my instructions admitting of no delay, I telegraphed to
Gen. Halleck, Commanding the Division of the Pacific, to carry
out your directions.

The enclosed is a copy of my dispatch to Gen. Halleck.[1]

I have the honor to be,
Very respectfully
your obt. svt.
U. S. Grant
General,

ALS, DLC-Andrew Johnson. On May 29, 1868, President Andrew Johnson had
written to USG. "Please immediately suspend, by telegraphic despatch, the
order relieving Col. Eddy as Chief Quartermaster for the Department of Oregon,
and designating Colonel Hodges as his successor, and report to me the reasons
which led to the change." LS, DNA, RG 108, Letters Received.

On June 6, Bvt. Col. Asher R. Eddy, San Francisco, telegraphed to USG.
"I am gratified and numerous friends here and Portland to know my late removal
was without your consent" Telegram received (at 2:55 p.m.), *ibid.*, RG 107,
Telegrams Collected (Bound); *ibid.*, RG 108, Telegrams Received; copy, DLC-
USG, V, 55.

1. On May 30, 11:45 a.m., USG had telegraphed to Maj. Gen. Henry W.
Halleck, San Francisco. "If there is an order relieving Col. Eddy as chief Qr.
Mr. Dept. of the Columbia, the President directs its revocation." ALS (telegram
sent), DNA, RG 107, Telegrams Collected (Bound); telegram sent, *ibid.*; copies,
ibid., RG 108, Telegrams Sent; DLC-USG, V, 56; DLC-Andrew Johnson.

To Maj. Gen. George G. Meade

(Cypher)   Washington, D, C,
                                        M̶June 1st 1868. [*10:00* a.m.]

Maj. Gn. G. G. Meade,
Atlanta Ga.

I would suggest that the military interpose no ~~interference with~~
obsticle to the meeting of the Legislature of Fla. Leave Congress to

reject or affirm their acts. I do not suggest ordering the legislature to meet, but mere instructions to the commander of the state that he do not interferes in the matter.

U. S. GRANT

General.

ALS (telegram sent), DNA, RG 107, Telegrams Collected (Bound); telegram sent, *ibid.*; telegram received, Meade Papers, PHi. On June 1, 1868, Maj. Gen. George G. Meade telegraphed to USG. "It will not be practicable to adopt your suggestion in regard to the Florida Legislature without some action on my part—When the election of State & County officers was ordered, I directed the returns to be sent to the Supdt of Registration instead of the Board of Canvassers, as provided in the ordinance of the Convention—The members of the legislature can not get their certificates of election, without my directing the returns to be turned over—My object was and is to retain control of the whole subject—because if the Legislature is permitted to convene, without orders from me, & without regard to the paramount authority which the Reconstruction laws vest in me—interminable confusion & conflict of authority will be sure to result.—So long as the reconstruction laws are in force, I should be opposed to the convening of the Legislature, except by my order & under my authority.—If these legislatures would confine themselves to simply acting on the 14th article, and then adjourning to await congressional action—I would not object so much, but once assembled they will do as they please—pass laws inconsistent with my powers & orders—tax ad libitum the State Treasuries, without any control & without any means of enforcing their acts except thro' me—Wheras if Congress will only act on the Constitution, and ~~declare~~ the authorise Dist Comdr to instal the elected Governments, on same terms, as if state was admitted—there would be no difficulty in the Govr elect calling together the Legislature and controlling their actions thru the veto. Unless therefore you send positive orders, I shall require the legislatures of Georgia & Florida to await action of Congress on the presented Constitutions of ~~the~~ those states" ALS (telegram sent), *ibid.*; telegram received (at 8:00 P.M.), DNA, RG 107, Telegrams Collected (Bound); *ibid.*, RG 108, Telegrams Received.

On June 2, Meade telegraphed to USG. "Official Returns of the Florida Election this day received shew, for the Constitution Fourteen thousand Five hundred & Sixty one (14561) votes—Against the Constitution Nine thousand five hundred and eleven (9,511) votes—Majority for the Constitution Five thousand and fifty votes (5050.) For the office of Governor—Harrison Reid received Fourteen thousand four hundred and twenty one votes—Geo. W. Scott received Seven thousand seven hundred & thirty one votes, and Samuel Walker received Two thousand two hundred & fifty seven votes." ALS (telegram sent), Meade Papers, PHi; telegram received (at 2:40 P.M.), DNA, RG 107, Telegrams Collected (Bound); *ibid.*, RG 108, Telegrams Received.

To Thaddeus Stevens

Washington, D. C., June 1st *1868.*

HON. THADDEUS STEVENS.
CH'RM'N COM. ON RECONSTRUCTION
HOUSE OF REPRESENTATIVES.
SIR:

I have the honor to acknowledge the receipt of your letter of 30th ult. asking to be furnished with the returns of the late election in Florida. The only information received in relation to the subject is the accompanying extract from a dispatch sent by Gen'l. Meade, Commanding 3d Military District.

Very respectfully
Your obed't. servant
U. S. GRANT
General.

LS, DNA, RG 233, 40A–F29.13. USG enclosed a telegram of May 8, 1868, from Maj. Gen. George G. Meade, Atlanta, to USG. "Col Sprague telegraphs— Election in Florida passed off without disorder—Judgeing from partial returns Constitution ratified by about three thousand majority and Reed ticket republican elected by a small majority.—The official Returns have been received in this state from all but one county & shew, Constitution ratified by 17,973 majority Bulloch elected by 7,279 majority—Senate 27 Republicans 16 Democrats 1 doubtful—House 95 Republicans 74 Democrats and 6 doubtful" ALS (telegram sent), Meade Papers, PHi; telegram received (at 9:30 P.M.), DNA, RG 107, Telegrams Collected (Bound); (at 9:00 P.M.) *ibid.,* RG 108, Telegrams Received. On May 30, L. R. Hibshman, clerk for U.S. Representative Thaddeus Stevens of Pa., wrote to USG. "Will you please furnish to the bearer the returns of the late Election held in Florida, for the use of the Reconstruction Committee" ALS, *ibid.,* Letters Received.

On June 2, U.S. Senator Lyman Trumbull of Ill., Committee on the Judiciary, wrote to USG. "Have you rec.d official information of the ratification of the constitution of Florida? The committee have under consideration the recognition of the Govt of that State, & desire any information you may have of the adoption of the constitution—" ALS, *ibid.,* Letters Received. On the same day, USG wrote to Trumbull. "The only information received at these Hdqrs. in relation to the matter is in the accompanying extract from a dispatch sent by Gen Meade, Comdg. 3d Mil Dist. I have no doubt of its ratification." Copies, DLC-USG, V, 47, 60; DNA, RG 108, Letters Sent. USG again enclosed the Meade telegram of May 8.

On June 3, USG wrote to Stevens. "Since my note to you of the 1st inst. in relation to the recent elections in Florida I have received from General Meade a telegraphic dispatch announcing the result there. I send you a copy of the same for your information." LS, *ibid.*, RG 233, 40A–F29.13. Also on June 3, USG wrote similar letters to Trumbull and U.S. Senator Henry Wilson of Mass. Copies, DLC-USG, V, 47, 60; DNA, RG 108, Letters Sent. For enclosures, see preceding telegram.

On June 1, USG wrote to U.S. Senator Benjamin F. Wade of Ohio. "I have the honor to acknowledge the receipt of Senate Resolution of date the 29th ulto, requesting the General of the Army to transmit to the Senate any reports and papers received by him since the 4th of May in relation to the late election in Arkansas upon the adoption of a constitution, and to reply that nothing whatever relating to the matter has been received at these Headquarters, since that date." LS, *ibid.*, RG 46, Senate 40A–G3, War Dept. Reports. On June 26, USG wrote to Wade. "In further answer to Senate Resolution of the 29th May 1868, I have the honor to transmit certain statistics received from General Gillem regarding the recent election in Arkansas." LS, *ibid.* On June 3, Bvt. Maj. Gen. Alvan C. Gillem, Vicksburg, wrote to USG. "I have the honor to transmit herewith for your information an official table, showing certain statistics, regarding the recent election in Arkansas, consolidated from reports of Registrars made in obedience to instruction from these Headquarters" Copy, *ibid.*, RG 393, 4th Military District, Letters and Telegrams Sent.

To Robert Bonner

Washington, D. C., June 3d *1868*

DEAR SIR;

Your favor of yesterday, in regard to Dunbar's matter, is received. The new Sec. of War is now very busy in finishing up business which has been hanging fire so long. Before I speak to him on the matter I will see you. This week I go to Annapolis to spend a few days with Adm.l Porter, and early next week to West Point, stopping a day in New York City on the way. I will see you then.

Yours Truly,

U. S. GRANT

To R. BONNER, ESQ,

ALS, Wayde Chrismer, Bel Air, Md. Robert Bonner, born in Ireland in 1824, a printer in Conn., purchased the New York *Ledger* in 1851, and created a cleverly advertised weekly newspaper specializing in popular fiction and celebrity articles. A noted turfman, Bonner owned the trotter Dexter. On Nov. 29, 1867, Bonner had written to USG. "I cannot help congratulating you on your testimony before the Impeachment Committee. It was *very good*; and will convince the country that it is not in military affairs alone in which you excel. Horace Greeley said confidentially to a friend of mine with whom he breakfasted the morning after it was published, that 'it showed General Grant to be a great man.' I think I comprehend the whole secret of Mr. Greeley's political course (although I do not bother my head with politics) more fully than most of the politicians. I still think that your present position as General, (as I took the liberty of saying to you when you was here) is better than that of President; but you must decide what horse you want to ride. Perhaps, you may look upon the Presidency in the same light as I look upon *Dexter*. Mr. Dunbar asked me the other day to write to you concerning the appointment of a Board of Officers to report upon his case. I very frankly told him that, *just at this time*, you, as acting Secretary of War, could not do anything about his matter that would not be likely to be perverted and used against you by political enemies; and I *say the same to you*, although I believe his system worth more to the country than he asks for it. But Congress is the power to take the responsibility. I know that your powerful individual influence he has already." ALS, USG 3. See letter to Hamilton Fish, Feb. 20, 1868.

On June 1, 1868, USG wrote to "C. H. Rogers" "saying he has been unexpectedly detained and will not be able to visit West Point at present, but will possibly be able to visit in a few days, and hoping that Mrs. Rogers will be restored." Robert F. Batchelder Catalogue 17 [1977], no. 212.

To Bvt. Maj. Gen. Robert C. Buchanan

Washington, D. C., June 5th *1868* [*12:15* P.M.]

GENERAL R. C. BUCHANAN
NEW ORLEANS, LA.

If the municipal officers recently elected take office by appointment from the District Commander before the new constitution has legally taken effect, they should undoubtedly be required to take the test-oath. But if they do not take office until the constitution has been approved by Congress and the State declared entitled to representation in Congress, then the officers would only be required to take the oath required by the constitution under which they are elected, because the reconstruction laws will have ceased to be operative in that State

U. S. GRANT
General.

LS (telegram sent), DNA, RG 107, Telegrams Collected (Bound); telegram sent, *ibid.*; copies, *ibid.*, RG 108, Telegrams Sent; *ibid.*, RG 393, 5th Military District, Telegrams Received; DLC-USG, V, 56. On June 3, 1868, Bvt. Maj. Gen. Robert C. Buchanan had telegraphed to USG. "Shall municipal officers elected at the late election be required to take the test oath or only the oath prescribed for all officers by the new Constitution   General Reynolds telegraphs Texas Convention organized & proceeding to business"   LS (telegram sent), DNA, RG 107, Telegrams Collected (Bound); telegram received, *ibid.*; (at 7:00 P.M.) *ibid.*, RG 108, Telegrams Received.

On June 6, Buchanan telegraphed to USG. "I have arrested S. B. Packard, Chairman Louisiana Board of Registration for issuing a proclamation, annulling my Special Orders No 121. fixing a date for installation of the newly elected State Officers & providing for the meeting of the General Assembly. I shall at once try him by Military Commission"   LS (telegram sent), *ibid.*, RG 107, Telegrams Collected (Bound); telegram received (at 4:00 P.M.), *ibid.*; (at 4:15 P.M.) *ibid.*, RG 108, Telegrams Received. At 8:00 P.M., Bvt. Maj. Gen. John A. Rawlins telegraphed to USG, Annapolis. "The following telegrams were sent here for you, by the Hon. Schuyler Colfax and explain themselves. General Buchanans order relative to the Meeting of the Louisiana Legislature has not reached here, but from the Newspaper report of it I infer the proclamation referred to in these telegrams are in violation of it   New Orleans June 6th 1868 HON SCHUYLER COLFAX   In consequence of proclamation issued by this board Genl Buchanan has arrested S. B. Packard chairman of the board of registration Please see Genl Grant & have him released   see senator wilson & other friends relative to the matter   Signed G. M WICKLIFFE   Member of the board   New Orleans La June 6th *1868*   HON S. COLFAX   Board has issued proclamation ordering Genl assembly to convene & civil officers inaugurated as provided by constitution   Genl. Grant must sustain the board in its action   Signed S. B. PACKARD Chairman"   ALS (telegram sent), *ibid.*, RG 107, Telegrams Collected (Bound); telegram sent, *ibid.*; telegram received, *ibid.*, RG 108, Telegrams Received.

On June 8, 10:30 A.M., USG telegraphed to Buchanan. "In view of legislation now pending relative to the admission of La, I would suggest suspension of all action in case of Packard's arrest and trial." ALS (telegram sent), *ibid.*, RG 107, Telegrams Collected (Bound); telegram sent, *ibid.*; telegram received, *ibid.*, RG 393, 5th Military District, Miscellaneous Records. On the same day, Buchanan wrote to USG. "In view of the recent occurrences in this city resulting in the arrest of the Chairman and members of the Board of Registration appointed by the Convention, and your telegram of this date, it becomes proper for me to make a detailed report of the case   In order to elucidate this matter fully I enclose a copy of the new State Constitution with my order announcing the result of the election for State officers Etc and a copy of the New Orleans Republican of the 7th inst, containing the proclamation signed by Mr. Packard, Chairman and a subsequent endorsement of it by the remaining members of the Board. It will be necessary to a full understanding of the case to give my reasons for deciding when the Constitution recently adopted by the people of the State goes into effect. . . . From the foregoing reasons it will be seen that my order was based strictly upon a legal construction of the act of Congress   That act gave me full authority to decide when the legislature should meet and authorized me to fix the date when the state officers should take their offices. The proclamation issued by the Board of Registration was in absolute defiance and contempt of the Authority vested in me by the reconstruction acts. By reference to Article 156. of the Constitution it will be seen, that the Board of Registration herein referred to, was only authorized to act in the event of the Commanding General of the 5th Military District, failing or refusing to act himself. Neither my predecessor in command nor myself failed or refused to act in any matters requiring action on our part. The functions of the Board of Registration appointed by the Convention were limited and determined by our refusal or failure to act. The contingency not having arisen, the Board has no legal existence even under the Constitution itself. Its assumption then of authority to issue a proclamation virtually countermanding my orders, was a violation of the reconstruction acts, was revolutionary in its character and had a tendency to impede reconstruction by creating disorders, instigating violence and by setting at defiance the authority of the Commanding General of the District. In its mildest sense it was an arrogation of authority expressly delegated by the reconstruction acts to the Military Commander, authorizing him to make removals and appointments. I therefore arrested, first, the Chairman and subsequently the other members of the Board and should have brought them to trial at once, but for the receipt of your telegram. In compliance with your suggestion I have suspended their arrest until the action of Congress referred to in your telegram shall be made known. Should Congress not sustain the action of the Board, their cases will yet be brought to trial unless you order to the contrary. During the interview at which the Board appeared before me in arrest, the Acting chairman, who is also one of the State Officers elect, stated 'You, General Buchanan, in your action with reference to this Election took charge only upon authority which we (the Board of Registration) agreed to delegate to you'—a remark that I allude to, only to show the spirit which animates this Board I send an officer with this communication in order that you may receive such verbal information relative to civil affairs in this State as you may desire" LS, *ibid.*, RG 108, Letters Received.

On June 11, 1:40 P.M., Rawlins telegraphed to USG, West Point. "The following dispatch has just been received, and answered as follows.—Packard probably did not get the dispatch until the address had been issued. . . . 'Time 9 30 a, m, cipher From New Orleans June 10th '68 Received June 11th '68 To GENERAL U S GRANT Commanding Armies U-S. On receiving your telegram I suspended action in the case of Packard and the other members of the Board of Registration. The Board, immediately after being released issued an address to the citizens of the State urging the State officers elect to disregard my orders, saying that they were illegal and not binding, and calling upon them to qualify on monday next, the 15th inst., and take possession of their offices. This, if attempted to be carried out may lead to serious trouble. I therefore request to be informed whether or not my orders in the case, sent to your Headqrs on the second instant are approved? Your approval or disapproval will settle the matter at once   (sgd) R. C. BUCHANAN Bt. Maj. Gen., Comdg.' 'Washington, June 11th 1868. BT. MAJ. GEN. R. C. BUCHANAN, Comdg 5th Mil. Dist. New Orleans, La   Your telegram of yesterday received. The orders you refer to have not been received at these Hdqrs. The following telegram was sent to Packard: (sgd) JNO. A. RAWLINS Chf of Staff 'Washington June 9th 1868. S. B. PACKARD. New Orleans. I am directed by the General of the Army to say to you that the subject of inaugurating civil government for La. is now pending before Congress, and he advises that you issue no orders or proclamations in conflict with orders issued by the Military Commander of the District, as such action on your part would be in violation of the reconstruction laws. (sgd) JNO. A. RAWLINS Chf of Staff.' " Telegrams sent (2—ditto marks expanded), *ibid.*, RG 107, Telegrams Collected (Bound); copies, *ibid.*, RG 108, Telegrams Sent; DLC-USG, V, 56.

On June 8, Mayor Edward Heath, New Orleans, and nine city officials had telegraphed to USG. "Genl Buchanan has, by an order, refused to permit the newly elected State legislative and Parish officers to take their seats at the time prescribed by the Constitution. By a subsequent order he has directed the newly elected municipal officers to take their seats on the tenth (10th) instant, five (5) days in advance of the time fixed by the Constitution. We ask a suspension of this latter order until a full statement of facts can be sent by mail. Many of the newly elected municipals, including the principal officers, cannot qualify" Copy, DNA, RG 108, Letters Received. On June 10, Heath telegraphed to USG. "I was forcibly ejected from the Mayors Office today, and Mr Conway installed by order of General Buchanan" Telegram received (on June 11, 9:15 A.M.), *ibid.*, RG 107, Telegrams Collected (Bound); *ibid.*, RG 108, Telegrams Received; copy, DLC-USG, V, 55. On June 11, Heath wrote to USG. "I deem it my duty to lay before you the acts of General Buchanan in relation to the Mayoralty of New Orleans, which have resulted in my forcible ejection from the same. About the time General Buchanan issued his order for the recent election, I had an interview with him, in which he stated that he would not pretind to say whether there was any authority for holding a municipal election or not, but that he should issue the order in accordance with what he und[erstood] to be the requirement of the reconstruction acts, and leave it to the people to decide whether they would hold such election or not, and to the courts, if any question arose, to determine as to the legality of the election. It is hardly necessary for me to state that an election took place in conformity with General Buchanan's order, and the result, as far as the State officers were concerned, declared by Special order No 121, postponing the time of said State officers entering upon their official duties till November next; and by a subsequent order Special No. 125, he declared the result of the municipal election, and directed that the newly elected officers should enter upon their official duties on the 10th inst. (yesterday), of all of which I advised you by telegraph of the 8th inst, a copy of which is herewith enclosed marked A It will be seen, by an inspection of the two orders, notwithstanding the State and municipal officers were elected under and in pursuance of the same authority, he has totally disregarded the provisions of the new Constitution which provides that the officers elected shall take their seats on the second Monday after the official proclamation of such election. See Sec 158, and, contrary to his announcement that he should leave the contest to the courts, he has forcibly interposed his military power to eject me from the Mayor's office, and installed the pretended Mayor, at a time when it is exceedingly doubtful whether a decision of the Courts can be reached before next Fall, owing to the close proximity of the adjournment of the courts. In an interview which I had with him this morning, upon reminding him of his previous pledge in case the election were contested, of leaving the matter to the Courts, he informed me that such is still his intention, and that too after having done me all the injury he can; and although I did not impugn his motives, he took occasion to remark that he was influenced, in what he had done, by no partisan feeling. I have instituted legal proceedings against Mr Conway as you will see by reference to a copy of the Crescent Newspaper which I send you herewith. I respectfully request you, therefore, General, in view of the circumstances above stated, that you will immediately reverse the acts of General Buchanan of yesterday inducting Mr Conway into the office of Mayor of this city, by an order directed to him to that effect. It may not be amiss to state for your information that M my attorney made an application to five of the six Judges resident in this city, before he found one who was ready to issue a writ against Mr Conway, and that the Judge who signed the process did so from a sick bed. I may add, in justice to Judge Leaumont, that he hesitated on the ground that he intends to contest the right of the pretended successor to *his* office, claiming it by virtue of the same election. The delay occasioned by the difficulty of getting the writ issued, gave Mr. Conway an opportunity to get possession of the office of Mayor through the aid of Genl Buchanan.—Hence the necessity of my appealing to you to undo his acts in the premises. If we are to contend here against the prejudices of the Judiciary and at the same time encounter an unfriendly exercise of their power by the Military, I fear that union people will have but little chance for maintaining their rights." ALS, DNA, RG 108, Letters Received.

On June 14, Heath wrote to USG. "Enclosed I hand the legal opinion of Judge J. S. Whitaker, to whom the matter was referred by me, touching the right to hold an election for municipal officers under the Reconstruction acts of congress and the Laws of Louisiana." ALS, *ibid.* The enclosure is *ibid.* On June 20, Heath and Thomas J. Durant telegraphed to USG. "Is the question of municipal officers still under advisement? Additional facts can be furnished if necessary" Telegram received (at 4:15 P.M.), *ibid.*, RG 107, Telegrams Collected (Bound); *ibid.*, RG 108, Telegrams Received; copy, DLC-USG, V, 55. On June 22, 12:10 P.M., USG telegraphed to Heath. "The question of municipal officers is not under advisement here. When the bill now pending before the President admitting La. and other states to representation in Congress, becomes, as it probably will, a law, and the state of La. has complied with its conditions, the matter of municipal officers will come under the control of, and become subject to the legal action of the civil authorities of the state." LS (telegram sent), DNA, RG 107, Telegrams Collected (Bound); telegram sent, *ibid.*; copies, *ibid.*, RG 108, Telegrams Sent; DLC-USG, V, 56.

On June 12, James E. Waldo, New Orleans, had written to U.S. Senator Richard Yates of Ill. "Many years ago we were acquaintd when I lived in Meredosia, and perhaps may be recollected now—It is now thirty nine years since I have lived in this City except the few years spent in Illinois—I feel that in that time I have pretty well become acquainted with this City and the situation of affairs here—I have all the time been engaged in business and have only devoted to politics that attention that seems to be the duty of every citizen—At this time I feel it to be my duty to write you and give you what I believe to be a true Statement of Political affairs here—You will doubtless have seen by the Newspapers that Gen. Buchannan forcibly ejected Mayor Heath from office on the 10th inst— and installed John R. Conway as his Successor—This was done by the General notwithstanding his pledge to leave the matter to the decission of the Courts—as Mayor Heath had served out a Quo Warranto against Mr Conway—What I would wish to call your attention to especially is the onesided, ultra partizan acts of the General—In the first place a few days previous to the election on the 17 & 18 of April last the General took the control of the Police Force of the City from Mayor Heath (who is made the head and given the control of the Police of the City by the City Charter) and gave it to Maj. J. J. Williamson, Chief of Police, who manipulated the force in the interest of the Democrats and *this act alone* gave the Democrats the City at that election—The next ultra partizan act of the General was the putting off the Republicans elected to state offices till Nov. although the Constitution required them to take office on the second monday after the official Promulgation of the result of the election—And the putting the Democrats elected to the City offices into office in two days although the Constitution required that they should take office on the second monday after official Promulgation &c—You will see at once that this kind of partizan maneuvering gives the Democrats the control of the whole State—Keeping the Republican State officers elected out of office till Nov. and putting the Democrats elected to the City offices at once into office takes the city from the Republicans and give it to the Democrats and continues the Democrats in possession of the State—Now it seems to me that the game is up for the Republicans—that they loose this state certain in Nov. next unless the State officers are installed within a reasonable time as they should be—and Mayor Heath is reinstated in office at once with instructions to leave the matter to the Courts to decide whether Mayor Heath or John R. Conway is intitled to the office—Let the Courts decide (as Buchannan & Hancock are in favor of the installment of Civil law) but let Mayor Heath be put back into the office from which a partizan General ejected him till it is decided—Also let Gen. Buchannan be instructed to give Mayor Heath the appointment and control of his own Chief of Police as the City Charter requires— these simple acts of justice being done there may be some chance in Nov. for the Republican party in La—But if it is not done I fear there is little chance of success—I have deemed it my duty to say this much to you—which is a true statement of facts of the case—Knowing your deep interest in the success of Republicanism and your intimacy with Gen. Grant who can order these things done—" ALS, DNA, RG 108, Letters Received. On June 22, Yates endorsed this letter to USG. ES, *ibid.*

To Bvt. Maj. Gen. Edward R. S. Canby

Washington, D. C., June 5th 1868 [*12:50* P.M.]

GENERAL E. R. S. CANBY
CHARLESTON S. C.

It is reported that since the issuance of your G. O. no. 84, current series, some of the railroads in N. C. have been mortgaged or otherwise encumbered to the prejudice of the state interests. Would it not be well to have this matter investigated and if true, then to issue another order prohibiting the officers of any railroad company in which the state is interested, from mortgaging their railroad and furniture, issuing bonds, giving trust-deeds, making or letting any contract or debt, the selling of any bonds, either state, county, or corperate, or any action which shall tend towards taking from state her present interest and control; and declare any action already taken tending to take away said interest or control from State of NC. null and void

U. S. GRANT, Gen'l

LS (telegram sent), DNA, RG 107, Telegrams Collected (Bound); telegram sent, *ibid.*; telegram received (misdated June 3, 1868), *ibid.*, RG 393, 2nd Military District, Letters Received. On June 5, Bvt. Maj. Gen. Edward R. S. Canby telegraphed to USG. "Your telegram is received. The matter has been undergoing investigation for some days and will be promptly attended to" Telegram received (at 1:45 P.M.), *ibid.*, RG 107, Telegrams Collected (Bound); *ibid.*, RG 108, Telegrams Received; copies (one sent by mail), *ibid.*, Letters Received; (misdated June 4) *ibid.*, RG 393, 2nd Military District, Letters Sent; DLC-USG, V, 55.

To Bvt. Maj. Gen. Irvin McDowell

(Cypher)   *Washington, D. C.*, June 5th *1868* [*11:00* A.M.]
MAJ. GN MCDOWELL,
VICKSBURG MISS.

Governor Humphrey, being a cadidate for re-election, and disqualified for taking his seat if elected, it would seem that he should not controll the state pending the approaching election. If removed I would suggest that the appointment of a politician be avoided by selecting off an officer of the Army to take his place. In this case I would suggest Gen. Kautz. It is a safe rule when removals have to be made to select Army officers in all cases. It gives provisional government over which district commanders have better controll.

U. S. GRANT
General,

ALS (telegram sent), DNA, RG 107, Telegrams Collected (Bound); telegram sent, *ibid.*; telegram received, *ibid.*, RG 393, 4th Military District, Letters Received. On June 6, 1868, Bvt. Maj. Gen. Irvin McDowell, Vicksburg, telegraphed to USG. "Will send a telegram by next mail to the cipher operator in Memphis in reply to yours of the fifth (5) inst. just received." Telegram received (at 6:55 P.M.), *ibid.*, RG 108, Telegrams Received; copies, *ibid.*, RG 393, 4th Military District, Telegrams Sent; DLC-USG, V, 55. On June 8, McDowell telegraphed and wrote to USG. "Immediately after the sudden death of his wife, Gen'l. Kautz left the District, with her remains, and will not return till too late for the purpose suggested   The Governor, in this State, is now without any control, patronage, power or funds; he has only bare prestige of his nominal office, and the loss of this would, I think, be more than made up by the prestige he would acquire of political martyrdom. In either case he would exert his personal influence, which is all he has against the adoption of the constitution, and that influence will only be increased by his removal. If I find I am all wrong in this view or you will telegraph me that you think I am, I will remove him and appoint Bvt. Maj. Gen. A. Ames as the most suitable officer I now have available for the place" Telegram received (sent from Memphis, June 10, received on June 11, 10:00 A.M.), DNA, RG 107, Telegrams Collected (Bound); (at 10:30 A.M.) *ibid.*, RG 108, Telegrams Received; copies, *ibid.*, RG 393, 4th Military District, Telegrams Sent; DLC-USG, V, 55. "The accompanying duplicate of a telegram sent to be forwarded by the Cypher Operator at Memphis is in reply to yours of the 5th recd. from him by mail! Will you not please have me furnished with a Cypher, that I may telegraph you direct? I am told Gen. Ord had one but took it away when he left—Both parties are exerting themselves to the utmost and the contest will be bitter and close. Yet I continue to be assured by loyal residents that the *constitution will be adopted*. Though there may be a doubt as to the members for the legislature. The anti-constitution party had a large barbecue in this vicinity Saturday, and tried to shake the faith of the colored voters but I am told without the slightest result." ALS, USG 3. On June 12, USG, West Point, telegraphed to McDowell. "No one would be more suitable for Governor than Gen Ames I leave it to your judgment however whether change should be made." Telegram received, DNA, RG 393, 4th Military District, Telegrams Received.

On June 15, McDowell telegraphed and wrote to USG. "I have this day removed Benj G Humphreys from the Office of Governor, and C. E Hooker from the Office of Attorney General, of the state of Mississippi and have appointed respectively Major General Adelbert Ames and Capt Jasper Myers to succeed them" Telegram received (at 3:00 P.M.), *ibid.*, RG 107, Telegrams Collected (Bound); *ibid.*, RG 108, Telegrams Received; copies, *ibid.*, RG 94, Letters Received, 775M 1868; *ibid.*, RG 393, 4th Military District, Telegrams Sent; DLC-USG, V, 55; DLC-Andrew Johnson. "I enclose, herewith, a duplicate of my telegram of this date, acquainting you of my having removed the Governor and the Attorney General of the State of Mississippi. I also send, herewith, the 'Daily Clarion',—a paper published at Jackson, Mississippi, of the 12th instant, giving a list of the public meeting at which the Ex-Governor and the Ex-Attorney General are to speak, and a letter from the paper's special correspondent, dated Corinth, June 8th, referring to the part taken by them in the present canvass. You will recollect I gave it as my judgment that it would not be well to make such removals at this particular time. I still think so; But on reading the 4th Section of the Act of July 19. 1867, it seemed to me that it was not a mere question, on my part, of expediency or propriety, but simply one of obedience to law. This Section says, among other things,—'*And it shall be the duty of such commander* [the District Commander] *to remove from office as aforesaid all persons who are disloyal to the Government of the United States,*' or (and now comes the part which applies to the case in point) '*who uses their official influence in any manner to hinder, delay, prevent, or obstruct the due and proper administration of this act, and the acts to which it is supplementary.*' In your letter of June 5th you refer to Genl. Schofield's course in removing from office in the 1st District, all who could not take the oath prescribed by Congress. I am led to believe I could not get half enough persons in this State, qualified to fill the various offices, who could take that oath, and I therefore—in the interests of good government—take advantage of what perhaps is an omission in the law— and do not require it of those retained in office. Section 9. of the act of July 19th 1867, says: . . . '*And all persons hereafter elected or appointed to office in said Military Districts, under any so-called State or municipal authority or by detail or appointment of the District Commander, shall be required to take and to sub-*

scribe the oath of office prescribed by law for officers of the United States.' It will
be seen the Act does not require the oath to be taken by those in office at the
time of its passage; nor, does it require that those then in office shall be removed
if they do not take it: but only that it shall be taken by all persons *'hereafter
elected or appointed.*' The 4th Section of the Act, quoted on the preceding page,
seems to provide for the question of removal. I am informed,—and all I see and
hear confirms it,—that the contest at the Election will be hot and close. The
Adoption—of—the—Constitution—party hope to carry the Election by not over
5.000. I have distributed the troops so as to give as much protection against
violence and intimidation as possible; and those interested say there are detachments at every post where they are needed." LS (brackets and ellipses in original), *ibid.* On June 19, 3:30 P.M., USG telegraphed to McDowell. "Give by
mail reasons for removal of Governor & Treasurer of Miss. for President who
calls for it." ALS (telegram sent), DNA, RG 107, Telegrams Collected (Bound);
telegram sent, *ibid.*; telegram received, *ibid.*, RG 393, 4th Military District,
Telegrams Received. On June 22, McDowell telegraphed to USG. "Reasons for
removal of Governor and Attorney General given in my letter to you of June
fifteenth 15 mailed June sixteenth 16. Has it been received" Telegram received
(at 3:30 P.M.), *ibid.*, RG 107, Telegrams Collected (Bound); *ibid.*, RG 108,
Telegrams Received; copies, *ibid.*, RG 393, 4th Military District, Telegrams
Sent; DLC-USG, V, 55. On June 23, 10:20 A.M., USG telegraphed to Mc-
Dowell. "Your letter of 16th received." ALS (telegram sent), DNA, RG 107,
Telegrams Collected (Bound); telegram sent, *ibid.*; copies, *ibid.*, RG 108, Telegrams Sent; DLC-USG, V, 56. On the same day, William L. Sharkey, Jackson,
Miss., telegraphed to USG. "You have been deceived, I think, by false representations, in ordering the removal of Governor Humphreys and Attorney General Hooker and hope you will revoke the order, or at least suspend it. Reply
[r]espectfully asked" Telegram received (at 2:35 P.M.), DNA, RG 107, Telegrams Collected (Bound).

On Feb. 26, Maj. Gen. Henry W. Halleck, San Francisco, had telegraphed
to USG. "In the present state of political feeling on this coast it is very desirable
that Gen McDowell be retained in command of the Department of California"
Telegram received (at 8:00 P.M.), *ibid.*; (on March 2, 4:00 P.M.) *ibid.*, RG
108, Telegrams Received; copy, DLC-USG, V, 55. On March 3, 10:30 A.M.,
USG telegraphed to Halleck. "You may retain Gen. McDowel until Ord arrives."
ALS (telegram sent), DNA, RG 107, Telegrams Collected (Bound); telegram
sent, *ibid.*; copies, *ibid.*, RG 108, Telegrams Sent; DLC-USG, V, 56.

On May 23, USG wrote to McDowell. "I will be pleased if you will assume
the Command of the 4th Mil. District, with as little delay as possible, and retain
it until after the election, which takes place in June. That over, if you should
desire it, I will favor authorizing you to spend the balance of the summer North."
Copies, *ibid.*, V, 47, 60; DNA, RG 108, Letters Sent. On June 4, McDowell,
Vicksburg, telegraphed and wrote to USG. "Arrived last night & assumed Command today" Telegram received (on June 4), *ibid.*, Telegrams Received; copy,
DLC-USG, V, 55. "I arrived here last night and assumed command of the
District this morning. I hasten to say I earnestly desire to avail myself of your
Offer to go north after the Miss. Election: and beg you will give me some duty,
for the time, in NewYork, that I may not be forced to the loss of a Leave of
Absence! It is thought that, though the election will be sharply contested, it
will be carried for the adoption of the constitution. Of this, however I have, as
yet, had no means of forming an opinion—There is every indication of a good

and profitable crop. And all with whom I have spoken say the negroes are working better than they have yet done since the War.—and are behaving well on the
plantations." ALS, USG 3.

To Bvt. Maj. Gen. Irvin McDowell

[June 5, 1868]

This will introduce to you Gen. Eggleston of Miss., candidate
for Governor under the reconstruction laws of Congress.[1] Gen. Eggleston served in our army during the rebellion, with credit. I
speak for the General a hearing upon the affairs of the State of
Miss., and that such consideration as may be fair and legal be
given to his suggestions.

I telegraphed to you this morning relative to the removal of
Gen. Humphrey and the appointment of Ka[u]tz! I do not believe
in the appointment to office of interested partisans, but it does not
seem to me fair that the offices should be held by men who . . . cannot qualify unless relieved from their disabilities by Congress.
Gen. Humphrey . . . presumes all the Acts of Congress, touching
reconstruction, unconstitutional, null and void. He yealds only to
force . . . What applies to him applies, no doubt, with equal force
to many other civil officers . . . Gen. Schofield, one of our most conservative district commanders . . . took the ground that all the officers in his district should qualify according to the requirements
of the reconstruction Acts of Congress and . . . commenced a wholesale removal. In that case it was impossible to appoint army officers.
Still, for Governor, and the most important state offices, I would
suggest army officers . . . I suggest Ka[u]tz because I have known
him from childhood . . .

Charles Hamilton Auction No. 46, Dec. 10, 1970, p. 42.
    On June 6, 1868, Bvt. Maj. Gen. Irvin McDowell, Vicksburg, wrote to
USG. "I have the honor to transmit herewith, for your information, an official
table showing certain statistics, regarding the election for the Convention in
Mississippi, Consolidated from reports of Registrars, made in obedience to instructions from these Headquarters." LS, DNA, RG 108, Letters Received. The
enclosures are *ibid.*
    On June 11, McDowell telegraphed to USG. "Can Genl. G. H. Thomas Be

authorized to lend me a few companies of Infantry for a few days. during the coming Election—" Telegram received (at 5:38 P.M.), *ibid.*, Telegrams Received; copy, DLC-USG, V, 55. At 8:10 P.M., Bvt. Brig. Gen. Cyrus B. Comstock telegraphed to McDowell and to Maj. Gen. George H. Thomas, Louisville. "Gen. G. H. Thomas has been authorised [to] lend you a few companies if he can spare them." "Gen Grant authorises you to lend a few companies of Infantry to Gen. McDowell for a few days if you can spare them." ALS (telegrams sent), DNA, RG 107, Telegrams Collected (Bound); telegrams sent, *ibid.*; copies, *ibid.*, RG 108, Telegrams Sent; DLC-USG, V, 56. On June 12, Thomas telegraphed to Comstock. "Can loan General McDowell five 5 Companies" Telegram received (at 1:20 P.M.), DNA, RG 107, Telegrams Collected (Bound); *ibid.*, RG 108, Telegrams Received; copy, DLC-USG, V, 55.

On June 16, McDowell telegraphed to USG. "I need, temporarily on account of the establishing of many small Posts for the election, more medical attendance than can be given by the Medical Officers or contract physicians now at hand. The Surgeon General has ordered no medical contract made except with those who can take the oath. I do not consider the temporary employment of a doctor as the creating of an office and I beg, in the interest of the service that no restrictions be allowed on such employment, except such as effect the health of the men. Please telegraph authority" Telegram received (on June 17, 9:20 A.M.), DNA, RG 107, Telegrams Collected (Bound); *ibid.*, RG 108, Telegrams Received; copy, DLC-USG, V, 55. On June 17, 1:45 P.M., Bvt. Maj. Gen. John A. Rawlins telegraphed to McDowell. "Under your authority as District Commander you can temporarily employ surgeons, but such employment must be paid for out of the reconstruction funds for your District. It is not deemed advisable to modify or suspend the Surgeon Generals order" Telegrams sent (2), DNA, RG 107, Telegrams Collected (Bound); copies, *ibid.*, RG 108, Telegrams Sent; DLC-USG, V, 56.

On June 22, USG wrote to Secretary of War John M. Schofield. "At the request of Gen. McDowell to be relieved at as early a day as practicable from duty in a southern climate, where past experience proves that he must undergo severe illness if left long, I respectfully recommend that he be relieved from the command of the Fourth Mil. Dist. and assigned to the command of the Dept. of the East." ALS, DNA, RG 94, Letters Received, 287A 1868. On June 23, McDowell telegraphed to USG. "Please apply to the President or suffer this application to go to him for my transfer next month to the command of the Dept of the East—that Dept forming part of the Div. of the Atlantic cannot now be commanded by any one senior to myself, and the present may be my only opportunity to have the station I most desire. General Gillem whose arrangements for the election and for the service generally have been admirable Will relinquish the indulgence granted him to succeed to the command here if desired" Telegram received (at 4:15 P.M.), *ibid.*, RG 107, Telegrams Collected (Bound); *ibid.*, RG 108, Telegrams Received; copy, DLC-USG, V, 55. On June 24, 9:45 A.M., USG telegraphed to McDowell. "Before receiving your dispatch I asked to have you relieved from the 4th Dist. and assigned to Dept. of the East in July. I think it will be done." ALS (telegram sent), DNA, RG 107, Telegrams Collected (Bound); telegram sent, *ibid.*; copies, *ibid.*, RG 108, Telegrams Sent; DLC-USG, V, 56. On the same day, McDowell telegraphed to USG. "A Million 1000000 of thanks" Telegram received (at 5:00 P.M.), DNA, RG 108, Telegrams Received; copy, DLC-USG, V, 55. AGO General Orders No. 44, July 13, assigned McDowell to command the Dept. of the East.

On June 24, McDowell telegraphed to USG. "The election has thus far gone on without disturbance. The revision of the registration in fifty eight 58 counties shows a net addition to the lists of seven thousand seven hundred and sixty five 7765 whites, and six thousand two hundred and eighty three 6283 colored voters. The four 4 counties yet to be heard from will not materially change the ratio— two of them having white and two colored majorities   There is much excitement and the contest will be close as there will be more of the white vote polled than of the colored" Telegram received (at 5:00 P.M.), DNA, RG 107, Telegrams Collected (Bound); *ibid.*, RG 108, Telegrams Received; copies, *ibid.*, RG 393, 4th Military District, Telegrams Sent; DLC-USG, V, 55.

On June 26, 1:00 P.M., USG telegraphed to McDowell. "The Bill entitling and admitting the State of Arkansas to representation in Congress is now a law and her Senators and Representatives have been admitted to Congress. Military authority under the reconstruction acts is therefore at an end in that State and everything appertaining to its government should be turned over to the civil authorities thereof at the earliest practicable moment." LS (telegram sent), DNA, RG 107, Telegrams Collected (Bound); telegram sent, *ibid.*; telegram received, *ibid.*, RG 393, 4th Military District, Letters Received.

On June 27, McDowell telegraphed to USG. "Please grant authority to District Commander to move District Head Quarters from this place during the sickly season" Telegram received (at 2:00 P.M.), *ibid.*, RG 107, Telegrams Collected (Bound); *ibid.*, RG 108, Telegrams Received; copies, *ibid.*, RG 94, Letters Received, 832M 1868; DLC-USG, V, 55. On the same day, USG favorably endorsed a copy of this telegram to Schofield. ES, DNA, RG 94, Letters Received, 832M 1868.

1. Bvt. Brig. Gen. Beroth B. Eggleston, former col., 1st Ohio Cav., settled in Lowndes County, Miss., presided over the constitutional convention in 1868, and campaigned unsuccessfully as Republican candidate for governor.

To Maj. Gen. Philip H. Sheridan

Washington, D. C., June 9th *1868* [*12:10* P.M.]

MAJ GN. P. H. SHERIDAN,

FORT LEAVENWORTH KANSAS,

Please suspend order removing settlers from Indian reservations in Kansas untill the matter is reported upon and it is known to be advisable to remove them. Please give your views at once.

U. S. GRANT
Gen.1

ALS (telegram sent), DNA, RG 107, Telegrams Collected (Bound); telegram sent, *ibid.*; copies, *ibid.*, Letters Received from Bureaus; *ibid.*, RG 108, Telegrams Sent; DLC-USG, V, 56. On June 9, 1868, Maj. Gen. Philip H. Sheridan telegraphed to USG. "In reply to your telegram of this date, I have to state that I had suspended the order of [r]emoval until the settlers could hear from Washington. Since that time, Bvt Lt Col Sheridan, who was engaged in removing the settlers, reports that all had gone off but about ten families. It is those who have remonstrated. If they are allowed to remain of course all the rest will go back. The trouble is that Congress has not ratified the treaty made the Sac and Fox Indians over a year ago, by which they were to remove and give up the reservation. The people have become impatient and have squatted on the indian lands in violation of right and justice The difficulty could be best settled by the confirmation of the treaty by Congress, otherwise these squatters should be put off. The treaty provides that the indians shall be removed before the land is occupied by white people. If Congress does not at once act and the order ejecting the squatters is suspended, the whole reservation will be covered by squatters in a very short time The land is excelent and immagration in that section of the state very large. I will forward Col Sheridans report by mail" Telegram received (at 4:30 P.M.), DNA, RG 107, Telegrams Collected (Bound); *ibid.*, RG 108, Telegrams Received; copies, *ibid.*, RG 107, Letters Received from Bureaus; (sent by mail) *ibid.*, RG 108, Letters Received; DLC-USG, V, 55; (2) DLC-Philip H. Sheridan.

On June 4, Governor Samuel J. Crawford of Kan. had telegraphed to U.S. Senators Samuel C. Pomeroy and Edmund G. Ross. "Lieut Col Sheridan has gone to the Sac & Fox Reservation with a military force to drive off the settlers in accordance with orders from Gen Grant to Genl sherman of Date Eighteen hundred sixty six *1866* and Eighteen hundred sixty seven *1867* will you please see Grant or the Secretary of War and have these orders revoked at once." Telegram received (on June 5, 3:15 P.M.), DNA, RG 108, Telegrams Received; copy, DLC-USG, V, 55. On June 5, Pomeroy and Ross endorsed this telegram. "We trust this report is incorrect,—please have such orders countermeded As we have a Treaty executed for the sale of these lands" ES, DNA, RG 108, Telegrams Received. On the same day, Crawford telegraphed to USG. "I do earnestly request that you suspend the execution of your orders to Gen Sherman of eighteen hundred sixty six 1866 and eighteen hundred sixty seven 1867 directing him to enquire into and remove settlers from indian reservations in Kansas until the facts can be reported by mail. Lt Col Sheridan is now engaged in this work. He has ordered the settlers to leave Sac and Fox reservation by Saturday next, which, if persisted in, will inflict great suffering upon these poor people, who will be thrown upon the prarie without any means upon which to subsist their families and no possible good can result to the government or Indians from the execution of this order. Please answer" Telegram received (at 3:30 P.M.), *ibid.*, RG 107, Telegrams Collected (Bound); *ibid.*, RG 108, Telegrams Received; copies, *ibid.*, RG 107, Letters Received from Bureaus; DLC-USG, V, 55. On June 10, Crawford wrote to USG. "Some time ago, as I am informed, an order was issued by you, directing Gen. Sherman to inquire into the circumstances, and to cause the removal of settlers from certain Indian Reservations in Kansas. In accordance with this order, and upon complaint of the Agent of the Sac & Fox Indians, Gen. Sheridan has sent out a detachment of troops to remove the settlers from the Sac & Fox Reserve. They number about Sixty families, and to drive them off at this time, causing them to abandon their crops and gardens, would inflict great suffering upon themselves and families.

A Treaty for this Reservation is now pending before the Senate, and if ratified will dispense with the neccessity of removing the settlers. I therefore respectfully ask that you revoke the order referred to, or at least suspend its execution until the Treaty shall have been acted upon by the Senate. Gen. Sheridan has suspended operations in the matter until the facts could be reported to you and an answer returned." ALS, DNA, RG 108, Letters Received.

On June 10, Sheridan wrote to Bvt. Maj. Gen. John A. Rawlins. "I have the honor to enclose, for the information of the General-in-Chief, reports in reference to squatters on the reservation of the Sac and Fox Indians—. My action was on the order of the President forwarded and endorsed from Army Headquarters. I am of the opinion that Congress should at once ratify the treaty made with these Indians, or if not, the settlers should be ejected." Copy, *ibid.*, RG 393, Military Div. of the Mo., Letters Sent. On June 15, Sheridan wrote to Rawlins. "Since my telegram of June 9th and reports forwarded to you on June 10th I have visited the reservation of the Sac and Fox Indians and examined the conditions of the treaty made February 1867. It appears by the terms of this treaty that the Indians agreed to give up their present reservation, select a new home in the Indian Territory, and after the ratification of the treaty they were to be allowed to remain undisturbed until their removal to their new homes. The treaty expressly stipulates this condition. The treaty has not been ratified nor have they, in consequence, selected their new homes, but their reservation has been encroached upon, their store houses, in some cases, have been taken possession of, their crops destroyed by the cattle of the squatters and much injustice done them. They all complain very bitterly of this violation of their rights and the bad faith of the Government with them. It is said the squatters are most of them men who follow squatting for a living and after residing for a short time on a claim sell out to other parties and go out and squat again under an assumed name. I do not see how the trouble can be settled except by ejecting the eight or nine families which still remain on the reservation in consequence of the suspension of the order putting them off. I had thought that when the treaty was ratified that the trouble would be ended, but it stipulates expressly that the reservation shall be kept intact, until the Indians move off, and as they have not yet selected a new home, it will probably be next spring before the removal can take place. I would recommend that the Government maintain good faith with this band; they cultivate the soil, are sensible and intelligent. There are about eight or nine hundred of these Indians. If they loose their crops by the cattle of these squatters, the Government will be obliged to feed them the coming winter. There will be no trouble in moving off the squatters still remaining." LS, *ibid.*, RG 94, Letters Received, 827M 1868. On June 20, USG endorsed this letter. "Respectfully forwarded to Secretary of War, in connection with previous papers forwarded 15th inst" ES, *ibid.*

To James A. Garfield

Washington, D, C,
June 19th 1868.

Hon. J. A. Garfield,
Ch. Mil. Com. &c.

Dear Sir:

In recommending a continuance of the same increase to the pay of officers of the Army given for the fiscal year just ending I did it on mature deliberation, and under the firm conviction that it is necessary to their decent support. The pay of the Army is now what it was at the breaking out of the rebellion, within a few dollars, which is offset by the income tax, whilst the cost of living has increased in a proportion familiar to every one.

Yours Truly
U. S. Grant
General,

P. S. The pay of all, or nearly all, who are employed by the Govt. except Army officers has been increased in the last seven years.

U. S. G.

ALS, DLC-James A. Garfield.

On May 25, 1868, U.S. Representative James A. Garfield of Ohio had written to Secretary of War Edwin M. Stanton. "I am directed by the Committee on Military Affairs to request that you will inform them whether in your opinion there is a necessity for the continuance for another year of the 33⅓ per cent. additional pay to officers of the army, which ceases under existing laws on the 30th of June next." LS, DNA, RG 107, Letters Received, M270 1868. On May 28, USG endorsed this letter. "Respectfully returned. Owing to the continued high prices of living it is my opinion that the 33⅓ per cent additional pay to officers of the Army should be continued, and I therefore renew my recommendation, made as Secretary of War *ad interim*, on the subject." ES, *ibid.*

On May 28, Bvt. Maj. Gen. John A. Rawlins wrote to U.S. Representative Elihu B. Washburne. "Personal . . . As a matter of justice as well as good policy I think Congress should at the earliest possible moment continue the 20 percent additional pay to the Department clerks and employes and in view of the fact that the General withdrew a recommendation of his for a continuance of it to the employees of the Military Department while Secretary of War ad interim you are the one who should move for its continuance. My reasons for this are—1st The reasons that originally induced its allowance, as well as the 33⅓ per cent to officers of the army, and that were used as an argument for the increase of the pay of Congress still exist. 2nd Congress has continued it to the clerks in its own immediate employ   3rd General Grant has renewed today his recommendation for the continuance of the temporily increased pay of officers of the Army. *4th.* Should this increased pay of officers of the Army, of Congress and its immediate employees be continued, and withheld from the Departmental clerks & employes it cannot be otherwise than damaging in the coming elections. *Last.* If you move for the continuance of it, being the *friend* of General Grant it will at once be inferred that he favors it, & will relieve him from the apparent discrimination against the clerks in which his renewal of his recommendation in favor of officers places him, and will insured those interested, of its success, and enlist their hearty support in the coming campaign beginning with the election here next Monday"   ALS, DLC-Elihu B. Washburne.

On Nov. 21, 1867, USG had written to U.S. Representative Robert C. Schenck of Ohio, chairman, Committee on Ways and Means, and other congressional chairmen. "My attention has been called to the fact that the Joint Resolution of 28th Feby /67 granting *twenty per cent additional compensation* to certain employees in the civil service of the Government at Washington expired on the 30th June last. Believing that the circumstances under which the additional compensation was given, and the reasons for giving it, have full as much force now as then, I earnestly recommend the subject to the favorable consideration of your Committee and of Congress." Copy, DNA, RG 107, Reports to Congress. On Dec. 14, USG wrote to Speaker of the House Schuyler Colfax. "I beg to withdraw my communication of the 21st November to the Committee of Ways & Means, and to the Committee on Appropriations of the House of Representatives, recommending an increase of *20 p. c* to the pay of the clerks &c. of this Department." Copy, *ibid.* On Dec. 18, USG wrote to Colfax reporting expenditures for additional compensation. Copy, *ibid. HED,* 40-2-63.

To George Wilkes

————

Washington
June 19th 1868

Geo. Wilkes Esq
Dear Sir

Your favor of the 5th May, enclosing copy of a letter from Genl Butler, wherein he desires to withdraw his response to an invitation to a reception at my house in Jan'y /65 is received. Of course I cordially accept the withdrawal of that letter, believing it to have been written under a misapprehension of the object of the invitation to which it was a response.

In regard to other matters in my report of the operations of the armies for the last year of the war to which Gen Butler alludes, I must decline to open discussion; but this does not debar him, or any other officer who feels himself aggrieved from making such written response as he or they may think necessary to their proper vindication

Yours Truly

U. S. GRANT

Copy, DLC-Benjamin F. Butler. George Wilkes, born in 1817 in New York City, cofounded the *National Police Gazette* (1845) and owned *Wilkes' Spirit of the Times*, a newspaper specializing in sports. See *PUSG*, 15, 404–5; *ibid.*, 16, 56. On May 6, 1868, Wilkes, Washington, D. C., had written to USG. "The enclosed correspondence between General Butler and myself touching matters in difference between himself and you, is herewith respectfully submitted. Acting without request from either of you, I have ascertained by the simple process of direct inquiry that the sole cause of the interruption of your social intercourse was, an answer returned by General Butler to a note of invitation to your house; and he, having learned, through me, that he acted therein under a misapprehension of your motive, has cheerfully desired to withdraw it. In regard to the Bermuda Hundred matter, you will perceive by General Butler's letter, that both of you substantially agree—at any rate that he has conceived of no offence and you have given none—and believing therefore, that the only real obstacle between you falls by the withdrawal of that note, I venture to hope, in common with the friends of both of you throughout the Country (which certainly includes the whole of the republican party) that your former personal relations are in an easy way of being resumed. I have only to add that if I have fallen into any error, in stating to General Butler the substance of your conversation with me, that you will permit me to correct it." ALS, DLC-Benjamin F. Butler. Wilkes enclosed a copy of a letter of May 2 from U.S. Representative Benjamin F. Butler of Mass. to Wilkes. "Your note did not receive an immediate reply because the pressing labors of the trial leave me scarcely time to meet the necessities of the routine of daily duties, and the subject of which it treats is one that ought to receive careful attention. That, what you have done in the matter has arisen from the most friendly motives, I do not doubt, and your thoughtful kindness is much appreciated. I agree with you that General Grant's command of the Army; our party relations; his high position as a man dealing with public affairs, which almost necessarily must bring us in official contact, would seem to render it convenient, at least, that no impediment should exist to social recognition each of the other even if supposed or real grievances to either, unexplained, or unredressed, should forbid more. Upon the explanation given in your note of the circumstances attending the sending of the card of invitation to his reception, from General Grant which was repelled by me in a manner which was intended to do, and did close social intercourse between us, it is clear that I mistook the object for which it was sent and misunderstood his purpose, and therefore ought not to have received or answered it in the manner in which it was done, and if General Grant desires or permits I will withdraw my answer thereto so that all cause of social offence may be at an end. The other matter spoken of by you scarcely needs further explanation. The phrase in General Grants report that my army was 'bottled up in the peninsula of Bermuda Hundreds,' which your note informs me was not intended to be by him offensively used, as the newspapers and vulgar minded men have declared, could of itself hardly be ground of offence, because on the 27th day of May 1864, long before General Grants report, at my own Head-quarters I applied the same epithet to my position and it was published in the correspondence from thence in the New York Times in a day or two after. The exigencies of the public service did indeed 'bottle up' the troops at the time under my command there, and of that and the reasons inducing it nobody can be more certain than myself save General Grant. That he did not think it a military fault or misfortune I am certain because he returned to me on the peninsula of Bermuda, i. e. to the 'bottle,' and put under my command on the 6th of June the 18th Army Corps which had been withdrawn from thence to reinforce the Army of the Potomac, and on the 10th of June sent me there the 6th Army Corps also, and in July ordered the 19th Army Corps to report to me for duty in the same 'bottle,' and on the 10th of August sent General Hancocks Corps on to the peninsula, i. e. into the 'bottle' to make a demonstration from thence against the works of the enemy on the North side of the James and on the 19th of August sent the 10th Army Corps out of the 'bottle' to aid General Hancock and the 2nd Corps to make an assault upon the enemy's works on Newmarket Heights which failed, and on the 29th of September allowed me to lead my whole 'Army of the James' out of the peninsula to the North side of James River to assault the same New-Market Heights and Fort Harrison a part of the defenses of Richmond both of which we carried after a hard fight and held as the most advanced posts of our forces till Richmond fell. It being so easy therefore to put Army Corps into and take them out of the 'bottle' again for military operations, and they and their stores and trains were so safe while there, that I did not need the explanation of your note to assure me that as a military man General Grant could never have intended any offence in the use of the phrase 'bottled up' in relation to my entrenched camp at Bermuda Hundreds. The position was indeed 'a bottle,' of refreshment to the Army of the Potomac when it got there as it was intended to be, furnishing that Army with supplies of subsistence ammunition and forage which is another instance of the propriety of the use of the phrase as an illustration of military affairs. If other supposed injustice done me in his Report can be as easily elucidated as this, there can be no reason why the most cordial relations should not be resumed between us as I do not hold this phrase as needing any explanation as only the ignorance of the Newspaper critics who seized upon it ever made it appear invidious. When General Grant makes known to me his desires to give opportunity for explanation of other matters of difference I will promptly point out to him such topics in his report wherein I think he has done me injustice and if he agrees with me as I believe he will upon reflection I see no difficulty in mutual satisfactory explanations which however I cannot even seem to seek from him as his position is such that would submit my motives in so doing to misconstruction while his own commanding place leaves it easy for him to do any needed act of reparation when brought to his attention without suspicion of any inducement save to do justice. There is one thing which I know he will accord to me in any event that while under his command I endeavored to serve the Country faithfully to the best of my knowledge and ability. With grateful thanks for your kind interest in my behalf . . ." LS and ADfS, *ibid*. See drafts of letters from Wilkes to Butler, April 12 (2), 14, 1868, *ibid*.; Wilkes to Caleb Cushing, June 21, 1868, DLC-Caleb Cushing.

On April 14, Mrs. Mora B. Fox, San Francisco, had written to Butler. "Gen U. S. Grant is indebted to me since last January one year ago, to the amount of four thousand dollars ($4000—) If you can succeed in inducing him to pay me this amount you shall be paid a liberal percentage—otherwise much scandal may be the result of the manner in which he is treating me." ALS, DLC-Benjamin F. Butler. Butler endorsed a copy of this letter. "Respectfully referred to General Grant for his information The application would seem to be some attempt to 'blackmail' which follows Gentlemen of position. I need not say that the original is at General Grants service if he desires it ~~to protect~~ himself against the author who is unknown to me" AES (undated), *ibid.* Whether Butler sent this to USG is unknown.

Between April and Aug. 1869, Wilkes forwarded five letters advocating his appointment as minister to Mexico or to China. DNA, RG 59, Letters of Application and Recommendation. A document labeled *"Extract"* may represent part of a letter from Wilkes to USG written in 1871. " 'It seems to me a little singular that if Genl Grant, holds me in such esteem, he should not have taken some opportunity to manifest it, even by a word or line during the two years of his administration. His administration has constantly had my support, and you will ~~b~~ bear in mind, that I ran under it as late as last Nov. on a Congressional nomination conferred upon me by his friends. As I write, the mail brings me my paper, of the 8th April containing a leading article sustaining his favorite measure. I may be excused therefore in expressing my surprise at what has occasioned surprise to a great many other ~~personal friends~~ persons, and also because Gen Grant was not left ignorant by my friends that some recognition of my services would be agreeable to them as well as to me. General Butler (between whom and the President I had then, recently effected a restoration of good feelings) called upon Mr. [W]ashburne as soon as that gentleman had been made Secretary of State, and indicated that the Mexican Mission would be the most agreeable form which any official compliment could take. Mr. W. replied that he would inform the President, but promptly added, that no pressure would be necessary in that quarter to insure a friendly action towards me. Subsequently Gen. Butler called upon the President, as also did Mr Sumner, (then chairman of the committee on Foreign Relations) as, likewise, did Gen. Logan and the two Senators of my state; all making the same application in my behalf. I have this, on their several information; and I have further been informed by Gen. Butler and General Logan that the late Secretary Rawlins warmly co-operated with them in the premises. I may also be allowed to add, in this connection, that I have reason to believe that Mr Fish was [infor]med by the late Mr. Stanton that *he* took a ~~personal~~ personal interest in my appointment. This seemed to combine all the warrant necessary to justify the friendly *action* of the President; while it may be said that it had been pretty well shown that my appointment would have been acceptable to the country, by the fact that it had been frequently foreshadowed by the press (as had also been my probable appointment to China) without eliciting disapprobation in any quarter—certainly none from any Republican paper. Through these endorsements Gen. Grant stood relieved of much of the responsibility which usually attaches to prominent appointments; while if he had any doubt of the approbation of the Senate, he had but to consult such members of that body as Messrs. Morton, Wade, Chandler, Howard, Wilson, Nye, Stewart, Sprague, and I may add, I think, all the Republican Senators; ex[ce]pt, perhaps one or two who had voted against impeachment. That secret enemies may have sought to prejudice me to Gen. Grant, I think it not unlikely but that he would decide against me on their statements, I am unwilling to believe. If he were really my friend, such a course would have been impossible;

while if he were not, the simplest sense of justice must have suggested an immediate reference of such calumnies either to myself, or to the distinguished gentlemen who had constituted themselves my representatives, and who were always at his side. It is not for me to speak, of the services by which I obtained the favor of the above-named gentlemen; but it is not improper for me here to say—that while I have never sought to profit by my position and while no friend holds even the humblest office through my application, I have made sacrifices in the interest of the present Administration, which certainly entitle me to its friendly recollection. Down to the opening of the rebellion in 1860 I belonged to the Democratic party, and held a position in the city of NewYork, which I have reason to believe would have sent me to Congress, whenever my ambition might have taken that direction. Besides, I was the owner, at the same time, of a very prosperous newspaper, the supporters of which, were in great part attached to the same political party. To take sides therefore, with the Republican party involved not only the necessity of constructing a new circulation for my paper, but the deliberate resignation of all political prospects, springing from my native city. I did not, ~~therefore~~, hesitate however to make these sacrifices. [Bu]t while I do not regret having done so, I am naturally puzzled that the Administration should ~~be~~ so steadily refuse to recognize them. Though now indifferent to office, it cannot be supposed, I am indifferent to this neglect, for under the contrary expectations of the public,—the neglect of the Government puts me under the ban of an injurious reflection, and works a penalty instead of a reward. It is plain, therefore, that however kind Gen Grant may feel towards me, his administration, has practically made itself my enemy, and it is equally plain, that if I still retained any wish for public life, I must regard his administration as an impassible barrier to any political future on my part. This is the view taken by my friends, and it seems to me, to be the only one of which the problem is susceptible. With no desire to trouble you further on this subject, . . ." Copy, USG 3.

To Lt. Gen. William T. Sherman

Washington, D. C., June 21st *1868*

DEAR SHERMAN,

Your kind favor, written from New Mexico, is received. You understand my position exactly. It is one I would not occupy for any mere personal consideration, but, from the nature of the contest since the close of active hostilities, I have been forced into it in spite of myself. I could not back down without, as it seems to me, leaving the contest for power for the next four years between mere trading polititcians, the elevation of whom, no matter which party won, would lose to us, largely, the results of the costly war which we have gone through. Now the democrats will be forced to adopt a good platform and put upon it a reliable man who, if elected, will disappoint the Copperhead element of their party. if elected.

This will be a great point gained if nothing more is accomplished.

I feel very grateful to the officers of our Army whose military achievements made my reputation as well as their own, to know that they support me in this new field. I do not expect, or want, active support but merely the satisfaction of knowing what your letter assures me of on your part. Officers who expect to make their Army their home for life have to serve under successive Administrations and should not make themselve obnoxious to any party likely ever to come into power. I shall not ask you to come to Washington until after November, and probably not then. For myself I expect to be away from here most of the time, but I shall keep within telegraph, and being within the limits of my Command will exercise it.

Present my kindest regards to Mrs. Sherman and the children.

Yours Truly

U. S. Grant

ALS, DLC-William T. Sherman. On June 7, 1868, Lt. Gen. William T. Sherman, Santa Fé, had written to USG ."I have just written you a letter on business and whilst I have a table to write on cannot deny myself the pleasure to tell you I have seen in the papers the notice of your nomination and acceptance as President of the U. S. I feel a little strange though this was a foregone conclusion. If you want the office of course I want you to have it, and now that you have accepted the nomination of course you must succeed. It is a sacrifice on your part, but one which I doubt not you feel forced to make. Surely it will give us four years and I hope eight years of calm, quiet, firm administration, during which all these ugly questions left by the war may be adjusted, and things be put on such a footing that the country will be allowed to grow, increase in wealth and population, and thereby emerge from all the fears now entertained by reason of the awful big public debt. I feel of course interested in your full success, not only in the election, but in the good you can and likely will do, in the new office. Though personally I would prefer to remain as now, I suppose I must contemplate a removal to Washington. Still even in this I shall not commit myself by word or act till you give me the hint. I would like as early a notice as possible that I may avoid all unnecessary expense. I have all my interests at St. Louis, and schools for the children. If I must change to Washington, it could be made better in the recess of schools than at any other time. If you intend to keep out of the way during the canvas, please let me know when you have made up your mind. If there be anything you want me to do I feel certain you will not hesitate to let me know. John Sherman will of course support you enthusiastically both on personal and party grounds, The Ewings seem to have interested themselves so with the President that I can't answer for them. It will depend on the personal character of the Democratic nominee. But they will not stand a copperhead, such as Pendleton, Getty is here, very well, and sends his best wishes—he expects his wife out in July." Copy, *ibid.*

On June 24, Sherman, St. Louis, wrote to USG. "I am this moment in receipt of yours of June 21, which gives me great satisfaction indeed. You appreciate our position exactly. and I do honestly believe you will be elected president. and that all parties will so far respect your person and antecedents—that we will enjoy more natural peace and stability than could be otherwise attained. You make more sacrifice than any one else. Dodge wrote me asking me to come out openly for you. I answered him fully and frankly pretty much after the terms used by you, that in giving up your present post for a four years office with its heap of personal abuse, you made a sacrifice that could not be accounted for except on the highest principles of patriotism, that all the leading men of the country know me to be your personal friend. that in case of your elevation I had a personal interest, one that would enable our joint enemies to impute my open assistance of your election to personal motives. and Concluded that I did not believe you wanted me to come out publicly as an [a]dvocate. Should the Democrats come out in July with a Candidate that occupies national ground as to the war. I must be neutral or silent because of the reason you assign; that professional officers of the Army, dependant on their salaries, must serve with ardor and fidelity any administration in power; and our whole experience in the past shows that the paties succeed each other from time to time, as by some law of Change and succession. I am so impressed however with the justness of our War, that should any Candidate like Pendleton, or Seymour be named I could not restrain my voice or pen from proclaiming to him, my open hostility: The War, no matter what its cause, or conduct was an epoch in our National history, that must be sanctified, and made to stand justified to future Ages. I must go to Genl Miles wedding next Tuesday. I propose to start via Cincinnati for Cleavland on Sunday. but will be ready to return on Wednesday. I see you contemplate a visit to Cheyenne an Denver, and some say you will leave Mrs Grant and the children on the farm at Gravois for the summer. Mrs Sherman has arranged to spend the summer at Lancaster Ohio, and is ready to start after the schools close here tomorrow—I must attend the exercises tomorrow—So I fear I may miss you here next week unless you stay here towards its close. I will endeavor to watch your movements & meet you here, or up the road. I am of course glad you will leave me here till November, as a summer in Washington would be a bore. as soon as the election is over, of which I feel no doubt as to the result, I will be ready to play any part you may assign me. I think we have steared clear of the Indian War, and gained very much by time, as your visit will prove. You could spend a Month or two about the head of the Railroad, and if you go out one, you should come in by the other, thus seeing the effect of both. If Mrs Grant is on the farm this summer. I and my Staff can be of use to her." Copy, *ibid.*

On June 27, USG wrote to U.S. Senator John Sherman of Ohio. "Knowing that you take great interest in all matters pertaining to the views and opinions of your brother, Gen. Sherman, I send you copy of a letter from him, written from New Mexico, and my reply to it with his response again." ALS, *ibid.* On June 28, John Sherman wrote to USG. "Your note with enclosures is rec'd. I am very much pleased with your correspondence with Gen. Sherman It is highly creditable to each of you. Your acceptance of the nomination is a sacrifice but I do not see how you could avoid making it. Your nomination was not made by our party but by the People and in obedience to the universal demand that our Candidate should be so independent of party politics as to be a guarantee of Peace and quiet. You are the only man in the Nation who can give this guarantee and that without pledges or platform   Gen. S. is entirely correct in saying that I will support you with all my heart—and I shall place it on the ground that all party questions are now settled by law & the result of the War—and what we want is an honest & faithful execution of existing law in a kindly spirit to the South. I do not doubt the result of the election. The Democratic party will not heartily support any one but a Copperhead. I hope they will select an open opponent of the War and let us frame a square & final fight on the issues of the War. The nomination of Chase would be a ridiculous termination of the party. They are too wise to make it. You will have the support of nearly all the patriotism of the Country and will be perfectly free to do what is just and right to all parties and sections"   ALS, USG 3.

To Nathan Grossmayer

Washington, D, C, June 22d *1868*

MY DEAR SIR:

Your favor of June 5th requesting to know how the money, thre Hundred dollars, presented by you to be given to the soldier who first planted the American Flag over Richmond, was awarded, is received. Other patriotic parties sent money for the same purpose making in all the sum of Four Hundred & sixty dollars. The manner of the fall of Richmond was such that there was no special merit in the mere running up of the flag, after entering the City by so large a force, and there was a great deal of merit on the part of thousands who contributed to make the feat practicable, so I awarded the money in three prizes, to soldiers in different parts of the Army. The enclosed are copies of letters forwarded to the brave soldiers who were awarded these prizes.

Yours Truly
U. S. GRANT
General,

TO NATHAN GROSSMAYER, ESQ.R
NEW YORK CITY,

ALS, American Jewish Archives, Cincinnati, Ohio. On June 5, 1868, Nathan Grossmayer, New York City, had written to USG. "Under date of September 12th 1864 I had the honor to forward to the Honor Edwin M. Stanton, Secr. of War, the sum of One hundred Dollars, with instructions that they might be presendet to the Soldier, who shall first unfurl our honored flag in the city of Richmond Va. In aknowledging receipt under date of Sept. 13. 1864 his Honor informs me that the said One hundred Dolls. have been forwarded by him to you with above instructions. Being desirous to know, *who* was the happy soldier—, and dessiring to preserve your answer for my children, I would thank you very much if you would please and let me have it in your own handwriting so as to be able to put it in frame" ALS, DNA, RG 108, Letters Received.

On Sept. 13, 1864, Secretary of War Edwin M. Stanton wrote to USG. "Enclosed herewith you will find a Treasury-Note for one hundred dollars which is remitted to you, at the request of Mr N. Grossmayer, a patriotic citizen of Washington, 'as a reward to the first men of our army who will unfurl the Stars and Stripes in the City of Richmond.' A copy of Mr Grossmayer's letter is herewith enclosed." LS, USG 3. The enclosure is *ibid.* On Sept. 21, USG wrote to Stanton. "I have the honor to acknowledge the receipt of your communication dated Sept 13, 1864, with the letter and contribution enclosed, of Mr. Grossmayer, 'a patriotic citizen of Washington.' The amount forwarded will be applied in conformity with his request." Copy, DNA, RG 107, Letters Received, Irregular Series. See *PUSG*, 15, 282–83.

To Bvt. Maj. Gen. Edward R. S. Canby

Cipher   Washington D. C.
                                                      June 26. 1868. [*1:00* P.M.]

GENERAL. E. R. S. CANBY,
CHARLESTON S. C.

The act to admit the states of North Carolina, South Carolina, Louisiana, Georgia, Alabama and Florida to representation in Congress became a law June twenty fifth 25, eighteen sixty eight 1868. Please notify the Governors elect of ~~your~~ the states in your District, for, under the act, the Governor elect may, if he deems it necessary, convene the Legislature thereof at an earlier date than that fixed by the law.

                                                      U. S. GRANT.
                                                      General.

Telegram sent, DNA, RG 107, Telegrams Collected (Bound); telegram received (at 1:45 P.M.), *ibid.*, RG 393, 2nd Military District, Letters Received. On June 26, 1868, Bvt. Maj. Gen. Edward R. S. Canby twice telegraphed to

USG. "The governor elect of this state has issued his proclamation convening the Legislature on the sixth (6th) of July Proximo" "Telegram received. The proclamation by the governors elect of both states have already been issued. The Legislature of North Carolina to meet on the first and of South Carolina on the sixth (6th) of July proximo" Telegrams received (at 1:35 P.M. and 7:00 P.M.), *ibid.*, RG 107, Telegrams Collected (Bound); *ibid.*, RG 108, Telegrams Received; copies (one of each sent by mail), *ibid.*, Letters Received; *ibid.*, RG 393, 2nd Military District, Letters Sent; DLC-USG, V, 55.

On June 27, USG signed a letter to Canby identical to the letter sent the same day to Bvt. Maj. Gen. Robert C. Buchanan. LS, DNA, RG 393, 2nd Military District, Letters Received.

On June 29, 4:00 P.M., USG telegraphed to Canby. "To avoid any question as to who shall exercise the offices of Governor and Lieutenant Governor in the States of North Carolina and South Carolina upon the convening of the legislatures of said States under the act of Congress passed June 25th 1868, you will appoint the Governor and Lieutenant Governor elect of North Carolina Governor and Lieutenant Governor of said State vice present incumbents removed; and the Governor and Lieutenant Governor elect of South Carolina Governor and Lieutenant Governor of said State, vice present incumbents removed. These appointments and removals to take effect at the date of the convening of said legislatures respectively." LS (telegram sent), *ibid.*, RG 107, Telegrams Collected (Bound); telegram sent, *ibid.*; telegram received, *ibid.*, RG 393, 2nd Military District, Letters Received. On June 30, Canby telegraphed to USG. "Telegram of the 29th received. The removals and appointments referred to are embraced in the general orders providing for the inauguration of the new State Government as soon as Legislatures have ratified the Constitutional Amendment. Instructions of the 27th, by mail, have also been received. A general order carrying out the provisions of the law, as they effect the military authorities, is in preparation, to be published as soon as the Legislatures have acted A draft will be sent to you before it is published." Telegram received (at 1:30 P.M.), *ibid.*, RG 107, Telegrams Collected (Bound); *ibid.*, RG 108, Telegrams Received; copies (one sent by mail), *ibid.*, Letters Received; *ibid.*, RG 393, 2nd Military District, Letters Sent; DLC-USG, V, 55.

On June 6, Canby forwarded to USG correspondence with the justices of the Supreme Court of N. C. concerning problems of assembling the court before Congress approved the state constitution. AES, DNA, RG 108, Letters Received. On June 15, Governor William W. Holden of N. C., Raleigh, telegraphed to USG. "Is there any objections to my convening the Legislature of this State on Wednesday the first 1 of July?" Telegram received (at 1:10 P.M.), *ibid.*, RG 107, Telegrams Collected (Bound); *ibid.*, RG 108, Telegrams Received; copy DLC-USG, V, 55.

On June 20, Canby telegraphed to USG. "Is the assembling of the Legislatures [o]f the states embraced in the act to [a]dmit the states of North Carolina South Carolina &c, is authorized [i]n advance of the full restoration of those states. I have regarded this law as dispensing with the oath of office prescribed by the act of July second 2 eighteen sixty [t]wo 1868 in the case of all members of [t]he Legislature who are not disqual[i]fied under the constitutional amendment, and, unless otherwise advised I propose to modify the orders heretofore given so as to conform to this construction." Telegram received (at 11:15 A.M.), DNA, RG 107, Telegrams Collected (Bound); *ibid.*, RG 108, Telegrams Received; copies (one sent by mail), *ibid.*, Letters Received; *ibid.*, RG 393, 2nd

Military District, Letters Sent; DLC-USG, V, 55. At 3:30 P.M., USG telegraphed to Canby. "Your construction of the law is concurred in and your proposed action approved" LS (telegram sent), DNA, RG 107, Telegrams Collected (Bound); telegram sent, *ibid.*; telegrams received (2—one at 3:15 P.M.), *ibid.*, RG 393, 2nd Military District, Letters Received.

On July 2, Canby wrote to Bvt. Maj. Gen. John A. Rawlins. "I have the honor to transmit a draft of the General Order which I propose to issue in relation to the states in this District, as they ratify the proposed constitutional amendment. I understand that the Reconstruction Acts do not become wholly inoperative until the proposed constitutional amendment becomes a part of the Constitution of the United States, as prescribed by the 5th Section of the Act of March 2nd 1867. I think it expedient and proper that all exercise of authority under those laws, should cease as to each state, upon the ratification, by its Legislature, of the constitutional amendment, except so far as to give force and effect to the law of June 25th. 1868, and then only in the case of unlawful and forcible opposition to the organization of the new State Governments. The other provisions are, in the main, directory, and conform, I believe, to the spirit of the General's instructions of the 27th ulto; except as to the 8th Section, which I have regarded as necessary, for the reason, that in both states there are several places captured or occupied during the rebellion, and where there are still large quantities of public property, the safety of which, might be jeoparded, if left subject to the jurisdiction of the local courts. If there should be anything in the provisions of this order that does not meet approval, will you please advise me by telegraph, as I presume that the ratification of the constitutional amendment will very soon follow the organization of the Legislatures in the two states." LS, *ibid.*, RG 108, Letters Received. On July 3, Canby telegraphed to USG. "The Constitutional Amendment was ratified by the Legislature of North Carolina yesterday and this morning the following instructions were sent to Commanding Officers in that State: 'You will abstain from the exercise of any authority, under the Reconstruction Laws, except so far as may be necessary to close up any unfinished business; and you will not interfere in civil matters unless the execution of the Law of June twenty fifth 25, eighteen sixty eight 1868, should be obstructed by unlawful and forcible opposition to the inauguration of the new state government. Detailed instructions, in orders, will be sent to you in a day or two 2. This, of course, will not interfere with any proper action in the case of insurrection or other disorder beyond the control of the Civil Authorities. In all such cases report your action at once, using the telegraph when the urgency of the case requires it.' " Telegram received (misdated July 4, received at 9:00 A.M.), *ibid.*, RG 107, Telegrams Collected (Bound); (2) *ibid.*, RG 108, Telegrams Received; copies (one sent by mail), *ibid.*, Letters Received; *ibid.*, RG 393, 2nd Military District, Letters Sent; DLC-USG, V, 55.

On July 11, Canby telegraphed to USG. "The Legislature of South Carolina ratified the Constitutional Amendment yesterday and instructions corresponding in effect to those given upon the ratification of the amendment in North Carolina have been sent to the Commanding officers in this State" Telegram received (at 10:50 A.M.), DNA, RG 107, Telegrams Collected (Bound); *ibid.*, RG 108, Telegrams Received; copy, DLC-USG, V, 55. On July 21, Canby telegraphed to Rawlins. "By the announcement by the Secretary of State that the constitutional amendment known as article fourteen (14) has been adopted, provided the original resolutions of Ohio and New Jersey are counted, it would seem that all the conditions imposed by the fifth section of the law of March 2nd 1867 have

been satisfied and that all authority under that law should now be formally remitted to the civil authorities of the two (2) states that constitute this District
This I propose to do unless it should be considered proper to defer it, until the
doubt expressed by the Secretary of State is removed. When the order is issued
will the designation of this command revert as of course to its former designation
'Department of the South' or will orders in relation to it be issued at Washington?" Telegram received (on July 22, 9:00 A.M.), DNA, RG 107, Telegrams
Collected (Bound); *ibid.*, RG 108, Telegrams Received; copies, *ibid.*, RG 107,
Letters Received from Bureaus; (sent by mail) *ibid.*, RG 108, Letters Received;
DLC-USG, V, 55. On July 22, Rawlins endorsed a copy of this telegram. "Respectfully forwarded to the Secretary of War. The reconstruction acts of Congress having become inoperative in the States of North Carolina and South Carolina, it is respectfully recommended that the 2d Mility District established under
the act of March 2d 1867 be discontinued." ES, DNA, RG 107, Letters Received from Bureaus.

To Bvt. Maj. Gen. Robert C. Buchanan

Washington, D. C. June 27th *1868*

BT. MAJ. GEN. R. C. BUCHANAN,
COMDG 5TH MILITARY DISTRICT,
GENERAL:

The act of Congress admitting the States of North Carolina,
South Carolina, Louisiana, Georgia Alabama and Florida to representation in Congress, passed June 25th 1868, declares that each
of said States shall be entitled and admitted to representation in
Congress as a State of the Union, when the legislature of such
State shall have duly ratified the amendment to the Constitution of
the United States proposed by the 39th Congress and known as
article 14, upon a certain fundamental condition fully set forth in
said act, except the State of Georgia, which has a further fundamental condition imposed upon it, also fully set forth in said act,
and to which the assent of the State is required to be given by a
solemn public act of the General Assembly of the State; that upon
compliance with the above conditions, the officers of each State,
duly elected and qualified under the constitution thereof, shall be
inaugurated without delay; but no person prohibited from holding
office under the United States, or under any State by section three
of the proposed amendment to the constitution of the United States

known as article 14, is to be deemed eligible to any office in either of said States, unless relieved from disability as provided in said amendment.

When therefore any one of said States shall have complied with said act of Congress and inaugurated its officers, military authority under the reconstruction acts of Congress will be at an end as to such State, and the terms of office of all military appointees in such State will be terminated. District Commanders should then transfer everything appertaining to the government of such State to its officers at the earliest practicable moment thereafter consistent with the interests of the public service.

Very respectfully
Your obedient servant
U. S. GRANT
General

LS, DNA, RG 393, 5th Military District, Miscellaneous Records.
On June 26, 1868, 1:00 P.M., USG had telegraphed to Bvt. Maj. Gen. Robert C. Buchanan. "The Act to admit the States of North Carolina, South Carolina, Louisiana, Georgia, Alabama and Florida to representation in Congress became a law June 25th 1868. Please notify the Governor elect of La. of this, for under the act he may if he deems it necessary convene the legislature at an earlier date than that fixed by the law." LS (telegram sent), *ibid.*, RG 107, Telegrams Collected (Bound); telegram sent, *ibid.*; telegram received (dated June 28), *ibid.*, RG 393, 5th Military District, Telegrams Received.
On June 27, 11:00 A.M., USG telegraphed to Buchanan. "To avoid any question as to who shall exercise the offices of Governor and Lieutenant Governor of the State of Louisiana upon the convening of the legislature of said State under the act of Congress passed June 25th 1868, you will appoint Henry C. Warmouth, (Govr elect) Governor of the State of Louisiana vice Joshua Baker, removed, and Oscar J. Dunn, (Lt. Govr elect) Lieutenant Governor of the State of Louisiana vice Albert Voorhies, removed. These appointments and removals to take effect at the date of the convening of said legislature" LS (telegram sent), *ibid.*, RG 107, Telegrams Collected (Bound); telegram sent, *ibid.*; telegram received (dated June 28), *ibid.*, RG 393, 5th Military District, Miscellaneous Records.
On June 29, Buchanan telegraphed to USG. "The Legislature met at noon, and after effecting a temporary organization, the Republican members of the House insisted on the test oath being taken, although your telegram of the 18th inst through Major Kieler was read to them. The Democrats then left—My opinion was that the oath prescribed in the constitution should alone be taken, but that was disregarded.—No one is recognized as a member of the House who cannot take the test oath, and I fear that trouble is brewing. In the Senate Lieutenant Governor Dunn refused positively to be governed by the opinion expressed in your telegram and when an appeal was made against his decision refused to

allow a vote to be taken on the appeal; declaring himself to be the sole judge of the oath required—HeHave you any orders to give in the case—" LS (telegram sent), *ibid.*, RG 107, Telegrams Collected (Bound); telegram received (at 6:00 P.M.), *ibid.*; (at 6:30 P.M.) *ibid.*, RG 108, Telegrams Received. On June 30, USG, Relay House, Md., telegraphed to Bvt. Maj. Gen. John A. Rawlins. "Instruct General Buchanan that the government of Louisiana is provisional and the Lieutenant Governor is bound by the decisions of the District Commander, right or wrong whilst it remains so." Telegram received (at 9:45 A.M.), *ibid.*, RG 107, Telegrams Collected (Bound). At 12:35 P.M., Rawlins telegraphed to USG. "Before receiving your dispatch from the RelayHouse the following had been sent to Buchanan. 'I have no orders at present to give, but I repeat to you as heretofore, that the members of the legislature of the State of La. are only required to take the oath prescribed by their own constitution, and are not required to take the test oath prescribed in the reconstruction acts. Meade and Canby are acting on this view of the case.' Would it not be best to wait and see if this will not have the desired effect, before sending yours from the Relay-House?" LS (telegram sent), *ibid.*; telegram sent, *ibid.* On the same day, USG, Martinsburg, West Va., telegraphed to Rawlins. "Your dispatch to Gen'l Buchanan will be sufficient for the present." Telegram received (at 2:40 P.M.), *ibid.*; *ibid.*, RG 108, Telegrams Received; copy, DLC-USG, V, 55.

On July 14, Buchanan wrote to Rawlins. "I have the honor to report for the information of the General Commanding the Army that I yesterday turned over the State of Louisiana to the Civil Authorities in accordance with the requirements of the Reconstruction Acts and his instructions of the ~~same date~~ 27th ult— The inauguration of the Governor took place at noon and the enclosed order was thereupon transmitted to him—I was not invited to be present on the occasion, but he had previously informed me that he would cause my order to be read to both Houses of the Assembly,—but it did not reach him in time—The legislation proposed and that already enacted by the new Legislative body is well calculated to alarm the thoughtful and moderate and exasperate to a great degree the heedless and discontented portion of the people—There are strong grounds for believing that serious riots and much disturbance will be the result, and in view of this probability, I respectfully request that special instructions be furnished me for my guidance in the use of my troops—Upon whose application and in what manner should such application be made in order to justify me in interfering to preserve the peace—So many of our Commanders of Posts have entered the service during the state of war, that full instructions for their guidance in time of peace are absolutely necessary." ALS, DNA, RG 107, Letters Received from Bureaus.

On July 18, Buchanan wrote to Rawlins. "I have the honor to transmit herewith enclosed a letter, with one enclosure, from his Excellency Governor Pease of Texas, addressed to Bvt. Major General J. J. Reynolds, Commanding District of Texas, asking that the same be transmitted to General Grant, and forwarded by General Reynolds to me. I deem it proper to submit therewith a few statements with reference to these communications, which relate to the subject of removals and appointments in the State of Texas. It will be observed from the enclosures that Governor Pease by implication and Messrs. Caldwell, Smith, Whitmore and Slaughter of the convention, by direct assertion, charge that I appointed Mr. Hodge to the mayoralty of Jefferson 'upon the petition of disloyal men' and 'at the instance of the entire rebel population.' Both implication and assertion, are false in fact, and without the slightest foundation. I appointed

W. N. Hodge, Mayor of the City of Jefferson, Texas, vice J. S. Elliott deceased, solely upon the recommendation, by telegraph of Judge L. D. Evans, Collector of Internal Revenue at Marshall, Texas, a member of the Texas Constitutional Convention I have yet to learn that Judge Evans is a disloyal citizen or is charged by any person whatsoever with being such. The petition of the one hundred and ninety six (196) citizens of the City of Jefferson, characterised in these letters as 'disloyal and as rebel sympathizers,' I never saw or heard of until after the appointment of Mr. Hodge had been made, when a copy of the original forwarded by the citizens to Governor Pease, was sent me. The gentleman recommended by Governor Pease and the four members of the Convention Mr Grigsby is is also a member of the convention at Austin, and if appointed Mayor of Jefferson could not discharge the duties of the office at present without resigning his seat in said Convention. Furthermore, on the 10th of June, nine days before the Governor's recommendation of Mr. Grigsby for the mayoralty of Jefferson, his Excellency upon a memorial signed by three (3) members of the Constitutional Convention—the first of whom was Mr. Grigsby—, asked for the removal of Judge Whitmore of the Criminal Court of the city of Jefferson and recommended the appointment of Mr. Grigsby to the vacancy thus to be created. In this connection I deem it proper to state the course I have pursued with reference to removals and appointments in Texas. I assumed command of the 5th Military District on the 25th of March and from that date until the 1st of July,—date of Gov. Pease's letter—I made eleven (11) removals and one hundred and sixty-five (165) appointments to civil and municipal officers in Texas. *Every one* of these removals and appointments was made upon the recommendation of Governor Pease and General Reynolds, *except in the case of Mr. Hodge.* And all of their recommendations for removals to the date referred to were approved by me and the removals made, save in eleven (11) cases presented in a letter of March 25th, 1868, which was referred back April 11th 'for proof to warrant the removals.' As nothing in relation to them has since been received, I conclude the required proof could not be obtained. Every recommendation for appointments made by them has been approved by me ~~and the~~ and the appointments made save in the case of the Mayoralty of the City of Jefferson, and in that of a Lieutenant of Cavalry who was recommended for an important Judgeship.— The papers in the latter case were returned with the suggestion that some competent and well qualified citizen be recommended instead, which was done, and the appointment made. Therefore—if inefficient and unworthy persons have remained in office or have been appointed to fill vacancies in Texas, and criminals *thereby* go unpunished and violence and murder abound, Governor Pease and General Reynolds are the parties solely responsible. From Governor Pease's letters recommending removals and appointments and from his general course as Chief Executive of the State of Texas, which has been closely observed by me since my assumption of the command of the District, I am led to believe that in general he pronounces an individual loyal or disloyal according to the political party with which he may be acting. If, of Governor Pease's political faith—which is simply that of self—the judgement is favorable—if otherwise it is unfavorable— I am therefore of the opinion that the best removal that could be made in Texas would be that of the Governor himself. I have observed that a report of a Committee appointed by the Texas Constitutional Convention on 'lawlessness and crime' has been transmitted to the President of the Senate and Speaker of the House at Washington, D. C., and that in said report the Commanding General of the 5th Military District is charged with being responsible for two hundred and twenty (220) or two-thirds of the entire number—of homicides alleged to have been committed in Texas since December 1st, 1867—. The following extraordinary language is used: 'Charged by law to keep the peace and afford protection to life and property, and having the Army of the United States to assist him in so doing he has failed—. He has persistently refused to try criminals rejected the prayer of the Executives of the State and the Commanding General of the District of Texas for adequate tribunals, and turned a deaf ear to the cry of tried and persecuted loyalists, and knowing whereof we affirm, and in the face of the civilized world, we do solemnly lay to his charge, the death of hundreds of loyal citizens of Texas, a responsibility that should load his name with infamy and hand his very memory to coming years as a curse and execration.' As will be seen by the facts previously stated by me, I have adopted with the few exceptions specified, *every recommendation of Governor Pease approved by General Reynolds, with reference to removals and appointments in Texas*, to which I will add, that every application for the appointment of a Military Commission in any special case has also been granted. I am therefore content to leave the question of responsibility for 'crime, outrage and violated law' in Texas to the sense of justice of the General of the Army and to Congress—to which the report above referred to has been transmitted." Copy, *ibid.*, RG 108, Letters Received. The enclosures are *ibid.*

To Maj. Gen. George G. Meade

Washington, D. C., June 29 *1868* [*4:00* P.M.]

GEN. G. G. MEADE
ATLANTA, GA.

To avoid any question as to who shall exercise the offices of Governor and Lieutenant Governor in the States of Georgia and Alabama upon the convening of the legislatures of said States under the act of Congress passed June 25th 1868, you will appoint the Governor and Lieutenant Governor elect of Georgia Governor and Lieutenant Governor of said State vice present incumbents removed; and the Governor and Lieutenant Governor elect of Alabama Governor and Lieutenant Governor of said State, vice present incumbents removed. These appointments and removals to take effect at the date of the Convening of said legislatures respectively.

U. S. GRANT
General

LS (telegram sent), DNA, RG 107, Telegrams Collected (Bound); telegram sent, *ibid.*; telegram received, Meade Papers, PHi.

On June 26, 1868, 1:00 P.M., USG had telegraphed to Maj. Gen. George G. Meade. "The act to admit the States of North Carolina, South Carolina, Louisiana, Georgia, Alabama and Florida to representation in Congress became a law June 25th 1868. Please notify the Governors elect of the States in your District, for under the act the Governor elect may if he deems it necessary convene the legislature thereof at an earlier date than that fixed by the law." LS (telegram sent), DNA, RG 107, Telegrams Collected (Bound); telegram sent, *ibid.*; telegram received, Meade Papers, PHi. On June 27, USG signed a letter to Meade identical to the letter sent the same day to Bvt. Maj. Gen. Robert C. Buchanan. LS, *ibid.*

To Charles W. Ford

Washington, D. C., June 29th *1868*

DEAR FORD.

I leave here to-morrow morning with my family for St. Louis. We will stop in Covington so as to reach St. Louis either Saturday[1] or Monday evening next. When I get to my farm, where I hope to spend several weeks, I have neither horses to spare from their farm work, nor vehicle to drive. Can you not secure for me a pair with an open carriage that is suited for me to drive myself or have a coachman drive as I like, which I can hire for the time I am out there? I take with me a good man to take care of horses and to drive, and on my place there is plenty of feed and pasture.

Yours Truly

U. S. GRANT

ALS, DLC-USG.

On June 23, 1868, USG had written to William Elrod. "I expect to be in St. Louis about the 6th of July and will keep house while there. If you can engage me a good white woman for cook during our stay I will be very glad of it. The woman who lived with Lewis Dent's family so long, if she is in the neighborhood, will suit." ALS, Don R. Stover, Maplewood, Mo.

On June 27, 11:20 A.M., USG telegraphed to J. T. Fulton, International Hotel, Niagara Falls, N. Y. "I will not visit Niagara going West. May do so returning late in August." ALS (telegram sent), DNA, RG 107, Telegrams Collected (Bound); telegram sent, *ibid.* On July 6, 10:20 A.M., Bvt. Brig. Gen. Frederick T. Dent telegraphed to William K. Patrick, Republican Central Committee, St. Louis. "Gen Grant says he can not now name day will be in St Louis— but prefers no demonstration" ALS (telegram sent), *ibid.*; telegram sent, *ibid.*

1. July 4.

Calendar

1867, OCT. 1.   To Maj. Gen. George H. Thomas. "Will you please direct your Quarter Master to receive from the bearer, H. G. Tachau, a pony which he will deliver, and take care of him until such time as he can be forwarded here to me. If the Quartermaster can forward him safely, at my expense, I would like him to do so."—ALS (addressed to "General"), Blumhaven Library & Gallery, Philadelphia, Pa. Listed as addressed to Thomas in Stan. V. Henkels & Son, Catalogue No. 1379, Oct. 15, 1925; Goodspeed's Catalogue 561, May, 1970. On Oct. 3, Thomas wrote to USG concerning a pony.—Jim Hayes, Antiquarian, List 29, Jan., 1985.

1867, OCT. 1.   Thomas H. Pearne, president, East Tennessee Wesleyan College, Knoxville, to USG. "Allow me to call your attention to the accompanying action of our Trustees. I was at a loss whether to send it to you or to the President. I hope you will favor us with your influence on behalf of this movement. The E. T. College is the product of loyal Methodism in East Tennessee. We have accommodations for 150 or 200 students as the law requires and we shall be greatly assisted in our good work if you establish the Military professorship desired in our institution."—ALS, DNA, RG 94, Letters Received, 633P 1867. The enclosure is *ibid.*

1867, OCT. 2.   USG endorsement. "The course of this young man since his appointment does not argue well for his fitness for the Army, and the remarks of Genl Grier, the Commanding Officer who forwarded his resignation,—viz: 'Lieut. Williams appears to exhibit so little fondness or aptitude for the profession of arms that I would recommend the acceptance of his resignation,' confirm this view. To the above it may be added that he has never served in the U. S. Army and that his loyalty is more than doubtful, it coming to me from a reliable source that he attempted to join the rebel army and once swam the Potomac River for that purpose. Before ordering his appointment it is deemed proper to submit to the President the above reasons for not doing so."—ES, DNA, RG 94, ACP, 3135 1874. Written on a letter of Oct. 1 from Alexander B. Williams, Georgetown, D. C., to President Andrew Johnson expressing regret that he had resigned a commission as 2nd lt., 3rd Cav., "in a moment of great despondency, . . . To my consternation the letter of acceptance arrived on the 27th. I started immediately for Washington, to see if any steps could be taken by my Parents, to prevent my unfortunate Act. General Grant on being appealed to, declared his willingness to rescind it, if it could be done. But unfortunately my place had been filled and given to another, appointed by your Excellency, and therefore nothing could be done that way. I was told my only hope was to apply to the President for a new appointment. . . ."—ALS, *ibid.* Johnson endorsed this letter. "If there is a vacancy let the appointment be made unless there is some good reason against it—"—AES (dated Sept. 2), *ibid.*

1867, OCT. 2.   To Secretary of the Interior Orville H. Browning. "I have the honor to send herewith for your consideration an extract from an In-

spection Report dated August 29th, 1867, by General Marcy, Inspector
General, U. S. A., relative to the Utes Indians and their agents Archuletta,
Sena and Garcia, and their present agent Arny."—LS, DNA, RG 75, Central Office, Letters Received, Miscellaneous. On Aug. 29, Bvt. Maj. Gen.
Randolph B. Marcy, Santa Fé, had written to Bvt. Maj. Gen. William A.
Nichols, adjt. for Lt. Gen. William T. Sherman. "It is said that there are
rich gold mines in the La Plata Mountains near the Animas River, and that
they cannot be worked without the protection of troops as the Utes who
range west of the locality are hostile. How this may be I do not know, but
all the Utes I met with on my route were friendly. In a talk I had with
'Cho-na-toh' and 'Pe-aste-cho-pe' the principal chiefs of the 'Capota' and
'We-we-nochee' bands of Utes which are said to number over seventeen
hundred souls, they expressed an earnest desire to remain at peace with our
people, but they did not appear satisfied with some of the men who had
been their agents. They said that Carson, Fifer, Mereure, Menzemares and
Labade, who at different times had been their agents, were all honest men,
who gave them all the presents that were sent out by the Government, and
that either of these men would be perfectly satisfactory to the tribe, but
that Archuletta, Sena and Garcia who had also been agents for them, were
not honest and they did not want such men. They said they did not know
much about their present agent Arny except that he had formerly been
agent for another band of Utes who did not speak well of him. They complain that he remains in Santa Fé instead of living near where they could
confer with him, and stated that they would much prefer any of the men
first named. I met these Indians nearly every day while I was in their country, and they were uniformly friendly, and I was greatly pleased with their
apparent honesty and candor. They brought into my camp a Government
horse that was abandoned by Col. Bergman last winter and wished to give
him up. This shows that they are sincere in their professions of friendship
and they should be kindly and fairly treated by Government Officials. They
do not want miners to come into their country or a military post established
beyond Camp Plummer, but if this was important it is believed that their
consent could be obtained for either or both objects. It was difficult for me
to make them believe that I was not there for the purpose of locating a post,
and they sent a delegation to their Agent at Santa Fé to ascertain what my
object was in visiting their country."—Copy, *ibid.*

1867, [*Oct. 2*].   USG note. "Direct Col. Parker to Sec. of Interior to examine Dismal swamp Canal. Withdraw paper refered to Chief Eng. on this
subject."—AN (initialed), DNA, RG 94, Letters Received, 553A 1867.
On Oct. 1, Secretary of the Treasury Hugh McCulloch had written to
USG. "If the interests of the Military service will permit, I have the honor
to request that an officer of the Engineer Corps may be detailed to this
Department for the purpose of making an examination and reporting the
condition of the Dismal Swamp Canal with his views as to the expediency
of a sale of the interest of the United States in said Company—Any ex-

penses incident to the performance of this duty will be paid by this Department on the presentation of proper vouchers—"—LS, *ibid.*

1867, OCT. 2.   Judge Advocate Gen. Joseph Holt to USG. *"Corporal Charles Wood,* was tried in June last by General Court Martial convened at Austin Texas, under the following charges. 1. Mutiny. 1. In joining in and exciting a mutiny against the authority of his commanding officer. This at Camp near San Antonio, Texas, April 9—1867. 2. In joining in and exciting a mutiny, with 1st Sergt. Harrison Bradford, Corporal James Lock and eight private soldiers of Co. E. 9th Cavalry, against the authority of his superior and commanding officer, in which 1st Lieut. E. M. Heyd, 9th U. S. Cav., was struck and severely wounded with a sabre, while in the discharge of his duty. This at time and place as above. 3. The same allegation whereby 2d Lieut. F. W. Smith was struck and severely wounded while in the discharge of his duties. Time and place as above. 2. Striking his superior officer. In striking with a sabre 1st Lieut. S. E. Griffin, 9th U. S. Cavalry while he was in the execution of his office as camp officer of the day, inflicting wounds thereby sufficient to cause his death. This at camp near San Antonio, April 9. 1867. 3. Desertion. In deserting immediately after the occurrence of the circumstances detailed above and remaining absent until arrested on the same day. The Court find the prisoner guilty under all the charges, and sentence him to forfeit to the United States all pay and allowances that are, or may become due, and to be hanged by the neck until dead, at such time and place as the Commanding General may direct; two thirds of the Court concurring. Genl. Mower approves the proceedings, findings and sentence, and forwards the record for the action of the President. The circumstances attending the revolt and homicide for which the prisoner was brought to trial have heretofore been considered by this Bureau, and brought to the attention of the Secretary of War, in a report made the 16th of July last, on the trial of private Irving Charles, Co. E. 9th Cavalry, sentenced to death, upon conviction under similar charges. In that case two members of the court, Bvt. Col. L. C Bootes, 26th Infty and Bvt. Lt. Col. J. F. Grimes, 26th Infty subscribed the following recommendation. 'We the undersigned, members of the General Court Martial, hereby recommend the prisoner to the Commanding General for mercy, in consequence of the mitigating circumstances as shown in the evidence for the prosecution and defence, setting forth the harsh and cruel treatment of Lieut. E. M. Heyd towards the men of Co. E. 9th Cav., and also in view of the fact as shown in the defence, that the Articles of War had never been read to the men of the company from the time of its organization until after the mutiny occurred.' In approving the proceedings Genl. Sheridan made the following endorsement. 'In view of the outrageous and cruel treatment of his men by Lieut. Heyd, 9th Cavalry, and their probable ignorance of the proper mode of obtaining redress, I respectfully recommend that the sentence be commuted to imprisonment for a term of years.' In the consideration of Pvt. Charles' case this Bureau remarked—'No more shocking illustrations of the brutal tyranny which an officer has it in his power to exercise over the men of his command, has ever been considered by this Bureau than the facts elicited on the trial of this prisoner show the conduct of Lieut. E. M. Heyd to have been, towards the colored soldiers of the company which it was their misfortune that he should command. That his savage treatment of three of the men of his company was the immediate occasion of the outbreak in which the prisoner took part, and that there was no pre-concert of action among the offenders at all deserving the name of conspiracy or meriting the punishment appropriate to the grave crime of mutiny, are facts equally established by the proof in this painful case. That the prisoner believed he was in immediate danger of life and acted as he thought in self defence under the influence of a terror inspired by the drunken ferocity of his company commander, and with no previous intent to resist by force the authority of his superior officers, this Bureau feels, after a careful study of the evidence, a strong conviction.' The above remarks are equally applicable ~~to the~~ to the case under consideration, in reviewing which, it has been deemed advisable to examine, in connection therewith, the record of the trial above referred to, to aid in obtaining a full and complete history of the unfortunate occurrences which resulted in the loss of two lives. The following facts connected with the acts of violence which led to the trial of the prisoner, are established by the testimony. On the morning of the 9th of April, three men of Co. E. were found to have left their nose-bags on their horses' heads after feeding them. Lieut Heyd had declared his intention to punish severely any soldier guilty of this act of neglect; and, discovering the fact on this occasion, sent his orderly sergeant to find and report the offenders. He did so and Lieut Heyd thereupon got three lariat ropes from his tent, and tied or caused to be tied the three men by their wrists to the branch of a tree, so that their feet swung more than a foot from the ground. He then went away to a drinking house and returned some half hour afterwards in a state of semi-intoxication. During his absence one of the culprits had released himself and run away. Perceiving this he sent his orderly sergeant with several men to find the fugitive, keeping the other two men meanwhile suspended by their wrists. In front of one of these was a stump just within reach of his toes, and the man naturally made efforts to reach and rest upon it. To prevent this, Lieut. Heyd got his pistol, and sitting down in front of his quarters, fired three shots at the man, without effect. After firing the third shot, he took his sabre and beat the man as he hung,—fifteen or sixteen blows with the flat of it, finally wounding him seriously in the side. These cruelties were seen by the whole company as they returned from watering their horses. The orderly sergeant, Bradford, immediately ordered the men of the company to dismount and to put on their sabres, saying he was going to march them up to Genl. Merritt's quarters to complain of the way in which Lieut Heyd treated them. The men obeyed, and the sergeant marched them in an orderly column, their sabres undrawn, in the direction of Gen. Merritt's tent, a route which led them past Lieut Heyd's quarters. It is in evidence that when the column was found, the sergeant gave the order to draw sabres, and that the prisoner, Corporal Wood, expostulated, urging that the sabres should not be drawn or the officers would think they were going to fight them. When the company got about thirty paces from Lieut. Heyd's quarters, that officer started out from the right of the regiment where Captain Purrington's tent stood, and came towards them. He ordered Sergt. Bradford to halt it, which he immediately did, leaving the men as they were en route, without dressing or facing them. The Lieut. ordered the Sergt. to come near him. The Sergeant stepped out about ten paces from the company and was asked by Lieut. Heyd 'where are you going with that company?' The Sergt. replied the he was going to report it to Gen. Merritt. The Lieut said 'what about?' The Sergeant answered, the way these men are treated. Lieut. Heyd said 'the way who treats them?' The Sergeant replied 'the way you treat them.' Lieut. Heyd demanded, 'what way?' The Sergeant answered, 'last night you cut one man to pieces with your sabre nearly; again this morning you tried to run your horse over one; and then this morning you tied up three men clear from the ground, and then stood off and shot at them and that would not do; and you went and punched and cut at them with your sabre as if they had been logs, and had their blood all running out of them, and that's what I'm going to report to Gen. Merritt, as I dont like to see these men treated so.' The Lieut. retorted 'I do them so, hey?' and the Sergt. replied 'Yes you do them so,' and these last remarks were interchanged three times. The Lieut. who had been standing with his hand on the hilt of his sabre, let it go and felt with both hands in the pockets of his blouse and trowsers in search of a pistol. Finding one after a moment's search, he dropped his hand with the pistol in it to his side, and then raised and lowered it three times successively, with an aim upon Sergeant Bradford. The Sergt. then advanced sabre in hand upon Lieut. Heyd, who immediately fired but missed. He then fired a second time striking the Sergt. in the mouth, the latter raising his sabre as if to disarm his opponent. A third shot was then fired, again taking effect; and Sergt. Bradford then knocked or cut him down. At this point Lieut. Griffin ran out with his revolver and fired on the Sergt who at once turned and made at him. Lieut Griffin shot a second time the shot striking Sergt. Bradford in the temple. The Lieut was then cut down by Sergt. Bradford and another member of the company who came forward at this moment, and received wounds in the head from the effects of which he died two days afterwards. Lieut. Smith then hurried up and shot Sergt. Bradford twice killing him instantly. Up to this time the men of the company remained perfectly quiet, but became greatly excited and terrified at the death of Sergt. Bradford,—four or five of them attacking Lieut Smith, and inflicting a slight wound on his arm. The company then dispersed and the prisoner escaped from camp, being subsequently captured the same day. It was claimed by the prosecution that the prisoner was the man who ran to the aid of Sergt. Bradford in his struggle with Lieut. Griffin, and that a wound he gave the latter was of itself sufficient to cause death. Lieut. F. W. Smith who took part in the affray, testifies that he heard a disturbance in camp and two pistol shots fired. Lieut Griffin and himself ran to the door of his tent and saw about fifteen men, as he states, attacking 1st. Lieut. E. M. Heyd with drawn sabres. Lieut Griffin went to the scene of disturbance, and he returned to his tent for a pistol: on coming out of the tent again, he saw Lieut Griffin standing with his pistol in his hand. Sergt. Bradford was standing in front of Lieut Griffin, and the prisoner Wood was standing to his right. He testifies that he saw them both strike Lieut. Griffin with their sabres, Sergt. Bradford striking him a direct cut on the top of the head, and Corpl. Wood directly across the head. The witness could not state how the prisoner was dressed. Anthony Baptiste testifies that he was a servant of Capt Purrington,—that he went out of the tent with his employer and saw company "E." marching towards the officers quarters. This witness then details the scene between Lieut. Heyd and Sergt. Bradford substantially as it has been set forth in this report. He further testifies that after Lieut. Heyd fired the first shot, Lieut. Griffin, the officer of the day, broke out of his tent and commenced shooting at the Sergeant. The Lieut. and the Sergeant then ran together in full charge, and struck ~~with~~ one another with such force as to cause Lieut. Griffin to fall backward. The Sergt. then struck him with his sabre and passed on by, when Lieut. Smith shot him. Then the prisoner upon seeing the Sergt. fall ran up and struck Lieut. Griffin with his sabre across the top of the forehead, and then ran back towards the company quarters. Private George Smith, Co. F. 9th Cav., and orderly for Lieut. Griffin details the circumstances of the affair up to the assault upon Lieut. Griffin, mainly as it has been given. In relation to that he testifies—'Lieut. Griffin was cut down, and the orderly sergeant was standing over him beating him on his back with a drawn sabre. Then I saw him cut him on his head from front to rear. Lieut. Griffin then called me—I started and went over to him and the orderly sergeant was coming towards me and I went back into the tent. Then I came out and just as I came out Corpl. Wood struck Lieut. Griffin with a drawn sabre. Lieut. Griffin was down at the time. The Corporal struck Lieut. Griffin across the top of the head from side to side. I picked Lieut. Griffin up and carried him to his tent. The front of the Lieut's shirt was all bloody—the brain was coming out of his head from the cut across the top of his head from side to side, given him by Corpl. Wood.' This witness testifies he was about thirty six feet from the prisoner when he saw him give the blow. Louis Brown a private in Co. E. testifies that when Sergt. Bradford struck Lieut. Griffin down, he saw the prisoner strike Lieut. Griffin with his sabre across the top of his head from side to side. The prisoner drew his sabre when he ran out of ranks to help Sergt. Bradford. Brown, The witness, further testifies that when Lieut. Griffin went to help Lieut. Heyd, the prisoner and Irving Charles went to help Sergt. Bradford. James Howard, bugler Co. E. 9th Cav., testifies for the defence, that he did not see the prisoner leave the ranks during the melee with the officers, to take part in it, and that he was so situated, standing near, that he would have seen him, had he done so; that when Lieut. Heyd shot at the Sergt. the prisoner went back to the company quarters. Private James Williams testifies that he saw the prisoner in the ranks on the left of the company just before Lieut. Griffin fell; that he should have seen him had he struck that officer, and is confident he did not. Corpl. Benjamin Garrett testifies that he was present during the mutiny, and that had the prisoner taken part in the assault on Lt. Griffin, he should have seen him; but swears he did not. That he saw Sergt. Bradford strike Lieut. Griffin two blows, one before and one after he fell. In response to a question by the court, this witness testifies that no one joined Sergt. Bradford to assist him, until after Lt. Griffin fell, when Irving Charles and Henry Johnson did so. Musician Richard Casin testifies, that when the disturbance occurred, he was standing on the right of the picket Line where he could witness the proceedings, and should have seen the prisoner had he taken part in the assaults, and swears he did not see him. He further testifies that Lieut Smith,—who, as a witness for the prosecution, had sworn he saw the prisoner strike Lieut Griffin a mortal blow,—caused the men all to fall in the ranks, after the mutiny, when he accused each one separately of striking Lieut Griffin. Upon the trial of Irving Charles, Lieut. Smith testified that when he had procured his pistol and went to the affray, Lieut Heyd was lying on his face, and several men were striking Lieut. Griffin with their sabres—among them he recognized Bradford and Wood. After a careful study of the testimony given in relation to this affair, so disgraceful in many features, this Bureau is led to the opinion that while the evidence strongly implicates the accused as having made an assault on Lieut. Griffin, yet there is room for grave doubt, and it is believed that he should receive the benefit of it. He made the following simple statement to the court. 'I am sorry for the charges that have been brought against me. I am innocent of the charges alle[g]ed against me except the charge of desertion. I deserted because I was frightened.' This Bureau is convinced that the findings of the court under all the specifications to the first charge are not justified by the evidence. The proofs fail to show that he joined in a mutiny, as alleged, the evidence being that the company stood quiet until Lieut. Griffin and Lieut. Smith approached. The men had fallen in by order of Sergt Bradford, in the belief that they were going to complain against the cruel tyranny of their officer, and with no other purpose. The suggestion of the prisoner—that the sabres should not be drawn or the officers might think they were going to attack them—exhibits, in a marked degree, a thoughtful intention on his part to have the proceedings orderly and quiet. While, as has been remarked, the testimony seems to bear against the prisoner under the second charge—(the assault on Lieut. Griffin)—yet, in view of the contradictions leaving the matter in doubt, the court would, it is believed, have been justified in acquitting him. The positiveness with which Lt. Smith in this case swears that he saw the prisoner give Lt. Griffin a wound which proved mortal, loses its weight when compared with the testimony given by him on the trial of Irving Charles, when he swore he saw several of the men assaulting Lt. Griffin with their sabres. The circumstances under which he was placed, the excitement which must have filled his mind in taking fatal part in the encounter, greatly weakens the strength of his testimony. The testimony in both cases shows that Irving Charles with another went to the relief of Sergt. Bradford; but it does not appear beyond a reasonable doubt, even, that that other was the prisoner. Had it been proved beyond all question, this Bureau would have placed the offence upon the same grounds with that of Irving Charles, who, it was proved, assaulted Lieut. Smith with his sabre, during the outbreak, under what is believed to have been great provocation, and what seems to have been over-mastering terror. The sense of cruel wrong which must have governed these men after the acts of Lieut. Heyd's brutal tyranny which they had experienced and witnessed, and the terror which must have inspired them when their Sergeant fell, would go far to mitigate punishment for any offences committed while they were so influenced. This Bureau has heretofore fully commented on the heartless and disgraceful conduct of Lieut. Heyd in the premises. In the case of Irving Charles, the sentence was remitted in the following terms:—'In view of the extraordinary circumstances developed by the testimony, showing that there was no disposition on the part of the prisoner either to mutiny or desert, but that his conduct and that of his company was the result of outrageous treatment on the part of one of the commissioned officers, and in view of the suffering he has already endured, the sentence will be remitted and the prisoner will be returned to duty.' It is advised that similar action be taken in the present case."—Copy, DNA, RG 153, Letters Sent.

On Oct. 14, Bvt. Maj. Gen. Edward D. Townsend endorsed papers concerning this matter. "July 18 1867 the Judge Advocate General addressed the Adjt General calling attention to the conduct of Lt Heyle as shown by the case of private Irving Charle[s] Co. E 9th U S Cavalry (Cold) who had been sentenced to be shot for '*mutiny*' & *desertion*   The Mutiny complained of arose from the treatment of the men by Lt. Heyle ~~and~~ which the Judge Advocate General characterizes as 'execrable cruelty' and deserving of an ignominious expulsion from the service. He calls attention to the case because there is no evidence in the Files of his Bureau to show that Lt Heyle had been arrested or brought to trial for his conduct   It was sent to Genl Sheridan from this office for report   It is returned with a statement of Bvt. Maj. General Edward Hatch in Command of the Regt. who expresses a very different opinion of the conduct of Lt Heyle, from that entertained by the Judge Advocate General. He thinks however it will be for the good of the service that Lt. Heyle be tried and he sends a copy of the charges which have been drawn up in order that a Court Martial may be ordered by the proper authority   Respectfully Submitted to Gen Grant" —ES, *ibid.*, RG 94, Letters Received, 927M 1867. On Oct. 16, Townsend endorsed the report. "The charges to be dismissed and reports filed."—ES, *ibid.*

1867, OCT. 2.   William S. Huntington, Washington, D. C., to USG. "I have the honor to submit herewith papers relating to the Gun Boat 'Little Rebel,' and beg the favor of your early consideration and reply"—Copy, DNA, RG 92, Letters Received. On Oct. 29, Bvt. Maj. Gen. Daniel H. Rucker, act. q. m. gen., wrote to USG. "I have the honor to return herewith, communication of W. S. Huntington Esq. dated October 2, 1867 enclosing application of Messrs R and J. Watson owners of the Gunboat 'Little Rebel' for release of the same, . . ."—LS, *ibid.* On Nov. 9, Act. Secretary of the Navy William Faxon wrote to USG. "I have the honor to return herewith the papers relating to the gunboat 'Little Rebel,' which were referred to this Department for further information. The Department has no information to communicate respecting the 'Little Rebel,' other than that contained in the papers, except that the vessel was, by order of the Department, sold at Mound City, Ills. November 29 1865. The Department is not aware that other vessels, similarly captured and condemned, have been restored, or that similar claimants have been compensated, under an executive order; and it would have no authority to entertain a claim in this case"—LS, *ibid.*

1867, OCT. 2.   John W. Meek, Rockport, Ark., to USG. "sometime ago, I wrote to the Honl Charles Sumner, asking him to use his influence to obtain for me an appointment to the National Military Academy, at West Point. He in reply, told me to address myself, directly, to the War Department; believing as I do, General, that I will receive some attention at your hands, I have concluded to act in accordance with his advice. I will merely state to you, General, as I stated to Mr Sumner; that I lost all I had, by reason of my loyalty to the United States, during the rebellion: and all I ask in return for all, is that I may receive an appointment to West Point. As to the truth of what I say, I refer you to J. E. Wallace Esqr. No. 7. Commercial place, New Orleans La: a gentleman of known loyalty. Hoping that you will condascend to reply to this, . . ."—ALS, DNA, RG 94, Unsuccessful Cadet Applications.

1867, OCT. 3.   To Secretary of the Treasury Hugh McCulloch. "At the instance of the Com'sy. of Subsistence U. S. A. I have the honor to request that the *Collector of Customs at New Orleans*, be instructed to deliver free of duties and charges the 50,000 pounds of Rio Coffee to Bvt. Maj. Genl. Beckwith, referred to in his letter of the 3d ult. addressed to the Col. at the Port of N. Orleans and by him transmitted to the Secy. of the Treas'y and a copy of which was rec'd. at this Dept. in your letter of the 9th ult. requesting the usual certification of use by the U. States. This coffee is a part of the cargo of the 'Mary Seymour' and was purchased for the use of the U. S. Army."—Copy, DNA, RG 107, Letters Sent to the President. On Sept. 9, W. H. West (for Asst. Secretary of the Treasury John F. Hartley) wrote to USG. "I transmit herewith a copy of a communication signed by

A. Beckwith Bvt. Major Genl. and C. S. U. S A—addressed to the Collector of Customs at the Port of New Orleans, and by him transmitted to this Department, requesting the free entry of 50000 pounds of Rio Coffee purchased for the use of the U. S. The paper referred to is respectfully submitted for your action. Before the Coffee in question can be admitted to entry free of duty, the usual certification from your Department that it is for the use of the U. S is necessary."—Copy, *ibid.*, RG 56, Letters Sent. On Sept. 2, 19, and Oct. 15, USG wrote to McCulloch requesting that the collector of customs, New York City, deliver shipments of coffee and sugar duty free.—Copies, *ibid.*, RG 107, Letters Sent to the President.

1867, OCT. 3.   To Secretary of the Treasury Hugh McCulloch. "I have the honor to enclose herewith an application dated September 16th from Ordnance Storekeeper Shoemaker for authority to deposit funds arising from sales of Ordnance Stores, in his safe. For the reasons given by him and the Chief of Ordnance it would seem to be a case for the favorable consideration of the Secretary of the Treasury."—LS, DNA, RG 56, Letters Received from the War Dept.; Df, *ibid.*, RG 156, Letters Received. On July 1, Capt. William R. Shoemaker, ordnance storekeeper, Fort Union, New Mexico Territory, had written to Bvt. Maj. Gen. Alexander B. Dyer, chief of ordnance. "I have the honor to transmit herewith, the Cash accounts pertaining to this Arsenal for the month of June ulto—I desire to call your attention to the fact that, small sums *arising from sales* are constantly accumulating here, there is no U. S. Depository in which to Deposit these amts, nearer than Santa Fe where I should have to remit at my own risk, therefore, I desire to have authority for carrying the funds refered to on my Account current as I have been in the habit of doing, & which practice I believe obtains in the other branches of the Service situated as we are"— ALS, *ibid.* On Oct. 12, McCulloch wrote to USG. "I have the honor to acknowledge the receipt of yours of the 3d ins't, with an enclosure, relating to special facilities for conducting the business of disbursements on account of the War Department   I enclose a draft of an order which has been prepared with a view to obviate a large number of difficulties arising in this business under existing laws. It will afford me pleasure to issue such order upon the receipt of your request to this effect or if you should desire a modification of its terms prompt consideration shall be given to your views upon their receipt."—LS, *ibid.*, RG 107, Letters Received from Bureaus. On Nov. 15, USG wrote to McCulloch. "On its receipt, your communication of the 12th ultimo, enclosing the draft of an order designed to obviate difficulties arising in War Department disbursements under existing laws, was referred to the several Bureaus, and I now enclose you a paper in which will be found certain suggestions for the modification of the terms of the order, which being approved by this Department, I ask may be adopted, if possible."—LS, *ibid.*, RG 56, Letters Received from the War Dept. The enclosure is *ibid.*

1867, OCT. 3.   Maj. Joseph H. McArthur, Dodgeville, Wis., to USG. "My Mother is at the point of death   may I delay obeying Special orders number forty two (42) for ten (10) days?"—Telegram received (at 1:05 P.M.), DNA, RG 94, Letters Received, 1391M 1867; *ibid.*, RG 107, Telegrams Collected (Bound). On the same day, Bvt. Brig. Gen. Frederick T. Dent wrote to Bvt. Maj. Gen. Edward D. Townsend. "The General says to give the delay asked for (by telegraph)"—ANS, *ibid.*, RG 94, Letters Received, 1391M 1867.

1867, OCT. 3.   John H. Sanburn, Knoxville, Ill., to USG. "I have the honor to call your attention to my application for a commission in the U. S. Army, placed on file in the war office early in 1866, and to ask that some action may be taken upon it. I also enclose a letter of recommendation from Brevet Brig Gen'l Charles. W. Drew and ask that it may be placed on file with my application. Should my application be favorably considered, and I receive an appointment to a colored regiment, I should have no hesitancy in accepting it, as all prejudice against colored troops was removed by serving with them."—ALS, DNA, RG 94, ACP, S1305 CB 1867. Sanburn enclosed a letter of Sept. 26 from Charles W. Drew, Chicago, to USG. "I have the honor to recommend to your favorable consideration, for a commission in the U S Army, John H Sanborn, formerly Captain, in the 76th U. S. Col'd Infantry,   He was in my command about eighteen months, during which time, I found him an energetic, faithful, and efficient Officer—"—ALS, *ibid.*

1867, OCT. 4.   To Mrs. Lucretia P. Baker. "Your favor of the 5th of September, by Express, accompanying a box containing branches &c. from the largest tree in California, and no doubt in the world, which too partial friends have done me the honor to name after me, is at had. Please accept my thanks for thus rembering me and also for the kind expressions of regard contained in your letter."—ALS, Mrs. H. L. Ford, Indio, Calif.

1867, OCT. 4.   Secretary of the Treasury Hugh McCulloch to USG. "I have the honor to inform you that the First National Bank of Norfolk, Va, has voluntarily ceased to be a Depository for Public Money, and in consequence thereof its designation as a Depository for the War Department is hereby revoked. I have therefore to request that you will cause the necessary instructions to be issued for the withdrawal of such funds as may have been deposited therein by the disbursing officers of the War Department."—LS, DNA, RG 94, Letters Received, 286T 1867.

1867, OCT. 4.   Secretary of the Navy Gideon Welles to USG. "Two deserters from the army, Robert G. Alludis and Henry Bellbraugh, having enlisted in the Navy under the name of Frank Weild and Henry Miller, respectively, have upon identification been given up to the army authorities, the first named of these men, Alludis or Weild being in debt at his delivery $68.96 and the latter $63—occasioned by authorized advances in money and clothing. I have respectfully to request that the amounts of indebtedness in these cases may be checked against the men on their army accounts and paid to the credit of the Navy."—Copy, DNA, RG 45, Letters Sent to the President.

1867, Oct. 5. USG endorsement. "Refered to Gn. Grier to report his views as to the discharge of the man named in this letter."—AES, DNA, RG 108, Letters Received. Written on a letter of Sept. 23 from U.S. Representative Samuel Shellabarger of Ohio, Springfield, to USG. "I am informed that H. C. Bretney was enlisted in the U. S. Cavalry service at Cinti while in a state of intoxication and that he is now at Carlisle barracks Pa. I know no other particulars. He and his parents are my constituents and I desire to earnestly request your attention to the case and that he may be mustered out if that can properly be done"—ALS, *ibid.* Additional material is *ibid.*

1867, Oct. 5. Bvt. Maj. Gen. Edmund Schriver, inspector gen., endorsement. "Disapproved by the Secy of War ad int."—AES, DNA, RG 94, Letters Received, 1413M 1867. Written on a letter of Sept. 30 from Bvt. Maj. Gen. Edward R. S. Canby, Charleston, to USG. "In the distribution of the means provided by private contribution for the relief of suffering in this city, two committees of ladies have heretofore been engaged. The first was composed of ladies (wives of officers stationed here) who made it their duty to visit and examine personally into the most of cases of reputed destitution and suffering and to superintend the application of the means of relief provided. The operations of this committee was directed but not limited to the Protestant population of the city. The other committee was composed of two of the Sisters of Mercy and was directed to the Catholic population but has not been limited to any creed or class. The duties assumed by these ladies are laborious and constant and to enable them to perform them properly each Committee has been allowed the use of an Ambulance and I recommend that this permission may be authorized and continued."—LS, *ibid.*

1867, Oct. 7. To Secretary of the Treasury Hugh McCulloch. "In reply to your comn of July 13 asking if this Department will transfer to the Treasury Dept the furniture of the Marine Hospital at Mobile when the hospital shall be relinquished by the military authorities, I have the honor to inform you that as the furniture will be needed for the new Post hospital lately erected at Mobile, the transfer cannot be made."—Df, DNA, RG 107, Letters Received from Bureaus; copy, *ibid.*, Letters Sent to the President. On Sept. 13, McCulloch had written to USG. "The Collector of Customs at Mobile having informed this Department of the intended removal of the Military Hospital at that port from the marine hospital building the latter part of this month, I have the honor to call attention to a letter addressed the War Department on this subject dated 13th July last, and to request as early a reply as practicable, in order that proper arrangements may be made for the marine patients now cared for by the Military Authorities."— LS, *ibid.*, Letters Received from Bureaus.

1867, Oct. 7.   USG endorsement. "Approved"—ES, DNA, RG 94, ACP, 1163M CB 1867. Written on a letter of Oct. 2 from Maj. Gen. George G. Meade, Philadelphia, to USG. "My attention has recently been called to the case of Col Henry S. Russell lately comdr the 5th Mass Cavalry, an officer of distinction & merit, who is justly entitled to receive promotion by Brevet, but whose case as far as I can learn has not hitherto been presented to the Dept—Col Russell entered the service in May /61 as 2d Lieut 2d Rgt Mass Infantry, and was in Decr 61 promoted Capt—in the 2d Rgt Mass. Inft—He was present in Aug—/62 at the battle of Cedar Mountain where he was made prisoner—In /63 on his release he was appointed Lieut Col in 2d Rgt Mass Cavalry, and in April /64 was appointed Col of the 5th Mass Cavalry which regiment he commanded in all the operations of the Army of the James till June 15th /64 when he was severely wounded in the attack on Petersburgh.—Altho not serving in the army under my immediate command, yet from his connection with Col Lyman of my staff, I had during the war much personal knowledge of the services of Col Russell, and feel satisfied; that no officer of his rank from Massachusetts, is better entitled to the acknowledgement of his services now asked—and I therefore beg leave to recommend that the Brevet of Brig General of Volunteers be conferred on Col Henry S. Russell 5th Mass Cavalry 'for faithful & meritorious services during the war & particularly for distinguished gallantry & good conduct at Baylers Farm before Petersburgh June 15th 64 where he was severely wounded' "—ALS, *ibid.*

1867, Oct. 7.   President Andrew Johnson endorsement. "Respectfully referred to The Secretary of War, ad interim, for his attention."—ES, DNA, RG 107, Letters Received from Bureaus. Written on a letter of Sept. 19 from M. H. Royston, former state treasurer, Austin, Tex., to Johnson concerning the removal of state officials by military order.—ALS, *ibid.*

1867, Oct. 7.   Mrs. Edward M. Holman, Holly Springs, Miss., to USG. "After much consideration as to the best method of getting redress for injuries sustained during the war it was kindly suggested to me by Col. Vedder Paymaster of the third District to become my own advocate making a plain statement of the facts & circumstances. Permit me to introduce my self as Mrs Holman widow of E. M. Holman. During your occupation of Holly Springs in 1863. my husband called upon you for advice in regard to his family residing 1½ miles from the Depot. You thought best to go to Memphis & gave us Tranportation   the Ticket I have to show if neccessary. I will not weary your patience by rehearsing the evershifting seenes through which we passed, as a family gradually descending from bad to worse, untill all was gone. Upon our return not a fence or house left of our

once pleasant home (250 acres) but 2 chimneys upon it—even the old
landmarks had been removed & a survey was necessary to reset fences.
After Van-Dorns raid the Federal Army done me great injury in unfencing
my Plantation—driving away my Stock, I had no protection papers, my
husband & Son being in the rear of the Army in charge of Stock & Horses
did not arrived in time   if I remonstrated the Soldiers would reply 'How-
dye good Union woman' so rare a thing to find Father & Son from Miss. in
the Federal Army. Haveing none but Rebel evidence I cannot say who completed the destruction after we left. Union Soldiers have often told me it
was camping ground for both parties in their raids. It was the only well
watered place this side of the Depot. I can prove by papers in my possession
1st Loyalty 2d undisputed Title to (250) Acres of Land—3d Drove away
by conscription—4th Confiscation by Confederate Authorities 5th My house
taken by Rebels Officers for HeadQuarters, attended by a Brigade to 'clean
us out' to use a southern phrase. Bressast works made upon my place at the
same time. 6th Visitations from Guerillas Bridge Burners—Cotton Burners
Scouts & sundry others favors for our Loyalty. 7th Unaided by Government. I supported myself &. 3 children in Memphis, paying over five
Thousand dollars for rent in the 4 years to Mansfield the Rebel Druggist,
while my property lay waste & open to plunder. A burning shame for loyal
people!!! My husband by profession a civil Eng. & R. Road Contractor,
have many testimonials in his favor from distinguished Engineers & R.
Road Directors. He was offered a high position on the Rebel fortifications
but always told me if he had to fight it would be on the right side. He was
a Free Mason & a very Scientific Man. He fled from Holly Springs in Aug.
1862,—upon arriving at Memphis met Morgan L Smith who gave him employment for a while was afterwards transfered to Gen Denver's Division.
He was Clerk in one of the Permit Offices (under Tomeny.) After the Surrender he came with our oldest son to his home for the purpose of repairing
the desolations but was taken with Congestive Chills & died very suddenly.
We came South to consruct the. Miss Central, R. Road, in 1853. have been
residents ever since. He was of Consumptive habit and choose this latitude
& Holly Springs as his home the air dry and bracing above all other Location in his estimation   He took his eldest Son with him in /62, E. E. Holman who served as (2) Lieut in the 1st Miss Mtd. Rifles and was to be
promoted as 1st Lieut at the surrender. We all think he done good Service
by the amount of property he brought in to the Government. Our loss has
been assessed at fifteen to twenty five thousand by competent persons. I
have shown several *proof papers* to the Military Gentleman who have kindly
offered to affix their names to what I have written   if needed I will send
them to Washington also present myself, but would prefer doing the business by others as my health is delicate. By giving this a carfull perusal and
returning an answer, you would greatly oblige your humble freind"—Copy,
DNA, RG 217, Southern Claims Commission, Claims Files, Miss., Marshall County, File 6968. Related papers include a letter of Feb. 23, 1870,
from E. E. Holman, Holly Springs, to U.S. Senator Adelbert Ames of

Miss. enclosing this copy of "a letter my Mother wrote to send to Genl Grant but did not."—ALS, *ibid.*

1867, OCT. 8.   USG endorsement. "Respectfully returned to the President with the information that there is no vacancy in any regiment of Cavalry at present"—ES, DNA, RG 94, ACP, C1076 CB 1867. Written on a letter of the same day from President Andrew Johnson to USG. "You will please appoint Fred G. Calvert, late Adjutant 1st Maryland Cav'y, and now private US General Service, to a 2nd Lieutenantcy in one of the Cavalry Regiments, if there is such a vacancy."—LS, *ibid.* On the same day, Johnson endorsed this letter. "Respectfully returned to the Secretary of War, ad interim, who will please cause this appointment to be made whenever there is a vacancy."—ES, *ibid.*

On Oct. 3, Fred G. Calvert had written to Johnson. *"Personal . . .* Necessity compels me to write a few lines trusting you will give them your kind consideration. I organized the Andrew Johnson Guards drilled them and enlisted myself (Commanded by Capt McBlair.)   at the expiration of my term of service I immediately went to Baltimore and recruited for the 1st Md. Cavy. I was given a 2d Lieut. position and afterwards promoted to Adjutant. I was compelled to leave the service on account of my Eye sight. I then made several ineffectual applications to you for your influence in obtaining a position After which I joined or enlisted in the General Service. I have always been a hearty supporter of you and your policy and always stood my ground when your doings were even hinted to. But there are men in this office who are doing every thing and lending their influence to defeat you and your policy. These are the men who are to be retained—and I am to be discharged. It is very hard for me, having a large family to support, and unable to work at my trade—printing—on account of my eyes. I appeal to you as a brother mason and ask your influence. I sincerely trust your excellency will consider my case."—ALS, *ibid.* On Oct. 16, Bvt. Maj. Gen. Edward D. Townsend endorsed this letter. "The within letter of Fred. G. Calvert is not only a palbpable violation of the regulations, which prohibit officers and soldiers from addressing the Executive except through intermediate authorities, but it contains gratuitous and *unfounded* statements, which make it a question whether the writer can be longer safely entrusted with the care of the public records now committed to him. The politics of clerks in this office is not known, and no inquiry has been made concerning them. With rare exceptions they were originally detailed from the *soldiers* who have been actively engaged in the war; and in discharging those whose services were no longer needed in view of the reduction in the public business, those *least efficient* have been selected, without regard to other considerations than military service in the War, except in cases where resignations have been voluntarily tendered. Mr. Calvert has been a good clerk in this office, and there has hitherto been no intention of discharging him."—AES, *ibid.* On Oct. 17, USG endorsed Townsend's report. "Respectfully returned to the President, inviting attention to the report of the Adjutant-

General—Since receiving the ~~above~~ within orders have been received, and executed, making Mr. Calvert a 2d Lt. of Cavalry. It is respectfully asked that authority may be given to Cancel his appointment."—ADf and ES, *ibid.* On the same day, Johnson endorsed this report. "Respectfully returned to the *Secretary of War ad interim.* From the report of the *Adjutant General,* it appears that *Mr. Calvert* has been 'a good clerk,' and his letter applying for retention in the General Service, to which the attention of the Secretary of War is invited, furnishes no ground for a belief that *Mr. Calvert* will not make a good officer of the Army. Unless the proper board of examination should find him mentally incompetent or physically disqualified for commission, you will please retain him as an officer of the Army."—ES, *ibid.* Calvert received an appointment as 2nd lt., 2nd Cav., as of Oct. 11.

1867, OCT. 8.   Secretary of the Treasury Hugh McCulloch to USG. "Enclosed I hand you a copy of a letter from Mr James Robb, which, although marked *private* and *confidential,* the writer, doubtless, would not object to your seeing. In fact, it seems from the last clause, that the letter would have been addressed to you instead of me if the writer had had the honor of your acquaintance. Mr Robb was formerly a banker in New Orleans, and is a gentleman of entire respectability, whose statements may be relied upon, and whose opinion upon the subject he refers to is entitled to much consideration."—ALS, DNA, RG 107, Letters Received from Bureaus. McCulloch enclosed a letter of Oct. 5 from James Robb, New York City. "Private and Confidential . . . The enclosed Publication which I cut from the Tribune of this morning—I deem it my duty to notice, and if possible prevent the success of a court attempt to injure the People of Louisiania. The law authorizing the issue of 4 millions dollars of 6% Bonds for Levee purposes has been before Mr Lamar and myself, and we considered the possibility of negociating them was arrested by a limatation of the price to 80 cents as provided by Law—as 6% Bonds of the State of Tenne promised to be equally good if not more responsible than Louisiania, now selling at 64 & 66%,   The assertion that the want of the signature of the late Govr Wells prevents a sale of the Levee Bonds is simply untrue. The Law however provides that the Levee Commissioners may pledge the Bonds for Loans giving the benefit of the interest to the Lenders—in which case, there being no limit or restrictions as to the mode and manner of there being pledged, the Bonds may be sacrificed, or not produce a third of their Value. The projectors of the Law Knew it was impossible to sell Southern State Bonds at 6%—and the clause giving the income of the Bonds to the 'Pledged' was designed to defraud the State by Legal enactment. I am informed that a large amount of claims are suspended which are alleged to be due for work done on Levees—and of an unjust character,   The claims will never be approved unless by authority of Govr Wells. The disposition of the 4 million of dollars of Levee Bonds—and the liquidation of excessive claims is the contending motive of those seeking to obtain the reinstation of Wells, and

I would not say this much if I did not feel warranted in my statement, and feeling a deep concern to protect the People of Louisiania from a great wrong being committed on their rights. There is a general prepossession against Southern securities, and in the present disposition of investors of Capital no considerable amount of Louisiania Bonds could be sold above 50 or 60%. The renewal of the Levees in Miss Arkansas & Louisiania is of the first importance to the people of those States as well as our entire country—but in their present circumstances it is quite impossible they can be restored, It can only be done with assistance granted by Congress. I am not personally acquainted with Genl Grant, nor am I sure he knows who I am, which is my apology for this tresspass on your time, otherwise I would have addressed him."—ALS, *ibid.*

1867, OCT. 8.   Silvester Bowlby, McKinney, Tex., to USG. "Having had the pleasure of your acquaintance in St. Louis County, Mo, at the time you and myself were living there, I take the liberty of writing you a short letter. As you will reccollect, I was at that time living on my brother-in law's (L. A. Benoist) farm near you   In 1859 I moved to this State & county, & have lived here since that time. Knowing that through your patriotic devotion to and military exertions for the government we love so well, you have saved the Union and us from the rule of some of the most despotic, unprincipled and self-serving men that ever tyranized over any people. Knowing, I say this much, and beliving that your soul swells with patriotic anxiety for our country's future well-being, I venture a few remarks upon the condition of affairs in this section of the country. At the close of the rebellion nine tenths of ~~the~~ our people were willing to submit to almost any conditions imposed upon them, many having no fears that they would or could be half so destructive of life, property, morale or liberty, as those from which they had just escaped. Especially did the Union men here look and see in their minds-eye that dear old Flag, returning to wave over us, with all the stars as bright and dazzling as of old. At that time, while giving thanks to the God of Justice for guiding you and your brave men in delivering us from under the yoke of bondage, little did we think, that so soon a love for the Union, Loyalty, & Liberty, would become a cause of persecution and reproach, yet I regret to state such has been the case & so continues to be. As soon as the Presidents' vetoe of the Civil Right's bill &c, became known, the rebels & Secessionists took fresh courage & since then have for the greater part of the time controlled things in their own way. After Congress passed the Military Reconstruction bills, they gave the Union men hope, and the enemies of the Government appeared to be willing to reconstruct under it, and we as a people were progressing very well, untill the President began to remove prominent officials, then the rebels rejoiced and begin again to take just as disloyal as during the rebellion. The removal of Sectry. Stanton and Gen. Sheridan (and especially the latter,) have emboldened the Secession element in this Section to declare that the whole plan of Reconstruction as passed by Congress, will be set aside by the

President and his adherents, and that they (the rebels) will be restored to all rights & privaleges, now withheld from them by the laws of Congress. Some of them have recently gone so far as to express publically joy at the untimely death of Gen. Griffin of this District. Untill the removal of Gen. Sheridan, the plan of Reconstruction was being carried out in this section with comparative satisfaction and quietly accepted as a final plan for the restoration of the rebel States into the Union; but since his removal the whole aspect has changed, the rebels now put on a bold front, & openly declare the President will soon resist the plan of Congress, even to the use of the army and navy, if necessary to overthrow the laws of Reconstruction. Having been Chairman of the Board of Registration of this County, I have had a favorable opportunity to become acquainted with the feelings of the citizens generally and I do not hesitate to declare, that those who are disfranchised by the laws of Congress and I fear many of those who have registered are not the proper element at this time for reconstruction. With the earnest hope that we may both live to witness a peaceful and permanent Union of the now distracted sections of our government I have the honor to remain, with many wishes for your welfare, . . . P. S. I would be pleased to receive a reply from you as an acknowledgment of this letter."—ALS, DNA, RG 108, Letters Received.

1867, OCT. 9.   To President Andrew Johnson. "I would be pleased to be permitted to appoint G. N. Whistler a 2d Lieut. in the Army. He is the son of Col. Whistler of the regular Army and the grandson of Col. Wm Whistler, of my old regiment, who died in the service."—ALS, DNA, RG 94, ACP, W979 CB 1867. On the same day, Johnson endorsed this letter. "Approved, and General Grant will cause an appointment to be issued for the son of his friend, Col. Whistler."—ES, *ibid.* See *PUSG*, 16, 552.

1867, OCT. 9.   To Secretary of State William H. Seward. "I have the honor to acquaint you that the request of Blacque Bey, the Turkish Minister to be allowed to purchase samples of certain arms from the U. S. has been complied with & that the Chief of Ord. has been instructed to do what is necessary in the case."—Df, DNA, RG 156, Letters Received; copy, *ibid.*, RG 107, Letters Sent to the President. On Oct. 3, Seward had written to USG. "I have the honor to bring to your attention the request of Blacque Bey, the Turkish Minister accredited to this Government, for samples of certain arms, now in use in our army, specified in the accompanied transcript, in translation, of the ministers communication. No objection is perceived by this Department to granting a compliance with this request."—LS, *ibid.*, RG 156, Letters Received. The enclosure is *ibid.*

1867, OCT. 9.   U.S. Representative John Hill of N. J., Boonton, to USG. "In March 1864 Geo. H. Smith late Capt. &C. of Vol. was Dismissed, for conduct unbecoming an officer—a young man who had borne an excellent character, but in an evil hour was led astray—and wrote an indecent letter

to a comrade and was dismissed on a/c of it—he came home much morti-
fied, left the Country and will not return until he can come home differently
than he went away—he is an only son of aged Parents who doted much on
him, and now mourn his absence, they ask that he may be reinstated, and
honorably discharged and I join with them in making this request, now
that the War is over, and the end for which he was punished, having been
accomplished, I feel it would be the saving of the young man, if he could
return home, a comfort to his parents, and I doubt not has learned a lesson
that he will remember all his life—I hope his case may receive favorable
consideration at your hands—and he be reinstated, and honorably discharged—The Papers are on Genl. Keltons desk, having been examined by
him, but not acted upon, as requested by me in July last—will you please
have them called up, and if possible help the young man out of his difficulty—"—ALS, DNA, RG 94, ACP, S878 CB 1864.

1867, OCT. 9. Bvt. Brig. Gen. Orville E. Babcock to U.S. Representative
Elihu B. Washburne. "Yours of the 6th is at hand. I hasten to send you a
reply, as I am about to leave the city and shall have no other opportunity. I
have not received the proceedings from you, but have read them in print.
I cannot see any objection unless it is on the subject of suffrage. I am one
of those who hope Genl Grant will not be the next President as I look upon
it as a great misfortune to him. I have heard no others than Porter and
Badeau, and they agree with me about the speech. While there is nothing
in it objectionable will it not be translated just now as given out to help
over the loss of Penn. & Indiana & Iowa   I leave here Friday and N. Y. on
Monday for the City of Mexico. I am going with Romero, and for some
gentlemen in N. Y. I take a leave of absence, and expect to be gone about
4 month—perhaps less perhaps more. I shall not leave N. Y. before Monday
evening and shall be glad for a letter from you, 'to whom it may concern'.
Please send it to Care Genl R Ingalls 17 State Street New York City. Annie
writes me that you have been up to see the boy, and herself. I am glad you
find them so well. I am more distressed at leaving them than anything else.
Genl Grant is very willing I shall go, and gives me splendid letters and
keeps my place on the staff while I am on leave to go—Sherman is here
and without doubt to see what they can do with him as 'Sect of War'. No
doubt now the Elections have gone as they have Mr J. will be on the *Ram-
page* again. Our people are all well. We shall be in our new house next
week.—It is rumored Erastus Corning will take McCullochs place,—No
other news.—I leave Friday. Kind regards to all in Galena.—I shall be glad
to hear from you while abroad. Mails will be forwarded through our Head
Qrs."—ALS, DLC-Elihu B. Washburne.

1867, OCT. 10. Cassius M. Clay, U.S. minister, St. Petersburg, to USG.
"In the absence of Colo Annenkoff, I sent the documents you were kind
enough to prepare, to the Minister of War D. Milutine, with permission to
use them if need be in the meantime. By note no-6154., 7th inst: General

Milutine responds, and among other things says: 'I do not doubt that our Government will be able to profit by the precious information ("indications") which these documents certainly contain: and in this connection I perform an agreeable duty in presenting you my sincere thanks for the kindness you have shown in asking them of General Grant: at the same time I beg you to be so amiable as to be the expounder ("l'interprète") of my sentiments of regard towards him.' Having thus performed this pleasant duty, I remain, General, . . ."—ALS, DNA, RG 107, Letters Received, C571 1867.

1867, OCT. 10. Orvil L. Grant, Chicago, to USG. "I have just reached home. Pay my note, will remit immediately"—Telegram received (at 3:18 P.M.), DNA, RG 107, Telegrams Collected (Bound).

1867, OCT. 11. USG endorsement. "Nothing further is known in reference to this officer. The brevet ordered should be for the battle of Shiloh."—ES, DNA, RG 94, ACP, M955 CB 1867. Written on a letter of Aug. 6 from John Hogan, Washington, D. C., to President Andrew Johnson. "I respectfully request that Col Madison Miller be honoured with Brevet rank for conspicuous gallantry in the field—1st at Wilsons Creek where as Captain in 1st Mo Inf he had to assume command & Saved the day—And 2d at Shilouh as Col of 18th Mo and in command of Brigade, he was most active & conspicuous unde[r] heavy fire; under orders of Genl Prentiss, until captured with his troops—I ask that he be honoured with a Brevet for such that his children may know his gallant conduct was duly appreciated by his country—"—ALS, *ibid.* Johnson endorsed this letter on Aug. 14. "Respectfully referred to the Honorable the Secretary of War. Let this Brevet be conferred upon *Col. Miller*, unless there is some reason unknown to me, why it should not be done."—ES, *ibid.*

1867, OCT. 11. USG endorsement. "Respectfully returned. It is not deemed just to other officers to brevet Capt Reeves to a higher position than that of Lt Col. for faithful and meritorious services during the war"—ES, DNA, RG 94, ACP, 581P CB 1867. Written on a petition from M. L. Patterson *et al.* to President Andrew Johnson recommending bvts. for Capts. Gaines Lawson and Thomas H. Reeves.—LS, *ibid.* Johnson received the letter on Sept. 28 and referred it to USG. "RESPECTFULLY REFERRED TO the Secretary of War, ad interim. Let these brevets be conferred, unless there is some reason why it should not be done."—ES, *ibid.*

1867, OCT. 11. To Secretary of the Interior Orville H. Browning. "I have the honor to transmit herewith accounts of Subsistence stores issued to Indians by various officers of the Subsistence Department of the Army during the months of May, June, July and August, 1867, not included in accounts previously transmitted, and to request that a transfer warrant may be drawn for the amount ($54.664 49/100,) on the appropriation for Subsistence

of Indians to the credit of the appropriation for Subsistence of the Army."
—LS, DNA, RG 75, Central Office, Letters Received, Miscellaneous. The
enclosures are *ibid.*

1867, OCT. 11.   To Attorney Gen. Henry Stanbery. "In compliance with
your request of October 7th I have the honor to send herewith all the title
papers relating the real estate of the United States at Harpers Ferry, furnished by the Chief of Ordnance and enumerated in the enclosed lists of
deeds and miscellaneous papers."—LS, DNA, RG 60, Letters Received,
War Dept. On Oct. 7, Stanbery had written to USG. "I have the honor to
request the early transmittal to this office of all title papers whatever, in
the possession of your Department, relating to the real-estate now held by
the United States at Harper's Ferry, Va. These are needed to enable me to
comply with a recent resolution of the House of Representatives, and will
be returned as soon as an examination of them can be had. It is understood
that the papers referred to are in the custody of the Chief of Ordnance."—
LS, *ibid.*, RG 156, Letters Received. On Oct. 11, Bvt. Maj. Gen. Alexander B. Dyer, chief of ordnance, wrote to USG. "In compliance with the
request of the Attorney General, in his letter to you of the 7th inst, I have
the honor to transmit the title papers of the U. S. to the land at Harper's
Ferry, contained in five bundles, with a list of contents; also nine bundles
of Miscellaneous papers having reference to the same subject, with a list of
the same."—ALS, *ibid.* On Dec. 5, Asst. Attorney Gen. John M. Binckley
wrote to USG. "I have the honor to return herewith all the papers relating
to the public property at Harper's Ferry, which were transmitted by you to
this office on the 11th of October last, in compliance with a request of the
Attorney General, of the 7th of said month."—LS, *ibid.*

1867, OCT. 11.   To Bvt. Maj. Gen. Benjamin W. Brice, paymaster gen.
"You are authorized to transfer Fifty thousand (50.000) dollars of the
reconstruction appropriation set aside for the 2nd Mil. District to the use
of the 1st District."—Copies, DLC-USG, V, 47, 60; DNA, RG 108, Letters Sent.

1867, OCT. 11.   Judge Advocate Gen. Joseph Holt to USG. "The papers
relating to the case of *M. A. McLaughlin, Captain 2d Cavalry California
Volunteers*, are respectfully returned with the following report. He was
dismissed the service in January 1864, in accordance with the sentence of a
General Court Martial convened at Camp Babbitt, Visalia, California, and
which convicted him of—Conduct unbecoming an officer and a gentleman.
The specifications, as amended by the court, of which he was found guilty—
were as follows, 1st In ordering, while Acting Quarter Master at Camp
Babbitt, a saddler to make a riding saddle and charge it to the United
States as a pack saddle. 2d In not taking this saddle up on his property
returns, and taking it for his own use and benefit, thereby unlawfully
realizing said saddle from the U. S. 3d In certifying to the correctness of a

certain voucher in favor of one Wm Oldgate for hay, said to have been delivered at Camp Babbitt, Cal., to the amount of twelve hundred dollars, the name of William Oldgate being fictitious. 4th In turning over in his list of outstanding debts, a debt, said to be due the said Oldgate for hay, of twelve hundred dollars, and certified voucher to that effect, to Lieut McK. J. Unger 2d Cal. Cav., who relieved him as Acting Asst. QuarterMaster at Camp Babbitt, with the understanding that the amount of said voucher was to be paid to him (Capt. McLaughlin) as soon as funds were to be placed to the credit of said Lt. Unger, the name of Wm Oldgate being fictitious. 5th In receiving from said Unger one thousand dollars in payment of the debt and voucher named in the preceding specification—6th In paying one J. Owens, a contractor, for fuel, $499 in lieu of $540. the amount due him (Owens) on account of wood furnished to the government, whereby he (Capt. McL.) realized from the United States or said J. Owens, the sum of $41. All the members of the court, in view of Capt. McLaughlin's high reputation, and in the belief that his conduct was owing to a misconception of his duties and accountability as Acting Asst. Qr. Master, signed a recommendation to the reviewing authority for the favorable consideration of the case. . . . After a careful review of all the evidence in the case, it is the opinion of this Bureau that, although it is evident that Capt. McLaughlin conducted the business of his position in an irregular and therefore improper manner, his offences—which rather consisted in conduct to the prejudice of good order and military discipline than unbecoming an officer and a gentleman—were unattended by any personal profit or criminality; and (in view of the animus by which he was governned) were scarcely sufficient to warrant dismissal from the service. It is recommended that the disability occasioned by his sentence be removed—"—Copy, DNA, RG 153, Letters Sent.

1867, OCT. 12. To Bvt. Maj. Gen. Edward D. Townsend. "Order Joshua Porter, deserter from Governor's Island, who now gives himself up, back to his Compy with loss of time he has absented himself from duty."—AN (initialed), DNA, RG 94, Letters Received, A577 1867.

1867, OCT. 12. USG endorsement. "Respectfully recommended. Mr. Hunter served as a volunteer in the Union Army during the rebellion."— AES, DNA, RG 94, ACP, 3594 1871. Written on a letter of the same day from Bvt. Maj. Gen. David Hunter, Washington, D. C., to USG. "I have the honor to request the appointment of Second Lieut. of Cavalry for Pendleton Hunter of Virginia.—"—ALS, *ibid.*

1867, OCT. 12. USG endorsement. "Approved."—ES, DNA, RG 94, ACP, B1959 CB 1867. Written on a letter of Oct. from William A. Brown, Washington, D. C., to USG. "I have the honor to lay before you, for your consideration, the following papers, being recommendations by the Governor and Adjutant General of Ohio, and others, for my promotion by

Brevet to the grade of Lieutenant Colonel. As you will see by the accompanying papers I entered the service as a medical officer in the early part of the late war, and served until its close. I participated in the surgery of Shiloh, Perryville, Stoneriver, Monocacy, Nashville, and other engagements of less importance."—ALS, *ibid.* Brown enclosed three letters addressed to USG.—*Ibid.* On Nov. 29, Brown wrote to USG. "I have the honor to respectfully lay before you, the following papers."—ALS, *ibid.*, Letters Received, B1100 1867. Brown enclosed four letters addressed to USG, including one of Nov. 27 from Lewis Wallace, Crawfordsville, Ind. "Permit me to call your attention to the case of Surgeon William A. Brown, formerly, if not now, of the 149th Ohio Vol. Surgeon B., I am informed, is applying for the medal of honor. He was with his regiment at the battle of Monocacy, where his conduct was above the praise of mere words. The particulars of his conduct on that occasion are given in full by Lt. Hildebrand in a letter dated of the 9th inst., addressed to you."—ALS, *ibid.*

1867, OCT. 12.   Act. Secretary of State Frederick W. Seward to USG. "On the 7th instant, Francis Clare Ford, Esquire, Chargé d'Affaires of Great Britain, addressed a note to this Department requesting, at the instance of the Governor General of Canada to be furnished with copies of some of the recent official Reports on surveys made of the Mississippi and Missouri rivers, for the use of the Department of Public Works of Canada. I shall be greatly obliged if you will cause the matter to be referred to the proper quarter with a view to supply copies of the documents in question."—LS, DNA, RG 77, Explorations and Surveys, Letters Received. On Oct. 25, Brig. Gen. Andrew A. Humphreys, chief of engineers, wrote to USG transmitting the reports.—LS, *ibid.* On Oct. 28, Secretary of State William H. Seward wrote to USG. "I have the honor to acknowledge the receipt of a letter of the 26th instant, from Bvt Brigadier General F. T. Dent, transmitting, at the request of this Department, copies of surveys of the Mississippi and Missouri Rivers for the use of the Department of Public Works in Canada. You will be pleased to accept my thanks for your prompt compliance with that request"—LS, *ibid.*, RG 107, Letters Received from Bureaus.

1867, OCT. 12.   Bvt. Maj. Gen. Edward R. S. Canby, Charleston, to USG. "In reporting upon Gov Orr's communication to His Excellency the President I have limited myself to correcting the misapprehensions into which he has fallen in relation to the order protested against but I think it right that you should be advised that in any of the orders issued in this District that were afterwards complained of were issued at the instance or to meet the wishes of the civil authorities or to supply remedies for wrongs that could not be righted in the present abnormal condition of these States. If the District Commander in regulating the details conformed his action to the laws of the United States and did not follow the local law much of which, in this State at least, has been stigmatized by one of its ablest jurists (Petigru) in his codification of the laws of the State as 'quite beneath the demands of the age and satisfactory only to those who live by its defects,' or if the action taken was found to run counter to public sentiment, it then became a matter of reproach and the burden of that reproach was thrown upon the military authority   In all cases when the action of the military authority was invited or because of manifest necessity it must be guided, under the laws of the United States by the judgement of the District Commander, and while he may seek and profit by the assistance of the ~~military~~ civil authorities, he cannot in the execution of the law commit that judgement to their keeping, for the responsibility rests upon him and not upon them. As already reported to you the order complained of was a modification not only of an existing order (32) but of the draft of an order that had been prepared to meet difficulties of execution that had been suggested by the civil authorities. In my conference with Gov. Orr the subject was very fully discussed. He could not have been ignorant of the operations of the order prohibiting imprisonment for taxes over due, for that order was issued at his instance see Circular of Apl. 12. 1867 herewith; its operation was manifested through his tax collectors, and he first called my attention to its operations. I found upon examination that under this order a great many whites and nearly all the blacks except such as were property holders had refused to pay taxes and that although some of these could not read and write they were 'well informed' and of good moral reputes and that even if the courts failed to exercise a proper discretion in rejecting those who were intellectually and morally unfit to serve as jurors, there could be under the order an injurious enlargement of the jury lists. Of the 212 colored persons in this District who have paid taxes for the current year 206 are property holders and the greater part of them have been so for years. If any of them are unable to read and write they are so by the force of law and not by their own volition. Moreover they have paid in this District a special school tax which has been devoted not to the education of their children but to to the education of white children. The suggestion made by Gov Orr in his communication to the President to make provision for colored jurors in cases in which colored persons were interested was made at the conference, but in common with several other questions that were then raised was postponed for further consideration."—ALS, DNA, RG 108, Letters Received. On Oct. 7, President Andrew Johnson referred to USG a letter of Sept. 30 from Governor James L. Orr of S. C. to Canby. —ES, *ibid.*, RG 94, Letters Received, 989S 1867.

1867, OCT. 12. Bvt. Maj. Gen. Oliver O. Howard, Bureau of Refugees, Freedmen, and Abandoned Lands, to USG. "I have the honor to request that Capt R. E. Johnston 43th U. S. Infantry may be retained for the present as an officer of this Bureau at Lexington, Ky. It is represented to me that his services are very necessary, and that his place can not be supplied by another detail. He is the officer of whom Mr. Davis of Kentucky spoke to you yesterday"—LS, DNA, RG 94, Letters Received, 214K 1867.

On the same day, U.S. Senator Benjamin F. Wade of Ohio, Jefferson, wrote to USG. "I enclose to you a letter from General Brisbin which will explain itself. I know Judge Goodloe Mathew Adams and Hiram Shaw and they are highly respectable and influential citizens of Lexington   Colonel Johnston seems to be the right man in the right place and I hope you will find it convenient to retain him on duty in the Bureau at Lexington"—LS, *ibid.* The enclosure is *ibid.* On Oct. 17, U.S. Representative George M. Adams of Ky. and William C. Goodloe, Lexington, telegraphed to USG. "We want Capt R E. Johnston Freedmans Bureau retained at Lexington. Can it be done. Answer"—Telegram received, *ibid.*, 583A 1867. On the same day, U.S. Representative Glenni W. Scofield of Pa. *et al.*, Lexington, wrote to USG. "We have been here for a week taking testimony in certain election cases. and have made the acquantance of many of the citizens who have been prominent in their attachment to the union and who have made sacrifices to maintain it, and we are satisfied that the union men here earnestly desire the retention of Capt R E. Johnson in charge of the office of the Freedmans Bureau in this city, and we believe that the public service and the best interest of the freedmen will be promoted thereby"—LS (three signatures), *ibid.*, RG 108, Letters Received. Capt. Robert E. Johnston, ordered on Sept. 25 to rejoin his regt. in Mich., was ordered on Oct. 17 to remain in Ky.—Copy, *ibid.*, Register of Letters Received.

1867, OCT. 12.   Bvt. Capt. Amos Webster to Bvt. Maj. Gen. William H. Emory. "General Grant desires me to say that he has just seen the President who is perfectly willing that the Review should take place on Thursday; instead of Wednesday"—ALS, USG 3.

1867, OCT. 12.   Eli Tyler, Ware, Mass., to USG. "Is there any certificates at Washington for me"—Telegram received (on Oct. 13, 10:10 A.M.), DNA, RG 107, Telegrams Collected (Bound).

1867, OCT. 13.   Henry J. Raymond, "Times office," New York City, to USG. "I am not much given to thrusting advice upon public men,—but I feel so much interest in the political prospects of the country that I am tempted to make one suggestion. Nearly a year ago, meeting you in the halls of the Ho. of Reps. I said that the people would look *to you* to get the country out of its difficulties, when it should get a little farther into them. They are doing so now. The recent elections mean YOU, and not much else. The people want a MAN, in whose patriotism, disinterestedness, and sound, sober judgment they have faith: they will trust him and follow his lead. They don't want opinions, nor professions—still less party commitments. Nothing in the world can prevent your nomination by the Republican party, as things are now. They dare not and cannot nominate anybody else. And when nominated—although the Democrats will run a candidate for the sake of keeping up their organization, you will get fully one third of the Democratic vote. Your election will create the new party which is to restore the

~~Uni~~ Union and rule the country for twenty years. All you have to do is to *stand still.* Say nothing, write nothing & do nothing which shall enable any faction of any party to claim you. Your strength is *in your self*—not in any party or in any platform. I trust you will excuse me for intruding upon you in this unceremonious way. I feel intense anxiety for your election—for I see in it the only way out of the difficulties and dangers that surround the country."—ALS, USG 3.

1867, OCT. 14.   To Secretary of State William H. Seward. "I have the honor to acknowledge the receipt of yr letter of the 10th inst. transmitting a copy of a comn from the U. S. Consul at London respecting a proposition by a Prussian to impart the secret of the fulminate used in the needle-gun cartridge, & to send herewith in reply a letter on the subject from the Chief of Ordnance,"—Df, DNA, RG 156, Letters Received; copy, *ibid.*, RG 107, Letters Sent to the President. On Oct. 10, Act. Secretary of State Frederick W. Seward had written to USG. "I have the honor to communicate, herewith, for your use and such action as you may deem expedient to take in the premises, a copy of despatch No. 452, dated the 28th ultimo, from our Consul at London in reference to a proposition offered by a Prussian, now in that city, who claims to have discovered the fulminate used in the Prussian needle gun; and wishes to impart his secret to this Government. I also hand you, herewith, a specimen of the fulminate which accompanied the Consuls despatch."—LS, *ibid.*, RG 156, Letters Received. The enclosure is *ibid.*

1867, OCT. [14].   USG note. "Telegraph to asertain the facts reported in this letter."—AN (initialed), DNA, RG 94, Letters Received, 782H 1867. Written on a letter of Oct. 12 from William L. Hirst, Philadelphia, to USG. "It is important, on a hearing before the Supreme Court on Tuesday next at 10 o'clock A M. to show the facts in relation to AN EXTRAORDINARY EVENT, said to have occurred at Fort Delaware. Certain papers, purporting to show, that the regular soldiers of Co.s K. & L. 4th Reg. U. S. Artillery *held an election* for Penna officers, of our City and State, on Tuesday last   Such an election is so illegal that it is believed no officer in your Army would ~~so~~ disgrace himself & the service by permitting such a fraud, and it is, therefore, supposed the papers are manufactured. I take the liberty, General, to request you, respectfully, to telegraph to the Commandant of that post for information, and to beg your telegraphic reply to me, in time for the hearing on Tuesday. I have no doubt that you will cheerfully afford your aid to throw light upon a subject intimately connected with the purity of elections. The papers sent to the Election Judges purport that 117 soldiers voted"—ALS, *ibid.* On Oct. 15, Bvt. Maj. Gen. Edward D. Townsend telegraphed to Hirst. "[I]n reply to your letter of October (12th) twelfth, [re]ceived yesterday, General Grant directs me to [se]nd you the following copy of telegram just [re]ceived from the Commanding Officer of Fort [D]elaware. 'Fort Delaware, Delaware, October. 14th 1867, GENERAL

E. D. TOWNSEND, Assistant Adjutant General   I was in Philadelphia when the election [o]ccurred here. Colonel Howard who was in [co]mmand reports that a citizen presented [hi]mself here with a commission from Governor [Ge]ary under the seal of Pennsylvania appointing [h]im to take the votes of Pennsylvania soldiers [at] this Post. Colonel Howard told him [th]at he was under the impression that such an [el]ection was not legal but as the man had a commission from Governor Geary he allowed him to take the votes. I add on my own authority that I have ascertained that a large proportion of the men voting had no vote in the state under any circumstances. It is said only thirty three (33) votes were polled while over a hundred were returned. No officers were concerned one way or the other in this election. (signed) C. H. MORGAN. Major 4th Artillery Bvt. Brig. Gen. U. S. A. Commanding.' "—LS (telegram sent), *ibid.*, RG 107, Telegrams Collected (Bound).

1867, OCT. 14.　USG endorsement. "Respectfully refered to the Q. M. Gn."—AES, DNA, RG 92, Consolidated Correspondence, A. H. Vance. Written on a letter of Oct. 8 from U.S. Representative Columbus Delano of Ohio, Mount Vernon, to USG. "I take the liberty of addressing you in behalf of my young friend *Alfred Vance*, who was recently a clerk in the Quartermaster General's Office, and now discharged from his late employment. Young *Vance* is the eldest of the children and only son of the late Col. *Joseph Vance* of this town who was killed in the battle of Arkansas Post, in 1863, while commanding his regiment the 96th O. Inf. and who left a family here, almost dependent on their personal exertions and industry for support and livelihood. Col, *Vance* was a man of extensive influence and possessed of the respect of all classes of citizens. His friends feel a degree of interest in the welfare of his widow and children that his noble character and example fully justifies[.] This son was placed in public employment for the purpose of assisting his mother which he has hitherto done to the best of his ability. I have known no case of public employment bestowed for public service, indirectly, of more merit than that of young *Alfred Vance*,   Under these circumstances, My dear Sir, I take the liberty of asking your personal attention and kind regard in his application for reinstatement to his clerkship in your Department. If I am correctly informed, he is altogether an efficient and competent clerk for the rank to which he was assigned."—ALS, *ibid.* On Oct. 12, Alfred H. Vance, Washington, D. C., wrote to USG concerning his case.—ALS, *ibid.*

1867, OCT. 14.　Benjamin J. Sweet, Chicago, to USG. "For reasons given below I respectfully ask that my brother, Elbert. E. Sweet. private in Batt. M. U. S. Art, who enlisted for three years at Chicago. Ill. about the month of April. 1867, and is now stationed at Fort, Jefferson, Dry Tortugas. may be discharged, and allowed to go to his home in Wisconsin. First. He enlisted without the knowledge or consent of his mother or guardian (his father being dead) and was not nor will he be 21. years old till the month of February. 1868. Second. He is one of three brothers, myself, John J. Sweet, and Elbert. E. Sweet, all in the service, during the late war. John. J. Sweet, was killed in battle, in the assault on Port. Hudson, being a member of Co. K. 4th Wis. Vol. Elbert, was huonorably discharged from the 1st Wis. Cav. after the war closed, and re-enlisted as above stated. During the war our father died   I reside in Illinois with my family, and our mother remains on the homestead in Wisconsin. Elbert. has been sick with yellow fever, and would be glad to return and remain at home. His mother is much broken in health, and suffers keenly from anxiety and ill health occasioned by his absence. If consistent with your views, it would confer a great favor, upon a family not lacking in duty to the Country, and gladden the heart of his mother, to order his discharge so that he may return home."—ALS, DNA, RG 108, Letters Received.

1867, OCT. 15.   USG endorsement. "Respectfully refered to His Excellency the President. I would not recommend this appointment because the applicant took no part in the suppression of the rebellion and there are a number of applications for the same appointment from those who did, and who have performed service in the Pay Dept. and who have now favorable endorsements from the Executive"—AES, DNA, RG 94, ACP, B1974 CB 1867. Written on a letter of Oct. 4 from Lloyd Brooke, New York City, to USG. "I have the honor to apply to His Excellency the President of the United States, through you, for the appointment of Pay Master in the Army from the State of Oregon, in the place of Pay Master Simeon Francis, who is to be retired, as I have been informed. I enclose herewith a telegram from the Hon. J. W. Nesmith, late Senator in Congress from Oregon. I could doubtless obtain and present recommendations from the present Senators and many citizens of that State, were it necessary. I have served in the Pay Department a long time, many years ago. I am therefore thoroughly familiar with the duties. I am a citizen and resident of Oregon. I have had the honor of being personally known to you, and therefore submit my claims for appointment without further remark, hoping you will deem me worthy of the place I seek."—LS, *ibid.* The enclosure is *ibid.* Brooke, former q. m. clerk at Fort Vancouver, had been USG's messmate.—See *PUSG*, 1, 275, 292, 297.

1867, OCT. 15.   To Secretary of State William H. Seward. "Major W. S. Beebee of the Ordnance Dept, a young officer who served with distinction during the late war goes to Europe for the purpose of improvement in his profession but more especially to exhibit a fuse of his own invention, wh has already been adopted for our military service. I have the honor, therefore to ask that you will ~~give~~ furnish the Major such letters as will afford him facilities in the countries which he shall visit, for obtaining audiences ~~from~~ that will ~~ensure him~~ contribute to the success of his undertaking"—Df, DNA, RG 107, Letters Received from Bureaus; copy, *ibid.*, RG 107, Letters Sent to the President.

1867, OCT. 15.　USG endorsement. "Approved for brevet Colonelcy."—
ES, DNA, RG 94, ACP, W464 CB 1864. Written on a letter of Sept. 26
from Joseph S. Wilson, General Land Office, Washington, D. C., to USG.
"I have the honor herewith to lay before you a letter of 24th inst. addressed
to you by Major General Meade, referring to my son, Lieut Col, Thos.
Wilson who was brevetted as Colonel and Brigadier General of Volunteers,
and recommending 'that Brevets of the same grade in the Regular Army be
now conferred' upon him, adding that 'his services in the field at "the Generals" Head Qrs 'having been such as to render this a matter of justice to
him.' It would be a satisfaction to me to learn that it is agreeable to you to
order accordingly."—LS, *ibid.* On Sept. 24, Maj. Gen. George G. Meade,
Philadelphia, had written to USG. "On my recommendation & for his services in the Field—the Brevets of *Col* & *Brigadier Genl*—were conferred on
Lt. Col Thos Wilson Capt. & Comy Subs U. S. A:—The recent order of
the War Dept having modified & materially lessened the value of Volunteer
Brevets conferred on regular officers, I have to recommend that Brevets of
the same grade in the Regular Army be now conferred on Lt. Col Wilson—
his services in the field at my Hd Qrs having been such as to render this a
matter of justice to him.—"—ALS, *ibid.* On June 20, 1868, USG endorsed
a copy of this letter. "Respectfully forwarded to the Secretary of War, with
recommendation that the brevet of Brig Genl. USA. be conferred upon Bt.
Col. Thos. Wilson Capt. and C. S., USA."—ES, *ibid.*

1867, OCT. 15.　Bvt. Maj. Gen. Edward D. Townsend to USG. "In compliance with your directions I have the honor to report that on the 19th of
August last I received from you the following 'memorandum of orders to
be published by Adjutant General of the Army without delay. Order transfer of Bureau for Exchange of Prisoners to Adjutant General's Department.
Removal of books and papers to War Department; discharge of officers
now in Bureau and all clerks whose services can be spared. Transfer of
Archive Office; discharge of officers and clerks in like manner.' In compliance with these instructions letters, of which those herewith enclosed are
copies, were addressed to Genl. Hitchcock, Commissary General of Prisoners, Genl. Breck, Assistant Adjutant General, on duty in this office, and Dr.
Francis Lieber, chief of the Archive office. These measures were taken for
the same reason and in the same manner that the duties of the Provost
Marshal General were turned over to the Adjutant General. In consequence
of the reduction in the amount of business which has of course ensued since
the close of the war, there was no farther occasion for employing so large a
number of officers and clerks as before. While the work is now superin-
tended by an officer already on duty in the Department, as many clerks
have been retained as are required to perform the duties. The private building occupied as an office by the Commissary General of Prisoners was given
up to the owner and the records distributed in other buildings in the occupancy of the War Department and thus so much rent was saved. The
records of the Archive office remain as they were and the work of recording

them goes on as before."—LS, DLC-Andrew Johnson. On Oct. 16, USG referred this letter to President Andrew Johnson.—AES, *ibid.* On Aug. 30, Francis Lieber, Washington, D. C., had written to USG. "My office as chief of the Archive Office having been abolished, I have several times endeavoured to wait on you, in order to take leave of you as the Secretary of War ad interim. Having not succeeded I now take the liberty of doing so in writing. My official connexion with the War Department being at an end I make bold to speak to you, in these serious times, as a simple citizen. General, the world was amazed, and the lovers of liberty rejoyced, when, after our civil war was concluded the greater portion of our large army under your command, was quickly and peacably disbanded. It had never been done before in history. The time may come when, what I do not remember having read of in history, the Military of a large nation ~~may~~ may protect a people's national character, their Country and their liberty against an aggressive executive. We firmly trust in you. May God protect you. I shall leave Washington to-morrow morning. General Badeau knows my direction in New York."—ALS, USG 3. On Oct. 19, Lieber, New York City, wrote to Col. Adam Badeau incorporating a newspaper clipping. "I found this moment the following in the N. York Times of this day: . . . 'PHILADELPHIA, Friday, Oct. 18. The *Morning Post* has the following special dispatch from Washington: Upon the retirement of Dr. LIEBER from the office of Rebel Records, he wrote to Gen. GRANT, congratulating him upon his success, and saying that it was rarely that history had ever devolved upon any man so many civil and military responsibilities. He said that he felt it was possible that a greater crisis was coming than that which ended at Appomattox Court-house, and he prayed he might be strong enough to accept the responsibility. Gen. GRANT's reply is said to be the most radical he has written. In it he says he trusts he may have strength to answer any responsibility that may devolve upon him, no matter how solemn it may be. He will not hesitate to accept it if the country demands it.' Whether this despatch really came from Washington, or not I do not know. No part of it came from me— directly or indirectly. I much disrelish newspaper correspondence, and if I follow my taste I shall say nothing about this communication; but you will do me a favour if you will inform me whether General Grant would wish me to state in the papers that he did not reply to my letter directly. I believe it had better be passed in silence, for you will observe that I would be obliged to say, if I say anything, that General Grant did not reply directly. If he wishes it however I shall do so. Please reply as soon as you can; for if I am to publish anything it ought to be soon. The results of the elections have turned every eye, at once, to General Grant, as if the command had been given: Eyes right!—To say the truth, I donot exactly know whether this is in the American drill book. It is in that ~~one~~ of the army in which I served and fought in early youth. . . . This very moment a person sent by the N. York Evening Post called on me to have 'the whole correspondence.' Of course he got nothing. You will do me the favour, I trust, to tell General

Grant that I am no leaky person; but I hope ~~it~~ this is not necessary."—ALS, *ibid.*

1867, OCT. 15.   Hughes, Denver, and Peck, Washington, D. C., to USG. "We have the honor to submit herewith the petition of John Burke with accompanying exhibits A. to H. From these papers it will appear that the petitioner in the month of August A. D. 1864 was placed in charge of the Military and detective police force of the Department of the Gulf. That as one of the perquisites of his office, he was entitled by virtue of existing orders to one half of the net proceeds of such confiscable or forfeitable goods as he should cause to be seized. That he did cause the seizure of such goods to the amount of Forty seven thousand, three hundred and eighty. four 24/100 ($47,384 24/100) dollars and the net proceeds to that amount were actually paid into the office of the Provost Marshal at New Orleans. That after the seizure of the goods and the rights of the petitioner had become established, an order was placed on the files of the Provost Marshals office at New Orleans reducing the allowance to one fourth instead of one half—While this fund of Forty seven thousand three hundred and eighty four 24/100 ($47.384.24/100) dollars was in the hands of the Provost Marshal he neglected to pay to petitioner the amount due him, but often promised it, and did in fact remove it from the funds of the Office and place it on deposit in his own name in the First National Bank of New Orleans—Soon after doing this, the Provost Marshal was suspected of, or charged with having procured money by illegal and improper practices—He was arrested, and it being supposed that this money deposited with the 1st National Bank had been corruptly obtained, it was also seized and removed to Washington City, where it now remains. The Provost Marshal was discharged from arrest and the charges against him dropped; so that the War Department holds the money seized, in trust for the real owner—The above facts are all proved in the most conclusive manner and it would seem to leave no doubt but that Mr Burke is entitled to receive his share of the Forty seven thousand, three hundred and eighty four 24/100 ($47.384 24/100) dollars. . . ."—LS, DNA, RG 107, Letters Received, 873H 1867.

1867, OCT. 16.   To secretary of war. "I have the honor to recommend the following appointments from Volunteers: . . ."—LS, DNA, RG 94, ACP, G619 CB 1867. On the same day, USG endorsed this letter. "Approved." —AES, *ibid.*

1867, OCT. 16.   USG note. "The Adj. Gn. will please give the Qr. Mr. directions to sell forage to Judge Edmonds so long as his horses are kept in the public stables."—AN (initialed), DNA, RG 94, Letters Received, A584 1867.

1867, OCT. 16.   Thomas Ewing, Sr., Lancaster, Ohio, to Thomas Ewing, Jr. ". . . Tell Grant we want him for President, and can elect him by common consent if he attaches himself to no party, and makes no pledges in advance   The moderate Republicans will nominate him, but they cannot elect without the aid of the conservatives, as the late elections have shown, and if he indorse the extreme Radical measures of proscription and negro supremacy we cannot vote even for him—He may do much, with the present congress to soften asperities and restore them to ~~restore~~ reason—He cannot fail to know, and can better than any once else impress it upon them, that the proscription of every man in the South who can read and write & cypher to the rule of three (for the reconstruction resolutions amounts to that) and placing the political power in the hands of plantation negroes, is simply anarchy or military rule—a people, white or black, deprived of all their men of intelligence, cannot establish or maintain a Republican government—Ohio could not—destroy our present organization—proscribe every man who has held office, civil or military, and it is doubtful whether we, with all our general intelligence could organize a free Goverment—Treat us with 600.000 negro votes from the sugar plantations, enough to make a majority and it were quite certain we could not, but must fall into anarchy— Gen Grant has relieved us of much unnecessary expense by his reforms in the war Department, but he will do much more if he will save us from the Congressional project of reconstruction and the expense of the standing army with which we must be charged until the bubble shall burst—"— ALS, DLC-Thomas Ewing. On Oct. 19, Ewing, Jr., Washington, D. C., wrote to his father. "Yr letter containing message to Gen Grant received. As I thought the letter one which it would do him good to ponder, I enclosed it to him. I will see him one of these days, before you get here, and ~~see w~~ report what he says about the Presidency & reconstruction. The Prest had a full talk with him Saturday last, as Sherman suggested he should have. The result I guess was not satisfactory to the Prest, as Gen Cooper the Prests confidential secretary & friend said yesterday that the Prest will surely make an appt of a Secy of War very soon—I have been talked of a good deal for Secy of War—and for various reasons I think it quite probable the place will be offered me if Grant goes out. I have no confidence in any change being made before the Novr elections, if at all. If Grant will agree to do the right thing in keeping Stanton out, & preventing the arrest of the Prest in the possible contingency of an attempt ~~to arrest the Prest~~ under an act of Congress after impeachment and pending trial, then the Prest ought by all means to keep him in. Grant wants to stay—there is no doubt of that. He has a chance there to change the regulations & practice of the Dept so as to throw as much power into the hands of 'the General' as possible; and he rules the whole army his own way—all which suits him exactly. Both the projects (of putting Stanton back, & of suspending the Prest under an act of Congress) are still seriously discussed & threatened but not with such emphasis as before the elections. Yet the Prest says he will make ready for both: by dismissing Stanton, & making sure his Secy of

War will stand by him. I appreciate your advice as to the Cabinet. If I should be tendered a place I would like to consult with you further before accepting or declining it. You will be here I am sure in time. Business good. Charley does well—"—ALS, *ibid.*

1867, OCT. 16.   Mrs. William Hudson, Washington, D. C., to USG. "I am a soldiers wife who has been out of employment for some time. He can obtain none. I am the only support of a widowed mother and her four children. I am in adverse circumstances and desire to find employment. I have thought of appealing to you to solicit your influence in obtaining for me a situation—how ever humble—it will be thankful—in one of the Departments. If you could do this you will confer a favor, for which I will be forever paryerfully thankful, and grateful. I humbly solicit an answer."—ALS, DNA, RG 107, Applications.

1867, OCT. 16.   U.S. Senator Alexander R. Ramsey of Minn., St. Paul, to USG. "Please transfer Robt. J McHenry from Company F. twenty ninth (29th) Infantry to tenth (10th) Infantry for purpose collecting money due him"—Telegram received (on Oct. 17, 8:40 A.M.), DNA, RG 107, Telegrams Collected (Bound).

1867, OCT. 17.   Brig. Gen. Andrew A. Humphreys, chief of engineers, to USG. "I have the honor to return herewith papers referred to the chief of Engineers for remark on the 11th of Oct. in relation to the application of the *Yerba Buena R. R. Co*—through its President, S. F. Butterworth—for permission to construct a Rail Road around the island of Yerba Buena, San Francisco Harbor, Cal., with the recommendation that Genl. Halleck be authorized and directed to protect the military reservations of the U. S. within the bay of SanFrancisco by all the means available for the purpose. The reservation by the President of the U. S. of land for military purposes is supposed to place it beyond all control or interference from any quarter which would render it useless for the intended object and virtually nullify the action of the President. The island of Yerba Buena is considered an important position for the defence of the harbor of San Francisco, and the possession of the whole island is necessary for this object. The Yerba Buena Rail Road Co. should not be allowed to construct any works whatever on or in front of it. Point San José is an important position in connection with the defence of the Bay and Harbor of SanFrancisco, and all intrusion upon the probable site of the works and the lines of fire should be prevented."—Copy, DNA, RG 77, Letters Sent Relating to Land. On Oct. 28, William B. Hyde, Washington, D. C., wrote to USG. "On Jan. 26th of the present year, a company was organized in San Francisco Cal. which under the title of the Terminal Central Pacific Railway Co. designed to extend the Pacific railroad from its present terminus at Vallejo Cal. to the island of *Yerba Buena* in the harbor of San Francisco, and now in military reserve. The particular desires of the Company with reference to the island, are to create thereon a vast Terminal R. R. Depot, with all of the necessary attendants and fixtures, to afford the greatest facilities to the commerce of our own Continent as well as the Asias. The Company is actuated by the belief that the fulfilling of this plan will not be inharmonious with the designs of the U. S. relating to San Francisco harbor defense, and entertain the hope that with our plan fully developed to the proper departments of our Govt. a favorable consideration may be given it. In my capacity as Chief Engineer of this Company, I submitted our project to the gentlemen of the U. S. Engineers to whom the interests of that Dept, for the Pacific coast are entrusted, asking for an informal judgment as to its merits. The opinion received strengthened the opinion of the Company that its plan *could* be carried out and harmonize with the designs of the Govt. Being authorized in connection with Mr. E. P. Flint to represent the Company in a petition to Congress for the grant or use of such portions of the Island of Yerba Buena as may not be needed for purposes of defense, and knowing that any Congressional action in our behalf must depend upon the favorable consideration of the project by the War Dept, I most respectfully request that the proper officers of the Engineer Dept. be authorized to report regarding the portions of said island of Yerba Buena necessary for harbor defense, and whether the remainder could not be applied, without detriment to the public interests, to the railroad purposes desired by the Company which I represent. The accompanying pamphlet and map are respectfully submitted for your consideration. Praying that this request may receive your most favorable attention, . . ."—ALS, *ibid.*, Letters Received. On Jan. 2, 1868, USG wrote to Speaker of the House Schuyler Colfax. "I have the honor to send, herewith, a report by the Chief of Engineers, dated Dec. 20th 1867 containing information called for by a communication from the Hon. G. W. Julian Chairman of the Committee on Public Lands, which Committee has under consideration a bill for the relief of the *Terminal Central Pacific Railroad* Co. to which the bill contemplates granting the island of Yerba Buena in San Francisco harbor."—Copy, *ibid.*, RG 107, Reports to Congress. On Jan. 4, USG wrote to U.S. Senator Henry Wilson of Mass., chairman, Committee on Military Affairs. "I have the honor to send, herewit[h] a report by the Chief of Engineers, dated Dec 20th 1867 respecting the relinquishment by the U S of title to *Yerba Buena Island* in California, to a RailRoad Co., a bill for which has passed the House of Representativ[es.]"—Copy, *ibid.* USG enclosed a report of Dec. 20, 1867, from Humphreys. ". . . It is to be remarked that the bill imposes no obligations upon the Company to build the proposed rail-road, nor to do any other thing. The grant is an absolute free gift, without a single condition, of four-fifths of an island, containing over one hundred (100) acres, in the middle of the harbor of San Francisco, one and a half miles from the city—with deep water, close up to the shore on all sides except one. The value of this gift, over and above the cost of work necessary to develope it, must be many millions of dollars."—Copy, *ibid.*, RG 77, Letters Sent. *HED*, 40-2-79.

On Feb. 7, 1868, Humphreys wrote to USG. "As recommended by the

Chief of Engineers in July last, Company "D." Engineers was transferred to the Pacific Coast and is now stationed at Fort Point San Francisco Harbor. . . . I beg leave therefore to recommend, that Company "D" Engineers be directed to take post under the orders of the Chief of Engineers on the island of Yerba Buena—in the Harbor of San Francisco, there to be instructed in its proper duties, to assist in the survey of that island, and to receive from him such other instructions and orders in the line of its service, as may be proper. . . ."—LS, DNA, RG 94, Letters Received, 44E 1868.

1867, OCT. 17.   Bvt. Maj. Gen. Joseph A. Mower, New Orleans, to USG. "Please authorize one carriage to be retained from sale ordered by G. O. number eighty eight (88) It being in use by attending Surgeon in this City and indispensable.—Full particulars by mail"—Telegram received (at 4:35 P.M.), DNA, RG 94, Letters Received, 1478M 1867; *ibid.*, RG 107, Telegrams Collected (Bound); *ibid.*, RG 108, Telegrams Received; copy, DLC-USG, V, 55.

1867, OCT. 17.   James P. T. Carter, secretary, Arizona Territory, Prescott, to USG. "By request of the fourth Legislature of this Territory, I send you copy of a concurrent Resolution adopted by that body."—ALS, DNA, RG 94, Letters Received, 652A 1867. The enclosure, requesting that Arizona Territory be made a military dept., is *ibid.*

1867, OCT. 18.   To Secretary of the Interior Orville H. Browning. "I have the honor to enclose herewith papers relating to the Indian Reservation on Mackinac Island, Michigan, and the buildings located thereon, for such action as may upon consideration be deemed proper"—Copies, DNA, RG 94, Letters Received, 751W 1867; *ibid.*, RG 107, Letters Sent to the President.

1867, OCT. 18.   To Secretary of the Interior Orville H. Browning. "I have the honor to transmit for the necessary action of your Dept. papers pertaining to a Military Reservation at *Ft. Wadsworth*, Dakota, Ty, established by Gen'l. Orders No. 41 of Oct. 1 /67 from Headquarters Dept. of Dakota, with the Presidents approval of the same."—Copy, DNA, RG 107, Letters Sent to the President.

1867, OCT. 18.   To Secretary of the Treasury Hugh McCulloch. "I have the honor to acknowledge the receipt of your communication of the 18th instant, enclosing letter of Hiram Dunn, late Collector of Customs at Plattsburg, New York, relative to Fenian arms seized and stored in Fort Montgomery, and to inform you that the same has been referred to the Chief of Ordnance, in whose custody the arms now are, with instructions to take the necessary measures to carry out your suggestions, in the event of the arms being given up or otherwise disposed of."—LS, DNA, RG 56, Letters Received. On the same day, McCulloch had written to USG. "I have the honor to transmit herewith a letter from Mr. Dunn, late Collector of Customs at Plattsburg N. Y., dated the 15th instant, relative to the fenian arms seized by him under instructions from this Department, and stored in fort Montgomery. The seizure was not made under the revenue laws, and this Department has no claim upon the arms, either for itself or its officers, nor does it hold itself responsible for the charges and expenses that may have accrued upon them. It is suggested that if the arms are delivered up, or disposed of provisions be made for the payment of charges &c by the parties receiving them, or from the proceeds."—Copy, *ibid.*, Letters Sent. On Dec. 5, McCulloch wrote to USG. "Herewith I have the honor to transmit you a copy of a letter this day received from the Collector of customs at Plattsburgh N. Y. reporting that the commandant of Fort Montgomery refuses to deliver the Fenian arms, stored there for transportation to Watervliet Arsenal, in accordance with the arrangement had with you on the 23d October last, unless the said Collector will receipt to him for them. The instructions given the collector by this Department were framed in the understanding that this Department had surrendered to the War Department all control of the arms, and directed him simply to co-operate as far as necessary with your officers in measures for the transfer to the Arsenal. The commandant of the Fort seems to labor under some misapprehension, and I will thank you, if you please, to instruct him in such manner on the subject as shall relieve the embarrassment now existing."—Copy, *ibid.* On Dec. 11, Bvt. Maj. Gen. Edward D. Townsend wrote to McCulloch that USG had ordered the transfer of arms.—Copy, *ibid.*, RG 94, Letters Sent.

1867, OCT. 18. To Secretary of State William H. Seward. "I have the honor to acknowledge receipt of ~~your~~ the letter of the Dept of State, dated the 7th inst, enclosing translation of a note ~~of~~ from the Netherlands Minister, of the 28th ultimo, requesting, for the information of his Government, information in regard to any trials ~~had~~ of breech-loading firearms subsequent to those ~~had previous to~~ of last winter, and to inform you in reply that the Chief of Ordnance reports that no trials subsequent to those named have been made, beyond the firing of a few service charges from each musket to test the arms and of ~~a~~ several thousand cartridges to test the ammunition—The Chief of Ordnance further ~~reports~~ states that reports received at the Ordnance Dept relative to such of the arms as are in ~~actual~~ service, are generally very favorable."—Df, DNA, RG 156, Letters Received; copy, *ibid.*, RG 107, Letters Sent to the President. On Oct. 7, Seward had written to USG. "I have the honor to inclose a translation of a note of the 26th ultimo, from Mr Mazel, the Netherlands Minister, who desires to procure for the use of his Government, information in regard to late trials of breech loading fire-arms which have been made under the authority of the War Department. I will thank you, if practicable, to cause proper steps to be taken to enable this Department to communicate the information sought by Mr Mazel."—LS, *ibid.*, RG 156, Letters Received. The enclosure is *ibid.*

1867, OCT. 18.   To Attorney Gen. Henry Stanbery. "At the instance of
the Chief of Engineers, U. S. Army, I have the honor to enclose a copy of a
letter dated the 14th instant, from the United States District Attorney for
the District of Massachusetts proposing a plan for removing the objections
set forth in your letter of the 18th June last to this Department, to the title,
proposed to be vested in the United States, to a portion of Long Island in
Boston Harbor. Your opinion as to the propriety of adopting the plan suggested is requested."—LS, DNA, RG 60, Letters Received, War Dept. On
Oct. 15, Brig. Gen. Andrew A. Humphreys, chief of engineers, had twice
written to USG concerning legal aspects of the matter.—Copies, *ibid.*, RG
77, Letters Sent Relating to Land.

1867, OCT. 18.   USG endorsement. "Return to Gn. Pope with suggestion
that Capt. Holliste[r] be brough before Court Martial on charge of 'Utter
worthlessness' and such other charge and Dist. Commander may prefer. If
not thotught advisable to bring him before Ct Mar enquire if his case will
warrant his being ordered before the Retiring Board. Law prohibits striking an officers name from the Army without trial."—AE (initialed), DNA,
RG 94, Letters Received, 1476M 1867. Written on a letter of Sept. 19
from Thomas W. Osborn and Sherman Conant, Republican party officials,
Tallahassee, to USG. "We have the honor to request that Capt. G. S. Hollister. of the 7th U. S. Infantry be ordered to duty out of the State of
Florida or retired from active service—for the following reasons—As an
officer of the United State he has thrown himself actively into the present
political campaign and is exerting himself in every way to disparage the
cause of liberty and of the policy of the Government. He is in the habit of dis-
paraging the the character of the men who served in the U. S. Armies during
the war also of advising against the liberty of the blacks and their privileges of free speech. His associations are with the lowest and most degraded
people of the Country and never with those of decent or respectable character, consequently no respectable person is able to counteract his influence
with those people with whom he associates   They are beneath the rest of
self respecting people and among them he labors against the policy of the
Government and throws the influence of his army rank and Uniform to
give force to his counsel. He is disapated in his habits. During the last
week has been continually drunk and conducting himself ~~with~~ without
respect or shame. Only last night was knocked down for telling a gentleman
he was a liar while this gentleman was defending the character of a brother
officer of Capt. Hollisters. For some cause which a Surgeon could better
explain than ourselves Capt. Hollisters head and face are now and have
been for a month disgusting to look at. In speaking of certain incidents we
do it to illustrate this mans general character. As for the illustration and
proof of his character we respectfully refer you to the record in the War
Department of Capt. G. S. Hollister 7th U. S. Infy. at one time Lieut. Col.
16th NewYork Vol. Cavalry. He is in our opinion a disgrace to the Goverment as well as to the service—We would Respectfully ask that he be

removed from the state."—LS, *ibid.* On Nov. 16, W. H. Hollister, New York City, wrote to USG. "Knowing as I do the value of every moment of your time an apology is necessary for this intrusion. My only excuse is a Sense of duty, which I owe to the family of which I am a member and an act of justice which I feel bound to perform. May I beg of you to read this letter and Enclosures   It is to ask no favor at your hands other than to request that no further injustice be done. Quite recently, papers have been sent from Col. John T. Sprague 7th u. s. Infantry to General Pope & through the latter, I presume to your department, regarding my brother, Capt. Geo. S Hollister. 7th. Infantry. Col. Sprague speaks of Capt Hollister in a manner derogatory to his character intimating that the service would be benefitted by his absence & recommending that he be dropped from the rolls of the army. I hope, General, that this will be the subject of thorough investigation by means of Court Martial   No inquiry of an impartial character is objected to by my brother nor by his friends, on the contrary, it is rather courted than otherwise. But what I wish to call your attention to, is the fact of reference by Col. Sprague to a matter fully investigated and passed upon by the War Department   I enclose herewith a copy of the Report of General Dix to whom this subject was referred for final action. This may have escaped your attention. I also send a copy of a letter written by General Dix to some officers of the 7th Infantry in reply to an inquiry by them upon this subject. I cannot believe that Col. Sprague is wilfully and intentionally persecuting my brother, but he is prejudiced against him through false and malicious statements made to him. This persecution ought to end. I think it sufficient to call your attention to this subject to feel that no further injustice be done Capt. Hollister. I contend and can prove that he is an Excellent officer & performs his duties faithfully"— ALS, *ibid.*

1867, OCT. 18.   USG endorsement. "Respectfully recommended."—AES, Atwood Collection, InU. Written on a letter of the same day from Bvt. Maj. Gen. Benjamin W. Brice, paymaster gen., to USG. "I have the honor to recommend that *Simeon Francis* Paymaster U. S. A be placed on the retired list of officers of the Army, as provided in Section 12 of the Act approved July 17th 1862, his age exceeding sixty two, being nearly seventy years. And I further respectfully recommend, if the President shall see fit to make the vacancy as above indicated, that *Isaac S. Stewart* late Addl Paymaster be appointed to fill the same."—LS, *ibid.*

1867, OCT. 18.   Bvt. Maj. Gen. Daniel H. Rucker, act. q. m. gen., to USG. "I have the honor to return herewith letter of A H. Hobson of Camden Ark, relative to destruction of his Printing Press and material by U. S. Troops, referred to this Office from the War Department 16th inst for report: The case is one of damages, to pay which the QrMr General has no appropriation, and over which he has no juris diction."—LS, DNA, RG 94, Letters Received, 1234M 1867.

1867, Oct. 18.   Governor John W. Geary of Pa., Harrisburg, to USG. "The friends of Lieut Chas C Crassen thirty fifth infantry stationed Victoria Texas are much worried lest he has become victim to yellow fever Can you inform me if he is alive or dead"—Telegram received, DNA, RG 94, Letters Received, P672 1867.

1867, Oct. 18.   Godwin and Crocker, attorneys, Portsmouth, Va., to USG. "We are requested by the personal representative of Wm H. Hardison dec'd to respectfully inquire whether the said Hardison was not entitled to some money for secret service rendered during the war—; and if so, whether it has been paid to any one."—ALS, DNA, RG 94, Letters Received, 493G 1867.

1867, Oct. 19.   USG endorsement. "Approved"—AES, DNA, RG 156, Letters Received. Written on a letter of Oct. 14 from Act. Secretary of State Frederick W. Seward to USG. "I have the honor to commend to your favorable consideration the enclosed transcript of a note of the 11th instant, from Baron von Gerolt, in which he communicates the wish of the Prussian Government to procure samples of the new Springfield muskets and Spenser's repeating carbines, together with a certain number of cartridges adapted to the use of these arms—"—LS, *ibid.* The enclosure is *ibid.*

1867, Oct. 19.   Secretary of the Interior Orville H. Browning to USG. "I have the honor to enclose, herewith a copy of an affidavit of Mrs Christiana Kiehl, and statement of Major General Jno. E. Wool U. S. A. in reference thereto, relating to a claim presented to this Department by the former, for depredations committed by Indians, and to respectfully request that a copy of so much of the report referred to by Gen. Wool as having been made to the War Department, bearing upon the claim of Mrs Kiehl, be furnished to this Department."—LS, DNA, RG 94, Letters Received, 95I 1867. The enclosures are *ibid.* On Oct. 16, Bvt. Maj. Gen. Edward D. Townsend had written to Christiana Kiehl, Washington, D. C. "A copy of Col. Wright's Report of an attack made by Indians at the Cascades on the Columbia River in 1856 is herewith respectfully furnished in accordance with your application by letter of the 7th instant"—ALS, *ibid.*, 270K 1867.

1867, Oct. 19.   Bvt. Maj. Gen. Edward R. S. Canby, Charleston, to Bvt. Maj. Gen. John A. Rawlins. "I have the honor to report for the information of the General of the Army, that I have suspended and as soon as a suitable and qualified successor can be appointed will remove Judge A. P. Aldrich of the Court of Common Pleas and General Sessions for the Southern circuit of this State. The order of the Judge in relation to juries in the Edgefield District will be annulled, but, as there may be other unfinished business in his court requiring judicial action to complete it, and to which no objection attaches,—I have thought it proper not to make the removal absolute until after he has had a reasonable time to complete the unfinished business. On the 7th instant Judge Aldrich, at the opening of the fall term of his court, for the Edgefield District, delivered an address to the juries and bar of that court, a copy of which (marked "A") is herewith transmitted. It will be seen by the Judge's letter of the 16th instant, a copy of which ("B") is also transmitted, that he admits that his address was 'correctly reported.' It will also be seen by the report of the clerk of the court ("C") that the expressed intention of the Judge was followed by an appropriate order for drawing the juries. I do not propose to remark upon the action taken by Judge Aldrich except so far as to invite attention to the manner in which judicial authority has been made subservient to the purposes of rebellion, and to indicate the relation between past and present action in their connection with this case. At an early period in the history of the rebellion a Judge of the United States Court then holding its term in this city paralyzed the judicial arm of the Government of the United States, within this jurisdiction, by laying off the robes of office and declaring his court to be adjourned forever. At a later period and in a different section of the country another Judge attempted to paralyze the Executive arm of the Government by a Judicial decision that the secession of South Carolina had dissolved the Union; that the officers of the United States were thereby absolved from their oaths of allegiance, and that there was no longer any constitutional, legal, or moral obligation resting upon the officers and soldiers of the Army to uphold the flag they had sworn to defend: and now, another Judge, avowing the same sympathies seeks, to the extent of his power and influence, to paralyze—the legislative arm of the Government by declaring that the Congress of the United States 'is an usurping body'; that he cannot 'lend his aid to support and perpetuate the tyranny of which we complain'— and by refusing obedience to orders issued under the authority of laws enacted by that Congress. The address of the Judge is a wail for 'our holy and lost cause'—and in his private relations might be entitled to some consideration for the frankness with which it is expressed; but in his official character it is difficult to reach any other conclusion than that his devotion is not to the Constitution of the United States, but to the constitutions that perished with the Rebellion, that 'deprived the people of the State of South Carolina of all civil Government.' I have endeavored to provide that there shall be no delay in the administration of justice by authorizing the Governor to assign one of the other Judges to hold the terms in the Southern Circuit until a successor to Judge Aldrich is appointed."—LS, DNA, RG 108, Letters Received. The enclosures are *ibid.*

1867, OCT. 19. George N. Corson, Norristown, Pa., to USG. "Is there no way this poor old Colored woman can be supported from the pay her faithless old husband will be entitled to from the Government. Her husband Robert Flowers is a man 55 years of age, was enlisted at Wilmington, Del, and the enclosed letter and endorsements theron will show you how much consolation this poor woman derives from investigations among officers who regard red tape as of more importance that the feelings of a poor old heart beneath a colored skin. Genl. trusting you may be able to answer the question, . . ."—ALS, DNA, RG 108, Letters Received. The enclosures are *ibid.*

1867, OCT. 20. Mrs. John W. Andrews, Philadelphia, to USG. "I now address you and ask you if you will be so kind as to awnser this letter i have writeing to my husband who is in the army or at least he was when he last wrote to me and that was on the 12th of aprial he then said that he was liveing and wreel and told me to be contented and wrote me a verey pretty letter and sent me his likenees my dear husband did not look as he always had done to me but i awnser his letter and i have different times since but recives no awnser to my letters i do not know what to think i cannot that my dear husband is dead for if i would i then know that i am left alone in this wide world to perrish i have neither father nor mother nor any relation but my husband and he knows how i am afflicked i have worked and tryed to get along but i cannt feel contented for i do not hear from him i did feel happy when i would get a letter and know that he was liveing and well but now i hear nothing Sir will you take pitty on me and find out if my husband is liveing or dead his name is John W Andrews Companey H fifth U S inft and he was in fort Summer New Mexico when he last wrote i send you the paper and envelope"—ALS, DNA, RG 108, Letters Received. On Nov. 2, 1st Lt. George McDermott, 5th Inf., reported that Andrews had deserted.—AES, *ibid.*

1867, OCT. 20. Thomas Claiborne, Nashville, to USG. "I have the honor to request that you will bestow a wholesome rebuke on Bvt Brigr Genl J W Davidson, who refuses to notice *two* letters I have written to him wherein, I have requested him to pay me the sum of One hundred & twenty five or thirty dolls (in gold) borrowed money) at Fort Fillmore N M. previous to the war. He then pledged me his masonic word for the return of it. Perhaps he regards the war as having 'wiped it out', yet, as debts due by southern men have been & are vigorously collected I cannot see why Bvt Brigr Genl J. W. Davidson can treat my just demand contemptuously *Twice* I have addressed him—he is silent—I turn him over to you—I believe he got my letters he justly owes me $125. in gold—can you make him pay it? I refer to Roger Jones, who knows me well."—ALS, DNA, RG 108, Letters Received.

1867, OCT. 21. USG endorsement. "Approved for Brevet Major General of Volunteers."—ES, DNA, RG 94, ACP, T482 CB 1867. Written on a letter of Oct. 14 from Maj. Gen. George H. Thomas, Louisville, to the AG. "I have the honor to recommend Colonel John Ely Veteran Reserve Corps, Brevet Brigadier General U. S. V. for the additional Brevet of Major General U S. Vols. for faithful and gallant conduct throughout the war. . . ."— LS, *ibid.*

1867, OCT. 21, 11:30 A.M.   To U.S. District Attorney Milton D. Browning. "Your letter just received. Papers asked for will be sent as soon as possible. . . . Copy for Gov. Stone, Desmoines Iowa,"—ALS (telegram sent), DNA, RG 107, Telegrams Collected (Bound); telegram sent, *ibid.*; copies, *ibid.*, RG 108, Telegrams Sent; DLC-USG, V, 56. On Oct. 19, Governor William Stone of Iowa had telegraphed to USG. "Please attend to subject of District Attorney Brownings letter of sixteenth (16th) inst promptly"— Telegram received (at 10:20 A.M.), DNA, RG 107, Telegrams Collected (Bound). See Bvt. Maj. Gen. Edward D. Townsend to Stone, Oct. 21, 11:30 A.M., *ibid.*

1867, OCT. 22.   To Secretary of the Treasury Hugh McCulloch. "Upon the recommendation of the Paymaster General I respectfully request that $2.768.00, standing on the books of the Assistant Treasurer at New Orleans, to the credit of Major George B. Simpson, Paymaster, deceased, and pertaining to the appropriation for 'Pay of the Army', may be repaid into the U. S. Treasury; and that the usual evidence of such repayment may be transmitted to me."—LS, DNA, RG 56, Letters Received from the War Dept. On Oct. 21, Bvt. Maj. Gen. Benjamin W. Brice, paymaster gen., had written to USG. "Major Geo. B. Simpson—Paymr U. S. A—died at N. Orleans on 4th Oct 1867—having then on deposit to his official credit with the Asst Treasr U. States at N. Orleans the sum of $2768.00—I have the honor to request that this sum may be placed to the credit of the Treasurer of the U. States for the purpose of being covered into the Treasy U. States to the credit of Major Simpson on account of appropriation for 'Pay of Army' "—LS, *ibid.*, RG 99, Letters Received. On Oct. 24, McCulloch wrote to USG acknowledging his letter.—LS, *ibid.*, RG 107, Letters Received from Bureaus.

1867, OCT. 22.   To Attorney Gen. Henry Stanbery. "At the request of certain of the Trustees of Norwich University, Northfield, Vermont, and in accordance with the recommendation of the Judge Advocate General of the Army, I have the honor to request your opinion as to the proper construction of so much of the 26th Section of the Act, approved July 28th, 1866, 'to increase and fix the Military Peace Establishment of the United States,' as forms the subject of the enclosed appeal from the decision of this Department upon the same."—LS, DNA, RG 60, Letters Received, War Dept. On Oct. 15, Bvt. Maj. Thomas W. Walker, president, Norwich University, Northfield, Vt., *et al.* had written to USG. "We have the honor to respectfully call your attention to the enclosed application to the Hon Attorney General for a decision in the matter therein referred to (marked A) and his answer thereto, also inclosed (marked B) and respectfully request that you will refer the same to the Attorney General of the U. S. or the President for decision as we think the former Secretary of war decided in this matter contrary to the meaning and intent of the 26. section of the Act of Congress approved July 28th 1867"—LS (three signatures), *ibid.*, RG

107, Letters Received, N118 1867. Section 26 provided education in military science at colleges and universities by assigning army officers to serve on the faculty.—*U.S. Statutes at Large*, XIV, 336.

1867, OCT. 22.   To Attorney Gen. Henry Stanbery. "I have the honor to enclose a certified copy of the decree of the U. S. District Court for the District of Virginia in the case of William E. Wood together with a copy of the bill of costs of the same, and to request that, for the reasons set forth in the Quartermaster General's letter of October 10th 1867, copy of which is also enclosed, the U. S. District Attorney for the District of Virginia be instructed to proceed, on behalf of this Department, to have the award— regarded as extravagant and unjust—reopened, and a new Commission (upon which the interests of the Government shall be represented) ordered: also, that upon the final decree he cause the bill of costs to be duly taxed, so that this Department shall not be called upon to pay any improper or unusual charges."—LS, DNA, RG 60, Letters Received, War Dept. On Nov. 7, Asst. Attorney Gen. John M. Binckley wrote to USG. "Referring to your communication of 22 ultimo, to the Attorney General, I have the honor to enclose a copy of our instructions of this date to District Attorney Chandler."—Copy, *ibid.*, Letters Sent. On Sept. 23, William E. Wood, Norfolk, had written to USG. "I have the honor to send to Your Dept. the Decree obtained from U. S. District Court for lands taken for Cemetery purposes near Fortress Monroe. . . ."—ALS, *ibid.*, RG 107, Letters Received, H345 1867. The enclosures are *ibid.* On Oct. 10, Bvt. Maj. Gen. Daniel H. Rucker, act. q. m. gen., wrote to USG concerning this matter.—LS, *ibid.*

1867, OCT. [22].   USG endorsement. "Approved"—AES, DNA, RG 94, Letters Received, 1013S 1867. Written on a letter of Oct. 10 from Col. Albert J. Myer, chief signal officer, to USG. "I respectfully recommend that the within issue as a General Order to the Army. In Submitting this recommendation I invite attention to the fact that the 'Manual of Signals' has been prepared by me, and has been published at my own expense. I am thus particular that there may be no imputation that I have recommended the purchase of a book prepared by myself without a full knowledge of the fact on the part of the Department."—LS, *ibid.*

1867, OCT. 22.   Bvt. Brig. Gen. Thomas M. Vincent, AGO, to USG. "I have the honor to request that the various claims for Subsistence, lodgings &c now on file with the records of the late Colonel L. C. Turner, Judge Advocate, may be returned to this office, as they are frequently required for reference in the examination of new claims. These accounts were rejected by this office as fraudulent and referred to Colonel Turner for the prosecution of the parties interested in their presentation. I would also request that this office be furnished with a list of such of these claims as are now in the hands of U. S. District Attorneys, with the name and residence of each attorney, so that in case any of the claims in their hands are required for reference, application can be made for them."—LS, DNA, RG 94, Turner-Baker Papers.

1867, OCT. 22. Bvt. Maj. Gen. Edward O. C. Ord, Holly Springs, to USG. "I reduce my Stations for Winter to six (6) in each State, Quarter Masters complain bitterly for want of funds, Vouchers unpaid for several months, Government credit suffering, Estimates in and approved by Quarter Master General Can I get sixty thousand (60000) dolls Sheltering fund for winter quarters? Much needed"—Telegram received (at 8:00 P.M.), DNA, RG 107, Telegrams Collected (Bound); *ibid.*, RG 108, Telegrams Received; copies, *ibid.*, RG 94, Letters Received, 1496M 1867; (sent by mail) *ibid.*, RG 108, Letters Received; DLC-USG, V, 55. On Oct. 24, Bvt. Brig. Gen. Frederick T. Dent wrote to Bvt. Maj. Gen. Edward D. Townsend. "The Sec. of War directs that the funds for Shelter to the amount of Sixty thousand dollars be furnished as requested by Gen Ord in the telegram herewith"—ALS, DNA, RG 94, Letters Received, 1496M 1867.

1867, OCT. 23. Governor Arthur I. Boreman of West Va. to USG. "In accordance with the Act of Congress approved July 2, 1862, entitled 'An Act donating Public Lands to the several states and territories which may provide Colleges for the Benefit of Agriculture and the Mechanic Arts' (see Acts 1861–62, p. 503.) the state of West Virginia has provided the necessary grounds and buildings and has established a College, with a full corps of Professors, such as the Act contemplates, at Morgantown in the county of Monongalia, and there are now in attendance at the College about one hundred and fifty students and the numbers are daily increasing. You will perceive by reading the 4th. Section of the Act of Congress that the College is required to teach 'Military tactics' and it is with reference to this matter that I address you. The Executive Committee of the College have made requisition on me for the necessary arms and ammunition to enable them to comply with this requirement of the law. I have supplied them with one hundred stand of Infantry arms which have remained here since the close of the rebellion. They also ask for Fifty stand of Cavalry arms (Carbines and sabres) One section of Artillery (Parrott Guns if practicable) and side arms for officers of one Company of Infantry. These the State has not; and it has occurred to me that, inasmuch as the teaching of 'Military tactics' is in obedience to an Act of Congress, and as it is probable that the Government has a surplus of the different kinds of arms and equipments that are needed, the War Department could and would furnish them on request. I may add that, if so furnished the arms will be well kept and taken care of, and will be forthcoming and returned whenever required. Will you be kind enough to say whether the desired arms will be supplied by the Department or not?"—LS, DNA, RG 156, Letters Received. On Oct. 29, Bvt. Maj. Gen. Alexander B. Dyer, chief of ordnance, endorsed this letter. "Respectfully returned to the Secretary of War, ad.-int. There is no authority of law or regulation for the issue of arms or other Ordnance Stores to any College, by this Department, and it should not be made. If the arms are required by the College they should be furnished by the State. They can be issued by this Department upon the requisition of Govr Boreman, approved by the Secretary of War. The amount due the State of West Virginia, on account of its quota for arming and equipping the Militia, exceeds the value of the arms and other stores, herein asked for."—ES, *ibid.* On Oct. 30, Bvt. Brig. Gen. Frederick T. Dent wrote to Boreman conveying this information.—Copy, *ibid.*, RG 107, Letters Sent. On Dec. 9, West Va. AG Isaac H. Duval wrote to USG. "By direction of His Excellency Governor Boreman I have the honor to enclose herewith requisition for Ordnance and Ordnance Stores for the use of the West Virginia Agricultural College at Morgantown W. Va. . . ."—LS, *ibid.*, RG 156, Letters Received. The enclosure is *ibid.*

1867, OCT. 24. To President Andrew Johnson. "I have the honor to recommend the appointment of Charles G. Fisher to be 2d Lt. in the Army."—ALS, DNA, RG 94, ACP, F155 CB 1868. On the same day, Johnson endorsed this letter. "Let the appointment be made as recommended—"—AES, *ibid.*

1867, OCT. 24. To Secretary of the Treasury Hugh McCulloch. "Upon the recommendation of the Paymaster General I respectfully request that $5.921.93, standing on the books of the Assistant Treasurer at New York, to the credit of Bvt. Lt. Col. A. D. Stewart, Paymaster, deceased, may be repaid into the U. S. Treasury on account of the appropriation for 'Pay of Army', and that the usual evidence of such repayment may be transmitted to me."—LS, DNA, RG 56, Letters Received from the War Dept. On the same day, Asst. Secretary of the Treasury John F. Hartley wrote to USG acknowledging this letter.—LS, *ibid.*, RG 107, Letters Received from Bureaus. On Oct. 23, Bvt. Maj. Gen. Benjamin W. Brice, paymaster gen., had written to USG. "Brv't Lt. Colo A D Stewart Paymaster, United States Army, died at NewYork on 17th inst, having then on deposit to his official credit with the Assist Treasurer U States at New York the sum of $5.921.93/100. I have the honor to request that this sum may be paid in to the credit of the Treasurer of the U States for the purpose of being covered into the Treasury U States to the credit of Brvt Lt Colo. Stewart on Account of Appropriation for 'Pay of Army.' "—Copy, *ibid.*, RG 99, Letters Sent. On Oct. 18, Brice wrote to USG. "A vacancy of Paymaster in the Army exists by the decease yesterday, in New York, of Bvt. Lt. Col. *A. D. Stewart.*—I have the honor to recommend *Wm. P. Gould* of Indiana, to fill the vacancy. The application of Col. Gould is very strongly endorsed by many distinguished gentlemen civil, and military, and the President has given favorable endorsement to the same. Col. G. was appointed additional Paymaster at the very beginning of the War, in 1861. And has faithfully discharged the duties of the office from that time, to the 1st day of the present month, when he was directed to be mustered out of service. He is eminently qualified by his intelligence, and his integrity, as well as by his long experience, and there is no name on the list of applicants whose appointment would be more eligable, or more deserving."—LS, *ibid.*, RG 94, ACP, P629 CB 1867. On the same day, USG endorsed this letter. "Respectfully recommended."—AES, *ibid.*

1867, OCT. 24.   USG endorsement. "Approved for brevet captaincy for Fort Fisher."—ES, DNA, RG 94, ACP, C1027 CB 1863. Written on a letter of Oct. 7 from Vice Admiral David D. Porter, Annapolis, to USG. "Second Lieutenant W. W. Clemens has written to me, requesting testimonials to enable him to obtain the same brevets in the regular army which were conferred on him in the volunteer Service. Mr. Clemens was under my command as Signal officer, in the North Atlantic Squadron, and acquitted himself with so much credit there, especially during the night attack on Fort Fisher, that I made the most favorable representations of him to the War and Navy Departments. I can say no more than I did then, and I think I said all that any officer could desire. Lieut Clemens is one of the finest young officers I ever met, unexceptionable in every way, and I think he will properly come under the order of the Adjutant General, herewith enclosed. I beg leave to refer you to my previous reports of this young officer, now on file in the Navy and War Departments."—LS, *ibid.*

1867, OCT. 24.   USG endorsement. "Respectfully recommended."—AES, DNA, RG 94, ACP, M1290 CB 1867. Written on a letter of Oct. 19 from Benjamin MacKall, Washington, D. C., to USG. "I have the honor to apply for an appointment. as Second Lieutenant in the United. States. Army."—LS, *ibid.* On Oct. 24, USG wrote to Bvt. Brig. Gen. John C. Kelton, AGO. "If appointment has not been sent to Mr. MacKall yet withhold is for further orders."—ALS, *ibid.*

1867, OCT. 24.   USG order. "At the request of the New York Sub-Marine Company, permission is hereby granted to the said Company to establish on Sandy Hook, New York Harbor, a station for the purpose of facilitating the saving of life and property from the dangers of the sea, at the spot or place designated by the report of the Chief of Engineers, dated 23d April, 1867, and subject to the following conditions, to wit:— . . ."—DS, DNA, RG 77, Letters Received. On Oct. 15, Samuel Samuels, New York City, had written to USG. "This company applied to the late secretary of war, for a life saving and wrecking station on Sandy Hook. The application was approved by him and referred to General Humphreys and by him to General Newton, who was to locate a position for us and to report, which we believe was favorable, and will be found on file. As the season is now rapidly advancing when life and property will be in great peril, we beg that early action may be taken in the matter."—ALS, *ibid.*, RG 107, Letters Received, N58 1867. On Sept. 3, U.S. Senator Zachariah Chandler of

Mich., Detroit, had written to USG. "Will Genl Grant be kind Enough to issue the order promised to Capt Samuel by Sy Stanton. You may recollect Capt S as the Man who Sailed the Yacht Henretta in the great race. I introduced him to you in Washington. He is a good Fellow & the is no possible objection to his project"—ALS, *ibid.*

1867, OCT. 24.   Bvt. Maj. Gen. Daniel H. Rucker, act. q. m. gen., to USG. "I have the honor to report that there are now in the possession of the Depot Quartermaster in this City two horses, claimed by Mr. Edgar T. Welles as the private property of his father, the Secretary of the Navy. It appears from the papers in the case, herewith enclosed, that early in 1865 Admiral Porter, U. S. N., shipped to the Secretary of the Navy three horses, which, it is stated, were taken at Fort Monroe, Va., by the U. S. forces used for army purposes. One of these horses, it appears, was subsequently delivered to the Navy Department by Gen. Rucker, then Depot Quartermaster. The remaining two could not be found; and the Secretary of War, July 8, 1865, directed the Quartermaster General to ascertain what had become of the horses, and to turn them over, if found, or have them accounted for by the responsible party. Subsequent inquiry failed to discover the whereabout of the horses, or that they had ever been accounted for; and the Quartermaster General thought they should be replaced from the stock on hand at Washington. No *written* order appears to have been given to turn said two horses to the Navy Department, as suggested by the Quartermaster General, to replace the two thus taken and used by the army. It does appear, however, that two horses were turned over to Secretary Welles from the Gisboro' Depot—by what authority is not known—and that the officer responsible for them considered them simply as a loan, and retained them on his papers. These animals have, since their transfer from the Gisboro' Depot for the use of Secretary Welles, been fed and groomed as public property, and are yet retained as such on the papers of the Depot Quartermaster. The transfer of the horses, and their use by Secretary Welles while they were kept and cared for at public expense, seems to have been irregular and unauthorized. In view of these facts, the Acting Quartermaster General does not feel at liberty to direct that these horses be delivered to Secretary Welles, but respectfully submits the case to the Secretary of War for his instructions."—LS, DNA, RG 92, Reports to the Secretary of War (Press). On Oct. 25, Bvt. Brig. Gen. Frederick T. Dent endorsed this letter. "Respectfully returned to the Quarter Master General. If the Hon. Secy of the Navy has a claim against the U. S. for private property taken for and used in the public service it must be presented and considered in the usual manner   The Secy of War ad int does not feel authorized to order the transfer of the public animals referred to within."—Copy, *ibid.*, RG 107, Orders and Endorsements.

1867, OCT. 24.   Joseph S. Wilson, commissioner, General Land Office, to USG. "I have the honor to inclose copy of a letter from Wm S. Smith Esqr

President of the International Ocean Telegraph Company dated New York Oct 16. 1867 applying for the information as to the steps necessary to be taken by the Company in order to acquire a title to the land on which buildings of Fort Delaney, near the mouth of Carloosahatchie River, Florida, are situated. As the land in question does not appear to have been surveyed by this Office, nor is there any evidence here of the Reservation for Military purposes at Fort Delaney, some buildings of which the writer states as having been sold by the United States to persons of whom the Company has purchased and now desires to buy the land upon which said buildings stand, it is supposed that if any sale of the buildings has been made it must have been by War Department under the provisions of an act of Congress authorizing sale of certain Military sites by War Department, approved March 3. 1819. U. S. Statutes at Large Vol 3 page 520. In order to enable this office to properly respond to the application made to purchase the land referred to I respectfully request to be informed of the condition of Fort Delaney, whether it has ever been formally reserved by competent authority for military purposes, if so when and its present status, in case it has been discontinued and abandoned by War Department whether the land formerly occupied by the Fort has been placed under the control of this Office under provision of an act of Congress approved Augt 18. 1856. Statutes at Large Vol 11. page 87."—LS, DNA, RG 107, Letters Received from Bureaus. The enclosure is *ibid.*

1867, OCT. 25.   Judge Advocate Gen. Joseph Holt to USG. "In July 1864 *William Cawfield, private 16th Vol Ky. Cavalry,* was tried by General Court Martial, and convicted and sentenced to death for the murder of Sergeant Berry, one of his comrades in arms. On the recommendation of General Schofield and Judge Advocate Burnett, who tried the case, this sentence was commuted to confinement at hard labor in the penitentiary for five years. A number of officers of the regiment to which the prisoner belonged and also of the 12th Ky. Vols., now apply to the President for his pardon on the ground that he has suffered enough—about three years confinement—for the crime of which he was found guilty. No attempt is made to deny his guilt, or to palliate it, except by the suggestion that 'the man slain was known as a coward and thief and so regarded' and had stolen the prisoner's money. The recommendation of Genl. Schofield and Major Burnett seems to have proceeded upon the belief that the evidence did not clearly show such malice aforethought as would constitute the homicide a murder. This view must have been entertained from a lack of comprehension of the full significance of the prisoner's words at the moment of firing the fatal shot. It was proved in the trial that just before the shot and while the prisoner was pointing his gun towards the deceased, he said to him, 'this is the second time you have had your hand in my pocket.' The import of this declaration finds a complete explanation in the petition of the officers referred to, addressed to the President, the language of which is as follows: 'About two months before the killing he (the deceased) had stolen part the money of said Cawfield, which he got back from him, and then told him if he ever stole his money again he would shoot him. A day or two before the killing he had received his wages and Berry knew it, and contrived in the night time while Cawfield was asleep to steal from him $130—which was found under his bed after his death. They occupied the same tent and Cawfield knew he had his money—and true to his word he forthwith did shoot and kill said Berry. Upon his trial he made no denial but quietly submitted to his fate.' This information, so frankly communicated, was no doubt furnished by the prisoner. The hiatus in the testimony, as given on the trial, is thus satisfactorily supplied. It now appears that the element of malice—for want of distinct proof of which the death sentence was commuted—was in fact present in the crime. Not only is the malice prepense avowed and set forth in the details of its history, but it is alleged that the deceased was deliberately killed in the execution of a previous threat. It may be added that the deceased, at the time he was murdered, was unarmed and unresisting; was begging the prisoner not to turn his gun towards him, and was endeavoring to dodge behind a tree to avoid the apprehended shot. The prisoner is therefore, in the fullest sense of the term, a murderer, and should have been punished as such. The petty theft, which the deceased is alleged to have committed, was an offense for which the law provided an adequate punishment, and it neither justified or palliated in the slightest degree, the taking of his life by the prisoner. It is recommended that the sentence as commuted be rigidly enforced. A copy of the original review of the record by this Bureau is herewith exhibited."— Copy, DNA, RG 153, Letters Sent.

1867, OCT. 25. Robert S. Wilson, Mill Point, Canada, to USG. "Although I have not the honor of being personally known to you, your high character for courtesy, induces me to hope you will excuse my troubling you, being a stranger in this country, & believing I am more likely to obtain the information I seek from you than any other. Previous to the Revolutionary War, a relative of mine, by name Ezekiel McComb, held the situation of Secretary to Sir Geoffrey Amherst, then I believe, Governor of the State of New York—I have a very interesting letter in my possession from that Ezekiel McComb addressed to my Grandfather (his uncle) Robert Wilson Merchant of Belfast, Ireland. he mentions in it a relative of his of the name of Stocton I presume a Brother inlaw—I am anxious to trace if any of his descendants are living and lately being reading Dr Russells letters to the 'Times' Newspaper of London, written during the late unhappy Rebellion in the *South*, in which he mentions meeting a *Genl McComb*, it struck me as a possibility that Genl McComb might be a descendant of the relative I allude to—from the style of the letter he must have been a person of respectable position & education—Might I take the liberty of asking, as you must be well acquainted with Genl McComb, of enquiring from him if my surmise is correct, or if he knows any thing of the party I allude to—I am well aware of your numerous avocations but perhaps you may be able to devote a few moments to *benevolence*, & obtain for me this information—All my family pretty nearly, have been in either Army or Navy for many generations, in the *British Service.* I lately took the liberty of writing to Genl Michel late Commander of the Forces in Canada respecting on only hunch, a retired Major, from whom I had not heard for nearly 20 years & I received a most courteous reply, & every information in his power to give. May I hope the honor of a reply & once more apologising for the intrusion, . . ."—ALS, DNA, RG 94, Letters Received, 791W 1867.

1867, OCT. 26. Bvt. Maj. Gen. John M. Schofield, Richmond, to USG. "Sufficient returns have been recd to show that a large vote has been polled with a decided majority for the Convention, Considering the exciting character of the contest remarkably good order prevailed throughout the State during the Election"—Telegrams received (2—at 11:35 A.M.), DNA, RG 107, Telegrams Collected (Bound); *ibid.*, RG 108, Telegrams Received; copies, *ibid.*, RG 393, 1st Military District, Telegrams Sent; DLC-USG, V, 55. On Dec. 13, Schofield reported the results of registration in the 1st Military District.—Copy, DNA, RG 108, Register of Letters Received.

1867, OCT. 27. Albert H. French, Concordia Ranch, Tex., to USG. "*Private* . . . The matter of the destruction of Fort Bliss by the river—& the offer of Concordia—has—or perhaps will come before you. Congress has I believe decided not to expend anything more at present in any of the southern states until they are reconstructed. Your influence would make in this an exception. I came here with Gen Carleton—was Capt—in the 1st Cala. Cavalry—Can refer to the Gen—or any Army Officer in NMexico as—to my record—have assisted to reconstruct this County of ElPaso, it is reconstructed—and *far distant from* the troubles of the state proper—& near New Mexico. Concordia is all I have. I belong in the state of Vermont and desire to take my family there, The result of the sale of Concordia would release me from my liabilities—and—place me in good Circumstances at home. As Concordia has been indorsed by all as a proper place to remove Fort Bliss; the property of a loyal man—and as it has been offered at a reasonable price, I beg of you to give it a favorable consideration. Excuse my pretention to address you on this subject—but I am sure you will listen as soon to a petition from this far off land as from a nearer point, . . ."—ALS, DNA, RG 107, Letters Received, F165 1867.

1867, OCT. 28. Cheme M. Levy, New York City, to USG. "I now beg leave to apply to you for my Commission as Capt A Q M having been nominated by President Lincoln on the 18th January 1864 and confirmed by the senate on 18th July 1864. I have applied by *letter* and *personally* to Hon E M Stanton for my Commission which he has refused me on account of some personal pique. I now at the suggestion of several of my military friends asks you to my commission made out and allow me to get an honorable discharge. I beg leave to refer you to Senator Pomeroy who is familar with every point connected with my case."—ALS, DNA, RG 94, ACP, L420 CB 1864. On Nov. 22, Judge Advocate Gen. Joseph Holt endorsed papers concerning this matter. "Respectfully returned to the Secretary of War, with expression of opinion that, when the sentence of dismissal of an officer is accompanied by disqualification from ever holding any office of trust or emolument under the United States, the disability so imposed, can only be removed, ~~can be only removed~~ by a formal pardon by the Executive. His appointment to a position by the President, cannot, it is conceived, be held to work a pardon by implication, as in the case of a reappointment of an officer who has simply been dismissed."—Copies, *ibid.*; *ibid.*, RG 153, Letters Sent.

1867, OCT. 28.   Samuel V. Niles, Washington, D. C., to USG. "I have the honor to invite your attention to the following facts: On the 6th of June, 1865, I filed in the office of the Chief of Ordnance, the claim of *Charles Spencer* of St Louis, Mo, for $5000, being for the value of an ordnance, or amory boat purchased from him by Capt W, F, Brink, acting ordnance officer of the district of Cairo, Illinois, and said boat was used on the Tennessee River, and was destroyed during a storm, March 20, 1862. The claim was ap approved by the chief of ordnance, June 16, 1865, for $4996, and sent to the 2nd Auditor, of the Treasury Dept, for settlement, who sent it to the 2nd Comptroller, and by him sent to the War Dept, where Mr C. A. Dana, Asst. Secretary of War, who had been chairman of the Claims Commission, sitting at Cairo, Ills, alleged that Mr Spencer had been paid for the boat, and recommended the prosecution of the claimant for an attempt at fraud upon the government! The papers in the case were forwarded to the U. S. District Attorney, at St Louis, Mo, and the case laid before the Grand Jury, which it is stated indicted Mr Spencer; but subsequently, upon the presentation of evidence proving the legality of the claim, the proceedings against Mr. Spencer, were withdrawn, and on the 21st of Dec, 1865, I filed in the office of the 2nd Comptroller, an official copy of an order of the U S District Court, to the effect that proceedings in the case had been withdrawn, and the papers were referred to the 'Claims Commission,' and Gen'l David Hunter informed me a short time ago that the claim had been allowed. As you have certified yourself that the claim was a just one, as the claimant is of undoubted loyalty, and in view of of the long delay to which Mr Spencer has been subjected, I respectfully ask that you will take up the case and dispose of it at your earliest convenience."—LS, DNA, RG 107, Letters Received, N122 1867.

1867, OCT. 29, 10:35 A.M.   To Charles H. Rogers, New York City. "Tell Mrs Rodgers she need not get for Mrs. Grant the articles she left word for. If already bought all right."—ALS (telegram sent), DNA, RG 107, Telegrams Collected (Bound). On Oct. 30, Wednesday, Rogers, Ravenswood, N. Y., wrote to Mrs. Elihu B. Washburne. ". . . Genl. Rawlins is said to have gone to Washington, passing Genl. Grant, who with Mrs. G—~~were~~

favoured us with a short visit, having arrived on Sunday evening from West Point: and left on Monday evening for home—. . ."—ALS, DLC-Elihu B. Washburne.

1867, OCT. 30. USG endorsement. "Respectfully forwarded to the President of the US."—ES, DLC-Andrew Johnson. Written on papers concerning the court-martial of Frank Ewing, civilian, accused of stating before a registration board at Newton, Miss.: ". . . 'If I had it in my power I would blow the whole of the United States Government to hell. This registration is a God damned humbug, and no true or honest Southern man could or would take that iron-clad oath,' . . . 'There is only one thing I would rather do than see you in the cotton field as a slave, and that I will do the first opportunity,' . . ."—Copy, *ibid.*

1867, OCT. 31. USG endorsement. "The Act. Sec. of War respectfully refers this to the P. M. Gn."—AE, DNA, RG 99, Letters Received. Written on a letter of Oct. 26 from Francis de Freitas, New York City, to Secretary of State William H. Seward. "As the Secretary of State I Respectfully address you, and do so with confidence from the fact of your known man attachment to the soldier who have put down the Great Rebllion—and also your known determination that justice shall be done to the most of the citiyons of the United States over whom you are the sworn Guardian For my character I Respectffully refer you to Mr Hatch Secretary of the State Illinois to Hon S. M. Cullom and to Hon John J. Weed to all of whom I am familiarly known. The object of my now addressing you, is to ask your favorable interposition in my behalf, under the following cercumstances which I claim is the case of the *most cruel opp0rission which has been meted out to any other cityon of the United States* a[nd do] not believe that you will *stand idly* by without protesting I was Orderly to General R. P. Buckland 3rd Division 15 Army Corps and other eminent Generals—with the responsible and dangerous duty of carrying Despatches—was wounded by a ball through breast taken out from my back, THE MOST DANGEROUS WOUND RECEIVED BY ANY ONE THROUGH THE WHOLE WAR, IT BEING ALMOST IMPOSSIBLE TO SURVIVE—and in addition a very dangerous wound by a pice of shell in my forehead—was captured by Rebels and in prison six months with heavy weight and chain—and sentenced to be shot, but ascaped at Richmond and what has been the action of the Governemt towards me for going through such Measureless Unspeakable and Illimilable Misery and Suffering to promote their interest? Answer. They have not paid me my common back monthly pay to the amount of $382 dollars *not gratuty* and deilayd for nearly three Long years I have had to work for them and find myself. Under such cercumstances of oppression far beyound that of the worst despot in the world, I entreat and beg of you to interpose your enfluence and address the President in aid of an Application which I sent him and which I am certain will be totally unheaded without your urging that monthly pay be instantly paid to me. For so doing your kindness and nobleness will be remembered with utmost warmth of gratituede by [me an]d by my numerous friends in Illinois inclusive of many Most distingushed Officers in the War, to our latest breath."—ALS, *ibid.* On Sept. 13, de Freitas had written to USG. "I have not yet received neather my back pay or my bounty and its is now over two years since I life the Hospital Jefferson Barricks Massouri. Please cause them to take up my case as I should like to go home in Europe. I have never got will of the wound through my breast and now should like to go home as I may never get well as I use to be—Hoping you will never forget your soldeir boys"— ALS, *ibid.* On Oct. 23, de Freitas wrote to USG. "General R. P. Buckland informed me by letter that he wrote to the Sec of War and enclosed three affidavits in referense to my case—Please have them looked up and the answer sent as he requested a[s] soon as possible—"—ALS, *ibid.* On Oct. 30, de Freitas wrote to USG. "I wrote you a few days since and respectfully requested a copy of the report made by the Paymaster against my claim for back pay and bounty—and also requested the answer to the affadavits which Genel R. P. Buckland (now M. C.) sent to the Secretary of War—but no answer to the above as yet reached me. General Buckland informs me that he will be in Washington about the 20 of Nov and I should like to have a copy of the report made by the Paymaster against my claim to send to him, as he will lay my case before the investigation committee which was appointed last sesson to investigation the Paymasters Generals Dept   Hoping you will cause a copy of the Report and answer to General Buckland letter to be sent to me immediately . . . I am sorry that you lift the city so soon when I called at the Hote you had gone"—ALS, *ibid.*

1867, OCT. 31.   William L. Burt, Boston, to USG. "Gov Andrew died at his house last evening at six (6) oclock. He was unconcious from the time of the attack the evening before. His family were all with him"—Telegram received (at 11:00 A.M.), DNA, RG 107, Telegrams Collected (Bound).

1867, OCT. 31.   F. U. Stitt, act. chief clerk, attorney gen. office, to USG. "I am directed by the Attorney General to transmit to you for your information, a copy of a letter received to-day from William Dorsheimer, U. S. Attorney for the Northern District of New York, in regard to the defense of certain soldiers indicted for murder at Plattsburgh, Clinton County, New York in the month of March last."—LS, DNA, RG 107, Letters Received from Bureaus. The enclosure is *ibid.* On Dec. 16, Attorney Gen. Henry Stanbery wrote to USG. "I have the honor to transmit herewith a copy of a letter from Wm Dorsheimer, U. S. Attorney for the Northern District of New York, enclosing the accounts of Messrs Stetson & Gay, Counsellors at Law, for services in the defence of Six soldiers indicted for murder at Plattsburgh, in March, 1867. Mr. Dorsheimer was authorized by this Office to employ special counsel in these cases under the approval of the Secretary of War, dated June 5, 1867."—Copy, *ibid.*, RG 60, Letters Sent.

1867, OCT. 31. U.S. Senator Henry Wilson of Mass., Hartford, to USG. "If possible please telegraph to Lieut M. C. Wilkinson forty second (42) Infantry now at Hartford Conn thirty (30) days leave of absence for special service"—Telegram received (on Nov. 1, 8:40 A.M.), DNA, RG 94, Letters Received, 808W 1867; *ibid.*, RG 107, Telegrams Collected (Bound). On Nov. 6, Wilson, Natick, Mass., wrote to USG. "*Private* . . . I met at the Young Mens State Convention of Christian Associations of Connecticut Lt Wilkinson now stationed at Sackett's Harbor. He was stationed in Hartford some time ago, had great influence there and the Christian Young Men of that city want to get a leave for him for 30 days if you can give it. If you can do so I hope you will do it for he can do great good there."—ALS, *ibid.*, RG 94, Letters Received, 808W 1867.

1867, [OCT.]. USG endorsement. "Refer to J. A. Gn."—AE (initialed), DNA, RG 107, Letters Received, P321 1867. Written on a letter of Oct. 26 from Gideon J. Pillow, Helena, Ark., to USG. "In 1862—When General Curtis occupied this place with an Army, he caused to be taken from my Plantations in this neighbourhood, about 200 very fine mules which belonged to me, and were private property. No steps were ever taken to confiscate or to change the right of property in the mules during the war. In Nov. 1865, after I was Pardoned by the President, I received information that my mules, were still held by the Government & were in the possession of the Quarter Master in St Louis. The Presidents Pardon, by express terms, restores to me all my rights of Property—(except to slaves & such articles—(if any)—as might have been sold under the Confiscation Law, by the judgement of a Court of Competent Jurisdiction. No Decree was ever rendered against me for the Confiscation of any thing I owned. Being satisfied under these facts, that I was clearly entitled to have my mules restored to me, I visited St. Louis, and applied to Genl Shurman to restore to me the mules. He promptly DECIDED that I was entitled the mules, & said they should be restored. He however, referred the application to his Quarter Master General,—for his opinion—The Quarter Master endorsed upon the application—that the right was clear, and that in his opinion, the mules ought to be restored. Upon the return of the application to General Shurman, he said 'I should have the mules'; but he thought it was best to Telegraph Mr Stanton,—the then Secretary of War, for permission to restore them—Upon my expressing doubts about getting the mules, if the matter was referred to the Secretary,—General Shurman, said the *matter* was *too clear*—that the Government could *not refuse* without *dishonoring itself.* General Shurman did Telegraph the Secretary, as I was informed, but I did not see him anymore, and was informed by an officer of his Staff, that he was sick, I remained at St Louis 2 or 3 days, and until I was informed by the staff officer above referred to, that the Secretary of War, had refused to permit the mules to be delivered to me—Thus the matter Still rests. The mules referred to were known to the officers of the Q. M. Department & to very many citizens of St Louis, and to many Freedmen (my former slaves)—who were then in the city, to be my mules. I could at that time, without difficulty have identified them—I do not know what has since been done with them, but I can still clearly prove, that they were taken from my Plantations by Orders of Genl. Curtis,—& General Shurman will confirm all my representations in regard to himself & his action. ~~Considering the matter of rights~~ Considering the rights too clear, even for the existance of a doubt,—and being satisfied that my application was never properly laid before the Secretary of War, or the President, and was never duly *Considered* by either, I make this application to you General—as acting Secretary of War—to have me *righted* & *justice* done in the premises Surely a great Government, will not do an act of *manifest injustice*, by witholding a *right*, from a citizen, because it has the powe[r]? You are familiar General with my past History and with my services to the Government during the Mexican War. It is known to all those who knew me,—that I was opposed to all those measures, which produced our late unhappy war, and used all my influence, to avert them, until war actually existed As a Soldier I know and admire you—As a man and statesman I confide in your sense of right and judgement, and I now appeal to you, as my last effort—to see me righted.—I am now, after a great but fruitless effort to restore my great losses by the War, living in *Poverty*—with a wife & nine children—7 of whom are daughters & five unmarried. At my time of life, and with so *large* and *helpless* a *Family* I cannot hope ever to better my condition. May I not General ask of you, as a personal favour to an old companion in arms, to answer this communication, & to take measures as will restore to me this right"—ALS, *ibid.* On Nov. 4, Judge Advocate Gen. Joseph Holt recommended the request be denied because Pillow "took an active part in support of the rebellion" and advised a claim be sent to Congress.—ES, *ibid.* See *HRC*, 43-1-677.

1867, [Oct.].   USG note. "Otis S Dimmick, Cavalry recruit. Order him before board for examination for 2d Lt. . . . Address Carlisle Bks Pa"—AN (initialed), DNA, RG 94, ACP, D581 CB 1867.

1867, Nov. 2.   To Secretary of the Interior Orville H. Browning. "In compliance with the request contained in your letter of the 14th of August, I transmit, herewith, lists of employés of this Department with other information for the Biennial Register. The necessary information ~~has not been received~~ from the Freedmens Bureau has not been recd. as soon as it reaches me, I will forward it to your Department."—Copy, DNA, RG 107, Letters Received from Bureaus. On Aug. 14, Browning had written to USG. "I have to call your attention to the Joint Resolutions of Congress approved April 27th 1816. and July 14th 1832, and to the proviso to the appropriation of March 3d 1851, for compiling, printing and binding the Biennial Register for 1867. (See Vols. 3. p. 342.—4-608.9-600) and to request that you will as soon as practicable after the 30th of September next, furnish this Department with as much of the information therein directed to

be inserted in the Register as relates to your Department."—LS, *ibid.* On
Oct. 2, Bvt. Maj. Gen. Daniel H. Rucker, act. q. m. gen., wrote to USG
transmitting a list of employees.—LS, *ibid.*, RG 92, Reports to the Secretary of War (Press). The enclosure is *ibid.* On Nov. 7, USG wrote to
Browning. "I have the honor to transmit herewith copy of letter of the
Quartermaster General of the Army of the 5th instant, inquiring when the
lists for the Biennial Register for 1867 will be required, and to request that
you will furnish this Department with the desired information."—Copy,
ibid., Letters Received from Depts. and Bureaus. The enclosure is *ibid.*
On Nov. 9, Browning wrote to USG. "I have received your letter of the
7th inst., inclosing a copy of a letter from the Quarter Master General's
office in relation to the Biennial Register, and in reply have the honor to
say, that while it is desirable to have the matter for the Register in the
printer's hands as soon as practicable, it is far more important that the
information contained therein should be complete, and the lists referred to
in Gen. Thomas' letter can be retained in his office as long as may be necessary to secure such completeness."—LS, *ibid.* On Nov. 27, Rucker wrote to
USG concerning the lists.—LS, *ibid.*, Reports to the Secretary of War
(Press). On Jan. 7, 1868, Browning wrote to USG requesting additional
lists.—LS, *ibid.*, RG 107, Letters Received from Bureaus.

1867, Nov. 2.   John Binny, New York City, to USG. "I send you Copy of
a letter forwarded this day to Mr Colfax, treating on the political situation.
I believe it lays down clearly the best mode of extricating the Republican
party from their present difficulties.—The late elections, demonstrate clearly
that the views of the extreme Radicals must be abandoned and that the
judicious Republicans should step forward again and control the work of
the Congress as they have done for the past eighteen months.—I believe
Providence will guide the nation safely through its present trials & perplexities"—ALS, DNA, RG 108, Letters Received. The enclosure is *ibid.*

1867, Nov. 3.   Lt. Gen. William T. Sherman, St. Louis, to USG. "At the
request of Mrs Curran Pope of Louisville Kentucky I write you in favor of
her nephew Mr Edward Tyler who is an applicant for a vacancy in the
Regular Army. I do not know the applicant, but suppose he will lay before
you his full history and claims. For Mrs Pope I know you and I should do
all that we can consistently with the interests of the Service. Her husband
was *I know* one of the best men of Kentucky, an old Graduate, and a very
refined Gentleman. Instantly on the breaking out of the Civil War, he resumed his Military Profession, raised a Regimt and served with it all the
time till he had to Succumb to wounds and death. No man ever gave up a
life with higher motives. Mrs Pope his widow still resides in Louisville,
and there is no request she can make of me that I will not fully consider. I
write this hastily as I am on the point of starting today for Omaha, and the
Plains."—ALS, DNA, RG 94, ACP, T523 CB 1867. See *ibid.*, T537 CB
1867.

1867, Nov. 4. Bvt. Brig. Gen. John C. Kelton, AGO, to USG. "I have the honor to submit the names of several persons appointed in the Army July 15, 1867, and previous thereto, who have either not accepted the appointment or have failed to appear for examination. As they have held appointments three months & a half without complying with their instructions, to the disadvantage of the service and to meritorious applicants for positions in the Army, it is respectfully suggested that their appointments be cancelled. Should any of these persons make satisfactory explanation of their delay they can receive new appointments."—LS, DNA, RG 94, ACP, W1065 CB 1867. The enclosures are *ibid.*

1867, Nov. 4. James C. Burbank, Chamber of Commerce, St. Paul, to USG. "The commercial and mercantile interests of the State of Minnesota and especially of the city of Saint Paul are deeply interested in the trade of the Government which legitimately belongs to this Military Department, it becomes the duty of this Chamber to make known to you that it will make known to you that it will make a saving to the Government to buy the supplies and material that is required by this Military Department, in Minnesota. The subsistence required is produced in this State and all other material can be furnished as cheaply here as at any other point in the United States, taking into account the additional expense of transportation. The mercantile and commercial interests of Minnesota can compete with the States of Illinois, Missouri or Iowa, and it is but a matter of justice that this State should receive the trade of this Military Department therefore we most earnestly request that the Secretary of War will issue an order directing the officers in the Military Department of Dakota to buy all supplies in the State of Minnesota when it is for the interest of the Government to do so."—LS, DNA, RG 107, Letters Received, R242 1867. On Dec. 26, Bvt. Maj. Gen. Daniel H. Rucker, act. q. m. gen., wrote to USG, and, on Dec. 27, Bvt. Maj. Gen. Amos B. Eaton, commissary gen., wrote to USG that preference was already given to local purchase.—LS, *ibid.*

1867, Nov. 4. Mrs. George H. Walker, Milwaukee, to USG. "As the Widow of the late Col Geo H Walker whom I doubt not you may recollect his accompanig you from Milwaukee to Chicago, and having had the pleasure myself of an introduction to you, I take the liberty of addressing you on a subject which is of great moment to me, now in my embarsed situation   When my husband was in Washington Sept 1866 he left with Genl E M Stanton a Claim for the Rent of Camp Reno which was used by the U S. Troops for two years I think from '62 to '64. The rent I believe amounting to five hundred dollars not quite sure as *I* never saw the claim, Genl S. presented it and in the mean time my beloved husband was taken from me, very suddenly, by death in the 20th Sept. Several papers have been transmitted to me which had to be made out, and questions answered by A G Miller U S. Judge and signed by two witnesses also certificate of my marraige etc all of which was done as directed. On the 9th of April last

I received notice it had been presented to the Claims Commission and stood No 918. Since which time I have heard nothing. It is a very small amount for Goverment but it is *justly* my due as tho it were so many thousands. Now Sir if thro your kindness or influence I could obtain it I should be forever very great ful to you, And may I ask your pardon for troubling you and be sure you would receive a widows most sincere thanks. I donot ask this as a favor from Goverment but really my due"—ALS, DNA, RG 107, Letters Received, W428 1866. On Nov. 7, Postmaster Gen. Alexander W. Randall wrote to USG. "The enclosed letter is from Mrs Col. Walker of Milwaukie Wisconsin. I think you knew him—(Col Walker)—Mrs Walker has been left destitute and is a most deserving woman. I know nothing about the claim she speaks of but venture to call your attention to it, as I do not know to what Bureau it should properly go—"—ALS, *ibid.* The enclosure is *ibid.* On Nov. 22, U.S. Representative Halbert E. Paine of Wis., Washington, D. C., wrote to USG. "I have the honor to apply to you for information respecting the claim referred to in the enclosed letter of Mrs Geo H Walker of Milwaukee for use of Camp Reno."—LS, *ibid.*

1867, Nov. 5.   USG endorsement. "Refered to Gen. Canby—for remark with the statement however that complaints from unreconstructed disloyal men is becoming so frequent that their cry is begining to be like that of the 'Boy & the Wolf.' Lest the Wolf may appear however this will receive notice"—AES (undated), DLC-Andrew Johnson; copy, DNA, RG 108, Register of Letters Received. Written on a letter of Oct. 23 from Governor Jonathan Worth of N. C. to President Andrew Johnson. "I do not know whether you interfere in any way with the action of Military Commandants. If not, this Communication will be useless except as a matter of personal information. A practice has prevailed in this State and still prevails, of having citizens arrested and imprisoned by Military authority upon charges often made by persons of bad character, the charges and the names of the persons preferring them, being Concealed from the party arrested. Several arrests have been made in this State and the accused transported to distant places of confinement, and detained as prisoners for months without preliminary trial, or notice of the cause of imprisonment. I have earnestly remonstrated against the iniquity of such proceeding to Gen'l Sickles and Genl Canby. To day I am informed that the Sheriff of Caswell Mr Jesse C. Griffith, a man of exemplary character, personal and political, has been arrested and carried a prisoner to Charleston, for some unknown charge preferred by one Wm Johnson, and one Tourgee, both of them men of the most detestable moral character. No form of Military Despotism can be more terrible to the orderly citizen than these summary arrests and imprisonments in Parts, distant from the homes of the parties arrested without preliminary trial. It gives mean partizan malevolence a feast, without fear of molestation"—ALS, DLC-Andrew Johnson. On Nov. 14, Bvt. Maj. Gen. Edward R. S. Canby, Charleston, submitted a report to Bvt. Maj. Gen. John A. Rawlins.—LS, *ibid.*

1867, Nov. 5.   Bvt. Maj. Gen. Christopher C. Augur endorsement. "Respectfully returned to Headqrs. of the Army. Fort D. A. Russell is but two miles from the city of Cheyenne and has one trader already. There is no occasion for another and I do not desire to have another appointed."—ES, DNA, RG 108, Letters Received. Written on a letter of Oct. 15 from Ross Cunningham, Washington, D. C., to USG. "With your permission I beg to present myself to you as an applicant for appointment of Trader at Fort D. A. Russell, D. T. Dept of the Platte, under recent Act of Congress Feeling that my knowledge and personal experience of camp and garrison life and the requirements of a military post on the Plains—will enable me to fulfill the duties &c. &c. I was connected with the Army of the Potomac from the commencement of its operations to suppress the rebellion and so remained till May 1863—when I entered the Headquarters of the Army as Clerk—where I am so still employed—and do respectfully refer to Genl Jno. C. Kelton, AAG. War Dept., as to my record and experience, and to the truth of the foregoing"—ALS, *ibid.* Cunningham enclosed a letter of recommendation of Oct. 16 from Bvt. Brig. Gen. John C. Kelton, AGO, to USG.—ALS, *ibid.*

1867, Nov. 5.   Bvt. Maj. Gen. John Pope, Atlanta, to USG. "I have only been delaying a re-trial of Capt Schaff until Yellow fever subsides in Mobile. Election in this state passed off without any disturbance whatever. Large majority for Convention & heavy white vote cast in middle & Northern Georgia"—Telegram received (at 11:40 A.M.), DNA, RG 107, Telegrams Collected (Bound); *ibid.*, RG 108, Telegrams Received; copy, DLC-USG, V, 55. On the same day, Pope wrote to USG. "I have the honor to acknowledge the receipt of communications to the President of the United States from Colonel C. J. Biddle, W. C. Patterson and Honorable S. J. Randall of Philadelphia concerning the case of Captain Schaff, Ordnance Department. U. S. Army   As I have hitherto reported to you Captain Schaff was arraigned and tried for shooting Colonel Shephard, immediately after the occurrence took place.—It was at the time supposed that the wound inflicted upon Colonel Shephard was a trifling one, and the charges preferred against Captain Schaff upon which he was tried were based on that belief.—The case was a very bad one, even under those circumstances and the sentence of the Court was therefore disapproved by me on account of its leniency and the Court ordered to re-assemble.—Subsequently Mr Shephard died, in consequence, it is alleged, of a surgical operation against which his physician had advised.—The reassembling of the Court has been delayed in consequence of the prevalence of Yellow fever at Mobile but will assemble in that city as soon as the Epidemic abates and proceed to the trial of Captain Schaff upon additional charges found necessary in consequence of the death of Mr Shephard.—The Civil authorities of Alabama have never applied to me for the person of Captain Schaff for trial before the Civil Courts nor should I surrender his person to them in the present state of excitement in Mobile, as I do not believe a fair trial could be had.—I expect the Court to assemble in the course of two weeks, but have been unwilling to send the necessary officers to constitute a Court to Mobile whilst Yellow fever was prevailing to an alarming extent in that City.—"—LS, DNA, RG 108, Letters Received.

1867, Nov. 6.   To Secretary of the Treasury Hugh McCulloch. "I have the honor to transmit herewith a letter of the Surgeon-General of the Army, dated the 5th instant, addressed to yourself,—respecting the prompt delivery of books and instruments to be imported for the Medical Department,— with the approval of this Department endorsed upon the same."—LS, DNA, RG 56, Letters Received from the War Dept. The enclosure is *ibid.* On Nov. 14, McCulloch wrote to USG. "I have the honor to acknowledge the receipt of your letter dated the 6th instant, covering the letter approved by you, of the Surgeon General of the United States Army, addressed to this Department under date of the 5th instant wherein the free entry is requested of certain Books and Instruments expected to arrive at the Port of New York every two or three weeks during the coming year, addressed to 'General Satterlee, Chief Medical Purveyor United States Army, New York City for the Surgeon General's Office.' It appears that the articles referred to are wanted for immediate use one arrival, that the request is made to avoid any possible delay and only in anticipation of the Special authority of this Department and with the understanding that duties are to be paid unless such special authority be obtained. The Department perceives no objection thereto, and the Collector at New York has this day been instructed accordingly."—Copy, *ibid.,* Letters Sent. On Aug. 29, Sept. 4, 27, Nov. 2, 18, 27, Dec. 12, 1867, and Jan. 7, 1868, USG wrote to McCulloch requesting that items addressed to Bvt. Brig. Gen. Richard S. Satterlee, chief medical purveyor, New York City, be delivered duty free.—Copies, *ibid.,* RG 107, Letters Sent to the President.

1867, Nov. 6.   To Secretary of the Treasury Hugh McCulloch. "I have the honor to enclose herewith a certificate of deposit for Five 62/100 dollars, deposited by Capt J. A. Smith, Corps of Engineers, with the Asst Treasurer of the U. S. at Boston, to the credit of the Treasurer of the United States, on account of the appropriation for fortification at entrance of New Bedford Harbor, with request that the amount be covered into the Treasury to the credit of the appropriation named."—Copies, DNA, RG 107, Letters Received from Bureaus; *ibid.,* Letters Sent to the President. On Nov. 5, Brig. Gen. Andrew A. Humphreys, chief of engineers, had written to USG. "I have the honor to transmit herewith the original of a Certificate from the Asst Treasr U. S. at Boston, Mass, dated Nov. 1st 1867, for $5.62/100 deposited by Bt Maj. J. A. Smith. Capt Enginers, to credit of the Treasurer of the US on account of the appropriation for 'Fortifications at entrance to New Bedford Harbor.' "—LS, *ibid.,* Letters Received from Bureaus.

1867, Nov. 6.   USG endorsement. "I join in the application for a clerk-ship in one of the Departments for Capt. Worth."—AES, DNA, RG 59, Applications and Recommendations, Lincoln and Johnson. Written on a letter of Sept. 18 from Bvt. Lt. Col. Wright Rives, military secretary for President Andrew Johnson, to Postmaster Gen. Alexander W. Randall. "The bearer—Mr H. A F Worth late Capt. 6th U S Infantry—is an appli-cant for a position in your Dept—Capt Worth is a graduate of West-Point and served during part of the war—with credit   He was wounded twice during the war—. As I belonged to the same regiment I of course—am well acquainted with him—and can bear testimony of his conduct as an officer and gentleman—I would be pleased to see him receive some appointment suitable to his condition."—ALS, *ibid.*

1867, Nov. 6.   Judge Advocate Gen. Joseph Holt to USG. "Asst Surgeon Mich'l Hillary, U. S. A. was tried at Fort Union, New. Mex. Sept. 4th last, under the following charges: 1. Conduct unbecoming an officer and a gen-tleman. 1. In that, while travelling on duty from Fort Stanton to Fort Sum-ner, N. M. he did take with him and allow to ride in a public ambulance, in which he did also ride, a Mexican woman of ill-fame, knowing her to be such. This between the 3d and 9th days of May, 1867. 2. Habitually occu-pying the same bed with said woman, knowing her to be of ill fame, and this in the presence of the enlisted men of his escort. This between Fort Sumner and Fort Stanton, N. M. between the 3d and 9th days of May, 1867. 3. In habitually eating or messing with said woman, knowing her to be of ill fame; this in presence of the enlisted men of his escort. Same place and date. 4. In sending for and instructing Corp. Kenney, of the 3d Cavy., the accused being then in bed with said woman, and not withdrawing while giving orders to said Corporal. This May 7. 1867. 5. In riding in an open Gov't waggon, in presence of several enlisted men and citizens, with a mexi-can woman of ill-fame, knowing her to be such. May 10. 1867. 1st Ad-ditional charge Conduct unbecoming an officer and a gentleman. 1. In sleeping and lying with Laucana Candellaria, a woman of ill fame, in the presence of several persons, at the Gov't. agency at the bend of the Pecos River, between Hatch's Ranche & Fort Sumner, on the night of the 1st May, last. 2. In transporting in a govt. wagon Laucano Candellaria, a woman of ill fame, and travelling openly with her as his companion. This between Tecolote and Fort Sumner, between the 27th of April and the 4th May, 1867. 3. In speaking of said woman as 'his lady,' with intent to deceive and to represent her as his wife. This at the Gov't agency May 1. 2nd Addi-tional charge. Conduct prejudicial to good order and military discipline. In that, when informed by Corpl. Kenney, 3d Cavy, comm'dg the escort, that his horses were not able to keep up with the accused's ambulance, at the rate he travelled, he did reply, 'Damn gov't horses; I never spare them, and never will;' or words to that effect. This May. 7. 1867. The accused pleaded not guilty to all the specifications & charges   The Court find him not guilty under the 3d spec. of Charge 1, and under the 3d spec. of the 1st addit. charge; guilty under the remaining specifications and under the three charges; and sentence him to be dismissed the service. Four out of the seven members composing the Court subscribe a recommendation to mercy in behalf of the accused, on the ground of his past character, as proven by a certificate in writing from Asst. Surg. E. McClellan, submitted by the accused. This certificate is to the effect that Dr. McClellan had had the accused under his command at Fortress Monroe in 1864 & 1865, and 'had always found his character to be of the highest standard.' Further, that 'when the yellow fever was raging at Newbern, N. C. in 1864, Dr. Hillary was one of that noble band of medical officers who endeavored to stop that fearful epidemic.' He ends by saying: 'I have always found him a gentleman in every sense of the word.' The proceedings, findings, and sentence are approved by Gen. A. J. Smith, commanding Dept. of the Mo., and are forwarded for Executive action. The certificate of Dr. McClellan, on which a part of the Court base their recommendation to clemency, is manifestly so vague as to be of little value as evidence. As proof of what the accused seeks to establish by its means, it is moreover clearly inadmissible. The facts alleged in the specifications are made out by abundant proof. At the Gov't. agency at 'the Bend,' where the accused halted with his escort for the night, he not only speaks of the woman with whom he travelled as 'his woman,' and 'his sleeping machine,' but he lies with her all night in a bed in the same room with the gov't agent or keeper, W. P. Calloway, his wife, and sister-in-law. On the march, he habitually ate and slept with the woman in his ambulance, and on one occasion summoned and gave orders concerning the march to Corporal Kenney, while lying in bed with her. His relations towards the woman were well known to every member of the escort. In defence, accused showed that the woman in question had been borne on the rolls as his servant for some months, and he alleges, without proof, that his attentions to her were in consequence of her illness. He accuses other officers in New Mexico of keeping mistresses, and denounces Dr. Weeds, by whom the additional charges were preferred, as a prying and peeping spy. However efficient may have been the accused's conduct at Newbern, N. C. in 1864, even if established by competent testimony, it is thought that the discipline of the army and the character & interests of the military service demand the enforcement of the sentence pronounced by the Court. If his indefinite accusations against others in the service be true, it is manifest that one so openly & shamelessly guilty as the Accused is shown to have been should be punished, as an example and warning to those similarly offending; and scarcely less evident too, that the grossness and indecency of his conduct must have been startling even, to those addicted to a like indulgence of their illicit inclinations. If on the other hand his statements against his brother officers be false, he has forfeited any right to a lenient consideration of his case which previous good conduct and devotion may have entitled him to. As an additional reason for the belief that the service will be benefitted by the dismissal of the accused, attention is invited to the shameful indifference to its interests which is exhibited in his answer to Corpl Kenney's remark in reference to the effect upon the horses of the escort of the undue speed at which he insisted upon travelling. It is in evidence that notwithstanding the Corporal's warning, the accused persisted in refusing to make a slower march, the result being that two of the five horses of the escort were seriously injured. It is believed that for this misconduct alone, a sentence of dismissal could scarcely be considered too harsh a punishment."—Copy, DNA, RG 153, Letters Sent.

1867, Nov. 6.   John Clark, Rochester, N. Y., to USG. "In case I could furnish information that would Lead to the recovery of ($5000 00) five thousand dollars in gold taken from the baggage of Jefferson Davis at the time of his capture by two soldiers would it be of any pecuniary benifit to me"—ALS, DNA, RG 56, Div. of Captured and Abandoned Property, Letters Received.

1867, Nov. 6.   Benjamin Moran, secretary, U.S. legation, London, to USG. "By direction of Mr: Adams I have the honor to transmit herewith a copy of a note conveying the thanks of the Trustees of the British Museum to your Department, for the Annual Report of the Secretary of War for 1866, recently transmitted to the above:named institution through this Legation."—ALS, DNA, RG 107, Letters Received, M557 1867.

1867, Nov. 7.   Bvt. Maj. Gen. Daniel H. Rucker, act. q. m. gen., to USG. "I have the honor to submit herewith the claim of the Trustees of the Presbyterian Church, at Harper's Ferry, West Virginia, for damages, etc, stated at $2,171.06. . . . It has been the custom of this Department to repair churches in loyal States where they have been occupied by the U. S. during the late war for hospitals, quarters, &c. . . ."—LS, DNA, RG 92, Reports to the Secretary of War (Press).

1867, Nov. 7.   2nd Lt. Joseph E. Griffith, Iowa City, to USG. "I have the honor to apply for Extension of leave of absence from Dec. 16th 67 to include the *Holidays*. These I have not spent at home since the war began & family reasons induce me to apply for this."—ALS, DNA, RG 94, Letters Received, 537G 1867.

1867, Nov. 8.   To Secretary of the Treasury Hugh McCulloch. "In reply to your letter of the 15th October, 1867, I have the honor to request that the following mentioned balances now standing on the books of the U. S. Depository at Chicago, Illinois, may be repaid into the U. S. Treasury, and that I may be notified of such repayment, viz: . . . It is presumed that you intended to call my attention to the Act approved 2nd *May*, 1866, Chapter 70, Statutes at large. I cannot find any Act approved on the 2nd *March*, 1866, which bears upon the subject mentioned in your letter to which this is a reply."—LS, DNA, RG 56, Letters Received from the War Dept.

1867, Nov. 8. To Secretary of State William H. Seward. "I have the honor to acknowledge receipt of your letter of the 6th inst, enclosing a transcript from a despatch of the U. S. ~~Belg~~ Minister at Brussels, relative to the proposed reorganization of the Belgian Army, and to request that the thanks of this Dept be conveyed to the Minister, for the valuable ~~and~~ military information embodied in his despatch."—Copies, DNA, RG 94, Letters Received, 1125S 1867; *ibid.*, RG 107, Letters Sent to the President. On Nov. 6, Seward had written to USG. "I take pleasure in enclosing herewith for the information of the War Department, a transcript of a despatch No. 465. of the 22nd ultimo from our Minister at Brussels, which relates to the reorganization of the Belgian Army."—LS, *ibid.*, RG 94, Letters Received, 1125S 1867. The enclosure is *ibid.*

1867, Nov. 8. USG endorsement. "Brevet Commissions are not given in any particular branch of the service, but in the Army, at large. If then an officer deserves a given brevet rank in the army at large, it is not seen that his transfer from one branch of the service to another can affect his merit in the army at large, or rightfully his brevet rank. If then he is to have the same brevet rank after transfer, to re-brevet him is an unnecessary form, and the old brevet should stand. The general principle that brevets fall with the actual commission on which they were based, is not deemed a correct one. If it were, an officer would lose all brevets at each actual promotion. The resignation of real rank in leaving the army is deemed a tacit resignation of all brevet rank. Maj. Carey is held to be BtLtCol. USA."—ES, DNA, RG 94, ACP, 1244 1879. Written on a memorandum of Oct. 31 from Bvt. Brig. Gen. John C. Kelton, AGO. "Captain *Asa B. Carey*, 13th Regt. of Infantry, received the brevets of Major for 'gallant and meritorious services during the war,' and Lieutenant Colonel for 'gallant and meritorious services in the war against the Navajos,' both to date from March 13. 1865. On October 5, 1867, Captain *Carey* was appointed Paymaster, U. S. A. and it is respectfully submitted that, by accepting the appointment in the Staff, and thereby vacating his commission in the Line of the Army, the brevets based upon his line commission fall therewith It has been decided in other cases that the brevet falls with the full commission on which it is based. All papers commendatory of Captain *Carey's* services are respectfully submitted to the General of the Army for his consideration in respect to conferring the brevet of Lieutenant Colonel on his grade of Paymaster with rank of Major."—DS, *ibid.*

1867, Nov. 8. Judge Advocate Gen. Joseph Holt to USG. "Bvt Major Genl. Geo. A. Custer, Lt. Col. 7th U. S. Cavalry, was tried in Sept. and Oct. last by Gen. Ct. Martial convened at Fort Leavenworth, Kansas, by order of the General-in-Chief, under the following charges: 1. Absence without leave from his command. In that Accused did, at or near Fort Wallace, K, on or about July 15th last, absent himself from his command without proper authority, and proceed to Fort Riley, K, a distance of about 275 miles; this at a time when his command was expected to be actively engaged against the Indians. Finding—Guilty. 2. Conduct to the prejudice, of good order and mil. discipline. 1. In that accused, immediately after his command had completed a long and exhausting march, and when the horses belonging thereto had not been rested and were unfit for service, did select a portion of said command, namely, three comm'dg officers and about 75 men, with their horses, and did execute a rapid march from Fort Wallace to Fort Hays; the said march being upon private business and without authority, and damaging the horses of the detachment. Finding Guilty 2. In that Accused, while executing an unauthorized journey on private business, from Fort Wallace to Fort Riley, did procure certain mules, belonging to the U. S., for the conveyance of himself and part of his escort. This July 17th. Finding. Guilty, but attach no criminality. 3. In that Accused, when near Downer's Station, K. July 16. 1867, after receiving information that a party of Indians had attacked a small party detached from his escort near said station did fail to take proper measures for the repulse of said Indians or the defence or relief of said detachment; and further, after the return of such detached party with report that two of their number had been killed, did neglect to take any measures to pursue such Indians, or recover or bury the bodies of those killed. Guilty. 1st Additional charge: Conduct prejudicial to good order and military discipline. 1. In that, while en route commanding and marching a column of his regiment, six companies strong, from the valley of the Platte River to the valley of the Smoky Hill River, did, when ordering a party of three officers and others of his command in pursuit of supposed deserters who were in sight leaving camp, *also order* the said party to shoot the supposed deserters dead and to bring none in alive. This on 'Custer's Cavalry column trail' 15 miles south of Platte River, 50 miles S. W. of Fort Sedgewick, Coldo July 7th 1867. Finding. Guilty. 2. In that Accused did order enlisted men of his command to be shot down as deserters, but without trial, and did thus cause three men to be severely wounded. This July 7. 1867. Finding Guilty. 3. In that Accused, after three of his command had been shot down & wounded by his order, did order said men to be placed in a Gov't wagon and hauled 18 miles; (neglecting and refusing to permit them to receive medical treatment). This July 7. 1867. Finding. Guilty—but attach no criminality. 4. In that Accused did order and cause the summary shooting as a deserter, but without trial, of one Ch. Johnson, 7th Cavy, whereby said Johnson was so severely wounded that he soon after, to wit: on the 17th July, 1867, at or near Fort Wallace, K, did die. This July 7th 1867. Finding. Guilty   The Accused pleaded not guilty under all the charges and specifications. The Court find the accused . . . 'To be suspended from rank and command for one year, and forfeit his pay proper for the same time.' . . . It is advised that the findings under these first two charges be approved, with the exception of the 1st specification under charge 2, which is defective in not alleging either time or place. The allegations under the additional charge are of a graver character. He is charged, and convicted by the Court, of having ordered the shooting down without trial of three enlisted men, on the supposition that they were deserters, one of the three dying ten days after, in consequence. The Court acquit the accused of the allegation of inhumanity in his subsequent treatment of the wounded men. . . . The findings under the specifications are thought to be in accordance with the evidence. It is for the Executive to determine whether the sentence as it now stands, shall be accepted as a Sufficient atonement for the offences committed by the Accused; or, if regarded as too lenient for the just punishment of his acts, the record shall be returned to the Court, if not dissolved, for reconsideration. It is true, the crime of murder; of which, unless his act be regarded as justified by imperative necessity, the Accused must be held to be guilty; cannot be adequately and legally punished by a military Court. Its appropriate punishment can be inflicted only by the civil authority of the Country, after a trial and conviction before a jury. Should Gen. Custer's act be considered as an unwarrantable exercise of lawless power, the result of habits of thought acquired while controlling in time of open war a large command, and when accustomed to the doing of those deeds of arbitrary energy which war sometimes necessitates, and not as justified by the peculiar and difficult circumstances under which this deed was committed, the sentence pronounced by the Court in this case is utterly inadequate, and measures should at once be taken for Gen. Custer's trial before a Court of competent jurisdiction. If on the other hand, it is believed to have been ordered to be done, in the exercise of a wise and conscientious discretion, by a commander fully alive to the grave character of the act, and yet convinced of its necessity with reference not only to the accomplishment of the objects of his expedition but to the actual safety of his command, the sentence as now recorded should be regarded as sufficiently rigorous for the breach of discipline committed by the accused; and its enforcement is respectfully recommended."—Copy, DNA, RG 153, Letters Sent. See telegram to Edwin M. Stanton, July 25, 1867; Lawrence A. Frost, *The Court-Martial of General George Armstrong Custer* (Norman, Okla., 1968).

On Feb. 14, 1868, Holt wrote to USG. "I have the honor to report that I have examined the extended communication, herewith returned, of Bvt. Major General Geo. A. Custer, published in the Sandusky Register of Dec. 28th. last,—in connection with the accompanying animadversions and comments thereon by Bvt. Major General J. W. Davidson, Bvt. Brig. Genl. M. R. Morgan, and Bvt. Lieut. Col. T. C. English, respectively, and the joint protest against said publication of all the members of the court which sentenced Gen. Custer, forwarded by Bvt. Major General Hoffman, the presiding officer of said court. Upon such examination, I am induced to concur in the views expressed by these officers, and to hold that Genl. Custer, in the manner of his thus appealing from his sentence to the public, in his misrepresentations in regard to the evidence in his case, in his attacks

upon the impartiality and justice of the members of the court, in his criticisms of the course pursued by Genl. Hancock, and in the language with
which he assails one of the officers who preferred charges against him, must
be deemed to have been at least guilty of *conduct to the prejudice of good
order and military discipline.* His accusations and insinuations are sometimes couched in cautious and indirect terms; and in order the more clearly
to set forth what are deemed to be his chief points of offence, specifications
have been carefully drawn, which are herewith submitted for the consideration of the General in Chief. It may be noted that, subsequent to the publication in question, Genl. Custer, as would appear from an article in the
within copy of the 'Leavenworth Daily Conservative', attempted to repeat
his communication in the latter newspaper. The comments of its editor
upon the subject are believed to indicate a no more than just and proper
appreciation of the proceeding."—LS, DNA, RG 108, Letters Received.
Numerous enclosures are *ibid.*

On April 15, Maj. Gen. Philip H. Sheridan, Fort Leavenworth, wrote
to Bvt. Maj. Gen. John A. Rawlins. "I feel a great sympathy for General
G. A. Custer, who was tried by a Court Martial some time ago and suspended for (11) eleven months. Custer has done many things which I do
not approve of.—especially the letter he wrote and had published, reflecting
on the court which tried him.—but I would be exceedingly gratified if the
General could have him pardoned. He feels very sensibly his punishment,
and I think would, if he were re-instated, make a better officer than if the
sentence was carried out to its full extent. He held high command during
the Rebellion and found some difficulty in adapting himself to his altered
position. There was no one with me whom I more highly appreciated than
General Custer. He never failed me, and if his late misdeeds could be forgotten, or overlooked on account of his gallantry and faithfulness in the
past, it would be gratifying to him and to myself, and a benefit to the service."—LS, *ibid.* On Sept. 25, Bvt. Maj. Gen. Edward D. Townsend telegraphed to Bvt. Maj. Gen. George A. Custer, Detroit. "The remainder of
your sentence has been remitted by the Secretary of War. Report in person
without delay [to] General Sheridan, for duty, Acknowledge receipt."—LS
(telegram sent), *ibid.*, RG 107, Telegrams Collected (Bound); copy, *ibid.*,
RG 217, Manning Collection.

1867, Nov. 8.   Bvt. Lt. Col. Thomas J. Treadwell, Washington, D. C.,
to USG. "I have the honor to submit, for your consideration photographs
of the design of Mr H. K. Brown of Newburgh New York, the Artist
named in the Resolution of Congress. Approved March 2nd 1867, to Execute an Equestrian Statue of the late Lieut Genl. Winfield Scott. The report of the Commission with accompanying papers was submitted to the
Secretary of War Aug 6th. The design submitted by Mr Brown merits
the approval of the Commission, but they recommend the following modifications. To omit the holsters, make the saddle cloth after the regulation

pattern—put the sash lower on the body so as to cover the lower buttons of the coat. Change the position of the bridle arm to make it more rested."—ALS, DNA, RG 107, Letters Received, T184 1867.

1867, Nov. 8. U.S. Senator George H. Williams of Ore., Washington, D. C., to USG. "I have the honor to submit for your consideration the enclosed letter from the Cashier of the First National Bank in the city of Portland—Oregon—Payments in the Department of the Columbia are now generally made by checks upon San Francisco & the parties receiving them are compelled either to send them down to SanFrancisco for collection at considerable risk & delay, or to sell them wherever they can at a considerable discount—It would be a great convenience & saving to those to whom the Govt makes payments in the Department of the Columbia to have them made in Portland & besides we feel in Oregon that we are subordinated to SanFrancisco in the transaction of business with the Govt when there is no necessity for it—If not incompatible with the public interests I hope that the Deposits for the use of the military in the Department of the Columbia madey be made with the First National Bank in Portland—That Bank is already the Depository for the Treasury Department & with equal propriety it seems to me should be of the War Department"—ALS, DNA, RG 107, Letters Received, W384 1867. On the same day, Williams wrote to USG on the same subject.—ALS, *ibid.*

1867, Nov. 8. Oliver E. Woods, Washington, D. C., to USG. "In april last I applied to the War Department for some compensation for the use of my inventions by the U. S. in order to enable me proceed on another tour of instruction to the troops of the commands of Genls. Sherman, Thomas, and Sheridan. I stated in my application the causes that operated in the fall of 1866, to almost wholly frustrate instruction to the troops, even although I visited for that purpose the Head Qrtrs, of Genls, Sherman, Thomas, and Sheridan. The construction given to the reports of the 1st Infantry operated to prevent compensation being awarded to me. I requested that a Board of Experts be directed to examine the practical operation of my accoutrement declaring my conviction that I could demonstrate that the adverse reports (if any) were due to lack of information and not to want of merit in my accoutrement. No such Board was in session and my request was not complied with. I will now state that my equipment was examined in 1864 by two Boards, one of which was appointed by the Qr. M. General, and the other by the Surgeon General. In 1865 it was examined by a Board established by the Scty. of War, and in 1866 it was examined by a Board convened at Fort Leavenworth by order of Major Genl. Hancock. This last Board witnessed the operation of the accoutrement on a body of troops the larger portion of whom were instructed in the use of the equipment, while the remainder were only partially instructed, nevertheless, this Board reported—as did *all* of the first mentioned—favorably to my plans. In addition to the above I have recently had my accoutrement before a Board of Officers convened by an order of the War Department, for the examination of Knapsacks, and accoutrements for use in the Army. I learn that this Board has reported, but on inquiry at the War Deptmt I was informed that no information in regard to the tenor of the report can be given me, until the report itself has been acted on by the Secretary of War. I now respectfully request that in case this last mentioned Board has also accorded merit to my plans that the Scty of War will permit it outweigh the alledged adverse reports and order *some* compensation given me for the use of my inventions on the equipments issued in 1866. Encouraged by the favorable reports that my accoutrements has from time to time received from Boards, and from soldiers who had it in actual service during the late war, I have expended much time and money on it, and at this moment I find myself seriously inconvenienced by the expenditures I have made. Troops that have not be instructed in my accoutrement, I respectfully submit ought not be regarded as competent judges of its merits."— ALS, DNA, RG 107, Letters Received, W386 1867. On Dec. 18, Woods, Philadelphia, wrote to USG at length about the same matter.—ALS, *ibid.*, W439 1867. See *PUSG*, 16, 49–51.

1867, Nov. 9.   USG endorsement. "Respectfully submitted to the President recommending that F. M. Malone be appointed 2d Lieut U. S. army. this recommendation is made in consideration of the troops furnished by Eastern Va."—ES, DNA, RG 94, ACP, M1375 CB 1867. Written on a letter of Feb. 21 from Frank M. Malone, Washington, D. C., to Secretary of War Edwin M. Stanton. "I have the honor to solicit an appointment as 2nd Lieutenant in one of the Regiments of Cavalry U. S, army having served as Captain, Co, A, 16th Va Vols from the 14th Sept 1862, to the 10th of June 1863,   Regiment mustered out of service by order from the War department. Enclosed please find recommendations from Gov. Peirpoint, Judge Underwood and Wm J, Cowing and others,"—ALS, *ibid.*

1867, Nov. 9.   To Secretary of the Interior Orville H. Browning. "I have the honor to transmit herewith accounts of subsistence stores issued to Indians by various officers of the Subsistence Department of the Army during the months of July, August and September, 1867, not included in bills previously transmitted; and to request that a transfer warrant may be drawn for the amount ($59,916 01/100) on the appropriation for subsistence of Indians to the credit of the appropriation for the Subsistence of the Army." —LS, DNA, RG 75, Central Office, Letters Received, Miscellaneous. The enclosures are *ibid.* On Nov. 7, Bvt. Maj. Gen. Amos B. Eaton, commissary gen., had written to USG transmitting these papers.—LS, *ibid.*, RG 192, Letters Received by Referral. On Dec. 11, USG wrote to Browning. "I have the honor to enclose herewith accounts of subsistence stores furnished to Indians by various officers of the Subsistence Department of the Army, at various points within the United States, during the months of June, July, August and September, 1867, and to request that a transfer-warrant for the amount,—$4,216 95/100, be drawn on the appropriations for Indian service to the credit of the appropriation for subsistence of the Army."—LS, *ibid.*, RG 75, Central Office, Letters Received, Miscellaneous. The enclosures are *ibid.*

1867, Nov. 9. To Secretary of State William H. Seward. "I have the honor to acknowledge the receipt of your note of the 22d Oct transmitting a copy of a request from the Danish Legation that drawings and explanations and apparatus of the System of Milt'y. signalling &c designed by *Col. A. J. Myer*, Chf. Signal Off. of the U. S. A. be furnished to the *Danish Govmt.*, and to acquaint you that the Chf. Signal Officer has been instructed to comply with the request, as far as is consistent with the interests of the service, on proper application being made therefor."—Copy, DNA, RG 107, Letters Sent to the President. On Nov. 4, Col. Albert J. Myer, chief signal officer, had written to USG. "I have the honor to acknowledge the receipt of a communication from the State Department of date October 22d 1867, covering the transcript of a note of date October 19th 1867, from Mr. *Dollner*, the Danish Charge d'affaires accredited to the United States, in which he makes known the wishes of his Government to procure drawings with explanations of the Signal System as arranged for the use of our Army. . . ."—Copy, *ibid.*, RG 111, Letters Sent.

1867, Nov. 9. USG note. "Gen. Kelton will please appoint John Williamson Dunn, ~~Hanover~~ Hanover, Ia, 2d Lt. of Infantry."—ANS, DNA, RG 94, ACP, D605 CB 1867.

1867, Nov. 9. Judge Advocate Gen. Joseph Holt to USG. "The application for pardon of John Pryor, formerly of the 6th Indiana Cavy, who is in confinement at Jefferson City, Mo., under sentence of a Gen'l Court Martial, is respectfully returned with the following report. He was convicted in August 1865, at Fort Snelling of Murder, and was sentenced to be hung. The sentence was confirmed by Gen. Pope in Sept. 1865. Application for pardon was made to the President by the prisoner's counsel, which was denied, and the execution of the sentence directed in Oct. 1865, but afterwards upon the representation of Hon. H. M. Rice, that the people of his section of the country were desirous for the commutation of the sentence, the President on the 25th Oct, same year, commuted it to imprisonment for life. Prisoner now states that the homicide was committed in defending himself against a parcel of rowdies; that he has always borne an exemplary character and that he did not receive justice at the hands of the Court which tried him, and asks to be relieved from further punishment. The circumstances of the case as shown by the evidence were as follows: The prisoner and one James L. Stilfex, a private of Co. B. 9th Mass. Infy. were a part of the guard of a train of gov't wagons, on the way from Fort Ridgeley to Fort Snelling, Minn. On the morning of July 29. 1865, the prisoner told the officer commanding the guard that Stilfex had stolen his pocket book, and that 'he was after him.' The officer forbade him to interfere with Stilfex, and said he would cause the pocket book to be restored if it had been stolen. The prisoner had his gun in his hand at the time of this conversation, & immediately went towards the wagon in which Stilfex was sitting. On getting within a dozen feet of the latter, the prisoner, demanding his pocket book, raised his gun & shot Stilfex through the body, killing him almost instantly, and wounding another man who sat next him. On the night before the murder was committed, the prisoner with several members of the command, was at the town of Chasta, Minn., and he there declared that Stilfex had taken his money, and that if he did not return it he would kill him. He was at that time intoxicated. The prisoner produced testimony in his defence to show that he bore a good reputation for quietness of conduct when sober, but his own witnesses, as well as those of the prosecution, prove that he was extremely quarrelsome, violent, and dangerous when under the influence of liquor, and had once before threatened to shoot a comrade. Several witnesses testify that he was somewhat intoxicated at the time of the homicide, but his Captain swears that he saw no signs of it. There is no evidence whatever that the prisoner's pocket book had been stolen. It will be seen that the statements now made by the prisoner are false, and instead of his offence having been committed in his own defence, he was guilty of a deliberate and premeditated murder. He was ably defended by counsel, and the record of the proceedings shows that the trial was conducted with the utmost fairness. It is advised that the sentence, as commuted, be enforced."—Copy, DNA, RG 153, Letters Sent. On Oct. 20, John Prior, Jefferson City, had written to USG pleading his case.—ALS, *ibid.*, RG 94, Enlisted Branch, PPR 1511-1865. On Oct. 25, USG endorsed this letter to Governor Thomas C. Fletcher of Mo., an endorsement later cancelled in the War Dept.—AES, *ibid.*

1867, Nov. 9.   W. K. Browne, New York City, to USG. "I take the liberty of addressing you in behalf of Mrs Elizebeth Fripp of St. Helena South Carolina, widow of the Late Capt. John Fripp. Capt in the U. S. service of the War 1812 and died at the advanced age of 76 years, in the year 1865 and who took no part what ever in the rebellion, his property fell in the hands of the Goverment, partly sold for taxes, and the balance still in their possession. This family is now in great destitution, and your Circular of Nov 5th 1867, relating to the return of the property having reached her, desires to be informed what steps will be necessary, and to whom the application must be made for its recovery."—ALS, DNA, RG 107, Letters Received, B23 1868.

1867, Nov. 9.   Thomas Cottman, Washington, D. C., to USG. "In visiting the Government Armory at Springfield I found the Regulation Musket 'reduced & reinforced' for the use of 'Cadets'. I would like to have one of them as a *speciman* to send to St Petersburg, Russia and would be very much obliged, for permission to obtain one for the object above named by purchase"—ALS, DNA, RG 156, Letters Received.

1867, Nov. 9.   George H. Stuart, Philadelphia, to USG. "Personal . . . A short time ago, Surgeon Geo. McGill *died of Cholera,* while in the discharge of his duties as an officer in the U. S. Army, on the Plains. He had been married about six months, and his wife, who accompanied him died of the same disease ~~before~~ a few days before he was suddenly cut off. His father Rev. Alex. T. McGill. D. D. an intimate and dear friend of mine and a Professor on a moderate salary in the Theological Seminary, Princeton N. J. was in Europe at the time of the sad event. It is the desire of the afflicted parents to have *the remains of their son exhumed and brought East for interment.* As Dr. McGill's means will not allow of the outlay required for such purpose, he would consider it a *very great favor* if the Government would order such a disposition of the body. The deceased had rendered hard, constant and faithful service for more than five years in the Army of the Potomac. It is supposed that the perilous exposure of that period made him an easy victim to the disease which so suddenly cut off himself and wife so far away from home and friends. Can you exert your influence to have the request of the afflicted father complied with. *I assure you such a favor would place me under* personal *obligations to you.* I have written to Surg. Gen. Barnes on the matter but anything you may do for its accomplishment will be gratefully remembered by the bereaved parents, . . ."— LS, DNA, RG 108, Letters Received. On Nov. 11, Bvt. Capt. Amos Webster wrote to Stuart. "Your letter of the 9th inst. is received   In reference to the same, the General-in Chief desires me to say that as a general rule the Government removes the remains of deceased officers of the army only, from the place of burial to the nearest express office and wishes to know if such an arrangement is satisfactory to you."—Copies, DLC-USG, V, 47, 60; DNA, RG 108, Letters Sent.

1867, Nov. 10.   George M. Willing, Princess Anne, Md., to USG. "By a telegram from San Francisco, Cal, I see that Major Clendenin Fort Mohave A. T. has recovered papers and other things belonging to my expedition from the Indians who killed James H. Stimpson & three others—as there papers & money and outfit belong to me, I desire that they be sent to me— if it comes through your department—the papers are of great pecuniary interest to me—as all my available means ~~were in~~ are tied up, until I get these papers—please give me the information as soon as you can as my pecuniary ~~means~~ condition arising from the massacre is extremely unpleasant, having almost to beg my way back from the colorado river—"—ALS, DNA, RG 94, Letters Received, 833W 1867.

1867, Nov. 10.   "A Subjugated Friend," Reardon, Ala., to USG. "Some time since, I wrote to you upon the subject of the Presidency. Since that time, Washburns speech in Illinois, did, for a time, shake the confidence of good men. The reputed authentic denial, by you, that Washburn was not authorised to commit you to any party, or policy, has put matters in *Statu quo* in the confidence of the quiet Sober people of the South, who are looking to you as the last hope of the Republic. The North has spoken, trumpet tongue, against negro sufferage & negro equality. We of the South are willing to endure confiscation & all the disabilities incident to a subjugated people; but, O, my God! save us the degradation of negro equality—of negro superiority? You Sir, can do it; you *alone* can do it. The Country *respects* you—The Radicals *fear* you: Your counsels, with the virtuous and the good, will be respected. . . ."—AL, DNA, RG 108, Letters Received.

1867, Nov. 11.   USG endorsement. "Respectfully forwarded to the President of the united states for his information."—ES, DLC-Andrew Johnson. On Nov. 7, Bvt. Maj. Gen. John M. Schofield, Richmond, had written to USG. "I have the honor to acknowledge the receipt of a letter addressed to the President by. *J. H. Gilmer* of Richmond, referring to General *O. Brown*, the Freedmans Bureau, and the late election in Richmond, which letter was referred by the President to you and by you to me, on the 2d instant. Whether considered with reference to the character of its author, or with reference to the character of the letter itself, I cannot regard that letter as worthy of any further notice than to say that, so far as I know and believe, its statements are without foundation in fact. But the receipt of this letter from the President, through you, makes it proper for me to anticipate the report which I have been preparing to forward at the proper time, so far as to forward at once copies of the correspondence upon the subject of the late election, between myself and the 'Conservative' Candidates for the convention. This I hope will be sufficient to disabuse the mind of the President, of any wrong impressions he may have received"—LS, DNA, RG 108, Letters Received. Extracts from a lengthy letter of John H. Gilmer to Schofield protesting election procedures appeared in the *New York Times*, Oct. 30, 1867.

1867, Nov. 11, 3:30 P.M.   To Lt. Gen. William T. Sherman, St. Louis. "Give Ninety days leave to Lt. Hesselberger, 3d Inf.y, now at Ft Dodge. Send leave by telegraph."—ALS (telegram sent), DNA, RG 107, Telegrams Collected (Bound); telegram sent, *ibid.*; copies, *ibid.*, RG 108, Telegrams Sent; DLC-USG, V, 56.

1867, Nov. 11, 10:45 A.M.   To Bvt. Maj. Gen. John M. Schofield. "You are authorized to be absent as requested in your dispatch of to-day."—ALS (telegram sent), DNA, RG 107, Telegrams Collected (Bound); telegram sent, *ibid.*; copies, *ibid.*, RG 108, Telegrams Sent; DLC-USG, V, 56. On the same day, Schofield, Richmond, had telegraphed to USG. "I respectfully request permission to be absent from my Command for a few days"— Telegram received (at 10:35 A.M.), DNA, RG 107, Telegrams Collected

(Bound); *ibid.*, RG 108, Telegrams Received; copies, *ibid.*, RG 393, 1st
Military District, Telegrams Sent; DLC-USG, V, 55.

1867, Nov. 11, 11:00 A.M.   To Maj. Gen. George H. Thomas, Louisville. "If Gn. Hamill has not gone to Lynchburg it will not be necessary
for him to go. Gn. Schofield has been directed to look after the interests of
the Govt. in the matter of Va & E. Ten. road."—ALS (telegram sent),
DNA, RG 107, Telegrams Collected (Bound); telegram sent, *ibid.*; copy,
ibid., RG 393, Dept. of the Cumberland, Telegrams Received. On Nov. 9,
Thomas had telegraphed to USG. "Mr Moffitt General passenger Agent of
the Virginia and Tennessee Rail Road is here & says that in the Election of
Officers of that road on tuesday next Wm Mahone will be Elected President
unless the Government interferes, This he claims will be detrimental to the
Government interests   The present management propose to pay five thousand (5000) dollars monthly if retained   If you have not acted upon the
matter I will send Col Hamill to Lynchburg to protect the interests of the
Government   Of course not to interfere in the Election"—Telegram received (at 2:30 P.M.), *ibid.*, RG 107, Telegrams Collected (Bound); copy,
ibid., RG 393, Dept. of the Cumberland, Telegrams Sent.

On Oct. 9, Bvt. Brig. Gen. Cyrus B. Comstock had telegraphed to Bvt.
Maj. Gen. Orlando B. Willcox, Lynchburg, Va. "The act'g Sec. of War
directs me to say that the United States will not allow a change in the
Presidency of the Virginia & Tennessee R. R. until the government claim
is satisfied or until further orders."—ALS (telegram sent), *ibid.*, RG 107,
Telegrams Collected (Bound); telegram sent, *ibid.* On Oct. 11, Willcox
telegraphed to Comstock. "Your instructions are fulfilled. the motion was
not allowed to change the Presidency of Virginia and Tennessee Rail Road
on any terms. They adjourned till November and appointed a committee to
go to Washington at once—Particulars by mail"—Telegram received (at
11:45 A.M.), *ibid.*; *ibid.*, RG 108, Telegrams Received; copy, DLC-USG,
V, 55.

On Nov. 11, 11:20 A.M., USG telegraphed to Bvt. Maj. Gen. John M.
Schofield, Richmond. "~~Does~~ What has been done in reference to election of
railroad officers for Va & E. Tenn. road?"—ALS (telegram sent), DNA,
RG 107, Telegrams Collected (Bound); telegram sent, *ibid.*; telegram received, *ibid.*, RG 393, 1st Military District, Telegrams Received. On the
same day, Schofield telegraphed to USG. "Your dispatch relative to Election of Rail Road Officers is rec'd, I forwarded to you on the sixth (6)
instant for your action a proposition from Mr G. C. Walker dated November second (2) to give bonds with ample security for the payment of the
claims of the United States and a copy of my order authorizing an Election
of Officers to take effect whe~~re~~n your prohibition is removed. If that proposition is not accepted by you Mr Walker proposes to pay the debt as soon
as the Election is held provided it result in securing to him and his friends
the control of the road   if it do not so result the Election will be void"—
Telegram received (at 1:20 P.M.), *ibid.*, RG 107, Telegrams Collected

(Bound); copy, *ibid.*, RG 393, 1st Military District, Telegrams Sent. At 2:30 P.M., USG telegraphed to Schofield. "The proposition of Va & E. Tenn. road to pay the govt. is accepted and as soon as bonds are filled all opposition to change of directory seases."—ALS (telegram sent), *ibid.*, RG 107, Telegrams Collected (Bound); telegram sent, *ibid.*; telegram received, *ibid.*, RG 393, 1st Military District, Telegrams Received.

On Nov. 11, Bvt. Maj. Gen. Daniel H. Rucker, act. q. m. gen., wrote to USG. "I have the honor to return herewith the letter of M. G. C. Walker, chairman of a Committee of the Virginia and Tennessee Railroad Company, dated Nov. 1st. 1867, to Bvt. Major General J. M. Schofield, referred to this office, with enclosures, on the 8th. instant, 'for immediate remark.' The Company proposes, as appears from the papers submitted, to elect new officers, President and directors, for the ensuing year, and if permitted so to do, proposes to pay the indebtedness of the Company to the Govt., as follows: . . . From the statements made by the chairman of the Committee and representations made to me, I am of the opinion that they intend in good faith to pay the debt of the company, and would recommend that they be allowed to elect officers in the manner proposed, and that the terms of payment proposed be accepted by the Govt., . . ."—LS, *ibid.*, RG 92, Reports to the Secretary of War (Press). On Nov. 12, Schofield telegraphed to G. C. Walker, Lynchburg. "Your proposition for the payment of the indebtedness of the Va. and East Tenn. Road to the Government is accepted by Genl *Grant.* As soon as the bonds are filed all opposition to change of directory will cease.—"—Copy, *ibid.*, RG 393, 1st Military District, Telegrams Sent. On Nov. 15, Governor Francis H. Peirpoint of Va. telegraphed to USG. "The bond to be executed to secure debt due from Virginia and Tennessee Rail Road has not yet come to hand, I am deeply anxious to have this matter closed"—Telegram received (at 2:30 P.M.), *ibid.*, RG 107, Telegrams Collected (Bound). On Nov. 18, Judge Advocate Gen. Joseph Holt wrote to USG. "Respectfully returned to the Secretary of War, with the expression of opinion that the within instrument is fully sufficient in law as a *joint* obligation of the subscribing parties; and, *so far*, is regarded as a substantial compliance with the recommendation of the Quartermaster General in regard to this proceeding. It is, however, the usual and more *convenient* form for the parties in such a contract to bind themselves severally as well as jointly. Unless it should be determined that the urgency of the case is such that the undertaking should be completed and the guaranty accepted without delay, it would be advised that an obligation expressly stipulating for a *several* as well as *joint* liability be substituted."—Copy, *ibid.*, RG 153, Letters Sent. On Nov. 19, 11:40 A.M., USG telegraphed to Schofield. "Notify the President elect of the Va & E Tenn. road that ~~their~~ bonds are accepted and no further obstruction will be interposed to. ~~their~~ his taking charge of the road."—ALS (telegram sent), *ibid.*, RG 107, Telegrams Collected (Bound); telegram sent, *ibid.*; telegram received, *ibid.*, RG 393, 1st Military District, Telegrams Received. On Dec. 18, Schofield telegraphed to USG. "The President of the Va & E. T. R R asks to know to whom to pay the January installments due the U. S. by that Road"—Telegram received (on Dec. 19, 8:15 A.M.), *ibid.*, RG 107, Telegrams Collected (Bound); copy, *ibid.*, RG 393, 1st Military District, Telegrams Sent.

1867, Nov. 11.   Judge Advocate Gen. Joseph Holt to USG. "The papers relating to the application for the pardon of John Ford, late private of the 20th Ill's Vols., who is now imprisoned in Jefferson City Mo., under the sentence of a General Court Martial for Murder, are respectfully returned to General Grant, with a copy of the original report in the case, made by this Bureau in May, 1864. Upon this report the President confirmed the sentence of imprisonment for life. Since his incarceration Ford has made thro' various sources, upwards of 20 applications for pardon, on each occasion giving a totally different account of the circumstances attending his offence, and in no instance making a statement of the affair which agreed with the facts as shown on his trial. His applications have heretofore been denied. The petition now presented is that of Mr. P. H. Riley, of Jefferson City, Mo., who states that the prisoner enlisted in the army in the earliest stage of the war, and served in the battle of Donaldson and others, and was a good and faithful soldier up to the time of committing the offence for which he is now suffering. Upon a reference by the General of the Army of this petition, Governor Fletcher of Missouri reports ~~reports~~ that he has obtained information from reliable and well informed persons, to the effect that Ford was a man of previous good character, and that since his confinement he has conducted himself to the satisfaction of the officers of the prison, who give him the highest recommendations. Gov. Fletcher recommends his pardon. Ford has now been imprisoned about three and a half years; and it is left for the Secretary of War, ad interim, to determine whether this punishment shall be accepted as a sufficient atonement for his crime."—Copy, DNA, RG 153, Letters Sent.

1867, Nov. 11.   Montgomery Blair, Washington, D. C., to USG. "Enclosed I send a letter from my brother in law Charles Woodbury who is an influential politician in New England—I send also copy of a note to Mr Reverdy Johnson which explains itself—I hope your attention was attracted to the leader in the World on Saturday—I have letters from influential Republicans who are still acting with the party expressing the hope that you will accept the Democratic nomination. That is the obvious way to beat both the Vallandinghams & the Phillips's   It would bring back the 'Era of good feeling'—as it existed in Mr Monroes time. There will be no opposition to you   The men who are regarded as most ultra Democrats as old Govr Pratt of Md when they really feel for the people of the South are most earnest for you in order to get the Southern people relieved from the most frightful of all dangers at the earliest moment   I solemnly believe that you alone can save us from a War of races & I doubt whether it will be in your power to avert it unless you take hold quickly and allow the men who love the constitution & the race who made it to rally under you immediately

You have saved the Union but your work is not complete till you restore the constitution"—ALS, USG 3. Blair enclosed a copy of an undated letter to U.S. Senator Reverdy Johnson of Md. "I have just received yr note post marked 9th inst asking whether it is true that I called on Genl Grant in relation to the article in the Chronicle and that he disclaimed it—The Statement is not correct—all that you see in the newspapers comes from my saying to a gentleman, who learning I know not how that I had seen Genl Grant, sought to learn his views from me—that neither I or any one else had a right to Speak for him"—ALS, *ibid.*

1867, Nov. 12.   USG endorsement. "It is recommended that Banks at the places named within be designated by the Sec. of the Treasury for the deposite of funds appropriated for the use of the Army."—AES, DNA, RG 56, Letters Received from the War Dept. Written on a letter of the same day from Bvt. Maj. Gen. William S. Ketchum to USG. "I respectfully suggest that the Secretary of the Treasury may be requested to designate, under the act approved 14 June 1866, Depositories for the safekeeping of public money entrusted to disbursing officers and agents of the War Dept, as follows: . . ."—LS, *ibid.* On Nov. 18, Act. Secretary of the Treasury John F. Hartley wrote to USG. "In compliance with your recommendation of the 12th inst. I have to respectfully inform you that the following National Bank Depositories have been specially designated for the reception, safe Keeping and disbursement according to law of the public funds intrusted for disbursement to any and all disbursing officers of the War Department; viz: . . ."—LS, *ibid.*, RG 107, Letters Received from Bureaus.

1867, Nov. 12.   To Secretary of State William H. Seward. "In reply to your inquiry of the 1st instant, if there has been a proclamation of the President or law passed by Congress restoring to citizenship deserters from the army and draft, I have the honor to transmit herewith copies of General Orders Nos 35 and 152, War Dept. 1865. [w]hich comprise all the information on the subject known to the Dept."—Copies, DNA, RG 107, Letters Received from Bureaus; *ibid.*, Letters Sent to the President. See *O.R.*, III, iv, 1229; *ibid.*, v, 126. On Nov. 1, Seward had written to USG. "I have the honor to submit to you for reply the following question. Has there been any proclamation of amnesty issued by the President or law passed by Congress restoring to citizenship those persons who deserted from the army. or the draft during the Rebellion?"—LS, DNA, RG 107, Letters Received from Bureaus.

1867, Nov. 12.   To Secretary of State William H. Seward. "At the instance of the Inspector of the Mil. Academy I have the honor to request that if practicable a copy of the 'Trial of John H. Surratt' be furnished for the Library of that Institution."—Copies, DNA, RG 107, Letters Received from Bureaus; *ibid.*, Letters Sent to the President. On the same day, USG wrote to Attorney Gen. Henry Stanbery. "At the instance of the Inspector of the Milty Academy I have the honor to request that if practicable a copy of '*Vol. 9. Opinions of the Atty. General*' be furnished for the library of that institution."—Copy, *ibid.* On Nov. 14, Seward wrote to USG. "In compliance with your request of the 12th instant. I have the honor to send herewith, a copy of the report of the trial of John H Surratt for the Library of the Military Academy at West Point."—LS, *ibid.*, Letters Received from Bureaus. On Nov. 15, Secretary of the Interior Orville H. Browning wrote to USG. "I have the honor to transmit, herewith, a copy of the 9th volume of 'Opinions of Attorneys General,'—in compliance with the request contained in your note of the 12th instant, which has just been received, by reference from the Department of State."—LS, *ibid.*

1867, Nov. 12. USG note. "The Adj. Gn. will issue order mustering Gn. Gregory out of service Nov. 30th Gens. Sickles & Scott Dec. 31st and if there are any other officers still retaining volunteer rank as high as Brig. Gn. they will also be mustered out. This will not apply to Gn. Howard."— ANS, DNA, RG 94, ACP, W1089 CB 1867.

1867, Nov. 12. To Judge Advocate Gen. Joseph Holt. "The Judge Advocate General of the Army will please furnish a copy of the order of the President disapproving the finding and sentence of Court Martial in case of Wm B. N. Cozens?"—ANS, DLC-Joseph Holt. On the same day, Holt wrote to USG. "On the report made by this Bureau in the case of *W. B. N. Cozzens*, is found the following endorsement of the President of the United States: 'After a careful examination of the facts and proceedings in this case, the finding and sentence of the Court are not approved. Andrew Johnson Executive Mansion. Sept. 5th 1867.' "—Copy, DNA, RG 153, Letters Sent.

1867, Nov. 12. To U.S. Commissioner Charles B. Norton, Paris. "I have the honor to acknowledge receipt of your letter of the 23d ultimo, with its enclosures, relative to the *Chalmers System* of *Iron Armor* for *Stone Forts*, and to inform you that the same has been referred to the Chief of Engineers for consideration. Be pleased to accept the thanks of this Department for your considerate attention."—Copy, DNA, RG 107, Letters Sent. On Dec. 20, Norton wrote to USG. "Since my last in reply to your favour, have received enclosed tracings of the Govt drawings of the Gibraltar Shields and Plymouth Forts—These I forward to the Department *strictly in confidence* as representations of the best efforts of the English Govt in their proposed defences against our 15 inch Gun—The improvements proposed by Mr Chalmers are shown in the tracing of the Gibraltar Shields. This gentleman is quite willing to go to the United States and arrange for building a target upon his principle provided his expenses are covered by the Govt—"—ALS, *ibid.*, RG 156, Correspondence Concerning Inventions. On Jan. 8, 1868, Brig. Gen. Andrew A. Humphreys, chief of engineers, wrote to USG. "I have the honor to return herewith the communication of Hon Mr. Norton, U. S. Commissioner at the Paris Exposition; on the subject of a system of armor for vessels and forts, with a report thereon by the Board of Engineers for Fortifications. The views of the Board are concurred in by me. It may be added that experiments have been made by us and are still in progress, upon a compound target prepared on a system similar to that of Mr Chalmers omitting the perishable material. These experiments have been incidental to those carried on at the Washington Arsenal, which have several objects in view, all of which they promise to attain; the results already arrived at are of an exceedingly interesting character. They are made at comparatively small expense"—Copy, *ibid.*, RG 77, Fortifications, Letters Sent.

1867, Nov. 13.   Judge Advocate Gen. Joseph Holt to USG. "Respectfully returned to the Secretary of War. There is in this Bureau no evidence whatever—as supposed by Major Gen Canby—connecting the within named Hine with a charge of 'subornation of perjury in relation to bounty frauds,' or, in any manner, with the subject of any such frauds. As it appears from the enclosed communication of Gen'l. Scott Asst. Commissioner for South Carolina, that Hine is an Agent of the Bureau of Freedmen, &c. employed thereby to investigate a class of frauds of this character, and bring the perpetrators to justice; it is advised by this Bureau that while so employed he should not be allowed to be interfered with, if it can be avoided, by the civil authorities or otherwise."—Copy, DNA, RG 153, Letters Sent.

1867, Nov. 13.   Samuel Cornell, "Prince of Peace," Westchester, N. Y., to USG. "having had a revelation three Mornings in succession stating that it is the will of the supreme being or Power that the Cannibal War is only to be spiritually as it would be too bad to have it carnally therefore I write this to you giving you the Plan to prevent it coming upon us carnally   the Plan is thus you must pretend to the President you are ready to carry out any order he may give you and it is right for him to give you an order to arrest the Radical part of Congress to have them tried for Treason. The Christian people wish you to make all the necessary preparations with the officers including Generals Meade sherman Sheridan shenk & Beauregard and all others you possibly can to get the soldiers all in readiness to carry out this plan as it is the very last chance of preventing the great Cannibal War coming upon us and we are satisfied the soldiers will be nearly if not all ready to do their duty as I believe there is very few that want to go to War again. . . ."—ALS, DNA, RG 94, Letters Received, C971 1867.

1867, Nov. 13.   U.S. Senator Lyman Trumbull of Ill., Washington, D. C., to USG. "In a suit pending in Ill. against the Ill. Cent. Railroad Co. it is supposed to be important to introduce in evidence a letter written by ___ Osborn, Pres. of the company to the Sec. of War about the 20th of Aug. 1861, acceding to the proposition of the Sec. of War for the use of the road for Govt purposes. I will be obliged if you will cause a certified copy of the letter referred to, to be furnished that I may forward the same to the atty. in the case—"—ALS, DNA, RG 94, Letters Received, 352T 1867.

1867, Nov. 14.   To Attorney Gen. Henry Stanbery. "I have the honor to request that you will instruct the US District attorney of ~~Missouri~~ Kansas to defend General G M Dodge—in any suits wh. may be brought against him for acts of his as a military officer in the service of the US during the war of the rebellion."—Df, DNA, RG 107, Letters Received, D243 1867; copy, *ibid.*, Letters Sent to the President. In Oct., U.S. Representative Grenville M. Dodge of Iowa, Council Bluffs, had written to Bvt. Maj. Gen. John A. Rawlins. "I see that the hounds are after me in the courts in Kansas   last march Mr Stanton orderd or obtain an order frm Atty Gen for Dist Atty to defend these suits   they are brought for acts or ordes of mine while in commd of the Dept of Mo and Dist of Territories and I believe in every case I acted under direct order of the Sec of War.   will you see the Sec of War and have gov't—defend the suits   one now pending I believe is of McMurty, Dodge and others—I enclose letter of Mr Fenlon   Mr Stanton I believe thought he was playing false and obtained the services of some one else—at any rate the Dist Atty should be orderd to defend the suits   I do not know as they have served on me in this one"—ALS, *ibid.*, Letters Received, D243 1867. On Nov. 18, Stanbery wrote to USG. "In accordance with the request contained in your letter of the 14th Inst., I have the honor to reply, that instructions have, this day, been forwarded to the United States Attorney for the District of Kansas, to take charge of any suits which may be brought against General G. M. Dodge, for acts of his as a military officer in the service of the United States during the war of the rebellion."—LS, *ibid.*, Letters Received from Bureaus.

1867, Nov. 14.   Secretary of State William H. Seward to USG. "I have the honor to enclose herewith for your information an extract from a dispatch No 14, of the 10th of October last, addressed to this Department by the United States Consul at Chihuahua, Mexico, relative to deserters from the Army of the United States."—LS, DNA, RG 94, Letters Received, 1127S 1867. The enclosure is *ibid.*

1867, Nov. 14.   Judge Advocate Gen. Joseph Holt to USG. "I have the honor to state that this Bureau has commenced to compile, and proposes— if authorized—to publish, as soon as its other duties may permit, a new edition of the 'Digest of the Opinions of the Judge Advocate General,' of which two editions have heretofore appeared. These editions—which were issued by the authority of the Secretary of War—have been widely circulated and largely used in the army, and have—it is believed—been of very considerable service in inducing a uniformity of practice in our military trials, and facilitating a proper and prompt administration of military justice. In the new edition it is designed to include—in addition to those already published —a selection of the opinions given by the Bureau upon questions of military law since March 1866, the date of the issuing of the last edition. The immediate occasion for the new issue is the fact that the last edition—of which copies continue to be applied for by officers, and to be furnished daily—is nearly exhausted. I have the honor, General, to request your formal approval of the publication of a new edition of one thousand to fifteen hundred copies of the said 'Digest'—in similar form and binding to the edition last prepared by the public printer."—Copy, DNA, RG 153, Letters Sent.

1867, Nov. 14.   Judge Advocate Gen. Joseph Holt to USG. "Respectfully returned to the Secretary of War; whose attention is invited to the enclosed copy of the most recent of a series of Reports, made by this Bureau in the within case of the Guerrilla, Samuel O. Berry. The application for pardon and release upon which this report was made was promptly denied by the President, as had been all previous applications. As set forth in the report, Berry was 'duly convicted of three acts of robbery and eleven distinct murders,' and his case was therein viewed as 'one of the most atrocious in the history of the guerilla warfare of the rebellion.' Surely the commutation of the death sentence of such a villian to an imprisonment for ten years in a penitentiary should be deemed to have been the utmost exercise of clemency of which such a case was capable; and this Bureau cannot refrain from an expression of profound surprise that Gen. Palmer, who approved the original sentence of this criminal, could have been induced to recommend his pardon at this time. He states indeed that he is 'not so much influenced by considerations of abstract justice as of comparative justice'; and bases his recommendation mainly upon the ground that as other criminals of this class—instancing 'Jim Davis' and 'Wells'—have been set free, there would seem to be no sufficient reason why the same proceeding should not be had in favor of Berry. But this argument is one of which this Bureau finds itself wholly unable to perceive the fitness or force. The cases of these convicts are far from being identical, and cannot, it is submitted, with any justice be disposed of *en masse*. Each application, on the contrary, should be treated according to its individual merits alone. The case of Berry indeed is one of a higher degree of criminality than either of the others mentioned —in so far as the commission of eleven murders involves a deeper guilt in law than that of a less number. Moreover, in the case of *Davis*, the remission of the unexpired sentence was based solely on the fact that he was afflicted with an epilepsy which was pronounced incurable by competent medical testimony and which was bringing him to a condition of idiocy. As to the case of *Wells*, it is to be added that there is no record whatever of his pardon to be found in the War Department; the last order issued therefrom in regard to him being one of June 9th 1866, in which the President approved a commutation of his death sentence to one of an imprisonment for ten years. This action is the same as that taken in the case of Berry; and yet

Wells was convicted of but a single murder. It is advised that the communication of Gen. Palmer be not favorably entertained."—Copy, DNA, RG 153, Letters Sent.

186[7], Nov. 14.   Col. Adam Badeau to Edward McPherson, clerk, U.S. House of Representatives. "General Grant directs me to express his thanks for the kind invitation conveyed by you to visit Gettysburg on the 20th inst, at the formal opening of the Soldiers' Orphan Home. It would give him great pleasure to avail himself of your courtesy, but imperative public business will detain him in Washington."—ALS, DLC-Edward McPherson.

1867, Nov. 15, 11:00 A.M.   To Capt. Daniel Ammen, New York City. "Will not be able to go to New York."—ALS (telegram sent), DNA, RG 107, Telegrams Collected (Bound). On the same day, Ammen had telegraphed to USG. "Will Genl Grant come on?"—Telegram received (at 10:20 A.M.), *ibid.*

1867, Nov. 16.   To Secretary of State William H. Seward. "In reply to your letter of the 6th inst. enclosing copy of one from the British Chargé d'Affaires, requesting the discharge from military service of *William Douglas*, a British subject, enlisted into the U. S. Army under the name of *Wm John Edwards*,—on the ground of minority, I have the honor to inform you that it appears from the records of the Dept. that the soldier named was enlisted at New York City on the 25th day of September, 1866, when he declared himself, under oath, to be 21 years of age, and no favorable action can therefore be taken in his case until it be shown that it comes within the provision of the law governing the discharge of minors, a copy of which is enclosed for your information"—Copy, DNA, RG 107, Letters Sent to the President.

1867, Nov. 16.   Robert J. Breckinridge, Lexington, Ky., to USG. "The undersigned respectfully represents, that he lately had two sons who were subaltern officers in the Army of the United States. The youngest of these Charles H Breckinridge, First Lieut in the 15th Infantry, died gloriously, on the 27th of August last of Yellow Fever, while in command of the post of Fort Morgan—below Mobile—which he refused to leave when the pestilence appeared—though he had leave of absence to go to Ky, our native state, to be married. The other son is Joseph C Breckinridge, Major by Brevet, and First Lieut in the 2nd Artillery of the Army of the U. S. now, and for more than two years past serving in California, in various situations—but at present I believe with his Battery in the Presidio of San Francisco, or recruiting in that city. The petition of the undersigned is that this surviving son,—if it is compatible with the interests of the public service, may be ordered to this Eastern Side of the Continent and put on duty, somewhere within reach of private and social duties which he has been obliged to neglect, almost wholly, since the late war commenced. And it may be considered a reason why this ~~petion~~ petition should be granted, that this young officer served uninterruptedly under orders from the Month of September 1861 to the present time—except while he was a prisoner of war in Charleston S. Carolina, and when absent on sick leave, after comeing out of that horrible confinement—A long service, and well performed, as is manifest by his rising, without outward influence, from a private Volunteer, at a very early age, through good conduct every where—but especially in the presence of the enemy.—I will add, that this petition is made, especially, because the struggle in this young officer's mind, between his love of his present profession, and his sense of duty to the last wishes of his lately deceased brother—and to the only parent of whom he ever knew any thing; seems to me to deserve, and to require some such mitigation of its rigorous conditions, for a reasonable time, as I have ventured to ask for. If General Grant can grant some relief, such in general as is asked for,—he will confer an obligation on two men, who have done their best for the same cause that he, by God's providence served so gloriously; two men, who never forget kindness."—ALS, DNA, RG 94, Letters Received, 1150B 1867. On Jan. 10, 1868, U.S. Representative James B. Beck of Ky., Washington, D. C., wrote to USG. "Enclosed find a communication to me, for you, from Rev Robert, J, Breckinridge of Danville, Ky. I have no doubt you know his reputation. The most eminent Divine in the West, The *most* decided Union man in Kentucky, his fame can hardly have escaped you, He is old, the loss of a most hopeful son by yellow fever last fall in the service of the United States has fallen heavily upon him, This son, & the one who is dead agreed when they entered the United States Army together that the one who died first should make the other his sole devisee; When Charles died he did so leave his property & the Father now desires Joseph to be allowed to come nearer home at least for a while to attend to it, & that he may see him once more. If he could be located at the Artillery School at Fortress Monroe or some where else this side of the Rocky Mountains, it would be a great obligation to his father & the young man, & I hope it may be consistent with your duty to do so—excuse the enquiry from me, a stranger. . . . Please notify me so I can advise Dr. B."—ALS, *ibid*. The enclosure is *ibid*.

1867, Nov. 18. To Secretary of the Treasury Hugh McCulloch. "In accordance with the suggestion of Hon. J. F. Hartley, Assistant Secretary U. S. Treasury, I respectfully request that the Assistant Treasurer of the U. S. at San Francisco, California, may be directed to repay into the U. S Treasury such balances as he now holds to the credit of W. F. R. Schindler, late Lieutenant A. A. Q. M and A. C. S. 2nd Infantry California Vols., and transmit to me the usual evidence of such repayment. Said balances are reported as amounting to $5.51 as A. A. Q. M, and $36.75, as A. C. S.; and as having accrued during the year 1862."—LS, DNA, RG 56, Letters Received from the War Dept. On Nov. 20, Asst. Secretary of the Treasury John F. Hartley wrote to USG. "In answer to your letter under date of the 18th inst: I have this day directed the balances now standing on the books of the Asst. Treasurer U. S. at San Francisco, Cal. to the credit of W. F. R. Schindler, late Lieutenant A. A. Q. M and A. C. S. 2nd Infantry Cal. Vols, to be deposited to the credit of the U. S. Treasurer, and the original certificates of deposit to be transmitted to you."—LS, *ibid.*, RG 107, Letters Received from Bureaus.

1867, Nov. 18. To Secretary of the Treasury Hugh McCulloch. "I have the honor to send herewith a communication from the Chief of Engineers respecting the rendering of accounts to the Treasury by disbursing officers of the Corps of Engineers, and recommend that his request be granted and that the same regulation be made to govern officers of the Ordnance Department."—LS, DNA, RG 56, Letters Received from the War Dept. On Nov. 16, Brig. Gen. Andrew A. Humphreys, chief of engineers, had written to USG concerning these accounts.—LS, *ibid.* On Dec. 16, McCulloch wrote to USG. "I have the honor to acknowledge the receipt of your letter of the 18th ultimo, enclosing a request of A. HA. Humphreys Brig. Genl of Engineers, dated Nov. 16 1867, that officers and agents disbursing for the Engineer Department be authorized to render their accounts quarterly instead of monthly in which request you concur. and desire also that the same regulation be made to govern officers of the Ordnance Department. After a full examination of the subject which has prevented an earlier reply, I am of opinion that the necessity for monthly statements of these two classes of accounts having now terminated, the rule prevailing prior to the late rebellion of stating and forwarding them quarterly should be reestablished, and in pursuance of the authority conferred upon the Secretary of the Treasury by the act of Congress approved July. 17 1862, entitled 'An act to provide for the more prompt Settlement of the Accounts of Disbursing Officers' the same is hereby authorized and directed; said accounts to be mailed however within the limit fixed by said act."—LS, *ibid.*, RG 77, Accounts, Property Returns, and Claims, Letters Received.

1867, Nov. 18. Governor Alexander H. Bullock of Mass. to USG. "I beg leave to commend to the favorable consideration of the War Department, the application of Lt Edwin R Clark 26th US. Infantry, for promotion. Lieut Clark served with credit during the war, and I have no doubt would do honor to a higher commission whenever he should receive one, and it gives me pleasure [to] call your attention to him"—ALS (press), Massachusetts State Library, Boston, Mass.

1867, Nov. 18. Henry L. Burnett, Cincinnati, to USG. "I have the honor to recommend that the sentence of the Court Martial in the case of F. W. Hurtt, late Assistant Quartermaster U. S. Vols., with the rank of Captain, as promulgated in 'General Court Martial Orders, War Dept., No 170, of date June 17th, 1864, 'dishonorably dismissing him from the service of the United States, with loss of all pay and allowances now due or to become due,' be revoked. I was the Judge Advocate of the Court Martial that tried

Capt. Hurtt and passed the above sentence; I am therefore familiar with all the facts in the case. I commenced the trial with the strongest convictions of the guilt of the accused, and used all the legal power of the Government at my disposal as a Judge Advocate, to demonstrate that guilt by valid proof. Capt. Hurtt being defended by two able counsel, I considered, under the circumstances, that I acted solely in the interests of the Government. My mind was, I confess, greatly prejudiced against Capt. Hurtt personally, from the publications against him in the daily papers and from the representations of those who made the investigations upon which the charges and specifications were based. When I commenced the trial, I knew personally little or nothing about the facts, relying upon the ability and truthfulness of the persons who had made the investigations and report to me. For nearly seven weeks I labored as hard as I ever did in any case—and that was with all the ability and physical strength I possessed—to find and bring into Court legal testimony to sustain the charges and specifications. In this, it will be seen by the findings of the Court, in the great majority of the essential elements of the specifications, I failed; not from want of effort or desire, but simply because the proof did not exist. The only instances in which I was able to trace money belonging to the Government into the hands of Capt. Hurtt, which he had not accounted to the Government for, were those set out in the 1st and 2nd Specifications to the 1st Charge; and, without the proof made, sustaining those Specifications, I am satisfied that no sentence would have been passed upon him, but he would have been acquitted. Since the trial, Capt. Hurtt has submitted to me the affidavit of D. J. Manly,—at the time of the transactions set forth in said Specifications, Cashier or paying clerk for Capt. Hurtt,—who swears positively that the money received for the Commissary stores described in said specifications, (and which he, Capt. Hurtt, was found guilty of embezzling and misapplying,) was properly returned and accounted for, and formed part of the item of $475 85, of his account Current for the month of April, 1863, as proceeds of sale of boxes, &c. Manly was absent during the trial, at Natchez, Miss., and, although subpoenaed, did not reach this city until after the trial closed. Had he been present and sworn to these facts, Capt. Hurtt could not have been found guilty of the 1st & 2nd Specifications 1st charge; and consequently the sentence, mainly based upon them, as a matter of abstract justice should be revoked. I came out of the trial, after as hard a struggle as I have ever had in any Court Martial case, with my conviction of Capt. Hurtt's guilt of the many offences and crimes charged against him by the Press and those who made the investigation, almost entirely swept away, and all personal prejudice gone; and I believe my experience was that of every member of the Court. During the whole trial the Captain was frank and courteous, rendering every help in the investigation of his papers and accounts, concealing and withholding nothing. Within a few weeks, I have gone through the Record very carefully, to refresh my recollection of the testimony, and this review has strengthened me in the conviction that the sentence should be revoked. That Capt. Hurtt, during his official career in the Quartermaster's Department, was guilty of irregularities and improprieties, there can be no doubt or question; but I believe the same could be truly said of a majority of the Volunteer Quartermasters of the whole army during the first two years of their experience. The proof was strong, as will be seen by the Record, that the Government never had in her service a more energetic, industrious and efficient Quartermaster than Capt. Hurtt during the time of his service:—for these reasons chiefly I make the foregoing recommendation."—LS, War Dept. Collection, NN. Five members of the court added concurring endorsements.—AES, *ibid.* See *HED*, 43-1-255.

1867, Nov. 18.   William W. Morrow, Fairview, West Va., to USG. "I have the honor to respectfully request an appointment as Detective under the supervision of the War Department. I was a Sergeant in 1st West Va Inf. (Three months men) was a First Lieutenant in the 1st W. Va Light Artillery—have been advised by many prominent officers in the W. Va State Government that I possessed the qualifications or rather particular cast of character necessary to make such an officer—I respectfully request a consideration of my claims to such a place, and hope that this application may not be thrown aside—without at least subjecting it to the approval or disapproval of any one from West Virginia in whom you have confidence—"—ALS, DNA, RG 94, Letters Received, 1683M 1867.

1867, Nov. 19, 3:07 P.M.   To Bvt. Maj. Gen. John M. Schofield, Richmond. "Complaints have been made of incindiary fires in Faquer Co. Va. and disposition to do violence to men for their political opinions   Send an officer to ascertain the facts and if necessary send a squad of soldiers to give protection."—ALS (telegram sent), DNA, RG 107, Telegrams Collected (Bound); telegram sent, *ibid.*; telegram received, *ibid.*, RG 393, 1st Military District, Telegrams Received.

1867, Nov. 19.   To U.S. Consul William L. Duff, Glasgow, Scotland. "In reply to your request of the 22nd October last for a certificate of the death of *Private James Hill*, Company "D," 1st Missouri Light Artillery, I have the honor to inform you that it appears from the records of the Adjt. Genl's Office he was mustered out of service with company "C," of that regiment, (to which he was transferred) July 11th 1865. Nothing further is known of him."—Copy, DNA, RG 107, Letters Sent.

1867, Nov. 19.   Judge Advocate Gen. Joseph Holt to USG. "Respectfully returned to the Secretary of War, with an expression of opinion that the firm of *Chenault & Co.* have no legal claim upon the Government for payment of the demand within submitted. It appears that when the rebels took possession of Lexington, Ky. in 1862, they seized 4500 barrels of pork and 200.000 pounds of bacon held by claimants, as owners and consignees. This property the rebels conveyed to 'Camp Dick Robinson,' at which point they were forced to abandon it by the approach of the United States forces under Gen. Buell. . . ."—Copy, DNA, RG 153, Letters Sent.

1867, Nov. 19.   Governor Samuel J. Crawford of Kan. to USG. "Herewith I transmit a resolution passed unanimously by the Regents of the Kansas State Agricultural College: 'Resolved that Brevet Major Gen. J. W. Davidson, U. S. A. is the unanimous choice of this Board as Professor of Military Tactics and that we most earnestly request the Sec. of War to detail him for this office in accordance with the Act of Congress, approved July 28th 1866; U. S. Statutes at Large, page 336, Section 26.' The Legislature of Kansas at its last Session passed the accompanying Concurrent Resolution, asking for his detail. All of which is respectfully submitted. Hoping this will meet your approbation & favorable consideration . . ."— LS, DNA, RG 94, Letters Received, 1243S 1867. Related papers are *ibid.*

1867, Nov. 20.   To Secretary of the Treasury Hugh McCulloch. "I have the honor to transmit herewith a communication from Bvt Major-Genl Canby, Commanding the Second Military District, concerning the distillation of grain in the States of North and South Carolina, and to request, for the information of that officer, your views upon the subject presented therein."—LS, DNA, RG 56, Letters Received from the War Dept. On Nov. 30, McCulloch wrote to USG. "I have to acknowledge the receipt of your letter of November 20 transmitting a letter and enclosures from Brevet Major General Canby, Commanding the Second Military District and requesting for the information of that officer my views upon the subject presented therein. General Canby refers to the existence of a military general order prohibiting the distillation of grain within that military district and wishes, before acting on an application for revoking that order, to be informed whether its continuance is desired 'as an aid to the revenue officers.' He expresses the opinion that if the order is rescinded the revenue laws will in future be observed. On receipt of your letter and the accompanying papers I referred them to the Commissioner of Internal Revenue whose application to General Sickles in April last would seem to have been one of the circumstances which induced the issue of the order in question, and requested his opinion on the subject. He replies 'I see no reason why North and South Carolina should any longer be made an exception to the regular method of administering the revenue law and I have no hesitation in saying that as far as this Office is concerned there is no objection to the revocation of the aforesaid order.' I fully concur in the opinion thus expressed by the Commissioner of Internal Revenue."—LS, *ibid.*, RG 107, Letters Received from Bureaus.

1867, Nov. 20.   To Secretary of the Treasury Hugh McCulloch. "I have the honor to request that the Assistant Treasurer at New Orleans may be instructed to transfer Three thousand six hundred twelve dollars and fifteen cents, deposited with him by Lieutenant Samuel B. Wallace, 1st Infantry, (now deceased) to his successor in Office, Lieutenant L. O. Parker, 1st Infantry. The above amount pertains to the Post Fund of Jackson Barracks, and the Regimental Fund of the 1st U. S. Infantry, and is not public money."—LS, DNA, RG 56, Letters Received from the War Dept. On Nov. 22, Asst. Secretary of the Treasury John F. Hartley wrote to USG acknowledging his letter.—LS, *ibid.*, RG 107, Letters Received from Bureaus.

1867, Nov. 20.   To Attorney Gen. Henry Stanbery. "As suggested by the Judge Advocate General I have the honor to transmit herewith papers in the case of B. Mackall, Jr., against General John C. McFerran, Deputy Quartermaster General, U. S. A., with a request that you instruct the United States Attorney of the District of Columbia to defend the Government's interests involved in the proceeding as set forth in the paper."—LS, DNA, RG 60, Letters Received, War Dept.

1867, Nov. [20].   USG note. "Have Capt. Delos Geary and N P Wright 147 N. Y. Vols been breveted? If not give them the brevet of Maj."—AN (initialed), DNA, RG 94, ACP, W1103 CB 1867.

1867, Nov. 20.   USG endorsement. "Mr. Houghton, Editor of the Galena Gazette has been one of the most zealous, and efficient supporters of the War in the Western Country and I think is among the most deserving of Govt. patronage. I hope it will be found practicable to restore to his paper the patronage herein asked for it."—AES, DLC-Edward McPherson. Written on a letter of Nov. 18 from U.S. Representative Elihu B. Washburne, Washington, D. C., to Edward McPherson, clerk, U.S. House of Representatives. "I was somewhat surprised to find that during my absence, the printing of the laws had been taken away from the Galena Daily Gazette. This is one of the oldest papers in the entire northwest and has ever been noted for the ability with which it has been conducted & for its patriotic and loyal course. Its editor, H. H. Houghton, Esq. has been connected with it *thirty two* years, and is the oldest editor in the State, and is held in the highest esteem by all the editors in the State. The publication of the laws was given to the paper by the personal direction of Mr. Lincoln, as a recognition of the great services of Mr. Houghton to the old whig and republican cause. in that part of the State which rolls up the big majorities. I hope, therefore, under the circumstances, you will give the publication of the laws for the next session to this paper."—ALS, *ibid.*

1867, Nov. 20.   Oliver Ames, president, Union Pacific Railroad Co., to USG. "Hon E. H. Rollins is hereby appointed Agent of this Company to settle any and all claims of the Co. against the United States for transportation of troops mails and other property; and to receive from the United

States from time to time the Bonds issued by them to this Co as per Acts of Congress—"—LS, DNA, RG 107, Letters Received, U20 1867.

1867, Nov. 20.   Montgomery Blair, Washington, D. C., to USG. "My brothers friends in Missouri wrote urging him to aid in getting Maj J K Robinson a place in the Army—They say that he is well recommended—by Genl Schofield among others—As my brother is not here as his friends in the Missouri suppose or likely to be I take the liberty of calling your attention to this case—I am well acquainted with the gentlemen who wrote to him & know their statements to be correct—"—ALS, DNA, RG 94, ACP, B2174 CB 1867.

1867, Nov. 21.   To Secretary of the Interior Orville H. Browning. "I enclose papers relating to the military reservation at *Cape Disappointment* in Wash'n T'y, with a request that you will inform this Dept. as to the present condition of that reservation and furnish a plat of the same with an official copy of the declaration, if it shall be found to have been a second time declared."—Df, DNA, RG 107, Letters Received, H399 1867; copy, *ibid.*, Letters Sent to the President. The enclosure is *ibid.*, Letters Received, H399 1867.

1867, Nov. 21.   To Attorney Gen. Henry Stanbery. "At the suggestion of Major General George H. Thomas, Commanding the Department of the Cumberland, the enclosed papers, dated November 14th, 1867, respecting the discharge by a United States Court of W. A. Milligan, a citizen of Tennessee and paroled rebel soldier, charged with violating his parole, are transmitted, with a request that the necessary measures be taken to put the question before the United States Supreme Court."—LS, DNA, RG 60, Miscellaneous Files. The enclosures are *ibid.*, RG 109, Union Provost Marshals' File of Papers Relating to Individual Civilians. See telegram to Edwin M. Stanton, July 23, 1867. On Dec. 6, USG wrote to Speaker of the House Schuyler Colfax. "In reply to the Resolution of the House of Representatives of December 5th 1867, asking for the report of *Genl. G. H. Thomas* in the case of one *Milliken*, a returned rebel, arrested for violation of his parole and released from military custody by Judge Twigg of the U. S. Court on writ of habeas corpus, I have the honor to inform you that on the 14th November—agreeably to the suggestion of Genl. Thomas, the necessary measures for putting the question before the U. S. Supreme Court were taken by sending the report to the Attorney General, in whose possession, no doubt, it yet remains."—Copy, DNA, RG 107, Reports to Congress. On Dec. 17, Stanbery wrote to USG. "I have had under consideration the case of W. A. Milliken submitted for my opinion by your letter of November 21st. It appears that William A. Milliken, formerly a soldier in the rebel service, committed an assault upon a Northern man at Lagrange, Tennessee, and the military authorities under orders of General Thomas commanding the Department of the Cumberland at Louisville, Kentucky, arrested Milliken, and held him in military custody with a view of putting him on trial by a military commission for a violation of his parole. The terms of Milliken's parole given on the first of May, 1865, are that he will not take up arms against the Government of the United States until properly released from the obligation of his parole, and he is permitted to return to his home, not to be disturbed by the United States authorities so long as he observes his obligations, and obeys the laws in force where he may reside. Milliken was arrested by the military authorities in September, and shortly thereafter, Judge Trigg of the United States District Court of Wwestern Tennessee granted a writ of *habeas corpus* upon his application. The return upon the writ by the officer having him in custody was as follows: 'Held as a military prisoner for violation of his parole.' On the full hearing of the case, Judge Trigg discharged the prisoner. The question submitted to me is, Whether there is any mode by which this case can be taken to the Supreme Court of the United States? It appears that when the argument upon the *habeas corpus* was begun, Mr. Justice Swayne of the Supreme Court of the United States was on the bench with the District Judge, but left the court whilst the case was in progress. If he had remained and a difference of opinion has arisen between him and the District Judge, then upon a certificate of such difference of opinion, that question might have been brought before the Supreme Court of the United States. The case seems to have been left to the decision of the District Judge alone, and it does not appear that any question of difference of opinion arising between the judges before Judge Swayne left the court, was certified in the case. I have carefully examined the Judiciary Act of 1789, the second section of the act of March 3, 1803, the act of May 31, 1844, the act of August 29, 1842, the act of March 3, 1863, and the act of February 5, 1867. None of these acts seems to have any application to such a case as that of Milliken, except the last mentioned act of February 5, 1867. . . . If Milliken were in military custody charged with a military offence, the provisions of the act would not apply. His discharge by *habeas corpus* would then be forbidden, and the right of appeal given by the act would not apply. From the facts which appear in the case, I am not prepared to say that Milliken was held in custody for any known military offence; for whether his confinement is put simply on the ground of a breach of his parole by committing the assault, or indepently of a breach of parole, for committing the assault alone, I am not satisfied that either way he could be held to have committed any military offence cognizable by the military authorities. So far as the parole alone is concerned, I take it to be clear that that has no legal obligation after the cessation of the war; and so far as the assault upon the Northern man is concerned, neither of them being in the military service of the United States, it was in no sense a military offence within the meaning of the statute. If, in this case, the final decision of the court had been that Milliken should be remanded to military custody, I think under the provisions of the second section, Milliken would have been entitled to an appeal to the Supreme

Court of the United States. Whether upon a final decision discharging him from custody, an appeal would lie in favor of the party or parties who held him in custody, is not so clear, for the act provides that upon a judgment of discharge the prisoner is to be at once set at liberty. This, of course, would end the case and there would be nothing left upon which an appeal could be founded or upon which a reversal of judgment could operate. But, aside from this, and upon the merits of the case, I do not see that any error was committed by the judge in discharging Milliken, or that it would be advisable, even if it were practicable, to bring the case before the Supreme Court of the United States with any expectation of reversing that judgment."— LS, *ibid.,* Letters Received from Bureaus. On Dec. 24, USG wrote to Colfax. "Since the date of my communication of the 6th inst in reply to a Resolution of the House of Representatives, dated Dec 5th 1867 respecting the report of Major *General G H. Thomas* on the case of one *Milliken,* a returned rebel, arrested for violation of his parole who was released on a writ of habeas corpus, the report has been returned to this Department by the Attorney General of the U. S. and it is now communicated in compliance with said Resolution."—Copy, *ibid.,* Reports to Congress. See *HED,* 40-2-75.

1867, Nov. 21.   To Cyrus Curtiss, chairman, N. Y. quarantine commission. "A communication from the *N. Y. Commission of Quarantine,* of the 13th October, asking the War Department to recommend to the President that a reconveyance of *Oyster Island,* for Quarantine purposes, be made to the State of N. York, has been received and in reply thereto, I have to inform you that as it is the opinion of the law officer of the Department that 'property of the United States cannot be disposed of through the will of any of the Departments, but only by Act of Congress,' the request cannot be complied with."—Copy, DNA, RG 107, Letters Sent.

1867, Nov. 21.   Judge Advocate Gen. Joseph Holt to USG. "Private Charles P. Blair, Co. K, 37th U. S. Infy, was tried Oct. 10th last at Fort Reynolds, C. T. under the following charges: 1. Desertion. In deserting, on or about Aug. 9th last from the place where he had been placed on duty, Coon Creek, Kansas, and remaining absent until arrested near Fort Larned, Ks, Aug. 16. 1867. . . . The prisoner plead guilty to the first charge; not guilty to the remainder. The Court convict him under every charge except the second; and sentence him 'to be shot to death by musketry at such time and place as the General commanding the Department may direct: two thirds of the members concurring therein.' . . . Desertion is well known to be now a crime of extensive and indeed dangerous prevalence among the troops on the frontier, and its suppression at any cost is loudly called for. The present case develops itself in the proofs as one of an unusually aggravated character, the prisoner leaving the entire party to which he belonged liable to massacre, by deserting his post as sentinel at a time when an attack by hostile Indians was far from improbable. Should the sentence as it now stands be commuted the Executive, in accordance with the suggestion of the Dept. commander, the punishment advised by that officer is regarded as in no sense too severe."—Copy, DNA, RG 153, Letters Sent.

1867, Nov. 22.   To Secretary of the Treasury Hugh McCulloch. "Upon the recommendation of the Chief of Engineers I respectfully request that the following mentioned balances to the credit of Captain J. St. C. Morton, Corps of Engineers, may be repaid into the United States Treasury, and that the usual evidence of such repayments may be transmitted to me;— . . ."— LS, DNA, RG 56, Letters Received from the War Dept. On Nov. 21, Brig. Gen. Andrew A. Humphreys, chief of engineers, had written to USG. "I have the honor to request that application may be made to the Secretary of the Treasury to cause the following amounts standing to credit of Capt. J. St. C. Morton, Corps of Engineers, to be covered into the Treasury to his credit as follows— . . ."—LS, *ibid.*, RG 77, Accounts, Property Returns, and Claims, Letters Received. On Nov. 25, Asst. Secretary of the Treasury John F. Hartley wrote to USG. "In answer to your letter, under date of the 22nd inst. I have this day directed the following sums Viz: $6000. and $30.350.77, now standing respectively on the books of the U. S. Treasurer, and Asst. Treasurer NewYork to the credit of Capt. J. St. C. Morton, Corps Engineers to be placed to the credit of the U. S. Treasurer, and the original certificates on account of the appropriations designated in your letter, to be sent to you."—LS, *ibid.*, RG 107, Letters Received from Bureaus.

1867, Nov. 22.   To Postmaster Gen. Alexander W. Randall. "I have the honor to send herewith a comn from the Qr. Mr. Genl of the Army, dated Nov. 21st 1867 with a request that his recommendation that *Postal facilities* between *Camp Logan* and *Canon City* be provided for by the Post Office Dept., be complied with, if possible."—Copies, DNA, RG 92, Letters Received; *ibid.*, RG 107, Letters Sent to the President. The enclosure is *ibid.*, RG 92, Reports to the Secretary of War (Press).

1867, Nov. 22.   Judge Advocate Gen. Joseph Holt to USG. "James A. Clifford, 1st Lieut. 3d U. S. Cavy, was tried at Fort Union, New. Mex. by Gen. Ct. Martial, under the following charges: 1. Drawing and lifting up a weapon against his superior officer, in violation of the 9th art. of war. In making an assault with intent to kill upon the person of Lt. Col. A. Duncan, 125th Col. infantry, by drawing and lifting up a pistol upon him, cocking it and pointing at him, saying at the same time,—'Get down on your knees, damn you, I will kill you,' or words to that effect. This without cause or provocation, at Albuquerque, N. Mexo, on or about May. 2. 1867. . . . The foregoing detail of the proceedings at his recent trial and of his conduct before the Court, is thought to establish the unfitness of Lieut. Clifford for a commission in the army, whatever be the degree of his responsibility for his acts. If sane, his demeanor before the Court was so unseemly, and his outrage upon his superior officer Lt. Col. Duncan, so criminal, that the sen-

tence as pronounced by the Court must be regarded as in no sense too severe. If insane, it is manifest that an officer capable of acts of violence so
savage and so dangerous, should be no longer entrusted with the command
of troops, or even permitted to go at large. It is therefore respectfully advised that the suggestion formerly made by a General Ct. Martial and now
renewed by Judge Slough, his Counsel, to be acted on by the Executive prior
to any definite action upon the proceedings of the Court; and that before the
accused is dishonorably discharged from the army in accordance with his
sentence; which if sane, or if his insanity be feigned, he richly merits; an
official inquiry be ordered into his mental health."—Copy, DNA, RG 153,
Letters Sent.

1867, Nov. 23.   USG endorsement. "Respectfully refered to the President
attention invited to remarks of J A General"—ES, DNA, RG 153, NN
1750. Written below an endorsement of Nov. 15 of Judge Advocate Gen.
Joseph Holt. "Respectfully returned to the Secretary of War; whose attention is invited to a copy of a report of this Bureau addressed to the Secretary
of War, on May 12th 1864, in which the facts in regard to the killing, by
the within-named Robert T. Bridges, of James Rhodes, a citizen of Georgia,
are fully set forth. Bridges, who was a lieutenant in the rebel army, was,
on being captured by our forces, tried for this murder, convicted and sentenced to be hung. Gen. Thomas approved the sentence and forwarded the
record for the action of the President. This Bureau—as perceived from its
report—recommended the enforcement of the sentence; and the late President, in General Court Martial Order, No. 198, of July 16. '64, confirmed
it and ordered its execution. He afterwards, however, respited the accused;
and on Feb. 22. 1865, he was specially exchanged as a prisoner of war, by
order of Gen. Grant. Subsequently on Aug. 23, 1865, the President, upon
a report of this Bureau of Sept. 30, '64, (on which action appears to have
been deferred;) ordered the sentence to be carried into execution, unless
the case had been otherwise disposed of. Meanwhile it *had* been disposed of,
by the exchange; as has been seen. It is now stated, in behalf of Bridges, by
the writers of the within communication, that an indictment is pending
against him in a criminal court of Georgia; and the President is urged to
grant him a special pardon for his crime. This Bureau can perceive no
sufficient reason for an interference with the ordinary course of justice in
this case. The accused, when brought to trial, will doubtless have an opportunity to interpose a plea of a former conviction; and even should this be
overruled, there is nothing shown to justify the belief that he would not
have a fair trial on the merits. In view, however, of his present *status*, as
that of a citizen indicted for the murder of a citizen by a civil court, it is
conceived that an application for his pardon would properly be passed upon
by the Attorney General and not by this Bureau. The province of the Bureau, as also of the War Department, in regard to the case would appear to
have rightly terminated with the final action and order above mentioned."—
ES, *ibid.* On Sept. 27, 1864, President Abraham Lincoln had endorsed

Bridges's file. "Will Judge Advocate General please reexamine this case, taking these papers in with the former recom.d,"—AES, *ibid.* On Sept. 29, Lincoln suspended Bridges's execution. See Lincoln, *Works,* VII, 540; VIII, 26, 29; Johnson, *Papers,* 7, 138.

1867, Nov. 23.   To 2nd Auditor. "Lt. Genl Wm T. Sherman U. S. Army has presented to this Department his account for disbursement of the sum of five thousand dollars, Secret Service Fund deposited to his credit with the Asst. Treas'r. of the U. S. at New York on November 3th 1866. His vouchers amounting to $3,111.24 are proper and sufficient and are approved and will be filed in this Office as it is not expedient to send them to the Accounting Officers. The balance $1,888.76 he has turned over to the Disbursing Clerk of the War Department, as per his receipt herewith, who will be held accountable for it to the Treasury of the United States. Lt. Genl. Sherman will therefore be credited with the sum of five-thousand dollars Secret Service Fund on the books of the Treasury, and his account closed."—LS, DLC-William T. Sherman.

1867, Nov. [23].   USG note. "Give Gn. Brisbin 20 days leave of absence"—AN, DNA, RG 94, 656A 1867.

1867, Nov. 23.   1st Asst. Postmaster Gen. St. John B. L. Skinner to USG. "I am directed by the Postmaster General, to call your attention to the enclosed copy of a letter, recently received at this Department, from Dover Arkansas, and to inform you, that in consequence of the statements therein made, he has been compelled to discontinue the Post Office. The Postmaster General earnestly desires that such a course may be adopted by the War Department as will justify the reestablishment of the Post Office at Dover Arkansas at an early day."—LS, DNA, RG 94, Letters Received, 756P 1867. On Dec. 19, Capt. Henry Clayton, 19th Inf., Dover, Ark., reported that Postmaster James Fondren of Dover kept a saloon at the post office, sold liquor to soldiers, and had fled after being indicted.—ES, *ibid.*

1867, Nov. 23.   Judge Advocate Gen. Joseph Holt to USG. "Respectfully returned to the Secretary of War. This is a claim made by *R. T Kirkpatrick,* for compensation for the use and occupation of land upon which Fort Dan McCook is situated, near Nashville, Tenn., and for material and property taken and destroyed by the military authorities in the construction of that Fort. Before the date of the order directing the claimant to vacate the property, a Board of Appraisers was appointed by Gen. J. D. Morgan to estimate the damages, which they placed at $20.523. It appears that this claim has been considered favorably by the Claims Commission, but that the order relieving Genl. Canby having left the Commission without a quorum, the conclusions reached were not formally reported. They are however set forth in a brief accompanying the papers in the case. From these conclusions this Bureau is constrained to differ, as, in its opinion, the War Department has no legal authority for the settlement of claims of this nature, which should, it is believed, be referred to the legislative branch of the Government for such action as may be deemed demanded. The question was carefully considered by this Bureau, in the examination of a similar claim, made by Dr W. P. Jones of Nashville, and a report made thereon in August 1866, (copy enclosed) to which attention is respectfully invited."—Copy, DNA, RG 153, Letters Sent. On Dec. 5, Absalom H. Markland, Washington, D. C., wrote to USG. "I respectfully ask that the papers in the case of R. T. Kirkpatrick claimnt for materials, &c used, by military order, in building fort for the defence of Nashville Tene be returned to me."—ALS, *ibid.*, RG 107, Letters Received, M577 1867.

1867, Nov. 23. U.S. Representative Thomas D. Eliot of Mass., Washington, D. C., to USG. "I received today a letter concerning a claim held by some friends of mine before the Government under a charter of a Steam boat, during the war, which was lost while in service of the War Department. The claim was made some time ago, has been investigated by the proper officers and upon inquiry at the Treasury Department I find that payment is delayed because in another case a doubt has been expressed whether payment can properly be made under a recent Act of Congress passed in February last. The question has been considered by the 2d Comptroller and also was referred to Judge Holt, from the War Department. And I am informed that the officers at the Treasury are now waiting for an opinion of the Attorney General. I called this morning at the War Department to inquire if any action had been had by the Attorney General and to ask if I may do so, properly, that the question may be referred to him, if it has not been done. I do not know the merits of the case on which the question has arisen; but the one in which I am interested is said to depend upon the decision in that case, and the claim is so just that I am anxious to avoid longer delay."—ALS, DNA, RG 107, Letters Received, E93 1867.

1867, Nov. 23. U.S. Representative William S. Lincoln of N. Y., Washington, D. C., to USG. "At a meeting of the Special Committee of the House of Representatives charged with the investigation of the affairs of the Paymaster General's office, held at their Chambers in Washington D. C. on the 22d day of November inst. It was *Ordered* that the Paymaster General be requested to furnish for the use of the Committee duly certified copies of all the *charges information* and *evidence* on file in his office of official misconduct on the part of Colonel *Thomas M. Winston* late Chief Paymaster of the 'Pay District of the Gulf,' together with a report of all the proceedings taken to investigate the truth of said charges or information; and the result thereof; also what *final action was taken thereon.*—And upon the same day it was further Ordered that the Paymaster General be requested to furnish for the use of said Committee the names of all the Paymasters on duty in the 'Pay District of the Gulf.' during the months of January and February 1866. In pursuance of the foregoing Orders I have the honor to request that the Secretary of War cause the before mentioned information to be furnished the Committee at as early a day as practicable—"—LS, DNA, RG 99, Letters Received.

1867, Nov. 25. To Secretary of the Interior Orville H. Browning. "In reply to your comn of the 6th inst. asking the transfer of certain frame houses on *Reservation No. 17* to the Interior Dept. for offices and work-shops, I have the honor to inform you that as those buildings are now occupied by the enlisted men, and laundresses of the 12th Infy. it is re-gretted that the necessities of the military service will not admit of a com-pliance with the request."—Copy, DNA, RG 107, Letters Sent to the Presi-dent. On Nov. 6, Browning had written to USG. "I am informed that upon reservation No 17, on which this Department has commenced the erection of the New Jail in and for this District, there are some small board houses, believed to belong to the War Department. The Architect, in charge of the building, has made application to this Department to have them placed at his service for offices and workshops. If belonging to the War Department, and not essential to its service, I would be pleased if you would issue the necessary order to transfer them to this Department for the purpose above named"—LS, *ibid.*, RG 92, Consolidated Correspondence, Washington, D. C. On Nov. 15, Browning wrote to USG renewing the request.—LS, *ibid.* On Nov. 22, Bvt. Maj. Gen. Charles Thomas, asst. q. m. gen., wrote to USG. "I have the honor to return the enclosed communication of the Secretary of the Interior of the 6th inst. requesting the transfer to his De-partment of certain Government Buildings on Reservation No 17 in this District, and to respectfully invite your attention to the report of Lieut N. W Deane A. R. Q. M—approved by Bvt Lieut Col P. W. Wallace Comd'g at Russell Barracks, from which it appears that the buildings referred to— are now occupied by the Laundresses and Enlisted men of the 12th US. Infantry, and therefore cannot be given up unless new buildings are pro-vided for the above named Regiment."—LS, *ibid.* On Dec. 2, Browning wrote to USG. "I respectfully invite your attention to the enclosed copy of a letter received by this Department from Mr Ebon Faxon Architect for the New Jail in relation to the urgent necessity for the removal of the buildings situated on Reservation No 17, selected as a site for the New Jail   I have the honor to request that as the space occupied by these buildings will be required for the erection thereon of workshops actually necessary for a speedy and proper construction of the New Jail authorized by law that you will cause the necessary order in the premises to be issued for their re-moval"—LS, *ibid.*, RG 48, Miscellaneous Div., Letters Received. On Dec. 17, Bvt. Maj. Gen. Daniel H. Rucker, act. q. m. gen., wrote to USG con-cerning this matter.—LS, *ibid.* On Dec. 21, USG wrote to Browning. "At the suggestion of the Qr. Mr. Genl of the Army, I have the honor to send herewith papers respecting the removal of the temporary building from Reservation No. 17, on which it is proposed to erect the *new jail for the Dist. of Columbia,* and for the reasons given in his comn. of the 17th inst., herewith request that the removal may be deferred until Spring. A return of papers is respectfully asked."—Copy, *ibid.*, RG 107, Letters Sent to the President.

1867, Nov. 25.   To Secretary of State William H. Seward. "I have the honor to acquaint you that instructions have been given to the Chief of Ord. to comply with the request of the British Chargé D'Affaires of the 14th Nov. 1867 transmitted in your note of the 16th inst., for *specimens of gunpowder* used in the U. S and for details as to its manufacture."—Copies, DNA, RG 107, Letters Sent to the President; *ibid.*, RG 156, Letters Received. On Nov. 16, Seward had written to USG. "I have the honor to invite your favorable attention to the inclosed copy of a note of the 14th instant from Mr Ford, Chargé d'Affaires of Great Britain, who has been instructed by his Government to obtain, for the use of Her Majesty's War Department, specimens of Gunpowder used in the United States Army, together with full details as to the working and the manufacture of the various samples sought."—LS, *ibid.* The enclosure is *ibid.*

1867, Nov. 25.   To Attorney Gen. Henry Stanbery. "At the instance of the Second Comptroller of the Treasury I have the honor to transmit the papers connected with the claim of Messrs Brott and Davis for the loss of a barge in the military service, requesting your opinion upon the question presented by the Comptroller, and in connection therewith beg to invite your attention to the opinion of the Judge Advocate General of the Army, furnished by invitation for the information of this Department."—Copies, DNA, RG 107, Letters Sent to the President; *ibid.*, Letters Received from Bureaus. On Oct. 3, Judge Advocate Gen. Joseph Holt had written to USG. "The accompanying papers relate to a claim for the value of the *Barge* '*Brott & Davis,*' impressed and seized, at New Orleans, in June 1864, by the Chief Quartermaster of the Department of the Gulf, and sunk and lost in the Mississippi River, while being used for the transportation of army teams. . . . In the present case the Barge, while being used as aforesaid, and in tow of a steamer, was found to be leaky; her load was then transferred to another boat, and she was abandoned in a sinking condition, near the River bank, where she was found on the next day sunk in ten feet of water, and a total loss. . . . The parties, whose loyalty appears not to be disputed, and whose claim is certainly meritorious, must—it is conceived— have recourse to Congress for relief."—Copy, *ibid.*, RG 153, Letters Sent.

1867, Nov. 25.   USG endorsement. "Respectfully refered to the Chief Eng. for his views in this case.—It is understood the application for the restoration of the rail-road iron refered to is in the Eng. bureau."—AES, DNA, RG 77, Accounts, Property Returns, and Claims, Letters Received. Written on a letter of Nov. 23 from Edward N. Dickerson, president, Florida Railroad Co., New York City, presumably to U.S. Representative Nathaniel P. Banks of Mass.—ALS, *ibid.* On Nov. 25, Banks wrote to USG.

"Mr Edwin N. Dickinson, President of the Florida railroad Company, has made application for the restoration ~~of~~ to the Company of a quantity of railroad iron, taken by the United States Army for the construction of Fort Clinch. The receipt of Major Sears, to whom the iron was delivered, with other papers in the case, is on the files of the War Department. The iron is still at the Fort, and has not been used for the purpose for which it was taken. I suppose there is no doubt of the facts stated in the accompanying letter, and I will be very glad if you will give instructions to have the case examined, and make such decision as seems to be proper. The iron is now needed for the completion of the road which is essential to the development of the industrial interests of that part of the country, as well as to the political restoration of the State. This iron is needed to complete the track at Fernandina, to the wharf, and therefore is necessary, to make the railway available to commerce. The parties will esteem it a great favor if ~~you~~ immediate attention can be given to the subject."—LS, *ibid.* On Nov. 30, USG wrote to Secretary of the Treasury Hugh McCulloch. "I have the honor to send herewith certain papers from the Honorable N. P. Banks and Edward N. Dickerson respecting the return of some Railroad iron used in the construction of Fort Clinch, Florida. As the iron belongs to the class of captured or abandoned property and cannot therefore be disposed of by this Department the subject is respectfully referred to the Treasury Department for such action as is deemed proper."—LS, *ibid.*, RG 56, Div. of Captured and Abandoned Property, Letters Received. On Dec. 4, McCulloch wrote to USG. "I have the honor to acknowledge the receipt of certain papers respecting the return to Edward N. Dickerson and others of a qantity of Railroad iron used in or about Fort Clinch, Florida; the papers being referred by you to this Department for the reason that the iron is supposed to belong to the class of captured and abandoned property—Upon examination of the documents submitted it appears that the iron has never been transferred to the custody of any Treasury Agent, but still remains in the charge of the military—As, for this reason, no action can properly be taken upon the petition the papers are herewith returned, as requested by claimant."— LS, *ibid.*, RG 77, Accounts, Property Returns, and Claims, Letters Received.

1867, Nov. [25]. USG endorsement. "Approved"—AES (undated), DNA, RG 94, Correspondence, USMA. Written on a letter of Nov. 25 from Bvt. Maj. Gen. Edmund Schriver, inspector gen., to USG. "I have the honor to recommend the following addition to the 21st paragraph of the Military Academy Regulations of 1866, viz:—'And shall further sign a written pledge, on his honor, that he will not in any manner improperly interfere with, harass, molest or injure new Cadets, nor compel or permit them to perform menial services or do for him anything imcompatible with their position as Cadets and gentlemen. And any Cadet declining to comply with the foregoing provisions shall be discharged from the Academy.' "— LS, *ibid.*

1867, Nov. 25. To Governor Jonathan Worth of N. C. "Your letter of the 22d ultimo to the President asking that the letter book of Governor Vance, and the papers captured with it be returned to you, has been referred to this Department, and in reply I have to say that the book and papers referred to are of such a nature as to require that they be retained in the custody of the United States. There are records of a few pardons in the letter book, copies of which are sent herewith."—LS, Governors' Papers, North Carolina State Archives, Raleigh, N. C.

1867, Nov. 25. Secretary of State William H. Seward to USG. "I have the honor to invite your attention to the inclosed letter of the 7th instant. from a catholic priest, M Torregiani, of England who desires to receive information concerning the estate of Michael Cleary, said to have been an Assistant Clerk in the War Department. Anything you can ascertain which may gratify the request of M Torregiani, I will thankfully receive and forward to him."—LS, DNA, RG 107, Letters Received from Bureaus. The enclosure and related papers are *ibid.*

1867, Nov. 25. Judge Advocate Gen. Joseph Holt to USG. "On February 11th. last, I had the honor to submit to the Secretary of War for his approval, a draft, prepared at this Bureau, of a proposed Act of Congress, framed for the purpose of remedying some of the chief and most embarrassing defects in our military code. . . . If, General, the legislation proposed and the views thus presented shall meet your approval, I have the honor to repeat the request that the draft of the Bill with this communication, duplicate copies of both of which are herewith contained, may be submitted to the Military Committees of the Houses of Congress, for action."—Copy, DNA, RG 153, Letters Sent. The enclosure is *ibid.*

1867, Nov. 25. Judge Advocate Gen. Joseph Holt to USG. "First Lieutenant B. F. Ryer, 2nd U. S. Arty, was tried at San Francisco, Cal. on the 3d of Oct. last, by Gen. Court Martial, under the following charges:—1. Conduct to the prejudice of good order and mil. discipline. 1. In that the accused, being at the time stationed at Fort Point, Cal'a, did on or about the evening of Sept. 25th, while in a state of intoxication, enter the Q. M. stables at Presidio of San Francisco and did without authority order the enlisted man in charge to hitch up the private buggy of the Q. M., and did insist on taking the same; and did take and retain said buggy until the following morning, when it was returned in a broken and damaged condition. . . . However the dismissal of Lieut. Ryer may be a thing to be desired, it is beleived the interests of the service, in the matter of the independence and efficiency of military courts, will be better subserved by a disapproval of the sentence in this case."—Copy, DNA, RG 153, Letters Sent.

1867, Nov. 25. U.S. Representative Nathaniel P. Banks of Mass. to USG. "Let me request your consideration of the application of Major.

Jno A. Brodhead of Mass. now Paymaster of Volunteers, for appt as paymaster in the Regular Army. He served during the war, bears an excellent
character and his record with the Paymaster General, is I believe without
blemish"—ALS, DNA, RG 94, ACP, 2621 1875. Other recommendations
addressed to USG are *ibid.*

1867, Nov. 26.   USG endorsement. *"Brevet Col. Blunt*, U. s. Engineers,
will repair to the City of Washington as soon as his duties will admit with
a view to giving testimony before the Commissioners appointed under Resolution of Congress approved July 26, 1866 to examine into *the claim of the
State of Massachusetts on account of Coast Defence.* On reaching Washington he will confer with Brevet Maj. Gen'l. *Jas. A. Hardie*, Inspector
Gen'l. U. S A   After completing this special service Col. Blunt will return
to his proper station."—ES, DNA, RG 94, Letters Received, 1058B 1867.
Written on a letter of Nov. 25 from Brig. Gen. Andrew A. Humphreys,
chief of engineers, to Bvt. Maj. Gen. James A. Hardie, inspector gen., concerning this matter.—LS, *ibid.*

1867, Nov. 27.   Maj. Gen. Oliver O. Howard to USG. "I have the honor
to request that when a change of Commanding officers transpires in the
State of Louisiana, the Military Commander of that State be also appointed
Assistant Commissioner of this Bureau, in order to make the two offices
coincident."—LS, DNA, RG 94, Letters Received, 320F 1867.

1867, Nov. 27.   Ambrose W. Thompson to USG. "The Board of Directors of the 'Hudson River West Shore Rail Road Company' have instructed
me to apply to the Secretary of War, for the right of way on the river front
of West Point, for locating the Rail Road, which, by the laws of the State
of New York, the company are authorised to construct on the West Shore
of the Hudson River. I therefore have the honor to make this application to
you, and forward herewith the Engineers map and Estimates of Cost, showing the several feasible projected lines, numbered 1. 2 & 3, and in behalf of
the company solicit the right over that line which may be least objectionable
to the War Department. I should also respectfully state, that economy in
construction, and early completion of the work are objects with the company, and if upon inspection of the lines, you find that no injury will result
to the public service, or by locating the road on the line ('No 1—water—')
the company would specially solicit that line to secure the objects named.—
In consideration of this grant the company are willing to enter into such
stipulations for reasonable reduction on Government transportation, as you
may deem proper, and to embody the same in an agreement or contract,
which Mr Bergholz is authorised to enter into—Trusting that this part of a
great route demanded by the increasing commerce of New York, may meet
with your approval, and that the grant may be made."—LS (press), DLC-
Ambrose W. Thompson. On Jan. 15, 1868, Bvt. Brig. Gen. Cyrus B.
Comstock wrote to William R. Bergholz. "The Surgeon General having

reported that to prevent injury to health at the post of West Point, all water spaces between the line of the Hudson River West Shore R. R, and the shore of the river should be filled up to the level of the Railroad and so graded that the new surface shall drain itself, Gen. Grant deems this the first and main condition with reference to your line No. 1, at West Point: As this condition might make it desirable to the company to change that location, he wishes to say that a tunnel whose general direction is from station 1615 to station 1655 would be still more satisfactory. . . ."—Copies, DLC-USG, V, 47, 60; DNA, RG 108, Letters Sent.

1867, Nov. 27.   Mrs. A. W. True, Washington, D. C., to USG. "With this I inclose a statement as nearly as I am capable what I suppose you may require to aid you in ariving at a just appreciation of my sons services in the army during the ~~the~~ past war   I may have failed in giving correct terms to what I wished to convey but I am sure what I have said is in substance true—I will only further add that ~~that~~ you may in a measure appreciate my loss, that I have brought those sons forward and attended principally to their education myself, their father having died when the two youngest were but lads. In doing so I sacrificed nearly all my available means. It was just at the point when they had become capable of rendering back to me for all my care and toil a greatful and happy return, that the Rebellion commenced—They like others left all, and went as they thought to the rescue of their country as you will see without the promptings of large bounties as was the case in after time—They endured the first and hardest experience of the war when all except Officers in high rank were uneducated in the science of warefare.—After my sons left for the army I with my own hands and heart commenced my labours for the relief as far as I could, of the suffering soldiers and their families   I spent nearly all my time as did many other ladies and only ceased when we were told that our services were no longer needed. I respectfully submit this to you hoping that you may be able to benefit me either by your authority or council"—ALS, DNA, RG 107, Letters Received, T194 1867.

1867, Nov. 28.   Bvt. Maj. Gen. John Pope, Atlanta, to USG. "I have before me, for my decision and orders thereon, the records of the trial by Court-Martial, of several soldiers for desertion, the sentence in each case being that the prisoner 'shall forfeit all pay and allowances that are or may become due him except the just dues of the laundress, to be indelibly marked on the right hip with the letter "D" one and one half inches in length, and ten days thereafter to have his head shaved and be drummed out of the service.' In the Digest of the Opinions of the Judge Advocate General p 194. (3), it is stated that 'the penalty of branding or marking, however mildly it may be executed, is regarded as against public policy and opposed to the dictates of humanity and consequently as not conducive to the interests of the service,' and 'it is conceived, therefore, that if reviewing officers should, in general, remit that part of a sentence of Court-Martial

which imposes this penalty upon the deserter they would materially promote the welfare of the Military Service.' My great respect for the opinions
of the Judge Advocate General and the fact that the decision quoted is
presumed to have the sanction of the War Department, induces me to call
the question of the propriety of marking deserters with the letter "D" to
your attention, and request your instructions in that respect. I need not say
to you that desertions from the Army now are of such frequent occurrence
as to demand the adoption of the most efficient means to prevent them. The
government is subjected annually to a vast expense in enlisting, clothing,
feeding and transporting a lot of vagabonds who enter the army with no
purpose of fulfilling the terms of their enlistment and desert whenever it
suits their convenience to do so; They are worth nothing while in the Army
and their desertion would be a good riddance were it not for the influence of
their example upon better men—Generally the only means of retaining them
in the Army is by keeping them in the guard house or military prisons.
This sort of life they find rather comfortable, than otherwise, as they are
clothed and fed and have but little, if any thing to do. They find it quite
convenient to leave the pinching cold and want of a Northern city to spend
a winter in the South and desert and return to the North in the Spring.
Should times become hard with them again they can re-enlist under other
names and go through the same process again. Now the only way to get
clear of these worthless fellows, seems to me, to be to put the 'ineffaceable'
brand of desertion upon them. The prospect of such a punishment will do
much to deter men from deserting and it will prevent all who have sufferred
its execution from re-enlisting. It is to be hoped that the knowledge that
desertion will be 'ineffaceably' punished will secure to the army a better
class of recruits and relieve it of the disgrace of its long roll of deserters.
Justice to the faithful men, of whom the army is largely composed, demands that some more efficient means of preventing desertion should be
adopted and rigidly enforced. The deserters not only impose upon the faithful men the performance of the duties which the deserters themselves should
perform but the extra duty of pursuing, capturing and guarding them. I
will await your answer before taking action in the cases now before me."—
LS, DNA, RG 94, Letters Received, 955W 1867.

1867, Nov. 29.   To Postmaster Gen. Alexander W. Randall. "I have the
honor to transmit herewith a recommendation of Nov. 12th 1867 from the
Com'dg Off. at *Ft. Jackson,* La., that a Post Office be established at that
post, and to request that the trader's clerk there be appointed the PostMaster"—Df, DNA, RG 107, Letters Received from Bureaus; copy, *ibid.,* Letters Sent to the President.

1867, Nov. 29.   USG endorsement. "Gen. Canby should be authorized to
retain the horses, for the service indicated, so long as the necessity for their
use exists."—ES, DNA, RG 94, Letters Received, 395Q 1867. Written on

a letter of Oct. 31 from Bvt. Lt. Col. Thomas B. Hunt, Charleston, to Bvt. Maj. Gen. Daniel H. Rucker, act. q. m. gen. "I respectfully call your attention to the enclosed Circular of September 28th 1866. In obedience to that Circular a large number of Horses were drawn from this Depot to mount Infantry in North and South Carolina for Scouting purposes. In obedience to G. O. No 88 A. G. O. Sept 21st 1867 I issued orders that all Horses belonging to the Quartermasters Department, except those mentioned in Par 6 of said order, should be immediately turned in. The A. A. Qr Mr of the different posts, report that many of these Horses are still used by the Infantry for Scouting purposes. I have allowed these Horses to remain in use for this purpose upon the advice of Bvt Maj Genl E. R. S. Canby Commanding 2d Military District, until the matter be decided at Washington. I therefore respectfully ask whether under G. O. No 88 they are authorized to be used by the Infantry for the purpose of Scouts."—LS, *ibid.*

1867, Nov. 29. USG endorsement. "It gives me great pleasure to endorse what Prof. Agassiz says in behalf of Mr H. Erni."—Copy, DLC-Carl Schurz. Written on a letter of Jan. 20, 1852, from Louis Agassiz, Charleston, S. C., "To the Trustees of the College at Huntsville. It gives me great pleasure, to testify that Prof. Erni has been known to me for many years as a distinguished student of chemistry, prior to his coming to this country. From the able professor of that science in the University in Zürich, and from other eminent scientific men of that faculty, I understood, that he was a promising investigator, likely to assume an independant standing among natural philosophers, before he had an opportunity of showing, as he has done afterwards, that he is equally able to teach and to trace original investigations. His attainments are not limited to the special department to which he has particularly devoted himself—chemistry and its application to the arts—; but natural sciences in their different branches, botany, zoology, and minerology, are equally familiar to him and his knowledge of modern languages enables him to trace the progress of these sciences in France and Germany as well as in England and this country, and from his amiable character the best influence is to be expected upon his pupils everywhere. I can strongly recommend him for a professorship in the new college at Huntsville. I expect with full confidence, that he will give entire satisfaction to the Trustees of that Institution."—Copy, *ibid.*

1867, Nov. 29. Bvt. Maj. Gen. Daniel H. Rucker, act. q. m. gen., to USG. "I have the honor to acknowledge receipt of Department letter of the 27th inst, requesting the filling without delay requisition of the Surgeon General for the 'Pullan Ventilator' tents, and to state, that on the 13th inst, General Crosman, Chf. Q Mr Dept, of the East, was ordered to prepare at once, 200 Hospital tents, with the 'Pullan Ventilator.' that being the number called for by the Surgeon General."—LS, DNA, RG 92, Reports to the Secretary of War (Press).

1867, Nov. 30.   USG order. "The Signal Corps being a temporary organization, and the law providing that 'officers of the Army, who may be
appointed in this Corps, may, after the rebellion, be restored to their respective regiments or corps, and receive the same rank and promotion as if they
had continued to serve therein,' appointments in the Signal Corps are not
considered as depriving any officer of the Army of any regular commission
held by him prior to such appointment."—Copy, U.S. Signal Center, Fort
Monmouth, N. J.

1867, Nov. 30.   Judge Advocate Gen. Joseph Holt to USG concerning
Private Louis Lark. "The within prisoner was tried at West Point, under
the charge of—Advising and persuading a soldier to desert. There being no
evidence to sustain the charge, the Court acquitted him. The proceedings
should be approved."—Copy, DNA, RG 153, Letters Sent.

1867, Nov. 30.   Judge Advocate Gen. Joseph Holt to USG concerning
Private James Lynch. "The within prisoner was tried at West Point, under
the following charges:—1. Conduct prejudicial to good order and military
discipline. In being drunk and disorderly in quarters after tattoo. 2. Disobedience of orders. In refusing to go to the guard house, and offering
resistance, when ordered to be confined by Sergt. O'Brien, 1st Sergeant of
the detachment. The testimony of Sergt. O.Brien is strongly in support of
the charges; that of all the other witnesses for the prosecution, as strongly
in acquittal. The Court acquit the accused. It is advised that the proceedings & findings be approved. The findings of the court convict Serg't.
O'Brien, by implication, of perjury; certainly of the grossest exaggeration
of the facts. In view of this fact, and of the circumstance that O'Brien
wounded the prisoner purposely with a bayonet while in the hands of the
guard, when, as the Court find, he was neither drunk nor disobedient, and
therefore was unjustly and causelessly ill-treated by the 1st. Sergt. it is
thought that some inquiry should be made into the character of Sergeant
O'Brien for temper and sobriety, and his general treatment of the men
under his control. Attention is respectfully directed to the case of private
Wells, which is herewith submitted, and in which the Court similarly disregard a portion of O'Brien's evidence."—Copy, DNA, RG 153, Letters
Sent.

1867, Nov. 30.   Maj. Gen. Oliver O. Howard to USG. "To be mustered
out under your order there will be about one hundred and fifty officers.
Now, the necessities of the Bureau will require me to employ these, or a
part of them, as civil agents. I have the honor to request that the attention
of the President be called to this subject again, with the view to the retention in the military service of such officers as may be necessary for the work
of the Freedmen's Bureau during its continuance. I should earnestly recommend it for the following reasons: 1st The difference of pay will not be

material under the present law, and the same officers cannot easily be retained under reduced compensation. 2nd The efficiency of the same men as officers of the army is double what it would be as civilians, owing to the respect their rank always gives them and the coöperation secured with other military officers of the regular service. If it be desired that the pay of these officers should be defrayed by the Freedmen's Bureau on and after January 1st 1868, this could be done by a simple order from yourself directing that the Bureau should assume the pay of these Volunteer officers. I can see no possible gain in the way of economy, efficiency, or necessity, by the muster out of these officers and the substitution therefor of civil agents. You are aware that the instant a volunteer officer could be dispensed with, or could be replaced by an officer of the regular service fit for the duties involved, such officer has always been recommended for muster out by me in the past, and will be in the future, as I do not wish to expend one cent more than is absolutely essential to the effective execution of the law. The great majority of the officers for whom I ask this favor are men who have been wounded in the service, many of them without arms or legs. Further, they are officers against whom very few complaints have arisen from any quarter. Petitions come to me from all parties for the retention of some of them in the military service. The law will admit of it, and I think good order and good Government will be promoted by it. I therefore earnestly recommend a reconsideration of this subject, and a revocation or modification of the order from the War Department, dated Nov. 26th 1867"—LS, DNA, RG 107, Letters Received from Bureaus. AGO General Orders 101, Nov. 26, required that all vol. officers be mustered out as of Jan. 1, 1868.—D, *ibid.*, RG 94, Letters Received, 887W 1867.

1867, Nov. 30.   To John B. Murray, New York City. "Your several letters of Octr 8th Nov. 5th & 8th respecting the revocation of the War. Dept. order prohibiting the Bureaus of the Dept. from transacting business with your firm, have been received & the whole subject has been referred to the Judge Advocate General to whom any further correspondence in the case may be addressed."—Copy, DNA, RG 107, Letters Sent. On Oct. 28 and Nov. 5, Murray had written to USG. "Will you have the goodness to forward to me your report upon the case submitted in my letter of 8th inst and also return to me the book of correspondence relating to it." "I again respectfully ask for a report on the case presented to you some time ago—and which is in the hands of Genl. Dent with the report of the Subordinate Officers of the Dept. As it affects the integrity & reputation of my house, my urgency may be excusable."—ALS, *ibid.*, Letters Received, M528 1867, M550 1867. On Dec. 6, Judge Advocate Gen. Joseph Holt wrote to USG. "The correspondence of *John B. Murray*, Banker, with the War and Treasury Department has been examined and carefully considered by this Bureau. It appears that on the 31st. of March 1862 Murray received payment of the account of Lieut. D. R. Franklin, 56th N. Y. Vols. whose resignation was accepted from Hd. Qrs.

Army of the Potomac on the 14th of the same month, amounting to $825.05. When the accounts of the Paymaster who made the payment (Maj. Prott,) were examined in the Second Auditor's Office, in April 1864, it was discovered that Franklin's name was not borne on the rolls of the regiment and that another person held the office, and performed the duties during the time for which he had secured payment. Mr. Murray was notified of the fact, and deposited the amount he had received with the Asst. U. S. Treasurer, in New York, subject to the final decision of the Auditor, and sought to collect evidence that Franklin had been legally mustered into service. It seems that Franklin's resignation was presented direct to Head Quarters and there accepted, without going through the regular channels where the facts in his case would have been brought to light. It was found at the War Department, upon comparing the resignation with other papers, that it had been drawn up in Murray's office. This circumstances was deemed to implicate Murray in the fraud which had been perpetrated by Franklin, and the order prohibiting officers from recognizing him in any transaction was published. Subsequently a copy of the muster roll of the company was received at the Adjutant General's Office, on which Franklin's name appeared as mustered into service July 31st. and resigned and discharged Sept. 27. 1861. The 2d. Comptroller allowed pay to Sept. 8th, the date on which Franklin's successor was mustered. It is clearly evident that Franklin is guilty of fraud, but the complicity of Murray is by no means established. The latter has been persistent in his efforts to have the order directed against him revoked, and has seemingly made frank and honest statements of his connection with the case, and has ever claimed that Franklin should be paid up to the date of his discharge. It can readily be perceived how Murray, who is a banker, could have been deceived by Franklin whose papers were pronounced good by the pay master who paid the account; and if he can satisfactorily explain the circumstances attending the preparation of the resignation, it is believed that the order against him should be revoked. It does not appear from the papers submitted that he has ever been called upon to exculpate himself from the suspicion attached to his connection therewith. The book of correspondence has been forwarded to Mr. Murray's address as directed by the Secretary of War."—Copy, *ibid.*, RG 153, Letters Sent.

1867, Nov.   U.S. Representative Sidney Clarke of Kan. endorsement to USG. "I think the above application is right, and that if the right of way asked for is granted, it will be alike conducive to the interests of the general public and of the government. I earnestly urge that the application be granted."—*HED*, 40-2-108. Written on a petition of Nov. 12 from the Leavenworth and Des Moines Railroad Co. requesting permission to cross Fort Leavenworth.—*Ibid.*

1867, DEC. 1.   Nicholas P. Trist, "*quondam* (at the same period) Comr Plenipotentiary of the U. S.,—who, by assuming the grave responsibility (rendered the more perilous to himself by its altogether doubtful success) of disobeying a peremptory order, did thereby liberate that Army from the certainty of an indefinitely prolonged detention in Mexico, wasting its energies & its substance in watching guerillas: thus restoring it to their Country, as a reserve for her own hour of need and of sore trial, and rescuing Her from the inevitable consequences of 'Permanent Occupation.' " "Near Chester," Pa., to USG, "*quondam* (in Aug & Sep. 1847) 2nd Lieut 4th Inf. U. S. A." "Doubly overburdened as U. S. Grant now is, by the charge of *two* posts, either one of which would demand the whole time and severely test the powers of endurance of any man, it must go against the conscience of any other man having a conscience to obtrude upon him with any personal concern of his own.—In the present case it certainly is most reluctantly—a reluctance so strong as to require motives of the greatest force to overcome it,—that I venture to do so, by asking of you, as a personal kindness, to read this, and then (if your public duties allow you time) to run your eye over the enclosed letters (copies) of *Henry C. Carey, S. M. Felton,* & *Robt Dale Owen:* which having done, to write & mail to me these five words, *Yes, I can & will,* or else the one word *Impossible,* as your reply to this enquiry: *Can you, & will you spare the time requisite* (a full hour or more) *for a perusal of the Memorial referred to by Mr Carey?* In case your reply be favorable, I will send it to you; and you will, after glancing your eye over it, do me the further kindness, to write me, *It will do,* or *It will not do,* as the expression of your judgment; and also, should it be presented to Congress, to do personally in speaking to your friends, whatever your judgment & feelings may dictate towards securing attention to it. Since those days when all eyes were anxiously turned upon me,—not because of anything in me, or done by me, but from the accident of position merely, from [m]y *chancing* to be the person occupying that position (*not* of my seeking, but forced upon me)—Since those Mexican days, we have met but once; that once, at a moment when the eye of the Nation was riveted upon you: Not, in your case as it had been in mine, through accident of any kind, but from the greatness of the deeds achieved by you. That one meeting was another accident, so far concerned me: it arose from the mere chance of my being with Mr Felton, Prest of the RR. Co from which I hold the employment that gives me a living, at the moment when, in order to pay to you the attention to which he deemed you entitled, he went to the Continental Hotel, inviting me to accompany him. But, if you have never seen me since, it has not been from any want of a fellow-feeling with the tens of thousands who have taken delight in personally testifying their gratitude for the services rendered by you in saving our Country from dismemberment, and the beautiful political fabric bequeathed to our guardianship from condemnation as an essentially worthless structure, sure to crumble to pieces at the first trial, bringing disgrace upon the fathers of the Republic as a set of visionary dotards, tampering in their foolishness with the destinies of mankind. If my own insignificant unit has never been added to those crowds, composed in great part of the most eminent of our

fellow-citizens in every walk of life, my absence is attributable, first to the
circumstances which make a slave of me as regards the disposal of my time,
compelling me still (at the age of 68) to sell it for a support, and the fragments of it which are left me never sufficing for the household demands
arising from those same circumstances; and even if this cause had not existed to enforce my absence, I should still have been kept away by a feeling
of *mercy*: by my being mindful of the fact, that people are so apt to forget,
that there may be such a thing as too much attention, in fine as *killing*
kindness. Although never its object myself, I have been closely connected
with those who were so, and so seen more than once the martyrdom thus
inflicted. This experience taught me that the truest way to show such feelings is often *not* to show them. Among all those thousands, there is not one
who *can* feel more deeply or warmly, or acutely (to speak of it as a matter
of feeling only) the value of that which it has been vouchsafed to *you*, to
be the most effective & conspicuous among the preservers of. Early in Decr
1860, just before the struggle began, I chanced to be in New York; and
there, at his table, a remark having been made to this effect: 'The Union is
gone, no hope left for it, the South will certainly secede, and it will have to
be acquiesced in,'—my feeling on the subject burst forth in these words: 'A
fifty years civil war first; and *one* of my reasons—only one of many—is,
that to acquiesce in Secession would be to doom our country to *endless* civil
war.'—And these words of mine were echoed by Winfield Scott—'Yes!',
said he, 'it *would* be endless civil war.' The conversation did not stop there.
'What would you *do*?' said the other, in a tone indicative of the sympathy
which afterwards became flagrant.—'*Do*!' I exclaimed, 'What *can* the Govt
do, but do its *duty*? Suppress the attempt, suppress it at all cost; and then,
bring the Leaders to trial for *Treason*: Arraign them, try them, convict
them, *sentence* them, and—PARDON them. For, *our* Government is strong
enough—the only Government that is, or ever was—to pardon the leaders
in treason; and it would be made stronger than ever by such proof of its
strength.' [So soon as we had risen from table, Genl S. took me to his office,
and placed in my hands those letters of his (copies, of course) to the Secy
of War & Prest, urging that the forts be manned. On returning them, I
said, 'Genl, this is the best act of your life; and, unless they be utterly de-
mented at Washington, it will be the greatest of all the services ever done
by you to our Country.'] Such having been, then, & throughout the whole
struggle, the state of my feelings on the subject, judge if there can be,
among the thousands who have been crowding around you, a single one
whose heart responds more earnestly to the service which you have done
her. On that one occasion of our meeting at the Continental Hotel, as we
walked away from that interview, I remarked to Mr Felton,—'One thing
at least is very clear: his head is a steady one, and does not turn giddy.
Here he is, knowing himself to be an object of enthusiastic admiration to
the whole country, and yet just as little elated, just as quietly natural, just
as simple & unassuming, as if he were *Corporal* Grant despatching business

with soldiers of his Company, instead of being Lieut Genl Grant, fresh from giving audience to a committee of "upper-tendone", sent to do him honor.'—Such was the impression which you made upon me on that occasion; and, to know the influence which that one trait has had upon my estimate of you, and my feelings towards you, one must know *me*; which *you* do not; which but very few do; which none do at all thoroughly, except a very few—a number which, even if it had been large originally, could not well have been otherwise than greatly reduced for one who has nearly reached the 'three score & ten.'—It is that estimate of you, & that feeling towards you, which have caused this to be written to U. S. Grant by his Fellow Citizen & Friend"—ALS (brackets in original), USG 3.

On Jan. 8, 1868, Trist, Philadelphia, wrote to USG. "The delay in transmitting the enclosed, written at my home on the 1st of December, (*Sunday* being the only day of the week, on which I can rely upon not being under hard pressure from office work, & the ceaseless interruptions to which that work is liable in the position I hold in the service of a R. R. Co) this delay has been caused by the fact, that the letters (copies) therein referred to, had got mislaid. It could not go without them, and therefore it had to wait till I could find them; or find time to procure others: no easy matter to one whose time is *sold*, and whose circumstances are such as to create a demand for such fragments of it as may be left, constantly arising at home, a rented dwelling in the country, where I am the 'only *man* about the place'; a part of the force, which might be exerted in doing man's work there, being unavoidably consumed in my morning & evening tramp, (generally at the 'doublequick,' which I am still 'good for,' at the age of 68) to and from the railroad station, a mile distant across the fields. And now that I am at length able to send that letter, I will add to it the enquiry,—*Did you get that Pipe?* I hope you did. But if not, then you will be at a loss to know what I mean. Therefore, I must explain. When that grand Fair of the '*Sanitary Commission*' (Ineffably glorious thing! That thing which never could have appeared on this Globe of ours, except as a spontaneous 'sucker' from the root of *American* Freedom). When that Fair was held here, *We*—I, & my wife & her sisters,—had no *money* to contribute. But we had some *relics*,—relics which, though of no marketable value, except *as* relics, might help a little towards making up that 'million dollars' which the Fair was to bring. Some were of *Thomas Jefferson*. (my wife's grand-father, with whom she had grown up, and with whom I also lived during the last years of his life, & whose nurse I was at the hour of death.) Some also of *James Madison*, 'the Father of the Constitution'; and its truest, profoundest, most lucid *expounder*—however fashionable it may be, now-a-days, to make a by-word of, & to scoff at, 'the Virginia Resolutions of '98,' among those who prove that *they* know *absolutely* nothing about the genuine 'State Rights' doctrine, by confounding it with that monstrous product of the *fungus*-breeding brain of Jno C. Calhoun; by feeding upon which, for thirty years & more, the whole South went mad. And some there were, of *Andrew Jackson*; the man who killed Calhounism, in its 'Nullification' form, but at the same time, (for want of *his* understanding the true State Rights doctrine—as I could show) gave to '*Secession*', for the whole Southern mind, & no small part of the Northern also, that tremendous power, intellectual and moral, which has come so nigh to breaking us up, and scattering to the winds all those magnificent hopes for Mankind which our Union had inspired & had justified.—Among these relics of 'Old Hiccory' was an old clay Pipe, often smoked by him in the White-House, whilst cogitating about 'the Bank' and other such little matters; and which, on leaving there, I brought away from that white-marble mantel-piece of the President's office, as a memento of the 'Old Roman' and of those days.—That old pipe was given to the Sanitary Commission, with a paper attached, stating whose it was, and respectfully suggesting that it should be raffled for, in the understanding that the winner should 'present it to *Unconditional Surrender Grant*, to be filled & smoked by him, for the first time, on the night (sure to come) when our Country shall be all a-blaze with illuminations, and every American heart shall be made to throb with delight at reading in letters, formed of stars of light, the inscription: *The Federal Union, it*—HAS BEEN—*Preserved*.' Thus much in explanation of my question,—*Did you ever get that pipe*?—There was also a pair of spurs, (brass) cast in the citadel of Mexico from mountings of captured muskets, to which I gave (so far as a suggestion could give it) the same destination, as a not inappropriate companion—after they should be substantially gilt,—for that sword of the New York Fair."—ALS, *ibid.*

On April 8, 1869, Trist wrote to USG. "Some four or five weeks ago, our fellow-citizen Mr Hitchcock (delegate from Nebraska, whilst a Territory) who has, for several years, manifested a friendly interest in my case, suggested to my son that the post of Commr for the settlement of Mexican Claims was one that would afford me the remunerative employment of which he knew me to have long stood in need. . . ."—ALS, DNA, RG 59, Letters of Application and Recommendation. Related papers are *ibid.*

On June 27, 1872, USG nominated Trist as deputy postmaster, Alexandria, Va. On Dec. 14, Trist, Alexandria, wrote to USG. "*Personal* . . . An opportunity presenting itself to render you a personal service, I gladly do so. It has reference to your daughter, who if she cultivates music & has a genuine fondness for it, will ever feel thankful for the opportunity so brought within her reach. There is another person also to be benefitted; a lady friend of my family, in whom we all feel a lively interest, knowing her to be a person of great worth & essential refinement of principle as well as manners. But the benefit to her is not my motive in the present instance: as her having Miss Grant among her pupils, though of course gratifying, would not affect her pecuniarily: for she is sure, wherever she goes, to have as many as she can find times for. Miss Anna C. Dyckmans, of Brussels, where she moved in the highest circles, is the lady referred to. . . ."—ALS (press), DLC-Nicholas P. Trist.

1867, DEC. 2. To Secretary of the Navy Gideon Welles. "At the suggestion of the Quartermaster General of the Army, I have the honor to request that the proposition of Adjutant General L. Thomas of July 9th, 1867, respecting a National Cemetery at Pensacola, Florida, herewith transmitted be acceded to by the Navy Department. A return of these papers is requested."—LS, DNA, RG 45, Letters Received from the President. On Dec. 11, Welles wrote to USG. "I have the honor to return herewith the proposition of Adjutant General Thomas, which was enclosed with your letter of the 2d inst. in referrence to a National Cemetery at Pensacola Fla. for the Army, and Navy, dead; also to transmit copy of a communication on that subject from Rear Admiral Jos Smith. Chief of the Bureau of Yards & Docks, whose views the Department requested—This Department approves of the suggestions of the Chief of the Bureau."—Copies, *ibid.*, Letters Sent to the President; *ibid.*, Subject File, Pensacola. Related papers are *ibid.*

1867, [DEC. 2]. USG note. "The Adj. Gn. will order transportation in advance to Surg. Carvallo to Ft Hancock Texas."—AN (initialed), DNA, RG 94, Letters Received, 906W 1867. An appended note indicates that War Dept. clerks interpreted "Ft Hancock" as a slip of the pen for "Gen. Hancock."—*Ibid.*

1867, DEC. 2. To Speaker of the House Schuyler Colfax. "I have the honor to send, herewith, for the consideration of the Committee on Appropriations, a communication from the Quarter-master General of the Army, dated Oct. 8th 1867 submitting plan and estimate for the repair and enlargement of the *wharf at Schuylkill* Arsenal, Pa, with a recommendation that the requisite appropriation of $15,000. be made therefor."—Copy, DNA, RG 107, Reports to Congress. See *HED*, 40-2-10.

1867, DEC. 2. To Speaker of the House Schuyler Colfax. "I have the honor to enclose, for the consideration of the Committee on Military Affairs, a communication of Nov. 14th 1867 from the Chief of Engineers, recommending the passage of a Resolution for the settlement of the accounts of certain officers and agents of the *Engineer Department*, in which recommendation this Department concurs—"—Df, DNA, RG 77, Accounts, Property Returns, and Claims, Letters Received; copy, *ibid.*, RG 107, Reports to Congress. See *HED*, 40-2-8.

1867, DEC. 2. To Speaker of the House Schuyler Colfax. "I have the honor to send, herewith, for the consideration of the Committee on Military Affairs, a draft of a Joint Resolution, explanatory of certain acts in relation to the *Armory & Arsenal at Rock Island*, Ill, with a recommendation of this Department that it be favorably considered by Congress."—Df, DNA, RG 156, Letters Received; copy, *ibid.*, RG 107, Reports to Congress. See *HED*, 40-2-6.

1867, DEC. 2. To Speaker of the House Schuyler Colfax. "In compliance with a Resolution of the House of Representatives of November 26th respecting buildings leased by the US. in New *York* & *Brooklyn*, I have the honor to send, herewith, a statement containing the information called for: Since the preparation of the statement an order for the reduction of the recruiting service will render the hiring of many of the rooms used for that purpose, unnecessary"—Copy, DNA, RG 107, Reports to Congress. See *HED*, 40-2-9.

1867, DEC. 2. To Speaker of the House Schuyler Colfax. "In compliance with a Joint Resolution of Congress, approved July 28. 1866—authorizing the Secretary of War to settle with the *Territory of Colorado* for the militia of said Territory, employed in the service of the U. S. in 1864 & 1865, I have the honor to send, herewith, a statement from the Adjutant General's Office, dated October 21, 1867, containing the information called for in the Resolution and the reason why it was not furnished before this time"—Copy, DNA, RG 107, Reports to Congress. For the enclosure, see *HED*, 40-2-7.

1867, DEC. 2. Judge Advocate Gen. Joseph Holt to USG. "Private George Wells, U. S. Mily. Academy, Detachment of Cavalry, was tried at West Point under the following charge:—Disobedience of orders. In that, when ordered by 1st. Sergt. Cornelius O'Brien, to harness a team of horses for Artillery drill, he did fail to obey such order; and when asked by said Sergeant why he did not harness up as ordered, he did reply: 'I don't give a damn for you or your order.' This at W. Point, Oct. 11th. The testimony of Sergeant O'Brien establishes the allegations against the prisoner in every respect, if that testimony is reliable. The Court reject O'Brien's statements touching the alleged insolent reply made by the prisoner, find him guilty of the remainder of the remainder of the specification, and sentence him 'to be confined 30 days in charge of the guard.' The evidence shows that the Sergeant ordered the Prisoner to harness up a certain team, and that the latter exchanged teams with another man. He was harnessing the second team, when the Sergeant came to him and demanded to know why he was not attending to the team assigned him. It is testified that these exchanges, though not frequent, were not unknown in the detachment, and that they had not before been interfered with. The prisoner answered that another man was harnessing the first team; whereupon the Sergeant told him he was to obey orders. His reply seems, from the testimony of the other witnesses, to have been: 'I don't give a damn which team I harness. The Sergeant immediately ordered him in arrest. His manner was probably offensive, and the Court deem him to have merited some punishment. The action of the Court in this and another case herewith submitted, however, tends to prove Sergeant O'Brien to be a man of violent temper, unreliable memory, indifferent regard for truth, and undue sensitiveness upon the point of the dignity of his rank. It is advised that the sentence be approved, and that inquiry be made into the 1st. sergeant's treatment of his men and his general fitness for a position of responsibility."—Copy, DNA, RG 153, Letters Sent.

1867, DEC. 2.   Judge Advocate Gen. Joseph Holt endorsement. "Respectfully returned to the Secretary of War. The within is the claim, amounting to $6000. of *John Handley* of Greenbriar County, West Virginia, for the value of certain property—consisting of a Dwelling House and Barns with the furniture, farming utensils, vehicles, provender, a horse, &c., contained therein—which were burned upon and destroyed by our military forces on 10th. January 1863. . . ."—Copy, DNA, RG 153, Letters Sent.

1867, DEC. 2.   U.S. Delegate José Francisco Cháves of New Mexico Territory to USG. "Enclosed, I have the honor to call your attention to a free translation of an extract of a letter received from Don José L. Perea, a resident of Bernalillo, County of Bernalillo, Territory of NewMexico, and one of the wealthiest, best and most influential citizens of the Territory.—You will perceive that if his information from his wagon master be correct, a great outrage has been perpetrated upon the rights of the property of three of my constituents. The trains of these gentlemen were legitimately on the road, carrying merchandise from the States to the Territory. About the middle of September last these trains were attacked by Indians at what is called the foot of the nine mile ridge on the Arkansas River, and lost nearly all of their mules. They were thus compelled to lay by until cattle or mules could be sent to them from NewMexico, and while so doing were a second time attacked by an overwhelming force of Indians, who fought them desperately for the greater part of one day, in attempting to capture the trains. It appears that on the 2nd ulto. the cattle arrived at the Buffalo (Sibolo) Station, where the trains had been subsequently transported to, and on the next day they left en route for NewMexico—And that on the 5th or two days afterwards, they were overtaken by an officer from Fort Dodge, who it appears had orders from his Commanding officer to destroy the spirituous liquors that they had in their wagons. This is all that I can gather from the reading of the letter of which the enclosed is a free and correct translation. In the transportation of merchandise from the frontier States to NewMexico, across the plains, I am not aware that there is any article, prohibited by the laws of the Country, to be so transported. And as regards the article of whiskey—The Government itself has transported it to the amount of hundreds of Barrells, to my own personal knowledge. The loss entailed by the order of the commanding officer of Fort Dodge upon Mr. Perea alone, who is but one of the parties thus far complaining, is by no means inconsiderable, and it appears to me but just that all of them should be refunded their losses, unless good and sufficient cause be shown by the officers to justify such a proceeding, as it is manifestly in conflict with that clause of the Constitution which provides that no citizen shall be dispossessed of his property without due consideration.—Hoping that this matter will receive a thorough investigation.—"—ALS, DNA, RG 107, Letters Received from Bureaus. Related papers are *ibid.*

1867, DEC. 2.   Governor John W. Geary of Pa. to USG. "Col. Gilbert W. Robinson, late Lieut. Colonel of the Third Maryland, is desirous of securing the position of Military Storekeeper, and wishes me to say a kind word for him, which I do cheerfully. He served in my command for nearly two years and I had frequent opportunity to observe his conduct as an officer and a man, and had it been otherwise than good and proper, I should not have to this letter subscribed myself"—ALS, Swarthmore College, Swarthmore, Pa.

1867, DEC. 2.   Edwin A. Merritt, N. Y. q. m. gen., to USG. "I have the honor to acknowledge the receipt of a copy of your order to the Quartermaster General U. S. A, dated October 22d 1867, in relation to the settlement for the clothing, camp equipage &c retained by the State of New York. I would respectfully represent that the order referred to, does not fully satisfy the conditions set forth in the application made to you and which I will briefly recapitulate. During the recent war, the United States from time to time turned over to the State of New York, quantities of clothing and other supplies for issue to U. S. volunteers. At the close of the war, a portion of such supplies was left on hand to be returned to the United States. Learning that the United States had in store a large quantity of such property rendered practically useless by the disbandment of the volunteer forces, it was thought best to issue a portion of that in my possession to the National Guard of the State, to secure its efficient and speedy equipment. All property received from the United States, with the above exception, has been returned, and accounted for to the Quartermaster General. In settlement for the property not returned, it is proposed to pay for the same at the average prices for the respective articles received by the United States at the several government sales, and in lieu of the return of the articles in kind. I would therefore most respectfully request such modification of your order as will authorize a settlement upon the proposed basis for all articles issued by the State of New York *since the close of the war.* The request for such equitable settlement was preferred on the ground that it would in all respects be just to both parties and also more convenient to the United States, in view of the large sales of such articles then advertised to be made. The deficiency could have been easily supplied at a cost to the State not exceeding the prices which were subsequently received at the government sales."—LS, DNA, RG 94, Letters Received, 593A 1867. On Jan. 4, 1868, Bvt. Maj. Gen. Daniel H. Rucker, act. q. m. gen., wrote to USG. "I have the honor to submit a copy of letter from the War Department dated Dec 3d 1867, directing the settlement of the account against the State of New York for clothing issued or furnished to it by the Government during and since the rebellion, and in connection therewith a list showing the average prices which were obtained at public sales for the articles specified. Your attention is respectfully invited to the accompanying list of prices for your approval, or other action, with a view to the settlement of the said accounts."—LS, *ibid.* Related papers are *ibid.* Between March 5 and 16, 1869, USG received at least six letters recommending Merritt for appointment as surveyor, Port of N. Y.; Merritt instead was appointed naval officer.—*Ibid.*, RG 56, Naval Officer Applications.

1867, Dec. 3.   To Attorney Gen. Henry Stanbery. "At the suggestion of the Quartermaster General of the Army I have the honor to transmit herewith a communication of November 30th, asking for an opinion respecting the source of means for payment of expenses which attend the examination by District Attornies of titles to land purchased by the United States, which I will thank you to furnish."—LS, DNA, RG 60, Letters Received, War Dept. On Nov. 30, Bvt. Maj. Gen. Daniel H. Rucker, act. q. m. gen., had written to USG concerning titles to land for cemeteries.—LS, *ibid.*, RG 92, Reports to the Secretary of War (Press). On Feb. 12 and 25, 1868, Rucker renewed his request through Secretary of War Edwin M. Stanton.—LS, *ibid.*, RG 107, Letters Received from Bureaus.

1867, Dec. 3.   USG endorsement. "Respectfully refered to the Chief Eng who will please cause an investigation and report from the senior Engineer officer at Portland, Me, on the subject treated of in the within."—AES, DNA, RG 77, Explorations and Surveys, Letters Received. Written on a letter of Nov. 28 from James L. Farmer, Portland, Maine, to U.S. Senator William P. Fessenden of Maine criticizing engineering work at Portland Harbor.—ALS, *ibid.* On Dec. 4, 1867, and Jan. 4, 1868, Brig. Gen. Andrew A. Humphreys, chief of engineers, wrote to USG concerning this matter.—LS, *ibid.* See *HED*, 40-3-1, III, part 2, pp. 849–50.

1867, Dec. 3.   USG endorsement. "Respy. referred to Lt. Gen. W. T. Sherman, who will take such steps as he thinks advisable for maintaining our treaty stipulations with the Indians. If troops are used, however, they will be under the command of their proper officers"—Copy, DNA, RG 108, Register of Letters Received. Written on a letter of Dec. 2 from Secretary of the Interior Orville H. Browning. "Asks that a Company of Cavalry be placed at the disposal of Supt of Indian Affairs, (*Thomas Murphy*) to remove persons who have settled on *Kansas Indians land*; occupied their houses &c. &c. in violation of law and treaty stipulations"—*Ibid.*

1867, Dec. 3.   To Speaker of the House Schuyler Colfax. "I have the honor to transmit, herewith, for the consideration of the Committee on Appropriations, a communication from the *Quartermaster General* of the Army, relative to the condition of the funds requisite to carry on the affairs of his department"—Copy, DNA, RG 107, Reports to Congress. See *HED*, 40-2-14.

1867, DEC. 3.   To Speaker of the House Schuyler Colfax. "In obedience
to the Resolution of the House of Representatives of the 26th ultimo, I have
the honor to transmit, herewith, a statement of the number of buildings,
rented or leased in the City of *Saint Louis* for military purposes; the annual
rent paid for each building and the names of the parties from whom rented"
—Copy, DNA, RG 107, Reports to Congress. See *HED*, 40-2-15.

1867, DEC. 3.   Judge Advocate Gen. Joseph Holt to USG. "Respectfully
returned to the Secretary of War. The within described premises called the
'*Adams House*' situated in Louisville, Ky., was in July 1861 vested in certain parties known as the heirs of R. C. Ballard deceased. At the date mentioned these heirs, being 'a mother married daughter and two female infants
went south.' In May '65, the Bank of Kentucky a creditor of R. C. Ballard,
bought in the property by virtue of a judgment in a chancery suit, commenced by the Bank, and obtained, as it is understood, the legal title. The
Military Authorities had occupied the premises as Head Quarters since
about July 1st. '64. . . ."—Copy, DNA, RG 153, Letters Sent.

1867, DEC. 4.   To secretary of war. "I have the honor to make requisition
for $5,000 of the appropriation for 'Expenses of the Commanding Gen-
eral's Office,' and request that the warrant be drawn in favor of Major Geo.
K Leet. A. A. G. of my Staff."—Copies, DLC-USG, V, 47, 60; DNA, RG
108, Letters Sent.

1867, DEC. 4.   To Attorney Gen. Henry Stanbery. "I have the honor to
transmit herewith a communication of November 27th, 1867, from Ex-
Governor Tod of Ohio, with a request that you will instruct the U. S.
Attorney in Ohio to make the necessary defence in all suits brought against
Governor Tod for acts done under the authority of the United States."—
LS, DNA, RG 60, Letters Received, War Dept. On Nov. 27, David Tod,
Youngstown, Ohio, had written to USG. "It becomes my duty to advise
your Department that I have again been sued, with others, by Dr. Edson
B. Olds for trespass and false imprisonment, committed in participating in
his arrest and imprisonment in Ft La Fayette N. Y. under and by virtue of
an order from your Department, dated Aug. 2. 1862, issued to and executed
by Wm Scott—This suit is pending in the Court of Common Pleas of Fair-
field County, Ohio, one of the Defendants being a resident of said County—
I have, of Course, employed Counsel—Messrs Hunter & Dougherty of Lancaster Ohio, and Benjamin F. Hoffman of this place. I assume, that your
Department will pay all necessary expenses I may be put to, in defending
the case; and I desire the co-operation and assistance of the Law Officer of
your Department—The former suit was certified up to the Federal Court,
under act of Congress, and there, on the 18th of Nov. 1866, was dismissed
for failure on the part of Plaintiff to enter Bail for costs; Hence, the case
has never been tried upon its merits—"—LS, *ibid.*, RG 107, Letters Received, T192 1867. On Nov. 22, Judge Advocate Gen. Joseph Holt wrote

to USG at length concerning excessive legal fees in the case.—Copy, *ibid.*, RG 153, Letters Sent. On Dec. 13, Stanbery wrote to USG. "In response to your request of the 4th instant, for the services of the District Attorney in the case of Hon. David Tod, late Governor of Ohio, enclosing a copy of Gov. Tod's letter to you, I have the honor to enclose herewith a copy of my instructions to the Dist. Attorney, in the premises."—LS, *ibid.*, RG 107, Letters Received from Bureaus. The enclosure is *ibid.* On Dec. 17, U.S. District Attorney Durbin Ward, Cincinnati, wrote to USG. "I am by letter advised by the Attorney General of the United States, that on your request to that effect he authorizes me to appear as the Atty of the U. States in defence of 'all suits brought against Governor Tod for acts done under the authority of the United.' He advises me, and such I understand to be the law that such consent and direction of the Attorney General 'is the proper authority for the District Attorney to appear in the suits, the *compensation* of the latter being a matter of *contract* between him and the head of the Department requesting his services.' I understand the nature of the suit now being prosecuted against Gov. Tod and it will I have no doubt be pressed with great vigor. In accordance with law therefore I have the honor to request that some amount be agreed upon as my fee. The Attorney General Mr. Stanbery knows me very well and has more than once been himself in like case. You may therefore consult him as to the compensation proper to be paid and I have no doubt I shall be satisfied with whatever you and he may fix upon. If you should prefer that I should indicate what I would think a fair remuneration so advise me and I will do so. The case growing out as it does of the arrest of Hon. E. B. Old & his imprisment in Fort La Fayette for an alleged political offence will of course involve much difficult law and a somewhat extended investigation—"—ALS, *ibid.*, Letters Received, W433 1867. On Jan. 9, 1868, Holt wrote to USG. "Respectfully returned to the Secretary of War; with the expression of opinion that the within 'request' of Hon. Durbin Ward, U. S. Attorney for the Southern District of Ohio, that 'some amount be agreed upon,' in advance, as his fee in the action of Olds vs Tod *et al.* cannot well be complied with; because of the inability of the Department to anticipate the extent of the services which may be required in the case. . . ."—LS, *ibid.*

1867, DEC. 4.   USG note. "Direct Gn. Emory to relieve Lt. Haskins, 5 Cav.y from arrest and to order him to his company subject to be tried any time within one year if his conduct hereafter should not justify the leniency shown in by releasing him."—AN (date on docket), DNA, RG 94, Letters Received, 670A 1867.

1867, DEC. 4.   USG endorsement. "Refered to the Paymaster Gen. for his views as to the propriety of suspending suit against Maj. McDowell untill further investigation is had into the cause of his loss of public funds and untill the return of his surities from Europe."—AES, DNA, RG 99, Letters Received. Written on a letter of Dec. 3 from W. S. Kermon, Washington, D. C., to U.S. Representative John A. Bingham of Ohio. "Permit me to call your attention to the following statement. Maj Malcolm McDowell formerly an Add. Paymaster in the Army has had a Settlement of his Accounts with the Goverment—having had a statement of differences from the Auditor & Comptroller they find an unaccounted for Amount of $17.500 in a Single item, which Maj McDowell never knew he had received and for which he can not now at present account for: as is the duty of the accounting Department a Suit is about to be instituted against him and his Sureties. this unaccounted for Amount Maj M. wants time to further investigate. He was a brave an efficient Officer in the field, and after he went in to the Pay Department was an active and Zealous one. There can be nothing said against his integrity as his reputation at home in the City of Cincinnati can be fully established his sureties Mr. James Frazier & Mr A. L. Moury of that City are both men of wealth what he wants is further time before suit is brought for investigation. the Goverment can lose nothing by a few months delay and he may be able to satisfy himself and the Goverment in relation to the Amount unaccounted if he can not he will be prepared to pay it in a very few months without suit or expense. Mr Frazier one of his Sureties is now in Europe, and will not be back for some months If he can not find this item he will pay it can it not be So arranged that time may be given him for further examination the Goverment can lose nothing by a temporary delay will you please see if an extension of a few months can not be had"—ALS, *ibid.* On Dec. 12, USG wrote to Bingham. "The letter of the 3d instant, of *W. S. Kermon*, Attorney for *Major McDowell*, late addl Paymaster, endorsed by you, was referred to the Paymaster General and by him to the 2nd Comptroller of the Treasy, to whom the Major's accounts with statement of differences has been transferred, and that officer has made the following remarks thereon, which are sent for your information. 'Major McDowell's accounts have not yet been finally revised in this office and when they shall have been I shall be very willing to defer the institution of suit, if thereby I can effect a prompt recovery of the amount justly due. (sd) J. M. Brodhead Comptroller' "— Df, *ibid.*; copy, *ibid.*, RG 107, Letters Sent.

1867, Dec. 4. To U.S. District Attorney E. C. Carrington. "I desire to ask your immediate attention to a suit concerning which on the ___ ultimo, I requested the Attorney General to take the necessary action—to guard the interests of the United States; being the case of *B. Mackall, Jr.* against *General John C. McFerran*, Dept. Qr. Mr. General, U. S. A. The suit is an important one. A copy of the letter to the Attorney General herein referred to, is enclosed."—Df, DNA, RG 107, Letters Received from Bureaus; copy, *ibid.*, Letters Sent.

1867, Dec. 4. To Speaker of the House Schuyler Colfax. "I have the honor to transmit, herewith for the action of Congress, a communication of the Inspector of the *Military Academy*, proposing certain legislation relative to that Institution, the adoption of which is earnestly recommended by this Department."—Copy, DNA, RG 107, Reports to Congress. See *HED,* 40-2-13.

1867, DEC. 4, 12:20 P.M.   To Charles W. Ford. "Tell Elrod not to come to Washington if he has not started yet. Write what he wants first."—ALS (telegram sent), DNA, RG 107, Telegrams Collected (Bound). On the same day, Ford, St. Louis, had telegraphed to USG. "Elrod leaves for Washington today"—Telegram received (at 11:25 P.M.), *ibid.*

1867, DEC. 5.   To President Andrew Johnson. "I have the honor to enclose herewith a comn from *John Cradlebaugh* dated Oct. 30th 1867 respecting the case of *H. K. Lawrence* late Paymaster, a defaulter. The records of this Department shew that the Record of the proceedings of the Chief of Engineers in his case was sent to the President on the 24th July 1864. If returned, the request of Mr. Cradlebaugh may be complied with."—Df, DNA, RG 107, Letters Received from Bureaus; copy, *ibid.,* Letters Sent to the President.

1867, DEC. 5, noon.   To Maj. Gen. Henry W. Halleck, San Francisco. "Let Babbit have his choice of duty."—ALS (telegram sent), DNA, RG 107, Telegrams Collected (Bound); telegram sent (misaddressed to Maj. Gen. Winfield S. Hancock), *ibid.;* copies, *ibid.,* RG 108, Telegrams Sent; DLC-USG, V, 56. On the same day, Bvt. Maj. Gen. Robert Allen had favorably endorsed a request of Bvt. Brig. Gen. Edwin B. Babbitt for assignment at the q. m. clothing depot in San Francisco.—Copy, DNA, RG 92, Decision Books.

1867, DEC. 5.   To Speaker of the House Schuyler Colfax. "In compliance with a Resolution of the House of Representatives of Nov. 26th 1867 I have the honor to send, herewith, a report from the Adjutant General of the Army, respecting the proceedings of this Department under the 7th Sec. of the Act of Congress approved March 2, 1867, relative to *California* or *Nevada Volunteers* discharged in *New Mexico, Arizona* or *Utah*—which contains the information desired"—Copy, DNA, RG 107, Reports to Congress. See *HED,* 40-2-24.

1867, DEC. 5.   To Speaker of the House Schuyler Colfax. "In compliance with a Resolution of the House of Representatives, dated April 16th 1866, I have the honor to send, herewith, a summary of the proceedings &c. of the trial of *Henry Wirz*"—Copy, DNA, RG 107, Reports to Congress. On the same day, Bvt. Maj. Gen. Edward D. Townsend had written to USG. "I have the honor to submit herewith a summary of the proceedings of the trial of *Henry Wirz,* prepared in this office by Lieut. *William Atwood* 19th U. S. Infantry late Bv't Major and A. A G of Volunteers, in compliance with Resolution of the House of Representatives of which the following is a copy: . . ."—Copy, *ibid.*, RG 94, Letters Sent. See *HED*, 40-2-23.

1867, Dec. 5.   Judge Advocate Gen. Joseph Holt to USG. "Captain P. K. Thomas, 3d Cavalry, was tried in Oct. last by Gen. Ct. Martial at Fort Union, New Mexico, under the following charges:—1. Wrongfully & knowingly selling government property. In that, on or about Aug. 21. '66, he drew from Captain Thayer, A. Q. M. at Fort Lyon, Colo Terry, one horse, property of the U. S., and did at Fort Garland, C. T., on or about Oct. 12. '66 sell said horse to Lieut. Whately, of the N. M. Vols. 2. Conduct unbecoming an officer and a gentleman. In defrauding Lieut. Whatley, New Mex. Vols., in the sale of a horse, in the manner follow'g: selling and delivering to him a horse which accused had drawn from Capt. Thayer, *Aug 26th 1866*, and giving him at the time of sale a certificate that said horse was his private property, which certificate had been given him the preceeding March by Col. Noble at Little Rock, Ark., with a different horse then bought by Accused for $90.00. The Court convict Capt. Thomas under both charges, & sentence him:—'To be cashiered, and to refund to the U. S. the value of the black horse sold to Lieut. Whatley.' . . ."—Copy, DNA, RG 153, Letters Sent.

1867, Dec. 6.   To U.S. Representative James A. Garfield of Ohio. "In compliance with your verbal request I send, herewith, copies of orders looking to *retrenchment* in the expenses of the War Department issued since I have been in charge of the *War Department.*"—Copies, DNA, RG 94, Letters Sent; *ibid.*, RG 107, Reports to Congress.

1867, Dec. 6.   To U.S. Senator James Harlan of Iowa. "In reply to your note of this date respecting the relative rank of *Capt. D. M. Sells*, 41st U. S. Infantry, I have the honor to inform you that the ignoring of Capt. Sells former service in the Marine Corps was in conformity to the law of Congress approved March 2d, 1867, which restricts the recognition of former services to army-service alone—The law is regarded as defective in not providing for the recognition of such prior service as that of Captain Sells, and also in prescribing that previous length of service alone *irrespective of the previous* rank held by officers shall govern in establishing future relative rank. Thus a former Brigadier General of *two* years distinguished services in the volunteer forces may be ranked by a 2d Lieut. of *three* years volunteer services in the event of their both holding the same grade in the Regular Army; a result not contemplated by the lawmakers."—Copies, DNA, RG 94, ACP, S392 CB 1870; *ibid.*, RG 107, Letters Sent. On the same day, Harlan, Washington, D. C., had written to USG. "In fixing the relative rank of Capt. Daid M. Sells, of the 41st. Regiment Infant, nearly two years of service in the Marine Corps was excluded. I respectfully request to be informed if this omission was an oversight, or the result of an official interpretation of the law so as to ex-clude such service in all cases."—ALS, *ibid.*, RG 94, ACP, S392 CB 1870.

1867, DEC. 7, 3:20 P.M.   To Bvt. Maj. Gen. John Pope. "Suspend your order regulating telegraph charges untill you refer your action, and grounds on which taken, to these Hd Qrs."—ALS (telegram sent), DNA, RG 107, Telegrams Collected (Bound); telegram sent, *ibid.*; copies, *ibid.*, RG 46, Senate 40A–F2, Messages; *ibid.*, RG 108, Telegrams Sent; DLC-USG, V, 56. On the same day, William Orton, president, Western Union Telegraph Co., New York City, had telegraphed to USG. "The following message has just been rec'd from our Superintendent at Augusta Ga. 'Genl Pope has issued an order forbidding the Manager of Atlanta Ga to charge the ten (10) cents tax on Government business. He also orders him to refund all heretofore collected. Shall he Comply? Signed J. VANHORNE' I respect-fully protest on behalf of this Company against the assumption by General Pope of the right to fix the rate at which our services shall be rendered either to the Government or the Public. At the same time I desire to say that we shall render cheerful obedience to any Military order having your sanction, but I appeal to the relations existing between this Company and your Department during the War as Conclusive proof of a disposition on our part to meet every requirement by the Government without the formali-ties of Compulsory orders. Our lines are at the service of General Pope with or without pay as he may decide best in respect to such services as he admits it proper to pay for we claim respectfully the right to make the same charge as that established for other business of like character"—Telegram received (at 2:40 P.M.), DNA, RG 107, Telegrams Collected (Bound); *ibid.*, RG 108, Telegrams Received; copy, DLC-USG, V, 55. On Dec. 9, Pope, At-lanta, telegraphed to USG. "I do not understand your telegram of the seventh. I have made no order whatever regulating telegraph charges nor concerning telegraph companies in any other manner. The corporation of this city by ordinance laid a tax on telegrams but the Mayor informs me that it was not intended to apply to official telegrams on United States busi-ness. I have accordingly ordered QuarterMaster not to pay this city tax. I send by mail correspondence with the Mayor on the subject"—Telegram received (at 1:00 P.M.), DNA, RG 107, Telegrams Collected (Bound); *ibid.*, RG 108, Telegrams Received; copies, *ibid.*, RG 46, Senate 40A–F2, Messages; (sent by mail) *ibid.*, RG 108, Letters Received; DLC-USG, V, 55. On the same day, Pope wrote to USG. "I have the honor to forward herewith official copies of all correspondence relative to the prohibition to pay the Corporation Tax of the City of Atlanta—in accordance with my telegram of this date—These Papers contain all the Orders that have been issued by me relative to the matter—I also enclose a copy of the City Tax Ordinance—"—LS, DNA, RG 108, Letters Received. The enclosures are *ibid.* On Dec. 20, Orton wrote to USG. "I had the honor to address you on the 7th instant a message relating to the reported action of Maj. Gen. Pope, in relation to the service rendered by this Company for the War Department at Atlanta, Ga. On the 10th instant I received from our manager at washington a copy of a message from General Pope addressed to you from Atlanta on the 9th instant, which I was advised was forwarded to me by your authority. It was as follows: . . . In order that the merits of the case may be fully understood I beg leave to submit the following statement: The municipal authorities of the principal cities south have, within the last year or two, levied very onerous taxes upon telegraph companies. The city of Macon, Ga., imposes a license tax of four hundred dollars per annum; Columbus, Ga., one hundred dollars per annum, and in addition thereto one per cent on gross receipts; Augusta, Ga, two per cent on gross receipts; Atlanta, Ga, twenty-five dollars license tax and one per cent on gross receipts; Richmond, Va, Five hundred dollars license; the State of South Carolina five per cent on gross receipts, in addition to the tax imposed by municipalities. All of these are in addition to the tax of three per cent on our gross receipts imposed by the Internal Revenue Law, which are paid directly to the Treasury. And when you become aware that it costs in actual expenses 70 cents to get every dollar we receive, if we assume that our taxes average but five per cent on gross receipts, you will see that is equivalent to 16⅔ per cent on net receipts. In view of these facts, and also that our business has shared in the general depression incident to all other kinds throughout the south, and that our aggregate receipts in that section were but little more than the aggregate expenses of performing the service, and keeping the lines in repair, it became necessary to devise some equitable mode of meeting the additional expense of this extraordinary taxation. A general advance of our tariff was not deemed advisable as the taxation was not uniform, and it was finally determined to increase our rates by the addition thereto of ten cents more than that charged before this local tax was imposed. And while we have no desire to increase the cost of telegraphic service to the Government we did not feel justified in exempting any class of business from the increase of rate. If, therefore, it is proper for us to charge a private citizen the present tariff from Atlanta to Washington, I submit if it be not equally proper to make the same charge on the messages of General Pope, provided they are paid for at all. Nor does it seem to me competent for his Honor the Mayor to say that the ordinance was not intended to apply to Government business. The tax is laid not upon the messages but upon the Telegraph Company in respect to its receipts for messages. Again: If it be proper to fix the rate which we shall charge for our service on official business done at Atlanta by military order, is it not equally proper to do so at all other points in that military district. In view of the facts above submitted I respectfully ask that we be permitted to charge the same rate for service rendered your Department as in the case of the public generally. Or, if this cannot be granted, that municipal authorities may be restrained from imposing excessive and unjust taxes upon our business. Or, finally, that whatever order is approved by you in respect to our charges at Atlanta shall be made to apply to all other places at which similar ordinances are in force. I beg to renew assurances of an earnest desire on the part of this Company to contribute by every means in its power, and without regard to specific compensation, in aid of your Department."—LS, *ibid.*, RG 107, Letters Received, W438 1867.

1867, DEC. 7.   Allen H. Conlan, Washington, D. C., to USG. "I have the honor to enclose statement relative to my recent Court-[Mar]tial, at No 18 State St. New York city, and [wou]ld most respectfully request that I may be reinstated as Hospital Steward U. S. Army. I would also state that after the finding of the court, my witnesses stated to me that they had been tampered with and intimidated by Capt. Huxford, 42d U. S. Inf. previous to the assembling of the Court for my Trial."—ALS (torn), DNA, RG 94, ACP, S41 CB 1868. On Dec. 10, Doctor W. Bliss wrote to USG. "I have the honor to state that Allen H Conlan late Hospital Steward U. S. A was for several months on duty at Armory Gnl Hospital while under my charge and was an active efficient & reliable non commissioned officer. He has recently been dismissed the service and feeles that injustice has been done his case   I would respectfully request that his case be carefully reviewed and that his past good character and service may have due weight in relieving him of the disability imposed by the courtmMartial"—ALS, *ibid.* On Jan. 7, 1868, Judge Advocate Gen. Joseph Holt wrote to USG. "Respectfully returned to the Secretary of War. *Allen H. Conlan*, Hospital Steward U. S. A., was convicted in October last, of 1st. Conduct to the prejudice of good order and military discipline; 2d. Disobedience of Orders; 3d. Breach of arrest; and was sentenced to forfeit all pay and allowances and to be dishonorably discharged the service. The specifications under the 1st. charge allege that Conlan 'said of his commanding officer, Capt. W. P. Huxford 42d U. S. Infty.—"I don't care a damn for him he has no control over me",' and 'of his commanding officer Acting Asst. Surgeon C. McFarlan, "I don't care a damn for him he has no control over me being a contract Surgeon" or words to that effect'; that he became 'intoxicated and failed to attend to the proper discharge of his duties'; that he 'did steal, or did, without authority, use or dispose of liquor supplied by the U. S. A. to the Hospital for the use of sick patients,' and that he sent 'without authority the Hospital attendant beyond the limits of the Post to procure intoxicating liquor for him'; . . . His offences, except that charged in the 1st Specification, scarcely merit dishonorable discharge from the service. He acknowledged before the court, and again in his petition, that he said that he 'did not care a damn for Capt. Huxford or Dr. McFarlan so long as he performed his duties in a proper manner and they were bound to sustain him in so doing.' He produced testimony to show that he made this remark under great excitement when the Matron had refused to obey his orders or assist him in the hospital. This, under all the circumstances is not thought to be so grave an offence that it may not be considered sufficiently atoned for in the punishment already suffered by him—loss of pay, allowances and position. Therefore, and in consideration of his former good character and faithful services, shown on his trial and by the testimonials presented in his behalf, the removal of the dis-

ability to re-enlist, and his reappointment are recommended."—LS, *ibid.*
USG endorsed "Approved" on the final page.—AES, *ibid.*

1867, DEC. 8. Bvt. Maj. Gen. John M. Schofield, Richmond, to USG.
"Steps have been taken by certain persons in Richmond to bring the question of Constitutionality of the reconstruction laws before the United States
Court for this District, with a view doubtless to ultimately getting the
question before the Supreme Court. I have sent Col. Burnham, Judge Advocate, to Washington to consult with the Judge Advocate General as to the
best mode of proceedure for us to adopt. Col. Burnham will also call upon
you, and I shall be glad of any suggestions or advice you can give me in the
matter."—ALS, DNA, RG 94, Letters Received, 1788M 1867.

1867, DEC. 8. Melchior Long, Tipton, Ind., to USG. "On or about the
1st of June 1862, I gave to the secretary of war information as to the location of a plantation owned by Braxton Bragg late a general officer in the
rebel army, I applied, I think, in the latter part of October, 1865. to the
President, to pardon Gen. Bragg and to restore to him if possible the property in question, provided he thought it not incompatible to the public
interest, the President through his private secretary acknowledged the appeal I then made and stated my appeal had been placed on file, . . ."—ALS,
DNA, RG 94, Amnesty Papers, La.

1867, DEC. 9. USG endorsement. "General Canby's recommendation is
approved. Brevets to date March 2nd 1867."—ES, DNA, RG 94, ACP,
2514 1872. Written on a letter of Dec. 2 from Bvt. Maj. Gen. Edward
R. S. Canby, Charleston, to Bvt. Maj. Gen. John A. Rawlins. "I find by the
Army Register for 1867 that the transfer of the Judge Advocates from the
Volunteer to the Regular Army has not been held to carry with it the brevet
rank confered upon them while in the Volunteer Service. Under the impression that the law by which they were transfered affected both the the ordinary and the brevet commissions alike I had abstained from making recommendations that would otherwise have been made and I have now the honor
to recommend that Major DeWitt Clinton, who served with me for nearly
four years, and Major E. W. Dennis, who is now on duty with me, may
receive the brevets of Colonel in the regular army, to date from the 13th. of
March 1865."—ALS, *ibid.* On Dec. 17, Bvt. Brig. Gen. John C. Kelton,
AGO, endorsed this letter. "Respectfully submitted to the General of the
Army with the information that the Judge Advocates, with rank of Major,
borne upon the Army Register for 1867, are not commissioned officers of
the regular army. The Judge Advocates to be selected by the Secretary of
War, Act of July 28. 1866, and authorized to be retained in service &c &c,
Act of Feb. 25. 1867, have not yet been selected nor authorized to be re-
tained permanently in service as of the regular army by the only process
known to law, that is, by nomination to and confirmation by the Senate.
The only commissions these officers now hold are their volunteer commis-

sions. The question of their nomination to the Senate for confirmation has been repeatedly brought to the attention of the Secretary of War, but never ordered. As there is nothing at present in the status of Judge Advocates to prevent their being mustered out of service as volunteers, it is respectfully desired that the question of the permanency of these officers, or of as many of them as it is desired to retain as Judge Advocates in the regular army may be definitely determined by nomination to the Senate for the action of that body."—ES, *ibid.*

1867, DEC. [9]. USG endorsement. "~~McAtee may be discharged so as to return with his children~~ . . . Make order for return of McAntee children"— AE (initialed), DNA, RG 94, Letters Received, 599G 1867. Written on a letter of Dec. 6 from U.S. Representative Adam J. Glossbrenner of Pa. to USG concerning transportation for orphaned children of George McAtee, 4th Cav.—ALS, *ibid.*

1867, DEC. 9. To U.S. Senator Benjamin F. Wade of Ohio. "In accordance with the Acts of Congress, approved April 21st 1808 & July 17th 1862, I have the honor to transmit, herewith, a statement of contracts made by the *Quarter Masters Department* from February 1st 1867 to November 30th 1867 and of those not received in time to be included in the last report."—Copies, DNA, RG 92, Letters Received from Depts. and Bureaus; *ibid.*, RG 107, Reports to Congress. On the same day, USG wrote an identical letter to Speaker of the House Schuyler Colfax.—Copies, *ibid.* See *HED*, 40-2-35.

1867, DEC. 9. H. B. Simonds, Greenville, Tex., to USG. "In behalf several widow women and Orphan children, who reside in this County, I wish to make you acquainted with some facts & ask your aid in their behalf should you think it possible to ascertain the facts necessary to learn the truth of the matter about which I write. In the winter of 1864 & 5, a company of men, who were opposed to the war, and who on that account, were the objects of suspicion, to the Confederate authorities, made preparations secretly, and left this county for Mexico, intending to make their way through to Calafornia. They were all residents of Hunt Co. Texas and their names were as follows . . . It was supposed by the families of these men that men from other Counties Joined them until their numbers were about forty. No trace of them has ever been found except one of their horses, ascertained to be one that was ridden by Thos J. Garrison was found on the Western Frontier, in Texas, on the route they expected to take. Vague rumors have reached their families that they were betrayed and all killed by Confederate spy companies, Others that they reached Mexico and also went to New Mexico. Lately however a report has reached here, from a man now in the state of Arkansas who says he saw them in Mexico and that they were making their way to Mexican mines, and the idea has gained some credence in the minds of their friends that they may have reached the mines and now if alive be kept at work their against their will   These men were all, I believe without an exception, sober, industrious honest men, who lived with and loved their families & friends. Every one who knew them is satisfied that they are either dead or confined in prison or mines. I have never supposed that any person Indian or White man was now imprisoned in the mines of Mexico. But, for the benefit of the friends of these persons, I write and ask you to give them such information as you have or can obtain, and if possible to learn something of these men. I have no doubt, but what a shrewd detective could ascertain something of what went with these men, if he could give it a thorough investigation. Now any facts that may be needed to prosecute the investigation will be promptly furnished by the friends of these men to the extent of their ability. Any communications can be addressed to Myself or Judge Harden Hart, at Greenville, Hunt Co. Texas. These men are or were thorough Union men and so are now all their friends living in this County. Please answer this letter as soon as possible, and it is thought advisable to investigate the matter, please give us directions how to proceed."—ALS, DNA, RG 94, Letters Received, 1284S 1867.

1867, DEC. 10.   To Attorney Gen. Henry Stanbery. "At the suggestion of the Quartermaster General of the Army, dated the 4th instant, I have the honor to send herewith papers in the case of the South-Western Iron Company, with a request that the proper U. S. District-Attorney be instructed to institute proceedings against the Company for the recovery of the value of rations furnished by the United States to the employés of the Chattanooga Rolling-Mill."—LS, DNA, RG 206, Letters Received from the Attorney Gen. USG enclosed a letter of Dec. 4 from Bvt. Maj. Gen. Daniel H. Rucker, act. q. m. gen., to USG, the second on the subject written by Rucker to USG that day. "I have the honor to transmit herewith the papers in the claim of the United States against the South Western Iron Company amounting to $4,855.86 for reimbursement of the value of the rations furnished the Employees at the Chattanooga Rolling Mill for a certain period subsequent to the date of the sale. The Judge Advocate General in a communication to the Secretary of War dated Nov. 27. 1867 expresses in reference to this claim the following opinion: 'As to the validity of this claim this Bureau can have no question, upon the evidence furnished. The liability of the Company is deemed to be very clear.' and 'But while satisfied that there is this valid claim against the Company this Bureau is equally satisfied that it cannot legally be offset against the liability to furnish the deed, inasmuch as the two obligations are of an altogether different nature and arise out of two separate and independent transactions.' In consideration of the fact that in the opinion of the Judge Advocate General this claim is just and a lawful charge against the South Western Iron Company and that the liability to furnish the deed for the transfer of said property as requested cannot legally be offset against the same, the Quartermaster General herewith respectfully recommends, that the proper officer of the Government be instructed to institute a suit against the South Western Iron Company for the recovery of the value of rations furnished to Employés at, the Chattanooga Rolling Mill subsequent to the date of sale amounting to $4,855.86." —LS, *ibid.*, RG 92, Reports to the Secretary of War (Press). A copy of Judge Advocate Gen. Joseph Holt's report to USG, dated Nov. 21, is *ibid.*, RG 153, Letters Sent. See *PUSG*, 15, 320–22. On Dec. 14, Asst. Attorney Gen. John M. Binckley wrote to USG acknowledging his letter.—Copy, DNA, RG 60, Letters Sent. On Dec. 17, Solicitor of the Treasury Edward Jordan wrote to USG. "The Attorney General has referred to this office, your letter of the 12th inst. with accompanying papers, relative to the claim of the United States against the South Western Iron company, for reimbursement of subsistence furnished the employees of the Rolling Mill at Chattanooga, Tennessee, from the 5th Oct, to 30th Nov. 1865, amounting to $4.855.86, and I have forwarded the papers to the U. States District Attorney for Southn Dis. New York, with instructions to institute the prooceedings against the said company, without delay, for its recovery."—Copies (2), *ibid.*, RG 206, Letters Sent.

On Sept. 20, Nov. 15, Dec. 15 and 26, Rucker wrote to USG concerning this matter.—LS, *ibid.*, RG 92, Reports to the Secretary of War (Press). On Sept. 28, Holt wrote to USG. "Respectfully returned to the Secretary of War. These Instruments are deemed to be substantially sufficient in law to convey the interests set forth therein; and the slight informalities which the contain need not be particularized. It may, however, be remarked that this Bureau is at a loss to understand why the Govt. should lease for a limited term real estate, which by an absolute deed taking effect at the same date, or on the day before, it conveys in fee to the same party."—Copies, *ibid.*, Decision Books; *ibid.*, RG 153, Letters Sent. On Jan. 4, 1868, USG wrote to Speaker of the House Schuyler Colfax. "I have the honor to send, herewith, for the consideration of the proper Committee, a draft of a Joint Resolution, having for its object the sale of the *Chattanooga Rolling Mill* property at Chattanooga, Tenn. and recommend its passage by Congress."—Copy, *ibid.*, RG 107, Reports to Congress. See *HED*, 40-2-77.

1867, DEC. 10.   To U.S. Senator Benjamin F. Wade of Ohio. "In reply to the Senate's Resolution of December 4th 1867, I have the honor to send herewith a communication of December 9th, from the Adjutant General of the Army, covering copies of reports and maps in the War Department, from the Commanding-Officer of the Military Division of the Pacific, concerning the reduction of the Military Reserve of Point San José, California."—LS, DNA, RG 46, Senate 40A–G3, War Dept. Reports. See *SED*, 40-2-11.

1867, DEC. 10.   Robin Sumner, Fort Dodge, Kan., to USG. "I am in Charge of a cemetery at this *Post*, & desirous of changing my *position*, among the reasons, being far from my connexions & most intimate friends, eleven years since I visited my only Sister in Boston. Perhaps it would be convenient to give me employment at Gettersburg. Sir their is many things I Could do if I had an opportetunity . . . P. S. Sir Black Kittle & Setanta White Cloud & other Indian Chiefs, are here to day & appear to be freindly.) Sir you may think it presumption in me to Address you if so please to forgive me   Lieut Hesselberger A. Q. M leaves for Washington City board st Metroplitan this day"—ALS, DNA, RG 94, ACP, S1583 CB 1867. On Feb. 28, 1868, Sumner wrote a letter received at USG's hd. qrs. on the same subject.—*Ibid.*, RG 108, Register of Letters Received. On March 9, Sumner, Ellsworth, Kan., telegraphed to USG. "Will you give me a situation or not"—Telegram received (at 9:00 A.M.), *ibid.*, RG 107, Telegrams Collected (Bound).

1867, DEC. 11.   To Attorney Gen. Henry Stanbery. "I have the honor to enclose herewith a communication of December 10th, 1867 from Messrs. Watterson & Crawford enclosing a letter from Charles Gould, of November 19th, with a power of attorney from John C. Fremont respecting the claim of the latter to United States property known as Alcatraz or Bird Island in California, with a request that you will give this Department your opinion in the matter."—LS, DNA, RG 60, Letters Received, War Dept. The enclosures are *ibid.*, RG 107, Letters Received from Bureaus. On Dec. 16, Asst. Attorney Gen. John M. Binckley wrote to USG. "With your letter of the 11th inst. the Attorney General received a power of Attorney executed by John C. Fremont, in favor of Charles Gould, of New York,—a letter from Mr. Gould of 19th ult. addressed to you,—and another from Messrs. Watterson & Crawford, of the 10th inst.—all which relate to a claim of General Fremont to the property known as Alcatraz, or Bird Island. But the nature, subject-matter, history, and present condition of the claim, appear no where in these papers, but as briefly recapitulated in the letter of Mr. Gould, in which, however, no question of law is stated, or shown to be involved. It will be observed that Mr. Gould, as attorney in fact of the claimant, requests 'that the claim be referred to the proper officer for investigation and decision'. Nothing appears in these papers indicating that the case has undergone investigation and decision. Its reference therefore to this office is of course premature. The Attorney General directs me to respectfully return the papers referred to, with the above explanation."—LS, *ibid.* On Jan. 2, 1868, USG wrote to Stanbery. "Referring to your communication of the 16th ultimo, respecting the claim of John C. Fremont, alluded to in a letter from Charles Gould of New York, I have the honor to acquaint you that the papers which you advised me were returned to this Department with said communication, did not accompany it."—LS, *ibid.*, RG 60, Letters Received, War Dept.

On Dec. 19, 1867, John C. Frémont, New York City, wrote to USG. "In the latter part of 1863 the military authorities at San Francisco, by order of Mr Stanton, forcibly took possession of certain property belonging to Mrs. Frémont on the north water-front of that City, and consisting of blocks 107, 108, & 178, and part of blocks 106, 109 & 177—making in all about twelve acres. This property was purchased and occupied by Mrs. Frémont in 1860, the property being then in the quiet and undisturbed possession of the former owners, who held under a title from the City of San Francisco. It was embraced in the four leagues of land belonging to San Francisco as a Pueblo, and the City's title to it had been fully confirmed by the United States Courts under the Act of Congress for the settlement of land titles in California. Mrs. Frémont left San Francisco at the beginning of the war after a years residence on the place which had been much improved by buildings and care of the grounds. From its position which is sheltered from the winds and the beauty of the views it was held to be the most beautiful position for a residence in San Francisco & was accordingly sought for from Mrs. Frémont who left it furnished & rented. Under these circumstances the government as above stated seized the premises. A writ of ejectment issued by the State Courts was disregarded by the officer in command. In the latter part of '65 I made formal application to the War Department for the restitution of the property. In his reply Mr Stanton did not claim possession by virtue of any title in the United States, and admitted fully Mrs. Frémonts right to have the property returned or paid for in the event it should be found necessary to the defense of the harbor, and in order to reach a decision promised to refer it to the Engineer Dept. and the Commdg. officer in California. This was accordingly done, and I learned that the Chief of the Engineer Dept. at Washington reported against the expediency of retaining these grounds in the permanent harbor defences. Subsequently I was informed by Mr Stanton, that Genl. Halleck had reported in favor of including these in the fortifications, and further claimed title for the United States. Of this report Mr Stanton declined to furnish me a copy, and I understand that the claim of the United States rests upon the ground that President Fillmore in 51–2, directed the whole northern front of the City to be reserved for military use. Mr Fillmore did this without the authority of Congress, or without any reference to that body, and his directions—so far as the property in question is concerned—were never acted upon until the seizure in '63. Upon the ground, now, that the original title of the City was perfect, that an order from Mr Fillmore was insufficient to appropriate it to public use, that its owner was loyal, that martial law did not exist there but that, not withstanding, the order of the Court was disregarded by the officer in command, and that we were illegally and violently ousted from possession by an order from the War Department, I ask, on the part of Mrs Frémont, that, under the same authority the government troops be withdrawn and she be re-instated in her former undisturbed possession of her property, and that reasonable compensation be made for its use and occupancy by the Government, leaving the question of damages for future decision."—ALS, *ibid.*, RG 77, Land Papers, Point San José. See *SED*, 43-2-26.

1867, DEC. 11.   John M. Brodhead, comptroller, to USG. "In the early part of 1864 a large sum of money—said to be $68,800—was stolen from

Major Benj. Malone A. P. M. U. S. A. then in this city: Col. Wm. Wood— a detective for the Treasury Department—apprehended two of the supposed thieves and recovered a portion of the money, which, he says he turned over to Major L. C. Turner of the Bureau of Military Justice. Will you please inform me how much money was so turned over to Major Turner, and what disposition has been made of it?"—Copy, DNA, RG 217, 2nd Comptroller, Letters Sent.

1867, DEC. 11.   U.S. Senator Edwin D. Morgan of N. Y. to USG. "I learn that Colonel Jay E. Lee, at present New York Military Agent, will apply for the position of Judge Advocate in the Army. I need not urge his professional fitness after the favorable testimonials he produces from Judge Davis, of the New York bench, and professor Dwight, of Columbia College law school, gentlemen for whose opinions I have great respect; but his experience acquired in the field and especially as Military State agent must render his appointment an eligible one, and I therefore cordially unite with his other friends in commending his application to your favorable consideration."—LS, DNA, RG 59, Applications and Recommendations, Lincoln and Johnson. Numerous letters addressed to USG on the same subject are *ibid.*

1867, DEC. 12.   To Secretary of the Treasury Hugh McCulloch. "In reply to your letter of November 29th, covering a telegram of November 26th to the Commissioner of Internal Revenue from the Assessor of the 5th District of North Carolina, respecting the removal of troops from Greenboro', I have the honor to acquaint you that Bvt. Major General Canby, Commanding the Second Military District, to whom your communication was referred, reports on the subject as follows: 'There is constant railroad communication between Raleigh and Greensboro' and the distance in time is only four or five hours. At Raleigh there will be four companies of Infantry. There is telegraphic communication between Greensboro' and Raleigh and between both places and this city. I cannot see any necessity for keeping troops at Greensboro' now that the election is over.' General Canby's views are concurred in by this Department."—LS, DNA, RG 56, Letters Received from the War Dept. On Nov. 29, McCulloch had written to USG. "I herewith transmit for such action as you may deem necessary a telegram addressed to the Commissioner of Internal Revenue by the Collector and Assessor of the Fifth district of North Carolina remonstrating against the removal of troops from the post at Greensboro on the ground that such removal would seriously interfere with the assessment and collection of the revenue"—LS, *ibid.*, RG 94, Letters Received, 1752M 1867.

1867, DEC. 12.   To Attorney Gen. Henry Stanbery. "I have the honor to enclose herewith a communication from the Quartermaster General of the Army dated December 9th, 1867, with an account against W. L. Dawson amounting to $8573 24/100 due the United States, and request that you will cause a suit to be brought against Dawson for a recovery of that sum."—LS, DNA, RG 206, Letters Received from the War Dept. On Dec. 9, Bvt. Maj. Gen. Daniel H. Rucker, act. q. m. gen., had referred the matter to USG.—ES, *ibid.*, RG 92, Reports to the Secretary of War (Press). On Dec. 13, Asst. Attorney Gen. John M. Binckley wrote to USG. "I have the honor to state that the communication from your Office of the 12th instant, enclosing information of a debt due to the United States from Wm. L. Dawson, has been referred, with its enclosures, to the Solicitor of the Treasury."—Copy, *ibid.*, RG 60, Letters Sent. On Dec. 14, Solicitor of the Treasury Edward Jordan wrote to USG. "The Attorney General has referred to this office, your letter of the 12th instant, transmitting account of Q. M. Department against Wm L. Dawson of Georgetown D. C. for $8573 24/100, and requesting suit thereon for the recovery of the same, and I have this day forwarded the papers to the United States Attorney for the District of Columbia, with instructions to institute the proper proceedings without delay."—Copy, *ibid.*, RG 206, Letters Sent.

1867, DEC. 12.   USG endorsement. "Respectfully refered to the Chief of Ordnance with authority to retain such employees as can be kept usefully at work untill Apl. 1st 1868."—AES, DNA, RG 156, Letters Received. Written on a letter of Dec. 10 from William W. Eaton *et al.*, Watertown, Mass., to USG. "We the undersigned would respectfully represent that we have been employed in the United States Arsenal at Watertown Massachusetts for some time, and have been notified within a few days, that we were to be no longer employed there, which is a matter of great distress to us and to our families. The winter has set in, and business every where is dull, and there is no prospect that we can find employment elsewhere, for the present, and probably not until the spring. We would also respectfully represent that we served our Country in the late rebellion, and were honorably discharged at the expiration of our respective terms of service, except those of us who were discharged for wounds or other disabilities contracted in the line of duty   We have endeavored to represent our case to Major Buffinton now in command at the Arsenal, but he has declined to hear us. We therefore throw ourselves upon your indulgence   We have been given to understand that men who served faithfully in the war would have preference given them in the Government service, over those who had given no service to the nation in its hour of peril. There are many persons kept in employ who have not served in the Army and who can perform the labor required no better than we can. We have been faithful in the discharge of our duties, and are not aware that we have been discharged from any cause whereof we are to blame. We therefore in the most respectful manner, and without in the least degree wishing to throw blame upon Major Buffinton, ask that we may be restored to our places of labor in the Arsenal that we may gain an honest living for ourselves and our families during the long winter months which are now upon us."—LS (10 signatures), *ibid.*

1867, Dec. 12. To U.S. Senator Benjamin F. Wade of Ohio and Speaker of the House Schuyler Colfax. "I have the honor to send, herewith, for the consideration of the proper Committee a communication of Dec. 9. 1867 from the Commissary General of Subsistence respecting an increase of the officers of the *Subsistence Department* of the Army, and to say that his views, as set forth therein are concurred in by this Department"—Df, DNA, RG 192, Letters Received, Special File, G124; copy, *ibid.*, RG 107, Reports to Congress. See *HED,* 40-2-37.

1867, Dec. 13. To Secretary of the Interior Orville H. Browning. "I have the honor to acknowledge the receipt of your communication of the 22d ult. transmitting copy of a resolution of the *Cherokee National Council* and letter to *Lewis Downing* their Principal Chief, requesting that the place of payment of monies due soldiers be changed from *Ft. Gibson to Tahlequah*, and in reply to transmit herewith a copy of a letter on the subject from Judge *John W. Wright*, Atty. for Indian claimants, with endorsement of the Paymaster Genl. thereon, from which it appears that this Dept. has no authority in the case."—Copy, DNA, RG 107, Letters Sent to the President.

1867, Dec. [13]. USG endorsement. "I would respectfully recommend that this appointment be authorized in case of vacancy occuring between this and Sept. 1st /68."—AES (dated Dec. 12), DNA, RG 94, Correspondence, USMA. Written on a letter of Dec. 13 from Bvt. Brig. Gen. John C. McFerran, deputy q. m. gen., to USG. "Genl G. R. Paul, who you know is blind, and retired—is exceedingly anxious to get his stepson, Alfred— Rogers to West Point—The General is Certainly a deserving old soldier, and owing to his misfortune, is unable to write, and exert himself to obtain what he wants—Wont you—if there is a vacancy—from those appointed, under your or the Presidents, orders, from 'at large' send one to Genl P. for his boy—It would make his old heart glad and thus give you one more Claim of enjoying—as I know you do—the pleasure & gratification of doing good to others—"—ALS, *ibid.* Alfred H. Rogers, USMA 1872, died in 1879.

1867, Dec. 13. USG endorsement. "As Lt. Wallingford now has higher real rank that he ever held in the Volunteer service this application is not approved."—ES, DNA, RG 94, ACP, 708P CB 1867. Written on a letter of Dec. 7 from U.S. Senator Samuel C. Pomeroy of Kan., Washington, D. C., to USG. "I have the honor herewith to inclose, for your recommendation, a paper numerously signed asking that Lieut. Wallingford of 7th U. S. Cavalry—be *brevet*[*te*]*d* Captain in the U S. Army—Not only since he entered the Regular Army, but while in the volunter service he distinguished himself—always—faithful, cool and determined. He won the approbation of his superior officers   I shall esteem it a personal favor if you recommend him for a *brevet* rank—"—ALS, *ibid.* The enclosure is *ibid.*

1867, Dec. 13. To Governor Reuben E. Fenton of N. Y. "I have the honor through you to request the passage of a law by the Legislature of the

State of New York ceding to the United States jurisdiction over certain land known as *David's Island, New York Harbor;* to be purchased by the Government for military purposes. The jurisdiction herein asked is essential to the objects of the General Government and has heretofore been granted in all cases where property has been acquired by the United States for military purposes—It is hoped therefore that this request will receive early and favorable consideration."—Copies, DNA, RG 107, Letters Sent; *ibid.*, Letters Received, N130 1867. On Dec. 16, Fenton wrote to USG. "I have the honor to acknowledge the receipt of your communication of the 13th inst. requesting the passage of a law by the Legislature of the State ceding jurisdiction to the United States over David's Island in New York Harbor. At an early day in the approaching session of the Legislature I will make your request the subject of a special message, and presume, it will receive favorable action."—LS, *ibid.* On Feb. 17, 1868, William Andrews, Brooklyn, wrote to USG. "Will you please to allow an officer of your staff to send me such information as may be possible in reference to Davids Island N. Y. (off New Rochelle)   I wish to know how long it has been occupied as a U. S. militay post, and on what terms, also use the Govt. will make of the Island if jurisdiction is now ceded by this State—I should like the information as quickly as possible, as I shall probably have to make a minority report from the committee on Federal Relations of the Assembly (of which I am a member)—and I desire to make it strong—in reference to your request while sec. of war *ad interim* to have Davids Island ceded to the Genl-Govt. A majority of the committee are 'peace democrats,' while I am decidedly of the war stamp, and I shall be able to beat them in the house— They are anxious not to allow to the Govt. too much power in view of the *'next civil war—'* "—ALS, *ibid.*, RG 94, Letters Received, 74A 1868. On March 14, USG endorsed this letter. "Respectfully forwarded to the Secretary of War"—ES, *ibid.* On April 16, Warren Leland, Albany, N. Y., telegraphed to USG. "There is danger that the Bill before the Legislature, ceding Davids Island to the Government, will be defeated. Will you telegraph the Governor, asking him to promote the passage of the Bill"— Telegram received (at 3:30 P.M.), *ibid.*, RG 107, Telegrams Collected (Bound).

1867, DEC. 13.   Jacob Weaver, Jr., Pittsburgh, to USG. "Allow me as a private citizen of the United States, after my respects, to extend to you my best wishes for your health and prosperity,   In common with the rest of your Fellow Citizens I notice your distinguished name coupled in connection with that of the next Presidency,   You now occupy the most exalted position in the public eye—an honor justly won, which is fixed and lucrative for life,   I can not but mingle my regrets with millions of your friends, fearing that you may be tempted to become a Candidate for the evanescent and momentary, honors which belong to the Presidency,   Your fame is already coeval with the world and will ever remain engraven upon the highest pinnacle of renown,   As it soars thus gloriously among the mightiest names recorded in human history, may I not join my voice to keep it there, above the spirit of party and out of the reach of political charlatans and demagogues   With sentiments of the highest consideration . . . (Please destroy when read)"—Copy, DLC-Andrew Johnson. Enclosed in a letter of the same day from Weaver to Robert Johnson.—ALS, *ibid.*

1867, DEC. 14.   To Speaker of the House Schuyler Colfax. "I have the honor to send, herewith, a communication of the 13th inst. with a report from *Genl Buchanan*, the Commissioner appointed by the President under the Act of Congress, approved July 25th 1866, respecting the claims of the *State of Iowa* for military supplies furnished by it."—Df, DNA, RG 107, Letters Received from Bureaus; copy, *ibid.*, Reports to Congress. On Dec. 4, U.S. Representative Grenville M. Dodge of Iowa, Washington, D. C., wrote to USG. "I learn from our State Agent Col Dewey that Gen Bucan-nin—is orderd—to New Orleans. He has the claims of Iowa nearly ready to report on and if allowed to delay his departure until the first of next week—he can submit and report on them so that our agent can go on to his settlement, if not it will be a month or more before we can, get the report Will it be asking too much to allow Gen Bucannan—to delay his departure until he submits that report—It will be a matter of great importin to Iowa. and if not a detriment to the service I urgently request that the delay be allowed—I write in the interest of Iowa solely and ask the delay on that account alone"—ALS, *ibid.*, RG 94, Letters Received, 443D 1867.

1867, DEC. 14.   Judge Advocate Gen. Joseph Holt to USG. "Private Daniel Coughlin, Co. D. 3rd U. S. Cavalry, was tried in November last, at Fort Union, New. Mexico, by General Ct. Martial, under the following charge:—Mutinous Conduct. In that prisoner, being at the time on a scout after Indians, and having been ordered by his Commanding Officer, 1st Lieut. Wm. P. Bainbridge, 3d Cavy, to deliver up his arms, did refuse to do so, and did in company with Private Walter Conners of Co. D. 3d Cavy, present and cock a loaded carbine and threaten to shoot the said Lieut. Bainbridge and Corpl. Bown of Co. D. same regiment. This on a scout between Plum Creek and Johnson's Ranch N. M. Sept. 5. 1867. Prisoner plead not guilty. The Court find him guilty, except of the threat to shoot Corpl. Bown; & sentence him: to be shot to death with musketry at such time and place as the Commanding General of the Army may direct:—two thirds of the Court concurring. General A. J. Smith, Commanding Dept. of the Mo., approves the proceedings with the following comment & recom-mendation: 'The offence having been committed in the presence of so many enlisted men, it is a matter of surprise that more witnesses were not called on the part of the prosecution. It is recommended that the sentence be com-muted as follows: To forfeit all pay and allowances due, to be dishonorably discharged the service, and to be confined in such Penitentiary as the Secre-tary of War may designate for the period of four years.' With the record of Coughlin's trial is submitted that of the trial of private Walter Conner,

Co. D. same regiment, tried four days later before the same court under the following charges: 1. Mutinous Conduct. In that he, while on a scout, &c. did in company with private Coughlin, draw and cock a loaded carbine on his Commanding Officer, Lieut. Bainbridge and on Corporal Bown, after he had been ordered to deliver up his arms; and did say to Lieut. Bainbridge, 'My name is Walter Conner, Bainbridge; Keep away from me or I'll shoot you.' This Sept. 5th 1867. 2. Disobedience of orders. The Court sentence him to be shot, under the same finding as in Coughlin's case. Gen. A. J. Smith approves the proceedings, and forwards the record, regretting that no more witnesses were called for the prosecution, 'particularly after the trial of private Coughlin on the same charge, in which similar contradictory evidence appeared;' and makes the same recommendation as in Coughlin's case. The recommendation in each case is concurred in by this Bureau, though a study of the evidence leaves no doubt of the guilt of both the prisoners, on the ground on which the Department Commander bases his suggestion. The testimony for the defence is, it is thought, clearly unreliable & worthless; but in trials of such importance, the prosecution should, and easily could, have established the facts alleged by more abundant, though not more positive and trustworthy, proofs."—Copy, DNA, RG 153, Letters Sent.

1867, DEC. 16. To Attorney Gen. Henry Stanbery. "At the suggestion of the Quartermaster General of the Army, I have the honor to send herewith his communication of the 16th instant and papers accompanying, respecting an injunction which has been issued against the sale of public buildings at York, Pennsylvania, and to request your opinion as to its legality."—LS, DNA, RG 60, Letters Received, War Dept. On the same day, Bvt. Maj. Gen. Daniel H. Rucker, act. q. m. gen., had written to USG. "It having been represented to this Office by Messrs Corcoran and Hay Attornies &C of York Pa. that there were a number of Government Buildings at York Pa. which were occupied by the US during the late war for hospital purposes, which were still standing and fast going to decay &C. Bvt Maj Genl Geo H. Crosman Asst Q. M. Genl. at Philadelphia Pa—was directed to thoroughly investigate the case— . . ."—LS, *ibid.*, RG 92, Reports to the Secretary of War (Press).

1867, DEC. 16. To Secretary of the Navy Gideon Welles. "I beg to enquire whether any prize proceedings were instituted against the blockade runner 'Virginia Dare', which is stranded on Debudeau beach, near the land of Mr. J. J. Middleton in the Georgetown, S. C., district"—LS, DNA, RG 45, Letters Received from the President. On Dec. 11, Bvt. Maj. Gen. Edward R. S. Canby, Charleston, had written to USG. "I have the honor to transmit a check on the Assistant Treasurer, City of New York, for the sum of Three hundred and five ($305) dollars, the proceeds of the sale of material recovered from the wreck of the Blockade runner—Virginia Dare. I do not know whether any prize proceedings were instituted against this vessel, but this can be ascertained by reference to the Navy Department. If none were, the money should be paid into the Treasury, as the proceeds of the sale of captured and abandoned property. In order that the proper disposition may be made of it, I have made the check payable to the order of the Secretary of War."—LS, *ibid.*, RG 107, Letters Received, C631 1867. On Dec. 20, Welles wrote to USG. "I have the honor to state, in reply to your letter of the 16th inst., that the Department is not aware that any prize proceedings have been instituted in the case of the blockade runner 'Virginia Dare.' The vessel is reported as having been chased ashore on the 9th of Jan: 1864, near North Inlet, S. C., by the U. S. Steamer 'Aries', and completely wrecked."—LS, *ibid.* On Dec. 23, USG wrote to Secretary of the Treasury Hugh McCulloch. "I have the honor to enclose herewith a draft on the Assistant Treasurer of the United States at New York, for three hundred and five dollars ($305 00/100) 'being proceeds of sale by the military authorities of materiel recovered from the wreck of the blockade runner "Virginia Dare," ' and to suggest that the same be covered into the Treasury as proceeds of the sale of captured and abandoned property, or otherwise disposed of as you may deem proper. The Secretary of the Navy informs this Department that he is not aware of any prize proceedings being instituted against this vessel, which was reported to the Navy Department as having been chased ashore by the United States steamer 'Aries' January 9, 1864 and completely wrecked. The papers pertaining to the subject ar[e] also transmitted herewith."—LS, *ibid.*, RG 56, Letters Received from the War Dept.

1867, DEC. 16, 11:15 A.M.   To Maj. Gen. Philip H. Sheridan, Somerset, Ohio. "I would like to see you in Washington as soon as it is convenient for you to come."—ALS (telegram sent), DNA, RG 107, Telegrams Collected (Bound); telegram sent, *ibid.*; copies, *ibid.*, RG 108, Telegrams Sent; DLC-USG, V, 56. On the same day, Sheridan, Zanesville, Ohio, had telegraphed to USG. "Will be in Washington on the eighteenth"—Telegram received (at 9:20 A.M.), DNA, RG 107, Telegrams Collected (Bound); copy, DLC-Philip H. Sheridan.

1867, DEC. 16.   To U.S. Senator Orris S. Ferry of Conn. "The Judge Advocate General has submitted to me your letter of the 12th instant, asking for a copy of the record of the Court Martial in the case of *Dorrence Atwater* with the final action thereon. In reply I have respectfully to inform you that in compliance with the Resolution of the House of Representatives, dated July 11. 1866, a copy of this record together with all the reports, orders and action in the case was furnished the House the 13th July 1866, and was published in a document of the House—I presume that the information you desire to obtain will be presented completely and in convenient form for examination by this printed document."—Copies, DNA, RG 107, Letters Sent; *ibid.*, Letters Received, W320 1867. See *HED*, 39-1-149.

1867, DEC. 16.   President Andrew Johnson to USG. "The Secretary of War ad interim, will please substitute the Pittsburg 'Daily Post' for the Pittsburg 'Daily Commercial', on the list of newspapers designated for the publication of advertisements for the War Department."—Copies (2), DLC-Andrew Johnson.

1867, DEC. 16.   Brig. Gen. Andrew A. Humphreys, chief of engineers, to USG. "The proposition of Lt. Genl. Sherman, to transfer 'Jefferson barracks' to the Engineers, and to take therefor the money appropriated for the new building for an engineer depôt in that vicinity, having been approved by the Secretary of War, and the transfer of the barracks having been made, the transfer of the money should follow. . . ."—LS, DNA, RG 77, Accounts, Property Returns, and Claims, Letters Received. See *HED*, 40-3-1, II, part 2, p. 22.

1867, DEC. 17.   To Speaker of the House Schuyler Colfax. "In relation to a Resolution of the House of Representatives, dated December 10th 1867, respecting the expediency of establishing an U. S. Arsenal at *Fort David Russell*, at Chiyenne, Dacotah Territory I have the honor to send, herewith, a report on the subject, from the Chief of Ordnance, dated December 17th 67"—Copy, DNA, RG 107, Reports to Congress. See *HED*, 40-2-64.

1867, DEC. 17.   To Speaker of the House Schuyler Colfax. "I have the honor to transmit, for the consideration of the proper committee, a copy of a report made by Col Houston, of the Engineers, dated Dec 9th and sent to this Department by the Chief of Engineers respecting the improvement of the *Pawtucket River*, R. I."—Df, DNA, RG 77, Explorations and Surveys, Letters Received; copy, *ibid.*, RG 107, Reports to Congress. On Dec. 17, Brig. Gen. Andrew A. Humphreys, chief of engineers, had written to USG. "I have the honor to transmit herewith for the information of the Hon. William Sprague, of the Senate of the U. S., a copy of a report made to this office on the 9th inst. by Bvt. Col. D. C. Houston in relation to a further appropriation for the improvement of the Pawtucket river, R. I., and respectfully return herewith the letter of Bvt. Brig. Gen. I. C. Woodruff, left by Senator Sprague at the War Department, and referred to this office for report. The object of the communication to Senator Sprague was that an official call might be made on the War Department by the Senate or one of its Committees for the report."—LS, *ibid.*, RG 77, Explorations and Surveys, Letters Received. See *HED*, 40-2-60.

1867, DEC. 17.   To Act. Consul Gen. John Wermuth of Switzerland. "In reply to your communication of the 5th instant, requesting, in the case of *Prvt. Charles Imhoff*, Co. F. 34th U. S. Infantry, that the forfeiture of pay for one year from October 1866, imposed by sentence of a General Court Martial, be remitted, I have the honor to inform you, that the Judge Advocate General, to whom the case was referred, reports that 'the sentence having been fully executed cannot now be remitted, and the amount of pay forfeited cannot be returned to Private Imhoff except by Act of Congress.'" —Copies, DNA, RG 107, Letters Sent; *ibid.*, Letters Received, S425 1867. On Dec. 5, Wermuth had written to USG. "*Charles Imhoff*, a Swiss, at present a Private of Comp. "F" 34th Regiment United States Infantry, stationed at Columbus, Miss, was placed in October 1866 before a Court Martial and sentenced to twelve months guardhouse and loss of pay for same period. It appears that the offence for which he received punishment, was connected, with many mitigating circumstances, so much so, that his superior officers appealed to Headquarters at Vicksburg to remit, at least portion, of the sentence passed. However no reply reached the command at Columbus and Private Imhoff has been advised to solicit the kind offices of this Consulate to intercede at Headquarters of the Army in his behalf, in order that the forfeiture of his pay may be remitted. It is stated that Imhoff's conduct since his enlistment has been most exemplary and the officers of his command are united in recommending the soldier to the kind consideration of the General Commanding the Armies. This Consulate would, therefore, most respectfully solicit the kind considerations of the General, in regard to Private Imhoff and to beg, that the forfeiture of his pay be remitted. The letter of 1st Lieut Allen Almy to the Comd'g Officer is herewith submitted"—Copy (unsigned), *ibid.* On Dec. 20, Wermuth wrote to USG. "This Consulate begs to acknowledge the receipt of communication of the 17th instant relative to the case of *Private Charles Imhoff*, Co "F" 34th U. S. Infantry. The undersigned has informed Private Imhoff of the decision of the Department, and embraces this opportunity to thank for kind attentions in the premises"—LS, *ibid.*

1867, DEC. 17. Jay Cooke, William G. Moorhead, and George H. Stuart, Philadelphia, to USG. "A leave of absence, say from 21st to 30th insts, if granted to Cadet Wm J. Volkmar of the Academy at West Point would confer a great favor upon a very meritorious young officer (whose conduct-record had for 1867 but one demerit) and would much oblige . . ."—LS, DNA, RG 94, Correspondence, USMA.

1867, DEC. 18. To Secretary of the Interior Orville H. Browning. "At the instance of Lieut. Genl. *William T. Sherman*, I have the honor to transmit for your information a copy of a com'n from *Capt. E. Byrne*, 10th U. S. Cav'y. relative to the killing of several *Osage* and *Kaw* Indians by the *Cheyennes* and *Arrapahoes*."—Copy, DNA, RG 107, Letters Sent to the President.

1867, DEC. 18. To U.S. Representative John A. Bingham of Ohio, chairman, Committee of Claims. "In compliance with request of the Committee of Claims of the 12th instant, I have the honor to transmit, herewith, a report of the Quartermaster General, with accompanying papers, comprising all the information known to this Department, pertaining to the claim of *Adam Hardt*, for re-imbursement of money advanced to a portion of the crew of the *Steamer 'John Raine'* "—Copy, DNA, RG 107, Reports to Congress. Printed as addressed to Speaker of the House Schuyler Colfax in *HED*, 40-2-62.

1867, DEC. 18.   William E. Chandler, Concord, N. H., to Bvt. Brig. Gen. Frederick T. Dent. "The. N. H. Republican Convention have unanimously nominated Gen Grant for President with cheers for his letter about Stanton & Sheridan"—Telegram received (at 4:10 P.M.), DNA, RG 107, Telegrams Collected (Bound). On Dec. 24, Chandler, Washington, D. C., wrote to Dent. "*Personal* . . . Please read the enclosed and submit to General Grant. The more unanimous the public sentiment in his favor and the more evident it becomes that he cannot refuse to be a candidate the better & safer for the country"—ALS, ICarbS.

1867, DEC. 19.   To Attorney Gen. Henry Stanbery. "The case of Grisar vs. Bvt. Major General McDowell, on the calendar at the present term of the Supreme Court, involves the title to the Military Reserve at San Francisco. A speedy decision is of importance to the public service and I therefore have the honor to request that you will procure the case to be advanced on the Calendar, so that a decision may be had as early as practicable."—LS, DNA, RG 60, Letters Received, War Dept.

1867, DEC. 19.   To Speaker of the House Schuyler Colfax. "I have the honor to send, herewith, for the information and consideration of the proper Committee, a communication from the Quartermaster General of Army, dated the 18th inst. respecting the hiring of a building to be used for all the military officers and for the storing of all army supplies necessary for the service in the *City of New York*. The recommendation by the Quartermaster General has been approved by this Department"—Copy, DNA, RG 107, Reports to Congress. See *HED*, 40-2-65.

1867, DEC. 19.   To U.S. Senator Henry Wilson of Mass. "In reply to your request, I suggest that the following section be added to the proposed Bill authorizing the sale of property of the United States at *Harpers Ferry*:— Sec. 2 And be it further enacted that the Secretary of War shall have power to convey by deed all those certain portions of the aforesaid property which have heretofore at various times been set apart by proper authority for religious, charitable, educational and town purposes."—Copies, DNA, RG 94, Letters Sent; *ibid.*, RG 107, Reports to Congress.

1867, DEC. 19.   To U.S. Senator Henry Wilson of Mass. "In compliance with your request, I suggest that the following clause be added to the proposed Bill 'donating a portion of the *Fort Leavenworth Military Reservation* for the exclusive use of a public road,'—'and the said road shall be and remain a public highway for the use of the Government of the United States free from tolls or other charge upon the transportation of any property, troops or mails of the United States' "—Copies, DNA, RG 94, Letters Sent; *ibid.*, RG 107, Reports to Congress.

1867, DEC. 19.   Judge Advocate Gen. Joseph Holt to USG. "James Dowd, private Co. C. 5th Infy., was tried Nov. 18. 1867, by General Court Martial convened at Fort Union, New Mexo under the following charges: 1. Drunkenness on duty. In that prisoner, while a member of the garrison guard, did become so much intoxicated as to be unable to perform his duties properly. This at Fort Wingate, Aug. 6. 67. 2. Sleeping on post. 3. Mutinous conduct, in violation of the 7th Article. In that, when ordered by 2d Lieut. Ennis, officer of the Day, to go with a sentinel thro' the sally port of the guard house, prisoner stopped in the guard room, and did then and there begin to excite mutiny among the prisoners. This Aug. 6th 1867. . . . Though the witnesses called for the defence, enlisted men on duty at the time at the guard-house, deny positively that prisoner's conduct was disorderly or mutinous as alleged, there can be little doubt that Lieut. Ennis's testimony is substantially correct. It is reasonable to suppose, however, that the heat of the sun, to which he had been for some time exposed without shelter, had much to do with prisoner's frantic conduct towards his officer. He deserves however, both as a warning and example, severe punishment; though the enforcement of the death penalty in his case would be an act, it is believed, of needless & cruel severity."—Copy, DNA, RG 153, Letters Sent.

1867, DEC. 19.   Lloyd J. Beall, Richmond, Va., to USG. "The Freedman's Bureau through its Agents in Florida has laid claim to certain lots as abandoned property within the limits of the town Pensacola bequeathed by the late Col. Arthur. P. Hayne to my wife, his only child—Col. Hayne was in no way engaged in the late conflict between North & South—but was a distinguished officer of the war of 1812, and Aid de Camp to Genl Jackson at the Battle of New Orleans—Mrs Beall has taken the oath of amnesty under the proclamation of 1865. Not knowing what other course to pursue, I have taken the liberty of laying the above facts before you, and ask that you will interpose your authority to have the property in question relieved from the claim set up by the Bureau"—ALS, DNA, RG 105, Land Div., Letters Received.

1867, DEC. 20.   USG note. "The Adj Gn may make the order assigning Maj. Wharton."—AN (initialed), DNA, RG 94, Letters Received, 708A 1867. On Jan. 28, Capt. Henry C. Wharton had been court-martialed for embezzlement and cashiered; on Aug. 16, his sentence was remitted.—*Ibid.*, 548P 1867.

1867, DEC. 20.   Bvt. Maj. Gen. John M. Schofield, Richmond, to USG. "I have the honor to transmit herewith a map, made from actual survey by an officer of the Engineers, showing the extent and location with reference to Fort Monroe of the tract of land which it has been proposed to purchase for Military purposes, especially for the use of the Artillery School at Fort Monroe. I also enclose an estimate of the values of the several portions of the tract in question with the names of the owners, and a proposition from Mr Joseph Segar to sell to the United States his farm containing about Three hundred and seven Acres, and constituting the main body of the tract referred to. This is the only proposition of sale which has been received. The other owners have generally declined to make propositions in such reasonable terms as to justify my recommendation of their acceptance. If the Government decide to acquire a title to the property the only practicable course seems to be, that adopted in the case of Arsenal property on Rock Island, Ills. Viz:—by an Act of Congress directing the Secretary of War to take possession of the property and appoint a Board of Commissioners to ascertain the values of the several parcels of land and award just compensation to the lawful owners thereof—"—Copy, DLC-John M. Schofield. See *HED*, 41-2-49.

1867, DEC. 20.   Lafayette S. Foster, Norwich, Conn., to USG. "*Private* . . . I have no doubt that you daily get letters from all parts of the country giving you a great deal of most excellent advice as to the course you ought to take in your present position—Any possible lull in this stream of correspondence is more than occupied by the pressing calls of very wise men who wish to give you the benefit of their counsel orally—Now General, I have no advice whatever to give—When you shall speak, how you shall speak, what you shall speak, or whether you shall speak at all, may, in my judgement, be safely left to your own decision. In politics I am a republican, not unobservant of passing events—The spontaneous uprising of the people in the various sections of the country to make you the next President of the United States, which you, under God, have saved from being dis-united, gives me the highest satisfaction—For you, I can readily see that it is a position not to be desired, but coming to you as it does, the people with united voice demanding it, you cannot refuse—The hearts of the people are with you and for you, and one may as well bid back the ocean wave, as stay the rising tide of public favor—I feel confident that your course will be as it has been, quiet, unostentatious, triumphant—"—ALS, USG 3.

1867, DEC. 20.   U.S. Representative Halbert E. Paine of Wis. to USG. "I beg leave to invite your especial attention to the enclosed letter from Gov Salomon. Maj Whittleseys Report had already come to my notice and I was favorably imppressed with his suggestions. But I hope it may be possible to furnish our State University with a suitable officer without awaiting further legislation. Under the auspices of the new President the Wisconsin University promises to take very high rank as a school and we are very anxious to secure the services of a competent officer as soon as possible—"—ALS, DNA, RG 94, Letters Received, 816P 1867. The enclosure is *ibid.*

1867, DEC. 21.   To Secretary of the Interior Orville H. Browning. "At the instance of the Qr. Mr. Genl. of the Army, I have the honor to transmit herewith, for settlement, two accounts in favor of the *Wash'n County* (Texas) *Railroad Co.*, for the *transportation of Indians*, amounting respectively to $9 22/100 and $11 79/100. These accounts have been disallowed as a charge upon the Qr. Mrs. Dept., for the reason, as set forth in the accompanying copy of the report of the Ch'f. Qr Mr. Dist. of Texas, that the Indians were not in the Military Service."—Df, DNA, RG 92, Consolidated Correspondence, Washington County Railroad Co.; copy, *ibid.*, RG 107, Letters Sent to the President. On Dec. 18, Bvt. Maj. Gen. Daniel H. Rucker, act. q. m. gen., had written to USG concerning this matter.—LS, *ibid.*, RG 92, Consolidated Correspondence, Washington County Railroad Co. On Jan. 3, 1868, Browning wrote to USG. "Your letter of the 21st ultimo, enclosing two accounts in favor of the Washington County (Texas) Railroad company, for the transportation of Indians, amounting, respectively, to $9.22/100 and $11.79/100, was received and referred to the Indian Bureau for examination and report. I now, transmit, a copy of a communication, dated the 31st ultimo, from the Acting Commissioner of Indian Affairs in relation to the subject of said accounts, for the payment of which this Department has no authority of law. They are therefore herewith returned, together with the accompanying copy of a report of the Chief Quarter Master, District of Texas, which were enclosed with said accounts."—LS, *ibid.*, Letters Received. The enclosures are *ibid.*

1867, DEC. 21.   USG endorsement. "Refered to Gn. Kelton to know if this man has heretofore been ordered before a 'Board.' If not leave this application on file untill apts. are again being made and then order him for examination."—AES, DNA, RG 94, ACP, M1388 CB 1867. Written on a letter of Dec. 20 from Maj. Gen. Oliver O. Howard to USG. "I have the honor to second and cordially endorse the application of 1st Sergt H. H. McConnell "A" Co. "6" Cav'y U. S. A. for an examination with a view to his promotion to a Lieutenancy. He comes to me highly recommended by gentlemen of high standing and influence. He is a young man, of good family, intelligent, finely educated, a gentleman in manners and bearing, and I think possesses all the qualities necessary to make him a good officer. Although he entered the ranks of the regular army as a private so recently as Sept. 1866, his uniform good conduct secured his rapid promotion through intermediate grades to the position of 1st Sergt and his application for examination is made at the instance of his superior officers stationed at Buffalo Springs and Austin Texas."—LS, *ibid.* No appointment followed.

1867, DEC. 21.   To Speaker of the House Schuyler Colfax. "At the suggestion of the Judge Advocate General, whose opinion is sent herewith I have the honor to transmit, for the consideration of the proper Committee, a letter from *Robert Buffum*, late of 21st Ohio Vols., who, with others, volunteered to perform a very hazardous service during the war of the rebellion in the State of *Georgia* in the Spring of 1862, as set forth in the accompanying report."—Copy, DNA, RG 107, Reports to Congress. On Dec. 18, Robert Buffum, Washington, D. C., had written to USG. "I have the honor respectfully to represent that on the 7th of April, 1862, General Mitchell, commanding a brigade of the fourteenth army corps, at Shelby-ville, Tennessee, called for volunteers to penetrate the enemy's country for the purpose of cutting his communications between the south and south-west, while he advanced upon Huntsville. Twenty-two men, of whom I was one, disguised as refugees, started on this expedition and penetrated as far as Big Shanty, eight miles from Marietta, where, finding no operator to telegraph about our movements, we seized a locomotive, and started down the road, cutting the railroad as we went along. Our purpose was to cut the communications between different parts of the enemy's country, and then join General Mitchell, who was to be at Huntsville Being pursued, we were compelled to abandon our purpose and take to the mountains, where all were subsequently captured, the rebels using bloodhounds to track us. We were carried to Chattanooga, Tennessee, where we were confined in a dungeon thirteen feet square, chained by the neck two and two; subse-quently we were taken to Dalton, Marietta, Madison, Knoxville, Lynch-burg, Libby prison, Castle Thunder, and Atlanta, where eight of the party were hung as spies. The approach of United States troops alone prevented the remainder sharing a similar fate. The full history of our proceedings will be found on file in the Judge Advocate General's office. The long im-prisonment, exposure, and cruelty with which we were treated while in the hands of the enemy, has so impaired my health and mind that I am in no condition to earn a livelihood for myself. I have a wife and three small children dependent upon me for support, and have no home or means of caring for them. My present object in making this statement is to solicit some immediate relief for my family. Congress has never legislated for our relief, and some of the surviving of this expedition are suffering for means. We believe that our past sufferings and hardships justly entitle us to the consideration of our country, but our families are in a suffering condition, and in want of immediate relief. I respectfully ask that the Secretary of War will afford me such relief as will enable me to support my family, and procure for them a home. . . . I request permission to accompany this state-ment to the Judge Advocate General, if it should be referred to him."—*HED*, 40-2-74, pp. 1–2. On Dec. 19, Judge Advocate Gen. Joseph Holt favorably endorsed this letter.—*Ibid.*, p. 2. For the Andrews Raid or "Great Locomotive Chase," see *O.R.*, I, x, part 1, 630–39.

1867, DEC. 21. U.S. Delegate Charles P. Clever of New Mexico Terri-tory to USG. "I have the honor to request that you issue a letter or warrant of appointment as a cadet at the West Point Military Academy, to Henry A. Carleton, the only son of General James H. Carleton of the Army. *Henry*

A. Carleton, was born at Fort Union, New Mexico, on the 21st day of June 1853, and he will, therefore, be sixteen years of age on the 21st day of next June. This young gentleman for whom I request this appointment, having been born in the Territory, I represent, has peculiar claims to my influence from *that* fact, and from the fact, that his father has served ten years in that Country, and became, from his labors and his successes with Indians there, identified as well with its history as with its interests. Henry A Carleton is a youth of excellent habits, and of a high order of intelligence. He has been two years in college, and is still there, and from his elementary and academic aquirements, will doubtless take a fair stand as a cadet. Should you cause the appointment to be made, please enclose it under cover to me."—ALS, DNA, RG 94, Correspondence, USMA. No appointment followed.

1867, DEC. 21.   Mrs. John Mountpleasant, Suspension Bridge, N. Y., to USG. "Is my brother Col Parker dangerously ill or is he still missing"— Telegram received (at 4:15 P.M.), DNA, RG 107, Telegrams Collected (Bound). See William H. Armstrong, *Warrior in Two Camps: Ely S. Parker Union General and Seneca Chief* (Syracuse, 1978), pp. 132–33.

1867, DEC. 23.   USG endorsement. "Respectfully returned to the President with the report called for. There is at present no vacancy—of Military Store Keeper, ordnance Department."—ES, DNA, RG 94, ACP, W56 CB 1869. Written on a letter of Dec. 13 from Inez Weston, Auburndale, Mass., to U.S. Senator James R. Doolittle of Wis. "In May last in presence of Hon. J. S. Black, the President promised to refer Capt. Chas. Weston's case to the Atty. Genl. After seven months of anxious Waiting, I have recd the enclosed letter! I entreat you to *see* Mr Johnson ask that he fulfil his promise, or, if hes has himself decided it—let me be so informed. His action in Col. Belgers case, *should* be a precedent in this. As one of the military committee tis proper I beg your aid. You left the Presidents office as I entered it—that passing glance *assured* me in you the wronged & unhappy will ever find a ~~generous~~ generous, zealous, advocate."—ALS, *ibid.*

1867, DEC. 23.   USG endorsements. "Under no circumstances would this officer be entitled to a higher brevet than that given to additional Paymasters retained in service; namely, a Lieut. Colcy. Under the actual circumstances in this case Major Wilcox is entitled to no brevets whatever." "Respectfully submitted to the President with reasons why the brevet requested should not be granted"—ES (the first as gen.), DLC-Andrew Johnson. Written on a letter of Oct. 17 from Secretary of the Interior Orville H. Browning to President Andrew Johnson. "I have personally known Col. Nathaniel G. Wilcox for a period of about thirty years, as an honorable and high-minded gentleman. He was nominated by President Lincoln to the Senate and confirmed while I was a member of that body—

on the 5th of August 1861, to the office of Addl Paymaster in the Army. His resignation of said office, took effect the 21st of February 1863. . . ."— LS, *ibid.* See Lincoln, *Works*, VI, 109–10.

1867, Dec. 23 and 24.   USG endorsements. "This officer was relieved from duty in the field by me while in the presence of the enemy. He cannot be brevetted Major General without injustice to others." "Respectfully submitted to the President, inviting attention to the endorsement of the General of the Army, before carrying out the orders in this case."—ES, DLC-Andrew Johnson. See *PUSG*, 11, 29. Written on a letter of Sept. 20 from Darius N. Couch, Taunton, Mass., to USG. "I beg to inform you that Brig Gen J. J Abercrombi late U. S. Vols Served in my Command in the Peninsular Campaign at the Battles of 'Fair Oaks' and 'Malvern Hill'. In both of these hard fought contests, I am able to state from personal observation that this Gallant Officer displayed marked gallantry. 'My "Div'n" ' was largely indebted for its successes on these days to the presence of Gen Abercrombi—"—ALS, DLC-Andrew Johnson. On Oct. 17, Nelson Cross, New York City, wrote to USG. "I am gratified to know that the Military friends of Brig Gen John J. Abercrombie, U. S. A. are making the endeavor to place his high merits as an officer, and particularly as a General in command of Volunteer Troops in the late war for the Union, properly before your Department, with a view of securing to him the deserved appointment of Major General by Brevet in the regular Army. I had the honor to command a Regiment in the Brigade of General Abercrombie, in the Army of the Potomac, during active hostilities, and I here take occasion to say unqualifiedly, that it was to his foresight and determined resistance, that the first day's battle of Fair Oaks was saved from disaster. It was through the suggestion of General Abercrombie that General Sumner was notified of the danger which threatened the advanced troops of the Army, whilst the battle was at the hottest, and when Sumner was conducted to the ground by a member of Abercrombie's Staff, it was Abercrombie's Brigade, even in an advanced position, that was resisting the concentrated charge of the Enemy to break our line, after Casey's Division had been swept from the field. During the subsequent Seven days of Battle, in which Abercrombie shared, his troops were handled with great skill and prudence. At Malvern Hills, it was by his command that the Troops of McGruder's command were charged and routed in their last endeavor to force our left centre. I do not say that I *believe* General Abercrombie to have been a discreet, able and brave officer, I *know* it, and am thankful that it is not too late to do him substantial justice, in the honor which his friends, more than he, desire to see conferred upon him, and as one of their number I earnestly request it may be done."—ALS, *ibid.*

On Dec. 14, Robert Patterson, Philadelphia, wrote to USG. "I venture to request you will do me the great favor to aid my Grandson J J Abercrombie Jr who is anxious to enter the Army—his application is now on file in the department—with recommendations from Officers under whom he served during the rebellion—Mr Abercrombie is the son of your old friend General John J Abercrombie—who with myself—will feel under very great obligations to you—if you will have the appointment promptly made—Pray present the cordial respects of Mrs Patterson & myself to Mrs Grant"— ALS, DNA, RG 94, ACP, A137 CB 1867.

1867, DEC. 23. Judge Advocate Gen. Joseph Holt to USG. "Samuel R. Honey, Capt. 33d Infy, addresses to Bvt. Brig. Gen. F. T. Dent, Asst. Adjt. General, under date of Dec. 19. 1867, a request that the Judge Advo. General 'be directed to review his opinion and action upon the record of the Gen. Court Martial by which I' (Capt. Honey) 'was tried in March last.' And he submits sundry affidavits and letters in support of his claim. . . . The very strong testimonials to his integrity, intelligence, and faithfulness in the service now submitted by him, from officers well qualified to form a reliable judgment upon such points, justify the opinion that this Bureau's estimate of Capt. Honey's culpability in the transaction, though seemingly in accord with the proofs which were then before it for its consideration and guidance, was in conflict with the tenor of his life for integrity & honor, as affirmed by officers of the highest rank and repute in the service; and it is but just to him, that this opinion, in the final disposition of his case, should find a place upon the records of this office."—Copy, DNA, RG 153, Letters Sent.

1867, DEC. 23. Samuel L. M. Barlow, New York City, to USG. "I enclose to you a copy of a letter just received from Col St Leger Grenfell now confined as a Prisoner at Fort Jefferson. I have taken some pains to ascertain the facts connected with his trial and am satisfied that he is innocent, and that he is now suffering an unjust Confinement—At the same time I know of no way in which I can aid in securing his release unless it be through some action of the War Department. May I ask that you will examine into his case and if the circumstances warrant it, that you will lay the matter before the President."—ALS, DNA, RG 108, Letters Received. On Dec. 5, George St. Leger Grenfell, Fort Jefferson, Dry Tortugas, had written to Barlow. "I have no better reason to give by the liberty which I take in addressing you & forwarding to your care the enclosed letters than that I have been requested to do so by Mr Joseph G. Eastland of San Francisco and that no one is more in want of the kind offices of some influential friend than I am. Mr Eastland in a letter dated '4th November Steamer Montana off Acapulco' says that he conversed with you about me and that you had kindly promised him to exert your influence at Head Quarters in my favor, and ends by begging me to lose no time in writing to you on the subject—I have therefore sent you a letter which I had already written to my ambassador, but had not despatched it, having waited to see whether Augustus Page or Mr Thornton would receive the appointment If the first I could count upon his most hearty cooperation with you, of the last I know very little, although I am personally acquainted with him having known him when he was British Chargé d'affair in Montevideo—if you approve of the Letter be so good as to forward it to Washington as also the one for Mr Ford—Mr Eastland mentions also Col Posten of the firm of Botts & Posten as being well disposed to assist me in obtaining my release— Is the Mr Botts alluded to any relation of John Minor Botts of Va? who wrote to me that he would willingly use his influence in my favor? During the war as Inspector General in Lees army I was enabled to serve him by protecting his property from our Cavalry marauders—Should you be able to spare time to make an effort for my release & require other influence than your own to back your exertions I beg to inform you that Mr Robert Henry Atty at Law, Chicago has had my case in hand from the beginning although I have not heard from him for 18 months—He told me that Burnet the Judge Advocate on my trial and four out of the eight officers who tried me had signed a petition to the President in my favor, as did Brig-Genl Sweet who was the cause of my arrest—Col. Wisewell formerly Military Govr of Washington is warmly disposed towards me—Archbishop Purcell of Ohio and Mr Montgomery Blair did what they could for me and several leading Democrats kindly also did the same—But Stanton & Holt were not to be persuaded, I was a Rebel and did not deny it, but Conspirator I never was as I will prove one of these days if Gods grants me life to get out of this Den—Messrs Pendleton and Vallandingham would have assisted me but in those days their protection was of no avail—Col or Judge Key of Cincinnati formerly Judge Advocate on Genl McClellans staff did his utmost to serve me, but all was of no use and unless you sir can influence the President to rescind my sentence I am afraid that I must wear out my life behind these prison bars—May God give you the disposition to exert your influence in my favor and under your efforts successful. You may boldly say that I am an innocent man not only innocent of being a party to the conspiracy but I was ignorant of the existence of it or any other conspiracy—I scorn the idea of being one of Jake Thompsons agents, I had nothing to do with them in any way whatever or any other Confederate agent—When I left the Con- federate service I left it entirely with the intention of returning to England and was not concerned in any of those plots—which were carried on near the Canadian Frontier—I wish to be sent for trial but before a Civil Court and not an assassination Commission—Excuse the length of this letter (but the subject to me is an engrossing one) and believe me sir that I look for- ward to your assistance with hope & gratitude . . ."—ALS, *ibid.* On Jan. 8, 1868, Judge Advocate Gen. Joseph Holt endorsed Barlow's letter. "Respect- fully returned to General Grant with a printed copy of the proceedings had in relation to the case of G. St. Leger Grenfell and his co-conspirators, and attention invited to the eight reports made by this Bureau, to be found on pages 645 to 653, of said copy. Grenfell's assertion of innocence in his communication to Mr. Barlow, has been repeatedly made heretofore, and it is believed that there is nothing now submitted by him, or in his behalf calling for further comment than has already been made in the reports alluded to."—ES, *ibid.* See *ibid.*, RG 94, Letters Received, 383M 1868.

1867, DEC. 24.   USG endorsement. "It does not appear that this officer has been in any battle during the war, nor that he has rendered any services deserving higher brevet rank than that he now holds. He could not with any justice be brevetted Maj Genl., unless every officer above him in the Qr Mr. Dept., first recieved that brevet, and that would be unjust to others"—Copy, DNA, RG 108, Register of Letters Received. Written on papers concerning Bvt. Brig. Gen. James A. Ekin "For brevet of Maj Genl. U. S. A. President of U. States recommending same be given if it is possible."—*Ibid.*

1867, DEC. 24.   USG endorsement. "Respectfully refered to Bvt. Maj. Gen. Canby with authority to give such leave of absence to Bvt. Brig. Gn. Burton as his physician may deem necessary, or to change his station to any post within any state occupied by his regiment except Ft Monroe."— AES, DNA, RG 94, Letters Received, 1135B 1867. Written on a letter of Dec. 19 from Montgomery Blair, Washington, D. C., to USG. "I enclose a duplicate certificate showing the condition of Genl Burtons health   It occurs to me to suggest for your consideration whether or not the Hd Qrs of his Regiment might not be transfered to Baltimore or to Georgetown where his daughter is at school   His pecuniary circumstances do not admit of his taking a leave of absence   I hope either by the suggestion I make or what is more likely through some suggestion of your own you will be able to provide for the General. You will not & ought not to let *humanity* or consideration for an individual to interfere with the Public interests. But where the Public do not require the sacrifice of life ~~even when the life~~ I am sure will study to save it & even to consider the pecuniary shorts of an old officer & aid him as far as you can to keep the position required to give the means of Educating his children—"—ALS, *ibid.* The enclosure is *ibid.*

1867, DEC. 24, 10:25 A.M.   To Lucius S. Felt, Galena. "Please have glassware sent also."—ALS (telegram sent), DNA, RG 107, Telegrams Collected (Bound).

1867, DEC. 24.   George C. McKee, Vicksburg, to USG. "Some time in July last, I forwarded an appeal from the decision of a Military Commission here in the case of Solomon Rothschild who was fined $200 00 & sentenced to Six months imprisonment for buying a pistol of a soldier. ~~Since~~ The fine has been collected & we want the money back. All the facts showing fully our rights were submitted with the appeal and if the case will ever be reached we have no doubt of the result. May I ask if any actions has been had upon the case?"—ALS, DNA, RG 107, Letters Received, M601 1867. On Jan. 10, 1868, Judge Advocate Gen. Joseph Holt endorsed this letter. "Respectfully returned. The question of jurisdiction now raised in this case is the same as that raised, when the case was heretofore considered by this Bureau, in its within report of Aug. 7th. last; and it is not deemed necessary to reconsider such question at this time. In view of the language of the Act of March 1863, providing a trial for the offence herein referred to by 'any court of competent jurisdiction'; and of the large and comprehensive authority vested in the District Commander by the Act of March 2, 1867, to convene in his discretion military commissions for the trial and punishment of all criminals, in the place and stead of any local civil tribunals; it is believed that no favorable action upon this application is called for or desirable."— ES, *ibid.*

1867, DEC. 26. Secretary of State William H. Seward to USG. "I have the honor to invite your attention to a copy of a communication of the 14th instant from Mr Ford, the diplomatic Representative here, of Great Britain, upon the subject of alleged ill treatment received by Henry Ansell, a British subject, at the hands of the officer in command of Fort Inge, Texas. I will thank you to refer the matter to the proper quarter for investigation and to make known the result to this Department."—LS, DNA, RG 94, Letters Received, 1236S 1867.

1867, DEC. 27. Jesse Root Grant, Covington, Ky., to Richard A. Wheeler. "While in Washington I recd your first late letter—I left there on the 20th, before the Great dinner came off—The truth is I have no great tast for such pagentry—But the great reason for coming then was that I had safe company, & at my time of life that is a matter of much consideration. Since my return home I have recd yours of the 20th, in reply to my snow bound letter of the ___ When I left home I could not find that fine picture I promised you—but left directions to have it sent by Capt Graham, who was to start two days after I did—He got it & changing cares at Parkersburg, he left it—He says he will get one of the same in Cincinnati and I will have a chance to send it by a M. C. last of next week—The Gen is receiving at this time a great many callers many of them on written introductions, but they are so very numerous that that there cant be much ceramony. But in your case I have asked him to be a little more free, & less formal. I got acquainted with several members from New England—All agree that N. E. will be for Grant almost as a unit, except Rhod Island, and there Spragues influence will be for Chase—Out here the people seemed to settle on Henry Wilson for the Vice President, but at Washington it is thought to be a matter of polacy to run a strong man in N York, so as to carry that state, which is regarded as doubtful, And Gov Fenton is the man suggested. The Gen says 'I do wish they would let me alone.' But they wont. He will be likely to be nominated by aclamation, and to be elected by a large majority of the electoral votes—But the great oposition to the Radical views on Negro enfranchisment will cause a large popular vote against a Republican nomination—And if a stringent Radical platform is adopted, the Copperheads will get some man of straw like Pierce or Buchanan, & run him in—And then I would not give much for our Union—The Union men at Washington seem to think that Gen Grant has published a platform fully sufficient And recommend none by the Convention—That is the best plan—

I will send you a copy of the Grant genealagy, which you will see I have slightaly altered & corrected   That makes it more strictly correct"—ALS, NHi.

1867, DEC. 28.   Bvt. Maj. Gen. John Pope, Atlanta, to USG. "Following telegram just recd 'I regret to inform you that Judge Busteed was shot and probably mortally wounded at Mobile this morning by District Attorney Martin. There was a Feud of a years standing between them about the occupancy of the Attorneys Office in the Custom House and the Judges refusal to let him exercise his functions   WAGER SWAYNE B. M G'."— Telegram received (on Dec. 29, 9:45 A.M.), DNA, RG 107, Telegrams Collected (Bound); *ibid.*, RG 108, Telegrams Received; copy, DLC-USG, V, 55. On Jan. 17, 1868, Bvt. Brig. Gen. Adam Badeau telegraphed to Richard Busteed, Mobile. "General Grant says: apply to General Meade for arrest of Martin; stating grounds of application."—ALS (telegram sent), DNA, RG 107, Telegrams Collected (Bound); telegram sent, *ibid.* On Jan. 25, Badeau wrote to Maj. Gen. George G. Meade. "General Grant directs me to refer to you the accompanying letter on the subject of the arrest and trial by military authority of Dist. Atty. Martin, for the attempt to kill Judge Busteed, of the U. S. Dist. Court. General Grant desires that you will give the arguments adduced their full weight and decide accordingly. He himself would not favor the interference of the Military Authority in this case, where both the accused and the object of his attack were officers of the civil government, unless it was manifest that justice could not be done through the civil courts."—Copies, DLC-USG, V, 47, 60; DNA, RG 108, Letters Sent.

1867, DEC. 30.   To Bvt. Maj. Gen. Edward D. Townsend. "You may assign Gn. Heintzelman to duty on the Retiring Board unless there is other detached duty where his services are more wanted."—ALS, DNA, RG 94, Letters Received, 996W 1867.

1867, DEC. 30.   USG endorsement. "Respectfully refered to the Pay Master Gn."—AES, DNA, RG 107, Letters Received, G7 1868. Written on a letter of Dec. 23 from Edward D. Gazzan, Washington, D. C., to USG asking the reinstatement of John F. Mackenzie, discharged as clerk in the Paymaster Dept.—ALS, *ibid.* On Nov. 1, U.S. Senator Charles R. Buckalew of Pa. had written to USG on this subject.—ALS, *ibid.*, B423 1867. On Jan. 11, 1868, Gazzan, Philadelphia, again wrote to USG concerning Mackenzie.—ALS, *ibid.*, G7 1868. Letters to USG by discharged clerks were written on Oct. 31, 1867, by Asaph Dodge; on Nov. 2, by Francis G. McNamara; on Nov. 5, by George A. Bartlette; on Nov. 8, by John H. Quail.—ALS, *ibid.*, B423 1867. On Nov. 5, Joseph W. Parker, Washington, D. C., wrote to USG also requesting reinstatement.—ALS, *ibid.*, RG 99, Letters Received.
   On Nov. 3, Mrs. S. C. Reeve, Washington, D. C., wrote to USG. "In

the dismissal of clerks under the Pay Master Generals Office, in your Department, there was one, whom I am sure if you were acquainted with the circumstances under which he was appointed, you would not sanction his removal—The appointment was made by the *special* request of our late President Lincoln under the following circumstances. At the time the attack was made by the Rebels on this City in the Summer of 1864, I was living near Fort Stephens on my little place, which was all that was left me by my late Husband, for myself & my childrens, only support—The house, which had just been repaired at much expense, was nearly entirely destroyed by the guns from our Forts, crops, farming utensils & *every* thing else, entirely destroyed, by our forces, & by the direction of the commanding Gen., & the President—when the distress I was reduced to, was made known to the President, he *immediately* requested Assistant Sec. Dana to give me an appointment under him, which I got a very efficient clerk to fill, & give me a portion of the salery, although small, it was something to relieve my great distress—Mr Dana consulted Sec. Stanton, & the appointment was instantly made— . . ."—ALS, *ibid.*, RG 107, Letters Received, R210 1867. On Dec. 11, Bvt. Maj. Gen. Benjamin W. Brice, paymaster gen., reported that Reeve's nephew had been given a clerkship in the Treasury Dept. "in answer to this appeal—"—ES, *ibid.*

1867, DEC. 30.   S. V. Yantis, Harpers Ferry, to USG. "The undersigned as President of the Shenandoah Bridge Company at Harpers Ferry, on the part of said company, respectfully asks your excellency to rescind the order taking from the said Company the use of the Ferry across the Shenandoah River at that place, lately issued by your department through the chief of ordnance Genl A. B. Dyer.— . . ."—ALS, DNA, RG 156, Letters Received. On Jan. 3, 1868, Bvt. Maj. Gen. Alexander B. Dyer, chief of ordnance, wrote to USG reporting at length on the subject.—LS, *ibid.* On Nov. 16, 1867, Dyer had written to USG on the same subject.—LS, *ibid.*, Letters to the Secretary of War (Press).

1867, DEC. 31.   USG note. "Col E P Cressey—order him to Carlisle Pa & then to his Regt in the spring"—AN (date on docket), DNA, RG 94, Letters Received, 721A 1867.

1867, DEC. 31.   President Andrew Johnson endorsement. "RESPECTFULLY REFERRED TO General U. S. Grant Secretary of War Ad interim; for his Consideration"—ES, DNA, RG 108, Letters Received. Written on a copy of a telegram of Dec. 31 from James B. Steedman, New Orleans, to Johnson. "Unless Wells is re-instated before twelve (12) O'Clock tonight the Levees Cannot be repaired on account of the Law expiring with the year"—Copy, *ibid.*

1867, [DEC.] 31.   B. C. Brown and others, Memphis, to President Andrew Johnson, USG, Albert Pike, and Robert W. Johnson. "Three hundred

300 negro militia are at Marion Ark robbing stores private houses stealing horses and insulting ladies   Have five 5 citizens in jail threatening to hang them and arrest others. They are building stockades and breastworks Will not the U. S. protect the people   fFor our standing we refer to Albert Pike and Robt W Johnson"—Telegram received (on Jan. 1, 1868, 11:00 A.M.), DLC-Andrew Johnson.

1867, [DEC.].   USG endorsement. "REFERRED TO Gn. Rawlins to examine and to advise Gn. Ord in the premises if advice is necessary."—AES, DNA, RG 108, Letters Received. Written on a letter of Dec. 5 from Liberty Bartlett, Little Rock, to "Friend Dawes." "There is but little in having a friend except at some time a personal use may be made of him, I come now for that use. Herewith enclosed I hand you a copy of a petition just sent to Gen—Ord for increase of salery and back pay for services rendered—The reasons therefor are set forth in the petition and accompyning papers— which I think ought to appear a sufficnt showing to grant the prayer asked— It appeared so to Gen—Smith in command here in this state through whome I sent the papers—But he expressed a doubt that Gen—Ord would act at all upon the queston of advance of saleries for want of authority—If such opinion had been formed, no case similar to this had been presented   I know not what his conclusion may be—but if it adverse for apparent want of authority you will see by my unofficial letter to him that he should withhold his decision until a further hearing may be had and some suggestion from Washington—Possibly Gen Ord may under the state of the case presented grant the petition, But he has appeared timid in the exercise of administrative authority and may need prompting or suggestions by some superor authority. He has however prorogued the Legislature, removed the treasurer and now holds the same under his own appointmnt—Now what I desire is that you will consider the petition and the reasons therefor and if found good and sufficent for any action to confer with Gen Grant or any other Departmnt with which authority is divided and if then it is so found to *suggest*—not to order—to Gen—Ord that the authority exists and lays in the Military Commandant to make such an order as is in the prayer of the petiton asked   I am somewhat anxious in this matter for the reason I have been so engrosed in the reorganization of the courts under the impresson that the Legislature would make a provision, that I have neglected my own personal interests, and unless Gen Ord grants this relief I may have to resort to that very liberal Bankrupt act your Congress passed last session— And I wish a dicision before the time expires—1st March—after which I would have to pay 50 per cent for a discharge   Really I would like the proposition settled for I can do far better—personally—in ~~other~~ other employments   The question is—Gen Ord having prorogued the Legislature should he now act in the place of it—I think he should where public justice require it for the administration of law and order   This eve—I have learnt that Maj. John Whytock U S. Dist—Atty—leaves in the morng—for Washington and N York by whome I will forward these papers as I am too late for the mail—I will give the Major a letter of introduction   He is a young man who received his law education in the office of Ex Prest Filmore was on Gen Grants Staff up to the fall of Vicksburg—After the organization of the courts here appointed prosecutig atty—and traveled over the circuit with me till displaced by the election last year—Is now U S. Pros Atty— and President of the Republican organization here—active and energetic. He can give you more of the 'reconstruction' movements in this state than I could write in many hours. Any introductions you can give him. or favors shown him would be greatfully acknowledged by me and may favor the Union cause here   Gen J M Thayer of the Senate was here on duty at the time of the reorganization of the State Govt in the Spring of /64. and I met him in meetings of consultation—I will call his attention to the matters submitted to you and if not considerd a matter of too little importance please confer with him   I see by the Adams paper you have taken up your family residence in the city of Washington for the session—Please extend my kindest regards to them"—ALS, *ibid.* The enclosures are *ibid.* USG endorsed a letter of Dec. 2 from Bartlett to Bvt. Maj. Gen. Edward O. C. Ord. "Refered to Gn. Rawlin"—AE (undated), *ibid.*

1867, DEC.   USG note. "Return discharg with statement that every place is full and more now."—AN, DNA, RG 107, Applications. Written on a letter of Dec. 9 from John Litten, Jr., Rush Run, Ohio, to USG. "Having been a Soldier in the Volunteer Service & My health being somewhat on the decline from Severe Exposure &c incident to a Soldiers life & Believing You to be a friend to a soldier, I without hesitation apply to Your honor for a position of Some Kind in the department. . . ."—ALS, *ibid.*

1867, DEC.   J. J. Christian, Staunton, Va., to USG. "I Know, that Such an Imperninent Letter as this to a genttleman of yur persesion & integerety will be Started to a recivd Letter from. me. one & who you never Kew nor heard of before, but I hope that you will give it your attention as much as to read it *at least* & parden me for intruding opon you for the favior that I am compelled to ask of you or Som one who has the power like yurself to help me & I believe after reading & hearing of what I hav to Say. that you will forgive me.—Even though you do not grant my request. I Stated above, that I was compelld to ask this favior. & I think that you will agree with me when I State to you my reasons for so doing,—now this is it. I had a Brother, who emigrated to Liberan. Some time in the fall of 1865, with a Wife & three (3) Children.   he died in (2) months after getting there, leving a helpless Wife & the (3) Children in an Open & a Strange World, With no relation or no one to Symathias with her, there, whatever. I Recivd in the fall of 1866 last year a verbial Message, that a certin man, had pas through the city Lynchburg, Va. direct from Libara, who emigrated from this Contry at the Same time My Brother & family did, in fact he was Slitley acquainted with them,   he reported the death of My Brother & of Seavel others that left Lynchburg & its viccinty   this coming to my hear-

ing *coming to me* by a friend from Lynchburg trouble me considably, but
not being certin that it was true, I tried to ~~make~~ console myself, & to force
myself to believe, the report was untrue, but in the 10th of Oct last, I
recived a Letter from the Widowd Wife, acquaiting me of her Sad fate
Since her hasban. had died, which had been ever Since they had arrived
there, Save (2) months asking me, to trie an aid her & her (3) Children
to retun to America. where we were, She also Stated to me, her distress
condition—Sayin that She didnot Know after Eating one meal, Where the
Next one would Come from, Now this Much Genl, you are aware is mor-
tifyin to the most brutish of Man Kind—Knowing as I do, that the poor
Girl, was always rais in her Mistress house as a Seimstress & never Knowing what hard work was, we were all formily Slaves, though we had very
good owners. they have promis to help me raise money to get her & the
children back to this contry, but they are poor & have don nothing in that
direction as yet. I have been trieing to Save Something in the way of money
to Send after her & the Children (3) but having a family to Surport myself, which Keeps me pritey businessy to help them, but I have Manage to
get about $25 00 dolls on the way to get them back to this Contry. Now
Gen.l I hope that you wont think that I am one of those paupers that are
all ways hangin Arround & opon the Charreties of the Goverment   While
I am, as poor, almost as any body, but this is the first accassion I ever had
to ask of it in any way whatever, although I was a Slave, up to your Crowing
& desissive Victory at Affomatox C. H. in this State. I hope Genal. that you
will favior me with answer soon"—ALS, DNA, RG 107, Letters Received,
C14 1868.

[*1867?*].   To Vice Consul Thomas Savage. "This will introduc[e] to you
Gen. C. B. Comstock, U. S. Army, who visits Havanna on a pleasure tour.
Gen. Comstock has served on my Staff since the siege of Vicksburg, and I
take great pleasure in asking for him your confidence and good offices."—
ALS (undated), WHi.

1868, JAN. 2.   To Secretary of the Interior Orville H. Browning. "I have
the honor to enclose herewith, for such action as you may deem proper, a
communication from *Col. Reeve*, the Milty. Commandant in *Montana*,
transmitting a petition of certain of the citizens, and other papers, relating
to the *liquor traffic* in that Territory."—Df, DNA, RG 107, Letters Received
from Bureaus; copy, *ibid.*, Letters Sent to the President.

1868, JAN. 2.   To Secretary of the Treasury Hugh McCulloch. "At the
instance of the Surgeon General of the Army, I have the honor to request
that you will instruct the *Collector of Customs at the port of New York* to
deliver free of duties and charges the *books* named in the enclosed memorandum, which were shipped by Gustave Bossanger, Paris, per Steamer
'Ville de Paris', in case marked '1. General Satterlee, New York.' "—Copy,
DNA, RG 107, Letters Sent to the President.

1868, JAN. 2. To Secretary of State William H. Seward. "I have the honor to acknowledge the receipt of your communication of the 18th ultimo, in which you call my attention to a letter, which at the suggestion of the Consul General of Switzerland, was addressed to the then Secretary of War by the State Department on the 21st of May, 1865, relative to the claim of Paul Chavannes, for property alleged to have been destroyed by order of Major General Burnside, at Knoxville, on the 19th of November 1863. In reply I have the honor to inform you that the claim, being for property destroyed in the theatre of war by order of ~~Major General Burnside for the better defence of Knoxville, on the night of November 19th 1863~~, a military commander for the public defence is one of a class, for the settlement of which by this department, Congress has as yet made no provision."— Copies, DNA, RG 107, Letters Sent to the President; *ibid.*, Letters Received from Bureaus. On Dec. 18, 1867, Seward had written to USG. "I have the honor to call your attention to a letter, which at the suggestion of the Consul General of Switzerland, was addressed to the then Secretary of War by this Department, on the 25th of May 1865, relative to the claim of Paul Chavannes for property alleged to have been destroyed by order of Major General Burnside, at Knoxville, on the 19th of November 1863."— LS, *ibid.*

1868, JAN. 2. To Attorney Gen. Henry Stanbery. "At the suggestion of the Judge Advocate General of the Army, I have the honor to transmit herewith the application and accompanying papers in the case of *Vigron Clement*, a civilian now in Libby Prison, asking the remission of the unexpired portion of his sentence."—Copy, DNA, RG 107, Letters Sent to the President.

1868, JAN. 2. Solomon Meredith, Helena, Montana Territory, to USG. "I would respectfully call your attention to the case of Capt Wm. G. Galloway 15th U. S. Infantry who has been cashiered on charges preferred by Brevet Major James C. Curtis for leaving his post for the purpose of getting married. I have some knowledge of Major Curtis and the course he has pursued towards those under his command. He is malicious and revengeful—using his official position to carry out his personal quarrels. I believe from the information I have that such has been his motives in this case. There is another sett of charges against Capt Galloway for chastising (physically) Major Curtis for insults offered his (Capt Gs) wife. I am familiar with the war record of Capt Galloway and can say that he was a gallant and efficient officer & though these indescretions are not excusable I think his sentence has been too severe. I would therefore ask that he be reinstated in the Army and the charges now against him be dismissed. From his services to our country he wishes to leave the Army honorably and I understand intends resigning should he be successful in his efforts to resume his position. My feelings for the Army are ardent and would not ask this of you did I not consider it an act of justice to a brave soldier. In this connection I beg leave to state that I believe Major Curtis has done great injury and injustice to the officers of the 15th Infantry. Together with his unpleasant disposition he never looses an opportunity to use his official position to avenge a private wrong or personal pique. His conduct has already driven several efficient officers to resign and his persecutions have been such that others deserving a better fate have been dishonorably dismissed. There is no doubt but his regiment suffers materially from these causes. I mention these things from no ill will but with a hope to see justice dealt out to all."—ALS, DNA, RG 94, ACP, G538 CB 1867.

1868, JAN. 3.   USG endorsement. "In compliance with the Presidents endorsement Lt. Daws should be brevetted Captain, if he is already a 1st Lt.; if not, as he declines a brevet of 1st Lt. the application is not approved."—ES, DNA, RG 94, ACP, R314 CB 1870. Written on a letter of Nov. 23, 1867, from J. H. Dawes, Fox Lake, Wis., to U.S. Representative Charles A. Eldredge of Wis. "I take the liberty of asking you to make some effort for procuring a Brevet promotion for my Brother—Lt. Wm J. Dawes 43d U. S. Infty. He entered the Volunteer Service as Captain in 8th Wis. and served in that capacity until he was severely wounded at the Battle of Corinth Miss. in October 1862. He was shortly afterwards transfered to the Veteran Reserve Corps, with same rank as before and being thus placed out of the line of promotion served for six years with the rank of Captain. He was however without solicitation given by the War Department the Brevet rank of Major of Volunteers for 'gallant conduct in the Battle of Corinth'. He was commissioned as Lieutenant in the Regular Army some time last Spring I think and is now on duty at Fort Wilkins Copper Harbor Michigan   By the Regulations of the War Department he is not allowed to use his Brevet rank in the Volunteer service, and it would gratify him and his friends if he could be Brevetted in the Regular Army as Colonel or Lt. Colonel. His long and faithful services as Captain V. R. C would seem to entitle him to such a compliment. There are on file in the War Department a large number of testimonials from his superior officers and others to which reference may be made if necessary to show the character of the services which he has performed. Any efforts which you can conveniently make in this matter will place me under renewed obligations"—ALS, *ibid.* On Dec. 28, Eldredge added a favorable endorsement; President Andrew Johnson added an undated one. "Let the Brevet be granted unless there is some good reason against it."—AES, *ibid.*

1868, JAN. 3.   USG endorsement. "In compliance with the President's order Lt. Deane should be brevetted 1st Lt. for siege of Port Hudson and Captain for faithful and meritorious services during war to date March 2d 1867."—ES, DNA, RG 94, ACP, D37 CB 1870. Written on a letter of Dec., 1867, from U.S. Senator James R. Doolittle of Wis. to President Andrew Johnson. "I have the honor to request that Lieut W W Deane, 12th US Infantry, receive a Brevet appointment as Captain in the Regular Army.

to date from the 13th Mar 1865   Lieut Deane was Captain of Vol's—and served faithfully throughout the war in active service."—LS, *ibid.* On Dec. 27, Johnson endorsed this letter. "Respectfully referred to the Secretary of War ad interim who will please confer upon Lt. Deane the Brevet rank asked for within."—ES, *ibid.*

1868, JAN. 3.   To Secretary of State William H. Seward. "As desired in your note of the 31st ult., I have the honor to acquaint you that the *longest ranges* obtained by the Ordnance Dept. from 8, 12 and 15 inch guns are as follows:—15 inch *Rodman* gun (smooth bore) 8,220. yards   12 inch Rifle gun 9,960. yards   8 inch Rifle gun 8,110. yards"—Copies (tabular material expanded), DNA, RG 107, Letters Sent to the President; *ibid.*, RG 156, Letters Received. On Dec. 31, 1867, Seward had written to USG. "I will thank you to inform me if six and a quarter miles is within the extreme range of cannon or rifle shot, and what is the extreme range of each.?"—LS, *ibid.*

1868, JAN. 3.   President Andrew Johnson to USG. "You will suspend until further orders the execution of the sentence of the General Court Martial in the case of Private John F. Ellis Co G. 5th U S Cavalry, as promulgated in General Orders No 91, Head Quarters Department of Washington December 20th 1867."—Copies (2), DLC-Andrew Johnson.

1868, JAN. 3.   Secretary of the Treasury Hugh McCulloch to USG. "I have respectfully to submit for your consideration the following Extract from a Report, by Edward Hartley Esq. Special Agent &c., of the examination of the U. S. Asst. Treasurer's Office at Philadelphia, Pa. and to request such action in the premises as will lead, as far as practicable, to a compliance with the suggestions of Mr. Hartley—'I would call attention to the fact that there are many old balances due disbursers which have remained undrawn since January 1st 1865. cumbering the books, some of them for a few cents only. Some of these disbursers are dead, some out of service and none are now disbursing. I recommend that the amounts [—] credit be transferred to General T[reasury] Account. I observe also among the b[alances] due, amounts due to Jas. Mc[—] F. H. Barral, J. McL. Hildt, [—] Rathbone and Samuel Dana who were Disbursing Officers under the Bureau of the Provost Marshal General discontinued more than a year since. I would suggest that these amounts be also transferred to General Treasury, on obtaining from the War Department, a list of checks drawn by them, in case none should appear outstanding'—"—LS (torn), DNA, RG 56, Letters Received from the War Dept.

1868, JAN. 3.   Secretary of State William H. Seward to USG. "It will give me pleasure to communicate to Dr Evans any reply you may find it convenient or proper to make to his request."—LS, DNA, RG 107, Letters Received from Bureaus. On Nov. 29, 1867, Thomas W. Evans, Paris, had written to USG. "For many years I have been much interested in the material connected with military hospitals—Knowing how much was accomplished in the United States during the late rebellion, by way of improving and perfecting the ambulance appliances previously used—the idea occurred to me of forming a *Collection* of all such special inventions, in the hope that some might be found of service in European armies, or at least that such a Collection might stimulate surgeons and military men in Europe to further efforts for the alleviation of the sufferings and miseries of war. This American Collection—created by my own personal effort—was exhibited in the Champ de Mars, during the continuance of the Exposition—Awarded with the highest honors it was in the power of the Imperial Commission to give, and universally regarded as the most interesting and valuable as well as most extensive collection of Ambulanc[e] and hospital material representing any Government or country, I have felt reluctant at the close of the Exhibition to break it up—In short I have fully resolved to establish it here in Paris *en permanence*, and to add to it whatever I may be able to obtain, which may render it a more complete and perfect exponent of the material improvements effected by military sanitary science at the present time—It is Sir, with this object in view, that I now write you—in the hope that I may be able to obtain from the Department of which you are the Acting Secretary, 1st Certain articles now in Paris, belonging to the United States Government, and classed with Quarter masters stores Viz: A Rucker's Ambulance, a medicine wagon, a wheeled litter, iron beds &c &c &c—2d Certain articles now in Paris and belonging to the United States—Medical Bureau—Viz: models of hospitals &c &c &c—I doubt very much if this material sent by the United States Government to the Paris Exposition is—commercially—worth reshipping—It is quite certain that the property belonging to the Quarter masters Department if sold either in Paris or New York would not bring one half the cost of a reshipment—Such being in brief the state of the case, I may ask, if it would be in any way incompatible with the original object, and ends had in view by the United States Government, when this material was sent to Europe, if it should *remain* in Paris, to form a part of such a permanent *Musée* as I propose to open to the free inspection of all interested in the special subjects it is intended to illustrate—Should ~~however~~ there seem to exist no serious objection to this disposition of the property of the War Department, before referred to, I presume there will be no difficulty in arranging all the necessary conditions precedent to its transfer to my hands—either with General Meigs who is now in Paris, or with Mr Beckwith the Commissioner General representing the United States at the Paris Exposition—Hoping the proposition I have suggested may meet with your approval, and that with me, you may see in it the means of extending in Europe not only a better knowledge of our country but also of the best ways and methods to be employed in a most important bran[c]h of military service"—LS, *ibid.* On Nov. 30, Bvt. Maj. Gen. Montgomery C. Meigs, Paris, wrote to USG. "Dr Evans the writer of the accompanying letter is an American Physician residing in Paris with intimate relations with a great number of persons in the highest positions Civil & Military in the principal European States   Dr Evans has heartily engaged in the Sanitary Cause. At great expenditure of time & money he has formed a Sanitary collection or museum which gained high prizes at the Paris exhibition. He has organized Sanitary commissions in several European states. He was present at Sadowa where he had the happiness to see great alleviation of suffering & the saving of many lives by the improvements which he had introduced in European Hospital & sanitary measures. All this is the result of his knowledge of the Sanitary measures which originated in our armys during the War & of his devotion to this great cause   You will recognise him as one who visited your head Quarters at City Point under peculiar circumstances & who rendered good service to his country while residing in Europe during the war. No better disposition can be made in my opinion of the articles sent to the Paris Exhibition by the Quarter Masters Dept than to place them at his disposal for his museum,   I recommend that this be done & also that his request be referred to the Surgeon General with authority to place in the museum such articles contributed by the Medical Department as it may not be important to carry again across the Atlantic. The collection is public though formed thus far at private expense & by the devotion of one man. Such is the origin of many great collections which now in the Cities of Europe are public property & open to all the world for instruction & improvement."—ALS, *ibid.* See *PUSG*, 12, 207.

1868, JAN. 3.   Secretary of the Navy Gideon Welles to USG. "I have the honor to return herewith, the letter referred by you to the Department in relation to the case of Margaret Bell, mother of William Bell, private Co. D. 99th Reg't N. Y. S. volunteers. A detachment of the 99th Reg't N. Y. S. volunteers was on board the U. S. S. Congress at the time of the attack on that vessel by the rebels March 8, 1862, but the Department has now no means of ascertaining whether or not William Bell was one of the detachment."—Copy, DNA, RG 45, Letters Sent to the President.

1868, JAN. 3.   Judge Advocate Gen. Joseph Holt to USG. "Bt. Capt. E. L. Palmer, 43rd Infantry, V. R. C. was tried in November and December last by Gen. Ct. Martial convened at Fort Wayne, Mich. by order of Gen. Grant, under the following charges: 1. Conduct unbecoming an officer and a gentleman. 1.—In asserting, in the presence of Lt. Jennings, 43d Infy., that another officer of the regiment had gone to Lieut. Col. Kiddoo, 43d Regt, and complained that enlisted men of the regiment had had criminal intercourse with his, the complainant's wife; which assertion was false and malicious. This at Sault St. Marie, Mich. Aug. 13. 1867. 2.—In asserting in the presence of one O. B. Lyon, citizen, and of A. B. Auchenleck, Ch. Engineer, Revenue Marine, that he, the accused, had been questioned officially by Col. Kiddoo in relation to some intercourse alleged to have taken place between Accused and a lady, the wife of a brother officer; and in reply accused had informed Col. Kiddoo that the alleged illicit intercourse had taken place, and offered to take him to the hotel and show him the room. All which statements were false and malicious, no such conversation ever taking place between Col. Kiddoo and himself. This at Sault St. Marie, Sept. 22. 1867. 3. In boasting to O. B. Lyon, and A. B. Auchenleck, aforesaid, that in a conversation with Col. Kiddoo, accused had said to him, 'God damn you, you cannot prefer charges against me because I saw you in criminal intercourse with this lady while her husband was looking on'; which statement was false and malicious. This Sept. 26. 1867. 4. In traducing the character of the wife of a brother officer. 5. In telling O. B. Lyon, citizen, a wilful falsehood in reference to the threatened removal of his horse from within the limits of Fort Wayne Reservation, to the effect that Gen. Robinson had ordered Col. Kiddoo to let Accused's horse remain. Charge 2. Conduct to the prejudice of good order & military discipline. Three specifications, alleging acts of insulting and indecent familiarity on the part of accused towards one Victoria Conta, an officer's servant. The accused pleaded specially to the specifications under the first charge, that they were vague, indefinite and uncertain, in that the lady said to have been slandered was not named. The Court overruled his plea, and very properly. The specifications as drawn convey to the accused, with abundant certainty, a knowledge of the offence for which he is brought to trial; and the introduction of a lady's name into allegations of the character of these, would result in no benefit to the accused; would be a needless and cruel invasion of the sanctities of private life, and is justly prohibited by every consideration of humanity, propriety, and common decency. The accused's motive in this act, and in a subsequent application for leave to publish the daily proceedings, which was most justly rejected by the Court, is believed to be sufficiently visible. The Court convict him under the first, second, and third specifications of Charge 1, striking out the word 'maliciously' in the third; reject specification fourth as indefinite and uncertain; acquit the accused under the fifth specification of charge 1, and under charge 2 and all its specifications, no proof being offered by the prosecution; and sentence him: 'to be dismissed the service.' . . . It is advised that the sentence be enforced."—Copy, DNA, RG 153, Letters Sent. See *ibid.*, RG 94, Letters Received, 61P 1868.

1868, JAN. 3.   Judge Advocate Gen. Joseph Holt endorsement on a record of a board of inquiry concerning "depradations committed by recruits at Omaha." "Respectfully returned to Genl. Grant, with an expression of opinion that the assessment of the damage caused by the recruits upon the officers in command of the several detachments, advised by General Townsend, would be warranted by their neglect and inattention to the duties of their situation. It is manifest that the depradation complained of would not have occurred, had the proper arrangements been made for the reception of the recruits by the Quartermaster's Department of the Dept. of the Platte, which had been notified of the anticipated time of their arrival."—Copy, DNA, RG 153, Letters Sent.

1868, JAN. 3. John W. Bowen, Bowling Green, Va., to USG. "Having learned much of your liberal feeling to southerners & that you desired all who have been deprived of their homes to inform you I beg leave to inform you that the whole of my lands lieing in Alexandria & Fairfax counties were confiscated or sold for Taxes without my receiving any notice. I left my home for the safety of my family in the commencement of the War carrying my wife & children to my wife's relations in Prince Wm Co, intending to return home myself: but getting into southron lines was forbidden a passport to return & hence had to seek employment South, to support my family. I went to Richmond became an assistant Surgeon: & have the satisfaction of knowing that, no Southron or Northern soldier placed under my care ever complained of my treatment: on the contrary all prefer me to any Surgeon North or South. The whole of my property was destroyed The houses on four tracts of land burned or destroyed all my stock of all kinds, as well as, farming-utensels, house hold furniture Library, Medecines &c &c were taken off or destroyed leaving me at the close of the War 61 years old, & with my family entirely destitute. We have suffered on in poverty ever since. often suffering for the necessaries of life, & almost destitute of clothing. We lost about seventy servants by Freedom; all of whom I doubt not are better off than we. If you can do any thing in restoring our lands (or compensating which I would prefer) you will confer on us a debt of grattitude eternal. Or if you can point me to any source where relief can be obtained a similar debt of grattitude will be confered on us. While we will ever remain under eternal obligations to you. . . . P S. Would I be asking too much, to beg a line from you."—ALS, DNA, RG 107, Letters Received, B1 1868.

1868, JAN. 4. To Attorney Gen. Henry Stanbery. "I have the honor to transmit herewith a copy of deed from the City of Boston to the United States for certain land on Gallup's Island, Boston Harbor, and to request, in accordance with the Joint Resolution approved September 11th 1841, your opinion as to whether the deed vests a valid title in the United States to the land therein described. The original is now being recorded at the office of the Register of Suffolk County."—LS, DNA, RG 60, Letters Received, War Dept.

1868, JAN. 4. To Attorney Gen. Henry Stanbery. "In reply to your letter of the 24th ultimo enclosing a communication of December 23d from E. W. Andrews, Esq., respecting certain suits of ejectment at Harper's Ferry, I have the honor to enclose herewith a report from the Chief of Ordnance on the subject, from which it will be seen that those suits may be abandoned. Mr. Andrews' letter is herewith returned."—LS (misdated 1867), DNA, RG 60, Letters Received, War Dept.

1868, JAN. 5. To Vice Admiral David D. Porter. "~~Your letter to~~ I will be at home now for some time. Will be glad to see you and Mrs. Porter.

Will you be down before the 8th?"—ALS (telegram sent), DNA, RG 107, Telegrams Collected (Bound).

1868, JAN. 6.   USG endorsement. "Respectfully returned to the President with the report that Harvey Tilden, Capt 16th Infantry was dropped from the rolls in February 1862 for drunkenness on duty and for conduct unbecoming an officer and gentleman in propo[s]ing that money should be given to him for the discharge of his duty as a mustering officer. These charges were supported by affidavits forwarded herewith."—ES, DNA, RG 94, ACP, 3559 1871. Written on a letter of Dec. 18, 1867, from Harvey Tilden, probably intended for President Andrew Johnson, whose office forwarded it to USG.—ES, *ibid.*

1868, JAN. 6.   To Secretary of State William H. Seward. "In compliance with your request of the 4th inst., made at the instance of Mr. Domingos Gonsalves de Magalhaens the Minister of Brazil, I have the honor to transmit herewith a copy of the report of the *Chief of Ordnance* of Oct. 23d 1866, embodying a report of a Board of Officers upon the comparative merits of *small arms.*"—Copies, DNA, RG 107, Letters Sent to the President; *ibid.*, RG 156, Letters Received. On Jan. 4, Seward had written to USG. "Mr. Domingos Gonsalves de Magalhaens, the Minister of Brazil here, who has recently returned from a visit to Rio de Janeiro, says that before he left there the Emperor requested him to endeavor to obtain a copy of a report of the board of ordnance of the comparative merits of small arms. It is understood that the report has been confidentially printed but not published. It is also represented that copies have been given to a few members of the diplomatic body. If this be so, I will thank you for one to enable Mr. Magalhaens to gratify the wish of his sovereign."—LS, *ibid.*

1868, JAN. 6.   To Secretary of the Navy Gideon Welles. "I have the honor to enclose herewith a communication of January 3d from the Quartermaster General of the Army and to request that the privilege of using the long United States naval wharf at Key West be accorded to this Department, if it can be done with due regard to the wants of the Naval service at that place."—LS, DNA, RG 45, Letters Received from the President. The enclosure is *ibid.* On Oct. 4 and 28, 1867, Bvt. Maj. Gen. Daniel H. Rucker, act. q. m. gen., had written to USG on this subject.—LS, *ibid.*, RG 92, Reports to the Secretary of War (Press). On Dec. 27 and Jan. 14, 1868, Welles wrote to USG. "The Department is informed that in the autumn of the year 1866, Commodore Jno. A. Winslow, commanding the Gulf Squadron, presented a bill amounting to $4.275.68 to the Quarter Master U. S. A. at Key West, Florida, for the use by the Quarter Master's Department of the Naval Wharf at that Station for one year ending 1st September, 1866, which sum was the interest on the cost of the wharf for the two years which it had been used by the army. Commodore Winslow states that the bill was referred by the Quartermaster at Key West to the

Quarter master's Department at Washington for settlement but on his leaving the station it had not been paid, nor had the arrears of tariff rates for transports, which had accrued for the prior six months been paid. As the Department incurred considerable expense necessary for the repairs of this wharf, it respectfully requests that directions may be given to have the amount refunded to the credit of the naval appropriation for 'Coal Depot at Key West.' " "I have the honor to acknowledge the receipt of your letter of the 6th instant, enclosing a communication of the 3d inst., addressed to you by the Quartermaster General of the Army, who desires the privilege of using the Naval Wharf at Key West. The Chief of the Bureau of Yards and Docks, to whom the subject was referred, reports, that there appears to the Bureau 'to be no objection to the use of the wharf by the Quartermaster's department of the Army, provided that the claim against that Department, already presented and amounting to the sum of $4,275 80/100 be paid, and also that the same wharfage fees be paid as are demanded from other parties. If the wharf referred to were used only as a temporary landing, no charge should be made, but for constant use rent should be collected, as the wharf will continually require repairs.' The Department approves of the views of the Chief of the Bureau of Yards and Docks, and consents to the use of the wharf by the Quartermaster's department on the conditions stated."—Copies, *ibid.*, RG 45, Letters Sent to the President.

1868, JAN. [6].   Secretary of the Treasury Hugh McCulloch to USG. "The Building now occupied by the Pay Master General known as, 'Corcoran's Building,' was surrendered by this to your Department at the solicitation of the then Secretary of War. In consequence of the many pressing demands made by the Heads of Bureaus for additional room & particularly from the 2nd Comptroller who certifies the accounts of your Department, I have the honor to request if not attended with serious inconvenience, that the necessary steps may be taken to restore the building to this Department."—LS, DNA, RG 107, Letters Received from Bureaus; copy (dated Jan. 8), *ibid.*, RG 56, Letters Sent.

1868, JAN. 6.   Judge Advocate Gen. Joseph Holt to USG concerning the court-martial of 1st Lt. Charles E. Drew, 34th Inf.—Copy, DNA, RG 153, Letters Sent.

1868, JAN. 6.   Brig. Gen. Andrew A. Humphreys, chief of engineers, endorsement. "Respectfully returned to the General of the Army. In time of war the garrisons of the sea coast defenses may consist mostly of newly raised troops, of either artillery or infantry; but there must be a nucleus of well instructed and experienced artillery for each work; and it is advantageous that the small peace garrisons be supplied from this arm if practicable. It is not to the public interest that they be derived from the engineer battalion, which is too small for the purpose of furnishing such garrisons and is moreover being instructed in the duties and exercises of sappers,

miners, pontoniers, &c, as prescribed for engineer troops by the act organizing them; and in the performance of some of the special duties of those
troops, duties that are inconsistent with that of a garrison in the sea coast
defenses of the Military Dep't under consideration. . . ."—Copy, DNA, RG
77, Fortifications, Letters Sent.

1868, JAN. 6. Samuel H. Sanders, Mount Airy, N. C., to USG. "Pleas
permit me to say that my object in writing to you thes few lines; is in regard
to the large amount of goverment armes that are Scatterd over the State of
N. C.   thare is now at least fifty or seventy fife thousan good No 1 goverment armes now in the hands of citizens who are willing to give them up at
any time Should they be wanted. &c   thes arms are of various Kinds consisting of good U. S. Springfield, and Enfield rifels; Sharps; Spencers and
Burnside rifels and navy Pisdols, & various other good guns.   most every
citizen has from one to two to five of thes guns, whitch belong entierly to
the goverment; &c. I prepose that if the goverment wants or wishes to have
thes arms taken up and deliverd at place to be agreed apon, that i will if
invested with the propper orthority and the necasary instructions and paid
a fair compensation for my trubble and my expences paid (which will be
light) I will gather up all of the goverment armes in the State of N. C or in
any amount of teritory assigned to me: &c. and will deliver the said armes
at any place the govrment may or so propper. I nead not say that if thes
thes arms ar taken care of by the goverment that Peradventure they may
saave the goverment of thousands of dollars. Pleas have the kindness to
inform me on this Subject at your earlist lesure and conveniance   P. S., As
a refferance i wish to Say that during the rebelion without ever serving in
any capasty of the army or navy of the Socalled confedracy I maid a ma-
racilous esscape out of the confedracy and Served twelve months in the
Federal army commanded by his excellancy Gen U. S. Grant. hoping to
bee informed by your noble advice . . ."—ALS, DNA, RG 156, Letters
Received. Related papers are *ibid.*

1868, JAN. 8.   To secretary of war. "I have the honor to forward a list of
recommendations for brevet promotions in the regular army, herewith."—
LS, DNA, RG 94, ACP, G3 CB 1868. The enclosure is *ibid.*

1868, JAN. 8.   To Secretary of State William H. Seward. "I have the
honor to acknowledge your letter of the 19th ult. enclosing copy of a com'n.
from the Chargé d'Affaires of Great Britain, requesting to be informed if
any steps have been taken for the trial of *Wm Barry*, an U. S. Soldier,
charged with the shooting of a British Officer, and to inform you that under
orders from this Dept. the soldier named was on the 24th Oct. last directed,
by the Comd'g. Genl. of the Dept. of Dakota, to be sent under guard to
Yankton, Dakota, and delivered, with a statement of all the facts and names
of witnesses, to the civil authorities for trial before the U. S. Court. No
further information can be afforded by this Department."—Df, DNA, RG

94, Letters Received, 567B 1867; copy, *ibid.*, RG 107, Letters Sent to the President. On Dec. 19, 1867, Seward had written to USG. "I have the honor to inclose a copy of a note of the 7th instant which Mr Ford, Chargé d'Affaires of Great Britain has addressed to this Department with a view to ascertain what steps have been taken by the proper authorities in bringing to trial one Barry, a sentry on board the steamboat 'Octavia', who is charged with having shot Captain Speer a British officer in the month of June last. I will thank you for any information regarding this case which may be in your power to communicate."—LS, *ibid.*, RG 94, Letters Received, 567B 1867. Numerous related documents are *ibid.* On Oct. 2, Bvt. Maj. Gen. Edward D. Townsend had telegraphed to Bvt. Maj. Gen. Alfred H. Terry. "General Grant disapproves the release of the soldier who shot Captain Spear of the British Army and directs that you cause him to be immediately arrested and brought to trial before the proper authorities.— Hasten the full report on the case. Please acknowledge receipt and report execution."—LS (telegram sent), *ibid.*, RG 107, Telegrams Collected (Bound).

1868, JAN. 8. USG endorsement. "Accept resignation"—AE (initialed), DNA, RG 94, ACP, S13 CB 1868. Written on a letter of Jan. 7 from Governor Ambrose E. Burnside of R. I., New York City, to USG. "My friend Mr Samuel Sloan of this city has a son in the 19th Infantry, who is in great trouble, and I fear is about to be cashierd—I know nothing of the circumstances, but I know his father and mother to be most respectable, and excellent people, and if the interest of service will permit a delay in his case until they can learn what is best for them to do I will be very glad— The young man says his superior officer has persecuted him—I hope for the sake of his parents, that he has done nothing dishonorable— . . . A letter will reach me here"—ALS, *ibid.*

1868, JAN. 8. To Speaker of the House Schuyler Colfax. "In compliance with the Act of April 2d 1794, I have the honor to transmit, herewith a report from the Chief of Ordnance of the expenditures, and the arms, and components of arms and appendages manufactured, and repaired at the *Springfield Armory*, during the fiscal year ending 30th June, 1867."— Copies, DNA, RG 107, Reports to Congress; *ibid.*, RG 156, Letters Received. On Jan. 4, Bvt. Maj. Gen. Alexander B. Dyer, chief of ordnance, had written to USG transmitting the information.—LS, *ibid.* See *HED*, 40-2-83.

1868, JAN. 8. To Speaker of the House Schuyler Colfax. "In reply to the Resolution of the House of Representatives of July 18. 1867. instructing the Secretary of War to ascertain and inform the House what quantity of *Swamp Land* heretofore granted to the States lately in rebellion yet remains undisposed of by said States, I have the honor to transmit herewith, reports from the Commanders of the five military districts on the subject, containing the information called for."—Copy, DNA, RG 107, Reports to Congress. See *HED*, 40-2-86.

1868, JAN. 8. To Speaker of the House Schuyler Colfax. "I have the honor to send, herewith, for the consideration of the proper committee, a draft of a joint Resolution, having for its object the sale of the site of *Fort Covington* in the City of Baltimore, Md. and to recommend its passage by Congress."—Df, DNA, RG 107, Letters Received, W436 1868; copy, *ibid.*, Reports to Congress. See *HED*, 40-2-88.

1868, JAN. 8. Secretary of State William H. Seward to USG. "I have the honor to enclose a copy of a Resolution of the House of Representatives, of December 19th 1867, calling upon the President to furnish certain information, under the impression that a portion of it can be obtained from your Department."—LS, DNA, RG 107, Letters Received from Bureaus. Seward enclosed a copy of a resolution requesting information on the acquisition of Russian America.—*Ibid.*

1868, JAN. 8. D. H. Byington, Northford, Conn., to USG. "I appeal to you for help in a matter Concerning My Son who is in trouble he Enlisted in the late rebellion and Served his time faithfuly and was honorably discharged soon after his discharge through the influence of liquor he was led to Enlist in the regular service from which he deserted and came home remaining and laboring with Me until about Six weeks since he was Arrested and taken to Governor Island and is now in Castle Williams awaiting his trial which he thinks the Sentence will be Severe he is now denied any Correspondence except occasionaly through the favor of the guard he is allowed no Clothes from government and put to hard work in the Cold with poor and scant rations he says he is so hungry sometimes, it seems he shall be Crazy and worst of all I am not permited to visit him to Carry him any food or Clothing now this seems rather hard in a Christian Country and under what is pretended to be a Christian government a poor heart broken father not allowed to visit his Son in prison I am a poor though respected Citizen and am a Member of the Church in this place and have endeavored all My life to do My duty towards God and Man I am likewise in poor health and dependent on the aid of My only son I have a wife and three daughters dependent on My exertions for support and now under these Circumstances they have taken My poor boy from Me he Enlisted before he was of age Contrary to law I suppose and had been drinking a thing which he very seldom does for he cant bear it it Crazys him he was probably enticed to it he says if it had not ben for liquor he should not have ben in his present situation and that is why he deserted he cant see how he is responsible for an act of which he did not realize the Consequences at the time I gave My Consent to his Enlistment in the late War becaus I thought it My duty and should probably have served Myself had health permited but in times of peace others must do the Army duty I am to poor to do it   I have not a dollar in the world and in feeble health at that   for Gods Sake for the Sake of all that is good on Earth Please give My Son his Discharge   if you cant discharge him Please Caus an easy Sentence and Me a Pass to visit him and Carry him Some little comfort of life   if it is necessary I can probably get any required number of Names to a Petition it is hard to serve three years in the rebellion and then three years more in Sentence and Cruely treated but I trust Mercy will be Shown him . . . My Sons Name on the roll is Thomas Barrington instead of Byington"—ALS, DNA, RG 108, Letters Received. On Jan. 21, Lt. Col. and Bvt. Brig. Gen. Henry D. Wallen, 14th Inf., Fort Columbus, endorsed this letter. "Respectfully returned to the *Adjutant General of the Army*, through Headqrs General Rect'g Service. Prisoners in confinement here are not allowed to correspond with or see their friends. These necessary restrictions were placed upon prisoners for the reasons, that by correspondence and visits the means were frequently provided, and arrangements made, for their escape from the Island. The prisoner, *Thomas Barrington*, is allowed the full Government ration, with the addition of fresh vegetables twice a week, and desiccated vegetables twice a week. The prisoners in confinement on the Island are not allowed to suffer for the want of clothing or fires; but they are required to labor. Private *Barrington* has served an enlistment of three years in the Army, & therefore knew all the requirements of the service. He is a deserter & thirty dollars have been paid for his arrest, & he is now awaiting transportation to his regiment, 17th Infantry. He could not have been drunk when he enlisted, as neither the recruiting officer nor Surgeon would have passed him in that condition."—ES, *ibid.*

1868, JAN. 8.   Governor Richard J. Oglesby of Ill. to USG. "I desire to recommend James W Jefferson of Decatur Illinois (my own home), who is now nineteen years old, with excellent habits and fine character, possessed of a first rate common school education in the higher branches taught in our State; the son of a widow with whom he lives. His brother was killed at Fort Donnelson in my old regiment. Another brother survived the war (Thomas Jefferson) who was your Orderly while you were Colonel of the 21s Ill Infty, serving in Missouri. I would recommend the appointment of James W Jefferson as a cadet at West Point and hope you will consider his wishes in this respect, and I will consider it a personal favor to me, and thank you for the same if you find you can consistently do so. His appointment will be no mistake and I feel sure he ought to have it   I take the liberty to enclose the accompaning letters of recommendation in his case"— LS, DNA, RG 94, Correspondence, USMA. No appointment followed.

1868, JAN. 9.   To Secretary of the Interior Orville H. Browning. "I have the honor to transmit herewith bills of Subsistence stores issued to Indians by various officers of the Subsistence Department of the Army during the months of September and October, 1867, not included in bills previously transmitted; and to request that a transfer warrant may be drawn for the

amount ($59,725 29/100) on the appropriation for Subsistence of Indians
to the credit of the appropriation for Subsistence of the Army."—LS, DNA,
RG 75, Central Office, Letters Received, Miscellaneous. The enclosure is
ibid.

1868, JAN. 9. To Bvt. Maj. Gen. Edward D. Townsend. "The Adj. Gn.
will please direct the Qr. Mr. Gn. to telegraph orders to the Qr. Mr. in New
York City in charge of the articles called for within to issue them to the agt.
sent by Gov. Smyth and to have the articles charged at the average rate
which the same articles are being sold for to be paid for out of the first
money due to the Assylums drawn from the Treas. on warrant of the Sec.
of War. If a portion of the articles come from the Medical Dept. give same
order to the Surgeon Gn."—ALS, DNA, RG 94, Letters Received, 14B
1868. On the same day, U.S. Representative Benjamin F. Butler of Mass.,
also president, National Asylum for Disabled Volunteer Soldiers, wrote to
USG. "I am grieved to inform you that the Board of Managers of the National Asylum for disabled volunteer Soldiers have had the great misfortune
to lose by fire on Sunday Evening last the principal building of the Home
at Augusta, Maine, with the entire loss of all furniture, beds and bedding.
I desire therefore to make application to you that you will allow the Quarter
master and Medical at New York to issue to the Asylum upon the requisition of Governor Smyth, local manager, who is now at Augusta, such
clothing, bedding and Stores, as may be required. The same to be received
by a special agent detailed for that purpose and the payments to be made
hereafter. The necessities for this issue are so great that I desire the orders
may be sent by telegraph. I assume that in Consideration of our misfortunes we shall be allowed to have the clothing and stores at the prices which
the same grade of clothing has been sold by the War Department."—LS,
ibid.

1868, JAN. 9. President Andrew Johnson to USG. "Will the Secretary of
War ad interim please furnish me with a certified copy of the telegraphic
despatch addressed to the Secretary of War on the 28th of July, 1866, by
Brevet Major General Baird, then commanding at New Orleans?—the copy
to be in the precise words of the despatch, as received in the Military Telegraph Office, at the War Department."—LS, DNA, RG 107, Letters Received from Bureaus. A copy was sent. "A convention has been called with
the sanction of Gov. Wells to meet here on Monday. The Lieutenant Governor and city authorities think it unlawful, and propose to break it up by
arresting the delegates. I have given no orders on the subject, but have
warned the parties that I could not countenance or permit such action without instructions to that effect from the President. Please instruct me at
once by telegraph."—Copy, DLC-Andrew Johnson. See *PUSG*, 16, 287–91.

1868, JAN. 9. Secretary of State William H. Seward to USG. "With a
view to answering a resolution of the Senate calling for information con-

cerning the joint military occupation of San Juan Island, I will thank you for a copy of any papers or correspondence on the files or records of your Department on the subject, of a later date than the message of President Buchanan to the Senate of January 30 1860. See Sen. Ex. Doc. No 10, 36 Cong. 1st Sess. On page 65 of that document is a copy of a letter from Governor Douglas of Vancouver to Lieutenant General Scott declining his proposal for a joint military occupation, without the express sanction of the British Government. It is understood that such sanction was subsequently given and that the joint occupation was carried into effect and has been since maintained; and it is important that I should be furnished with any information showing how these proceedings were consummated."—LS, DNA, RG 94, Letters Received, 30S 1868. See *SED*, 40-2-29; *HED*, 40-2-226.

1868, JAN. 9.   Bvt. Maj. Gen. Benjamin W. Brice, paymaster gen., to USG. "The fraudulent practices, the nature of which will be set forth in a report which I am preparing, and which will be transmitted to you as soon as the evidence of new facts now being inquired into shall reach me, I urgently recommend that an order be issued through the Adjutant General, suspending *W. E Sheldon*, a Claim Agent in New York City, from further practice in the Bureaus of the War Department."—Copy, DNA, RG 99, Letters Sent.

1868, JAN. 9.   U.S. Representative James A. Garfield of Ohio to USG. "I have the honor to transmit herewith the memorial of Walter B. Plowden, asking compensation for his services as a scout, and request that you will inform me if this is a claim that can be settled in your Department, and if not, that you will give me any information you may have respecting its merits as a claim upon Congress for a special relief act. A return of the papers is asked"—LS, DNA, RG 107, Letters Received, M18 1868. See *HED*, 40-2-109; *HRC*, 40-3-13.

1868, JAN. 10.   To Secretary of the Interior Orville H. Browning. "I have the honor to send herewith a communication from the Collector at St. Augustine, Fla., dated Dec. 17th 1867 respecting the *Seminole Indians* in that State, which has been forwarded to this Dept. by Bvt. Maj. Genl. John Pope."—Df, DNA, RG 94, Letters Received, 1864M 1867; copy (misaddressed to William H. Seward), *ibid.*, RG 107, Letters Sent to the President.

1868, JAN. 10.   To Secretary of the Treasury Hugh McCulloch. "I have the honor to acknowledge receipt of a letter from the Treas'r. of the U. S., dated the 17th December last, concerning the management of the funds of the *Qr. Mr's. Dept.* at *Santa Fe*, New Mexico, and to enclose for the information of that officer copies of a letter of the Qr. Mr. Gen'l. of the Army, dated the 6th inst., and of a letter of Bt. *Lt. Col. M. J. Ludington*, the U. S.

Qr. Mr. at Santa Fe, on the subject."—Copy, DNA, RG 107, Letters Sent
to the President. On Jan. 6, Bvt. Maj. Gen. Daniel H. Rucker, act. q. m.
gen., had written to USG. "I have the honor to return herewith the letter of
the Treasurer of the U. States dated December 17th 1867, to you, on the
subject of managing the funds of the Qr. Mrs: Dept: at Santa Fé, N. Mexo,
referred to this Office, and to report that a letter on the same subject dated
November 8th 1867, was received from the Treasurer of the U. States enclosing a copy of correspondence between him and the Designated Depository at Santa Fé, suggesting that a reasonable charge be made for drafts
on the Atlantic cities. . . ."—LS, *ibid.*, RG 92, Reports to the Secretary of
of War (Press).

1868, JAN. 10.   To Secretary of State William H. Seward. "I have the
honor to return, as requested, the despatch, No. 74 of Oct. 1st 1867 of the
U. S. *Vice Commercial Agent at Acapulco*, Mexico, with its accompani-
ments, ref'd. to this Dept. in your letter of the 26th ult., concerning the
refusal of the military authorities at San Francisco to refund to him the
expenses, amounting to $66 25/100 in gold., incurred in the arrest and
safe-keeping of two deserters from the Army of the U. S., and to inform you
that the Qr. Mr. Genl. of the Army has been directed to instruct the proper
officer of his Dept. at San Francisco to pay the account as rendered, upon
its presentation by the Vice Commercial Agt. or his authorized agent."—
Copy, DNA, RG 107, Letters Sent to the President.

1868, JAN. 10.   To Speaker of the House Schuyler Colfax. "I have the
honor to return herewith, for the action of the Military Committee, a petition of certain members of the late *Militia of Memphis, Tenn*, referred to
this Department by Hon. Isaac R Hawkins, M. C on the 12th December
last—accompanied by official copies of papers on file in this Department,
containing, it is believed—all necessary information on the subject"—Copy,
DNA, RG 107, Reports to Congress. See *HED*, 40-2-92.

1868, JAN. 10.   To Speaker of the House Schuyler Colfax. "I have the
honor to transmit, herewith, for the consideration of the proper Committee,
a communication, of January 2d 1868 from the Chief of Ordnance suggesting that action be taken for the removal of the *St Louis Arsenal* to the Jefferson Barracks reservation, in which suggestion this Department concurs."
—Df, DNA, RG 156, Letters Received; copy, *ibid.*, RG 107, Reports to
Congress. For the enclosure, see *HED*, 40-2-94.

1868, JAN. 10.   William Dennison, Columbus, Ohio, to USG. "If you
read the N Y Tribune, you may have seen an editorial paragraph in the
last tuesday's number, of my favoring the nomination of Chief Justice
Chase for the presidency. The Statement was doubtlessly made on an unauthorized telegram in the Cincinnati Commercial which I corrected by
note published in that paper last Monday. Having on several occasions in-

dicated to you my expectation of your being the Successor of Mr Johnson, I feel it due to myself, in view of the Tribune Article, to say, that I heartily favor your nomination by the Republican National Convention, nor do I doubt of your nomination by that body. The current of popular opinion is, and has long been, as unmistakeably in favor of your election as it was for Mr Lincoln's in 1864. Large as will be your personal sacrifice in accepting the presidency, I hope you will not hesitate to make it, in compliance with the patriotic wish of the Country."—ALS, USG 3.

1868, JAN. 10. George W. Johnes, clerk, Committee on Claims, U.S. House of Representatives, to USG. "By direction of Hon: Jno. A. Bingham Chairman, Com. of Claims, House Repr. I have the honor to state that a Bill (H. R. 60) 'Authorizing the payment of the rewards offered by the President of the United States in April, 1865, for the capture of Jefferson Davis,' with memorials and claims of sundry citizens lately officers and soldiers of the Volunteer forces of the United States, is referred to this Committee for examination and report, and to request that you will order to be sent to the Committee the following additional information, if the same can be conveniently furnished, from your Department, viz: I The names and rank of the seven officers and one hundred and twenty eight men of the Fourth Michigan Volunteer Cavalry who, under Command of Lt Col. Benj. D. Pritchard, actually captured Jefferson Davis, near Irwinsville, Georgia, on the 10th of May 1865. II The names of the twenty men who accompanied Lt Joseph O. Yeoman (First Ohio Volunteer Cavalry, Col. B. B. Eggleston) disguised in rebel clothing and who met and joined Davis' escort in his flight, marching two or three days with his party and who first gave the direct intelligence, as it has been claimed, which led to his capture. Any other information, or further report, on the subject of distributing the reward offered for the capture of Jefferson Davis, which you, or any Officer of your Department, may be pleased to make will be acceptable and valuable   The printed evidence, now before the Committee, referring to the specific information requested is herewith enclosed."—ALS, DNA, RG 94, Letters Received, 30C 1868. Related documents are *ibid.* See also *HMD*, 39-2-82.

1868, JAN. 10. John A. Strain, Perry County, Ala., to USG. "In a few words I will give you an idea of the situation of this county, and South Alabama generally. Starvation is on us, both white and colored. Only a portion of the blacks worked last year and a full majority of them subsisted by pillage and stealing—the cattle and hogs are now about all stole and eat up by the freedmen—cribs of corn are broke open by them publickly—the white people are grossely insulted by them, and the Ladies now fear to step out of doors unless guarded. But few freedmen will contract to work the present year—they roam through the country, and take what they want wherevr they find it.—But, all this is not the worst of our condition—threats, serious threats are made of a general insurrection—Their secret leagues have concerted a scheme of action in the event the action of the late convention is not adopted that will devastate our whole country and drench our once happy homes in blood—We pray for relief. unless protection is given us by the powers of the government the scenes of San Dominga will *very shortly* be enacted in Alabama—These are truths for your consideration."—ALS, DNA, RG 94, Letters Received, 163M 1868.

1868, JAN. 11.   To President Andrew Johnson. "In reply to a Resolution of the House of Reps. dated March 15th 1867, asking for various *information concerning the Ordnance Dept.* and its transactions, referred by you to the Sec'y. of War, I have the honor to send herewith a Report of this date by the Chief of Ordnance on the subject."—Copy, DNA, RG 107, Letters Sent to the President. For the enclosure, see *HED*, 40-2-99.

1868, JAN. 11.   To Attorney Gen. Henry Stanbery. "As suggested by the Chief of Engineers whose letter of the 10th inst. I enclose herewith, I have the honor to request that you will give the requisite instructions to the Dist. Atty. of Iowa, respecting the legal business connected with the improvement of the *Des Moines rapids* of the Miss. River referred to in Genl. J. H. Wilson's letter of the 6th inst. also enclosed."—Copy, DNA, RG 107, Letters Sent to the President. On Jan. 10, Brig. Gen. Andrew A. Humphreys, chief of engineers, had written to USG. "I respectfully transmit herewith a copy of a letter received at these Hd. Quarters from Bvt. Maj. Genl. J. H. Wilson, Lieut. Col. 35th Infantry, asking that the U. S. District Attorney for the District of Iowa be instructed by the proper authority to take charge of such legal business in connection with the improvement of the Des Moines rapids of the Mississippi river, as the circumstances may require, and beg leave to request that the matter be referred to the Attorney General of the United States for such action as he may deem proper."—Copy, *ibid.*, RG 77, Explorations, Letters Sent.

1868, JAN. 11.   Secretary of the Treasury Hugh McCulloch to USG. "Herewith I have the honor to transmit a copy of a letter from the Comptroller of the Currency of this date calling attention to an order issued by General Canby, imposing upon all Banks in his military district a tax of two per cent on their gross profits, which is believed to be in conflict with the provisions of the Currency Act of June 3, 1864, (Sec. 41—provisoes,) so far as it relates to National Banks established under the authority of that Act. I would request that the attention of General Canby be drawn to the matter, and that his order be so modified as to relieve National Banks from any tax other than that contemplated by the Section of law above cited."—Copy, DNA, RG 56, Letters Sent.

1868, JAN. 11.   Judge Advocate Gen. Joseph Holt to USG. "Brevet Captain George O. McMullin, 1st Lieut. 3rd Cavalry, was tried at Fort Union,

New Mexico, in December last, under the following charges: —1. Wrongfully selling government property. 1. In that Accused, while Act. comm'y
of subsistence at Fort Marcy, did corruptly sell to Thomas McDonald,
eleven sacks of flour, U. S. property, without proper authority, receiving
therefor $65—which money he appropriated to his own use. This the 29th
May, 1867, at Santa Fe, New. Mexico. Guilty, eleven being reduced to ten.
2. In delivering or furnishing to Thos. McDonald 44 gals. vinegar, property of the U. S., in satisfaction of a private debt, and without a proper
order. This June 21. 1867. Guilty. 3. In corruptly selling to R. M. Stevens,
one sack of bacon, U. S. property, without a proper order; receiving therefor $20, which he has not accounted for, but appropriated. This between
April 1 and July 17. 1867. Guilty. 4. Corruptly selling to R. M. Stevens,
20 farregas of corn, U. S. property; receiving therefor $80., which he ap-
propriated. This between the 4th & 17th of July. 1867. Guilty. 5. Corruptly
selling to G. O. Bachman twenty sacks of corn, U. S. property; receiving
therefor $60.00 which he appropriated. This July 17. 1867. Guilty, *twenty*
being reduced to seventeen, and sixty to thirty by the court. . . . This Bureau, in the presence of the many proofs of Capt. McMillan's deliberate &
habitual dishonesty, cannot, without a violation of its plain duty in the
premises, do otherwise than express its conviction of the Accused's unfitness for longer retention in the service. It recommends a rigid enforcement
of the sentence."—Copy, DNA, RG 153, Letters Sent.

1868, JAN. 13. To Secretary of the Interior Orville H. Browning. "In
reply to your com'n. of the 28th Dec. 1867, enclosing copies of certain
papers pertaining to a case of mail robbery pending at Wheeling, W. Va.
and requesting that *John E. Davis*, Co. H. 2d U. S. Cav'y. be ordered to
that place as a witness for the Govmt., I have the honor to inform you that
by special Orders A. G. O. No. 526 Dec. 21st 1867, he was directed to
report in person to *E. M. Norton*, U. S. *Marshal at Wheeling* W. Va., and
on the same day the Comd'g. Genl. Dept. of the Platte was directed by
telegraph to order him to report to the Marshal by Jan'y. 8th 1868. The
receipt of the telegram was acknowledged Dec. 23d 1867, by the Com'dg.
Genl. Dept. of the Platte, who reported that he had ordered Davis to report
as directed."—Copies, DNA, RG 94, Letters Sent; *ibid.*, RG 107, Letters
Sent to the President. On Dec. 28, 1867, Browning had written to USG.
"I enclose herewith a copy of a communication addressed to this Depart-
ment by E. M Norton Esq Marshal of the United States for the District of
West Virginia in which he states that 'John E Davis, Company H. 2d U S
Cavalry, stationed at or near Fort Russell Dakota Territory, is an important
Witness in mail robbery case to be tried here on the 5th January next,' and
requests that he be ordered to attend at Court at that time. I also enclose a
copy of a letter from B H Smith Esq the District Attorney of the United
States, wherein he states that said Davis is a 'material and important' Wit-
ness in the case   I have the honor to request that you will be pleased to

cause the necessary orders to be issued, directing said Davis to report to the Marshal of the United States at Wheeling, as a Witness on behalf of the Government in the case referred to."—LS, *ibid.*, Letters Received, 116I 1867.

1868, JAN. 13, 3:00 P.M. To Maj. Gen. Winfield S. Hancock. "Your action in instructing General Reynolds to make no more appointments by delegated power is approved, but I think it judicious to confirm the removals and appointments already made by him"—Telegrams sent (2), DNA, RG 107, Telegrams Collected (Bound); copies, *ibid.*, RG 108, Telegrams Sent; DLC-USG, V, 56.

1868, JAN. 13. Secretary of the Treasury Hugh McCulloch to USG. "I have the honor to enclose herewith a copy of a communication addressed to this Department by Henry S. Wells Esq., of New-York, who has contracted to remove the obstructions to navigation in the channel of the Savannah river, placed there by the so-called Confederate Government during the late rebellion. It is very important to the interests of all persons engaged in business at Savannah that these obstructions be removed at the earliest possible period, and I have the honor to request, if no objection to such action occurs to you, that you will instruct the proper Department commander to investigate the facts stated by Mr. Welles relative to the delay and injury caused by the rapid passage of vessels while obstructions are being raised; and if his statements are found to be correct, to take all proper and necessary measures to abate the evil complained of, and to enable him to comply with his contract."—Copy, DNA, RG 56, Letters Sent Relating to Restricted Commercial Intercourse. See *HED*, 40-2-123.

1868, JAN. 13. Postmaster Gen. Alexander W. Randall to USG. "I have the honor to inform you that inquiry has been made by the French Office respecting the delivery of a packet posted at Lyon on the 19 of July by M. Denare Ronat, and addressed to 'M___ The Minister of War, at New York' and alleged to have contained 25 hundreths of white cotton fabric.—The Postmaster of New York can find no trace of said packet in his office and thinks it was undoubtedly forwarded to Washington, D. C. I request that you will please inform me, for the information of the French Office, whether, or not, said packet has been received at the War. Department.—"—LS, DNA, RG 107, Letters Received from Bureaus.

1868, JAN. 13. Maj. Gen. Winfield S. Hancock, New Orleans, to USG. "The act creating Field Officers Courts has become almost inoperative. In few instances—in only two within the limits of my command are there field Officers present with their regiments, of inferior rank to the post commanders. They themselves are the post commanders, and could therefore only be detailed by higher authority. But the next higher authorities are the District commanders; and District Commanders, as such, are not authorized to appoint courts; their commands not being recognized as established subdivisions of the army. The great convenience of Field Officers Courts can not be disputed, and I therefore beg to call your attention to this subject, with the view, if you think proper, of procuring the passage of a supplementary act to the effect that, in the event of their being neither brigade nor post commander, a field officer's Court may be ordered and the proceedings reviewed and acted upon by the officer next superior in command to the field officer detailed"—LS, DNA, RG 94, Letters Received, 723A 1866.

1868, JAN. 13. Bvt. Maj. Gen. John A. Rawlins to Maj. Gen. Oliver O. Howard. "General Grant directs that an order be prepared relieving General Gregory as Assistant Commissioner for the State of Maryland, and detailing the senior officer in command in said district to act as Assistant Commissioner."—LS, DNA, RG 94, Letters Received, 18A 1868. On the same day, Howard wrote to Rawlins. "In accordance with your request I enclose the appointment of General Gregory. According to Sec. 3d of Bureau Law passed July 16. 1866, General Gregory's appointment as Assistant Commissioner for Md. would have been made by the President, if he, Gen Gregory had been a civilian. But he was detailed as a mil. officer. When mustered out he was simply continued temporarily under Sec. 4 by a reappointment in accordance with that Section, as 'an officer of said bureau,' under the power given to the Sec. of War 'to fill vacancies, until other officers can be detailed in their places without detriment to the public service.' The President can, if he so choose, detail an officer of the Army, or appoint a civilian by & with the advice & consent of the Senate, to take Gen. Gregory's place. It was contemplated by the Sec-of War, & has been so ordered, to assign the Senior officer on duty in Md. to take effect Feb. 15th proximo. Gen. Gregory is an excellent [off]icer, faithful in the discharge of duty, and as there is no complaint against him, I advised his retention for a month longer to give him time to get other business."—LS, *ibid.,* 78F 1868.

1868, JAN. 13. U.S. Representative James K. Moorhead of Pa. to USG. "I wish to know whether the Government will send home the remains of Army Officers who died of the yellow fever—Capt S. Watson Black died in Texas (at Hempstead I think) Capt Lancaster has been kind in giving his orphan sisters information & will see to sending the body home, if ordered to do so by the Dept, or will attend to it for the friends if proper arrangements are made—Capt Black was of the 17th U S Infantry. His father Col S W Black was shot through the head, and killed instantly, at the head of his Regiment, 62d Pa V at Gaines Mill. Since then the mother of Capt Black has died, leaving only two orphan sisters, the entire remnant of the family— They are from my District, the girls still reside in Pittsburgh—The Col was one of my particular friends. I feel therefore anxious that the body of Capt Black should be sent forward to Pittsburgh by an order from the

Department, but if that can not be done, I wish to know it soon, so that I may make the proper arrangements and have it done myself—If the order is given have the body sent to the care of Major W J Moorhead Pittsburgh Pa—an early reply will oblige"—ALS, DNA, RG 94, Letters Received, 53M 1868.

1868, JAN. 13.   John Wise, Lancaster, Pa., to USG. "In the early part of June 1861 Captn Whipple of The Topographical Department of U: S. Service issued an order to me to furnish him a Balloon of a certain size and quality to be finished before the middle of July. I fulfilled the contract and delivered the Balloon. Gen. S. Cameron then Sec. of War requested me to come to Washington and take charge of the Balloon for the purpose of Army Observations. On my arrival at Washington I was ordered to report to Gen. Scott who ordered me to report to Maj Bache of Topl Beauro and by him was stationed at the Columbia Armory to await orders. On the saturday previous to the first Bull Run Battle I recd an order to fill the Balloon with gas and proceed to Centreville, under Signal Officer Captn Myers. I filled the Balloon and under an escort of 20 men and an Army Waggon proceeded on the way towards centreville. Having to cross Tellegraph Wires, potomac river, canals, and woods, the onward progress was naturally slow, and the following morning at sunrise having got within hearing of the Battle's volleys, Captn Myers ordered us forward, with the Balloon hitched to the tail end of the waggon, and in our hurry onward the Balloon was damaged by being rushed between some tall trees in our way. After this battle I made observations from Georgetown and arlington heights. I then addressed a communication to Maj. Bache stating what should be done in order to make the Balloon thoroughly effective for War purposes. Upon this I was requested to write to Morris Taske & Co. upon the authority of the Dept for an estimate of cost for a Locomotive Gas generator to be used for the decomposition of water and rapid production of Hydrogen Gas These Gentlemen furnished a comparative Estimate and spoke favorable of the design with an approval of I. C. Cresson of Philadelphia, to whom I referred as being qualified to judge of its merits. The Topl Depts plead a limitation of their appropriation & therefore did not feel disposed to incur an expense of six or seven thousand dollars. Upon this I addressed a note to Captn Woodruff and Maj. Bache that if these requisites and proper assistants were not furnished, and an Official appointment given me, I would leave washington, as I had then exhausted all my private means in the expenditure of assistants and subsistence. I could not get a moments interview with the Sec. of War—he being overun with pressing business, and the Topl Depts doing nothing of itself, not even allowing me to employ any person at the Govts expense. I left Washington after twenty eight days Balloon service—and that the most laborious Balloon service mentally and phisically, that I had ever performed. The records of the Topograpical Dept show the service. I never got a single cent of my personal expenses reimbursed—not a cent of compensation, and I think the government ought to allow me a fair reimbursement for my expenses actually incurred—a Bill which the Topl Dept said they could not pay, as there was no authority for it to do so. These are the main facts in the case, and I submit them to your judgment whether I should not have a return of my actual outlay, if not a fair professional salary for my services."—ALS, DNA, RG 77, Accounts, Property Returns, and Claims, Letters Received. See F. Stansbury Haydon, *Aeronautics in the Union and Confederate Armies* (Baltimore, 1941), I, 57–81.

1868, JAN. 14. To U.S. Representative William A. Pile of Mo. "I have the honor to forward herewith the draft of a bill providing for the saile of the public property mentioned in our recent conversation on that subject"—Copies, DLC-USG, V, 47, 60; DNA, RG 108, Letters Sent.

1868, JAN. 14. Henry D. Cooke, Washington, D. C., to USG. "At the request of the writer, Capt. John Corson, of the Capitol Police, I have the honor to forward his application enclosed, and to commend him as a worthy and reliable gentleman, whom I believe would satisfactorily discharge the duties of the position he seeks."—ALS, DNA, RG 94, ACP, C478 CB 1868. Cooke enclosed an undated letter from John Corson to USG requesting appointment as q. m.—ALS, *ibid.*

1868, JAN. 14. A. D. Matthews, St. Louis, to USG. "I was employed by Genl. S. G. Burbridge about a year ago, to collect several thousand dollars, from Mr E. J. Curly, who got a claim allowed during the latter part of last session of Congress for about $34,800. I went on to Washington about the time the claim was allowed, and from what I learned and observed there and what I have learned since I am fully convinced that the claim was wholly fraudulent, or if not wholly so, that part justly due Mr Curley could not have exceeded $1000, or $1500. If the Government has investigated the matter and has not succeeded in establishment of the fraud it must be on account of the neglect of the person representing her, or because he has been thrown off the proper track. I understand that the papers and evidence in the case have all been published. I have endeavored to obtain a copy of these papers but have so far failed. If you can procure a copy for me, and send it to me, I have no objections to rendering such assistance as is in my power, if not inconsistent with my former relations to Genl. Burbridge. That gentleman has however assured me that if there is anything wrong it will not compromise him, but notwithstanding I did not wish to take any steps without first seeing the papers."—ALS, DNA, RG 107, Letters Received, M31 1868. See *SRC*, 39-1-133.

1868, JAN. 14. L. Perrine, q. m. gen. of N. J., Trenton, to USG. "Application was made, on behalf of the State of New Jersey, to the Secretary of War, on the 18th of February, 1864, for the use of the Bergen Heights arsenal, situated in the city of Hudson, county of Hudson, State of New Jersey, to be used by this State as an arsenal and drill-room, during the pleasure of the Secretary of War, 'upon condition that the authorities of this State will put and keep the building in good repair, and place a suitable person, subject to the approval of the Secretary of War, to take good care of the premises.' This application was referred to the Quartermaster General United States army, who, under date of April 8, 1864, directed the quartermaster at New York to turn over the govenror of New Jersey the premises upon the conditions named. Owing to some delay in the execution of the transfer, it was rented in 1865 to some parties in New York for a cattle yard. Application was again made on the 22d of March last, in reply to which I was informed that the property had again been leased to the same parties. I understand that the lease for these premises will expire on the 1st of April next. By direction of the governor, I have to request that you will cause the said property to be turned over to the State upon the conditions and for the purposes specified. I beg to state, upon the information of the authorities of Hudson county, that the property as occupied at present is an intolerable nuisance. The house is occupied by prostitutes and other disreputable characters, and the grounds by drovers for cattle yards. It is pleasantly situated on the main street of Hudson city, almost in the centre of the town. This statement is made at the request of the authorities of Hudson city and county, who feel agrieved that the government maintains a nuisance in their midst. Copies of the correspondence herein referred to are herewith enclosed. By order of the governor."—*HED*, 40-2-307, pp. 3–4.

1868, JAN. 14.   M. G. Ramsey, Manchester, S. C., to USG. "I wish you to communicate with Gen Potter who commanded in S. C. during the latter part of the War. & to inform him of my privations, do not think it presumptoous in me to address you thus. as I am entirely ignorant of Gen Potters address. You will please say to Gen P. that I am destitute of allmost everything. he will no doubt reccollect the name as he dined in my Mothers house in his raid in Sumter dist. S. C. I think I am entitleed to his sympathies for I being almost an invalid who took *no* part in the war, but was stripped of everything I had, even down to my little childrens clothing I beg you my dear sir that you will commnicate these facts to Gen P. & consider them strictly confidential as I amshamed to be compelled to ask assistance under the circumstances. hopeing that soon we may be blest *soon* with *permanant peace* I subscribe my self . . ."—ALS, DNA, RG 108, Letters Received. On Jan. 29, Lt. Col. Joseph H. Potter, Fort Sedgwick, Colorado Territory, endorsed this letter. "Respectfully returned with the information that I never *raided* through South Carolina during the rebellion. I never was in South Carolina. This letter must have been intended for some other person."—ES, *ibid.*

1868, JAN. 14.   A. C. Richards, Washington, D. C., to USG. "The police force of this District are to give a ball to-morrow (Wednesday) night for the *benefit of the poor* of this District, and they desire to obtain the use of several *U. S. Flags* to decorate the hall (Odd Fellow's) in which the ball is to be given—Understanding that it requires an order from you to obtain the use of the flags from the Armorey Square Depot I have to request that you will give the necessary order—The flags if obtained will be carefully cared for and promptly returned—"—ALS, DNA, RG 107, Letters Received, R9 1868.

1868, Jan. 15.   USG endorsement. "Respectfully forwarded to the Secretary of State"—ES, DNA, RG 59, Letters of Application and Recommendation. Written on a letter of Dec. 18, 1867, from B. R. Raines, M. D., Bureau of Refugees, Freedmen, and Abandoned Lands, to USG. *"Personal . . .* I enclose herewith, recommendations from Genl. W. E. Strong and Col A. P. Ketchum endorsed by Generals Sherman and Howard, (to which your attention is invited) and have the honor to ask your favorable endorsement if you feel warranted in doing so upon the recommendations of these officers *so well known to you.* This together with my services under you while in the 'West' is my only apology for asking this favor"—ALS, *ibid.*

1868, Jan. 15.   To Bvt. Maj. Gen. Edward D. Townsend. "Direct Bvt. Col. H. C. Wood, A. A. G. to report to Gn. Pope for duty, and Bvt. Brig. Gn. Geo. D. Ruggles, A. A. G. to report to the commanding officer, Dept. of the East for duty."—ALS, DNA, RG 94, Letters Received, 22A 1868.

1868, Jan. 15.   Lucy Abbott, St. Augustine, Fla., to USG. "My uncle and guardian James D. Stark, a union man, and not until he found he would be forced into the Confederate service, did he take part in the revolt—had in his possession a portion of my property amounting to several thousands of dollars, of which owing to his losses, will not be able to restore but little From a plantation in Volusia County some of his slaves came here bringing with them two mules, which they used for a time, and then were taken by the commander of this post, and have remained here in possession of the garrison. Reduced from a good competency, my mother, a widow, and myself endeavor by constant labor to earn a livelihood, we find it hard indeed. The right to the mules, such as it is, was released to me by my uncle who was their owner—I write this frank statement, on the truly distressing situation in which two women find themselves, to ask that this little property be given up to me for our benefit. I feel General, that I am appealing to one of noble and generous impulses—to one who thought it not unmanly to weep at the downfall of an opponent, and cannot believe he will disregard the prayer of the unfortunate orphan."—LS, DNA, RG 107, Letters Received from Bureaus. Additional papers are *ibid.*

1868, Jan. 15.   Robert A. Maxwell, Philadelphia, to USG. "Presidential tasks well done. Drive while Stanton refreshed pursues reformation"— Telegram received (at 11:20 A.M.), DNA, RG 107, Telegrams Collected (Bound). On Oct. 15, 1867, Maxwell had telegraphed to USG. "Colored

and other classes requiring Enfranchisement could lend Rail Roads col-
laterals"—Telegram received (at 12:10 P.M.), *ibid.*, RG 94, Letters Received, 1460M 1867; *ibid.*, RG 107, Telegrams Collected (Bound). For
more on Maxwell's incoherent messages, see Lincoln, *Works*, V, 499; VI,
331–32, 475–76.

1868, JAN. 15.   Mguth-thew ("American Eagle") and Nahn-daum (Sa-
chem), Washington, D. C., to USG. "The delegates from the Ma-hic-kon
Indians, a Tribe originally discovered upon the East side of the Hudson
River, are pleased to take you by the hand. We have often heard of your
fame—It is as broad as the air. You are the great War Chief of the Whites,
and stand at the head of your warriors—We represent here that ever peaceful and faithful band, the Mo-he-con-nuk Tribe, whose war hatchet and
bow have never yet been raised against an American White—During all
wars, thro which this country has passed, the braves of this tribe have stood
by the side of your men, and have lain their bones along by the side of your
fallen ones—During the Revolution, the tribe had its Capt. Yokum, whose
daring feat brought destruction upon Brittish Storehouses & supplies at
Charleston Massachusetts, when no White brave could be found to undertake the work—In the war of 1812, we had out Capt. Au-pau-mut, with a
brave band of warriors, whose heroism told no inconsideral part in the victories achieved against the enemy of that time—And when they heard of
the late Rebellion, their spirits were stired to exhume the tomahawk so long
buried, and to string the bow, and 42 of our warriors, out of 400 souls were
upon the 'War Path', to represent the tribe, who fought in your severest
battles, and endured the hardships—of your long campaigns   All those who
survived, returned to speake well of the Great War Chief in whose presence
we now stand—This small tribe with all its unfailing friendship and loyalty,
has been harrassed and driven. When they have attained a good home, their
White neighbors have covetted and wrenched the same from them, and
when a poor one has been gained, necessity has forced the Tribe to call
upon their Great Father to change and give them a better one—Today we
are upon that very errend—But among the desturbances of your Counsel-
ors, and council fires, our matters sink into nothing. The [B]lack Man's
cause is the all absorbing theme   The suffering Indian, whose ~~rich~~ fertile
soil ~~and~~, great waters, and rich mines, that have blessed the Americans, and
given him the welth of today, finds scarcely a place in the thoughts and
plans of your wisest ~~Counselors~~ men   We are sorry to see your differences,
when our Great Father has always told *us*, to live in Peace and harmony—
But we trust the time is not far distant, when the troubled waters will be
assuaged to a calm, and the Indian can paddle his canoe upon its peaceful
surface without being swamped. Accept, General, our sincerest thanks for
your past kindness to our warriors, ~~and~~ & May you ere long be the great
Leader & Father of this Country, blessing the Red Man in his lonely
haunts—"—LS, USG 3.

1868, JAN. 16.   Bvt. Brig. Gen. Adam Badeau to Secretary of State William H. Seward. "Genl Grant directs me to forward you the accompanying letter in compliance with your request of last night, and to ask that you will send it, with your own letter, to Gen. Upton, so that he may be able to use both communications abroad."—ALS, Seward Papers, NRU.

1868, JAN. 17.   USG endorsement. "Respectfully refered to the Q. M. Gen. for employment if there is a vacancy."—AES, DNA, RG 92, Consolidated Correspondence, Mrs. Angroine. Written on a letter of Jan. 14 from Margaret A. Chanler to Julia Dent Grant. "The bearer, Mrs Angroine, is very desirous to get a position for her son, as watchman of stores under government, or some similar position—The man has served for several years in the army and is now honorably discharged—She wishes to tell you about him herself, and I write to certify that she is a perfectly respectable, hard working & *very poor* woman, so that if it is in your power or inclination to aid her, you are assisting a really deserving and worthy woman. I was disappointed yesterday in not finding yourself or Miss Fish at home—Please give my love to her, & believe me . . ."—ALS, *ibid.*

1868, JAN. 17.   Bvt. Maj. Gen. John A. Rawlins to [U.S. Representative Grenville M. Dodge of Iowa]. "No steps have been taken to perfect your proposed Army bill which is herewith returned—Upon consulting the General ~~refer~~ with reference to it, he says that it is his earnest wish that Congress do not legislate for any reduction or change in the present status of the Army. That so long as we are compelled to maintain military occupation of the South we shall need Every man we have, and that when the necessity for such occupation ceases, he can under the Existing laws deplete the army as fully as can be done by the proposed bill and that it is his positive intention to do so, unless in the meantime Exigencies should arise rendering such a course impolitic—Existing laws or orders do not prohibit the detailing of officers to duty into the civil service of any branch of the government, but in the contrary has always been permitted hence nothing special can be gained by the proposed bill except to give the details a more specific direction—Existing laws also warrant the consolidation of regiments as proposed, and which the General intends to enforce as soon as circumstances will admit—If it becomes necessary to meet any proposed reduction of the army or radical change in its organization, the General thinks this bill would fully meet the case."—Copy, Dodge Papers, IaHA.

1868, JAN. 18.   USG endorsement. "Respectfully forwarded to the Secretary of War, with request that copies be sent to the Secretary of the Interior."—ES, DNA, RG 107, Letters Received from Bureaus. Written on reports of Indian attacks in Dakota Territory and Tex.—Copies, *ibid.*

1868, JAN. 18.   USG endorsement. "I knew the applicant years ago as an excellent soldier in the old Regular Army and earnestly recommend him for the appointment of Ordnance Sergeant."—AES, DNA, RG 94, ACP, G16 CB 1868. Written on a letter of Jan. 18 from John Gorman, private (serving as War Dept. messenger), to Secretary of War Edwin M. Stanton requesting an appointment as ordnance sgt. after serving fifteen years in the U.S. Army.—ALS, *ibid.*

1868, JAN. 18, noon.   To Bvt. Maj. Gen. Edward R. S. Canby, Charleston. "Suspend ~~the~~ Seriffs sale of W. B. Skellengers lease and proper in Nash Co. N. C. ~~an~~ in favor of J. J. Jones until the matter can be investigated by you."—ALS (telegram sent), DNA, RG 107, Telegrams Collected (Bound); telegram sent, *ibid.*; telegram received (at 12:30 P.M.), *ibid.*, RG 393, 2nd Military District, Letters Received.

1868, JAN. 18.   Bvt. Maj. Gen. Daniel H. Rucker, act. q. m. gen., to USG. "I have the honor to acknowledge the receipt of a letter addressed to you by Mrs Louisa A. Byrne, widow of Dr Byrne of the Army, with your endorsement of this day, asking a Clerkship for her. It would afford me great pleasure to comply with your request, if in my power, but the law allows only 30 female copyists to this office, and I regret to say there is at present no vacancy. It is proper to add that such appointments are made by the Secretary of War. The letter of Mrs Byrne will be filed and receive special and kind consideration when a vacancy occurs."—LS, DNA, RG 92, Miscellaneous Letters Sent (Press). Louisa Albert Byrne, widow of Surgeon Bernard M. Byrne, eventually held a clerkship in the Q. M. Dept.

1868, JAN. 18.   Maj. George K. Leet to Bvt. Maj. Gen. Andrew J. Smith. "A report has reached these Headquarters to the effect that one Indian was killed and several women wounded at Fort Gibson, I. T., on New-years eve, by shots fired by soldiers into a ball-room, in which were assembled Cherokee Indians and some Army officers   You will cause an investigation to be made and report the facts to these Headquarters. Special attention is invited to the Act of Congress No. 1, published in Gen. Orders No. 15 H. Q. A., AGO., February 15th 1862—copy enclosed."—ALS, DNA, RG 108, Letters Received. On March 5, Maj. Gen. Philip H. Sheridan endorsed this letter to Leet, enclosing reports from 2nd Lt. George T. Cook, 6th Inf., and Capt. Henry E. Alvord, 10th Cav.—ES, *ibid.* "In obedience to endorsement from Head Quarters Post of Fort Gibson, I. T. upon the accompanying papers, I have the honor to submit the following report of my investigation of the circumstances attendant upon the shooting of Jesse Bushyhead, a Cherokee Indian, on New Year's eve—I having been on that date 'officer of the day.' New Year's eve Mr Jesse Bushyhead gave a party in the second story of a Store occupied by him in the town of Fort Gibson. After the breaking up of this party which took place about one o'clock A. M., Mr Bushyhead with others who had been with him during the night, proceeded to a house of doubtful character, situated about half a mile from his Store, where they found a party composed of an inferior class of Indians and Negroes, Indian Scouts and Quartermaster's employés. Mr Bushyhead as well as his associates had been drinking during the evening. At this house more liquor was obtained and so riotous did the men become that the women present, with one exception, fled—fearful of the consequences likely to ensue. Shortly after, Mr Jesse Bushyhead was shot, and such of the party as were able dispersed, fearful of Military arrest. This affair took place about three fourths of a mile from the Military Reserve and beyond any points visited by the officer of the day. Owing to the universal fear of being known to report to the Military authorities the affair did not come to my knowledge until after eight o'clock A. M. of the first ultimo, when an Indian, Lawson Runyon, came to me and made a statement of the circumstances, accusing an Indian Scout, James Ross, with having fired the shot. Upon this statement I arrested the said Ross. He is now in the hands of the Civil authorities awaiting trial. Although I have made strict inquiry I can find no one who states that there were any United States Officers or soldiers present at the time the shot was fired, or indeed, at anytime during the night. The Surgeons who attended Mr. Bushyhead inform me that he lived until about four o'clock P. M. of the first ultimo, and up to the time of his death was perfectly conscious. When interrogated as to who shot him he declared himself unable to tell, stating that he had not the slightest idea by whom it was done, but did not once infer that United States soldiers had any hand in the affair. The Commanding Officer of the District at that time—Col De L. Floyd-Jones, 6th U. S. Infantry, ordered a partial investigation made by an Officer, who was assisted by Mr William Ross, late Chief of the Cherokee Nation, to ascertain whether the grounds for holding the Indian, James Ross, were sufficient. These gentlemen assure me that they elicited nothing to lead them to the opinion that there were any Officers or soldiers near the house. The occupants of the house positively assert that there were none present during the night. They further state that when the first party came they brought a demi-john containing liquor. The Commanding Officer ordered a search for the person from whom the liquor was obtained. It was found to be an Indian living about two miles from town. He was arrested, turned over to a United States Marshal by whom he was taken to Van Buren, Ark., and, although undisputed proof of the sale of liquor was elicited upon trial, was released. I am informed by an Officer present at the trial that the Commissioners decided that an Indian could not be held for selling liquor to an Indian—that he must be detected in the act of introducing the liquor into the Indian Territory. As Mr Bushyhead was a prominent young man, unusual endeavors have been made by the Cherokee authorities to obtain witnesses but with indifferent success. In conversing with Mr William Ross, ex Chief, I asked what he supposed the reason to be. His reply was to the effect that he could conceive no reason except the fear of being personally in peril of their lives should those acquainted with the facts offer their testimony. This supposition is sustained by a recent attempt at murder the circumstances of which have been partially brought to light since the commencement of this investigation; and as it forms part

of the history of the shooting of Mr. Bushyhead and also shows the demoralized condition of the people and the defective system of Cherokee law, I
take the liberty of including the principal points in this report. Reilly Keys,
an Indian of property and influence, while riding from Fort Gibson towards
his home, overtook a Creek Indian, about a mile from town, with whom he
had ridden but a short distance when the Creek fell to the rear and shot
him. It being near a house and the wounded man calling loudly for assistance, the would-be assassin fled. This occurred on the fifth instant. On the
eighth instant the Creek was captured and taken before Keys who immediately identified him. The prisoner then acknowledged his guilt, but explained that it was a mistake on his part, he having been *hired* to shoot an
Indian named *Starr*. The person identified as having employed him was
after some delay arrested. Both were then brought to the Military authorities for confinfinement, as no steps can be taken in the matter by the Civil
authorities unless Keys dies. I am informed that there is no criminal law by
which an Indian can be tried for shooting another should the shot not prove
fatal. The general opinion expressed is, and I deem it correct, that as the
Indian, Mr Starr, whom the Creek was employed to kill, is expected to be a
prominent witness at the trial of James Ross for the murder of Mr Bushyhead, some interested parties attempted by his assassination to rid themselves of his testimony. Similar cases of shooting in the most cowardly
manner are by no means of infrequent occurrence. Some pass unnoticed,
others go through the form of a trial, but I am not aware of an instance in
which a party has been punished during the past six months. The civil law
is almost powerless. It does not provide any officer of the grade known in
the States as 'Justice of the Peace.' To make a legal arrest it is necessary to
go to the Court House of the Nation and make deposition before the Clerk
of the Court, thereby giving ample time and opportunity for the escape of
guilty parties. The deposition is the indictment. Upon it the prisoner is tried
before a Judge by a jury of twelve. The moral effect of the presence of the
Military authorities, who upon application of prominent citizens frequently
arrest and hold parties guilty of crime until civil warrants can be procured,
seems to be the only check upon these excesses, as no legal authority can be
obtained for arrest by civil law within twenty miles of this Post. After a
thorough investigation, I am of the opinion that no Officers or soldiers were
in or around the building in which Mr Jesse Bushyhead was shot at anytime during the night of December 31st 1867. I append hereto an official
statement by Captain H. E. Alvord, 10th U. S. Cavalry, of such facts as
came to his knowledge while conducting the partial investigation ordered
by the Commanding Officer of the District—"   "Since the latter part of
November, 1867 I have been stationed at Fort Gibson, Cherokee Nation,
Indian Territory in command of company "M" of my regiment and since
the middle of December, 1867 have also commanded the detachment of
U. S Indian Scouts serving at the Post of Fort Gibson. I heard of the shooting of Jesse Busheyhead, a merchant of the town of Fort Gibson at the
house of a colored man named Foster, on the night of the 31st of December,

1867 and on the 1st day of January, 1868 Private James Ross of the Det. of Scouts under my command, was arrested by order of the Post Commander and confined in the Guard House on charge of having shot Busheyhead. A few days later, Colonel D. L. Floyd-Jones, Comdg. the Post and District requested me to informally investigate the facts of the murder in connection with Will. P. Ross—one of the most prominent Cherokee citizens. The civil law of the Cherokees provides for no preliminary examination of any kind in criminal cases,—Private Ross had been arrested upon the affidavit of one man, he of doubtful character, the civil authorities had taken no action in the premises and Mr. Ross and myself understood that the purpose of the investigation we were requested to make was to ascertain what evidence could be produced of the criminality of the scout James Ross and whether it was sufficient to warrant his being kept in confinement by the military authorities. No testimony was taken under oath but a number of persons were examined by Mr. Ross and myself and we from all the evidence adduced became satisfied of the following facts:—1st That the murdered man was in a room at a low resort on the outskirts of the village near this post not on the reservation with about a dozen other men—and all intoxicated—2nd. That on the night named no officers, soldiers or citizens connected with the U. S. Army—were at or near the house at which the murder was committed, except three or four Indian Scouts (James Ross among the number) and one or two employees of the Qr. Mr. Department— and that they were all absent from their camps without leave. 3rd That as all the persons in the room at the time the pistol shot was fired which killed Busheyhead were under the influence of liquor—it is exceedingly doubtful whether, should they try to do so any of them would be able to give a correct statement of the circumstances in connection with the murder. 4th That while the evidence against Private Ross is not sufficient to even render it probable that he is the guilty party—it is more than likely that a regular trial of any suspected person will bring forth testimony which it is impossible to obtain by an informal investigation and therefore that a trial by the proper civil tribunal of the Nation. of the scout Ross who, notwithstanding his previous good character seems to be the party most suspected by the community—will be the best means of securing justice to all concerned. Mr. Ross and myself consequently united in recommending to the civil authorities of the Nation that they demand Private James Ross of the military authority and proceed to regularly try him for the murder of Busheyhead and to Colonel Floyd-Jones that Private Ross be held in confinement a sufficient length of time to enable the civil authorities to issue a warrant for his arrest."—DS, *ibid.*

1868, JAN. 19. Matías Romero to USG. "I have had nothing from you for some time. Since I wrote you my last letter, President Juarez invited me to enter his cabinet, by accepting the Treasury Department. After a mature deliberation I concluded to accept it, supposing that I could render in this very dificul position under the present circumstances, some more effective service to my country than in any other place. I assure you that it is only with very great reluctance that I have given up my position in Washington and the idea of returning for good to the United States—a country to which I am almost as much attached as to my own—, but I think it is my duty to remain at home as I believe I can do here more good. I may however return to Washington for a few days to present the President my letters of recall and attend to some private business. Should hereafter occur any thing of importance which will require my presence in the United States, I would willingly and cheerfully return. Mr Lerdo de Tejada remains and will remain in the cabinet as Secretary of State. Gen. Diaz is expected today in this city. Matters remain quiete at home and we have every chance to restore permanent peace and consolidate our government. With my mother and sister's and my own best regards and wishes, for yourself and family, I remain . . ."—ALS, USG 3. On Feb. 3, Romero wrote to USG. "I have not been favored with any of your letters for over two months. I hope this is not for indisposition of yourself or any of your family. The last intelligence from the United States seems to us rather alarming. We sincerely hope that next steamer may bring us more satisfactory advices and information to the effect that the past excitment has subsided. I have been only two weeks in the Treasury Department, and yet, I am very much encouraged to hope that it is not so difficult to restore Mexican finances to a sound and healthy basis. All we need for this, besides keeping the public peace, is honesty and perseverance, and I am disposed to have both. In my report to Congress, which was prepared in great haste, and a copy of which I enclose to you, you will see that our financial condition is quite hopeful. The reported disagreements between President Juarez and Gen. Diaz amount to nothing. The Gen. has just left for Oaxaca after having paid me a visit of ten days in this city. We discussed quite freely political affairs, and although he does not entirely agree with Mr. Lerdo de Tejada, our Secretary of State, and is somewhat disposed to hear the leading members of the opposition, yet, there is not the slightest danger of his turning against the Government or in any way disturbing the public peace of the country. We have now, as you very likely know, a few little disturbances in Yucatan, Guerrero and Sinaloa but they are quite insignificant and by no means enough to give us any serious uneasiness   With my best regards for your health and happiness and begging of you to present my compliments to Mrs. Grant, I remain . . ."—ALS, *ibid.* On March 9, Romero wrote to USG. "The last news we heard from the United States, are very exciting. We are extremely anxious to hear other developments and really hope that peace will not be disturbed in your country. I read with great interest your correspondence with President Johnson about your surrender of the War Department to Mr. Stanton. I had made all my preparations to leave VeraCruz on the 12th instant for New York, but our Congress having extended their session, I found it impossible to leave just now, and have been obliged to delay my trip until about the end of next May   We have had lately a little incident here, which I am affraid may be reported with some exageration

in the United States. Admiral or General J. Napoleon Terman who is somewhat known in the North, was once in our service and took afterwards service with Maximilian. The President thought he ought to be sent away
under the annesty proclamation. Terman I believe claimed to be a citizen
of the United States. The President I believe will be disposed to send him
quietly away and even to pay his expenses   In the meanwhile newspaper
men have taken hold of this incident and they will make great deal of noise
about it. Gen. Diaz does not like to leave this country under the present
circumstances   Matters go on very satisfactory and we progress every day
in the work of consolidation   We are paving the way to settle our old
difficulties with European nations by paying off the debt we owe to their
subjects. With my kindest regards to yourself and family and my best
wishes for your health and happiness, . . ."—ALS, *ibid.* On March 28,
Romero wrote to USG. "I have not been favored with any of your esteemed
letters. I suppose you have been engaged more than usually with the political events in the United States   We feel here great deal of anxiety to learn
what is going on in Washington. I have very little doubt that President
Johnson will be impeached, and I hope too that this event will not upset the
public peace of the country. I would like very much that we could have
telegraphic communication with the United States, so that we could hear
the news every day. Matters progress well in Mexico. My faith in the future
of my country is not at all shaken. We have little difficulties to contend
against, but I hope we will be able to overcome them all in the course of
time. Senor Vallarta the Ministe[r] of the interior has just come and has
taken possession of his Department. We have had lately some rumors about
reported intentions of the English to blockade our ports. I place very little
credit in such rumors. My only fear would be that the United States might
find envolved themselfes again in a civil war. That is the only case in which
our peace might be endangered. I am anxious to go to the United States
and I might do so about the end of April next. I beg of you to present my
kindest regards to Mrs. Grant your children and Mr. Dent, and to believe
me most truly, . . ."—ALS, *ibid.* On April 28, Romero wrote to USG. "It is
a very long time since I have not received any of your favors. I suppose
your engagements at Washington, scarcely leave you time for any thing. I
have heard from my brother that yourself and family are well, at which we
all rejoyce here very much. We have been watching with the deepest concern, the course of affairs in the United States. We are quite glad to see
that there is no danger of any disturbance on account of the probable impeachment of President Johnson. We are progressing on very favorably
here. Public peace has been restored in the States of Guerrero and Sinaloa
with very little difficulty. A few bands remain about Tulancingo and Pa-
chuca; but they are of very little account and they will soon be disposed of.
I never saw the country in such good condition, as it is now. We can make
all our expenses without exacting any thing from any body, and we even
are paying quite largely our public debt. Our Congress will adjourn on the
31st of next month. If possible I will leave VeraCruz by the 1st of June or

as soon as I can after that. It will afford me great pleasure to find you at Washington. With my best regards for your self, Mrs. Grant, and your children, I remain . . ."—ALS, *ibid.*

1868, JAN. 20.   Bvt. Maj. Gen. John Pope, Pomeroy, Ohio, to USG. "Just as I was leaving Washington I handed you a letter from Gov. Brown of Ga. which contains matter worth your immediate consideration. He indicates rather than states that Gnl Meade is opposed to holding an election in Georgia for state officers and a Legislature at the same time the Constitution is voted on—I gave this subject anxious consideration before I made the order for Alabama & I consider such election not only in all respects desirable but nearly essential to Reconstruction for two or three reasons which I will give you—1st As you are aware the steps in reconstruction are the assembling of a Convention & framing of a Constitution; The submission of that Constitution to a vote of the people; If adopted by the people, its transmission to Congress & its approval by that body; *then the adoption of the Constitutional amendment by the Legislature elected under the new Constitution*—Now if there be no Legislature in existence when the Constitution is sent back accepted by Congress, what is to be done?—There is no authority except in the Convention itself to order an election of Legislature & state officers—Therefore in this case the Convention must reassemble at great trouble & expense merely to order an election attended with heavy expense & great excitement, an election which the Convention is as competent to order now as at any other time—So also if there be no Legislature in existence to do the final act required under the Reconstruction acts, great delay is unavoidable in consummating the final step of reconstruction,—a delay which ought by all means to be avoided—Again the Convention being the only authority competent to order such an election at all, of course it can order the election whenever it pleases & if Genl Meade refuses to allow his Boards of registration to receive the votes at the same time & places the Constitution is voted on the duty is imposed on the Convention to appoint the its own judges of election for the purpose, thus occasioning great confusion & unnecessary expense by the presence at the same time & places of two setts of election officers, conducting two elections—As a matter of course the Convention in Georgia as in Alabama will order the election for Legislature & state officers at the same time the constitution is voted on, for very sufficient reasons to them—1st to avoid delay in consummating the the final act of Reconstruction, 2nd to avoid the expense & excitement of again calling together the Convention & a separate & different election; & 3rd in order that as full a vote as possible may be had on the question of ratifying the Constitution—Every body understands that the fuller the vote, the larger will be the Union majority, and it is needless to say that the fullest possible vote can be got out by having a general election of state & County officers at the same time with the vote on the Constitution—Gov Patton's objections, as I told you are opposed to common sense & are simply the fruits of his insane desire to be a candidate for Gov of Ala, which he

cannot be until his political disabilities are removed by Congress & therefore he wishes to postpone the election for state officers—this may seem a
hard judgement but it is true as Genl Meade may ascertain by a little enquiry in Ala—The Convention will certainly order the election in Ga, as
was done in Ala & the only question is, will Genl Meade allow his Boards of
Registration to receive the Votes at the same time they are receiving the
votes on the Constitution, or will he force the Convention to appoint election
officers of its own to do the work & thus be the occasion of expense, confusion, & unnecessary excitement?—I am sure if I could have ten minutes
conversation with him on the subject I could convince him I am right—I
studied the whole subject very carefully before I made the Ala order—Genl
Meade as I gather from Gov Brown's letter & the Genls. despatches to you,
seems to think that the election for Legislature & state officers is to be ~~made~~
ordered by him—This is a mistake—He has no power to order such elections
& indeed he has no power to order an election on the question of ratification
of the Constitution—These orders are by law, the province of the Conventions & the only orders he is required to make or empowered to make are
simply for the *conduct* of the election—The time is fixed by the Convention—Of course if the Constitution is not ratified by the people or accepted
by Congress, all elections under it fall to the ground—If the people do not
like the Candidates nominated by the Conventions (as Gov Patton represents) they can easily nominate others—In short Genl, I consider it in all
respects desirable that the election for Legislature & state officers be held
at the same time the Constitution is submitted to popular vote and I have
no doubt the Convention in Ga will order this to be done—I trust that Genl
Meade will permit his officers conducting the election for ratification to
receive the votes for state officers also—I can see no good result from refusing but I think I *can* see great harm—I had a conversation with Genl
Rawlings on this subject & I think we agreed on the views I have expressed
to you—Will you talk with him about it & do what you may think judicious
to influence Genl Meade to assent to them—I am perhaps meddling with
what does not now concern me officially but I need not say how deeply I am
interested in the result in the District which I commanded—This interest
must be my excuse for these suggestions and I feel sure that Genl Meade
will accept it—I shall be detained here a day or two by the illness of one of
my children & then will go direct to Detroit—Will you please accept my
thanks for your kindness, & consideration for me—"—ALS, USG 3.

1868, JAN. 21.   F. D. Butler, New York City, to USG. "Is Gen Sheridan
in the City? Answer"—Telegram received (at noon), DNA, RG 107, Telegrams Collected (Bound).

1868, JAN. 21.   A. Q. Withers, Holly Springs, Miss., to USG. "For some
time past several of my Friends being well known to my many misfortunes
in the late War have urged me to present to you and others the same to see
if you would approbate by recommendation that an appropriation be made

me by special enactment by the Congress of the United States. that I may be enabled to support my now dependent Family of a bed ridden wife & seven children five of whom are Daughters Varying in ages from 4 to 14 years. I here give you a sumery in part my losses by the late War and assert here & can establish the fact by a Majority of the Citizens of this County that I took a public & decided stand in opposition to Sesession & do to this date although disfranchised having served several years in our State Legislature prior to & after the Ordinance of Sesession was past. being at the time a Representative. . . . Now General. I have given you in part a sumery of my losses & have not mentioned those of the Confederate forces for they too gave me a corresponding blow as they too burnt for me 368. ba cotton & impressed several horses. I say this that most of this property was made by arduous toil. I owned at the commencement of the War 73 slaves most of whom I raised. Some 30 of them are now on one of my farms. & with my efforts to work them as freedmen both of us have lost by it. they in debt to me far more I fear than they will ever pay. I am now in my advanced age reduced to *Poverty*. Some help will again star[t] me. and with my ambition & energy can yet make a support for Family. I appeal to you in the name of them. & your humanit[y] to recommend to Congress or devise some Means by which I may regain a portion of my losses a grateful heart will throb with em[o]tion. you have doubtless received many such appeals & of course they [beco]me more or less a bore to you. I do not feel that I am or should a[sk] too much of the goverment to pay me at least one half my losses b[ut] a fourth would set me up then I could demonstrate possibly better than any man in this county the availibility of Freedmen & be wi[th] them a benefactor as engaging their esteem & confidence. What I desire you to do is to Name some Member of Congress (as a[n] unknown to me) who would with your recommendation introduce a Bill for my special relief. when I would write out one & send to yo[u] for your recommendations that the same do pass. am I asking too much. answer me if the above be consistant with your view[s.] . . . Note, the within can & will be testified to by numerous witnesses b[oth] white & Black if nessessary as hundreds know most the facts as name[d.]"—ALS, DLC-Elihu B. Washburne. On Sept. 27, 1874, Withers wrote to USG concerning Reconstruction policy.— ALS, DNA, RG 60, Letters from the President.

1868, JAN. 23. Martin Morrisey, Washington, D. C., to USG. "I beg leave to state that I was an employee at Arlington Natl Cemetery for over two years—that I was discharged from there on the 4th of this month on account of a reduction of force—that I served over 3 years in the Army, during which time my heath suffered to an extent that now seriously inconveniences me—that I have four small children and a wife dependant on me for support. And finally that I am, owing to my premature discharge, at this inclement season of the year, without the means to furnish the common necessaries of life. I would respectfully call your attention to the inconsistency, let alone the injustice, of the re-employment of a colored man since I was discharged, who has *never been in the Army*, and is reported in comfortable circumstances. The fact that he has not been in the Army is sufficient to warrant his discharge, and that he was employed at all to call up the honest indignation of the discharged soldier. I feel that after your well known wishes, not to say orders on the subject of employing discharged soldiers, and these only, you will be surprised to learn that there are other colored men, four of them, who are still employed there. who have not been in the Army. Comment is unecesary. The destitute soldier and his family suffering for want of the common necessaries of life. The soldier that fought by your side compelled almost to beg, while the worthless civilian is sheltered with a solicitude charitable to behold were injustice not mixed with it. I therefore respectfully ask to be re-appointed, and if reduction *is necessary*, that it fall on those who have no claim to retention."—ALS, DNA, RG 108, Letters Received. Additional papers are *ibid.*; *ibid.*, RG 92, Consolidated Correspondence, Martin Morrisey. On Feb. 3, Bvt. Maj. Gen. Daniel H. Rucker, act. q. m. gen., wrote to USG. "I have the honor to return the letter of Martin Morrisey, of the 23d January last, asking to be re-instated as an employé at Arlington National Cemetery, and complaining that civilians are employed instead of soldiers. This letter was referred to Gen. J. C. McFerran, in charge of this branch of the Department, for report, and by him referred to Bvt. Lt. Col. A. P. Blunt, A. Q. M, for report without delay. Col. Blunt reports as follows: 'Asst Qr Mr's Office, Lincoln Depot, Washington, D. C. Jan. 30, 1868. Respectfully returned to Bvt. Brig. Gen. J. C. McFerran, Depy Qr Mr Gen. U. S. A., with report, that I have not re-employed any colored men at the Arlington Cemetery since the discharge took place on the 4th instant, but I have sent one man—a discharged soldier that lost one of his legs in service—there to be employed; nor is it my intention to employ an additional force at that Cemetery until the Spring opens, as the interest of the service does not require it. All the employés retained—excepting four colored men—are discharged and mostly disabled soldiers—and the four colored men were retained because they lived in the vicinity, and had old and helpless parents to take care of. I have ordered their discharge, however, and sent four discharged soldiers to take their places. (Signed) A. P. BLUNT, Bvt. Col. & A. Q. M. U. S. A.' The foregoing is transmitted with the following endorsement by Gen. McFerran: 'Respectfully forwarded to the Qr Mr Gen'l. It is the rule at the Depot to give preference, in all cases where it can be done in justice to the Gov't, to discharged soldiers, and to disabled ones, when they can perform the duties required. (Signed) J. C. McFERRAN, Depy Qr Mr Gen'l, Bvt Brig. Gen. U. S. A. Depot Qr Mrs Office, Washington, D. C. Jan. 31, 1868.' "—LS, *ibid.*, RG 108, Letters Received.

1868, JAN. 24. USG endorsement. "Respectfully returned to the Secy of War. I concur in the recommendations of the Chief of Engineers."—ES,

DNA, RG 94, Letters Received, 800P 1867. Written on a letter of Nov. 23, 1867, from Brig. Gen. Andrew A. Humphreys, chief of engineers, to USG. "I have the honor to acknowledge the reference to the Chief of Engineers, for remark, of the letter of Major General H. W. Halleck, Com'g Military Division of the Pacific—of the 15th ulto., calling the attention of the War Department to the importance of mounting some heavy guns on Point Defiance, Puget Sound. I recommend that the following armament be provided by the Ordnance Department, and sent as soon as practicable to the Pacific Coast. . . ."—LS, *ibid.*, RG 156, Letters Received. See *SED*, 50-1-165, pp. 65–67.

1868, JAN. 24, 12:30 P.M.   To Maj. Gen. Winfield S. Hancock. "Have you received report from Lt. William Hawley, Comdg. Post of Marshall, Texas, of a riot at that place on December 31st 1867. If so you will forward the report to these Headquarters."—Telegrams sent (2), DNA, RG 107, Telegrams Collected (Bound); telegram received (misdated Jan. 25— marked as sent at 11:30 A.M.), *ibid.*, RG 393, 5th Military District, Telegrams Received. On Jan. 24, Maj. William P. Wilson, New Orleans, telegraphed to USG. "Gen Hancock is absent in Texas, Lt Hawleys report has been rec'd. Lieut Col Wood first Infantry has been ordered to Marshall to investigate,   Report Will be forwarded as soon as received"—Telegram received (on Jan. 25, 8:40 A.M.), *ibid.*, RG 107, Telegrams Collected (Bound); *ibid.*, RG 108, Telegrams Received; copy, DLC-USG, V, 55. On Jan. 21, Hancock, New Orleans, had telegraphed to USG. "I leave here for Texas this morning. I expect to go to Galveston and Austin Texas. Will be absent from eight to ten days"—Telegram received (at 1:00 P.M.), DNA, RG 107, Telegrams Collected (Bound); *ibid.*, RG 108, Telegrams Received; copy, DLC-USG, V, 55. On Feb. 1, Hancock telegraphed to USG. "I returned from Texas last evening"—Telegram received (at 3:40 P.M.), DNA, RG 107, Telegrams Collected (Bound). On Feb. 10, Hancock forwarded to USG reports concerning the Marshall riot.—*Ibid.*, RG 108, Register of Letters Received. U.S. Senator Henry Wilson of Mass. favorably endorsed to USG a letter of March 1 from W. B. Moore, *San Antonio Express*, to Wilson. "Enclosed I send you an extract from the Express. The whole rebel press in Texas are encouraging the murdering rebels in their belief that Hancock will sustain them in their proscriptive measures against loyalists. Scipio McKee a colored man in employ of the Union men, organizing Loyal Leagues, was in Marshal with Judge Caldwell and he reports the colored people of that region in more abject slavery than during the war he is one of the most reliable unexciteable men, Having organized more than 30 leagues many of them in regions where the life of a negro is of less consequence than a dogs. If you want affidavits I can send them. For Gods sake send us Sheridan and relieve us from Hancock."—ES and ALS, *ibid.*, Letters Received. Moore enclosed a clipping. "THE MARSHALL RIOT. —Colonel Wood, of the staff of Gen. Hancock, who was sent to Marshall to investigate the late riot at that place, in which Judge Caldwell figured so conspicuously, returned to New Orleans on the 3rd. Col. Wood, says the Picayune, reported the affair very much exaggerated, and that the trouble was nothing more than an ordinary election squabble, which might occur, and which often does occur everywhere throughout the country.—Houston Telegraph. General Hancock is a better judge of human nature than President Johnson, as is evinced by his selection of tools. To call the riot at Marshall an 'election squabble' requires extraordinary discipline and we give Col. Wood credit for being a good soldier."—*Ibid.* See *HED,* 40-3-1, III, part 1, pp. 254–58.

1868, JAN. 24, 3:30 P.M.   To Maj. Gen. George G. Meade. "Order issued authorizing you to draw forage in Philadelphia."—ALS (telegram sent), DNA, RG 107, Telegrams Collected (Bound); telegram sent, *ibid.*; copies, *ibid.*, RG 108, Telegrams Sent; DLC-USG, V, 56.

On Jan. 27, Bvt. Maj. Gen. Thomas W. Sherman requested "permission to forage, his authorized horses by requisition to the Q M at Ft Adams R I. for the month of Jany."—DLC-USG, V, 44. On March 3, USG endorsed this letter. "Respectfully forwarded to the Secretary of War. Jan 24. 1868. I directed the Adjt General to issue an order granting Maj Genl Meade permission to draw forage in Philadelphia Penn for his authorized number of horses during his absence in command of the 3d Mil District. Subsequently the written application of Gen Meade, which is enclosed herewith, having the endorsement of the Acting Q M General was received. In his endorsement upon the application of Bvt Maj Genl Sherman the A Q M Genl remarks 'that in view of the Act of Congress appd July 17, '62 which allows forage to be issued only for such horses as are kept by Officers at the place where they are on duty, the A Q M Genl can not recommend that Genl Sherman's request be granted'   In my opinion the Act of Congress referred to by the A Q M Genl does not contemplate that an Officer temporarily transferred to another station shall be deprived of his allowance of forage at his permanent station; as in this case, during such temporary absence therefrom, but was intended to apply only to Officers regularly relieved at one station and ordered to another. I therefore recommend that General Sherman's request be granted."—Copy, *ibid.*

1868, JAN. 24.   Secretary of State William H. Seward to USG. "I have some important papers to submit to you upon a subject in which you have taken a proper and patriotic interest, and I shall be pleased if you can favor me with a visit at the Department to-morrow or Monday."—Copy, Seward Papers, NRU.

1868, JAN. 25.   USG endorsement. "Respectfully forwarded to the Secretary of War, with the recommendation that the model within named be referred, for examination and report, to the Ordnance Board, now in Session in this City, of which Gen. Hagner is president"—ES, DNA, RG 94, Letters Received, 27G 1868. Written on a letter of Jan. 16 from Jacob L. Gebhart to Secretary of War Edwin M. Stanton. "Through the Ordnance Committee and Head Quarters of the Army. Your petitioner Jacob L. Gebhart of Illinois would represent that he has a model gun breech loading field piece known as the Beaupré Gun, that has been examined by the ordnance committee and Genl. Grant, which your petitioner believes will overcome all objections to field and heavy ordnance breech-loaders, That he has expended all his money in getting up this model, and now asks the Hon, Secy of War, that a gun of any calibre desired by the Government may be made at the expense of the Government under your petitioners supervision, for the purpose of testing the efficiency and durability of the same made after this model."—ALS, *ibid.*

1868, JAN. 28.   To [Maj. George K. Leet]. "I wish you would find 'Appendix' to Maj. Whittlesey's report on 'Military Colleges' and deliver it to him. It is probably on file in the Adj. or Insp. Gen. Depts."—Stan. V. Henkels, Catalogue No. 1194, June 8, 1917, no. 483.

1868, JAN. 29.   To Bvt. Maj. Gen. Edward D. Townsend. "You will please issue Special Order leaving Maj. L. H. Marshall, 23d Inf.y. awaiting orders in this city to give him an opportunity to settle his accounts with the Treasury."—ALS, DNA, RG 94, Letters Received, 41A 1868. On Aug. 4, 1867, Maj. Louis H. Marshall, 23rd Inf., Portland, Ore., had telegraphed to USG. "I request an order to Washington to settle accounts. ⚓Recommended F Steele Brevet Major General"—Telegram received (at 8:40 P.M.), *ibid.*, ACP, M460 CB 1868; *ibid.*, RG 107, Telegrams Collected (Bound); *ibid.*, RG 108, Telegrams Received; copy, DLC-USG, V, 55.

1868, JAN. 29.   To Bvt. Maj. Gen. Edward D. Townsend. "You will please order Maj. J. Stewart, 4th Arty.—to Fort McHenry for duty."— ALS, DNA, RG 94, Letters Received, 40A 1868.

1868, JAN. 30.   USG endorsement. "Respectfully forwarded to the Secretary of War."—ES, DNA, RG 94, Letters Received, 672M 1868. Written on an undated letter from William A. Carter, Fort Bridger, Utah Territory, to Bvt. Col. Henry A. Morrow, 36th Inf., Fort Bridger, requesting military protection for miners on the Sweetwater River.—ALS, *ibid.* On Jan. 28, Lt. Gen. William T. Sherman endorsed this letter. "Respectfully referred to the General Comdg the Army. The place herein indicated is Indian Country and if we Establish a Post there, the Indian Bureau will charge us with making war. We cannot prevent people going there in the numbers stated, and whatever is done should be by order of the President."—AES, *ibid.*

1868, JAN. 30.   Bvt. Maj. Gen. Daniel H. Rucker, act. q. m. gen., to USG. "Your note of this day relative to the reduction of pay of Saml D. Smith Fort Walla Walla, W. T., is received. Upon an examination of the Rolls of Brevet Lieut Col H. C. Hodges Chief Quartermaster Department of the Columbia for July 1867 it appears that Mr Smith was employed during the month of July at $100 per month—in charge of Government property at Walla Wall[a.] Also from his Rolls for August 1867, that the rate of pay of Mr Smith was reduced to $50—although no order or reason for this reduction is reported. I respectfully enclose a copy of a letter sent to Brevet Major General R Allen to day in relation to this subject."—LS, DNA, RG 92, Miscellaneous Letters Sent (Press).

1868, JAN. 30.   Bvt. Maj. Gen. John M. Schofield to USG. "Genl Barry is quite earnest in his desire to be relieved from all duty outside of the Artillery School, and says his duties as Sub-district commander accupy much time that ought to be devoted to the School. In deference to his wishes I am willing, if you deem it expedient, to relieve Genl Barry from command of the Sub-district; and place an other officer in command with Head Quarters at Norfolk. The Quartermasters depot for this department is at Fort Monroe and hence ought to be excepted from the operation of any order making that a separate post. With this exception there is no serious objection to the proposed change"—Copy, DLC-John M. Schofield. On Feb. 3, Maj. George K. Leet wrote to Schofield. "General Grant directs me to say in reply to your communication of the 30th ulto., that he has been of the opinion for some time past, that it would promote the interests of the Artillery School to have General Barry relieved from his duties as Commander of the Sub District. The General has refrained from suggesting this change however, fearing it might embarrass you in executing the reconstruction laws. As you now express your willingness to spare Gen. Barry, Gen Grant will be glad to see the change you propose effected."—Copies, DLC-USG, V, 47, 60; DNA, RG 108, Letters Sent.

1868, JAN. 31.   USG endorsement. "Respectfully returned to the Secretary of War—I approve the 2d section of Gen. Humphrey's Bill, and so much of the 1st section as provides for two principal musicians for the Battalion of Engineers, also the item of appropriation; but I do not think a Commissary Sergeant of a regiment of any arm of the service is required—" —Copies, DNA, RG 77, Letters and Reports; *ibid.*, RG 233, 42A–D1. Written on a letter of Jan. 9 from Brig. Gen. Andrew A. Humphreys, chief of engineers, to USG. "I have the honor to enclose herewith two sections of a proposed law, and an item of appropriation, upon which legislation is needed, for the service of the Battalion of Engineer Troops. . . ."—Copies, *ibid.*

1868, FEB. 1, 2:30 P.M.   To Mary K. Sullivan, Cumberland, Md. "If subpoenied I will have to go."—ALS (telegram sent), DNA, RG 107,

Telegrams Collected (Bound); telegram sent, *ibid.*; copies, *ibid.*, RG 108, Telegrams Sent; (dated Jan. 31) DLC-USG, V, 56.

1868, FEB. 3.   To AG. "Extend the leave of absence heretofore granted Brig. Gen. G. A. H. Blake, 1st U. S. Cav.y to the 1st of June 1868."— ALS, DNA, RG 94, Letters Received, 45A 1868. Probably on April 1, USG wrote to the AG. "The Adj. Gn. will please order Gn. Blake & Lt. Hall to accompany first batch of recruits to the Pacific Coast. If no recruits are going there put them under orders to join their regiments by July 1st /68"—AN (undated, received on April 1), *ibid.*, 137A 1868.

1868, FEB. 3.   To AG. "Please give Gn. Howard a list of officers of the Invalid Corps now on duty with their companies, to select from such officers as he may want to be detailed for duty in the Bureau of R. F & A. Make the detail he asks for being careful however to leave one officer to a company."— ALS, DNA, RG 94, Letters Received, 49A 1868.

1868, FEB. 3, 2:15 P.M.   To Maj. Gen. George H. Thomas. "Certainly— go and take such officers with you as you like. I regret that I cannot be with you."—ALS (telegram sent), DNA, RG 107, Telegrams Collected (Bound); telegram sent, *ibid.*; copies, *ibid.*, RG 108, Telegrams Sent; DLC-USG, V, 56. On the same day, Thomas, Louisville, had telegraphed to USG. "I respectfully request authority for myself and portion of my staff to be absent for a few days for the purpose of attending the meeting of the officers of the old army of the Cumberland, at Cincinnati on the sixth instant. The Head Quarters will be left in charge of competent hands"— Telegram received (at 1:40 P.M.), DNA, RG 107, Telegrams Collected (Bound); *ibid.*, RG 108, Telegrams Received; copies (sent by mail), *ibid.*, Letters Received; DLC-USG, V, 55.

1868, FEB. 4.   USG note. "Order Capt. Gageby, 27th Inf.y, to join his regiment at the expiration of his present leave of absence, or as soon thereafter as practicable. He is now at Johnstown Pa."—ANS, DNA, RG 94, Letters Received, 46A 1868.

1868, FEB. 4.   USG note. ". . . Wallach and Davenport to please send by the bearer a Box for myself and family for this evening . . ."—Parke-Bernet Galleries, Sale No. 1802, Jan. 28–29, 1958, p. 27. James W. Wallack, Jr., and Edward L. Davenport, managers of Wall's Opera House, presented Kate Reignolds in *Marie Antoinette.—National Intelligencer*, Feb. 4, 1868.

1868, FEB. 4.   Cassius M. Clay, U. S. minister, St. Petersburg, to USG. "Under pressure from Washington I have resigned my post of Minister here, to take effect on the first day of April next: as I desire to be present at the Republican Convention on the 20th of May: and cast my influence, however small, in your favor as the candidate of the Union party for President. As early as 1862, before the question was made in the Ud States, I took ground against the extinction of state sovereignty by rebellion. Mr Lincoln followed in the same views. I think now the Union party would have been stronger, and wounds of our war would have been healed sooner, if that position had been followed by the Republican policy. I for a long time hoped that President Johnson would have succeeded in carrying over the mass of Republicans to that theory. But having failed, whether through want of the proper temper, or from the inherent difficulties of events, I was not willing to follow him into the camp of the enemies of the union, and of those principles of Enlightened liberty, and Constitutional equality of rights, to which I had devoted, my fortune and life. The acknowledgement of the belligerent rights of the Confederacy by the proclamation of the blocade of the Southern ports (a great mistake of Mr Seward, which greatly strengthened the South at home and abroad,) gives color to the doctrines of the Radicals, and makes the Reconstruction policy at least plausible, as holding the South as conquered territory: and therefore absolutely under the controul of Congress, subject to like Constitutional restrictions as are applicable to other territory of the nation. Be this as it may, the life of a nation is the highest law: and it seems to me now that we have gone too far in that direction now to return with safety. *But I should desire to see all the whites of the South, free to vote.* The sooner the Union party returns to the *normal conditions of our Constitutional action the better.* The Freedman's bureau, the army (except as held in aid of the local civil law) should as soon as possible cease to exist in the South. They, the whites and Blacks, once readmitted into the Union should be as soon as possible left to themselves to organise and reorganise the constitutions and all the rights of states to suit themselves. Otherwise, it seems to me, we make the Southern disaffection by central domination *chronic*—a Poland, an Ireland, and a Hungary! Consistently with the safety of the Union, great magnanimity should be shown to the South—trusting to time to cure the wounds of terrible war. Next in importance to reconstruction is the currency and debt questions. The public faith must be kept, not only to the letter, but the spirit. As our population increases about one hundred per cent in every twenty two and one half years, and our wealth about four hundred per cent in the same time, we shall be four times as able to pay our bonds off twenty years hence as now. Prudence thus would dictate that we should be in no hurry to pay the principal: whilst at the same time a small portion of that principal should be paid off yearly for the moral effect. As to the currency we should return to a specie basis as soon as possible, without causing so much pressure as to favor repudiation among the tax-payers. A national paper currency equivalent to specie, and every where receivable alike would in itself, I think, more than repay us for all our pecuniary losses in the late war: not only by its financial facilities, but by its moral effect in consolidating our Union. Excuse me, my dear general, for the liberty I have taken in these suggestions. They will show you what a dispasionate looker-on, from out of the spere of party heat, thinks of the situation of our public affairs: From an aggregate of such hints, coming from many quarters, your good sense will suggest the true policy; which your patriotism will no doubt well insure in action."—ALS, USG 3.

1868, FEB. 6. William G. Moore, secretary to President Andrew Johnson, to USG. "The President directs me to request that you will inform him if Major General Meade has made application to be relieved from the command of the Third Military District."—ALS, DLC-Andrew Johnson. On the same day, USG endorsed this letter. "Respectfully returned to His Excellency, the President of the United States with the information that no request has been made by Maj. Gen. Meade, known at these Hd Qrs, to be relieved from duty as Commander of the 3d Mil. Dist."—AES, *ibid.*

1868, FEB. 6. "Col De Bar" to USG. "It suits all"—Telegram received (at 3:00 P.M.), DNA, RG 107, Telegrams Collected (Bound).

1868, FEB. 7. M. A. Shaffenburg, Washington, D. C., to USG. "I take the liberty to submit the following statement.—In the month of August 1867 I was recommended by the Post commander at Fort Reynolds Col. Ter. with and by the consent of the officers, then stationed at said Post, for the appointment of Post trader, agreeably to an order for Post commanders to designate the proper person for such appointment.—Simultaneously with notification of my recommendation having been forwarded, I was requested to move a stock of goods to said Post. After erecting such building, necessary to store such goods, then required by the command I took an assortment of goods to the Fort.—I carried on the business of Post trader for two months (& I have every reason to believe to the satisfaction of officers & men), when I received an order from Genl. Hancock, then commanding the Deptmt of Missouri, that Clough and Nichols were appointed Post traders for said Post & no other person in the capacity of Post trader would be permitted to remain on the reservation, which order I obeyed, by at once abandoning the reservation. In consideration of these facts, which have worked great loss & damage to me, I would most respectfully ask, that I be reinstated as Post trader at said Fort, or receive a like appointment for some one of the other Posts on the Plains.—In addition to my indorsement, already above mentioned, I would respectfully refer you to the Hon. E. G. Ross U. S. Senator from Kansas, Hon. G. S. Orth M. C. Indiana and Hon. G. M. Chilcott M. C. Colorado—"—ALS, DNA, RG 108, Letters Received. On Feb. 17, Bvt. Maj. Gen. Andrew J. Smith, Fort Leavenworth, endorsed this letter. "Respectfully returned to Bvt Lieut Col Geo. K. Leet. A. A. G Headqrs. of the Army, (thro Hdqrs. Mil. Div of the Mo) I respectfully recommend that Mr M. A. Shaffenburg be not appointed a Trader at Fort Reynolds or at any other post in this Department. Mr Shaffenburg obeyed, literally, Gen. Hancock's order to remove his goods from the reservation of Fort Reynolds, but not its spirit; he established a trading establishment immediately across the river on some unoccupied swamp land and continued to trade with the troops. There are other reasons, which it is not considered necessary to mention at this time, why Mr Shaffenburg should not be appointed a Trader. An investigation is now being had into the conduct of certain officers of the Army with reference to purchases and contracts made by the United States at Fort Reynolds, in which Mr Shaffenburg is understood to have been interested."—ES, *ibid.*

1868, FEB. 8.   To 2nd and 3rd Auditors. "This will be delivered to you by Capt. R. C. Rankin, late of the 7th Vol. Cavalry (Ohio), who wishes to settle unsettled accounts grown out of his services du[r]ing the rebellion, and the capture of his company papers by rebels troups. I have known Capt. Rankin from my boyhood, and also know personally of his services during the rebellion. I hope facilities will be given to him to settle his accounts while here and that he be furnished information how to proceed."—Quoted in R. C. Rankin newspaper article, Ripley, Ohio, July 27, 1885, unidentified clipping in DLC-August V. Kautz.

1868, FEB. 8.   Charles Ziegler, New Orleans, to USG. "I most respectfully apply to you General, that you may Issue an Order to the Millitary Authorites here, to allow the Body of Dr. Geo. S. Grinder Late of the. U. S. A. in Actif service who Diet November 25th 1867. with Yellow fever in this City, be Disentred and sent to his Heartbrocken Mother, who wishes to hav her Son near her, at her home in Creagorstown, Fredrick, County, Marryland."—ALS, DNA, RG 94, Letters Received, 37W 1868.

1868, FEB. 10.   To AG. "I would like to have Gn. French placed on duty either on the Retiring Board or elsewhere temporarily."—ALS, Northwestern University, Evanston, Ill.

1868, FEB. 11.   USG endorsement. "Respectfully referred to the Chief of Ordnance with recommendation that if the Department have these old guns on hand they be sold to the Oregon, Cal and Mexican steam ship Co."—ES, DNA, RG 156, Letters Received. Written on a telegram of Feb. 8 from Ben Holladay, San Francisco, to Bvt. Brig. Gen. Orville E. Babcock. "Obtain order to have delivered here by the Navy or Ordnance Department four (4) twelve (12) pounds long guns & two (2) twenty four (24) pounds Carronades, needed for the Steamer for the Mexican Government   Cannot be obtained here from private persons—"—Telegram received (at 10:10 P.M.), *ibid.*

1868, FEB. 11.   Governor Ambrose E. Burnside of R. I. to USG. "Please allow me to present to you my friend, Major Raymond H. Perry, who was an efficient and gallant officer during the late war, and has since done excellent service in the fifth military district, under General Sheridan, to whom he is well known. He is the son of Hon. James D. W. Perry, of this State, one of my oldest and best friends. Any kindness shown him will be remembered."—*SRC*, 41-2-234, pp. xxxiii, 256.

1868, FEB. 12.   To President Andrew Johnson. "I have the honor to return herewith Resolution of the Senate of the U. S. of February 4th, with copies of the papers in my custody bearing upon the subjects therein referred to."—LS, DNA, RG 46, Senate 40A–F2, Messages. USG transmitted papers concerning instructions given to Bvt. Maj. Gen. John Pope and Maj. Gen. George G. Meade, 3rd Military District.—See *SED*, 40-2-30.

1868, FEB. 12.   Benjamin Moran, secretary, U.S. legation, London, to USG. "Referring to the Note I had the honor to address to you on the 20 of December last under instructions from Mr Adams, I now inclose a continuation of the paper by Captain Ross, which I then sent at his desire to your address—"—Copy, DNA, RG 84, Great Britain, Miscellaneous Letters Sent.

1868, FEB. 12.   Edwards Pierrepont, New York City, to USG. "I expected to have seen you before this—The public matters in which you bore so conspicuous a part induce me to say, that you need no affidavits to make people believe you speak the truth—Your *real* friends were never so firm as now— *No one* doubts you—no matter what newspapers say when they have party ends to serve. You will be made President—I know you do not want, it, but you cannot refuse it"—ALS, USG 3.

1868, FEB. 13.   USG endorsement. "Respectfully forwarded to the Secy of War, with recommendation that the request of Mrs. Johnson be granted."— ES, DNA, RG 94, Letters Received, 17J 1868. Written on a letter of Feb. 4 from Mary E. Johnson, Fort Monroe, Va., to USG. "Hoping you will pardon the liberty I am taking in addressing you on the following and I hope I am not asking too much for you to give it your earnest consideration, I am the widow of the late William H Johnson who was 22 years in the U S Army,   He died at Black Creek, Florida in the year 1840, from the effect of wounds received during the Florida war   at his death I was left in a very destitute condition but up to the last few months have striven to support myself without asking assistance, but now I am unable to do anything for myself owing to sickness and old age,   I am 79 years of age and the I wished to ask you is to be allowed a ration for the remainder of my days, this is the first time I have ever appealed to the Government for aid and I hope that my request will be granted,   General Barry has kindly given me quarters inside the Fort for myself and daughter, and if you consider my request favorably I shall be enabled to pass the remainder of my days in comfort whereas no I am in absolute want; Enclosed you will find recommendation from General Nichols"—ALS, *ibid.* A letter of Feb. 11 from a different Mrs. Johnson, Washington, D. C., to USG requesting assistance in paying her rent is *ibid.*, 16J 1868.

1868, FEB. 14.   USG endorsement. "Respectfully forwarded to the Secy of War for his information."—ES, DNA, RG 94, Letters Received, 218M 1868. Written on a report of Jan. 16 by Maj. Robert M. Morris, 6th Cav., Buffalo Springs, Tex. "I have the honor to submit for the information of the Major Gen. Comdg. the facts (as near as I could ascertain) relative to a massacre which took place on Clear Creek on the 5th and 6th inst. by Indians, tribe unknown to me. On the evening of the 8th inst. Judge Wade and a citizen named Shannon reached this Post and informed me that a raid had been made upon the Settlement at Clear Creek, that they had killed or captured most of the settlers there, these persons were unable to tell me the course of the trail or even the general direction of it. The next morning I left with them for Montague, accompanied by Lieut. Bothwick 6th Cavalry, two non. commissioned officers and eight Privates, which town I reached that evening   I remained the following day and night: the information which I elicited was as follows. An uncertain number of Indians variously estimated at from 45 to 100, attacked the settlement on the 5th and 6th instant, killed & carried into captivity the following named. *Killed.* One man named Leatherwood. One man named Parkhill, One named Mowasco. One man named Fitzpatrick, man name unknown   One Woman Mrs. Fitzpatrick and a child named Chigog. *Carried into Captivity.* Four Women and 6 children. I left the detachment as a guard to Montague and its vicinity, with strict orders to the Sergeant (Sergeant Swift,) to repel any attack which might be made, and that if his small force was inadequate to compell all able bodied citizens to assist in the protection of their homes, the citizens professed to me their perfect willingness, to assist him in every way possible. I returned to this Post, and should have sent a party to attempt to intercept them, but, having heard from reliable information, that the greater part had passed out, and having but twenty four effective horses, I knew that it was useless, as they had five days the start of me from Clear Creek." —Copy (tabular material expanded), *ibid.*

1868, FEB. 14.   USG endorsement. "Respy. forwarded to the Secretary of War—It is respectfully recommended that the enclosed estimate by Genl. [Mea]de be referred to Congress for action with approval—"—Copy, DNA, RG 108, Register of Letters Received. Written on a letter of Feb. 10 from Maj. Gen. George G. Meade, Atlanta, to USG. "My attention has been called to the want of funds for executing the re-construction Laws in this District—Enclosed you will find an estimate from which you will see that at present there are outstanding unpaid liabilities accrueing prior to Dec 31. 67 amounting to $56.750.00/100. and that after paying the current and incidental expenses at this point for the month of January, there remains in the hands of the disbursing agent only the amount of $798.55. It is true

that there is in the deficiency Bill now before Congress an appropriation
for this District amounting to $97.000.00/100, but of this amount already
$56.750.00/100 are expended; leaving $40.250. for future demands—A
sum as far as I can judge totally inadequate—I have therefore directed the
Disbursing Agent to make an additional estimate for anticipated liabilities
up to June 30. 1868, and I find it will require the sum of $87.701 00/100
in addition to the $97.000 now proposed to be appropriated—to enable us
to pay off all debts, and have sufficient means to meet future wants—There
are many considerations that induce immediate action in this matter—The
last elections both in Alabama and Georgia have not yet been paid, and
some of the obstacles encountered in the recent election in alabama, where
in some counties not a single man relied on to carry on the election came
forward, is due in a great measure to Registrars Judges and Clerks of
election not having been paid for their services at the previous election. I
find also it has been the custom to charge to the Quartermasters Department many expenditures that in my judgement strictly speaking are legitimate charges against the Civil Service Fund—these expenditures are of
course made by the Military Authorities, but they unfairly swell the expenditures of the Army, and diminish the cost of Re-construction. These
items are principally for transportation of officers and men and for Military
Commissions. I have directed these items to be embraced in the estimate
and they form the bulk of the increased amount asked of Congress. I beg
you will give your immediate attention and influence to this important
matter as it is a great embarrasment in carrying out the laws to be without
funds, not only creating as I have stated dissatisfaction but in many instances proving an insurmountable obstacle."—Copy, Meade Papers, PHi.
See *HMD*, 40-2-123.

1868, FEB. 14.   To AG. "Please make the order heretofore published giv-
ing Bvt. Brig. Gn. Geo. B. Dandy Q. M. Sixty days leave of absence, from
~~Jan.y~~ Nov. 1st /67 date from March 1st 1868."—ALS, DNA, RG 94,
Letters Received, 63A 1868.

1868, FEB. 15.   USG endorsement. "Respectfully forwarded to the Secretary of War, with recommendation that these papers be submitted to the
Secretary of the Interior, for such action as he may deem necessary in the
case."—ES, DNA, RG 107, Letters Received from Bureaus. Written on a
letter of Dec. 22, 1867, from Maj. and Bvt. Col. Alexander Chambers,
Fort Randall, Dakota Territory, concerning a projected expedition of citizens from Yankton, Dakota Territory, into the Black Hills.—ALS, *ibid*. On
Feb. 3, 1868, Lt. Gen. William T. Sherman, Washington, D. C., wrote to
Bvt. Maj. Gen. Alfred H. Terry. "I have the honor to acknowledge the
receipt of your letter of January 28th, 1868, reporting that the people about
Yankton are on the point of organizing an expedition into the Indian coun-
try selected by the late Peace Commission for the exclusive use of the
Northern Indians, and asking instructions. You will please give public

notice that the project is forbidden, and if any person then persist in moving upon said district of country, or even go there to explore, or to travel across on the pretense of finding shorter and better roads, you will use force to prevent them. The whole question is now before Congress, and pending their action, you will take care that it does not become complicated by the action of any people whatsoever."—Copy, *ibid.*, RG 108, Letters Received. On May 13, U.S. Senator Alexander Ramsey of Minn. favorably endorsed to USG a letter of May 6 from P. B. Davy, Winona, Minn., to Ramsey. "I wrote you a few days Ago from Blue Earth City asking you to interest yourself in a Claim I hold against the Government, I again take the liberty to ask your assistance in a matter of the most vital importance—not only to myself, but also to the State of Minnesota—You are aware of my projected Expedition to the Northern Black Hills—which if successful (in my Opinion) would prove of incalculable benefit to the state of Minnesota by Establishing A route through Minnesota to Montana lessening the distance Over three hundred Miles Over the southern route now travelled—Also settling the Black Hills Country which is known to Abound in Mineral and pine timber—whose trade would naturally pass through Minnesota to the Eastern Markets—together with that of Montana—when this route is opened which it will be, this summer if my Expedition is permitted to proc[e]ed there—By the recent treaty with the Indians at Fort Laramie (though the Indian Peace Commission.) I Cannot learn that the Black Hills Country is sett apart as a reservation—in fact I know it was not the intention of the Commission to in Clude that country in the reservation—'at least'—Genl Sherman—So Expressed himself to the Hon M. K. Armstrong of Yankton D. T—at St Johns Iowa a short time ago—My expedition, now numbers hundreds and my desire is; to proceed peaceably into that Country—I ask no aid at the hands of the Government—and no assistance in the Event that I get into difficulty—By the Order (Enclosed) you see I am prohibited from Carrying out the object—As there are no Explanations with the order, I am at a loss to know—whether where the Commanding Officer of S—E—Dakota received his instructions from—and would respectfully Ask you to ascertain, and if it Emanates from Washington—to use your influence to have it recinded—The Expedition is now Enroute for Yankton from different portions of the Country—and on arrival will be greatly disappointed to find the Government—arrayed in opposition to their wishes—Many are preparing to accompany the Expedition destined to the Sweet water Mines— which country is now opened But, by the Conditions of the order, will be prevented from Crossing the Missouri River into the Indian Country— Please do what lays in your power—'Senator', to Assist me in this matter— And I shall be grateful toward you *whether successful or not* Please write Me at Yankton D. T."—AES and ALS, *ibid.*

1868, FEB. 15. USG endorsement. "Respectfully forwarded to the Secy of War for instructions"—ES, DNA, RG 107, Letters Received from Bureaus. Written on a letter of Feb. 3 from Samuel B. Reese, Union Pacific

Railroad Co., Cheyenne, Dakota Territory, to U.S. Representative Grenville M. Dodge of Iowa. "I apply to you to see if somethig cannot be done to keep men from building shanties and selling whiskey along the line of Road. Our ties and timber is in danger of being burned by drunken men who are intised into whiskey Ranches Robed of their mony and put out incensed at somebody. Cannot something be done to stop it and prevent its spread in the future. We want to build more than three hundred miles of road this year. This whiskey business unless stoped will be a serious drawback to the progress of the work   I go to Joliet for a few days   may go to N Y"—ALS, *ibid.* On Feb. 12, Bvt. Maj. Gen. Christopher C. Augur endorsed this letter. "Respectfully referred to the genl in chief for information—The Country referred to is ~~indian~~ undoubtedly 'indian county' though within the organized territory of Dakota. How far the military authorities may interfere with persons claiming to be settlers, but in truth mere vendors of liquors, is not settled by any law or orders within my knowledge. Similar questions are constantly arising, and it is important that military commanders shall have some competent decision as to what are their duties."—AES, *ibid.*

1868, FEB. 17.   To George W. Greene acknowledging "the first volume of the life and services of Gen (Nathaniel) Greene which you have done me the honor to contribute to my library. The services of General Greene in establishing a free government on this Continent which has cost us so much blood and treasure for the last five years to maintai[n], cannot be otherwise than interesting to a patriotic people now."—ADS Autographs, Catalogue No. 10 [*1987*], p. 9.

1868, FEB. 17.   Bvt. Lt. Col. George K. Leet endorsement. "Respectfully referred to the Adjutant General for compliance with the foregoing instructions of the President."—AES, DNA, RG 94, Letters Received, 32K 1868. Written on a letter of Feb. 8 from Francis P. Blair, Jr., to President Andrew Johnson. "On behalf of Capt James Kelley 34th U. S. Inft stationed at Columbus Mississippi I apply for a leave of absence for 4 months to take effect from the date of leaving his command at Columbus. Capt Kelley has very important private business which demands his personal attention. He is a friend of mine & I am very anxious to save him"—ALS, *ibid.* On Feb. 15, Johnson endorsed this letter. "RESPECTFULLY REFERRED TO the General Com'd'g, the Armies of the U. S., who will please grant Capt Kelley leave of absence for four (4) months, to take effect from the date of leaving his command."—ES, *ibid.*

1868, FEB. 17.   Bvt. Lt. Col. George K. Leet endorsement. "Respectfully referred to Bvt Maj. Gen. E Schriver, Inspector General."—AES, DNA, RG 107, Letters Received, H408 1867. Written on a letter of Feb. 1 from Elizabeth Irish (for Hannah Horsman), London, to USG. "In consequence of the Notice in the London Newspapers that all Claims to Property in the

South must be sent in before the 1st of January I wrote to you one the Subject on the 23rd and 26th of November last informing you that my late Husband Mr John Horsman died posessed of Property near Charleston Virginia and in Texas   I would feel extremely obliged if you would let me know if there has been anything decided upon in the matter   I beg you will pardon me for troubling you with another letter but I am so very anxious to have my late Husbands affairs settled and I am not in a position to advance money for Law Expenses to proceed against Mr Donnelly who has taken posession of my late Husbands Effects   he (Mr Donnelly) is a Clerk in the employ of Messr J. L Peters 50 North Fifth Street St Louis . . . Please address Mrs Hannah Horsman Post Office Burton Crescent Tavistock Square London"—ALS, *ibid.* On Nov. 23, 1867, Hannah Horsman had written to USG. ". . . I beg to give you Notice that I Claim as the Lawful Wife of Mr John Horsman the property Situate near Charleston Virginia and in Texas   My late Husband John Horsman died in St Louis Mo about October 1866   he had been Married to a Lady in America 8 years who died in the September previous to my Husband's death, a circumstance I knew nothing of until after his death   He bought a Farm near Charleston Virginia in 1860 and lived there until he was driven off in time of the War, I was informed he held Confederate Bonds at that time,   he went back after the War but could not collect any of his things together, . . ."—ALS, *ibid.* Horsman's letter of Nov. 26 to USG essentially duplicated her earlier letter.

1868, FEB. 17.   Bvt. Lt. Col. George K. Leet endorsement. "Respectfully referred to Brevet Major General A. C. Gillem, Comdg 4th Military District, for investigation and report."—AES, DNA, RG 94, Letters Received, 420M 1868. Written on a letter of Feb. 6 from Elias Harrell, Fayetteville, Ark., to USG. "Articles of Impeachment having been preferred against me in Feb. 1867, by the House of Representatives of the Ark. Legislature, I was notified to appear before the Senate, and answer the charges in March. I appeared and filed a plea to the Jurisdiction of the Senate, alleging that many of the members were inelligible under the Reconstruction act of Congress. The managers demurred to my plea, and argued, and the Senate unanimously decided that the reconstruction act was unconstitutional and void.—The Gen. Assembly then adjourned, (against my remonstrance) until July, and notified me to appear and answer on the 11, July, 1867, previous to that time Gen. Ord issued an order prohibiting, or forbidding said Legislature to re-assemble in July, that order was enforced, and the Gen. Assembly did not convene. I am of the opinion that at the time the Legislature was desolved by order of Gen. Ord, that all business before that body ceased to be of any force, and was void.—I applied to Gen. Ord, and to Gov. Murphy to be reinstated, or for some disposition to be made of the case. Gen. Ord informed me that no change would be made by him in the Judgship of the 8th Judicial Circuit, Ark., I received no answer from Gov. Murphy. I learned while at Little Rock in last month, that Gov. Murphy had referred the matter to Gen. Ord,—and that Gen. Ord had referred the matter back to Gov. Murphy. and Gov. Murphy refused to do any thing in the premises, and continues yet to hold me in suspension, and to recognize his appointee, William Story as Judge, under a commission to serve only during my suspension, and certainly I was, (if the law governed the case) relieved from impeachment the moment the court before whom the case was pending, ceased to exist. I solicit your attention to this short detail of facts.—If it is proper for you to re-instate me in the Judgship 8th Judicial Circuit, Ark, I hope you will do so at once. If you desire to see the Articles of Impeachment I will send you a copy, and answer. I desire to have a determination of the case. If I am to be continued a victim to rebel malice, and vituperation their charges sustained, only, by falsehood and base calumny, I wish to know it. If there is, or may be, any tribunal that will decide the case, I desire to be informed. I hope to hear from you soon, shall be pleased with any disposition that you may see fit to make of case."— ALS, *ibid.* On March 13, Governor Isaac Murphy of Ark. endorsed this letter. "Respectfully returned—with the following remarks—The statement of Judge Harrell is correct—The Governor refused to interfere because the Law Gave him no power—his duty is to enforce the Law not to make or interpret—The Legislature makes—the judiciary interprets   The appointment of Judg Story was made to continue until the impeachment '*was determined*'   See Goulds Digest page 595 sec 4   The Senate continued the case & in the mean time the Legislature is desolved by order of Gen Ord. was that, a determination of the impeachment? It seems to me that this is a judicial question for the determination of the courts—not of the executive— Judge Herral should have applied to the supreme court. If his view is right he would have been restored by Judgment of the court"—AES, *ibid.* On March 27, Bvt. Maj. Gen. Alvan C. Gillem, Vicksburg, endorsed this letter. "Respectfully forwarded to the *Adjutant General of the Army,* Washington *D C.* Attention is respectfully invited to endorsement hereupon of His Excellency Isaac Murphy Governor of Arkansas, of date March 13th 1868, in which I entirely concur."—ES, *ibid.*

1868, FEB. 18.   Bvt. Lt. Col. George K. Leet endorsement. "The Adjutant General will grant Lt. Wells permission to delay joining his regiment for one month from the 17th inst."—AES, DNA, RG 94, Letters Received, 82P 1868. Written on an unaddressed communication of President Andrew Johnson. "If, consistently with the interests of the service, General Grant can allow 1st Lieutenant Daniel T Wells, of the Eighth Infantry, one month's delay, from the 17th instant, within which to join his command I should be pleased to have the permission granted."—DS, *ibid.*

1868, FEB. 19.   USG endorsement. "Respectfully returned to the Secretary of War with recommendation that the Committees on Indian Affairs be furnished with copies of these papers."—ES, DNA, RG 94, Letters Received, 798P 1867. Written on a letter of Nov. 21, 1867, from Maj. Gen. Henry W. Halleck, San Francisco, to the AG transmitting a report of

Bvt. Lt. Col. Robert N. Scott concerning Indians near the boundary between Alaska and British Columbia.—ES, *ibid.* The enclosures are *ibid.*

1868, FEB. 19. Bvt. Maj. Gen. John Pope, Detroit, to USG. "I write you this unofficial letter as I prefer to learn your wishes on the subject of it without making any official application until I do—I wish very much to remove the HdQrs of this Dept to Milwaukee for many reasons—some of which you doubtless will understand—I find it impossible to get myself a house here & I find beside that the political atmosphere is not very different from that of Atlanta—Personally I would like above all things to remove to Atlanta and officially I see no reason why it should not be done—The lease of the public offices here are about to expire with no prospect of renewing them   The Chief Commissary of the Dept is already stationed in Chicago by orders from Army HeadQrs. & does the business of the Dept as well there as he could here—There remain here the Chief Q. M & Medical Director who could as easily do what they have to do here, at Milwaukee— I would make an official application to you but that I prefer to know your decision in this way—If there be any objection to taking the Chief Q. M from here (though I can imagine none) I can leave him & the Medical Director & take only the a. a. g—the business of this Dept is very small & by no means of a character that it could not be as well done in Milwaukee as here—At all events if you do not object I would like temporarily (for the Summer) to move to Milwaukee with my a. a. g. Will you please telegraph me what you decide about it"—ALS, DLC-Cyrus B. Comstock. On Feb. 24, Pope telegraphed to USG. "Please consider my letter of nineteenth (19th) canceled"—Telegram received (at 11:00 A.M.), DNA, RG 107, Telegrams Collected (Bound); *ibid.*, RG 108, Telegrams Received; copy, DLC-USG, V, 55.

1868, FEB. 19. John S. C. Abbott, New Haven, to USG. "For a long time I have been engaged in writing the Life of the present Emperor of France, a copy of which I hope you will allow me the privilege of sending to you when published; for I am sure that the character of Napoleon III. is not generally understood in this country. I have recently laid aside that work however to write the Life of General Grant. I have been led to this from the deep conviction that in the present state of our country that it is a matter of great importance that General Grant should receive the nomination to the Presidential chair, and should be elected by a triumphant majority. I am somewhat familiar with my theme; as I have written the History of the Civil War, and have given more than a hundred lectures, in our leading cities upon 'Grant And The War,' and have also many months ago written two brief sketches of his military career, for different publishers Our plan is to prepare a duodecimo book of three hundred pages, neatly executed, with several maps and three steel engravings. The book is to be published by B. B. Russell and Co of Boston and to be sold by subscription at one dollar and a half a copy. I wish to make it eminently readable, so that there may be an extensive demand for it. Avoiding the language of eulogy, I give a simple and, as far as possible, a glowing narrative of those great achievements which Providence has enabled General Grant to accomplish. I also make it my endeavor to render a just tribute to those of your subordinate officers who have so nobly cooperated with General Grant in his patriotic labors. For several weeks I have been at work upon this History with the concentration of all my energies. We hope to publish early in April   It has seemed to me that courtesy required that I should communicate these facts to you. I can not fear that the measure will meet with your disapproval. I am very deeply impressed with the conviction that Providence has placed General Grant and our country in such a position, that it is a matter of more moment than the human mind can well imagine, involving the interests of millions living, and millions yet unborn, that General Grant should be our next President. Upon this subject however I say nothing in the History. I simply give the record of his life, so shaping the narrative that intelligent men can not but see that God has endowed ~~him~~ General Grant with those qualities which in the present crisis, peculiarly qualify him for the Presidential Chair. If General Grant, through his friends can send me any documents, throwing light upon events which have occurred since the War, I shall be very grateful. There will be about 26 chapters. I am now writing the 10th having just finished the battle at Spottsylvania Court House. The first six chapters are already in print. It has never been my privilege to meet General Grant. But I feel as [we]ll acquainted with him and as strongly attached to him as if he had been my neighbor and friend for years."—ALS, USG 3.

1868, FEB. 20.   To AG. "Unless there is something not known of by me to prevent it direct Lt. Col. Sykes, Bvt. Maj. Gen. to report to Gn. Hancock to take command of 20th Inf.y, the regiment to which he is entitled to be promoted; and Capt. and Bvt. Col. H. W. Freedly to report for duty with the regiment to which his promotion carries him."—ALS, DNA, RG 94, Letters Received, 78A 1868.

1868, FEB. 20.   Maj. Gen. Oliver O. Howard to USG. "As one of the Trustees of the Peabody Fund, I have the honor to place before you the following facts, to wit: There is a school established upon Lookout Mountain by a christian gentlemen of N. Y. City, Mr. C. R. Robert. When you receive this letter, I hope you may endorse it over to the Agent, Dr. Sears, and I trust that the calling of his attention to the subject involved, may bring about some good. When I passed through the South, I visited this school, and found there very few scholars—few indeed of those that I wished expressly to give assistance to, namely the children of soldiers of our Army from Southern States, and the children of those who were driven from their homes, and had their property utterly destroyed on account of their adherance to the Government of the U. S. In many cases these children are so ostracised now, that they are driven from the established schools in the localities where they live. I went to Nashville and issued an order, directing that a limited number of such children be looked up, and transported to this school. My order had the desired effect, and an interest has grown out of it, which shows itself in Tenn., La., and the portions of N. C. that are not too distant from this institution. Mr. Robert has invested a sum of $40,000 or $50,000 in this enterprise, and has thus far supported the teachers and superintendents, and paid nearly all the expenses himself, the scholars that have paid or been able to pay anything, being small in numbers. The school is not, of course, limited to the class I have named but the flag of the country waves over the building, and therefore without a word being spoken, it necessarily draws from the loyally disposed. Now I can assist this school the coming year by the issue of rations to the destitute; that is, to those who are beneficiaries, and I can pay perhaps $2,000 from a fund that can be properly devoted to this subject. I understand Mr. Sears has been to this school. I wish he could give it a reinspection under present circumstances, and remember it with a view to the great good that it is accomplishing. Now if he can manage to devote a certain amount to these beneficiaries, say $50 each, and limit the number, say to 50 or 75 persons carefully selected, this sum to be granted for two years or longer, I believe results the most desirable will be produced, and by that time the school will become so well known, and so prosperous, that it will be self-supporting. I may not have suggested the proper mode of granting it assistance; but I will cooperate with your agent in assisting these poor refugees who are so worthy, and have been our true friends, and who are now deprived almost altogether of educational advantages for their children. This school in Lookout Mountain is the only one for refugees, for which I should ask assistance of this kind. Enclosed please find several letters from young people, who have been refused admittance for want of means to pay their expenses."—Copy, Howard Papers, MeB. See Martin Abbott, ed., "A Mountain School in Tennessee: Some Reconstruction Letters," *Tennessee Historical Quarterly*, XVII, 1 (March, 1958), 72–73. On July 24, 1867, Howard had written to USG introducing Christopher R. Robert and inviting USG to visit the school on Lookout Mountain.—LS (press), Howard Papers, MeB.

1868, FEB. 20.   Private Henry E. Vaness, Springfield, Mass., to USG. "I inlisted into the servace of the *U S* at Cincincinati Ohio on the 6th day of Nov last by Brevt Capt C. S. Newlin who Detaled me on his Recruting Party where I served fathfuly untill the 24th day of Dec when by special Orders from you our officer was closed & we wer ordered to Report to *Coln* Woods at Newport Bks Ky on the 26th for duty but on the 24th I was arrested on a charge of Larceny said to of ben commited in this state of which I am not Guilty   they brought me hiere without giving any notice of it to any officer or any one els   I wrote a line to Capt Newlin & paid a Police officer to deliver it but insted he broak it open and I hav it now   I told the officer Mr Peas of this City that he had no write to bring me away without notifying my officers to which he seid I was no soldier   he reported hiere that I was only a runer for a Recruting office   I hav served my Country honestly and fathfuly for many yeares and now all I ask is my Rights   if they had a right to bring me hiere as they did I will say no more but stand to it like a soldier   if not I apply to *you* the *Commander* of the *U. S. Army* to se that I hav my Rights   I wrote to Genl Butterfield who Refured it to the Comdg—officer of Newpt Bks Ky. from whom I hav not yet herd   Capt Newlin having gon to his Regt I now of no one but you to apply to for my Rights   I should be very thakful to heare from you as regards my Confinement Pay &c   by giving me the required instructions you will confer a great favor upon youre humble servt . . . pleas Direct in care of Frederic Bush"—ALS, DNA, RG 108, Letters Received. F. D. Bush, "Turnkey-Jail," endorsed the letter with a statement that Vaness, charged with stealing a horse, was imprisoned with *"evidence enough to convict sure—"*—AES, *ibid.*

1868, FEB. 21.   USG endorsement. "Respectfully forwarded to the Chairman of the Military Committee of the Senate with the recommendation that the promotion of N. H. Davis to be Lieut Colonel and Asst. Inspr. General be confirmed in accordance with the custom of the service—Col. Davis has been an efficient officer of the army for more than twenty years and is entitled to the promotion by seniority.—If there is anything to disqualify him for this promotion it can be made the subject of a Court Martial, and thus avoid punishment without trial—I will state, however, that I know nothing in his case to justify a Court of Inquiry much less a Court Martial—"—Copy, DNA, RG 108, Register of Letters Received. Written on a letter of the same day from Bvt. Col. Nelson H. Davis concerning congressional opposition to his confirmation.—*Ibid.*

1868, FEB. 24.   Sgt. Peter McKenna, 12th Inf., and thirteen others to USG. "We have the honor to report to you; that on yesterday the 23rd Inst, and this morning; we have *witnessed with grief, and mortification a repetition* of the outrages committed upon the *dead bodies of our Union Soldiers,* in this Department; which after being disinterred, are brot to the beach; (instead of the proper Wharf,) and *left below tide water*; and without any guard, or care whatever; have been permitted to float in and out upon the waves until in Some cases the boxes; the lids of which were only fastened with Six Small nails; were bursted open, and the bones lost in the Surf. This conduct has been repeated, and witnessed by the most casual observers. It is really Shocking, and repugnant to our most common humanity. In the name of our dead Soldiers; and common country we appeal to you for redress. . . . N. B. The above work refered to, is under the care of Employes of the Department Quarter Master, So we are informed Since the above was written."—DS, DNA, RG 108, Letters Received. Accompanying papers dispute the charges.

1868, FEB. 26.   USG endorsement. "Respectfully forwarded to the Secretary of War. Gen. Sherman's recommendation in Lt Col McCoy's case is approved. Bt Lt Col. McNutt is recommended for brevet of Colonel."—ES, DNA, RG 94, ACP, S229 CB 1868. Written on a letter of Feb. 21 from Lt. Gen. William T. Sherman, St. Louis, to Bvt. Brig. Gen. Cyrus B. Comstock. "Recent occurrences have drawn my attention to a subject that I ought not to have overlooked—One of my Aids, Lt. Col McCoy, has been with me from Shiloh till now, always, on every march and at every Battle, and has not a Brevet in the Regular Army, and only the lineal Rank of 2nd Lt 2nd Inf—& Bvt Lt Col. of Volunteers—Now as long as I live & hold my present commission I can protect him, but if I should die, or be legislated out; his interests might be jeopardised. He holds the position of Aid on my staff with Rank & pay of Lt Col which is as high as in my judgmt officers should be brevetted. Above that Rank promotion should be by selection out of the particular arm of service. But if you make up a list of Brevets, put in McCoys name for Brevets in the Regular Army, for 2nd Lieut up, to Lt Col, and for the dates & events, you can use—Shiloh—Vicksburg, Atlanta, and Bentonville, for the four grades. McNutt of the Ordnance Corps a class mate of mine, also wants the Brevet of Colonel if he cant get that of Brig Genl—I would, like to gratify him also."—ALS, *ibid.* On Feb. 25, Comstock wrote to Sherman. "Your letter recommending that McCoy be breveted Lt. Col. & McNutt Colonel is just received and the General has approved the brevets. As the Gn only sends papers thro. the Sec of War, it is possible that there may be delay in conferring the brevets, till the present complication is unravelled. Everything is quiet in town today & no new developments, though the story is that Thomas is to apply for a quo warranto, today."—ALS, DLC-William T. Sherman.

1868, FEB. 26.   To Maj. Gen. Henry W. Halleck. "Several citizens of Washington Territory, have telegraphed here that an effort is being made to have Fort Steilacoom, W. T. abandoned by the military. I do not suppose you have had any intention of giving up the occupation of that post, but write to learn your views in the matter. Do not abandon the post before reporting and receiving acquiescence from here."—Copies, DLC-USG, V, 47, 60; DNA, RG 108, Letters Sent; *ibid.*, RG 393, Dept. of the Columbia, Letters Received. On March 21, Halleck wrote a letter received at USG's hd. qrs. "Reports relative to re-garrisoning Fort Steilacoom—and the reason for his withdrawing the garrison—Has instructed Gen Rouseau in the matter—Acknowledges reciept of letter of Gen-in-chief of date Feb 26."—*Ibid.*, RG 108, Register of Letters Received.

1868, FEB. 27.   USG endorsement. "Respectfully forwarded to the Secretary of War."—ES, DNA, RG 94, Letters Received, 222M 1868. Written on a letter of Jan. 16 from Maj. Henry Douglass, 3rd Inf., Fort Dodge, Kan., to Bvt. Brig. Gen. Chauncey McKeever. "I have the honor to report that a Govt. train loaded with stores to Fort Lyon and Ft Reynolds, sent out by Major Inman Chief Quartermaster District, stopped at Cimmaron Crossing on the 12th instant and was visited by Indians, who said they were on a war party against the Utes   The statement of the Wagon Master, Frank Origon, is to the effect that the Indians drove the teamsters from their fire by presenting their revolvers and ordering them to leave, they 'went through' the wagons, and, if any man tried to prevent them, they pointed their revolvers at him—they took the rations of the men, leaving them but little. The Wagon Master said that the Indians called themselves Cheyennes. The Agent of Stage Co, who corroborated the statement of wagon Master, says that the Indians visited the Ranche at Cimmaron Crossing and being noisy and threatening they contrived to get them out of it and closed the door. The Indians (through a Mexican Interpreter) said that if they were not allowed to enter the Ranche they would fight,   Mr Wright, proprietor of the Ranche, told them that if they (the Indians) wanted to fight, he was ready for them. They then went to the train and, to use his words 'went through' it. They staid 24 hours and then left going up the river. The Agent said the Indians called themselves Arrapahoes. I respectfully state that I re-rationed the train for 10 days and sent an escort of one N. C. Officer and fifteen men to guard the train as far as Fort Lyon, with instructions to act purely on the defensive; but not to allow molestation on the part of Indians in any manner whatever. The Wagon Master says that the number of Indians who assumed this hostile attitude was 25. His own men were unarmed."—Copy, *ibid.*

1868, MARCH 2.   USG endorsement. "Respectfully forwarded to the Secretary of War."—ES, DNA, RG 94, Letters Received, 123C 1868. Written on a letter of Feb. 18 from Lt. Col. and Bvt. Brig. Gen. James H. Carleton, 4th Cav., New York City, to Bvt. Maj. Gen. Lorenzo Thomas. "I beg through you to call the especial attention of the General-in-chief and of the War Department to recommendations made to the President by the Indian Peace Commissioners in their Report dated the 7th ultimo, and published by the House of Representatives, marked 'Ex. Doc. No. 97.' The recommendations to which I refer are numbered 9. and 11. and are to be seen on page 22. of that Report. They relate to the removal of the Navajo tribe of Indians from their present position at the Bosque Redondo to some point further east. The military authorities are well aware that I have had great experience with that tribe, and that I necessarily know somewhat of their temper. I made or rather, continued war upon them and sent all who surrendered as well as all who were captured from the fastnesses of their native country to the point on the open plains where they now are. This was done after nearly two centuries of almost continued war with them waged under the Spanish, the Mexican and the United States governments. They were promised that the Reservation at the Bosque Redondo should be their home. If you will send for the Report of the *Congressional* Committee, you will see the printed reports of all that was promised to them. Little by little they have become partially weaned of the love for their ancient homes in the mountains—and have begun to regard their new location as their home for the future. At the Bosque Redondo a great many Navajo children have been born who of course have no knowledge and consequently no longing for the old Navajo Country; whilst at the same time aged Navajoes have died; and thus gradually comes about a change in the tribe looking towards a time when they will be completely reconciled to live east of the Rio Grande. In my opinion it would be acting in bad faith to that very interesting people to move them again. For the present, at least, to attempt to do so would result in their scattering by detail, until you would find them nearly all back again in their native country. Then you would be sure to have another protracted war which will cost millions of money, to say nothing of the renewed murdering and robbing of the inhabitants of New Mexico, which would certainly at once take place. Test the cost of the wars with this tribe for the last twenty years, to say nothing of the acts of violence and rapine which they have committed on the people—and make a comparison of that cost with what it costs to feed these Indians—and you will be sure to see that what I have repeatedly said—'*you can feed them for one fourth of what it will cost to fight them*'—is true, and easily proved to be so by the logic of figures. Many contend that they should be removed and placed upon a Reservation in the Old Navajo Country! There is no *one* piece of irrigable land in that country for this tribe. Even if there were, you could not keep them upon it. They would escape into the neighboring mountains—and soon be back to their ancient haunts, and to their accustomed business of killing the people and running off their stock. If you will see my testimony before the Congressional committee, you will see in full my reasons why they should not go back to *that* country to say the least. The increased cost of transportation in supplying them in that country would alone feed them where they are. It is true, that *at* the Bosque Redondo, wood for fuel is scarce: but *up* the river it is abundant;—and in the summer-time, the Indians should be taught to cut and ~~run~~ float down to the Reservation a years supply. This can *easily be done.* It is also true that at that place good land and a plenty of water are found—sufficient in all respects for the wants of the whole tribe. These you cannot find on any unclaimed lands in New Mexico at any other point. It would be well to have this very serious matter duly considered and weighed before any steps are taken looking to any removal of this powerful tribe. General Kit Carson who served with me in New Mexico, is now in Washington. I am sure if this letter is read to him, that he will agree entirely with my views in the premises. I have felt it to be my duty to give *the* War Department my ~~thoughts~~ thoughts on this subject."—ALS, *ibid.*

1868, MARCH 3.   USG endorsement. "Respectfully refered to Maj. Gn. G. H. Thomas for investigation and report. If thought advisable release the prisoner from confinement until authorized to discharge or restore him to duty."—AES, DNA, RG 108, Letters Received. Written on a letter of Feb.

15 from William Parker, Wenona, Ill., to Col. R. Plumb. "With reference
to the case of Angelo Welles, who is now confined in the Guard house of the
45th infantry Veteran reserve corps at Nashville as a Deserter I will state
the following facts as furnished me by his Mother   1st He claims entire
innocence of ever enlisting, but that he was simply a clerk   2d He claims
that he was arrested by a man named Taggart of Tonica Ill. through
Malice, to prevent his Marriage. 3d He and his father were both prisoners
at Andersonville, at which place his father died and he reached home with
his health very much impaired, and he is not now able to do a soldiers duty
4th His Mother is now a widow and depends on him for a portion of her
support. 5th He served four years in the volunter army during the war
Under all the circumstances I think if the matter is presented to the proper
parties, that an order can be procured for his release, and you will confer
a great favor on the widow, who is almost heartbroken, and a betrothed in
the same state of feeling, if you will present the matter and urge his immediate discharge   I enclose you a letter from Mrs W. written to the Captain
of his company which you are at liberty to show or not, as you think best"—
ALS, *ibid.* The letter returned with an endorsement stating that Private
Angelo P. Wells, 45th Inf., had "deserted from confinement" on March
3.—ES, *ibid.*

1868, MARCH 4.   Private Charles Bohm, 6th Inf., Fort Macon, N. C., to
USG. "Hoping that you will excuse my whriting to you y take the liberty of
stating my case to you. I wars tried before a General Court martial at
Charleston S. C. on the 5th day of March 1867 and sentenced for 2 jears
hard labor to this place. I have a Mother over sixty jears old to support, y
am her only son and so she has no help from any body. I serve during the
war unter your command in the twenty-fourth Armychops and be willen
and take my oath to do the same again and to defend you so long as there
is a drop of blood in my body. I am in confinment now twelve (12) months.
In stating to you this foue lines y humbly pray to you for pardon or remit-
tance of my sentences and you will oblige myself and my sickly and helpless mother. Hoping to heret from you soon . . ."—ALS, DNA, RG 108,
Letters Received. On March 27, Judge Advocate Gen. Joseph Holt endorsed this letter. "Respectfully returned to Gen. U. S. Grant commanding
the armies of the United States with report that it appears from the record
of private Bohn's trial, that he pleaded guilty to 'conduct prejudicial to
good order and military discipline', and was sentenced to be dishonorably
discharged with loss of all pay and allowances, and to be confined at hard
labor for two years. He has been imprisoned under the sentence a little
more than a year. He represents that he has an aged mother to support, who
is sick and helpless; and prays for pardon. His offence consisted in forging
the name of the Qr. Mr. Sergeant, Shaar, of his Company, to an order on a
firm in Columbia, S. C. by means of which he obtained groceries to the
value of five dollars. His present story of a destitute mother is received
with distrust, as upon his trial, he made no effort to influence the court in

mitigation of punishment by any statement whatever. No reason appears why his sentence should not be fully enforced."—ES, *ibid.*

1868, MARCH 5. USG endorsement. "Respectfully returned to the Secy of War with recommendation that Genl Dodge's request be granted"— Copy, DLC-USG, V, 44. Written on a letter of Feb. 24 from U.S. Representative Grenville M. Dodge of Iowa, Washington, D. C., "requesting that an order be issued, allowing the Co. to enter upon that porition of the Mil Reservation at Fort Sanders, selected for the depot."—*Ibid.*

1868, MARCH 5. USG endorsement. "Respectfully forwarded to the Judge Advocate General with the recommendation that Col. Merrill be appointed Judge Advocate vice Montgomery resigned."—AES, DNA, RG 94, ACP, M103 CB 1863. Written on a letter of Feb. 28 from Capt. and Bvt. Lt. Col. Lewis Merrill, 2nd Cav., Omaha, to Bvt. Maj. Gen. John A. Rawlins. "I have the honor to apply to be appointed Judge Advocate, with the rank of Major. I have heard that a vacancy has occurred in that Department, by the resignation of Major Montgomery. I beg to call attention to the recommendations which have heretofore been made in my case, when applying for appointment to the Inspector Generals Dept."—LS, *ibid.* On June 29, USG wrote to Secretary of War John M. Schofield. "I have the honor to respectfully recommend that Brevt. Lieut-Colonel Lewis Merrill, Captain 2d U. S. Cavalry, be appointed Colonel by brevet in the U S Army for gallant and meritorious services during the war, to rank from March 13th 1865."—LS, *ibid.*, Treasure Room.

1868, MARCH 5. Lt. Gen. William T. Sherman to USG. "The Bearer of this Lt Howgate now of the 20. U. S. Infantry, formerly of the Volunteer Army, writes me that he proposes to write a history of the Services of the Signal Corps of which he was formerly a member, and wants access to the necessary public Records. I commend him to your notice, and that you give him such facilities as consist with the Rules of your office."—ALS, DNA, RG 94, Letters Received, 538S 1868. On March 19, Bvt. Brig. Gen. Albert J. Myer, chief signal officer, wrote to USG. "Second Lieutenant H. W. Howgate, 20th U. S. Infantry, has applied to me for facilities to aid him in compiling the Service of the Signal Corps during the war, and he brings to me letters favoring his plans from Generals Thomas and Sherman. The compilation is one which ought to be made, and will be of interest and of value to the general Service of the Army. With the view of giving Lieut. Howgate an opportunity to collect material for his work, I recommend that leave of absence for Sixty days be granted him. Lieut. Howgate's address is,—Romeo, Macomb Co, Michigan."—LS, *ibid.*, 191S 1868.

1868, MARCH 5. "Officers and friends," New Orleans, to USG. "The fireman of this City, whom nine tenths are Ex Rebel officers and Soldiers of the late defunct Rebel Army, had their Anual (pow wow) or Cebration yesterday, they halted in front of our Genl Hancocks head Qrs. and cheered him three times. And then Sang this burlesque, which pleased no officer present only our Comdg General. If there cannot be a Stop put to Such indecency and disloyalty, as is now in vogue and constantly on the increase, we the Subordinate officers on duty at Head Qrs and elswhere in this city will in a body, ask to be transfered to other fields of duty, and if our request is not complied with, Self respect will compel us to resign our Commissions in the US Army, these Genl Grant, are humiliating facts, and facts only—"—AL, USG 3. Written on the reverse of a printed "Democratic Campaign Song!" See William C. Carroll to U.S. Representative Elihu B. Washburne, March 6, DLC-Elihu B. Washburne.

1868, MARCH 6. President Andrew Johnson endorsement. "Referred to General Grant, Commanding the Army of the U. S., for attention."—Copy, DNA, RG 94, Letters Received, 495M 1868. Written on a letter of March 5 from Secretary of the Interior Orville H. Browning to Johnson. "I have the honor to transmit herewith a copy of a communication dated the 4th instant, from the Commissioner of Indian Affairs, and copies of letters enclosed therein, from Thomas Murphy, Supt. of Indian Affairs, and I. L Butterfield, a licensed trader with the Arapahoe and Cheyenne Indians, in relation to whiskey being furnished to members of said tribes, by parties at Fort Dodge, Kansas. I respectfully request that the attention of the Military authorities may be called to the subject and proper measures adopted to suppress the traffic in liquor, which is said to be carried on from that Fort."—Copy, *ibid.* On April 25, USG endorsed this letter. "Respectfully forwarded to the Secretary of War, inviting attention to Major Douglas' report, and Gen. Sheridan's endorsement dated 13th Ap. '68."—ES, *ibid.*

1868, MARCH 10. USG endorsement. "Respectfully forwarded to the Secretary of War. The recommendation of the Judge Advocate General is concurred in and it is further recommended that Major Elderkin be ordered to resume his duties at Richmond, Va."—ES, DNA, RG 94, Letters Received, 1823M 1867. Detached from accompanying papers. On March 11, Bvt. Maj. Gen. John M. Schofield, Richmond, wrote to USG. "If Brevet Majo[r] Wm A Elderkin C. S. i[s] exhonerated by the Court of Inquiry, recently appointed to investigate his case, I respectfully recommend that he be restored to his former position of Chief Commissary of this Department. I make this recommendation solely as an act of justice to Maj Elderkin, he having been relieved from duty here solely for the purpose, as I understand, of enabling him to appear before the Court of Inquiry. Lt. Col. Penrose, who is an excellent and very acceptable staff officer, does not wish to be r[eg]arded as standing in [t]he way of Maj Elderkins restoration to his former position. Both of these officers are equally and entirely acceptable to me."—ALS, *ibid.* On March 12, USG endorsed this letter. "Respectfully forwarded to the Secretary of War, approved. Attention is invited to my endorsement of March 10 /68 in this case."—ES, *ibid.*

1868, MARCH 10.   Maj. Gen. Oliver O. Howard to USG. "A scout I sent
into Virginia at your request reports as follows: Mosby lives at Warrenton—his farm, four miles from Warrenton in the mountains—colored family one mile from farm reports that Mosby has sent up a number of horses—
has a quantity of saddles and some small-arms at the farm. Mosby's men
have been trying to buy up guns wherever they can. The scout saw a young
man in a cloth factory at Buckland, ~~Fauquier~~ Prince William County, who
had a gun. He saw one of Mosby's men trying to buy the gun—three persons came to buy the same gun—seven men came into Buckland, all with
muskets in their hands. Mosby sent word to a man at this place to be ready
to report at a moments warning. Mosby tried to enlist another young man
named John Bayse, who lives near Buckland; tried to get him to put Mrs
Chappel and her son out of the way. This the young man utterly refused to
do, and he would not join his band. Mosby declares he intends to prevent
'all d—d niggars and yankees' from reenforcing the friends of Congress, if
any trouble should occur at Washington   At New Baltimore Mosby made
the threatening speech reported some days ago. Some thirty or forty emigrants—Irish mostly—have come to Warrenton recently; said to be Mosby's
recruits, from New York. Scout saw four who go under the name of Mosby's emigrants. A man by the name of Riley, from New York, lately bought
a farm near Warrenton; is riding day and night, visiting rebels, and is
saying he will soon get the colored people out of there. Mosby came to
Washington on Thursday last to see how men were going to act there. He
is just now in Leesburg. Scout visited a Union League. Colored men think
Mosby is reorganizing his command. His men say colored men shall not
vote   The foregoing statements are corroborated by a letter from Buckland of a confidential character. The writer says they have a goodly force
of loyal colored men; and thinks that all that would be necessary to head off
Mosby, would be to arrest him for breaking his parole if possible, and give
them a commissioned officer with a few soldiers, as a nucleus around which
the loyal could rally. I think Mrs Chappel, her son, and Mr. O. C. Nichols,
can be relied on for information, though they are a little exposed in the
midst of so many unscrupulous men. The above statements are all I have
been able to gather."—LS, DNA, RG 108, Letters Received. On March 16,
2nd Lt. and Bvt. Capt. William V. Richards, 11th Inf., Warrenton, Va.,
wrote to Bvt. Col. Samuel F. Chalfin. "I have the honor to report that I
arrived at this place with my command at 4.30 P M March 13th, and immediately took possession of and finally rented a building known as the 'Old
Episcopal Church', a delapidated structure used in part by negro families
Having quartered my command—I instantly proceeded to carry out the instructions of the Bvt Maj Genl Comdg. I have carried on my investigation
to my entire satisfaction and respectfully report the same to the Comdg
Genl for his information. Immediately on my arrival in town I met and was
introduced to Mosbey. He said 'I see you have some troops with you. I hope
Forneys article about me is not the cause of your being sent here'   I told

him I was sent here to preserve quiet between [t]he whites and blacks, which was readily received from the fact that on last Sunday night there had been rather a serious disturbance between a few drunken white men and some negroes. I noticed Mosbey looked disturbed, and laughingly remarked it to the gentleman, (Mr James a very highly respectable gentleman whom I had picked up an acquaintance with on the cars, and who resides here)   he Said 'it is not because you are here but because the Col has got a very sick daughter and he had sent for a eCatholic Priest and expected him on this train, but was disappointed.' I made some cautious and incidental enquiries from Mr James as to the business of Mosbey and drew out of him without exciting suspicion his 'Mosbeys' late movements. I jokeingly remarked that at Gordonsville some citizen had remarked that we were sent here to look after Mosbey and to prevent his raising a band of men to to recommence hostilities.   he laughed at the idea and said there was no more peaceablefull man citizen in our midst at present than Col Mosbey, and that the first that any of the people here ever heard of this thing was from the 'Washington Chronicle. Not knowing my man I made allowance for his statements.   he did most of the talking and I did not suffer myself to be influenced one way or the other by them. I next met a negro-teacher named mMorse, a white man from Massachusetts whom I found to be extremely Radical, a member of the Loyal League, and a man very active in securing any information against the white people here. I examined him critically on the Subject of Mosbey, and found that he knew nothing of the Charges against him, except what he saw in the Chronicle, and the Scout whom the Govt sent here had given him instructions to to watch Mosbey and report anything that might go to corroborate the rumor about him. I found from Morse that the Scout had told him that he the Scout had been unable to find out anything more to lead to suspicion. I have sent reliable negroes to the farm spoken of in the communication given me, and find from the negroes on the place, that there have been no horses collected on it, no saddles nor has Mosbey been there much himself. I also met here a Merchant named Patterson, who was formerly in the Union Armey, and is now in business here.   this man is very intelligent & keen very hostile to the people down here but for the sake of his business keeps quiet. IIe is young and well acquainted with all the young men in the town. He came to me voluntarily to inform me in regard to certain people here. I guardedly examined him as to Mosbey but he was positive that he was doing nothing overtly or covertly. I placed more reliance on this mans knowledge than any I have met, as from the mans character and association I am sure he would know if any thing were going on. I made careful enquiries as to the importation of foreigners or strangers to this place, and find that Mosbey is the agent of the Emigration Society here: that he has lately secured four Scotchmen to work for Governor Smith. These Scotchmen are the ones that had the row with the negroes on the Street Sunday night. And these are all the men who have come here under the auspices of Mosbey. Mosbey passed through Washington on his way to Baltimore on professional business three weeks ago: he remained in

Baltimore seven days, but except that time I learn he has been here all the time for some months, quietly practicing the profession of the Law. Lieut Vinal arrived here last night   we conferred together, and both came to the conclusion that this rumor was an entire canard. No one here seems to have suspected any such thing nor had they ever heard of it until they saw it in the Chronicle. I am perfectly satisfied that the rumor did not start from here. That Mosbey is bitter in his feelings I have no doubt. Nor have I any doubt that he sometimes makes hostile remarks but I can get no one to repeat any that he ever did make. In my judgement, there is not one iota of cause to suspect any hostile demonstration from him   The parties named in your letter of instructions to me do not live here, but I have ~~not~~ learned who they are. Mr Nichols or Nicholas, is a mail carrier from some point on the O & A R. R to Buckland   Mrs Chappel has been a teacher of negroes, and is not particularly admired nor does she particularly admired the people with whom she resides   Her son is a young fellow sharing his mothers antipathies. I have no doubt some young man in their neighborhood has told them he was 'going to fight with Mosbey'   In fact I am so informed, and that their suspicion and this rumor started from that   There are residing in this place rather an unusually large number of young maen for so small a town. In drunken ~~rebels~~ revels they some times get abusive but as far as I can ~~get~~ learn the law is rigorously administered and justice secured to both classes   The colored people here have for advisors men of very weak calibre and no judgement. I refer to Northern white men sent here to teach and influence them   The Loyal League embraces nearly all the negroes of the place, and the white people also have a political organization which I imagine is pretty extensive. In conclusion I would say that law and order seems prevail that as far as I can learn by observation the feeling between the races is in the main amicable infinitely better than the feeling exhibited in Richmond, and that the troubles that do occur are attributable to drunken broils but their occurrence are not frequent. Lieut Vinal the Military Commissioner of this Division concurs with me in this opinion"—Copy, *ibid.*

1868, MARCH 10.   William E. Chandler and Edward H. Rollins, Concord, N. H., to USG. "The Republicans of New Hampshire, by a triumphant majority of over four thousand, demand that you shall be nominated and elected to the Presidency, in order that reconstruction may be achieved on a loyal basis, and peace and prosperity secured to the country."—*National Intelligencer*, March 13, 1868.

1868, MARCH 11.   USG endorsement. "Refered to Lt. Gn. Sherman."—AES, DNA, RG 108, Letters Received. Written on a letter of Feb. 20 from Private Charles King, 13th Inf., Camp Cooke, Montana Territory, to USG. "It is not until the proper channel has been obstructed, through which memorials and petitions should pass in transit to superiors; that your humble servant deigns to thus informally Communicate his letter of grevences— Conceiving then; 'no undue temerity in the motive which prompts this appeal, I, would most respectfully ask the Commanding General, to restore my citizenship; by virtue of expiration of term of enlistment,—notwithstanding I, am in durance, pending sentence for a trivial offense and one which I, have fully attoned for by long previous Confinement"—ALS, *ibid*. King had been convicted of desertion.

1868, MARCH 12.   Maj. Gen. Oliver O. Howard to USG. "Enclosed please find the information that I referred to this morning"—LS (press), Howard Papers, MeB.

1868, MARCH 12.   Frederick Sawyer, Charleston, S. C., to USG. "The State Nominating Convention have expressed their preference for General Grant as President"—Telegram received (at 11:00 A.M.), DNA, RG 107, Telegrams Collected (Bound).

1868, MARCH 13.   USG endorsement. "Respectfully forwarded to the Secretary of War, with the request that these papers be submitted to proper Committee of Congress."—ES, DNA, RG 108, Letters Received. Written on a letter of March 4 from Lt. Gen. William T. Sherman, St. Louis, to USG. "Several gentlemen of this city, personally known to both of us, interested in the Union Pacific Railway, Eastern Division, have frequently spoken to me and have now addressed me a letter, which I enclose herewith, in which they virtually ask our assistance in their efforts to extend their Road westward to a point where it will reach timber and coal, and where their Road will be of additional military advantage to us. You probably remember that, by the first charter of the Pacific Road, it was designed for this Branch to start from the State line near Kansas City, to follow the main valley of the Kansas River to the mouth of the Republican Fork (Fort Riley), and up that Fork to a point in its valley abreast of Fort Kearney, and thence to make a junction with the other branch of the Pacific Road in the Valley of the Platte at the 100th meridian. Subsequently the route was changed, with the consent of Congress, and the Directors were allowed to build their road up the Smoky Hill Fork; since which time it has in a measure ceased to be considered as a feeder or branch of the Omaha Pacific Road, and has become a separate or independent Road altogether. By the terms of the original act or charter, this Company receives $16,000 per mile of road *finished*, and when the location was changed from the Republican to the Smoky Hill, no increase of subsidy was made, so that this subsidy will cease to be paid, when the extension amounts in distance to the length of the line originally provided for. This Road is now finished 335 miles out from Kansas City, and the Company calculate that their subsidy will enable them to reach Fort Wallace, which is about fifty miles beyond their present terminus (Coyote). Without the aid of additional subsidy the Road will however stop at Fort Wallace, which is in the midst of that wide tract of prairie, devoid of wood, coal and everything useful except buffalograss. Ultimately, the Company designs to build this road, via New Mexico to California, substantially along the 35th parallel or Whipple Route, but in the present financial condition of the country, they hardly expect Congress at this time to give them the same subsidy which has been secured by the Main Omaha Road. Still, to them and to us, the termination at Fort Wallace will be very awkward, because the point is simply nowhere, being a mere naked spot in a limitless wilderness. It seems that the Company has secured iron and materials to build during this year a couple hundred of miles, if they can only obtain from Congress a subsidy of $16,000 per mile for, say, 250 miles beyond Fort Wallace. At the Cheyenne Wells 40 miles west of Fort Wallace, the proposition now is to branch; one Road to go to Cedar Point, 100 miles west towards Denver, where are reported to exist beds of coal, and considerable pine and cedar wood; the other branch to go in the direction of New Mexico to Fort Lyon, 70 miles southwest of Cheyenne Wells. All I need say is that the completion of this Road during the present year to Fort Lyon would be a most important event to the military interests of that frontier, and the completion of the other branch to coal and wood would also be most important to all the interests along the Valley of the Smoky Hill, chiefly so to us, who have to guard that line, and to provide for the wants of the necessary garrisons. It seems to me that we can with great propriety recommend to Congress at its present session to extend their subsidy to this Company at the present rate for 250 miles more, the aggregate being $4,000,000, in bonds. This Road is a military necessity and will very much stimulate the settlement of that region of our public domain. I therefore simply transmit to you the letter in question signed by Jno. D. Perry, President, with the foregoing remarks, and the expression of my opinion that this Road is in most competent hands. I believe the Company to be both able and willing to faithfully execute any contract or obligation they may make with the Government."—LS, *ibid*. The enclosure is *ibid.*; *HED*, 40-2-222.

On April 27, 1866, Sherman had written to U.S. Senator John Sherman of Ohio. "The Railroads now in course of construction from Kansas City and Omaha to the westward necessarily are rivals for Governmt aid and patronage. Present Laws seem to contemplate their coming together on the 100th Parallel of Longitude, after which I understand Governmt aid will be given *only* to one Road. In my judgmt the Roads will not come together till they reach the Rocky Mountains on the parallel of Denver, and even then new discoveries and new interests may force them to continue on separate Routes. I know that our Military interests would justify both routes so long as private parties are willing to give their money and work to the Enterprise. The Road from Omaha in my judgmt will never get to the South of the Platte, and the one from Kansas should, and must keep straight up the Smoky hill. No good could result from forcing this Road up the Republican Fork to make a junction on the 100th Parallel. I understand that new legislation in Congress will be necessary, and some modifications as to time. I think you will do right to favor both roads, Equally as long as they are managed so as to increase the chances of making 'westing' leaving the matter of their uniting to be determined by new facts and interests as they arise. I have watched the progress well as we have so large an interest, and am satisfied that as much progress has been made as possible—Mr Shoemaker in charge of the Construction of the Kansas River line, is a man of great experience and undoubted ability. I wish you to favor the companies all you can and leave them to choose the locations most to their private interest, the Governmt being only interested to have the Roads make as much to the West as possible, and in as short time as the work can be well done."—ALS, DLC-Andrew Johnson. On June 30, USG endorsed this letter. "I most heartily concur in the views expressed by Gn. Sherman as to the importance of the Smoky Hill route for a Pacific railroad. It give between two and three hundred miles more of road in communicating with N. Mexico and materially shortens the distance from St. Louis to the Pacific." —AES, *ibid.*

1868, MARCH 14. Kate Shaw, Ocean View, Calif., to USG. "I know from the many and arduous duties that you have to perform, that your time is fully occupied and every moment of value to you, yet do I respectfully ask a few minutes for the consideration of the following letter. I am entirely ignorant whether I use such language as I should or not but you will certainly pardon me when you know that I am but a young girl—and that I have undertaken this business without the knowledge of anyone. I knew of no friends or acquaintances to whom I could apply with the least hope of success—therefore, I must of necessity come to a stranger and, General Grant, hearing of you as a good, kind gentleman, I have taken the liberty of applying to you, in behalf of my brother—to ask of you—to procure for him an appointment as cadet to the U. S. Military Academy at West Point. You, no doubt, think that I, a complete stranger, to you, am exceedingly rash and impertinent in thus troubling you by the asking of such a favor— having no claims, whatever, upon you for such preferment. But what could I do? I have no excuse whatever to plead, but my great anxiety that my brother should have the opportunity to acquire the education he so ardently desires, and also, my belief that you could have the power to procure for him the cadetship which would be the fulfilment of our fondest wishes. I am so anxious that my brother should receive a military education—first, because to become a good soldier in the Army of his country, has been his dream by night and his hope by day for many years; secondly; because I think, and it has been the testimony of others more competent to judge, that he has the real talent or genius required in military life. When but a child he delighted in the study of all the, to others, dry and uninteresting 'Tactics,' which he could procure. He arranged and drew plans for all sorts of battles, camps and fortifications which he could read of or imagine. He received no encouragement, either, from a member of his family—for Papa and Mamma knew they should not be able to give him the necessary education for the successful prosecution of the life he had chosen for himself, and therefore tried to turn his attention away from the subject which seemed so wholly to engross his mind. But all in vain! When the War began he plead earnestly to enlist, young as he was, said he 'I know that I can do *something* for my country, I know I am young, but I do not look so—I am so tall and large they will never think of my being too young to go, and beside Father, Mother I feel that I was *born* to be a *soldier*, so I can get along *somehow* if you'll *only* let me go'! But father thought he was entirely too young to go *then*, but promised him if the War lasted until he was sixteen that he might enlist—in the meantime he was to work, learn all he could and *wait*! He immediately joined a militia company in town—all of the members of this company were men who for years had been in military companies, yet at the first election of officers, which occurred soon, they elected my brother 1st Cor. of the company, which position, I presume he filled more than satisfactorily for at the next annual election they elected him Lieut. but he respectfully declined *that* or *any* office—and gave as his reason for declining the honors conferred upon him—that he was the youngest member of the company, and there were others better fitted to fill the offices than he. But the men said he *should have* an office for he knew as much 'drill' as the Capt. When he found the men so determined, he consented that they might re-elect him Corporal he would again try to fill that position to the best of his ability—He was unanimously elected! He was then but thirteen years of age but very large and strong, so the men supposed him to be eighteen at least, for he was always rather silent, so that the men were never informed by him of his true age. Next year he was elected 1st Lieut. in which office he served one year, the Capt. of the company then moved af away from the State, and the men of the company offered him the Captaincy. he thanked them for the honor done him but told them he had decided to withdraw from the company and organize a company to learn the 'Zouave Drill.' A Major D— who had just 'come from the War' and professed to know all about this particular kind of drill engaged to take them new company under his special protection and learn them all he could. So Major D— was elected Captain, my brother Lieut. After the first two months the Major was scarcely ever present at the regular drills so that my brother really had the command of the company, which command he retained until we moved from that place, which we did four months since. Although there were several other companies in town, the 'Zouave Cadets' were the prize company of the place and pronounced by officers of the regular Army exceedingly well drilled. I hope, dear sir, that I have not wearied you by this recital. I have only tried to give you some account of my brothers life thus far. He is now in his seventeenth year, and as you know, the days of the War were num-bered faster than the years of his life and he was not permitted to be in the War, which was a very sore disappointment to him. But, perhaps, it was best that he did not get to go, as he was then too young to have long endured the hardships and privations of a soldiers life for any length of time. He is firm in his determination to join the Army as soon as he is twenty-one, at all events. He has had to work hard in the past, with scarcely any time for study, and will have, in the future, the same 'hard row to hoe' unless you have the great kindness to procure him a cadetship to West Point—then by the time he reached his majority he would be fully fitted to become a soldier in the Army of the United States—If his life is spared, it is our hope and belief that, if he could have the right kind of education and training—he will make a soldier that will be an honor to the country to which he belongs, and surely, dear General Grant, you will never have to regret having aided my brother to get an education. If I only knew how, I would plead *so earnestly*, I would *beseech* that if you *have* the power to aid my poor brother you will use it for his sake! My brothers name is Waller Riggs Shaw. If you are so kind as to answer this sending my brother notice of his appointment, write to my address, K. Shaw, Ocean View, Cal. as I know not *where*, my brother's address may be by that time. If you do not procure the cadetship for my brother, please write my to that effect, as soon as possible as you know not *how* I shall wait for an answer to this application. Please excuse this lengthy communication, and whether you shall accede to my request or not I shall ever remain your firm friend and well-wisher,"—ALS, DNA, RG 94, Unsuccessful Cadet Applications.

1868, MARCH 17. USG endorsement. "Respectfully forwarded to the Secretary of War. Lieut. Genl. Sherman's recommendation is approved."— ES, DNA, RG 94, Letters Received, 706M 1868. Written on a letter of Feb. 26 from Lt. Col. and Bvt. Maj. Gen. Innis N. Palmer, Fort McPherson, to Bvt. Lt. Col. Henry G. Litchfield, adjt., Dept. of the Platte. "I desire to call the attention of the General Commanding the Army to some matters concerning the Light Battery "C", 3d Artillery, stationed at this Post, and to beg that some measures may be taken to insure the usefulness and efficiency of both Officers and men of that Organization. The commander of this Battery Captain & Bvt Col. D. R. Ransom, is a gentleman in all his instincts, his record during the war was perfectly good as far as I know, but it is my firm beleif that he has lost all force of character and all power of properly controlling his command by the excessive use of liquor. Twice, within about three months, he has been totally incapacitated for any duty by reason of delirium tremens and I see not a glimmer of hope of his changing his habits in that respect. The Senior 1st Lieutenant and the 2nd Lieutenants attached to this Battery are intelligent officers and anxious, I have no doubt, to make the command what it should be—a school of practice—for the officers and men, but they are not permitted to have any voice in the matter, and I do not think that either of the Lieutenants have been to a dozen drills since they have been attached to it. One of the 1st Lieutenants, Lieut *Fine*, is so constantly steeped in intoxicating drinks that he is perfectly worthless and a shame to the service. He has, I think, no knowledge of his duties as an officer and I am forced to the beleif that he is partially imbecile in consequence of his habits. These Light Batteries are among the Most important commands in the army, and I presume it was intended that they should be schools for the officers of the regiment to which they belong. They should be commanded by sober, intelligent and

zealous officers who do not require to be watched or goaded on to their
duties. It is true that I, as Commanding officer, can give my orders and I
can, by constant watching, see that they are obeyed, but I cannot furnish
that zeal and pride in the service that a Battery Commander should have.
Neither can the respectability of such an organization be kept up if the
short comings of the Captain and the disgraceful conduct of one of the
Lieutenants is made subject for common talk among the enlisted men. I
would therefore respectfully urge that another Captain be transferred to
this Battery, and I would then also urge that 1st Lieutenant Fine be ordered
before the Army Retiring Board with a view to having him wholly retired
for incapacity resulting from dissipated habits, and for utter worthlessness
as an Officer. If this cannot be done I should think it best to order the Battery to some post in the East where some of the Senior officers of the 3d
Artillery could give his personal attention to it"—ALS, *ibid.* On March 12,
Lt. Gen. William T. Sherman endorsed this letter. "Respectfully forwarded
to the HeadQrs of the Army, to be laid before General Grant *personally.* I
regret to say that this Report is too true about Col Ransom who commands
that Battery, C 3rd Artillery one of the oldest & best Batteries in the Army.
I recommend that you simply order the Colonel of the 3rd Artillery to
transfer Ransom away, and another Captain say Piper to the Company C,
and have him report for duty as soon as possible to General Augur, at
Omaha. The other officer Lt Fine shall be tried, and dismissed unless he
reforms, at once."—AES, *ibid.*

1868, MARCH 17.   Edwin A. Jones, Las Cruces, New Mexico Territory,
to USG. "I wish you would inform the Sitizens of new Mexico. what you
keep. one or Two Companes of Solders out here for. if it is to draw their
pay and for the hoffisers to ride around in govment ambulan[ces] get drunk
&c&c. they do the thng up to the handle.   but, as a protection to the Sitizens. they are useless in the first [—].   they wont hunt Indians and in the
next place their is not enough of them and they dont Know how.   neither
do the offices wish to Know   on Thursday last their was Thirteen Sitizens
Killed about ¼ of mile from Tularosa incldig amirican women and mexicans.   if you ar not *albe* to protect us, why not offer from fifty to five
hndre[d] $50 to 500 Dolles per head for them Indians and I will warant
you that their will be no more Indian Massacrees and people will be able to
trabe thrugh the Country without fear. 'If' you cannot protect us you had
better sell out and we will try and protect our Selves."—ALS, DNA, RG
108, Letters Received. On April 28, Maj. and Bvt. Lt. Col. Andrew W.
Evans, Fort Selden, New Mexico Territory, wrote to hd. qrs., District of
New Mexico. "I return herewith the letter of Edwin A. Jones written from
Las Cruces N. M. March 17/68 to Genl U. S. Grant, and abusive of the
Military in New Mexico; referred to me for report. The assertions in the
first paragraph of this letter are evidently false. No officers in New Mexico,
so far as I have observed, ride in Gov't ambulances, except when authorized
by orders. Upon my tour of inspection I have seen but one officer under the

influence of liquour, and he was in arrest awaiting sentence. There are in the 3d Cavalry, at least, many officers & soldiers of long experience in this country, and fully acquainted with the ways of Indians & how to hunt them. At this very moment Co K, 3d Cav'y from Ft Selden is pursuing Indians at Tulurosa, as well as troops from Forts Stanton & Craig. The present disposition of troops in New Mexico is probably as judicious as could be made. With so small a force it is impossible to post soldiers everywhere, and therefore impossible to anticipate all Indian outbreaks. It is true that a party of Indians laid in wait above Tulurosa and killed several passers on the road, in March; not all on the same day. The offer of a large reward for scalps, instead of preventing Indian massacres, would be the direct cause of the murder of many peaceable & friendly Indians & Mexicans by such men as the writer of this letter. The generality of the Americans who live in these Mexican towns, sunk to the level of the lowest order of the natives, is of a very bad class. The Commander of this Post, Col Tilford, has repeatedly offered to the citizens near him, arms, ammunition, rations & even horses, if they would accompany him in pursuit of hostile Indians, and has never yet succeeded in persuading one of them to such a step. Their principal occupation in the neighbourhood of Posts is selling whiskey to soldiers, and purchasing their arms & clothing. I cannot learn that there is any such man as *Edwin A. Jones* known here, and the signature is probably fictitious; but the handwriting bears a wonderful resemblance to that of one Ed. J. Owen of Las Cruces (which I have seen), whose father-in-law was killed at the Tulurosa affair spoken of; but who refused & neglected to go & fetch in the body."—ALS, *ibid.*

1868, March 20. USG endorsement. "I am not aware that Greenes name was ever mentioned to or by me in Col. McAlisters presence, and nothing has ever been said to or by, me relative to his confirmation. I was not aware, before reading this, that he was awaiting confirmation."—AES, DLC-John Sherman. Written on a letter of the same day from Bvt. Brig. Gen. John C. McFerran, deputy q. m. gen., Washington, D. C., to Bvt. Brig. Gen. Frederick T. Dent. "A Col. McAlister, a claim agent in this city, offered to bet $50. day before yesterday, in the presence of General Brice, that he, McA., would have the nomination of Henry H. Green (my brother-in-law) as Assessor of Internal Revenue for New Mexico, now before the Senate, rejected, and said General Grant would oppose it. General Brice told him that he doubted that, as Genl. Grant had signed a recommendation for Green, for that very place.—Yes, said McAlister, but he said he only did it to please you (Genl. Brice.)—Brice replied, You are mistaken—the General signed it at the request of McFerran, and without my ever having spoken to him on the subject. Now, I do not beleive one word of all McAlister said.— Gen'l. Grant never did go back upon any one, and least of all, upon as old a friend as I am.—I am so satisfied of that fact, that were it not that this same statement might, and I beleive, will be used, to reject Mr. Green, I should never think of it a second time.—Now to contradict such a statement if made, I want you to show this to Genl. Grant, and ask him to endorse on the back of it, whether it is true or not. If he has had reasons to change his mind about Green's fitness for the office, I shall be satisfied by his just saying so. I am not well to-day or I would go over and see the General in person."—LS, *ibid.*

1868, MARCH 21, 12:30 P.M., and MARCH 24, 2:00 P.M. To Bvt. Maj. Gen. Joseph J. Reynolds, New Orleans. "Give escort if practicable to party of Miners now at Corpus Christi to Northern part of Texas where they propose to settle;" "J. M. Moor is the name of the party at Corpus Christi in favor of whom orders were given to furnish escort to Northern Texas."— ALS (telegrams sent), *ibid.*, RG 107, Telegrams Collected (Bound); telegrams sent, *ibid.*; telegrams received (on March 21 and 24), *ibid.*, RG 393, 5th Military District, Telegrams Received.

1868, MARCH 21, 2:00 P.M. To Maj. Gen. Philip H. Sheridan. "Please relieve Chaplain Van Wyck from arrest and order him to report to the Adj. Gn. Washington. He is at Fort ~~Riely~~. Harker."—ALS (telegram sent), DNA, RG 107, Telegrams Collected (Bound); telegram sent, *ibid.*; copies, *ibid.*, RG 108, Telegrams Sent; DLC-USG, V, 56. On the same day, Sheridan, Fort Leavenworth, telegraphed to USG. "Chaplain Van Wyck was released from arrest some days ago, on the receipt of the charges against him, which were disapproved at these Head Quarters. An Inspector Genl was at once sent to investigate the trouble who returned last night after an amicable settlement of the difficulty. I will order him to report to the Adjutant General as designated"—Telegram received (at 7:25 P.M.), DNA, RG 107, Telegrams Collected (Bound); copies (one sent by mail), *ibid.*, RG 108, Letters Received; (2) DLC-Philip H. Sheridan.

1868, MARCH 23. Harry D. Cook, Ill. State Agency, Washington, D. C., to USG. "At the request of Geo S. Thompson Eq of this City I address you this note, and take pleasure in stating that I have been acquainted with Mr Thomson for the last three years and have on several occasions called on him for explanations and information in reference to claims of soldiers in his charge. I have always found him ready to give all necessay information, and statements made by him have always been found to be correct. I have no reason whatever to suspect any intention or design on his part to do any thing that would injure his client or the Government. I believe him to be a man of integrity [a]nd Good business capacity"—ALS (press), IHi.

1868, MARCH 23. John McNally, New Orleans, to USG. "I am an old Soldier having served in the regular army under Maj. Genl. Taylor and Maj. Genl. W. Scott throughout the mexican War and was severly wounded at the 'Belen gate' going into the City Mexico which rendered me unfit for active labor   I have a certificate of merit Signed by the late President J. K.

Polk and W. L. Marcy then Secretary War Which is recorded in the adjt Genl. office in Washington I am a pensioner of the united States but received none since 1861—I have always been Loyal to the Goverment.— Col. A J. McGonnigle post Qr. Master for Maj. Genl. P. H. Sheridan appointed me in 1866 Captain of the U. S. Dispatch Boat 'Ella Morse' Which some of your staff officers recollects the boat—when they vistted this city and Texas—on the 11th Feby. last Col. Batchelder Post Qr. Mr. for Genl. Hancock removed me from the boat and placed another man in my place that was not very loyal untill Genl. Butler made him so in 1862   I. have recommendations from Genl. W. F Smith Genl. Gordon Granger Genl. Hurlbut and Genl. Sherman who lost his leg at Port Hudson—General. Genl. Reynolds will be here in a few days from Texas and if you would be so kind as to have me placed in my position by the Genl. or Col. Tompkins Chief Qr. Dept of the Gulf I have a wife and Six Children to Support and the times is very hard in New Orleans at present—When Genl. Sheridan left this city I lost my best friend"—ALS, DNA, RG 108, Letters Received. On April 1, Bvt. Col. Richard N. Batchelder, New Orleans, endorsed this letter. "Respectfully returned to Hd. Qrs. 5 Milty Dist—with the information that Mr McNally was not employed by the Q. M. Dept. but by the Contractor—(for Running—Manning & Victualing the US. Stmr Ella Morse—) who was required to remove him on account of incompetency and inefficiency"—ES, *ibid.*

1868, MARCH 24.   Lorenzo Dow, The Intertropical Co., New York City, to USG. "I had the honor some weeks since, to write you at the suggestion of the Hon. E. G. Ross. concerning the survey of the Darien. I presume that public business of great importance has caused it to be overlooked. I write again at Mr. Ross' suggestions to propose to undertake the survey under your directions and secure two surveys with the appropriation of Congress—One, that route indicated by Admiral Davis from the bay of Caledonia and the other, that indicated by Gogorga last winter. Two expeditions should start each under the direction of such officers as you may appoint. The two parties should be accompaied by a compenent man with a corps of natives, who knows how to use them & in the case of Gagorgos [—] Mr. Richman who first discovered the route. I believe that a complete & exhaustive examination can be made immediately of those two routes, for the sum appropriated by Congress & that by next winter a report can be ready that woul[d] settle one way or the other the f[eas]ability of those routes. I have no peculiar qualifications for undertaking the work except an acquaintance with the country, the climate, & the requirements of an expedition in tropical woods and a very great interest in a work so great & important and one so little considered. Mr. Ross writes that he will call on you to speak of the matter. If I can be of service I am desirous to act."— ALS, Seward Papers, NRU. On April 1, Bvt. Brig. Gen. Adam Badeau wrote to Secretary of State William H. Seward. "General Grant directs me to submit to your consideration the enclosed communication from Mr L. Dow, relative to the Survey of the Isthmus of Darien."—ALS, *ibid*. On the same day, Seward drafted an acknowledgment addressed to USG.—ADf, *ibid*.

1868, MARCH 24.   Jesse Root Grant, Covington, Ky., to USG. "A gentleman from the city, asking me to call your attention to the case of Stephen Hagen an enlisted Soldier, now at Carlile Barracks—It seems that he was an Orphin boy under 17 years of age—of steddy sober habits—He was learning the shoe making business—And was of delicate constitution—He has an Older brother in Cin who wishes to get him out of the army, that he may finish his Traid—The papers in this case were handed to you by Gen S. F. Cary—You better give them an early attention, & if not too detremental to the interest of the servis, grant him a discharge"—ALS, DNA, RG 108, Letters Received. On April 9, Bvt. Maj. Gen. Edward D. Townsend endorsed this letter. "Respectfully returned to General U. S. Grant, Commanding Armies of the United States. J. R. Grant Esqr calls attention to the application for the discharge of Stephen Hogan, Company "C" 3d U. S. Cavalry, on the ground of minority. From the enclosed application referred to, it appears that this soldier was in his seventeenth year of age at the time of his enlistment—December 8th 1865—and that he enlisted without the consent of his Guardian. It appears from the records of this office that Private Hogan enlisted December 8, 1865, and deserted the service at Camden, Arkansas, April 11th 1866, since which time his name has been dropped from the records of said Company. As this soldier is a deserter at large, and as the case does not come under the law governing the discharge of minors (copy enclosed), the soldier being over 18 years of age at the time of the application no favorable recommendation can be made by this office."—ES, *ibid*.

1868, MARCH 27.   President Andrew Johnson endorsement. "Referred to the General commanding the Army of the United States, for consideration and report"—Copy, DNA, RG 108, Letters Received. Written on a letter of March 26 from Secretary of the Interior Orville H. Browning to Johnson. "I have the honor to transmit herewith a copy of a report of the 17th inst., from the Commissioner of Indian Affairs, and accompanying letter from J. B. Bassett, Agent for the Chippewa Indians of Minnesota; in relation to the removal of said Indians to Leach Lake, and respectfully invite your attention to the consideration of the proposition to transfer the military post, Fort Ripley, to the vicinity of said lake, therein contained."—Copy, *ibid*. Copies of the enclosures are *ibid*. On April 23, Lt. Gen. William T. Sherman, St. Louis, wrote to Bvt. Lt. Col. George K. Leet. "I have the honor to acknowledge the receipt of the letter of the Hon. O. H. Browning, Secretary of the Interior, of March 26th, enclosing one of the 17th from N. G. Taylor, Commissioner of Indian Affairs, and another of March 10th from J. B. Bassett, U. S. Indian Agent, all referred to me by your endorsement of March 27th 1868. Fort Ripley is an old post, erected at considerable cost many years ago, designed for the protection of the Chippewas. To remove it to Leach Lake will involve its entire abandonment and the building of another post at a cost beyond our means. It seems to me that the Chippewas will not be permitted to stay long at Leach Lake, so that the expense incurred by the War Department in this transfer will be out of all proportion to the interests involved. The opinions of the several Indian Agents relative to the use of military posts at or near the Indian Reservations vary so widely, that I cannot recommend these changes until the Interior Department settles down to some stable policy, looking to the permanent establishment of the Indians on Reservations such as were recommended by the Peace Commission last fall. Besides Fort Ripley we have already in Minnesota proper, Forts Abercrombie, Wadsworth and Ransom, all soon to be pushed away by the progress of settlement; and I cannot sanction the building of any other Post thereabouts, unless Congress make express provision for it by an adequate appropriation of money. This question should be referred to General Terry, who commands the Department of Dakota, but he is now absent with the Peace Commission at Fort Laramie, and I venture to return you the papers with the above remarks."—Copy, *ibid.*

1868, MARCH 28.   USG endorsement. "The case of Mrs Taylor is one of extreme hardship, but it does not appear that any remedy can now be afforded by the Military authorities. It is one of a large class of cases in which relief justly due cannot be afforded loyal sufferers at the South during the War without legislative action. It is recommended that the papers be transmitted to Congress for such disposition as in its judgment may be appropriate."—ES, DNA, RG 107, Letters Received from Bureaus. Written on papers concerning Mary A. Taylor, widow of Charles Taylor and sister of Col. and Bvt. Maj. Gen. Orlando B. Willcox, who requested compensation for property seized in Tex. by C.S.A. authorities in 1864.—*Ibid.*

1868, MARCH 29.   Count Otto von Bismarck, Berlin, to USG. "Baron Gerolt has transmitted to me a copy, which you have been kind enough to inscribe to me, of the history of your military career. I hasten to return you my hearty thanks for a work which promises me the enjoyment of reviewing in a succinct shape that gigantic struggle the varying phases of which I did follow, at the time, with intense interest. It will be a permanent source of gratification and pride to think that I am owing the volume, now open before me, to the kind and sympathetic feelings of the very man who took Vicksburg and Richmond. May peace, restored by you, afford equal scope to your powers with equal benefit to your country and may the present interchange of friendly sentiments between us, prove a good augury for the continuance of those relations so happily established between America and Germany."—LS, CSmH.

1868, MARCH 31. Governor Alexander H. Bullock of Mass. to USG. "I take pleasure in introducing to you Mrs. Sarah F. Ames, of Boston. This accomplished lady and artist will probably make to you some request as to a sitting for your photograph, to aid her in the modelling of a bust which she designs to prepare. I beg to say that, in addition to her other works of art, there is in this State House a bust of President Lincoln made by her last year at the order of the Legislature, which receives great commendation. I commend the lady to your confidence."—LS (press), Massachusetts State Library, Boston, Mass.

1868, [MARCH]. Bishop E. R. Ames and E. A. Manning, secretary, to USG. "The following Report and accompanying Resolution on the State of the Country were unanimously adopted by the New England Annual Conference of the Methodist Episcopal Church during its regular session, held in Boston, March 28th 1868. The vote, by which the Report and Resolution were adopted, was by the rising of each member in his place and its announcement was greeted by the vast audience present with enthusiastic demonstrations of applause. The number of Ministers composing the Conference is (201) two hundred and one. In certification of this action, above stated, we hereby affix our signatures."—LS, USG 3. "The Committee on the State of the Country respectfully report: We give thanks to our Lord and Saviour for leading our nation through the blood and fire and vapor of smoke which for four years enshrouded us in its sulphurous canopy. We especially praise His name that in this hour of national agony the greatest crime of history perished from the face of the land. We rejoice that in carrying forward the work of national regeneration the Congress of the United States has been so faithful to the will of God in building up our ruined State organizations on the only just and enduring foundations of the equal and fraternal oneness of man. We deeply regret the constant and violent hostility of the President of the United States to the action of Congress and the will of the people in respect to this duty, and that it has compelled his impeachment for high crimes and misdemeanors before the Senate of the United States. We hereby heartily and solemnly approve this action of the House of Representatives, and trust the Honorable Senate and the Chief Justice of the United States in this most important trial will magnify our laws and make them honorable in the eyes of all the nations. We cordially approve the action of Ulysses S. Grant, General of the Army of the United States, in yielding up the keys of his office as Secretary of War *ad interim* to the regular Secretary immediately on the decision of the Senate as to the right of occupancy. We also commend his whole action in this critical history as inspiring confidence in the Republic, and as showing to all nations that in America her first generals are obedient to law, in both drawing and sheathing the sword of victory. We most gratefully recognize the sagacity, courage and faithfulness of Hon. Edwin M. Stanton, the Secretary of war. We honor his great services during the war, and those equally valuable which he has rendered in this one last struggle with the Slave Power. May

God preserve him in his high trust until the rebellion, whether in the White House or in its Southern departments, shall be utterly put down. As our nation has been conducted through this long, perilous, and bloody controversy by the Spirit of God through the prayers of his church, we request the members of our churches and all Christians to be unwearied in their supplications that the consummating of the conflict now going forward, may be conformed to all its previous steps, and obtain for us as a nation the continued and crowning blessings of God. Resolved, That a copy of this report be sent to the Secretary of War, the Speaker of the House of Representatives, the President of the Senate, and the Chief Justice and General of the Army of the United States."—Copy, *ibid.*

1868, [*March*?]. Anonymous to USG. "Well General I suppose this will have to be so! I suppose you will have to be *Our next President.* I am very sory for it! sory for the countrys Sake, for we need you where you are! Especially sory for your Sake, for your present place is for life, & in it the measure of your glory is full; & will so remain unless indeed (, as now in Maryland), patriotism becomes disgraceful, & disloyalty becomes honorable! Yet, Iit must be so! for I believe yours is the only name that will render triumph sure! And the possibility of failure is fearful to contemplate. For then, the progress in a wrong direction which has prevailed since Mr Johnson a[cc]eeded to power, will continue, and soon the Comonwealths, the Statesmen, the Generals, the Soldiers, & the Capitalists who did most to sustain the Govt, & put down the Rebelion, instead of being held in grateful rememberence, & honored, will be spurned & abused, as they are to day in the Comonwealth where I write! The party now in power here through the infimous treachery of Thomas Swan will not nominate a man to office of responsibility unless he has done some glaring act against the Govt. See the doings of their late nominating conventions, specially in the case Gill, & Dobin, Parnel & others. The hostility of these two first names to the Govt was unmistakable all thro. the war, but their doings were not so glaring, or vulgar as these Scott & others, they were not imprisoned, & therfor they could not be placed upon the bench. When this becomes general, the Publick Debt will be repudited, the Rebel debt be paid! &. &. &. 'Oh God! spare the Republick!' The Goodly heritage of our Fathers! As I am no politician, I withhold my name & subscribe myself, *Loyalty* P. S Tho. not a politician, I love my country with a fervor no language can express!"—AL, USG 3. Written below a newspaper clipping mentioning that the Md. Republican Convention had endorsed USG for president.

1868, APRIL 2. USG endorsement. "Respectfully forwarded to the Secretary of War. I concur in the recommendation of Maj. Gen. Halleck."— ES, DNA, RG 94, Letters Received, 136P 1868. Written on papers concerning a treaty made by 1st Lt. Richard C. Dubois, 14th Inf., with Apaches in Arizona Territory, which Maj. Gen. Henry W. Halleck endorsed on Feb. 19. "The action of Lieut. DuBois in this case, so far as concerns the issues of rations, tobacco &c, &c, to these Indians, is not only unauthorised, but in direct violation of the orders of the Division Commander. In this matter he has not only exceeded his own powers, but also the powers which it was possible for the Dept, or Division Commander to confer upon him. Nevertheless, as he has acted in good faith and for the good of the Country, even at the peril of his own life, and in such a way that great advantages may, possibly, result to our Government, in the pacification and settlement of the vast region of Country, now occupied by these Apaches, I respectfully recommend that the quasi treaty of Lieut DuBois be approved by the War Dept. and authority be given for the issues pro-~~vided~~mised by him. I fully concur in the marginal notes and endorsements of Gen. McDowell   Respectfully forwarded to the Adjutant General of the Army."—ES, *ibid.*

1868, APRIL 2.   U.S. Senator Reverdy Johnson of Md. to USG. "I do not how better, to comply with the request of Mrs Creighton's letter, than by sending it to you, with her son's statement, & hoping that something may be done for his release"—LS, DNA, RG 108, Letters Received. Johnson enclosed a letter of March 18 from Catherine Creighton, Baltimore, to Johnson, and a letter of Jan. 28 written for Michael Creighton, Camp Kelly, Tex., to his mother. "Pardon my long Silence towards you, but I ca[n] asure you that it was not through neglect but an act of Shame for I have bin guilty of a crime known as disertion, but I was compeled and drove to it, by Sever treetment for when we was at fort mason we had not anuf to eat, and we had more manual labor to performe than a lot of men who work on the rail Road, instead of doing a Soldiers duty witch I enlested for. So I come to the conclusion that I couldnot put up with it no longer So I resorted to witch I have alredy Stated, and I feel concientious that I done no wrong for I would of Stuck to my bargin, if I had of resived what the guvement had of Stuck to thairs   well mother I will informe you of my whair abouts and how my health is   well I am in the guard hous at this post in Irons and treeted like a dog, for they work me every day and I am unable to informe when I will get a trial as the Cort dose not Set but twice a year, and thair is but a poor chance for hopes—but I wish you would try and See Mr Sidney Johnson or the Rail Road president and give them the whole acount of my misfortune and See if I cannot get out of this for I am ancious to get free for I am more like a laborer than a Soldier   this Mr Johnston is a congressman and he may try to get me off   you try and See and use your best efforts in my behalf and whrite to me as Soon as you can and Let me know how you make out for I am ancious to hear if aney thing can be done in my behalf.   well mother my health is very good never was better, as I hope this may find you as it leaves me—Mother I hope you will not think hard of me for not whriting Sooner, but I couldnot under the Sircumstances, for I was expecting to get home Safe, but failed to—for I was arested near auston, and Lodged in the guard house, ear I knew that I was in danger— well now mother I must comence to bring my hasty letter to a close for the present hoping to be rememberd very kindley to all who knows me also I wish you to Resive my very best Love and wishes for your well fair and prosperity in this world and when we come to die may we be prepaired to meet in heaven, is the wishes of your Son, and now I must comence to bring my Epistal to a Close by informing you to Direct your letter to Michal Craighton Co G 4th U S Cav Camp Kelly *via* Fort Chadburn Texas"—*Ibid.*

1868, APRIL 3.   Lt. Gen. William T. Sherman, Chicago, to USG. "I introduce to you the Bearer of this letter Hon C. C. Shackelford, of Canton Miss, whom I met during the war, & of whom I have heard since. I believe him to be a fair, and just man willing to do the right, and capable of doing much good to his Country."—ALS, DNA, RG 60, Records Relating to Appointments. On Dec. 14, 1874, Charles C. Shackleford, Washington, D. C., wrote to USG requesting appointment as district judge in Ark., submitting several letters of recommendation addressed to USG including that of Sherman.—ALS, *ibid.*

1868, APRIL 4.   To Miss Olie A. Childs. "Enclosed I send you a button from one of my coats worn in the rebellion, as requested in your letter of the 19th of March. Excuse me for not being more prompt in complying with your request."—ALS, Luella Rayman, Chicago, Ill.

1868, APRIL 7.   Maj. Gen. Oliver O. Howard to USG. "I will send you a copy of the conversation as soon as I can prepare it. I was not in the office when your note arrived"—LS (press), Howard Papers, MeB.

1868, APRIL 8.   To U.S. Delegate George M. Chilcott of Colorado Territory. "Referring to your communication of Jany. 27th 1868, to Gen'l Grant enclosing a letter from Mr. W. F. Stone relative to an anticipated encroachment upon the land of 'old Charley Antrobus', near Fort Reynolds, C. T., I have the honor to inform you that a report has been received from the Commanding officer at Fort Reynolds which shows that Mr. Antrobus had no grounds for complaint. A copy of an order requiring squatters to vacate the reservation was served upon Mr. Antrobus but there was no intention to disturb him in the possession of any land to which he is justly entitled"—Copies, DLC-USG, V, 47, 60; DNA, RG 108, Letters Sent. Entered in letterbooks as signed by USG, but content indicates a possible staff signature. See *ibid.*, RG 94, Letters Received, 414M 1868.

1868, APRIL 8.   Maj. Gen. Oliver O. Howard to USG. "I desire to [reco]mmend, for the brevets of 1st Lieut[en]ant, Captain, and Major, 2nd Lieut Ernest Hoffman, 35th U. S. Infantry,—late Maj and Additional Aide-de-Camp U. S A.—now on duty in the Engineer Department, with General J. H. Wilson   Major Hoffman was in my command and upon my staff as chief Engineer for a long time, and I was particularly gratified with his zeal and ability. He displayed a thorough knowledge in his department, and I know of no one, whom I think more worthy of this recognition of valuable services. He has also served with distinction in Europe."—LS (press), Howard Papers, MeB.

1868, APRIL 8. Henry Debbille, "Chairman Campaign Committee," New Orleans, to USG. "The Constitution to be submitted seventeenth (17th) and eighteenth (18th inst provides for election of Municipal Officers of this City. The act of Congress late passed authorized it. The Rebels are urging General Buchanan to order otherwise. He submits question to City Council. They advise against election. Loyal men wish it. Without election for Municipal Officers ratification of Constitution is doubtful. We are orga-nized—have expected election 'as Buchanan has ordered it'. Have prepared and are sanguine of success"—Telegram received (on April 9, 8:30 A.M.), DNA, RG 107, Telegrams Collected (Bound); *ibid.*, RG 108, Telegrams Received; copy, DLC-USG, V, 55.

1868, APRIL 9, 11:00 A.M. To Maj. Gen. George H. Thomas. "Send Lt. Kennedy, 25th Inf.y at Columbus Ky. leave for twenty days unless his com-pany is under marching orders without any other officer."—ALS (telegram sent), DNA, RG 107, Telegrams Collected (Bound); telegram sent, *ibid.*; copies, *ibid.*, RG 108, Telegrams Sent; DLC-USG, V, 56.

1868, APRIL 9. Bvt. Maj. Gen. John A. Rawlins to Bvt. Maj. Gen. Dan-iel H. Rucker, act. q. m. gen. "Can you without inconvenience furnish me with an unofficial approximate statement of the reduction of expenses in the War Dep't during Gen. Grant's administration of that Dep't., caused either by his own orders or the execution of orders existing upon his assumption of that office. I have the permission of Gen. Grant to prefer this request, and will feel greatly obliged if you can grant the information sought"—LS, DNA, RG 92, Letters Received. On May 12, Rucker wrote to USG supply-ing the information.—LS, *ibid.*, RG 108, Letters Received.

1868, APRIL 9. Louis C. d'Homergue, New Orleans, to Bvt. Maj. Gen. John A. Rawlins. "As a matter of interest in the Political History of Lou-isiana I take the liberty of enclosing a most extradordinary document, it is in reference to the coming Municipal elections of this City. On the adjourn-ing of the Louisiana Constitutional Convention and in accordance with its provisions, the Commanding officer of this District issued his order for a general election to be held in this state and city 'for state, judicial, parish and *municipal officers*' in accordance with the Supplemental act of Con-gress, which says 'voters may vote for all elective officers provided for by said constitutions.' And the document in question wh provides by Art 154 for said Municipal election. Said Article I have the honor to enclose. The doubt if any existed as to the legality of City elections should have been considered prior to the issuing of the Military order for such an election, and not await the result of a most liberal re-opening of Registration during which almost every *white* man offering to do so was allowed, and inspite of which sho[we]d a clear majority for the Republicans. Then the question is mooted whether a City election is legal or not—and to shift the responsability of a decision, the question is referred to the Mayor of the City and by him to the Council, neither of whom have nothing to do with the question. The majority report of the commitee is the document which I mention as enclosing, it is such a report as one would expect, knowing these parties, as they not being candidates for office desire to perpetuate their 'tenure of office,' even at the sacrifice of the triumph of their party. The importance of a Municipal election here is as important for Republicanism as it is in the state, for this City owing to being the center of commercial, political and money influence of the State, it is easey to see what influence it can have on the balance of the State body political. For these reasons and especially now that all preparation has been made these elections should undoubtedly be held at the time designated; both political parties have named their municipal tickets, the Republican ticket is composed, with few exceptions, of representative men, right from the heart of the party, and it can be elected. This last fact, it is possible, may have something to do with the talk about postponing the election, and it certainly justifies the Republican party, in desiring that the election should be held. On the near approaching eve of my departure of Louisiana, the whole interest I have is to see the crushing out by this means of the last vestige of Rebel power and arrogance. And as I deemed this a matter which might possibly interest you General I have taken the liberty of addressing this to you."—ALS, USG 3. A newspaper clipping is enclosed.

1868, APRIL 9. Thomas Jewell, Washington, D. C., to USG. "I regret that I find it necessary to make complaint of, and ask tangible redress for a gross outrage which was committed on my property, lying adjacent to this City, in Alexandria County, Va, where I reside, on yesterday, the 8th inst. during my absence from home, by a party of soldiers from Fort Whipple, numbering some fifteen or twenty men, who came upon my premises with Cart and mule, and axes, and proceeded to cut down & remove a flag staff standing within the enclosure of Fort Smith, which flag staff, with the fort, became my property by purchase from the Government at the time the forts around Washington were dismantled and sold. These men in their attempt to take down this pole allowed the same to fall heavily upon the ground, when it was shivered to fragments. My wife, the only grown person upon the place at the time, except a colored man, discovering this proceeding when too late, accosted these men with the enquiry as to the authority under which they were acting, when they replied that they had received their orders from Colonel Van Tassin, in command of Fort Whipple. Learning of this outrage upon my arrival at home, I proceeded with my wife to the headquarters of Col Van Tassin, but was informed that he was absent in Washington. I learned there however that these men had acted under the orders of their Colonel.—I beg leave to represent, in addition to the

foregoing particulars, that Fort Smith, or what remains of it, is located on
my property, that the timber of which it was constructed was taken from
my land and was worth a very considerable amount of money, it being a
very large fort; that before the building of the Fort my dwelling house
worth some six or seven thousand dollars and my barn, worth $3500 more
were pulled down to afford an eligible site for this Fort; that the materials
of which these buildings were composed, were carried off and used, so far
as they were available, in the construction of other buildings for the use of
the Goverment at Freedman's Village or elsewhere, which said buildings
were afterwards sold by the Government for its own benefit; and that in
addition to these losses there were others to a large amount not now necessary to enumerate, for which I have not received one penny's compensation.
As I have stated above when the Forts were sold I became the purchaser of
the one at a cost of $1106—thus actually paying the Government for what
was fairly my own property. My object now is to obtain redress from this
Colonel in the shape of money indemnity for the property he has caused to
be destroyed, and for the further object of making him feel that the people
of the section in which I live have rights which he must not invade. He has
no more right to commit a trespass upon me than has any other man and if
he has not intelligence enough to know this, it is time he was taught it, and
I know of no better mode of doing that than by requiring him to indemnify
me. I have repeatedly refused to sell the Flag staff in question, having been
offered $25—for it last July, preferring to keep it just as it stood. I would
not have taken $100—for it, which amount it would now cost to erect a
similar pole. I now respectfully ask that the sum of $50—, one-half of its
value, may be stopped out of Colonel Van Tassin's pay to satisfy me for
this loss and for his high-handed and outrageous trespass upon my premises. . . . P. S. It may be pertinent to state that all through the war I was
an uncompromising Union man, and that all my energies were given to the
putting down of the rebellion."—ALS, DNA, RG 108, Letters Received.
On April 10, Jewell wrote another lengthy letter to USG on the same
subject.—ALS, *ibid.*

1868, APRIL 10.   USG endorsement. "Respectfully forwarded to the Secretary of War, with recommendation that the attention of the Surgeon
General be called to this subject."—ES, DNA, RG 94, Letters Received,
200P 1868. Written on a letter of Feb. 22 from 1st Lt. Foster E. Parsons,
31st Inf., Fort Stevenson, Dakota Territory, to USG. "I have the honor to
request, that an opportunity be afforded me, to place before the War Department. for its consideration; two inventions; which, if adopted by the
government, I am confident would be of great service, especially to the
army. The first is a stove, which, after fair trial in my own house during
this severe winter, has satisfied me, that the same room can be warmed with
it, by the use of but little more than one half the fuel, necessary to produce
comfort with the stoves now in use by the government, at military posts.
The second is a bedstead, four of which, when folded, can be placed in a

box 3 ft long, 24 inches wide. and 16 inches deep, which makes it easy of transportation; or it can be as easily transported without boxes. It is entirely of wood except the hinges by which the parts are held together. In transportation none of the parts need ever be removed, excep a slight head and foot board, which act as Keys to hold it firm when ready for use; and there is no part of it but that can be repaired when necessary, by the most ordinary carpenter. My observations since entering the army, have led to this invention, and I feel confident, that the Hospital Dept. would be much benefitted by its introduction. I have taken the necessary steps to have drafts prepared, with the view to making application for pattents; but having a desire that the army shall be benefited by them, I make this application hoping that the government will grant them favorable consideration."— ALS, *ibid.*

1868, APRIL 10, 10:00 P.M. To Bvt. Maj. Gen. Robert C. Buchanan, New Orleans. "Report your opinion and reasons if you recommend removals of City Council and street Commissioner, by Mail."—ALS (telegram sent), DNA, RG 107, Telegrams Collected (Bound); telegram sent, *ibid.*; telegram received (at 9:45 P.M.), *ibid.*, RG 393, 5th Military District, Telegrams Received. At 4:00 P.M., Buchanan had telegraphed to USG. "Petition relative to the removals in the Boards of Aldermen and of the Street Commissioner received. Is it intended that I shall take action on it, or simply report my opinion."—LS (telegram sent), *ibid.*, RG 107, Telegrams Collected (Bound); telegram received (on April 11, 8:30 A.M.), *ibid.*; (on April 10, 7:30 P.M.) *ibid.*, RG 108, Telegrams Received.

1868, APRIL 11. To Secretary of the Interior Orville H. Browning. "Referring to your communication of 9th inst to the President enclosing application of the Commission appointed by the Presdt. to negotiate a treaty with the great and little tribes of Osages, for, Escort, Ambulances and flags referred to me by the President with directions to 'give the necessary instructions in this case and notify the Secy. of the Interior of his (my) action thereon,' I have the honor to inform you that the papers have been sent to Lt. Gen. Sherman, Comdg. Mil. Div of the Mo St. Louis Mo. for compliance with the President's instructions"—Copies, DLC-USG, V, 47, 60; DNA, RG 75, Letters Received; *ibid.*, RG 108, Letters Sent. On April 9, Browning had endorsed a "letter of Hon N. G. Taylor and other Commissioners, designated as such by the President to negotiate a treaty with the Great and Little tribes of Osages—requesting to be furnished with a military escort—and means of transportation as long as may be required—and to be furnished with 6 American flags, same to be presented to the Osages after close of negotiations."—*Ibid.*, Register of Letters Received. On April 10, President Andrew Johnson endorsed this letter. "The General will give the necessary instructions and notify the Sec of Interior of his action—unless there should be good reasons why the request of the Indian Commissioner should not be complied with—in which case the General will make them known to the President."—Copy, *ibid.*

1868, April 11.   President Andrew Johnson to USG. "I ~~will~~ If not incompatible with law or detrimental to the interests of the service, I should be pleased if you ~~will~~ would direct Captain Daniel G. Thomas, Military Storekeeper at Washington, to loan to Messrs N. D. Larner and E W W Griffin, under such conditions as he may deem necessary, a reasonable number of flags for use at the celebration of the Knights Templar, to take place in this city on the evening of the 15th instant"—Copies (2), DLC-Andrew Johnson. On April 13, Bvt. Brig. Gen. Orville E. Babcock favorably endorsed this letter to the Q. M. Dept.—DNA, RG 108, Register of Letters Received.

1868, April 13.   USG endorsement. "Respectfully forwarded to the Secretary of War, with recommendation that the accompanying extracts from Gen. Davis' report be furnished the Secretary of the Treasury, the Secretary of the Interior, and the Surgeon General respectively."—ES, DNA, RG 94, Letters Received, 154P 1868. The report on the condition of the Military District of Alaska is *ibid.* See also *ibid.,* 279P 1868.

1868, April 13.   USG endorsement. "Respectfully forwarded to the Secretary of War"—ES, DNA, RG 107, Letters Received from Bureaus. Written on a letter of March 31 from A. Siemering & Co., publishers, *San Antonio Express,* to Bvt. Maj. Gen. John A. Rawlins. "Enclosed please find correspondence with civil bureau in Texas. In addition we would beg leave to state that our publication of the registration list of Mason County was within the time of the spirit of orders, and our paper has a circulation in that County of over a hundred, to one of the Austin paper. Circular No 2, accomplished nothing but the gratification of Genl' Hancock's spite against the 'San Antonio Express' "—LS, *ibid.* On April 17, 20, and May 8, USG endorsed similar communications from Siemering & Co. and J. B. Roudanez & Co., publishers, *New Orleans Tribune.*—ES, *ibid.* On May 19, Thomas J. Durant, Washington, D. C., wrote to Rawlins. "I have received several letters from Mess. J. B. Roudanez & Co, proprietors of the Neworleans 'Tribune'; a newspaper published by them in that city, in relation to one of the ordinances of the late constitutional convention in Louisiana, the terms of which Mess J. B. R & Co feel that they have some right to complain of. They inform me that they have addressed a letter to General Grant accompanied by a copy of the journals of the convention containing the ordinance, and explaining to him the mode in which they feel themselves aggrieved by it, together with a prayer to him for relief. It appears that the constitutional convention could not command ready money to defray its various obligations, and among others those incurred for printing incurred towards Mess J. B. Roudanez & Co, the official printers of the convention. The expedient was therefore resorted to, of providing that the warrants or orders issued by the convention in favor of its creditors, acknowledging indebtedness and directing payment, should be received by all collectors of state taxes in payment as money, but in the ordinance making these provisions, the warrants issued in favor of Mess J. B. Roudanez & Co, the proprietors of the Tribune for printing were excepted and it was declared that these should not be received for taxes; the consequence of this distinction is such that while warrants receivable for taxes are sought after and readily disposed of by the holders, the warrants received by Mess. J. B. Roudanez & Co cannot be made use of at all; a result equivalent in their case to a refusal of payment. Mess J. B. Roudanez & Co think that General Grant under the powers granted him by the reconstruction acts might afford them relief, and if he concurs in that opinion, I sincerely hope that he will do so."—ALS, *ibid.*, RG 108, Letters Received.

1868, APRIL 13. Thomas J. O. Wooden, Livonia Station, N. Y., to USG. "I am encouraged on account of our beloved Bishop E. S. Janes of N. Y also Hon Horice Greely of N. Y. to ask a favor of you   If you Should be so Kind as to grant it, I may never be able to repay you, But our Kind Heavenly Father can do it. I have a Son 17 years old last Feb. 8th—He is now Prepaired to enter College But has a great desire to enter our Military School at West Point. Will you secure him admission there?—His name is—Irving. J. Wooden. I am a Member of the East Genesee Conference of the Methodist Episcopal Church, now stationed as above. Was chaplain of the 161 Regt. N. Y. vol.—Went south with Gen Bank's Expedition—Suffered much with the climate while there, probably never regain my former health.—Was I a Politiction I might Possibly get assistence through our member—but you know how all *that* goes. Dear General, do me the favor to reply at your earliest convenience, ..."—ALS, DNA, RG 94, Unsuccessful Cadet Applications.

1868, APRIL 14. USG endorsement. "Respectfully forwarded to the Secy of War with the opinion that this matter should be left to the judgement of the Commanding Officer of the Dist of Texas."—Copy, DLC-USG, V, 44. Written on a letter of "Bvt Maj Genl. R. C. Buchanan, Comdg 5th Mil Dist, dated New Orleans, La. April 4th 68, forwarding copy of part of letter to the A. G. O. (Feby 18th) relating to arming and organizing of citizens in Texas for frontier defence, to which he has received no reply. Submits also Circular letter from Genl. Reynolds, authorizing the enrollment of citizens for the above purpose at certain frontier posts; states that he entertains doubts of the legality of this circular under existing laws."— *Ibid.*

1868, APRIL 15. Maj. Gen. Philip H. Sheridan, Fort Leavenworth, to USG. "While in Chicago recently, in a conversation with Mr. McFeeley of the Com'y. Dept, I found that he had been neglected in the list of brevets, & he has been so timid in asking for himself as to have never brought it to

your notice. He served with you in the Vicksburg campaign, & I believe
with satisfaction, & now finds himself in Bvt. rank below many of his
juniors. If he could be made a Brig. Genl. by Bvt. to date from 13th Mch.
1865, I believe it would be only a matter of justice. I have taken the liberty
of forwarding to you this note, in furtherance of this end, & in the hope
that he may receive the appointment."—ADf, DLC-Philip H. Sheridan.
Sheridan enclosed a formal letter addressed to the AG.—ADf, *ibid.* On
April 21, USG favorably endorsed this letter.—DNA, RG 108, Register of
Letters Received.

1868, APRIL 15. Governor Francis H. Peirpoint of Va., Richmond, to
USG. "I most respectfully call your attention to the following order of Majr
Genl Schofield, commanding the District of Virginia, dated February 14th
1868, in regard to Inspectors of Tobacco in the state. . . . 1st I charge that
this order was issued by Gen Schofield with intent to evade and nullify the
Act of Congress passed March 2d 1868, which declares that no person shall
be appointed to office under the provisional Government, 'who would be
disqualified from holding office under the provisions of the third article of
said Constitutional Amendment.' . . . I further charge that this order was
made to give the benefit of valuable offices to persons, who are disfranchised
under the proposed amendment of the Constitution, and who cannot take
the oath prescribed by law for officers of the United States; thereby defeating and annulling the law, and tending to defeat reconstruction in Virginia.
The intent of Congress was to place the offices in these States under the
control & influence of Union men. . . . The office of Tobacco Inspector is
among the most valuable in the state. It has ~~there~~heretofore been sought for
its income, and political influence. It brings the inspector in contact with
the producer and purchaser, in addition to the number of laborers he em-
ploys and hopes to control at elections. This labor is principally performed
by colored men; last fall many were turned out of employment for voting
the Republican ticket. The Republicans, fully aware of these facts, determined to procure positions in these tobacco Warehouses, both for political
influence and to protect the colored man in the free exercise of his franchise
at the coming election. The Conservatives, or late Confederates, determined
on the other hand, that they would if possible, retain this power and influence. Both parties made application to Gen Schofield for the appointment
of their favorites. The General informed the Republicans that he could not
appoint their men, but he would appoint none but Radicals to the inspector-
ships. The Confederates knew Gen: Schofield's disposition to yield to their
manipulations, and went to work in earnest. They determined that good
Confederates should, substantially, enjoy these offices. But the inspector
must take the oath prescribed by Congress; therefore some person utterly
incompetent must be hired to receive the appointment and hand it over for
a price, or for no price, as he was a man of standing or otherwise. But it
was expensive to buy two; and so the General assumed the lawmaking
power, and declared he would annul the law of the State, and require but

one inspector instead of two; the other he would *call* a deputy, & suspend
the laws of Congress which requiringed him to take the oath, and the fees
should be divided as stipulated at the time of appointment; hence this extraordinary order. This statement is demonstrated by the appointments of
Gen Schofield under it, and since its publication. . . . The office of City
assessor became vacant in Richmond last Winter   There were numerous
applicants among the Republicans of Richmond for the place. Gen Schofield
refused to appoint any of them. He sent to Ohio, & imported his brother, a
mere adventurer without property at home, & appointed him to this valuable
office. This brother, as I am informed from a reliable source, has denounced
the members of the Constitutional Convention, in the presence of conservatives, in the most offensive terms, and, from the company he keeps, I judge
him to be a democrat or conservative. I am informed he has four deputies,
one of them a reputed Union man; another, an old citizen former who is
appointed inspector at one of the tobacco warehouses in the city, but who
does not discharge the duties of that office; another a young man who was a
lieutenant in the Confederate force employed in the defence of Richmond &
a clerk in one of the Confederate Departments in Richmond. The fourth one
was for a while the order clerk of the famous Gen Winder in Richmond
during the War   The Lunatic Asylum at Williamsburg, at my request
came, rightfully, under the control of Gen Schofield. The Superintendant,
Dr Garrett, was a Union man before the war, resided on his farm, and took
no part in the rebellion. Was decidedly in favor of reconstruction and was
acceptable to the Union party in his section; he was an accomplished and
efficient officer, as appeared by written report, placed in the hands of Gen
Schofield, by an able committee appointed by myself to investigate the condition of the Institution. Gen Schofield's officers by his order took charge of
the Institution, and turned out Doctor Garrett, & put in his place Dr Pet-
ticolas of Richmond, who was a Surgeon in the Confederate Army and
distinguished for his bitter Anti Union sentiments. They also appointed an
assistant physician who was an assistant surgeon in the Confederate Army.
General Schofield had the most unquestionable assurances from the well
informed parties of the ability and efficiency of Dr Garrett. There is no
doubt that this act was procured by recommendations of active secessionists
who surround Gen Schofield and are his advisers in similar cases. . . . I
will furnish the names of witnesses to prove all the facts set forth in the
above papers"—ALS, DNA, RG 108, Letters Received. On April 23, Peirpoint wrote to USG. "On reflection, I find that the statement I submitted to
you through the Hon Messrs Hubbard & Shanks, was not as full as it should
have been, to show the intent of Gen Schofield to invade violate the law of
Congress & the laws of Virginia, and to give the benefit of the tobacco in-
spectorships in Virginia to Confederates who cannot take the oath required
by law for officers of the United States. . . . I find that the 'whisky ring' at
the Custom House connected with Judge Underwood's Court,—the Freedman's Bureau, and General Schofield with the 'Conservatives' around him,
have formed a common alliance to place strangers in all the important

offices, state and federal; determined that no Virginian, whatever may have been his devotion to the Union, shall have a place of ~~honor or~~ profit. General, I do not desire to enter into a contest with these influences. The Freedman's Bureau, backed by the Federal Treasury and by the Army strikes down, and tries to disgrace every Union man that stands in their way. This is considered a combination too strong for me to contend against. Gen Brown, the head of the Freedman's Bureau, is using the whole power of the Bureau for political purposes and against Union Virginians, and under his administration that is all the purpose it serves now in Virginia. It would be useful in the hands of a proper party. These things I desire to communicate to you, believing that you take a deep interest in the welfare of the country, and ought to know them. Then, I shall communicate them to Congress and the Country. I shall then, have discharged my duty in this behalf."—LS, *ibid.*

1868, APRIL 16.   To Secretary of War Edwin M. Stanton. "I have the honor to inform you that the communication from the Treasurer Central Branch U. P. R. R. Co., for an escort for a surveying party, forwarded through the Hon. O. H. Browning, Secretary of the Interior, has been referred to the Commanding General of the Military Division of the Missouri, with instructions, to furnish the escort if practicable."—LS, DNA, RG 107, Letters Received from Bureaus. Written to accompany a "communication of E. H. Nichols, Treasurer Central Branch U. P. R. R. Co. of April 13th (inst)—requesting a military escort for protection of surveying party from attacks of hostile Indians while running the line by way of Republican Valley via: Fort Kearny to unite with U. P. R. R. near Plum Creek."—*Ibid.*, RG 108, Register of Letters Received.

1868, APRIL 16.   To John Rogers. "I have the pleasure to acknowledge, and thank you, for the receipt of the Statuets of President Lincoln, Mr. Stanton and myself, which come duly to hand."—ALS, Rogers Papers, NHi.

1868, APRIL 16.   Bvt. Maj. Gen. Alexander B. Dyer, chief of ordnance, to USG. "I have the honor to acknowledge your application and that of your Chief of Staff of 13th inst and respectfully to inform you that orders will be given to Bvt Maj Gen Ramsay to send to your Head Quarters the two Cadet Muskets and ammunition asked for as soon as they shall be received from Springfield Armory from whence they have been ordered this day"—Copy, DNA, RG 156, Letters Sent.

1868, APRIL 17.   To Secretary of the Interior Orville H. Browning. "In reference to your letter of date 16th inst. to the President, and by him referred to me, requesting a military escort to be furnished Agent Pratt during his visit to the Cherokee Country, with accompanying papers, I have the honor to inform you that the letter and enclosures were this day referred to Lt. Gen. Sherman Commanding Military Division of the Missouri, with directions to furnish the escort if practicable."—Copies, DLC-USG, V, 47, 60; DNA, RG 108, Letters Sent. Written on a letter of April 16 from Browning "enclosing copies of letters from N. G. Taylor, Commr of Indian Affairs of 15th inst. Thos. Murphy, Supt. Ind affairs of 7th inst., and Indian Agent Jno. G. Pratt of 3d inst—requesting that a Military escort and transportation be furnished Indian Agent Jno. G. Pratt during his intended visit to Cherokee Country for purpose of paying the Delaware Indians the residue of money due to them for lands and improvements purchased by the Missouri River R. R. Co.—Sec of Int. approving the request—"—*Ibid.*, Register of Letters Received. On April 17, President Andrew Johnson endorsed this letter. "Referred to the Gen-in-ch. who will give the necessary instructions in the case, and notify the Sec of Interior of the same—unless there should be good reasons why the request should not be complied with—in which case Gen Grant will please make them known to the President—"—Copy, *ibid.*

1868, APRIL 20, 10:10 A.M. To Vice Admiral David D. Porter. "Your letter just rec'd. I will be home all week and glad to see you any day."—ALS (telegram sent), DNA, RG 107, Telegrams Collected (Bound); telegram sent, *ibid.*

1868, APRIL 20. President Andrew Johnson to USG. "If it can be done without detriment to the interests of the service, I would be pleased to have Captain John S. Wharton, of the 14th Infantry, and at present stationed at Camp Lincoln, Arizona, ordered to report for duty to Major General Hancock, commanding the Military Division of the Atlantic."—LS, DNA, RG 94, Letters Received, 202P 1868.

1868, APRIL 20. William G. Moore, secretary to President Andrew Johnson, endorsement. "Respectfully referred to the General commanding the Army of the United States."—AES, DNA, RG 108, Letters Received. Written on a letter of Jan. 22 from F. C. Adams, Washington, D. C., to Johnson. "I beg to call your Excellency's attention to the fact that the officer Commanding the Department of Washington, Brevet Maj: Genl: Emory, having Conducted himself towards the undersigned, at a place of public amusement in this City, in a maner unbecoming a gentleman, and an officer, and being properly rebuked therefore, armed himself with a revolver, and went about the City threatening to shoot the undersigned 'at sight.' Also that the said Genl: Emory did on the morning of the 13 inst, at the banking-house of Messers Riggs & Co, draw said weapon 'a revolver' on the undersigned, and threaten to shoot him, and all under pretence of defending himself against an unarmed Citizen. The undersigned respectfully submits to your Excellency whether such Conduct on the part of an officer of the Army does not stamp him unfit to hold so important a Command; and he also prays that such action may be taken as the Case demands. . . . N. B. This note will be handed you by my friend Mr Binkley, 'asst atty Genl' "—LS, *ibid.* On March 27, 1869, William B. Franklin, Hartford, wrote to USG. "Capt. F. C. Adams of Washington served on my Staff, during the campaign of the Army of the Potomac of 1862. He was an efficient and valuable officer, and is a man of culture, and of literary reputation & ability. I believe that he would serve the United States well in any capacity, and particularly in a diplomatic or consular position. I cordially recommend him for appointment in such position."—ALS, *ibid.*, RG 59, Letters of Application and Recommendation. On April 9, U.S. Representative Nathaniel P. Banks of Mass. endorsed this letter. "Captain F. C. Adams was an early and honorable soldier of the Army, and by his excellent character and honorable career as a citizen and scholar, merits the favor of the Administration. I very cordially join in the recommendation given him by Major General Franklin, under whom he served, for his appointment in the diplomatic service of the Government, and hope that he may be permitted to serve the country in that capacity as faithfully as he has in the civil and military service"—ES, *ibid.* Adams wrote an undated letter to USG. "May I ask the appointment of Secy of Secretary of Legation to London—if the place has not been filled?"—ALS, *ibid.*

1868, APRIL 20. Judge Advocate Gen. Joseph Holt to USG. "Brevet Major Andrew Sheridan, Captain 3d Infantry, was tried by a General Court Martial at Fort Leavenworth, Kansas, in December and January last, under the following charges & specifications: 1. Absence without leave. In this, that he, being an officer of the garrison of Fort Dodge, Kansas, did absent himself from the Post without authority, on the 30th day of July, 1867, and did remain absent until the 23d day of October following. 2. Conduct to prejudice of good order and military discipline. In this, that he, being the second officer in rank in the garrison of Fort Dodge, and the commanding officer, Major Henry Douglas being confined to his bed with cholera, did require or induce the acting post adjt., Lieut Reade, to issue an order in the name of the commanding officer, granting him a leave of absence for seven days; said order further directing that a non-commissioned officer and ten privates should accompany Maj. Sheridan as an escort to Fort Harker, the Acting Assistant Quartermaster at the Post to furnish the necessary transportation; which order was without the approval or authority of Major Douglas. 2. In absenting himself while the cholera was prevailing among the troops at the Post; thereby deserting and disheartening the troops. 3. In taking the escort referred to in first specification to the 2d charge, without authority of the commanding officer. 4. In failing to turn over the sum of $37.77, belonging to the company fund, to the officer who relieved him. The Court found as follows:—Of Specification to charge 1st, guilty, excepting the words '30th day of July', and the words '23d day of October;' and substituting therefor the words, '6th day of August,' and the words '23d day of September,' when the medical certificate of Dr. J. Neil takes date. Of Charge 1st—guilty. Of specification 1 to charge 2nd—Guilty. Of specification 2 to charge 2nd Not guilty. Of specification 3 to charge 2nd Guilty. Of specification 4 to charge 2nd Not guilty. Of Charge 2nd.— guilty. He was sentenced to be suspended from rank and pay proper for the period of eleven months. The proceedings were approved and the sentence confirmed by Bvt Maj. Gen A. J. Smith. After a careful examination of the record of Major Sheridan's trial, this Bureau is of opinion that the findings and sentence by the court were erroneous, and that he cannot be deemed guilty of the offences with which he was charged. . . . A report upon this case has been delayed, for the reason that the record of the trial was out of the Bureau for the purpose of having it copied, at the request of a brother of the accused."—Copy (tabular material expanded), DNA, RG 153, Letters Sent.

1868, APRIL 20. Brig. Gen. Andrew A. Humphreys, chief of engineers, to USG. "I am informed by Major G. H. Elliot, Corps of Engineers, that he has authorised the construction of a temporary closing wall in the upper tier of the Fort at Fort Point, San Francisco harbor, Cal., by which three gun casemates of that work can be used for additional prison rooms. The matter is presented by Major Elliot as an emergency, and his action will be approved therefore by me. But I desire to ask your attention to the point that the casemates of a seacoast battery should not be used for prison purposes, beyond those rooms which are provided for that purpose in the plan of the work, or for the keeping of prisoners other than those of the garrison. In this case, I suppose that prisoners pertaining to the garrisons of other posts have been sent to the Fort at Fort Point, because they are easily guarded there. While this is for the present a convenience, it is obvious that the casemates of the Fort are subject to be needed for defense at any time, and when the occasion arises for their use the embarrasment for the want of them will be increased by the presence in the work of extra prisoners requiring the care of the garrison. No seacoast fortification should be used as a depot for prisoners."—LS, DNA, RG 108, Letters Received.

1868, APRIL 21. USG endorsement. "Respectfully forwarded to the Secy of War, with the opinion that the R. R. Co. should be allowed a reasonable time to turn in and account for this property, and that the property not turned in or properly accounted for should be paid for by the Company."— ES, DNA, RG 92, Letters Received. Written on a letter of April 18 from William J. Palmer, treasurer and director of surveys, Union Pacific Railroad Co., Washington, D. C., to USG. "I have the honor to state, that the Q. M. Deptmt has filed with the 3rd Auditor of Treasury, a stoppage against this Co amtg to $29.947 37 for transportation &C issued by your order of May 2/67, to aid in our surveys through New Mexico & Arizona to California. I inclose copy of application to Sectry of War, dated Apl 18/67, for Escort &C, covered by your indorsement to Genl Sherman directing same to be granted & providing that proper receipts should be taken therefor. The surveys extended through the year & have only now been completed; during this time there has been of course no opportunity to account for this property, as it was still being used. On Febry 6/68. the Actg Q M. Genl referred the matter the matter to you, asking if the stores so issued, were to be paid for & if not how they were to be accounted for? Febry 15/ 68, you returned the paper, with the information that they should be *paid for*—The Q. M. Deptmt then filed the stoppage. When this information was returned, it was doubtless without your original indorsement at hand & only intended to cover the general principle that property received & not properly accounted for, should be paid for. As fast as our Engineers reached California portions of the property were turned in & proper vouchers received from Quarter Masters or Post Commandants—Already some of these receipts have reached me here & others are En route & will soon arrive—Two divisions of the Engineer Corps, returned overland & are now in the vicinity of New Mexico—As soon as possible, they will turn over the remaining stores, when we shall be prepared to account for all transportation &C. received under your order. The Sectry of War has applied to the Q. M Deptmt for all the papers in the case, among which will appear your indorsement that this property 'should be paid for.' In view of this I have the honor to request that you will call the attention of the Sectry to your first indorsement, Explaining that it was Expected these stores would be returned to the Govtmt & recommending that a reasonable time be granted this Co. to so account for them on the final return of all the Engineer parties & that meantime the *cash stoppage* be held in abeyance."—LS, *ibid.*

1868, APRIL 22. USG endorsement. "Respectfully forwarded to the Secretary of War, with recommendation that the report be referred to the Secretary of the Interior."—ES, DNA, RG 75, Kiowa W841. Written on a "Statement of Tosh-o-na a Camanchee Chief at Fort Arbuckle, I. T., March 6th 1868" prepared by Col. and Bvt. Maj. Gen. William B. Hazen, special inspector. "This chief says he is the only Comanchee that has ever tried to live as white men live. That for the past ten years he has in good faith lived near the friendly tribes with all of his people numbering some 250. That for all that time he has been friendly with the white people, has planted corn and tried to live like them. That ten years ago and on several occasions since, he has been promised by his agent, a house of good quality, such as are built for the other chiefs, and that no steps have ever been taken to built it for him. That by treaty stipulations his people were to receive flour, Sugar, Coffee, seeds and implements. That his agent Colonel Leavenworth gives them only Corn meal and that no implements have as yet been given them—that they dont want corn meal, that they can raise it themselves, that it is not what was promised, that he believes it is not what the United States (the great Father) intends shall be given them, but that the agent is giving them meal in place of flour by his own will. That he wishes all these things which have been promised him, but more especially the house which he has waited ten years for, be now given him. That he wishes this written out and placed before the Indian Commission which he under-

stands is soon to meet, with the request that they instruct Colonel Leavenworth to fulfill all the promises that have been made him. By consultation
with Gov. Harris of the Chickasaw nation and Captain Rife Commanding
post of Arbuckle, I find the statement of Tosh-o-na to be substantially
true"—Copy, *ibid.*

1868, APRIL 22.   To Governor Ambrose E. Burnside of R. I. "Yes I shall
be at my office tomorrow morning"—Telegram sent, DNA, RG 107, Telegrams Collected (Bound). On the same day, Burnside, New York City, had
telegraphed to USG. "Can I meet you at your office tomorrow forenoon?"—
Telegram received (at 1:00 P.M.), *ibid.*; *ibid.*, RG 108, Telegrams Received.

1868, APRIL 23, 12:25 P.M.   To Maj. Gen. Henry W. Halleck, San
Francisco. "If Capt. Stevenson, 8th Cav.y has surgeons certificate permit
him to have leave to come East."—ALS (telegram sent), DNA, RG 107,
Telegrams Collected (Bound); telegram sent, *ibid.*; copies, *ibid.*, RG 108,
Telegrams Sent; DLC-USG, V, 56. On April 25, Halleck telegraphed to
Bvt. Maj. Gen. Edward D. Townsend. "Capt Stevenson has not the cer-
tificate required by regulations to permit him to leave the Division   does
Gen Grant intend that the leave be granted without the proper certificate"—
Telegram received, DNA, RG 94, Letters Received, 220P 1868. On April
27, Townsend endorsed this telegram to USG.—ES, *ibid.* On May 1, 1:00
P.M., USG telegraphed to Halleck. "Give Capt. Stevenson six months leave
without certificate if you think proper"—Telegrams sent (2), *ibid.*, RG
107, Telegrams Collected (Bound); copies, *ibid.*, RG 108, Telegrams
Sent; DLC-USG, V, 56. On May 12, 11:50 A.M., USG telegraphed to
Halleck. "If you have not done so, give Capt. Stevenson leave of absence—"
—Telegrams sent (2), DNA, RG 107, Telegrams Collected (Bound);
copies, *ibid.*, RG 108, Telegrams Sent; DLC-USG, V, 56. On the same
day, Halleck telegraphed to the AG. "Captain Stevenson has leave of absence and has gone east"—Telegram received, DNA, RG 107, Telegrams
Collected (Bound); *ibid.*, RG 108, Telegrams Received; copy, DLC-USG,
V, 55.

1868, APRIL 23.   James White, New Orleans, to USG. "I have been in
the service of the United States since the rebellion broke out, as scout,
guide, &c,   I have the honor to apply to you through Major General P. H.
Sheridan for a letter or recommendation by which my retention in the employ of the Government may be rendered a matter of greater certainty. The
constant changes in this District may without some good recommendation
from the proper source, dispose of me altogether and if I posessed a letter
from General Grant would feel safe in my present position. I have the honor
to enclose a pamphlet which so far as it goes will gives you an idea of my
services. I apply to you through General Sheridan as he is best acquainted
with my services, and I feel confidant does appreciate them; his recommen-

dation therefore I hope will be satisfactory."—ALS, DNA, RG 108, Letters Received. On April 28, Maj. Gen. Philip H. Sheridan endorsed this letter. "The applicant was employed by me as a scout from 1864. to Sept 1865 I found him an honest capable intelligent man being zealous & success-ful—"—AES, *ibid.* White enclosed *James White, Scout and Guide of the Union Army* (n. p., n. d.).

1868, APRIL 24.   USG endorsement. "Respectfully referred to the Chair-man, Committee [on] the Judiciary U. S. Senate, heartily concurring [in] the recommendation of General Canby—"—DNA, RG 108, Register of Letters Received. Written on a letter of April 15 from C. W. Dudley re-questing "pardon and removal of political disabilities—same being strongly recommended by Genl Canby—"—*Ibid.*

1868, APRIL 24.   P. C. Williams, Washington, D. C., to USG. "I beg leave to submit for your consideration the enclosed deiscription of a new army and marine night telegaping lamp—I will be most happy to waite on and exibite the workings of the Lamp—to any Officer you may appoint for that purpose"—ALS, DNA, RG 111, Letters Received.

1868, APRIL 27.   USG endorsement. "Respectfully returned to Secretary of War, inviting attention to the indorsement of Bvt. Maj. Gen. R. C. Buchanan, commanding Fifth Military District."—*HRC,* 51-1-1822. Writ-ten on papers concerning Davis B. Bonfoey.

1868, APRIL 27.   Maurice W. Wall, New York City, to USG. "Permit me to call your attention to the enclosed affadavit. I have written the Officer on four differant occasions asking for the return of my money but he failed even to reply to my communications,   I think that an officer of the United States Army would Subject himself to punishment for keeping money loaned him when he was SICK & IN NEED,   I leave the matter as a last re-sort in your hands, feeling confident that you will See justice rendered in the matter, a[n]d can confidently refer you to the house of H. B. Claflin & Co. N Y. City for my character & &c. Where any reply you may See fit to make will be most thankfully received"—ALS, DNA, RG 94, Letters Re-ceived, 199A 1868.

1868, APRIL 28.   Bvt. Maj. Gen. Edward R. S. Canby, Charleston, to Bvt. Maj. Gen. John A. Rawlins. "On the morning of the twenty fifth (25th) Brevet Major Lyman fortieth (40th) Infantry, with a detachment of his company attempted to capture Riddick Carney of Pitt County North Carolina, with his party who are charged with several murders. On reach-ing the house Major Lyman found it barricaded and the party prepared to resist. Being refused admittance forced an entrance and was immediately shot and badly wounded. A sergeant and a private of his ~~company~~ detach-ment were killed by the desperadoes who fired from the house. Carney and

his son George Carney were killed by the troops and his son-in-law White-
hurst badly wounded. Carney is the man who while in arrest for murder in
January eighteen sixty six (1866) murdered Lieut Kenyon of the twenty
eighth (28th) Michigan Volunteers, and made his escape from the guard"—
Telegram received (at 9:00 A.M., misdated April 29), DNA, RG 107,
Telegrams Collected (Bound); *ibid.*, RG 108, Telegrams Received; copies
(one sent by mail), *ibid.*, Letters Received; DLC-USG, V, 55.

1868, APRIL 30.   To Secretary of War Edwin M. Stanton. "I have the
honor to recommend that Brevet Major General A. P. Howe be relieved from
duty in the Freedmen's Bureau, and ordered to report to the Commanding
Officer 4th Artillery, for assignment to duty with his regiment."—LS, DNA,
RG 94, Letters Received, 202A 1868.

1868, [*April*?].   Petition to USG. "We the undersigned Citizens of San
Antonio Texas recommend that Sergeant Dwyer Co "F" 35th U. S. Infantry, who has been indicted before the Grand-Jury of Gonzales County
for murder in killing D. *Cunningham*, while said *Cunningham* was escaping from the Guard, he having been arrested on suspicion of having fired
upon the troops—be ordered before a Military tribunal for trial. Escaping
from a *Military Guard* is not considered a civil Offence, *killing* is; and as
the killing is said to have occurred under Military orders, the Sergeant
cannot be acquitted if 'Civil Law' is enforced.—Public sentiment in rebel
circles, where the trial would be had (Gonzales County) is intensely em-
bittered towards the troops who shot D. *Cunningham*, and orders having
been issued to turn said Sergt over to the civil authorities, we deem it improbable that he will be able to obtain a fair trial."—DS (fifteen signatures),
DNA, RG 108, Letters Received. Related papers are *ibid.*

1868, MAY 1.   Bvt. Maj. Gen. Daniel H. Rucker, act. q. m. gen., endorse-
ment. "Respectfully returned to General U. S. Grant, Com'dg Armyies of
the U. S. with the following information, Steamer 'Nassau' was chartered
Nov 11/62 by Col J. W. Shaffer—Q. M. of S. P. Griffin—for $300. per
day—at New Orleans, La; chartered May 8/63 by Capt A. N. Shepley
A. Q. M. of S. L. Clapp, Atty, at $300 00 per day, chartered Oct 13/63 by
Col S. B. Holabird, Chf Q. Mr, at. New Orleans. La, of S. P. Griffin for
$200 per day,   The records of this office show payments made by Col
Holabird, for services amounting to *$66.308.00*—to Mr Griffin and to his
Att'y, Mr Clapp.—The '*Nassau*' was purchased by Col Holabird Dec 4th
1863, for $45,000—of Mr Griffin and was lost in December 1863, on
Brazos Bar."—AES, MH.

1868, MAY 1.   Thomas J. Durant, Washington, D. C., to Bvt. Maj. Gen.
John A. Rawlins. "Some time ago, I spoke to you of the removal by order of
Major General Hancock of Mr. Alphonse Oubre, Sheriff of the Parish of
St. John the Baptist, in Louisiana. I stated that no cause had been assigned

for that removal: further that Mr Oubre was a man of entirely respectable character; that he was a native of that parish, and of one of the old planting families; that, as such, it was remarkable that he had adopted Republican principles and was a zealous advocate of the congressional plan of reconstruction. For all these reasons I considered he should have been restored to the place General Hancock removed him from. No action has been taken by General Grant on my request. I now have the Honor to submit to you an official certificate, enclosed herein, from the Board of Registration of the Parish of St. John the Baptist, showing that at the recent election, Mr. Oubre received 1215 votes for the office of Sheriff against 465 polled for his opponent. Mr Oubre was a candidate on the Republican ticket. On this statement I again respectfully renew the application I formerly made that Mr Oubre be restored to the office of sheriff of that Parish of St John the Baptist, La."—ALS, DNA, RG 108, Letters Received. The enclosure is *ibid.*

1868, MAY 2.   To Secretary of War Edwin M. Stanton. "I have the honor to request that Commissary Sergeant G. C. Lyon, 26th U. S. Infty., be honorably discharged the service. Sergt. Lyon served with distinction during the late war and when mustered out was a field officer of one of the Michigan Vol. regts."—Copies, DLC-USG, V, 47, 60; DNA, RG 108, Letters Sent.

1868, MAY 2.   Maj. Gen. Philip H. Sheridan, Fort Leavenworth, to USG. "The Kansas branch of the Union Pacific Railroad will in a short time be completed to a point about (30) thirty miles distant from Fort Wallace, Kansas. At this point the Government subsidy ceases, and the work ends. I would respectfully urge on you the importance of the Government continuing its aid at once as far as Fort Wallace, and afterwards, to Fort Lyon, C. T. The road could be finished to Fort Wallace about July 1st and to Fort Lyon in time for the spring freight to New Mexico in 1869. I know that pecuniarily it would be to the advantage of the Government to help this road: certainly as far as Fort Wallace, and, also, to Fort Lyon. But in addition, it almost substantially ends our Indian troubles, by the moral effect which it exercises over the Indians, and the facility which it gives to the military in controlling them. I have not had a single depradation in my Department since I assumed command and I have the greatest desire to maintain this peaceful condition of affairs. I have made a great deal of personal exertion by visiting nearly every Post in the section of country in which the Indians were hostile last year, and in all interviews with the Indians was led to believe that we may be able to preserve the peace during the coming summer. No one unless he has personally visited this country can well appreciate the great assistance which this Railroad gives to economy, security and effectiveness, in the administration of Military affairs in this command."—Copy, DLC-Philip H. Sheridan. See *HED*, 40-2-277, part 2.

1868, MAY 2.   Bvt. Lt. Col. George K. Leet to U.S. Representative James K. Moorhead of Pa. "General Grant directs me to acknowledge the receipt of your communication of 2nd inst., enclosing an application from Hon. John Wood for the transfer of his son to some other regiment and to say in reply that the desired transfer can only be made upon the mutual application of Lt. Wood and officer of equal rank in some other regt. without expense to the Government."—Copies, DLC-USG, V, 47, 60; DNA, RG 108, Letters Sent. On the same day, Moorhead had written to USG. "Enclosed find letter of Hon John Wood who was a member of Congress from the 5th District of Pa in the 36th & 37th Congress I believe—If without detriment to the public service, you can comply with his request I will be much gratified by your doing so. Please let me know the result of this application—"—ALS, *ibid.*, Letters Received. The enclosure is *ibid.* USG endorsed this letter. "Answer transfer will have to be with officer of same rank on mutual application of both, without expense to the Govt."—AES, *ibid.*

1868, MAY 4, 10:20 A.M.   To Maj. Gen. Henry W. Halleck, San Francisco. "Order Lt. Converse, 14th Inf.y, before Medical Board in San Francisco."—ALS (telegram sent), DNA, RG 107, Telegrams Collected (Bound); telegram sent, *ibid.*; *ibid.*, RG 94, Letters Received, 242P 1868; copies, *ibid.*, RG 108, Telegrams Sent; DLC-USG, V, 56. On May 8, Halleck telegraphed to the AG. "If General Grant means Retiring Board for Lieut Converse please detail Generals Ord and Fry in place of McDowell and Townsend."—Telegram received, DNA, RG 94, Letters Received, 242P 1868; (2—at 2:30 P.M.) *ibid.*, RG 107, Telegrams Collected (Bound); copy, *ibid.* On May 12, USG endorsed this telegram. "Respectfully forwarded to the Secy of War with recommendation that Gens. Ord and Fry be detailed as members of the retiring board at San Francisco, in place of Gens McDowell and Townsend."—ES, *ibid.*, RG 94, Letters Received, 242P 1868.

1868, MAY 5.   To Secretary of War Edwin M. Stanton. "I have the honor to recommend the discharge of Private George Gresham, Co. "C." 5th U. S. Arty."—Copies, DLC-USG, V, 47, 60; DNA, RG 108, Letters Sent.

1868, MAY 5.   Bvt. Maj. Gen. Edward D. Townsend to Bvt. Maj. Gen. John A. Rawlins. "In reply to your inquiry of April 25. '68. I have to inform you that the records of Rebel Prisoners of War, on file in this Office show that the number of prisoners, captured by the Armies of the Potomac, and the James from May 1. 1864 to April 9. 1865, amount to Sixty six thousand, five hundred and twelve (66,512.) 245 flags, 251 guns & 22633 small arms."—Copy, Bender Collection, Wy-Ar.

1868, MAY 5.   Joseph E. Brown, Atlanta, to USG. "(Private) . . . I entertain no doubt that you will receive the nomination of the Republican party for the office of President, and I have made up my mind to give you an active zealous support. After a very bitter canvass we have carried the late election in this state. We have ratified the Constitution by a handsome majority, and have elected Hon. R. B. Bullock Governor, with a safe working majority as we think in both branches of the legislature. Now if the Governor elect can be inaugurated soon, and the legislature be permitted to assemble, and put the wheels of the new government in motion which will secure the patronage and power of the state government to your friends, we can carry the state for you in November by a safe majority. But, if this is not permitted or if the legislature is called together and the governor elect is not permitted to be inaugurated, and to control the legitimate patronage and influence of the Executive, but it is left, as at present, in the hands of the *so called* democracy we shall be defeated in this state in the Presidential election and thrown into a hopeless minority. Allow me to illustrate. The Western and Atlantic Railroad, is the property of the state, and is under the control of the Governor, and when properly handled is worth one thousand to fifteen hundred votes in an election. In the late election the Road now under the control of the Military government, but managed by the Superintendant appointed by Provisional Governor Jenkins, was used with telling effect in favor of General Gordon for Governor, and reduced the Republican majority at least fifteen hundred votes in the state. This influence will be continuously used to strengthen our opponents till Governor Bullock is inaugurated. While his other patronage under the new State Constitution is very large, it will be of no service till he comes into office. We have but little over five months to come, before the election. Within that time a government is to be organized and its power made effective, or we must meet inglorious defeat. I have conducted many a political canvass in this state and it has been my good fortune never yet, to experience defeat. I am unwilling that the coming election shall form the exception. I see what is necessary to success now, but I am powerless unless Congress or the Military Commander will accelerate the inauguration of the new government, that it may be controlled by the friends of your election. I am aware that the government must be Provisional till we have complied with the terms of the Sherman Bill, but let the officers of the Provisional government be placed as soon as possible in the hands of our friends. Let the government elected go into operation in all its parts as soon as possible, as Provisional, and let it become permanent so soon as we have complied with the terms. If any of our friends who have been elected are not eligible let Congress relieve them at once. This is absolutely necessary, as we are obliged to have earnest, fearless, native white men, to lead, or the democracy will control a large part of the freedmen. Please excuse this hasty letter . . . P S. This letter will be handed you by Mr Blodgett, who understands my views on this question."—LS, USG 3.

1868, MAY 6.   To Helen Barrett, St. Louis. "My family expect to occupy Wishton Wish this Summer."—ALS (telegram sent), DNA, RG 107, Telegrams Collected (Bound).

1868, MAY 8. USG endorsement. "Respectfully forwarded to the Secy of War, with the recommendation that Department Commanders be invested with discretionary power to approve requisitions and order the issue of ammunition to proper State or Territorial authorities, to be used by frontier settlers in protecting themselves against Indians."—ES, DNA, RG 94, Letters Received, 279A 1868. Written on a letter of April 27 from Kan. AG J. B. McAffee to U.S. Senator Edmund G. Ross of Kan. "Gov Crawford applied to General Grant & Sec Stanton for Ammunition with which to provide the frontier Settlers so as to protect themselves and recd assurance from both that an order would be issued to the Dept Commander to approve a requisition for the same I made application and received the following reply. Will you please see General Grant at *your Earliest convenience* and have the order issued and confer a great favor on the frontier Settlers . . . P. S. I feel *certain* that you will do your *whole duty* as a Senator in the Johnson case but regard your position as a very trying one to have the press wading in and you occupying a position in which you cannot say anything Patience is a great Christian virtue and these times furnish ample opportunities for the exercise of it"—ALS, *ibid.*

1868, MAY 8. To John A. J. Creswell. "The presence of a gentleman from New York, who I have engaged to meet on Saturday evening, will prevent my spending Sunday with you as I had promised myself the pleasure of doing. If nothing occurs to prevent I shall do myself that pleasure however the following Saturday, leaving here on the train which starts about 12 m. It is probably Washburne will go with me at that time."—ALS, deCoppet Collection, NjP.

1868, MAY 8. Judge Advocate Gen. Joseph Holt to USG. "Seven of the late officers of the 1st Regt. Conn. Cavalry, comprising two ex-Colonels, one ex-Lieut. Col, two ex-Majors, and the late Surgeon and Chaplain of the regiment, petition for the revocation of the orders dishonorably dismissing from the service, Major Geo. O. Marcy and Lieut. A. V. Burnham. They state that Major Marcy enlisted at the beginning of the war, and by his courage, intelligence, and uniform faithfulness, rose steadily in rank till he reached the office of Major; that that he commanded the regiment in some of its most trying experiences, and no one of its officers was more universally admired and beloved; that Lieut. Burnham also rose from the ranks; that he was connected with the regiment nearly three years; was never discharged from duty for a single day, and was always ready for any duty. The petitioners express the opinion that these two officers were not intentionally unfaithful, and ask that the stigma resting on them may be removed. They ask this not only in behalf of the sufferers, but for the sake of the regiment, that their yearly reunions may not longer miss two comrades so endeared. The statement of Major Marcy, accompanying this petition, sets forth, that in the Autumn of 1864 he commanded his regiment in the Shenandoah Valley. On the 16th of October 1864, he was detailed with his regiment for picket duty on the extreme right of the army. On the night of the same day the picket line was changed; the main line being posted a mile and a half further to the front, leaving one small body of men at a very exposed and isolated position in the rear of the extreme right. He visited this post in the night about nine o'clock, and, in view of its exposed situation, determined to remain there during the night. The reserve of this picket was at the house of a Mr. Cartwell; and after seeing everything properly disposed of for the night, he lay down upon a lounge and fell asleep. He was awakened by firing at the outpost, when he went out and joined the reserves. The post was attacked by a large body of infantry and cavalry under Gen. Rosser, of the rebel army, and after a stout resistance, most of the guard were captured. Major Marcy claims that by his resistance, the real design of the enemy to surprise the union camp, was thwarted, as his force was the only body between them and our cavalry camp. Major Marcy succeeded in effecting an escape from his captors two nights afterwards; and after six days wandering and severe suffering, he made his way into the national lines. He was much disabled, and was granted a leave of absence, though he claimed his discharge in view of the fact that his term of service had expired. When he reached Hartford, he presented himself at the mustering office and was mustered out of service, and a discharge given him. This was on the 4th day of November, 1864. Three weeks afterwards he was notified that he had been dismissed from the service, for 'being captured by the enemy while asleep on picket.' He urges that his three years faithful service entitles him to a revocation of the order dismissing him. The facts above recited are believed, after an examination of the papers relating to the case in the office of the Adjutant General, to be true; and it is deemed obvious that upon the merits of the case Major Marcy is entitled to have his request granted. It is further remarked that this Bureau has uniformly held that the government, after having formally mustered an officer out of service and granted him an honorable discharge, cannot legally revoke the muster for the purpose of dismissing him, unless such officer has procured his discharge fraudulently. Lieut Burnham states that while on picket duty Oct. 31. 1864, he went from his reserve post to a house about two hundred yards distant to purchase a canteen of milk; that he was not absent from his command more than five minutes; that his line was in the rear of the camp, and was not in front of the enemy. On his return to camp he was arrested, and remained in arrest until dismissed for disobedience of orders, Nov. 14. 1864. It appears that charges were preferred against him, and that for the purpose of making an example Gen. Custer recommended his summary dismissal. While this *officer* was technically guilty of the offence for which he was dismissed, it is believed that inasmuch as the object of his punishment has been answered, his previous honorable record should be taken at this time into consideration. It is therefore advised that in the case of Major Marcy, the order dated Dec. 13th 1864, dismissing him, be revoked, and that his honorable discharge of Nov. 4, 1864, be confirmed; and that the order of dismissal in the case of Lieut. Burnham, of Nov. 23. 1864, be also revoked, and he receive an honorable discharge as of the date of its issuance."—Copy, DNA, RG 153, Letters Sent.

1868, MAY 9.   USG endorsement. "Respectfully forwarded to the Secretary of War, approved."—ES, DNA, RG 94, Letters Received, 119L 1868. Written on a letter of May 6 from Bvt. Maj. Gen. John Pope, Detroit, to USG. "I have the honor to request that Brevet Brigadier General Joseph R. Smith, U. S. Army, (retired) resident in this city, may be ordered to report to me for assignment, temporarily, to such duty as he may be able to perform. So many officers have recently been ordered from the regiment in this Department for service in the Bureau of Refugees, Freedmen and Abandoned Lands, that there are really not sufficient officers for detail to make the investigations, obtain the evidence &c., required in the numerous cases of volunteer deserters, pension and other claims referred here for action from the War Department. I trust, therefore, this request may be granted." —LS, *ibid.*

1868, MAY 13.   Bvt. Lt. Col. George K. Leet to U.S. Senator James Harlan of Iowa. "General Grant directs me to acknowledge the receipt of your communication of 7th inst., enclosing letter from Mr. Sydenham, and to inform you that all applications for trading permits are referred to Dept. commanders for their action. Your letter will be sent to Gen'l Augur in whose command Fort Kearney is located. Enclosed herewith I return Mr. Sydenham's letter, as requested."—Copies, DLC-USG, V, 47, 60; DNA, RG 108, Letters Sent. On Feb. 20, 1867, Moses H. Sydenham, postmaster, Fort Kearny, Neb., had written to Secretary of War Edwin M. Stanton asking permission to open a store.—ALS, *ibid.*, RG 94, Letters Received, 210S 1867.

1868, MAY 16.   Bvt. Brig. Gen. Cyrus B. Comstock to Maj. Gen. George G. Meade. "I enclose a letter from Samuel Walker, candidate for the governorship of Florida, to Gen. Grant, in reference to alleged ill treatment of Col. L. Billings and also copy of a letter from Billings to Capt. Corse, for writing which it is alleged Billings was arrested. Gen. Grant wishes you to make such investigation as you deem necessary."—Copies, DLC-USG, V, 47, 60; DNA, RG 108, Letters Sent.

1868, MAY 16.   Walter B. Scates *et al.*, Chicago, to USG. "The undersigned, late officers of the 13th Army Corps, take the liberty of enclosing for your information a copy of the proceedings of a meeting of the officers and privates of the Corps to form a social reunion   At the same time we request your acceptance of a Badge adopted for the Corps. Alow us the expression of the earnest hope and desire of meeting you at Indianapolis on

the next reunion of the Corps on the first Wednesday of October 1868—
and to enjoy with our late military chief a social season"—DS, USG 3.

1868, MAY 18.   USG endorsement. "Respectfully forwarded to the Sec-
retary of War, with recommendation that the request of Hon. Leonard
Myers be granted"—ES, DNA, RG 94, Letters Received, 14M 1868.
Written on a letter of May 16 from U.S. Representative Leonard Myers of
Pa., Washington, D. C., to USG. "I ask as a *personal favor* that Lt Alman's
remains be sent to his wife in Phila   He was a gallant soldier—a private in
Texas when the war commenced rose in the Volunteers afterwards from
2nd Lt to be Major & then at *my own request* was appointed in the regular
army"—ALS, *ibid.* On June 14, Myers wrote to USG. "You were kind
enough at my personal request to direct that the bodies of Lieutenants
Rothermel and J. Alman should be sent north to their families as soon as
the commanding officer judged it convenient. My friend Samuel H. Rothermel, the father of Lieut. Rothermel, writes me that no action has yet been
taken. I shall esteem it a great favor if you will again send directions in
regard to both these cases. Col Sinclair is coming east this summer, and
Mr. Rothermel informs me will be glad to bring the body of his son. A
favorable reply will much oblige . . ."—ALS, *ibid.*, RG 107, Letters Received from Bureaus. On June 22, USG endorsed this letter. "Respectfully
forwarded to Secretary of War, inviting attention to previous papers, forwarded 18th May."—ES, *ibid.*

1868, MAY 19, 2:00 P.M.   To Governor Andrew J. Hamilton of Tex.,
Briggs House, Chicago. "General Reynolds has been directed to furnish
escort if necessary"—Telegrams sent (2), DNA, RG 107, Telegrams Collected (Bound); copies, *ibid.*, RG 108, Telegrams Sent; DLC-USG, V, 56.
On May 15, Bvt. Lt. Col. George K. Leet had written to Bvt. Maj. Gen.
Joseph J. Reynolds. "The members of the Constitutional Convention of
Texas represent that without an escort their lives would be in jeopardy in
travelling to Austin, where the Convention is to be held. If in your judgement an escort is necessary to protect them from violence, General Grant
desires that you will furnish it."—LS, DNA, RG 393, 5th Military District,
Letters Received.

1868, MAY 19.   Bvt. Maj. Gen. Edward D. Townsend to Bvt. Maj. Gen.
John A. Rawlins. "In compliance with your request of the 22d ult. I have
to transmit herewith statement from the Regimental Records on file in this
Office, showing the losses sustained by the Army of the Potomac, in killed,
wounded and missing, from May 5th 1864 to April 9th 1865, also statement from the Regimental Records on file, showing the losses sustained by
the Army of the James in killed, wounded and missing from May 5th
1864, to April 9th 1865, together with the Recapitulation showing a total
of losses sustained by both Armies during the period above named."—LS,

DNA, RG 108, Letters Received. The summary gave figures of 12,663 killed, 49,559 wounded, and 20,498 missing.—*Ibid.*

1868, MAY 20. Susan Lottier, "Colored," Richmond, Va., to USG. "I respectfully make application for a Fourlough of 30 days for my son, Prv Samuel D Lottier Co B 39th Regt U S Infty, now stationed on Ship Island. I should not make this application but for my ill health, and great desire to see my darling boy—Grant this request, and you will cheer up his aged and enfeebled mother"—ALS, DNA, RG 108, Letters Received. On June 5, 1st Lt. George E. Ford, Ship Island, Miss., endorsed this letter. "Respectfully returned. Private Lottier was assigned to the company, as a Recruit, Dec. 13th 1867, having been enlisted during the month of October 1867. I do not think it would be judicious to give any man a Furlough with permission to visit a point at a distance from his Company, until he has served a sufficient length of time to become familiar with his duties as a soldier."—AES, *ibid.*

1868, MAY 21. Mallory, Young & Anderson, attorneys, Memphis, to USG. "We enclose You a Series of Interogatories, to which we desire Your answer: in order to use them as evidence in the Case of Brinkley vs Wiggin now pending in the Municipal Court of this City. This Case is a peculiar one involving a principle of law which it is verry important to a large portion of our people to have finally adjuodicated—The facts are briefly as follows: In the Year 1860. the Plaintiff Brinkly—Leased to the Defendent Wiggin a Certain Store House in this City for a term of Five Years at a Yearly rental of Twenty five Hundred Dollars, which he paid in quarterly installments up to July the 1st 1862, About this time, Brinkley who resided in this City left with his family—went South and took up his residence within the lines of Rebel Military Occupation When the Military forces of the U. S. Goverment occupied the City of Memphis Some time in the months of June or July 1862, all the property of Brinkley remaining here was seized as 'abandoned' under a Military order which we suppose was issued by Yourself. Wiggin the defendent in this Case was ordered to vacate the Store House which he occupied or to pay rent for the Same to an Officer to the U S Goverment—which latter alternative he accepted—and took receipts from said Officer for the amount which he paid extending over a period of about one Year. . . ."—D, DNA, RG 108, Letters Received.

1868, MAY 23. To Joseph Thurman. "Some week or so since I received your check for Twenty-five dollars and some cents, . . . It is barely possible that I may have endorsed the check, which was made payable to my order, so that it can be collected by any man into whose hands it may fall."—James Lowe, Catalogue 19 [1982], no. 43; Swann Galleries, Inc., Public Auction 1529, May 3, 1990, no. 285.

1868, MAY 23.   A. C. Bailey, Oregon City, to USG. "Esteeming you as a man of high Standing, both in private & publick. holding the highest position in the Military department, knowing that you have great influence, I commend to you consideration a letter received from my brother who is a priviate of Co. F. 8th U. S. cavelry, & to ask your aid in the matter together with your influence with the Secretary of War, in procuring his discharge from the Services,   Sometime last fall I wrote to you a letter together with an affidavit. drawn up by Gov Woods praying for his discharge for reasons Set fourth in affidavit. I received an answer in return Stateing the kind of affidavit—& what I had to do in order to have any notice taken,   I set to work & got an affidavit & filled out the instructions & Sent it on about three weeks ago to the Sec. of War. Since Which time I have recived a letter from my brother, which made the blood chill through my veins, and my dear Sir, Shall I entertain an idea, that our Government is so debased that She will allow her citizens to be treated as my brother has been treated I would ask if we have no law whereby we can obtain justice. I Saw Gov. Woods afew days ago & showed him the letter   he read it & has promised to give me all the aid he could.   he agreead to write to you & the Sec. of War. also, to Canyon City to F. Adams Atty at Law & to see the commander of this department. I will now give you my brothers letter word for word. Camp Logan Apr. 30th 1868   MY DEAR BROTHER   You will be greatly astounded when you have finished reading my letter, & you will agree with me, that I, your Brother has been the victim of as base, & disgracefull treatment as ever darkened the annals of barbarin History, but to the point. I have been cruely lashed worse than a negro ever was, to confess a crime that before my God, I am innocent of, as innocent as your-self. they accuse me (my Officers) of Stealing a carbine from the quarters at night & flogged me on the bare back, tied to a tree ¼ mile from camp, at midnight, to force me to confess a crime that I am entirely innocent of Capt D. Seward, & 1st Sergt Smith did that foul deed, & to Save my bleeding back more strips, I acknowledged that I had taken my own Carbine from the Qrs. but had replaced it aftewards. (O, My God if I could of but been there)   No confession of the crime they impute to me   You will see the articls of War, Expressly forbids flogging, but I was taken out at night & away from the Camp tied striped, & flogged, to be forced to confess the crime, & afterwards be tried for it, & I am now in close conf't. & Still they do not know who took the carbine. Capt D. Seward told me that day, that 'he would cut my guts out if I didnot tell him where the carbine was, by 8. O'clock, & after I was tied to the tree, Sargt Smith told me, he would flog me untill I confessed to the crime. And when walking back to camp, he, Sergt. Smith told me 'not to say any thing about the flogging & he would not,'   after being tied the Capt. walked of how far I do not know. I have plenty of proof to the above.   the guard saw the Strips on my back when I returned. Do all that you can for me, & do it quick. for we are (the company) are under ordes to go to Nevada and if you try you can do a great deal ~~for~~ that will place me under lifelong obligations to you. I was flogged on the night of Apr. 28. 1868. Yours as Ever PETER BAILEY   accompanying the above was as follows   May 1rd 1868   Your letter of April 25th just received & contents noted   no time to write more. Yours affectionate Bro. PETER J. B.—By W. T. W,   Gen—for the Sake of an only Sister, who is almost constantly weeping for her brother. O give thy aid.   he is but 17 years old the baby of the family. Give thy influence for his delivery, & to bring justice upon those two Scoundrels, Seward & Smith,   with this I shall close, hoping that you will give it your amediate attention"—ALS, DNA, RG 108, Letters Received. On Sept. 30, Bvt. Col. John P. Sherburne, Camp McDermit, Nev., wrote to the adjt., Dept. of Calif. ". . . On my arrival at Fort Churchill, I learned that Private Bailey had not arrived at that post, as ordered—so I proceeded to Camp McDermit—As soon as the investigation commenced I learned that he deserted the service of the U. S. on the 25th of July 1868—I however proceeded with the investigation— and herewith enclose the statement of Bvt: Maj: Seward—and the testimony under oath of 1st Sergeant William Smith—Sergeant Tish S. Jackson and Sergeant Fred S. Hawley, all of Co. "F" 8th U. S. Cavalry—By reference to the retained company rolls, I find that Private Bailey, and Private Stout,—alluded to in the testimony,—deserted at the same time, towit— July 25th 1868—Lance Corpl. Sharp & Private Stafford a few days after— I have failed to find any evidence to corroborate the statement made by Bailey, that he was whipped on the night of April 29th 1868—on the contrary, the evidence goes to prove that his statement is without foundation—"—ALS, *ibid.* The enclosures are *ibid.*

1868, [MAY 24].   To H. Bernd, Danbury, Conn. "Please forward to my address, pr. Adams Ex. One Thousand 'Colfax' segars to collect on delivery."—ALS (facsimile), Marjorie P. Morgan, Westerly, R. I. Date taken from postmark accompanying the frank of Speaker of the House Schuyler Colfax.

1868, MAY 25.   Judge Advocate Gen. Joseph Holt endorsement. "Respectfully returned. to General Grant. The crime with which the Indian scout 'Makegebandumanee' is charged, having been committed before he entered the service as a scout, the military authorities have no power to bring him to trial for its commission. He should be held in custody, however, until the civil authorities of Nebraska are notified of the facts in the case and demand his possession, in accordance with the provisions of the 33d Article of War."—ES, DNA, RG 94, Letters Received, 608M 1868. Related papers are *ibid.*

1868, MAY 25.   Maj. Gen. Oliver O. Howard endorsement. "Respectfully forwarded to Genl. U. S. Grant USA. I think Genl Carlin's recommendation a good one to check the lawless proceedings which he reports and recommend that the within copy be referred to Genl. Geo. H. Thomas. If a company can be located at Columbia alone, the other places can be reached in cases of necessity"—Copy, DNA, RG 105, Endorsements. Written on a report of May 16 of Bvt. Maj. Gen. William P. Carlin "suggesting a military force be sent to Columbia, Pulaskie and Franklin—enumerating cases of bad conduct of the Ku Klux Klan."—*Ibid.*, RG 108, Register of Letters Received. On June 3, Maj. Gen. George H. Thomas, Louisville, wrote to Bvt. Lt. Col. George K. Leet. "I have the honor to acknowledge the receipt of extracts from the report of Bvt. Major General Carlin Asst Commr Bureau R. F. & A. L. for Tenn. with endorsement by order of the General in chief dated May 25th 1868. You are respectfully informed, that a copy of the report was sent to me by General Carlin and upon his request and that of his Excellency Gov. Brownlow, a Company of Infantry was stationed at Columbia Tenn. in April and is still there. It is hoped that the presence of troops in that lawless district may have a moral effect in preventing disturbances and outrages, but under existing orders they can be of but little service physically, as they can only aid the civil authorities, who do not appear to be zealous in their duties as conservators of the peace."— LS, *ibid.*, RG 105, Letters Received.

1868, MAY 25.   Allen Dunn, Twin Springs, Kan., to USG. "I had a son, James Allen Dunn, who was born the 7th of June 1845, who on or about the 10th of July 1862, (being then about 17. years and one month old,) left home without my knowledge, or consent, and joined the 6th Regiment of Kansas Volunteers at Fort Scott, Kansas in Capt. H. M. Dobyns' company E. under Col. Judson, and though I tried frequently by writing to get him out ~~by~~ could not succeed. I wrote to Col. Judson, to the Secretary of War, to President Lincoln. Went twice to Fort Scott but ~~th~~ Captain Dobyns would not give him up, and finally on the 5th of April 1864, he was one of the Escort which was sent with Surgeon Fairchild from Fort Smith, Arkansas, to Roseville, about 40 miles East of that place, where ~~and~~ he was killed, about 8, or 9 ~~miles~~ miles from that place. The escort of 25 being attacked by several hundred of the enemy, as stated in a letter from Capt. Dobbins to me, a copy of which I send you, the original being in the second auditors office of the U. S. Treasury. I could, not do without the service of my son, having no good health and totally unable to make provision for my family, (a wife and one Daughter). When he was killed being then not 19 years of age, his horse and equipment fell into the hands of the enemy. I have no property, land, or stock, am in my 70th year, and from *want of means* have not been able to prosecute the claim before our government, as it requires me, so agents inform me, to take out letters of administration. The value of the horse and property lost when he was, killed as I am informed by some of the soldiers is as follows. Horse $100. . . . in all, 176.70 The horse and equipments were all his own. Besides this also he had lost another horse which by reason of its poverty had been left on some of the marches, and had been found and was taken by the enemy at Mazard prairie on the 27th of May, or June, so Capt. Dobyns told me, in his life time. I wish to know whether you could give me permission to get a horse saddle and bridle from those which have been turned out of service or to be sold at Ft Leavenworth. I got th Bounty and additional Bounty due my son. But the first bounty was given in part to a man who had sold him a horse. If you have authority to let me have a horse saddle and bridle, you would confer a great kindness on a poor man. My last Voucher or certificate was numbered if I recollect correctly 428.227. if you wish to see the statement in full for my procuring th bounty. If you can grant me my request address to me at Twin Springs, Linn County, Kansas."—ALS, DNA, RG 108, Letters Received.

1868, MAY 25. George O. Yeiser, Frankfort, Ky., to USG. "I have just recd a letter from my brother P D Yeiser of Paducah which I herein Send— he States that I can possibly obtain thro. you an appointment, for my brother J D Yeiser (a practising physician residing near AFlorence Alabama) as Surgeon at Post Paducah   My brother is a regular graduate of Medical School Louisville Ky and has been practising medicine in Southern Ky for 6 or 8 years & had a good practise   Moved to Ala in 1865. where he now resides   He has practised in my family & I really think there is no better physician   He is now & has always been an an *unconditional* Union man—I do not write this to have the present incumbent displaced, just for my brother, but, that in case, there is a vacancy, or change, to have you to assist my brother in procuring the situation as Surgeon Paducah Ky tho, if you feel any delicacy in the matter would not urge it on you   If necessary can obtain for my brother any desired recommendation   Any thing done by you will be highly appreciated . . ."—ALS, DNA, RG 108, Letters Received. The enclosure is *ibid*.

1868, MAY 26. To Secretary of War Edwin M. Stanton. "Will you please authorize the Qr. Mr. Dept. to loan to the Wesley Chappel Congregation, Methodist Church, Ten (10) large, and Eight (8) small National flags, to decorate the church with, on the occasion of their Sunday school festival. The Rev. Dr. Ames, pastor of the church, will be pleased to get the order for them so that they can be obtained when called for."—ALS, DLC-Edwin M. Stanton.

1868, MAY 26. To Bvt. Maj. Gen. Alexander B. Dyer, chief of ordnance. "Will you please send from the Washington Arsenal a detachment of ordnance soldiers with one gun and ammunition to fire a national salute—to report to the Supt. of the National Cemetery at Arlington at 11, A. M., on Saturday the 30th of May, the detachment to return with the gun after firing the salute."—Copies, DLC-USG, V, 47, 60; DNA, RG 108, Letters Sent.

1868, MAY 27. U.S. Representative James K. Moorhead of Pa. to USG. "The enclosed letter came here during my absence at Chicago—I fear that it is too late now for any thing to be done—The writer of this letter is entirely truthful & trust worthy—If Snyder has not been executed yet, I hope the execution will be delayed and some milder punishment ordered—Please let me know what has been done—"—ALS, DNA, RG 108, Letters Received. On May 14, Charles Porter, Huntingdon County, Pa., wrote to Moorhead. "I have taken the liberty of adressing you on a subject of life and death. from my former early acquaintance with you I concluded you were the relyable person I could write to. John Snyder of this Township is sentenced to be shot on Saterday next at Jacksonville Mississpaa for desertion it is said that it is the third time he has deserted—David Snyder his Father had five children three sons and two daughters his two oldest sons were bothe lost in the army during the war. one was killed in battle and the other died in the Hospital. his youngest son John who is sentenced to be shot on saturday next ran away from his parents in 1866 and enlisted at Harrisburg in the regular army. he was under age—His mother is nearly distracted about him She is a Christian woman—If you would be so good as to use your ifnfluence with the powers that be at the seat of Goverment to have at least the time extended I would insure unto you the reward of the blessings & prayres of a Christian Mother"—ALS, *ibid.* On June 3, Bvt. Maj. Gen. Alvan C. Gillem, Vicksburg, endorsed this letter. ". . . Private John Snyder, Company "E," 5th U. S. Cavalry, has been found guilty of the charge of desertion, and sentenced to be confined at hard labor at the Military Prison at Little Rock, Arkansas, for one (1) year. It is presumed that this is the soldier referred to within, as he is the only one of that name in the District who has been tried for desertion."—ES, *ibid.* On June 9, Bvt. Lt. Col. George K. Leet wrote to Moorhead. "Referring to your communication of may 27th /68 with enclosure, relative to John Snyder, an enlisted man of the U. S. Army, whom it was supposed was under sentence of death, at Jacksonville, Mississippi, for desertion, I am directed by General Grant to furnish the following information. The papers were referred from these Headquarters to the Commanding General of the 4th Military District, which command includes the State of Mississippi, who now returns them endorsed as follows: . . . It may be added that the death penalty for desertion is only inflicted in time of war."—Copies, DLC-USG, V, 47, 60; DNA, RG 108, Letters Sent.

1868, MAY 27. John Stokell, Portsmouth, N. H., to USG. "I have a Private account against Brvt Major Edmund Pendleton of about $80.00 and also an account Against Co "I" 3d Regt of U. S. artillery of which this Pendleton has had Command while it was Stationed here at Fort Constitution in this Harbor of about $202 00 the Private bill of his was for meats Poultry &Co furnished his table for about 3 months and the Company account was for Potatoes and other Vegetables furnished the Company. brvt mjr Pendleton having Command, of Course had the money Paid him from Lieut Charles Humpheys Commisary, and instead of Paying me for the Goods I had furnished the Company he Kept the money and appropriated it to his own use. I have Tried in Vain to get the money from him although he has faithfully Promised to pay the Same more than 20 times, and I have been waiting now Since January 1st and have not Received one Cent yet. the Company has now Gone from this Harbor to Fort Warren in Boston Harbor. I have been advised by Prominent men in this City to Lay the matter before you. I have Delivered these Goods and ought to have my Pay for them. as Every officer Stationed here with the Company are willing to Certifiy to, among whom are Genl Gates. Lieut. Charles Humpheys Brvt Major Bartlett and all the officers who have been Stationed here the Past Year—I have Stated the Case Just as it is and most Respectfully ask your attention to the matter. as I am Doing a Small Business and to be Kept out of So much money Such a Lenth of time Causes me no Little Embarrassment. hopeing that you will Investigat the matter at your Earliest opportunity . . ."—ALS, DNA, RG 94, P661 CB 1867. On Oct. 18 and 28, 1867, Edmund Pendleton, Berkeley Springs, West Va., had written to USG that his dismissal as 1st lt., 3rd Art., for absence without leave resulted from illness, and both USG and President Andrew Johnson (on Nov. 11) endorsed a recommendation for Pendleton's reinstatement.— AES, *ibid.* Pendleton's reinstatement was revoked as of July 9, 1868.

1868, MAY 27. George A. Trenholm, Charleston, S. C., to USG. "The Kindness of your reception when I had the honor of being introduced to you in Washington, encourages me to take this liberty. It is to introduce to you my son Mr Wm L. Trenholm, and to bespeak for him, if possible, a similar reception. It is proper for me to say that he enjoys my entire confidence, and I may without presumption add, the respect and goodwill of our whole community, and is entirely worthy of the honor of this introduction. He visits Washington on business of importance, in which perhaps it may accidentally happen that your good opinion of him may facilitate his progress; I venture to hope therefore that he may be so fortunate as to obtain it, and commending him again to your favorable consideration . . ."—ALS, DLC-George A. Trenholm.

1868, MAY 28. Bvt. Maj. Gen. William A. Nichols, adjt. for Lt. Gen. William T. Sherman, St. Louis, to USG. "I have just received the following telegram from General Sheridan dated Fort Leavenworth today: 'There has been much bad conduct on part of the Cheyenne Indians within the last week. They burned the traders store at St Aral the nineteenth (19th)— were insolent and threatening to the officer commanding the detachment of troops there. A party attacked a citizen camp at Coyale on the twenty sixth (26th)—wounded one man and drove off the stock. They have created much excitement and alarming the upper country. The Ossages also took a hand in the murdering business, a short time ago, at the mouth of the mouth of the Little Arkansas and killed and scalped two 2 white settlers—These indians are now holding council with the Commissioner of Indian Affairs."— Telegram received (at 4:00 P.M.), DNA, RG 107, Telegrams Collected (Bound); *ibid.*, RG 108, Telegrams Received; copies (one sent by mail), *ibid.*, Letters Received; DLC-USG, V, 55. On June 2, USG endorsed to Secretary of War John M. Schofield a letter of May 27 from Maj. Gen. Philip H. Sheridan to Nichols discussing these events in greater detail.—ES and LS, DNA, RG 94, Letters Received, 677M 1868.

1868, MAY 29. Bvt. Brig. Gen. Frederick T. Dent to Charles W. Ford. "I have just heard that you had interested yourself in trying to secure for Proff W D Fielding the possition of Asst Superintendant of Pub Schools in St Louis and am highly gratified at the news as I have known Fielding for many years as an instructor of the youth of Missouri to him or his father a large per cent of the young men of St Louis and St Charles Counties are indebted for their rudiments and progress I feel confident that Mr Fielding is in every way Competent and faithfull and it would be a source of gratification to hear that he is elected"—ALS, DLC-USG.

1868, [MAY]. USG endorsement. "Judge Dent, my brother-in law, has lived in the state of Miss. some four or five years, and understands the condition of public feeling there, and the means necessary to secure peace and harmony, as well as almost any Citizen of that state. His views given in this letter express about what my information confirms about the necessities in the present Canvas."—AES, Providence Public Library, Providence, R. I. Written on a letter of May 28 from Lewis Dent, Washington, D. C., to William M. Burt, Boston. "The constitutional convention of Mississippi having completed its work, is about to adjourn and submit the constitution framed, to the people of the State. In other Southern States it has not been a task of extreme difficulty to ratify the new constitutions, but in Mississippi, it will be clearly seen upon reviewing the situation, to be not only difficult but delicate and to be successfully accomplished only through the most skillful management and the most plausible presentation of the principles lying at the basis of the plan of reconstruction. Mississippi has long been known as a democratic State, the home of Jefferson Davis, the persistent and determined opponent of liberal ideas and as one of the most zealous adherents to the cause of the rebellion. Relatively it contained, with perhaps one exception, less original loyalty to the nation than any other State. Like South Carolina, Mississippi gloried in her disloyalty and struggled to rival her Atlantic Sister in her bold and treasonable official utterances. And what She was at the commencement of the war through the treacherous policy of Mr Johnson She is to day—not perhaps openly but in Spirit and covert purpose. With nearly all the civil offices, both federal and State, in the possession of the friends of the President, she will wield a strong power to defeat the ratification of the constitution and the election of loyal men to congress. There are but few large cities in the state The country is sparsely settled and the inhabitants in masses difficult to reach. The whites, in a large majority are poor and ignorant and deeply predjudicial against what are called radical ideas. The plantation interest, for several years, has suffered fearful losses on account of the failure of the crop.

The once wealthy and intelligent among the few who remained loyal to the last, and who would gladly see the State restored to the union upon almost any terms can render but little assistance, for they have no money and but little influence,. If therefore the constitution is to be ratified, if loyal men are to be elected to fill the State offices and loyal men are to be sent to the Senate & House of Representatives; if the plan of reconstruction is to be accepted in good faith and if the State is to be carried for the Repablican party in November, it is evident that much aid is to come from without and that what the state cannot itself furnish must be obtained elsewhere. It is fortunate that the 4th military Dist. is commanded by an officer in full Sympathy with the plan of reconstruction. But that of itself is not enough. The State must be thouroughly canvassed & the Rep. party compactly organized. Able, moderate, judicious & at the Same time, sound Republican speakers must be heard, in all the principal cities towns and political centers of the State. Clubs must be formed in every ~~halmets~~ hamlet & efforts made to put them under good party discipline. All this will require money and Mississippi has no money. The men by whom the State is to be brought back into the union, are at the lowest stage of poverty. What she asks, therefore from her friends at the north is, materiel assistance in the shape of contributions of money, to aid in the thoroug canvassing of the State and organization of the party. It will take no large Sum. A few thousand dollars, judiciously expended at the proper moment will restore the State to the union under a constitution harmony with the most advanced ideas of national policy. This Statement of facts and personal appeal is made with the knowledge that you are deeply interested in the Success of the congressional plan of reconstruction & election of loyal men to congress & that you have expressed a desire to assist, in aiding so patriotic & worthy a purpose. Trusting that the friends of national unity and freedom at the North will extend a generous hand, to the friends of the same great principles at the South . . ."—ALS, *ibid.*

1868, June 1. Bvt. Maj. Gen. Lovell H. Rousseau, Louisville, to Bvt. Maj. Gen. John A. Rawlins. "I desire to visit my family now at Saint Paul, Minnesota, and to adjust family affairs; this will require several weeks. For this purpose I hope to be allowed to delay starting to my command for five or six weeks, and respectfully request the proper order in the premises. . . . P. S. My address will be St Paul Minesota."—LS, DNA, RG 94, Letters Received, 217R 1868. On June 6, Bvt. Lt. Col. George K. Leet endorsed this letter. "Approved."—AES, *ibid.*

1868, June 1. Bvt. Lt. Col. George K. Leet to U.S. Senator Simon Cameron of Pa. "Referring to your application in behalf of Sgt. David McConaghy of the 19th U. S. Infty., who is now undergoing sentence of a Court Martial, for the crime of desertion, General Grant directs me to say that he recommended to the Secretary of War, on the 3d of April last, the remission of the unexecuted portion of the sentence. The attention of the

Secretary will again be called to this case."—Copies, DLC-USG, V, 47, 60; DNA, RG 108, Letters Sent.

1868, JUNE 1.   Richard Dunn, Fulton, N. Y., to USG. "I wish an appointment to the U. S. Military Acedamy at West Point. Am 21 year old, served in the last war. Was a prisoner at Andersonville 11 month. Am now attending school at Folley Seminery"—ALS, DNA, RG 94, Unsuccessful Cadet Applications.

1868, JUNE 2.   USG endorsement. "Respectfully forwarded to the Secretary of War."—ES, DNA, RG 94, Letters Received, 896M 1868. Written on a letter of May 28 from Maj. Gen. Philip H. Sheridan, Fort Leavenworth, to Bvt. Lt. Col. George K. Leet. "I have the honor to forward, herewith, for the information of the General in Chief the report of Brevet Colonel G. A. Forsyth, Acting Assistant Inspector General, Department of the Missouri, on the claim set forth by the Governor of the Chicasaw Nation for the expenses incurred in calling out a company of 'Rangers' to protect his people from the incursions of the wild Indians. There have been no depredations committed upon the Chicasaw Nation that would warrant the calling out, or mounting, of a Company of 'Rangers', and, when this Company was called out there was no intention of asking the Government to assume the expense. The whole affair is, I think, the work of Mr Leavenworth, Indian Agent, and other interested parties"—LS, *ibid.*

On May 22, Sheridan wrote to Bvt. Maj. Gen. William A. Nichols, adjt. for Lt. Gen. William T. Sherman, St. Louis. "The Indian Agent, Col Leavenworth, now stationed near or at Fort Cobb, Indian Territory, has given great annoyance to the troops and is constantly jeopardizing the peace and quietness of the frontier. He has asked for troops from Fort Arbuckle two or three times, and as many times either sent them back or changed his mind. He now calls for all the cavalry, Infantry and artillery at Fort Arbuckle and proposes to call out four hundred (400) Chickasaw Indians to meet some emergency, but which from the report of Colonel Forsyth now at Arbuckle, is intended to protect and help to consume some (500.000) five hundred thousand dollars worth of goods now being shipped by speculators and traders to Fort Cobb or vicinity. I feel satisfied from what I have seen of this man myself, and many others know of him, that he is an improper person to have in his present place."—Copy, *ibid.*, RG 75, Kiowa, W896. On June 13, USG endorsed this letter. "Respectfully forwarded to the Secretary of War, with request that this matter be laid before the Secretary of the Interior. I concur in the views of General Sheridan"— Copy, *ibid.* On June 17, Sheridan wrote to Bvt. Maj. Gen. John A. Rawlins on the same subject.—Copy, *ibid.*, RG 393, Military Div. of the Mo., Letters Sent.

1868, JUNE 2.   USG endorsement. "Respectfully forwarded to the Secretary of War"—Copy, DNA, RG 94, Correspondence, USMA. Written on a letter of May 22 from E. P. Dorr, Buffalo, to USG. "I have the honor to enclose to you, some papers relating to an application from Stephen J. Mulhall to the Hon. Sect. of War. U. S.—to be appointed~~lication~~ to the Military Academy at West Point. He has asked me to aid him. I would say that I knew him a Boy before entering the Army & his Father also—who is an old Soldier, having served many years in the Regular army, U. S. an excellent worthy man—Stephen is a first rate, splendid Boy; of excellent character & habits, a natural soldier, from love of the profession. The writer promised & gave him a gold watch for his good services during the War. We think him very deserving & meritorious, & if Gen. Grant, would hand this enclosure & letter to the Hon. Sect, of War. we hope he will have him appointed."—ALS, *ibid.* On May 26, Maj. Gen. George G. Meade, Atlanta, endorsed this letter. "Respectfully forwarded through Gen-in Chief to Honl Secy War.—I have known Capt—E. P. Dorr for many years & there is no man whose recommendation would have more influence with me. I therefore most earnestly recommend the appt of young Mulhall—whose papers are I presume on file in the War Office.—"—Copy, *ibid.*

On June 28, 1869, Stephen J. Mulhall, Auburn, N. Y., wrote to USG. "I have the honor respectfully to ask leave to present this note of grievance to his excellency for his kind Consideration   my son Stephen J Jr received a Conditional Appointment to the U S. Military Academy at West Point NY. for the class of 1869   he reported on the 3rd June and remained at the Academy until after the examination but was found defecient in his studies & rejected. Now I very respectfully ask his excellency to reapoint him, for the following reasons to viz   First his Father is an old soldier having served in the Mexican War & also through the recent rebellion is now superanuated from long service & disabilities   (second) the boy served all through the rebellion and was promised the Appointment by the lamented President Lincoln on conditions that he would be a good boy   the latter were the grounds which he received his appointment from President Johnson and not through any political agency. I am sorry to have to write such a [l]ong letter. but I must further state the boy Could not get relieved from military duty to attend to his studies in proper season to gain admission but I am fully satisfied if he should be so fortunate as to be reapointed he would be able to master the full Course by the 1st of septr. next. hoping his excellency will give this matter a favorable Consideration . . . P S I enclose discharge & Appointment which please return"—ALS, *ibid.*

1868, June 2, 11:55 a.m.   To Maj. Gen. Philip H. Sheridan. "Direct the transfer of Capt. Cochrane, deranged, now at Fort Union, to Pittsburgh Pa. in charge of Maj. Paul & brother, now on their way out to take charge of him. Maj. Paul will leave Pittsburgh to-morrow ~~for Fort Union~~ West. You may direct Capt. Cochrane to be brought to the end of the rail-road at once to meet his escort there."—ALS (telegram sent), DNA, RG 107, Telegrams Collected (Bound); telegram sent, *ibid.*; copies, *ibid.*, RG 108, Telegrams Sent; DLC-USG, V, 56. On June 3, Sheridan, Fort Leavenworth, telegraphed to USG. "Your telegram with reference to Lieut Coffman, deranged, received. Lieut Robinson was ordered on the eighth 8 of May to take Lieut Coffman in an ambulance to the end of the track U. P. R. R. E. D."— Telegram received (at 4:00 P.M.), DNA, RG 107, Telegrams Collected (Bound); *ibid.*, RG 108, Telegrams Received; LS (sent by mail), *ibid.*, Letters Received; copies, DLC-USG, V, 55; (2) DLC-Philip H. Sheridan.

1868, JUNE 2.   Bvt. Maj. Gen. Edward D. Townsend to Bvt. Maj. Gen. John A. Rawlins. "In reply to your inquiry of this date, I have to inform you that from the records of this Office it appears that the total number of prisoners surrendered by General Lee, and paroled at Appomattox Court House Va April 9. 1865, was Twenty-seven thousand, four hundred and sixteen. (27.416.)"—LS, DNA, RG 108, Letters Received.

1868, JUNE 2.   Christopher C. Andrews, St. Cloud, Minn., to USG. "One of the benefits to the country which we may expect from the national canvass about commencing is the *instruction* of the popular mind in the principles of the government, as well as the cultivation of a national spirit. It is important that the ballots shall represent *convictions.* I venture to recommend that you impress upon committees and influential public men the importance of circulating extensively among the people the ablest and best Republican newspapers. If possible every voter who reads should be supplied with a good campaign paper from now till November."—ALS (press), Andrews Papers, Minnesota Historical Society, St. Paul, Minn.

1868, JUNE 3.   USG endorsement. "Respectfully forwarded to the Secretary of War for instructions."—ES, DNA, RG 108, Letters Received. Written on a telegram of the same day from Bvt. Maj. Gen. Edward R. S. Canby, Charleston, to Bvt. Maj. Gen. John A. Rawlins. "Bushy Head and five 5 other Cherokee Indians from North Carolina, who claim to have been in the service of the United States during the rebellion, have applied to me for transportation to Washington. I have declined to give this until it is ascertained from the Commissioner of Indian Affairs that it is desired they they should come to Washington. Will you please ascertain this and whether the transportation, if furnished, will be refunded by the Indian Department   They represent that their business is important and I telegraph because they are now at Columbia far from their homes and without means"—Telegram received (at 11:40 A.M.), *ibid.*; *ibid.*, RG 107, Telegrams Collected (Bound). On June 5, 11:00 A.M., Rawlins telegraphed to Canby. "Secretary of Interior says the presence of Cherokee Indians referred to in your telegram of 3d is not required here & he will not sanction payment of transportation expenses"—Telegrams sent (2), *ibid.*; copies, *ibid.*, RG 108, Telegrams Sent; DLC-USG, V, 56.

1868, JUNE 3.   Alexander Todd, U.S. Assay Office, New York City, to USG. "When does George W Dent start for California?"—Telegram received (at 1:15 P.M.), DNA, RG 107, Telegrams Collected (Bound).

1868, JUNE 4.   Emilie S. Baker, Cartersville, Ga., to USG. "Because of my distresses in this as yet wretchedly rebellious South I addres you At this time upon a matter of much import to myself, and the revered old Uncle (Mr Tompkins) with whom I reside. A matter that my Uncle Communicated to General Logan, and in which reply from General Logan, he informed us that he had called upon you and you had informed him You would have it immediately attended to—but hearing nothing, seeing nothing appertaining to it at present from Genl Meade in Atlanta I take the responsibility of advising with you about it, it being none other than this That at the time Gen Sherman Evacuated Cartersville knowing my Uncle would be killed by the Rebels if he remained here, we refugeed North the Fall of 1864, and by Gen Shermans advice to Uncle in Cincinatti Ohio, we returned here November of 1865, and on that return between here and Chattanooga a very valuable Box was lost, containing thousands of Dollars of value to us, on which we paid the full freight   This Railroad has received the papers that it was shipped here, & it is lost on this Western & Atlantic road. The Superintendent has said he would pay the bill, the amount my Uncle estimates his loss at—yet does not pay the $1600—(Sixteen Hundred) and as we need the money very badly—we desire its payment immediately that we can go to Missouri and make a home for here tis impossible to remain, for as our Union Army destroyed Cartersville on Shermans March to the Sea, and consequently my Uncles business Houses was burned down, which on his return Home here deprived him from his having a House to do business in, and having so great Expenses while gone North a Refugee, and on coming back property not desired by strangers to settle here among these wretched Rebels, & each returned rebel again had his own Property, as we returned here only to sell out and then since our return have been persecuted shamefully by these Rebels because we REFUGEED North & again dragged into these unlawful rebel courts & openly robbed of hundreds of Dollars—that now with all of this large amount of Property my Uncle owns South, (though now unavailable till Georgia is again loyally back into the Union), a year yet, may pass, before he can sell, and he doing no business, till we are actually reduced to such a condition, that we have not the necessaries of life, and as a Lady accustomed to have what I want—I am suffering physically for many things   We cannot collect a debt, these courts will do a Union man *no* justice with a *Rebel* jury, and then must I starve, while living in a large House & owning Houses & lots & lands elsewhere? It appears so, and without your orders, to Gen Meade to make the Superintendent pay us the loss of that Box on this Western & Atlantic RR., we never *shall* get it, for they will first go to the Civil Courts to law (although they told Uncle they would pay it) before they WILL pay it, and as military law is still here and we know, we know WELL we cannot get justice, even after Georgia is back in the Union, as the Juries will still be Rebel we desire that you order Gen Meade to order them to pay it for if we lost it by Refugeeing North, as loyalists to our Country, should not you loyal General [see] that loyal person get paid their damages back again to them—when they, the Rebels were so careless as to lose, or rob them of their effects on their return Home South? I think so & who are we to look to for the restitution of our Property at the hands of these rebels, if not to Congress under some Consideration, & under the within mentioned subject, to yourself as chief Commander, over the Military Districts South— where the rebel, will not do Justice to the loyal man, which loyalist has sacrificed so much for his country—See what the Nation does for yourself, it is promotion, after promotion—& now to the highest seat in the Nation— as a loyal General in the Union Army, one in whom we now have a holy trust, that like the departed Lincoln that your adminision as coming President of these United States you will carry us as safe through the present pending crisis of our country which is as bad if not worse, than the past late Civil: as he did through the war while pending And consequently the Nation looks to you now, as its only relief—will you not then give us your entire aid by ordering Gen Meade to request the Superintendent of the Western & Atlantic Railroad to pay us over 1,600$ for the loss of our valuable Box? Pray do for us all you can for we greatly desire the means to go west west to Missouri because we cannot longer live here, put upon as we are, & insulted by these rebels & doing no business; & we will wait to sell our Property till better times, for I cannot starve longer—without an income where is our support? Leaving ourselves at your mercy & hoping you may restore us our money—"—ALS, DNA, RG 108, Letters Received.

1868, June 5. To Secretary of War John M. Schofield. "I have the honor to recommend General Horatio P. Van Cleve, late BrigadierGeneral of Volunteers, for appointment as Military sStorekeeper, Q. M. Dept., USA., to fill the vacancy now existing in that Department."—LS, DNA, RG 94, ACP, 1167 1874.

1868, June 5. Judge Advocate Gen. Joseph Holt to USG. "The papers relating to the death of Private Charles Lehman, Co. B. 35th U. S. Infy, are respectfully returned with the following report. On the night of the 1st of January last, the deceased, in company with other soldiers, was in a drinking saloon in Indianola, Texas, between the hours of ten and eleven o'clk—being absent from their quarters without permission. They had been drinking, and talked so loudly as to attract the attention of Captain Frederick W. Bailey and Lieut. C. A. Dempsey, of the 35th regiment, as they passed the place on the way to their quarters from a supper given in Indianola by Act. Asst. Surg. Santoire. These officers entered the bar-room and attempted to arrest the men, who, fearing punishment if recognized, ran out—passing a short distance down the street and turning off into the first alley they reached. They were pursued by the officers, who were pre-

vented by darkness from distinguishing them in the alley. At the command
of Capt. Bailey, Lieut. Dempsey fired upon them with a pistol, inflicting a
wound on Privt. Lehman, of which he died on the 3d of January. The officers heard no cry, and were not aware until the next day that the shot had
taken effect. Bvt. Brig. Gen. Hatch, under whose direction an investigation
of the circumstances has been had, expresses the opinion that no blame
attaches to Lieut. Dempsey, and regrets that Capt Bailey did not content
himself with ordering a check roll-call, which would have caused the detection of the offenders, instead of endeavoring to intimidate them in the
method taken. Gen. Hatch thinks it is shown that intimidation only was
intended, by the fact that the night was so dark that it was not perceived
that any of the party had fallen. He makes no recommendation. After careful examination & comparison with each other of the statements of Capt.
Bailey and Lieut. Dempsey, and of three of the comrades of Lehman, this
Bureau is constrained to differ from the opinion expressed by Gen. Hatch—
that no blame attaches to Lieut Dempsey for having obeyed the order of
his commanding officer. That order was clearly unnecessary and illegal;
and the prompt obedience he rendered with such a fatal result is deemed
highly culpable. It may be said, however, in his behalf, that the order came
upon him suddenly, in the heat and excitement of a chase; and that under
such circumstances he had no time for deliberation. In this view it is believed he should have the benefit of the doubt raised as to his criminal
responsibility, and should not be proceeded against formally. It is thought,
however, that such action should be taken by the General Commanding the
Army as would signify to the service disapprobation of the disregard of
human life evinced in the part borne by Lieut. Dempsey in the transaction
under consideration. As to the case of Capt. Bailey, it is deemed that more
stringent action is demanded. This officer, in his affidavit, sets forth that
when the deceased and his comrades fled from the Saloon, they were several
times commanded to halt. Lieut. Dempsey, in his statement, is not only
silent on this point—so important to his own vindication—but his narrative
is incompatible with it. Private Ryan who was close by Pvt Lehman when
the fatal shot was fired, swears that he heard no such command given.
Private Brill makes no statement whether such command was issued.
Private Schindler swears, that as the men ran from the saloon he heard
some one cry 'halt' once. Capt. Bailey also swears that shortly after Lieut.
Dempsey fired, he heard another discharge of firearms near the same place;
but as such a fact is not mentioned by any of the others, but little credit is
given to it. Indeed the inference cannot be avoided that Capt. Bailey, in
seeking to exonerate his conduct, has resorted to statements which, as has
been indicated, are not only unsupported by the statement of his subordinate, Dempsey, but at variance with the general tenor of the testimony in
the case. When it is considered that the only offence committed by the deceased was an absence from his quarters in company with some of his
comrades, without permission, at a time universally devoted to social meet-

ings and conviviality; and that he was shot down while simply seeking to avoid recognition and attempting to reach his quarters, the Act of Capt. Bailey appears one of wanton disregard of human life, which, the honor of the service demands, should receive the condemnation of the government. It is therefore recommended that he be immediately brought to trial before a General Court Martial for the homicide, under the charge of manslaughter, to the prejudice of good order and military discipline."—Copy, DNA, RG 153, Letters Sent.

1868, JUNE 5.   Bvt. Lt. Col. George K. Leet endorsement. "Respectfully referred to MajorGeneral W. S. Hancock, Commanding Mil. Div.n of the Atlantic, who will direct the CommandingGeneral Dept. of the East to make a thorough investigation, and if the rumors of a contemplated invasion of Canada from our no[r]thern frontier are found to have any foundation in truth, to report the same to the President of the U. S. through the proper channel for instructions."—ES, DNA, RG 107, Letters Received from Bureaus. Written on a letter of June 1 from Secretary of State William H. Seward to Secretary of War John M. Schofield transmitting a report of possible Fenian activity.—LS, *ibid.* Related papers are *ibid.*

1868, JUNE 5.   Maj. Gen. George H. Thomas, Louisville, to USG. "I have the honor to request that the name of Brt Col. John Mendenhall Capt 4th Arty may be placed upon the list of applicants for the next vacancy for Inspector General U. S. A. Colonel Mendenhall was on duty with General Brannan Chief of Arty Army of the Cumberland whilst you were at Chattanooga in the winter of 1863 & 64 an[d] and until the close of active operations. He was chiefly engaged in the personal inspection of the several Batteries belonging to that Army, and always perfor[me]d his duties with promptness, intelligence, and efficiently. He was regarded by General Brannan as amost efficnt and reliable Inspector which estimate of his qualifications I am unable from personal knowledge of the manner in which he discharged his duties to endorse fully."—ALS, DNA, RG 94, ACP, T118 CB 1864. No appointment followed.

1868, JUNE 6.   Bvt. Lt. Col. George K. Leet endorsement. "Respectfully referred to the Adjt. General. It is understood that the Secretary of War desires that this detail be made. If the information on this point is correct the General of the Army withdraws his disapproval on a previous application for the detail of this officer."—AES, DNA, RG 94, Letters Received, 154M 1868. Written on a letter of June 5 from Bvt. Brig. Gen. Albert J. Myer, chief signal officer, to USG. "I respectfully recommend that First Lieutenant J. Harrison Hall, 1st. Cavalry, be ordered to report to the Chief Signal Officer of the Army for duty."—LS, *ibid.*

On May 12, Myer had written to USG. "I respectfully recommend that First Lieutenant J. Harrison Hall, 1st. Cavalry, now at Dayton, Ohio, be ordered to report to the Chief Signal Officer of the Army for duty."—LS, *ibid.*, 381S 1868. On May 14, Leet endorsed this letter. "Respectfully referred to the Adjutant General for report."—AES, *ibid.*

1868, JUNE 7.   George G. Gunn, New Orleans, to USG.   "you must excuse me for Writing to you but under the circumstances perhaps you Will   Genral Grant I have ben in the united states servis 4 years during the War and during that time I beleave that I done my duty to my country Why I Write to you is because I nead assistance   sience the War I ha[ve] ben layed up With the rhumatis and have not ben able to Work for a living I. have to beg   it is hard for me to doe so but such is the case   I Was a member of the second R I Regement   I have some Bounty money coming to me but I doe not know When I shall get it   my discharg papers ar in Washington at preas[en]t   now Genral I am no imposter   Will you be so kind as to Releave me or eaven to leand me a little money   if you Would I Will neaver forget you   It is hard for a man that has fought for his country as I have done to have a try to Work for his vitals as I am doeing at preasent   I Wish you Would Write soon to me and direct to post ofice Neworleans   if I could get some light employment under goverment it Would doe me veary Well   I have no trade   I have ben a Salor but I can not goe to sea eney more   I am at preasent living on the bounty of thoes that I fought against but they doe not know that   Genral grant for god sake send me something if it is only transportasion from heare to New york . . . If you think you can see my discharg in Wasington   Will you Write soon"—ALS, DNA, RG 105, Letters Received.

1868, JUNE 8.   USG endorsement. "I do not recommend the creation of the Office of Inspr of Cav.y."—AES, DNA, RG 94, M162 CB 1868. Written on a letter of June 3 from U.S. Representative James A. Garfield of Ohio to Secretary of War John M. Schofield. "Some weeks since I addressed a letter to the then Secretary of War, asking his views upon the expediency of providing by law for the appointment of an Inspector of Cavalry with the rank of Colonel, a bill for that purpose having been referred to the Committee on Military Affairs. Thinking that the letter, which has not been answered, may not be brought to your notice, and desiring to report upon the bill at an early day, I have the honor to call your attention to the subject."—LS, *ibid.*

1868, JUNE 9.   To Secretary of War John M. Schofield. "I have the honor to recommend the discharge of private Eben Smith, Company K, 36th U. S. Infantry,"—Copies, DLC-USG, V, 47, 60; DNA, RG 108, Letters Sent.

1868, JUNE 10.   Maj. Gen. Philip H. Sheridan, Fort Leavenworth, to Bvt. Maj. Gen. John A. Rawlins. "I wish to respectfully call the attention of the Government to the great necessity of connecting the Military Depôt of Fort Leavenworth with the several lines of the Union Pacific Railroad for the construction of which the Government is now giving large subsidies per mile. In my letter of the 6th instant I represented that the Leavenworth Lawrence and Galveston Railroad Company be compelled to connect with this post giving reasons for same. I now desire to impress on the Government the necessity of having the Central Pacific Railroad, which is to connect Atchieson with the Union Pacific Road near Fort Kearney, extend from Atchieson down the river to this post. This would place the Post of Fort Leavenworth, which is the great distributing point in the west, in complete connection with all the lines extending across the Continent and will be of great and lasting benefit to the public service. I think it very reasonable for the Government to insist on these conditions. By engrafting the first condition in the ratification of the Osage treaty and insisting that the Central Pacific Railroad Company be compelled to extend down from Atchieson to this Post, a distance of about twenty five (25) miles, the result which I ask for will be accomplished. If it is not done, this Depot will be within the hearing of the whistle of the Locomotive and at the same time crippled in the facilities which it affords for quick work and economy. The Government has here seven thousand acres of land. It will in course of time be the great central point for the administration of the Military command of the West, and will, with scarcely a doubt, have transferred here the Cavalry Recruiting Depot from Carlisle Pa, and will grow in importance as the great Military center and Depot of the West."—LS, DNA, RG 107, Letters Received from Bureaus.

1868, JUNE 11.   Maj. Gen. Winfield S. Hancock, Washington, D. C., to USG. "I have the honor to inform you that a review of the troops composing the Garrison of Washington will take place at Lincoln Barracks on Thursday, the 18th instant, at 11 o'clock A. M., unless prevented by unfavorable weather, when it will be deferred to the first suitable day thereafter. Yourself and Staff are respectfully invited to be present on the occasion."—LS, DNA, RG 108, Letters Received. On June 17, Bvt. Maj. Gen. John A. Rawlins wrote to Hancock. "I have the honor to acknowledge the receipt of your note of the 11th inst. informing General Grant of the review of the troops composing the garrison of Washington on Thursday, the 18th inst., and inviting him and staff to be present on the occasion and to say that the General was, at the date of its receipt and has been ever since, absent from the City. Should he return in time and be able to attend as invited he no doubt will notify you at the earliest possible moment"—Copies, DLC-USG, V, 47, 60; DNA, RG 108, Letters Sent.

1868, JUNE 13.   Bvt. Maj. Gen. Edward O. C. Ord, San Francisco, to Bvt. Maj. Gen. John A. Rawlins. "I beg to call attention of the General Commanding to the enclosed reports. Men and Officers in this Department are much discontented at the miserable manner in which they are compelled to quarter themselves for want of funds, and proper material—The Department Quarter master, General Kirkham, informs me that his estimates for building material and forage have just been cut down One Hundred Thousand Dollars ($100 000) these estimates being based on the forage and material absolutely necessary at current rates to keep the troops where they have been sent for the protection of the frontiers; that the troops and horses cannot be kept there without the money, and that his estimates have been sent in up to date; yet he has only been furnished with funds to include the month of February, last—This delay adds largely to the amount we have to pay for all sorts of supplies, and leaves the troops in the desert districts of Arizona, and Navada, exposed to the weather or under much covering; increasing desertions, which as General Kirkham reports have in some cases exceeded 50 per centum in a year—If the Secretary of War would let me have a Hundred—or even Fifty—Thousand Dollars of the Sheltering Fund, I would see that it was expended in making the men more comfortable, and I am sure it would save that amount in preventing desertion, and by giving additional efficiency to the troops—"—LS, DNA, RG 94, Letters Received, 460C 1868.

1868, June 14.   Bvt. Maj. Gen. Edward R. S. Canby, Charleston, to Bvt. Maj. Gen. John A. Rawlins. "On the 3d inst and during the late election, a trifling difficulty occurred at the polling place at Barnwell Court House, in the course of which W. J. Mixson, Republican Candidate for County School Commissioner was shot, and mortally wounded, (since reported dead), by A. V. Eaves, the present Clerk of the Court of Barnwell County The shooting occurred in the presence of the Sheriff who made no attempt to arrest the criminal, and it is alleged positively refused to make the arrest when applied to; and a Magistrate who was applied to refused to issue a warrant unless bonds to prosecute were first given. Eaves and his two accomplices Harley and Brown remained at Barnwell C. H. from 11 o'clock in the morning until after night and then fled. There were no troops nearer than Aiken, and they could not reach the place until after the murderers had made their escape, but I think that I am in possession of information that will secure their arrest. About 10 o'clock on the evening of the 4th inst. Mr. S. W. Dill, one of the County Commissioners elect of Kershaw County was murdered by a party of men supposed to number from five to nine. Ten shots were fired, killing Mr Dill, and dangerously, probably mortally wounding his wife. A colored man (Nestor Ellison) was killed while attempting to make his escape from the house. No arrests were made by the civil authorities. A detachment of troops was at once sent by Lt. Col. Edie, the Commander of the Post in the limits of which Kershaw County is included, to Camden the county seat, and as soon as the news reached me, a detective was sent to aid in the investigation of the matter and the arrest of the criminals. Six persons, (four white and two colored), suspected of being implicated in the murder, have been arrested by the military authorities, two of whom have since been released. In both these cases the murders were purely political, and without any provocation so far as can be learned. —In the first case, if not planned, advantage was taken of a trifling affray to carry out a premeditated purpose.—In the second case there is no reasonable question that the whole was premeditated, and carried out by persons who were intimately acquainted with Mr. Dill's house, his personal habits &c. Both of the murdered men were South Carolinians; Mr. Mixson had served in the Confederate Army and lost an arm in that service, and both, as native Unionists, were specially obnoxious to the Rebel element for the reason that they were regarded as traitors to that cause.—The County Officers of Kershaw and Barnwell have been removed, and will be replaced by the Officers just elected, so far as they can qualify."—LS, DNA, RG 108, Letters Received. On June 18, USG endorsed a copy of this letter to Secretary of War John M. Schofield.—ES, *ibid.*, RG 94, Letters Received, 774M 1868.

On June 12, Bvt. Maj. Gen. Robert K. Scott, Charleston, wrote to U.S. Representative James M. Ashley of Ohio. "I notice by this mornings paper, that you offered a resolution in the House, yesterday, relative to the murder of Solomon Dill, County Commissioner, and member of the Legislature, elect, from Kershaw District, in this State. I fear that this resolution may by implication convey to the country at large the idea that Congressional action in the matter was thought necessary because of an existing want of confidence in the willingness of the Commanding General of this Military District to use every effort to discover, arrest and punish the murderers. Against the justice of such a construction of this resolution I desire to bear testimony, as I know that in this, as in every other case of similar nature, Brevet Maj. Gen'l. Canby has acted most promptly and energetically."— Copy, *ibid.*, RG 108, Letters Received. On the same day, Canby endorsed a copy of this letter. "Respectfully forwarded to Headquarters of the Army. —I had noticed in the morning papers the action taken by Mr. Ashley in the House of Representatives but it had occurred to me that it would have the construction placed upon it by Gen. Scott. My own experience has satisfied me that the public offer of a reward, operates simply as a motive to the guilty parties to get out of the way, and I have uniformly been more successful in the arrest of criminals by working quietly. In this case the detectives reported by telegraph on the 10th inst. the arrest of six of the persons, implicated in the murder, but the detailed report sent by mail, has not been received and is probably delayed by the late storm. A Judge Advocate goes up to Camden tomorrow to prepare the cases for trial, which will be ordered so soon as he is ready. So far as I can now judge the murder was purely political. I will send a full report so soon as I get the detailed report from Camden."—Copy, *ibid.* On the same day, Scott wrote to USG. "Permit a soldier to tender you his earnest congratulations upon your nomination to the highest position within the gift of the people. May the perseverance and energy which animated you during the late conflict, inspire your friends in the ensueing struggle, and enable them to overcome at the ballot box, the foes you conquered in the field. In my humble way no effort will be spared towards bringing about that desired end."—LS, USG 3.

On June 17, Canby telegraphed to USG. "One of the city morning papers contains a sensational paragraph in relation to outrages in Kershaw County in this state. Col Edie in reply to an inquiry from me has just telegraphed from Camden that there is no foundation whatever"—Telegram received (at 4:00 P.M.), DNA, RG 107, Telegrams Collected (Bound); (at 2:00 P.M.) *ibid.*, RG 108, Telegrams Received; copies, *ibid.*, RG 94, Letters Received, 932M 1868; (sent by mail) *ibid.*, RG 108, Letters Received; *ibid.*, RG 393, 2nd Military District, Letters Sent; DLC-USG, V, 55. The clipping read: "Fearful Outrage in Kershaw District—Two Citizens Hang[ed] and one Killed—We learn, upon authori[ty that] we consider indisputable, that dispatches were received in Columbia Monday night from Camden, stating that an outbreak had occurred amongst the negroes in that vicinity, in the progress of which several of the most prominent citizens were forcibly incarcerated, and two of them hung, and that the Sheriff of the District, in a futile effort to command the peace, had been fatally shot. It appears that the company of Federal soldiers which had been sent to that point at the earnest solicitation of the citizens to quell the disturbances which were threatened in consequence of the killing of S. G. W. Dill last week, had received notice that they were to be relieved by a company from Columbia, and without waiting for the relief to arrive, had started from Camden. The negroes taking advantage of their absence, rose *en masse* and committed the horrible outrage to which we allude. At this hour it is impossible to learn more of the details or the names of the victims, and we await with solicitude further reports of what seems to us to possess every probability of truth."—DNA, RG 108, Letters Received.

1868, June 15.   Speaker of the House Schuyler Colfax to USG. "Allow me to introduce to you Capt John C. Conner, 41st U. S. Infantry, a son of a valued friend of mine in Indiana, & whom I commend to you as every way worthy of your esteem. He served during the whole War & will explain to you his business."—ALS, OCIWHi.

1868, June 16.   U.S. Representative Grenville M. Dodge of Iowa to USG. "I desire to call your attention to the case of General P. E. Connor, formerly commanding in Utah. I am informed that there has been reports made of his administration, derogatory to his character and integrity as a man and a soldier. I am certain they were made under misapprehension of facts, and through a determined and designed effort of his enemies, to mislead the officers who made them. All these charges were laid before me, while the General was in the service, were investigated by me and found to be based entirely upon false grounds. I desire you to look at his report, (made to you and myself when I took command of that country,) and your response thereto. If there ever was a soldier under me who I believe worked for the good of the government, it was Connor. A great amount of calumny and opposition was heaped on him all over the Plains, because he did his duty fearlessly. You can scarcely have an idea of the condition of affairs on the Plains, when I went there and called him to take command of a portion of that country, to obtain, if possible, an honest administration of affairs there—there was so much demoralization that it took months to even bring matters back to respectability.—Gen. Connor ably seconded all my efforts, exposed the corruption, broke up the rings, and thwarted their efforts in all directions, lending me all aid possible. His endeavors, of course, made him countless enemies—Again, his administration of affairs in Utah was not in accordance with the views of the Mormons, and brought down on him their ill-will. If you ever visit that country you will find that whilst the Mormons opposed him, his straight forward and manly course, commanded the respect of all right minded men west of the Missouri River. After a soldier has served as faithfully and ably as General Connor has, it is very hard for him to retire to civil life with any stigma resting upon his name, and I hope you will give him the opportunity to meet and answer any and all charges resting against him—I feel that I owe it to Gen. Connor to say, that in all my service I never knew any officer who had so many complaints made against him, all of which I examined closely, and many personally, and I never knew an officer, under similar circumstances, who showed so clean a record; and I do believe that he has done nothing that will in the least reflect on his integrity as an officer or soldier. He may have made mistakes, but if so, they were of the head and not of the heart, and who, of all of us who were in the war, did not?"—LS, DNA, RG 108, Letters Received.

1868, JUNE 18. USG endorsement. "Respectfully forwarded to the Secretary of War, inviting attention to the new regulations for the government of the 'Soldiers' Home,' and recommending their revision. That portion of the regulations which places the Secretary & Treasurer beyond the control of the Governor is, in my opinion, entirely wrong in principle, and in effect would undoubtedly be detrimental to the interests of the institution. In conclusion I respectfully recommend that Gen. McIntosh be retained as Governor of the Home."—ES, DNA, RG 94, Letters Received, 470S 1868. Written on a letter of May 2 from Bvt. Maj. Gen. John B. McIntosh, governor, Soldiers' Home, Washington, D. C., to the board of commissioners, resigning his post.—ALS, *ibid.*

1868, JUNE 18. U.S. Representative William S. Lincoln of N. Y., Washington, D. C., to USG. "I have the honor to enclose herewith a letter from Gen. I. S. Catlin who is now stationed at Louisville Kentucky—and who on account of his health desires to be transfered to Brooklyn N. Y.—or some other point north where he can engage in the Recruiting service or some other useful service and at same time regain his health—Gen. Catlin I have known personally for many years—He was one of the first to enter the army in 1861—and was faithful and brave to the last—He lost a leg in front of Petersburg and was otherwise injured in that campaign—He is a man of education and influence in the State of NewYork where he is well known—

I most cordially endorse him and respectfully ask that if there is any service in the Northern States to which he can be assigned it may be done"—ALS, DNA, RG 108, Letters Received. The enclosure is *ibid.*

1868, JUNE 19. To Secretary of War John M. Schofield. "I respectfully recommend that Wm S. Coyner, who has recently been appointed a 2d Lt. in the Army, from Ohio, be authorized to go before any Surgeon, in good standing, in Delaware, Ohio, to be examined for admission into the service. Mr. Coyner was appointed to the Army more than a year ago and passed his examination, except physically, then. He, with three brothers, & his father, served in the Union Army during a great part of the rebellion, and being Virginians [w]ere compelled to leave their state, ~~at the close of their service~~"—ALS, DNA, RG 94, ACP, C145 CB 1868. On June 20, Bvt. Brig. Gen. John C. Kelton, AGO, endorsed this letter. "All the facts having been stated in this case to Genl. Grant he withdrew his recommendation and desires that the applicant be examined as usual in such cases."—AES, *ibid.*

1868, JUNE 19. USG endorsement. "Respectfully refered to Hon—H. Willson Chm.n Mil—Com—of the senate—I unite with Gen Meade in recommending the removal of all disabilities in the case of P. M. B. Young to the end that he may be able to take his seat in Congress—"—Copies, DNA, RG 108, Register of Letters Received; (undated) *ibid.*, RG 233, 40A–F29.15. Written on a letter of June 3 from Maj. Gen. George G. Meade, Atlanta, to "Gen.l," presumably USG. "This letter will be handed to you by Gen'l Young late of the confederate army—Gen'l Y—commanded a brigade of cav—in Lee's army, and his name and feats were very familiar to me during the war, but since I have been here it gives me pleasure to say I have derived great satisfaction from my intercourse with him—I wish you to talk with him, and you will find he is all right and it is just such men as he we want down here, as their influence & example are most powerful—I should like to see Gen'l Young disabilities removed & he allowed to take his seat in Congress—not that he would be a republican, tho I dont know that he is not but I know he is loyal to the Union and will do as much to uphold it, and the flag as if the rebellion had never existed—Hoping you may have it in your power to aid him— . . ."—Copy, *ibid.*

1868, JUNE 22. USG endorsement. "Respectfully forwarded to the Secretary of War."—ES, DNA, RG 94, ACP, B406 CB 1868. Written on a letter of Nov. 1, 1867, from Edward J. Brooks, Washington, D. C., to USG. "I have the honor to state that in May 1861, I was a 1st Lieut & Adjutant 7th US Infantry and was dropped from the Rolls for disloyalty by an order from the then Secretary of War Hon Simon Cameron—My situation at that time, was somewhat peculiar surrounded by influences, of a family nature extremely difficult to resist, and threatened with the loss of a large property by my wife's relatives if I remained in in the Army, I one day, after more than ordinary pressure had been brought to bear, was weak and criminal enough to yeild to threats and persuasions, and write certain letters, to a relative, enclosing my resignation to be forwarded if the State seceded, and also an application to Jefferson Davis for a position in the rebel army—Twenty fours after the letters had left my possession General, I would have given my right arm to regain possession of them—After I had thus committed myself, beyond power of recall, my judgment and my conscience continually warned me of my fatal error—After mature reflection, no earthly consideration could have induced me to espouse the rebel cause— In the following August I participated in the skirmish before the town of Mesilla Arizona, and was then wounded, when our command was surrendered at San Augustine Springs, I was then and there offered a commission as Colonel of Texas troops, and in the presence of nearly all the Officers of the Command, and my whole Company, I refused & rejected it with scorn— In the following September, I received the order dropping me from the Rolls. Had I been truly disloyal, General my first impulse, and probably first act, would have been to go South & join the rebel army—Acknowledging as I did fully the justice of my punishment, I could only bow my head to the blow and submit—For more than six years, I have endeavored faithfully to perform my duties as a loyal citizen, and encouraged others to do likewise—Such feeble aid, as my position permitted, to the Union Cause, was cheerfully & hopefully given—I raised at a heavy expense nearly 400 men, and consented to their transfer to fill up a partially organized Cavalry Regiment in Arkansas, I have been at all times and under all circumstances ready & willing to do all in my power to uphold the integrity of the Union—For more than six years General, I have suffered such anguish as perhaps but few men ever experience, I was proud of my position, and of a military record commenced during the Mexican War, but alas! so disgracefully ended—I was ambitious, and in common with my brother Officers longed for glory & distinction—In an unfortunate hour, the weaknesses of my nature reigned supreme, but I overcame them, but all too late to escape punishment, disgrace and a total overthrow of all hopes for the future—I have a family growing up, and it is a source of unspeakable pain to me to feel that my boys, shall forever bear the stain of disloyalty stamped upon their brows, through the misdeeds of the father   General. I have been weak & criminal but the error has been expiated by six long years of disgrace—But that I was not advised of my exchange as a prisoner of war until, my family was in such a condition as to require my presence, I should have again entered the Army as a private soldier, and endeavored to wipe out the stain by true & faithful service in the good cause—In conclusion General, I ask if possible that the order dropping me from the Rolls for disloyalty be rescinded, and my resignation accepted to take effect from same date, and that the letter now on file in the War Department may be returned to me that I may be enabled at least to destroy such damning evidence of my weakness, and criminality"—ALS, *ibid.*

1868, JUNE 22. USG endorsement. "Respectfully forwarded to the Secretary of War."—ES (undated), DNA, RG 107, Letters Received from Bureaus; copy, *ibid.*, RG 108, Register of Letters Received. Written on a letter of June 20 from L. Mitchell, "of the old 4th," Washington, D. C., to USG. "As a stranger, I beg pardon for the liberty I take in directing these few lines to you, but knowing you as a friend to the soldier, and also, that if justice is to be done to a class of men, who have faithfully done their duty & freely shed their blood for the preservation of this Republic, it can only be done by appealing to you, & through you to the U. S. Congress; shall be my apology for so doing. The various Bounty Bills passed by Congress, makes no provision for the soldiers, their wives & orphans, who have served in the regular army, during the whole period of the late War, and never received one cent of State or Gov. Bounty; it is true, that none was promised to them & consequently none due, but this is equally true with those, who received the bounty promised & now receive additional. The regular soldiers as you Genl. know were true & loyal, fought the Battles of the Republic, had to serve five years & therefore no chance for re enlistment, as those, who enlisted during the progress of the War, the soldier of the regular Army had to serve during the whole period, received not one cent of State or Gov. Bounty, had no State Agents to look out for their interests, their families received no aid or suport from State or Gov, & yet the very Govt, to whom they properly belong, does nothing for them, but even seems to exclude them from every thing. The Vols Soldiers first enlisted for one year & received for that State & Gov. Bounty at the expiration of that time, re-enlisted & received Bounty, so in many cases he received nearly one thousand dollars bounty, some more, some less, his family was taken care of to some extent, by the State he credited himself, while the regular soldier, who fought nearly in all the Battles of the Rebellion from Rolla Mo. under Genl. Lyon, up to the close, does not get one cent. The Bounty Bills gives additional Bounty to those who received it & to those who received none, and have the best claim therefore, it gives none, particularly is that true of those soldiers who enlisted in 1859 and 60 & had to serve for 5 years, unless sooner killed or otherwise disabled. Alas for Republics!—I am *not* capable to present *our* case to you Genl with more eloquence, but I can only state the facts in a plain manner, and trust, that you Genl will at least bring the case to the notice of the U. S. Congress; a Congress which has rendered itself forever memorable by its efforts in behalf of the downcast and the wrong always, ought to do itself the justice to consider the just claim respectfully urged."—ALS, *ibid.*, RG 107, Letters Received from Bureaus.

1868, JUNE 22. Lt. Gen. William T. Sherman, St. Louis, to USG. "Am just back from New Mexico via Forts Lyon and Wallace. Will make full report by mail within a day or so."—Telegram received (at 1:15 P.M.), DNA, RG 107, Telegrams Collected (Bound); *ibid.*, RG 108, Telegrams Received; copy, DLC-USG, V, 55. On June 25, Sherman wrote a lengthy report to Bvt. Maj. Gen. Edward D. Townsend.—LS, DNA, RG 94, Letters Received, 809M 1868. On June 29, USG endorsed this report. "Respectfully forwarded to the Secretary of War inviting special attention to the subjects of this communication. I concur fully in the views and suggestions of Lt Gen. Sherman expressed herein."—ES, *ibid.*

1868, JUNE 23.   To Secretary of War John M. Schofield. "I have the honor to recommend the discharge from service of Wm. B. Lewis, an enlisted man in Co "K" 12 U. S. Infantry"—Copies, DLC-USG, V, 47, 60; DNA, RG 108, Letters Sent.

1868, JUNE 23.   To Lt. Gen. William T. Sherman. "Relieve Paymaster Ihrie from all duty except his appropriate duties as Paymaster."—ALS (telegram sent), DNA, RG 107, Telegrams Collected (Bound); telegram sent (dated June 24, sent at 12:10 P.M.), *ibid.*; copies (dated June 24), *ibid.*, RG 108, Telegrams Sent; DLC-USG, V, 56. On June 24, Sherman, St. Louis, telegraphed to USG. "I think that Pay master Ihrie has long since been relieved of all duties except those of Pay master. General Sheridan reported so to me, March seventh 7 last, but I will repeat your orders to Genl Sheridan, in whose Department Denver is"—Telegram received (at 3:30 P.M.), DNA, RG 107, Telegrams Collected (Bound); *ibid.*, RG 108, Telegrams Received; copies (one sent by mail), *ibid.*, Letters Received; DLC-USG, V, 55. On the same day, Bvt. Lt. Col. George K. Leet endorsed to the AG charges against Maj. George P. Ihrie.—AES, DNA, RG 94, Letters Received, 327H 1868. Telegrams exchanged between Ihrie and President Andrew Johnson in July concerning these charges are in DLC-Andrew Johnson.

1868, JUNE 23, 3:30 P.M.   To Bvt. Maj. Gen. George Stoneman. "Yes." —Telegrams sent (2), DNA, RG 107, Telegrams Collected (Bound); copies, *ibid.*, RG 108, Telegrams Sent; DLC-USG, V, 56. On the same day, Stoneman, Richmond, had telegraphed to USG. "Can I have an interview with you on Friday"—Telegram received, DNA, RG 107, Telegrams Collected (Bound); *ibid.*, RG 108, Telegrams Received; copy, *ibid.*, RG 393, 1st Military District, Telegrams Sent. On June 26, Stoneman wrote to USG. "I have the honor to recommend the passage of an Act of Congress authorizing and directing the Commanding General of the 1st Military District to order an election in Virginia within sixty days after the passage of the Act, for the ratification or rejection of the Constitution framed by the Convention recently assembled in that state and that at such election the section of said Constitution embracing an additional oath of office be submitted separately; also that section 9 of the Act of July 19th 1867, prescribing an oath of office in the Military District be repealed. I have also the honor to recommend that an appropriation be made at the earliest date to carry out this election, the amount to be based upon communication of my predecessor."—Copy, *ibid.*, RG 107, Letters Received from Bureaus. On the same day, USG endorsed this letter. "Respectfully forwarded to the

Secretary of War. I heartily concur in Genl. Stoneman's recommendation."
—Copy, *ibid.*

1868, JUNE 23. To William J. Brigham. "I have the pleasure to acknowledge the receipt of your book . . . Geology of the Hawaiian Islands and to
thank you for it. I shall take pleasure in examining . . ."—Kenneth W.
Rendell, Inc., Catalogue 89 [1973], no. 70.

1868, JUNE 23. Brig. Gen. Andrew A. Humphreys, chief of engineers,
to USG. "I transmit herewith for your information a copy of a letter and
enclosure, received at these Head Quarters from Bvt. Brig. Genl. J. H.
Simpson, in relation to charges of disloyalty made against the employés
upon the Patapsco River improvement & other works under his direction."—
LS, DNA, RG 108, Letters Received. The enclosure is *ibid.*

1868, JUNE 23. 2nd Lt. Joseph W. Wham, Fort Mason, to USG. "I have
the honor to state that on the 21st inst this Post was visited by Bvt Brig
Genl C. H. Tompkins Chief Q. M. Fifth Military District, The conversation turned on Politics, and in the course of his remarks he said that Jefferson Davis and George Washington were both traitors and both fought for
the same purpose, he did not insist on Washington and his followers beig
traitors but made that statement in palliation of Jefferson Davis's course
during our late struggle, and said further that he would just as leave give
Davis a Government Contract as Lincoln were he living, such is the sub-
stinence of what he said, if not the exact words, many similar remarks were
made but God knows these are enough. I have made this report because I
cannot sit quietly by and here a man because he is a *Superior Officer.* com-
pair, that *Fiend* of *Hell.* Jefferson Davis with the Immortal Washington,
had I done so I would have expected that my *dead brother* who sleeps beneath the *cold clay* of *Andersonville* would have risen up and *rebuked* me
I send this through Genl John. A. Logan M. C. for an Endorsement as to
my veracity"—LS, DNA, RG 108, Letters Received.

1868, JUNE 23. Governor Ambrose E. Burnside of R. I., Cleveland, to
USG. "I wrote you today about the case of John McCauskland thirty third
(33d) Infantry now under sentence at Rome Georgia for desertion. Hope
you will discharge him I spoke to you of his case"—Telegram received
(at 12:55 P.M.), DNA, RG 107, Telegrams Collected (Bound); (at 12:15
P.M.) *ibid.*, RG 108, Telegrams Received; copy, DLC-USG, V, 55. On
June 27, USG endorsed Burnside's letter. "Respectfully forwarded to the
Secretary of War—with recommendation that the unexpired portion of the
sentence in this case be remitted, and the man discharged from the service—"—Copy, DNA, RG 108, Register of Letters Received. On June 29,
Burnside, New York City, telegraphed to USG. "Can you inform me if any
action has been taken in the case of McCauland of which I wrote you from
Cleveland? Please answer to twenty six 26 Exchange Place NewYork"—

Telegram received (at 11:20 A.M.), *ibid.*, RG 107, Telegrams Collected (Bound). On July 6, Burnside, Providence, telegraphed to Bvt. Maj. Gen. John A. Rawlins. "I wrote Gen Grant from Cleveland about John McCausland deserter from Thirty Third 33 Infantry now confined at Rome Georgia Has anything been done for him"—Telegram received (at 2:40 P.M.), *ibid.*; *ibid.*, RG 108, Telegrams Received. On July 9, 3:30 P.M., Rawlins telegraphed to Burnside. "McCauslands discharge has been ordered"— Telegrams sent (2), *ibid.*, RG 107, Telegrams Collected (Bound); copies, *ibid.*, RG 108, Telegrams Sent; DLC-USG, V, 56.

1868, JUNE 23.   W. W. Goldsmith, former act. asst. surgeon, Louisville, to USG. "I have the honor to most respectfully invite your kind attention to the following statement in regard to my Nephew T. D. Godman and request if possible that he be given an appointment to the Military academy at West Point. Thomas. D. Godman is a great Grand Son of. Rembrandt. Peale. the artist late of Philadelphia and also a ~~great~~ grandson of Dr John D Godman the naturalist. Mr Godman enlisted in Oct 1861. in Co. a. 15th Regt. Ky Infty when only 14 years of age serving with gallantry with that Regt. until May 14th 1864 when he was admitted to the Jefferson~~ville~~ U S Gen Hospital at Jeffersonville Indiana. for a wound recieved at the battle of Resacca Georgia May 14th 1864,   Subsequent to the battle of Chickamouga Mr Godman was recommended by Col M C Taylor for an appointment to the Milatary acade but never recieved it. While at the Hospital he went before the board of examiners for commissions in the US Col Troops of which Major J Ham Davidson was president and was recommended ~~fand~~ found qualified for a 1st Leutenancy in the 12th US Col Heavy Artillery, but as that Regt was shortly after Mustered out of Service he did not recieve his appointment,   He is at present a private in Co. K. 2nd U S Infantry and clerking at the Head Quarters of Genl Burbank at Louisville Kentucky. He is temperate intelligent and has ever been active and prompt in the discharge of his duties. of good social standing in Society and as he has served faithfully during the war, and is well recommended, I respectfully submit the above,"—ALS, DNA, RG 94, Unsuccessful Cadet Applications.

1868, JUNE 23.   Francis Lieber, New York City, to USG. "Yester-day the enclosed Resolutions—no longer merely proposed, but adopted—were bought to me with the request of communicating them to you, which I do with the greatest pleasure, because they contain my sentiments too. We did not slight small squads when our Country was in danger, and you will not slight these resolutions though they donot come from a mass meeting by the many thousand. The German Republicans are very earnest, very active, and very liberal, in the present election movement. Let me add, General a fact which will not be wholly uninteresting to you, at this very moment, that the President Dr Jacobi, is a Jew, and I believe Dr Schuetz, the Chairm of Ex Com. is also one. Whether he is a Jew or not, he is a most excellent man and ardent Republican, who has drawn up the Resolutions. He will travel and speak all over the State, without being paid for it, as is now often the case—and he ~~is poor~~ has but small means   I mention this, to show you his zeal as a Republican. Permit me to add ~~the~~ a copy of a paper which I have caused to be printed for private distribution. If you find time to read it, you will find that it bears upon our present situation and the question of your election. No matter who will be your opponent the question will be: *You and the Nation* ~~and~~ or, the *Democats and* a *hashe* of *puny State Sovereignties.* My paper though very brief, perhaps artificially brief, contains nevertheless the results and fruits of a long and checkered life of study and experience. May God give us victory. I shall work in my sphere as ardently as any one."—ALS, OFH.

1868, JUNE 24.   Thomas W. Conway, New Orleans, to USG. "Is it your intention to allow the First Infantry to remain forever in this city? The officers and men of that regiment are corrupted by years of association with the rebels of this community. Daily the officers are to be seen drinking whiskey and parading the streets with the worst men of the rebellion. *We who fought* for the flag are ashamed of this regiment, and *we* are of opinion that it would be a good thing for you to send it away—far away, and send another in its stead."—ALS, DNA, RG 94, Letters Received, 1007M 1868. Formerly chaplain, 79th Colored, Conway served as La. superintendent of schools.

1868, JUNE 26.   USG endorsement. "Respectfully returned to the Secretary of War; with recommendation that Gen. Roberts be detailed as requested"—ES, DNA, RG 94, Letters Received, 77N 1868. Written on a letter of June 13 from Theodore D. Woolsey, president, Yale College, to Secretary of War John M. Schofield requesting the assignment of Bvt. Brig. Gen. Benjamin S. Roberts as military instructor at Yale.—ALS, *ibid.*

1868, JUNE 26.   Bvt. Maj. Gen. Edward O. C. Ord, San Francisco, to USG. "I think you wish to distribute a fair share of the Government purchases to the Merchants and Manufacturers of this Coast—I find that the Woolen Mills here, can furnish clothing, far superior to anything sent out, and at nearly the same price when the cost of transportation in coin is considered—By comparing the price list of goods made here and tho[se] sent out you will see that Drawers (knit and flannel)—flannel Shirts and Blankets, are actually cheaper than those from the East—The troops who pay for these articles much prefer the California made, and have, since they learned the difference complained bitterly at having to pay for an inferior and almost worthless article, when they can get a good one for nearly the same money—I believe it is only necessary to call the atten[tio]n of the Secretary of War to this matter, and he will direct that the troops be su[p]plied with what they prefer, especially as it will add to their efficiency, and costs the Government *nothing*—"—LS, DNA, RG 107, Letters Received; DfS (dated June 25), Ord Papers, CU-B.

1868, JUNE 27. USG endorsement. "Respectfully forwarded to the Secretary of War."—ES, DNA, RG 94, Letters Received, 180D 1868. Written on a letter of June 23 from Jesse E. Dent, Columbia, S. C., to USG. "Permit me to ask at your hands the favor to have the enclosed petition and papers asking that my disabilities be removed—placed in the hands of the proper authority for their consideration, and that you give like direction to papers which may be forwarded to you from Mr John C Dent at St Louis Mo touching this subject."—ALS, *ibid.*

On Feb. 18, 1881, Dent wrote to USG. "I am personally a stranger to you but I think you may have heard of me through your brother in law Col. John C. Dent with whom I became acquainted under the following circumstances. Col. Dent was arrested during the late war in the latter part of 1863 in Mississippi by Gen. Polk's command and was transferred to this state and placed as a prisoner in charge of Gen. M. L. Bonham then Governor of this State. Gov. Bonham committed him to my charge, I being then the Sheriff of Richland County, and I held him as a prisoner of war in my custody for about nine months. About twelve or fifteen days before Gen. Sherman reached Columbia I received an order directing me to ~~receive~~ turn over Col. Dent to the Confederate authorities at Richmond for exchange. I held Col. Dent under very embarrassing circumstances but my treatment of him was such as to elicit his most grateful acknowledgments, and when he was removed from my custody for Richmond, he handed me a very flattering open letter to Gen. Sherman and his officers, who were then supposed to be on the march to Columbia requesting them to give me and my family all the protection and aid in their power in return for my kindness to him. This letter I handed to Gen. Stone who was in command of the first detachment that formed in the Streets of the city of Columbia, and asked for his protection, which he promptly furnished by detailing a sufficient guard to protect my residence and family. This guard remained with me until morning, and did all they could under the Circumstances. I mention these facts so that your memory may be refreshed and that you may remember who I am. If any confirmation of these facts is necessary I beg to refer you to Col. Dent himself—In 1872 and again in 1876 I was elected Sheriff of Richland County on the Republican ticket, and by the Republican Party. I was a candidate for reelection in November last and was elected—but I was counted out and my opponent counted in. I was counted out by the Democratic Party. I am now making application to the President of the United States for the U. S. Marshalship of the District of South Carolina. If you can consistently do so, I will thank you if you will aid me in this matter with the President. I respectfully refer you to Judge Bond and Ex Governor Chamberlain who is now practicing law in the city of New York. These gentlemen know me and my politics. If it would not be too much trouble for you, I would be pleased if you would furnish me with Col. Dent's address. He will verify every thing I have said about him in this letter."—ALS, *ibid.*, RG 60, Records Relating to Appointments. On Feb. 20, USG endorsed this letter. "Please endorse on this what you think of the writer and send it to the Atty. Gen. Washington after the 4th of March."—AES, *ibid.* On March 7, John C. Dent, St. Louis, endorsed this letter. "During my stay as prisoner of war at Columbia, S. C under Sheriff Dent for over ten months, I found Mr D always kind & attentive to all federal prisoners & my self, and we fully thought his polaticks were with us, so far as he dare express them, I am satisfied from my knowledge of Mr D that he is a good reliable man, & fully deserving the position he asks"—AES, *ibid.*

1868, JUNE 27. USG endorsement. "Respectfully forwarded to the Secretary of War."—ES, DNA, RG 107, Letters Received from Bureaus. Written on a letter of June 18 from George D. Newburg, Cherokee County, Kan., to USG. "you Will Pleas Excuse Those few Lines for it seemes that it is the Last Resort. knowing that you Can have some Barring on the minds & Action of Congress knowing that you Led our men on to victory in the Rebelion & also Believing that you are—the same nows then that you Want the people to have their Rights the Rights that our Ansestery faught for & also that our People faught for under the Comand of your Hon. Person in the last War, & knowing that there is About 4.500 inhabitance Now Located on this Neutral land of Which the Boys in Blue are in the majority of the Adults males & that they have spent their all in improving their Clames & Now have Ben sold out to A Mr Joy inbehalf of A RR. Company it seemes As Though the soldiers have No friends in Congress & that there is No Dependance to Be put in any of the Government Authorities or at Least the Mager part of, them as there Has Ben partittion after partitt[ion] Goten up & Numerously sighned Stating the facts in in Regards our Rights Being Trampled up on By the secretary & members of Congress & Now to Cap the Climax I see that there has Be A. Nother Treaty made of the osage lands Consisting of 8 milion Acres for 6 milion &. 6 hundred Thousand Dollars But A Little trifle Above the price that the settler has to pay in homesteading Lands in other parts of the state & had that of Ben Bought By Government & Alowed to of Ben Homesteaded it Would of Ben settled up 10 times As fast & it Would also secured the settler in his improvements Which he Will ultamatly Loose or pay an Extravigant price for his land Where Bye those Land sharks Will Pocket millions of money that Rightfuly & Justly Belongs to the poor & for the Want of Which Hundreds of poor Children Will Have to suffer & As I have Ben through this part of the Country A Great Deal & know the sentament of the settlers they Would as quick take up their muskets to fight for their Homes & their Rights as they Did in the Rebelion & knowing the Influance that you have With Congress & Being satisfied that you Will not Let such Groce an outragae Be imposed on the people & By Request of Numerous of your suporters I Drop you those few lines hoping that in the Name of heaven that there Can Be some means

Reached to obtain the Rights of the settlers on the frontier Especialy those
of the two Tracts of land mentioned Namley the Cherokee Neutral Lands
& the osage Lands Which Are Being thickley settled & should Government
officials Do their Duty as their oath Requires them two Do & Buye those
Lands outRigt & iff they Dont let it Be homesteaded Allow them to Buye
their Clames at As Reasonable figures as Required of the Rail Road Co,
they Could soon improave their Clames Anough more to pay Government
in taxes 10 fold What they Get from R R. men & Before 3 years more
Would pass there. Would Be ten men here in those parts I spoke of to one
New Making A Nother Great Item in favor Both of the Government & the
thousands of Poor that are yet in the Eastern states renting Where they
Will have to Remane iff there isent something Don for their Relief   Hoping
that you ~~Woulde~~ Wont let A moment pass till you Try & Do all in your
Power for the Poor of the frontier By Which iff you Acomplish Will make
A Great standard in your next political Carier I Remane As Ever Respect-
fuly your obedient servent in Behalf of the people of the Cherokee Neutral
Lands Kansas . . . N. B Pleas to let me know the Rsult Direck to Baxter
springs Kansas"—ALS, *ibid.*

1868, JUNE 27.   USG endorsement. "Respectfully referred to the Commissioner of Pensions."—ES, DNA, RG 108, Letters Received. Written on
a letter of June 18 from Alice L. Varney, Hudson, Ohio, to USG. "Pardon
the liberty I take in addressing you thus—but knowing that you stand as
Gen-in-Chief in the Military Dep't it seemed quite as practicable for me to
apply to you. My desire is to obtain a pension for my noble, faithful but
disabled husband, Mr S. J. Varney. Of Course you would require a statement of facts on which to found such a favor, and I will give them briefly
as I can. . . ."—ALS, *ibid.*

1868, JUNE 27.   USG endorsement. "This recommendation is cheerfully
concurred in."—AES, DNA, RG 107, Letters Received from Bureaus.
Written on a letter of June 18 from Maj. Gen. Oliver O. Howard, Washington, D. C., to USG. "I earnestly recommend that the disabilities of Dr. E. H.
Smith of Richmond Va. be removed. His reputation for doing his whole
duty fearlessly & cheerfully reaches me often from the most trust-worthy
sources—Perhaps your endorsement of this request would be enough—"—
ALS, *ibid.*

1868, JUNE 27.   Jennie Stewart, Brownsville, Ohio, to USG. "My Husband belongs to the 13th US infty Fort Benton an I implore you in the
name of an afficted wife and Children to write me by what means he can
reach home by ferlough or discharge . . ."—ALS, DNA, RG 108, Letters
Received.

1868, JUNE 28, 5:30 A.M.   To Bvt. Maj. Gen. Robert C. Buchanan. "If
the services of Lt. Allen Smith can be spared please give him sixty days

leave of absence."—ALS (telegram sent), DNA, RG 107, Telegrams Collected (Bound); telegram sent, *ibid.*; telegram received (on June 29), *ibid.*, RG 393, 5th Military District, Telegrams Received.

1868, JUNE 28.   A. B. Carlin, Mayfield, Ky., to USG. "At the time in which you commanded the Union forces Stationed at Paducah Through your Orders a Mill (Saw. & flower) Situated one & ahalf miles East of Mayfield on Mayfield's Creek was consumed by fire, in the early part of December 1861. ~~then~~ property then belonging to Mr Hudgens who fled South. in Nov. of the same year. I the undersign was in the North from 1860, until the Spring of 1862, at which time I went to Nashville Tenn. where I remained as a peaceful and law abiding citizen until last fall, at which time I came to Kenty. to inherit what was left me of my Mother & Stepfather (Mr & Mrs Hudgens. My reason's for addressing you on this occasion are ~~Simp~~ Simply to know whether or not I can be remunerated for the loss of that Mill, which cost thirty five thousand dollars ($35000.) and if so in what Manner must I proceed, as I would like to have some means to aid us in Our ~~pre~~ present Campaign, to defeat Democracy forever—I being the only Surviveing heir to the Said Estate and there being nothing but land left me, I cannot find a Market for the Sale of the Same, and am anxious, to get all I can in money to assist the defeat of Democry Please inform me on what I may depend and Greatly oblige one of your wellwishers in the Cause."—ALS, DNA, RG 107, Letters Received from Bureaus.

1868, JUNE 28.   Dennis H. Mahan, West Point, N. Y., to U.S. Representative Elihu B. Washburne. "*Private* . . . Here is a little matter, that perhaps may demand immediate attention, which after hearing it you can best decide upon. In a conversation, last evening, with a lady, the wife of an officer now stationed here, she gave me a statement of a conversation that she had had, within a day or two, with the wife and mother-in-law of another officer, also stationed here, who (the two women) belong to that most bitter sect of the Secesh Copperheads, those residing in Washington and Georgetown D. C. This conversation between the women was on the subject of Lieut. Ledyard—a grandson of the late Gen. Lewis Cass—who has been here about a year, as an assistant professor of the French language; and who has just been ordered away from here to his company. It seems, that, for the last six months, Cadet Grant has been under the instruction of Ledyard; and that, during this time, some difficulties occurred between them, of the merits of which I am not accurately cognizant; and which perhaps are of not much importance; the gist of the matter being this: It is a very unusual circumstance to relieve an officer on duty here, who has been here so short a time as Ledyard has been; except for something very grave; as incompetency, or some vicious habit; and as Ledyard is an excellent French Scholar, and of unexceptionable habits, being a communicant of the

Episcopal Church, the ground assumed, and now spread abroad, to account for this official action, is, that L. has been put into this mortifying position, in some way, direct or indirect, through Grant's influence; and to prevent this son from coming under the instruction of L. during the coming year. All this of course is put in the most odious light for Grant that women's tongues can put it in. Now I happen to know, that both Lieut. Ledyard and his father are most bitter enemies of Gen. Grant. Why, except that both are violent copperheads, I know not. They, of course, will gloat over such a chance as this to vilify him the more; although I suspect you will find, upon inquiry, that Grant has not even heard of the order for relieving Ledyard from here. How will it do for you to call and see Gen. Grant, and suggest to him to have this order countermanded, *by instructions in his own hand*, no matter what the grounds upon which it was based? I leave the thing in your hands as seeing its bearings better than I can."—ALS, DLC-Elihu B. Washburne. On July 2, Mahan, New York City, wrote to Washburne. "I received, when just leaving home yesterday, on some business here, your note in reply to mine. Since writing my first to you, I wrote another to you on the subject of Lieut. Ledyard, that I thought of sufficient importance, on account of his connections, to merit some attention from Gen. Grant; who, I suppose, knew no more of his being relieved from duty at the Military Academy than you did. Since then, I have tried to find out from the Adjutant of the Academy, Major Boynton, who, from having had General Grant's son, now at the Academy, in his family, is on somewhat intimate terms with him, why Ledyard was   He either could not, or would not give me any definite clue to it; but, in the course of conversation, told me, that whilst the General was here, he said, in his presence and that of some other officers, that the father of Ledyard, for some reason that he could not find out, had expressed himself in terms of the bitterest hostility to him; and that the son, equally without cause known to him, had, by his actions, shown the same spirit, as, in never having called to pay his respects to him, and in passing him without recognizing him as his superior officer. Now however unjustifiable and in fact punishable this may be on the part of Ledyard, Gen. Grant cannot descend to notice it, but must treat it with the contempt which alone it merits from him. But, more than this, he must not even be suspected of having noticed it. On this account it is, that, although I have no question, Ledyard was relieved for satisfactory reasons, still, as it may give the Gen's enemies another handle of abuse, I think the course I suggested in my second note to you, would be well timed. The General you are aware has many enemies in the Army, particularly among the officers of the old Army of the Potomac. His own ways and those of his wife have injured him with not a few. For instance, he has with his family been on a visit here at West Point several times before this Summer. In these visits they were called upon by the whole community there, and yet these calls were never returned until this Summer   Now this kind of thing wont do among women. There ~~were~~ are many ladies there, who in birth, education and all that constitutes ladyhood are inferior to none in this country; and who, in the republic of social intercourse, will submit to no terms of inequality. I mention these things to you as a *trusted friend* of Grant. My own wife was one who determined to pay no more calls until her own was returned. Well, it was returned on Mrs G's last visit. What was the result? Whilst I was talking to the General on indifferent things, the two women happened to strike a common chord of sympathy, about some motherly apprehensions respecting their respective daughter's healths; and parted, I know on the part of my wife, with feelings of deep interest in Mrs Grant's fears; which in her were only apprehensions, whilst my wife had experienced all the painful realities of the case. Let me say to you one word on a topic that regards your own acts. It was with more than painful feelings that I saw your name in the *yeas* on the Cobb resolution. Depend upon it that, although bolstered by such articles as we find in that panderer to all base things the N. Y. Herald, of to-day. It will cost Grant, if he sanctions it, the support of more truly patriotic men than you can imagine. I have never gone to the polls in my life, and never shall so long as I hold my present position; but I may say to you candidly, that if Grant accepts that resolution, I would sooner give my vote to Pendleton, copperhead as he is, than to Grant. I can better trust a man all whose antecedents have been consistently denationalizing, for I then know where to find him, than one who could not look his private creditor in the face, should he do such a thing to him, as Cobb's resolution proposes to do to public creditors; put what gloss on it party may. You will perhaps say this is the raving of a bloated bond holder. Well it is to this extent. During the Rebellion, during the darkest days of it $ two thousand dollars (2000) came into my hands. Without a thought of security, I at once invested it in U. S. 5/20s. I have not looked at the face of the Bonds to this day. I did the same for my wife later. She owns two thousand five hundred, for my sister in law, who owns fifteen hundred. For my child's nurse, who owns four hundred. Now if the country cannot pay off a debt contracted for so priceless a treasure. I and my wife for two will give our investment *gratis*, to satisfy those whiners, who are now crying out against a burthen which every true patriot might well glory in bearing with fortitude, if they will only spare us and our children the shame of hanging our heads, where once we could boast of the proud and spotless name of American Citizen. . . . P. S. The other matter *confidential* there is no hurry for. It was merely to suggest circumspection on the part of yourself and others of the Gen's friends where I have some suspicions it may at least do no harm."—ALS, *ibid.*

1868, JUNE 29.   To Secretary of War John M. Schofield. "At the request of Gn. L. P. Graham I recommend that he be left off the Board for revising Cavalry Tactics. I have no special recommendation to make for a substitute but would suggest that some young Cavalry officer be taken who served with Cavalry during the rebellion."—ALS, DNA, RG 94, Letters Received, 193G 1868. See *ibid.*, 184G 1868.

1868, JUNE 29.   USG endorsement. "The facts set forth in this letter and
in the enclosed copy of affidavit of Comdr Henry Walke of the seizure and
loss of the unfinished steamer they state to conform fully to my recollection
of the same."—Copy, DNA, RG 108, Register of Letters Received. Written
on a letter of William B. Campbell. "Presents claim for loss of *unfinished
steam-Boat* (no name) which was siezed for military purpose by Capt
Henry Walke U. S. Navy by order of Genl Grant and was sunk while
being towed and totally lost."—*Ibid.* On Aug. 23, 1867, Bvt. Maj. Gen.
Daniel H. Rucker, act. q. m. gen., had written to USG. "I have the honor
to return herewith communication of W. B. Campbell Esq. dated July 19.
1867 requesting information relative to his claims Nos 871 and 872, filed
with commission at Cairo Illinois which has been referred to this office for
report. These claims are for value of a Steamboat hull taken at Caledonia
Illinois, by the United States forces in October 1861., amounting to $81,468
65/100, and for injury to property by United States troops amounting to
1083.00   Total $82,551.65   It appears that these claims were submitted
to the Cairo Commission of which the Hon. C. A. Dana was chairman, but
were dismissed for want of jurisdiction. The papers in the claims are herewith respectfully transmitted."—LS, *ibid.*, RG 92, Reports to the Secretary
of War (Press).

1868, JUNE 30.   Bvt. Maj. Gen. Robert C. Buchanan, New Orleans, to
USG. "I have the honor to recommend my Aide-de-Camp 1st Lieut. George
Baldy. 39th U. S. Infantry, to receive the following appointments by Brevet
for Gallant and Meritorious Service in the Field, whilst in the Volunteer
Service, viz: To be Captain by Brevet, to take effect July 28th 1866—for
gallant and meritorious Service in New Mexico, Colorado, and on the
Plains, whilst Adjutant of 3rd Colorado Volunteers. To be Major by Brevet,
to take effect 28th July 1866, for gallant and meritorious Services at Battle
of Bayou Metia, under General G. W. Davidson, in the Campaign which
resulted in the Capture of Little Rock Ark. To be Lieutenant Colonel by
Brevet, to take effect July 28th 1866, for gallant and meritorious services
in the Field at Morganza, whilst Acting Inspector General of Division. All
of these Brevets to take effect from July 28th 1866 Lieut. Baldy's date of
appointment in the Regular Service. In the Volunteer Service 1st Lieut.
Baldy has held successively the Grades of Lieutenant and Adjutant—
Major,—Lieut. Colonel—and Colonel—and whilst holding the latter commission, he received the Brevet of Brigadier General of Volunteers, for
gallant and meritorious services in the Field, to date from March 15th
1865. I have recommended 1st Lieut. Baldy for three Brevets, from the
fact that he is first for promotion to a Captaincy in his Regiment—I also
have the honor to recommend for appointment by Brevet, my Aide-de-Camp
Captain Isaac D. de Russy 1st U. S. Infantry To be Major by Brevet, to
take effect   for faithful and meritorious services during the War."—LS,
DNA, RG 94, ACP, B310 CB 1868. On July 22, Bvt. Maj. Gen. John A.
Rawlins endorsed this letter favorably.—ES, *ibid.*

Index

All letters written by USG of which the text was available for use in this volume are indexed under the names of the recipients. The dates of these letters are included in the index as an indication of the existence of text. Abbreviations used in the index are explained on pp. xvi–xx. Individual regts. are indexed under the names of the states in which they originated.

		DATE DUE	